W9-BBT-352

42-118711

ordered 7/2/59   Magee

reordered 1/16/60

THE CENTURY HISTORICAL SERIES
William E. Lingelbach, *Editor*

THE LATIN AMERICAN REPUBLICS

980
M

THE
LATIN AMERICAN
REPUBLICS

A History

DANA GARDNER MUNRO

William Stewart Tod Professor of Public Affairs
Princeton University

SECOND EDITION

New York

APPLETON-CENTURY-CROFTS, INC.

Wingate College Library

Copyright, 1950, by

APPLETON-CENTURY-CROFTS, INC.

*All rights reserved. This book, or parts
thereof, must not be reproduced in any
form without permission of the publisher.*

594-10

Copyright, 1942, by D. Appleton–Century Company, Inc.

PRINTED IN THE UNITED STATES OF AMERICA

vi   PREFACE

Preface

It is hardly possible to write an adequate history of the Latin American Republics today, because we know so little about some phases of
their development. Scholars have done much work in the colonial period, at least in Spanish America, but less attention has been paid to
the evolution of political institutions and the relationship between social
classes in the period since independence. It is especially difficult to
compress the story into one short volume. Many persons who have
taught or written about the history of Latin America have wished that
it were possible to deal with the subject in broad outline, without con-
fusing the student with details about so many different countries. It is
impossible, however, to get away from the fact that the countries are
different, in their geography, in the makeup of their populations, and
in other factors that have shaped their development. Each individual
country must receive some consideration if we are to have a faithful
picture of the story of the American community as a whole.

In this new edition, parts of the text have been rewritten to include
the results of recent research. Other portions, dealing with more recent
events, have been revised to omit material that seems less significant today than it did eight years ago. An effort has been made to group the
twenty republics by areas and to discuss briefly the peculiar conditions
and problems of each area. The story of each country, and the story
of inter-American relations, have been brought down to date. It would
be inappropriate, in a general history, to discuss current political problems in detail, but the most important recent events in each country
are at least noted.

To avoid the accumulation of footnotes, sources of information are
not generally cited in the text. I wish, however, to acknowledge my
indebtedness to the numerous American historians who have given
us authoritative studies of the various aspects of Latin American history
and civilization. Most of the more important books in English are men-

v

11579

tioned in the reading list at the end of this volume. I have also relied heavily on some of the Latin American historians: Levene, Galdames, Henao and Arrubla, Zavala, Acevedo, Amunátegui Solar, Arguedas, Basadre, Varnhagen, Gonzales Guinán, Reyes, and many others.

D.G.M.

Contents

Maps

ACKNOWLEDGMENT

The map of Indian tribes on pages
20 and 21 is a modification of a similar
map in W. S. Robertson, *History of
the Latin-American Nations* which in
turn is adapted from maps by J. W.
Powell, C. Thomas, J. R. Swanton,
and A. E. Chamberlain. The maps on
pages 125 ("Latin America in 1800")
and 235 ("Territory under Dispute
in the War of the Pacific") have
also been adapted from similar maps
in the Robertson book.

Maps

ACKNOWLEDGMENT

The maps of Indian tribes are
based on a reconstruction of a similar
map in W. S. Robertson, History of
the Latin-American Nations which in
turn is adapted from maps by A. F.
Bandelier, C. Thomas, J. R. Swanton,
and A. L. Kroeber. The map on
"Countries under Dispute in the Area
of the Pacific" is similarly based,
and the "Countries under Dispute
in the Area of the Pacific" is here
also been adapted from similar maps
in the Robertson book.

Part I

~~~

THE SPANISH COLONIES

1

Before the Conquest

THE twenty independent republics below the Rio Grande are called "Latin American" because of their historic relationship to three of the Latin nations of Europe. Eighteen of them were colonies of Spain. Brazil was Portuguese; Haiti was French. All owe their official language, the culture of their upper classes, and much of their political and social tradition to the European mother countries. In most of them the better educated and more influential families are largely of European descent.

This is not true, however, of the population as a whole. There are only a few countries—Argentina, Uruguay, Costa Rica, and perhaps Chile—where people of European descent are greatly in the majority. In Brazil and the Caribbean, a substantial part of the laboring classes are the descendants of Negro slaves. Elsewhere they are Indian or part-Indian; and in the highlands of Mexico and the Central Andes, where populous civilized communities existed long before the Spaniards came, there are still millions of people who retain the languages and to some extent the customs and social organization of the period before the Conquest. It is impossible to understand the history of the Latin American nations or their political and social problems today without knowing something of the Indian heritage.

The ancestors of the American Indians were probably mongoloid tribes that crossed the Behring Strait from Asia, perhaps 10,000, perhaps 20,000 years ago. They were a primitive people, living by hunting and fishing, with no domestic animals except the dog. They had no iron, and they had not discovered the wheel. Coming presumably in successive waves of immigration, they spread throughout the continent from Hudson's Bay to Tierra del Fuego. At the time of the Spanish conquest, they had developed varying degrees of civilization and many different languages, but the race was "singularly uniform in its physical traits, and individuals taken from any part of the continent could easily be mistaken for inhabitants of numerous other parts." [1] There were many similarities in social organization, customs, and religious beliefs. Nearly all cultivated maize, beans, cotton, and tobacco where the climate permitted, and all depended mainly on polished stone weapons and instruments, though copper, gold, and silver were used to some extent.

The migrants had been compelled to adapt themselves to a great variety of physical environments, and these had done much to determine the character of the culture that each group developed. In any study of Latin America geography is a factor that must constantly be borne in mind. In the tropics, where most of the Indians settled, and where a majority of the people of Latin America live today, variations in altitude and rainfall have an even greater effect on the conditions of human life than in the temperate zones. Regions like the hot plains of the Amazon with their excessive rainfall offered little encouragement for the evolution of a higher civilization, but in the highlands of Mexico and the Central Andes a cooler climate and more moderate precipitation favored the establishment of settled agricultural communities. It was in these regions that the first advances toward civilization seem to have taken place.

We know almost nothing of the long period when the predecessors of the Maya and the Incas were developing the indigenous food plants on which their civilization rested and were gradually changing from nomadic hunters to settled farmers. The continuous archeological sequences thus far discovered seem to take us back hardly more than two thousand years,[2] to a time when the Indians were already living in permanent villages, cultivating corn, beans, and cotton, and making pottery. It was from this "archaic civilization," extending throughout most of the highland region from Mexico to Peru, that the later more advanced cultures evolved. The evolution seems to have taken place independently in two great centers, one in the Middle American region and the other in the Central Andean highlands and the nearby valleys along the Pacific Coast. The people of each region knew little or nothing of the other, for the mountains and jungles of the Isthmus of Panama

---

[1] Brinton, *The American Race*, p. 41.
[2] Kroeber, *The Maya and Their Neighbors*, p. 474.

and northwestern South America were then as now a formidable barrier to intercommunication.

Middle America: The Maya

At several places in southern Mexico and northern Central America there are impressive groups of pyramids and ruined temples, evidently the remains of ceremonial centers to which the people of the surrounding country came for religious observances. The people who used them had already attained a high civilization a thousand years or more before the Spanish conquest. Their size and their magnificence show that they were built by large, well-organized communities. There were a number of independent cultures in the Middle American region, but there had clearly been much interchange of ideas and techniques.

The most notable, and perhaps the oldest, of these early cultures was that of the ancient Maya who occupied a hot, humid belt of land extending from northwestern Honduras across Guatemala into the southern part of Yucatán. Why an advanced civilization should have flourished in this region where few people would wish to live today, is a mystery. It is clear, however, that the area once supported a large population, for at site after site, buried in the tropical jungle, we find the ruins of massive, skilfully built stone temples and beautifully sculptured monuments. Among the monuments are the series of *stelae* which were erected in many of the centers at the end of each period of five or ten years. Sometimes as much as thirty or forty feet in height, these monoliths bear row after row of intricate glyphs which show that the Maya had a system of writing superior to that of any other American people. Some of the word signs, and especially those standing for dates and numbers, can be deciphered, because they were still in use in Yucatán at the time of the Conquest, and it has thus been possible to read parts of the inscriptions. They indicate that the Maya had a remarkably accurate calendar and an astonishing skill in mathematical and astronomical calculation. They had learned to use the mathematical quantity of zero and a system of numeration by position some centuries before these concepts had come into use in the old world.[1]

We know little of the ancient Maya beyond what we can learn from the monuments. The dates on the *stelae* tell us something, though archeologists disagree as to their correlation with our own chronology.

[1] Morley, *The Ancient Maya*, p. 275.

The earliest date thus far found has been translated as 328 A.D., which would indicate that the Maya culture was flourishing before that time. The similarity of the architecture and the glyphs at the various sites seems to indicate that there was constant intercourse and probably a close political and religious connection between them. The absence of pictures of weapons and warlike subjects suggests that they were peaceful communities, little troubled by civil strife or foreign invasion. The sculptures show clearly that religion was the subject most important to the people who made them, and bear out the tradition of the later Maya that their ancestors were ruled by priests. They tell us little of customs or social organization or historical events.

The dates on the monuments throughout the southern region cease suddenly at about the same time, probably in the eighth or ninth century of our Christian era. Apparently what is sometimes called the "Old Empire" ceased to exist. Whether its inhabitants were driven to seek new homes by a pestilence, or by foreign enemies, or simply by the superior attractions of other regions, it is impossible to say. Some authorities have suggested that the *milpa* system of agriculture, the clearing of small patches in the forest which are cultivated for a few years and then abandoned to weeds and brush, had exhausted the arable land just as it is still impoverishing agricultural areas in some parts of the Caribbean. Whatever the cause, the center of Maya culture seems to have moved at this time to the northern part of the Yucatán peninsula.

The people of this "New Empire" were even more skilled in architecture than their predecessors, though their sculpture never attained the perfection of the monuments in the ancient cities. They had the same system of writing, not only carving records on stone but keeping histories and genealogies in books of maguey fiber. Only a very few of these have survived and only a part of their contents can be deciphered. We know something of the history of the later Maya, however, not only from magnificent archeological remains like those at Chichén Itzá but from traditions still extant at the time of the Conquest. For a long period Yucatán seems to have been ruled by a confederation of the three chief cities, Chichén Itzá, Mayapán, and Uxmal, but at the end of the twelfth century A.D. this broke down and the leaders fell to fighting among themselves. It is probable that this strife, combined with hurricanes and pestilences, brought about the decline in the Maya culture which was noticeable by the end of the fifteenth century.

The Maya were nevertheless among the more advanced of the American peoples at the time of the Conquest. They still made fine pottery and textiles, and continued to use their elaborate calendar and system of writing. Their agricultural methods were primitive, as they probably always had been, for land was plentiful and they were able to supplement their food supply by hunting. In Yucatán, the great majority of the people lived in simple wooden huts, well adapted to the needs of a population that frequently moved from place to place in search of new lands. In the highlands of southern Guatemala and Chiapas, on the other hand, there were populous nations of Maya stock which had stone-built cities and well-organized governments. All of the later Maya peoples were ruled by hereditary chiefs who seem to have had more power than the priests.

The Aztecs

In the sixteenth century, the most important Indian civilization of Middle America was not in the Maya area but in the region around what is now Mexico City. Mexico, north of the Isthmus of Tehuantepec, is a great triangular plateau, flanked by mountain ranges that fall off sharply to a narrow coastal plain on either side. The most fertile portion is the southern apex of the triangle, in the Valley of Mexico and the nearby highlands. This region, with its high altitude and an invigorating climate, had long been the home of populous communities whose culture was similar in many respects to that of the Maya. The civilizations that produced the great ceremonial centers at Teotihuacán and Monte Albán seem to have flourished and declined at about the same time as the "Old Empire," to be succeeded after a century or two by another high culture centering around Puebla. This was perhaps the "Toltec" empire, of which traditions survived among the Aztecs. Its influence extended throughout Central Mexico and into Yucatán, where some of the "New Empire" cities were ruled by chiefs of Mexican origin. This culture also declined, probably as a result of barbarian invasions, for at the time of the Conquest most of the people who lived in Central Mexico were by their own account descendants of nomadic hunters who had come into the region from the north. These newcomers had retained their own language, called *Nahua*, but they had absorbed much of the civilization of the older inhabitants and had gradually built up a new culture of their own.

The Aztecs, the most powerful of the Nahua tribes at the time of the

Conquest, had probably entered the Valley of Mexico in the thirteenth century. Finding the best lands already occupied by stronger peoples, they settled in a small area surrounded by marshes and water in the lake region in the center of the valley. Here they built their city of Tenochtitlán, or Mexico. At first they maintained a precarious existence by fishing, hunting, and growing such scanty crops as their limited territory permitted, but it was not long before their warlike qualities made them welcome allies of their stronger neighbors in the continual struggles between the cities of the lake region. The inaccessibility of Tenochtitlán gave them an advantage over the people of the more exposed cities on the mainland, and this was increased by the construction of a causeway that penned up the waters flowing through the nearby marshes, so that the city came to be entirely surrounded by a large lake. About the beginning of the fifteenth century, the Aztecs defeated the people of Azcapotzalco, who through their aid had acquired a temporary supremacy over the other tribes of the valley. Soon afterward Tenochtitlán joined with Tezcoco and Tlacopán in a confederacy that extended its conquests into other parts of the plateau and into the lowlands of the coasts. When the Spaniards reached Mexico, the Aztecs and their allies were dominant from the Pánuco River and Lake Chapala to the Isthmus of Tehuantepec.

This territory was not, strictly speaking, an "empire." The confederacy was a partnership for military purposes between three cities that used their superior power to exact tribute from other peoples. There was constant warfare, and some nearby tribes, like the Tlascalans, who played an important part in the Spanish conquest, had never been subjugated. Even the cities that paid regular tribute were largely independent in the management of their internal affairs. The Aztecs and their allies sent officials among them to supervise the collection of tribute and possibly to watch for signs of revolt, but in most cases these officials had no other governmental authority and were not supported by resident garrisons. The three cities that were members of the confederacy had entirely separate governments, and each might engage in private wars on its own account. It was only when they engaged in joint operations that the Aztec war chief assumed the leadership of the combined armies.

The Aztec capital Tenochtitlán, in the midst of the lake and accessible only by three long causeways, excited the wonder and admiration of the Spanish conquerors. It was apparently the home of some sixty thousand families when it was first visited by Cortez.[1] At its center were several imposing public edifices including the great temple of the tribe and the *Tecpán*, where the war chief, with his numerous family and a great host of officials, lived and dispensed hospitality. Less important temples and public buildings were scattered throughout the city. The houses were of stone or adobe, many of them built on piles in the water and accessible only by boat. The inhabitants were supported not only by the product of their own lands but by the tribute paid by other cities. This took a great variety of forms—slaves, pottery, textiles, feather work, gold ornaments and other works of art, as well as food. The city also carried on an active commerce with other parts of the "empire" and with regions not yet conquered, sending out carefully organized trading expeditions which also obtained much valuable military information. The safe return of these expeditions was celebrated with feasts and religious observances and the merchants themselves were accorded the respect due to men who had been successful in a dangerous and difficult undertaking.

There were many other large cities in the lake region and elsewhere in Central Mexico, though few of them were so populous or so wealthy as Tenochtitlán. The Nahua had made great progress in the arts of civilization since their wandering ancestors had entered the valley only a few centuries before. They were skilful workers in gold and silver and they made weapons and other articles out of copper and copper alloys, although the limited supply of metals forced them to rely mainly on stone as material for weapons and utensils. They showed much skill also in their architecture, their stone carving, their painting, and their pottery. They wove textiles from maguey fiber and cotton and made paper from maguey fiber. There were artisans especially trained in each craft, and those following certain callings such as the gold and silver smiths, were highly honored.

The people of Central Mexico were of several racial stocks and spoke many different languages, but there seems to have been a general similarity in their social organization and religion. We know something about their institutions, and especially about those of the Aztecs, from the reports of Spanish chroniclers and from the very small number of Indian manuscripts preserved after the Conquest. The government, in Tenochtitlán at least, seems to have been relatively democratic. The

[1] Merriman, *Rise of the Spanish Empire*, Vol. III, p. 470. Vaillant, *The Aztecs of Mexico*, pp. 122, 234.

people of this city-state were divided into twenty clans, or *calpulli*, and
it was the clan, rather than the individual, that owned most of the
land. A part of each clan's holdings was apportioned among the heads
of families, in accordance with their needs, and other portions were
cultivated, either coöperatively or by hired labor or slaves, for the
support of the officials and the priesthood.

Each clan had its own temples and its own gods, though all joined
in the worship of the great tribal gods also; and each received its share
of the war prisoners for sacrifice and of the tribute from subject cities.
Within the clan, a council of old men, probably the heads of families
or of households, exercised supreme authority, except on the rare occasions when all of the members met to consider an especially weighty
question. The council elected two chief officials: the *Teachcauhtli*,
who led the troops of the clan in time of war and was responsible for
the maintenance of order and the military education of the young men,
and the *Calpollec*, the principal civil official. The latter collected the
taxes and distributed the land and the clan's share of the tributes, keeping written records with colored plats to show the lots held by each
family. Both officials administered justice in minor cases, but more
serious matters were reserved for action by the council.

For the government of the city as a whole the *Tlatocán*, composed of
representatives of the clans, met about once in twelve days to decide
questions of general interest. Matters of very great moment were reserved for consideration by a grand council in which not only the
members of the *Tlatocán* but a number of other important officials and
priests participated. The city, like the clan, had two principal executive officers: the *Tlaca-tecuhtli*, or war chief, and the *Cihua-cohuatl*, who
was in general charged with the administration of civil affairs, though
he was also a war leader. They were assisted by a great number of other
officials who were supported by tribute from conquered towns or by
the product of lands set aside by each clan for their benefit. Each of the
four quarters of the city had its own military chief, and there was a
large organization to collect and distribute tributes and other revenue.
There was also a class of honorary chiefs, or *tecuhtin*, who had acquired special distinction in battle or had earned the title by going
through severe penances. These were treated with the greatest respect,
and the officials and war chiefs seem always to have been chosen from
among their number.

The *Tlaca-tecuhtli*, the principal war chief, was the representative of the city in dispensing hospitality to strangers; and Montezuma, who held the office when Cortez entered Mexico, so impressed the Spaniards by the ostentatious reception which he gave them that they thought they were dealing with a monarch of the European type. In reality he was not an "emperor" but an elected leader, subject probably in important matters to the decisions of the tribal council. The war chief, however, seems usually to have been chosen from among the members of certain powerful families, and his authority may well have been increasing in the years just before the Conquest. In other respects too, military conquests and the rising wealth and power of a few influential groups seem to have been breaking down such democratic institutions as the Aztecs had formerly enjoyed, for much land taken from conquered enemies in the vicinity of Tenochtitlán was cultivated by serfs for the benefit of powerful Aztec leaders—an arrangement that was later used by the Spaniards for their own benefit.

Nearly all of the activities of the Nahua communities were closely connected with religion. There were a multitude of gods. Some of them, like the war god Huitzilopochtli, were apparently tribal deities whom the Aztecs had worshiped before their arrival in Mexico. Others had been taken over from the more civilized earlier inhabitants of the valley. Of these, the most interesting was Quetzalcoatl, the god of the arts, who was also worshiped by the Maya under the name of Kukulkán. The priests, of whom there were said to be five thousand in Tenochtitlán alone, were educated in special schools in the temples where they were subjected to rigorous discipline and trained to an austere life. One of their principal occupations was the study of astronomy and the calculation of the dates of the numerous religious festivals, for the Aztecs had an intricate calendar which bore a marked resemblance to that of the ancient Maya. The priests also prepared the religious and historical manuscripts, but in a system of writing far inferior to that of the Maya. They had a few conventional symbols but in general they recorded events and ideas pictorially, much as the North American Indians did.

The religious festivals were celebrated in a way that horrified the Spanish conquerors. Human sacrifices were practised to some extent by many of the American peoples, but nowhere did they assume such gruesome form as at Tenochtitlán. Nearly all of the Aztec festivals were celebrated by the immolation of numbers of war prisoners or women or children, whose bodies were usually eaten after the sacrifice by the priests and the populace. Wherever the first Spanish invaders went, they found the temples noisome with the smell of blood. One of the chief purposes, and often the sole purpose, of the frequent wars that the Aztecs waged against neighboring peoples was to obtain victims for sacrifice, and every youth must capture a prisoner before he attained full standing as a warrior.

Religion was thus a dominant influence in the Aztec culture, as it had been apparently in the earlier cultures of Mexico. It has been said that nearly all of the great achievements of the Middle American Indian civilizations took the form of "material religious expression." [1] Their art and architecture, their calendars, their mathematical knowledge, and even their remarkable systems of writing, were used chiefly in connection with the worship of the gods. They had made less progress in the organization of society and in improving the conditions of daily life among the masses of the people.

The Incas

On the west coast of South America, the Indians had achieved more efficient political and economic systems and a far greater skill in building public works of practical utility. The more civilized peoples lived in regions where large communities could exist only by organizing themselves to overcome geographical handicaps and to make the most of a relatively small amount of good land. One of these was the rainless desert of the Peruvian coast, where the antarctic current affords a relatively cool climate but where agriculture is possible only in the valleys of the rivers coming down from the Andes. Here elaborate irrigation systems had existed from very early times. There were other populous communities in the adjacent highlands. The Andes, in Peru and Ecuador, form two or three generally parallel chains, snow-covered at their summits, but enclosing fertile valleys where every foot of arable soil was being cultivated at the time of the Conquest. A third center of population was the great, almost level Bolivian plateau, twelve to fourteen thousand feet above sea level. Much of this was too arid for agriculture, but was well suited to the llamas and alpacas which formed the pastoral wealth of the inhabitants, a hardy race who had adapted themselves to the cold and the high altitude which makes life cheerless and uncomfortable for persons accustomed to other climates. At the time

[1] Vaillant in *The Maya and Their Neighbors*, p. 296.

of the Spanish conquest, these three regions, extending for more than two thousand miles from north to south, formed one empire ruled by the Incas of Cuzco.

We know very little about the history of this area before the time of the Incas. The domestication of the llama and the alpaca, and the development of the potato and other useful plants from very different ancestral varieties, must clearly have been the work of many generations of people who had already emerged from a state of savagery. Archeological investigation has shown that there were advanced cultures at an early date in different parts of the Andean area, but their origin and the relationship between them is still obscure.

The earliest high civilization in South America, so far as we can judge from the evidence now available, existed in the coastal valleys of what is now northern Peru. The Chimu, whose capital was at Chan-Chan near the modern city of Trujillo, were a powerful nation when they were conquered by the Incas in the fifteenth century, and their tradition that their ancestors had long enjoyed an advanced form of culture is substantiated by the archeological remains in their territory. At about the same time, perhaps, that the Maya were bringing to perfection the architecture and sculpture of the "Old Empire," the early Chimu were living in large and well-organized communities, portraying much of their daily life and occupations on pottery of exquisite workmanship. A different type of fine pottery is found in graves of about the same period in Nazca and other valleys farther south.

At a somewhat later time the center of civilization, and perhaps of political power, seems to have shifted to the highlands. At Tiahuanaco, in the cold, bleak region south of Lake Titicaca, there are remains of impressive temples or palaces built of great blocks of stone cut and fitted together with marvelous accuracy. Vestiges of similar "megalithic" masonry are found at several places in the highlands north of Lake Titicaca, especially in parts of the walls of the great fortress at Cuzco, and other remains, including designs on pottery, seem to show that the cultural influence of Tiahuanaco reached many places on the coast. The city was very possibly the center of a great empire foreshadowing that of the Incas. When it flourished and why it fell we can only guess, for the Peruvians knew little or nothing of the history of its ruins at the time of the Spanish conquest. The archeological evidence indicates that its fall was followed by a period of general cultural decline. On the coast a higher type of civilization soon reappeared, but the people of

Wingate College Library

the highlands seem to have reverted to more primitive conditions, under the rule of a great number of petty local chieftains.

Among these, perhaps, were the Incas of Cuzco, a fertile valley in the mountains north of Lake Titicaca, where something of the civilization of Tiahuanaco may have survived. The Incas believed that their ancestors, claiming to be children of the Sun, had come into the valley from outside and had persuaded its people and those of other districts nearby to accept their rule. Their traditions indicated that the family had ruled at Cuzco some four hundred years before the Spanish conquest. They had early begun to expand their domain first in the basin of Lake Titicaca and later in the valleys north and west of Cuzco. At the beginning of the fifteenth century their empire was still a relatively small state but three great rulers who immediately preceded the Spanish conquest extended its frontiers until it included present-day Ecuador and much of Chile and northwestern Argentina, as well as the greater part of modern Peru and Bolivia. The coastal regions, which had been powerful independent kingdoms, became one of the most important parts of the Incas' realm.

The conquered territories were not merely tributary states, like those dominated by the Aztecs, but integral parts of a highly centralized kingdom. The Incas seem from the beginning to have shown an astonishing statesmanship in consolidating their conquests. Their dominance was effectively secured by building fortresses and roads, and the loyalty of each group of new subjects was obtained by skilfully harmonizing their political and social system with that of the empire. In most cases the former rulers were allowed to remain in power, under the supervision of the Incas' representative, and local customs were interfered with as little as possible. The inhabitants were required, however, to learn *Quechua*, the language of Cuzco, in order to simplify the problem of administration, and this is the prevalent tongue in the Andean highlands today. The process of assimilation was doubtless made easier by the fact that the more important parts of the Andean region were occupied by tribes of a similar culture and closely related languages, and also by the great prestige which the Incas acquired as their power grew.

The *Sapa Inca*, the ruler of the empire, was an absolute monarch whose claim to descent from the Sun invested him in the eyes of his subjects with a divine character which strengthened his temporal power. When he was not leading the army or engaged in long tours of inspection in outlying parts of his domains, he lived in great state at Cuzco, surrounded by a numerous court and a large harem. Among the later Incas, at least, the heir to the throne must be the son of the monarch by his own sister—a custom evidently adopted to enhance the sacredness of the royal family in the eyes of the people. The other princes of the royal blood, including all legitimate descendants of former rulers, formed the high nobility from whose ranks were selected the principal military and civil officials and the chief priests. They, with the other descendants of the original inhabitants of Cuzco, were entitled to call themselves Incas and to wear the large ornaments in the lobes of their ears which led the Spaniards to call them *orejones*. Many of the special privileges that they enjoyed were also enjoyed by the *curacas*, the hereditary chiefs of conquered provinces, whose children were usually educated at Cuzco to imbue them with a spirit of loyalty. Below these were a host of minor officials, charged with the supervision and control of the political and economic life of the people of the empire.

The social and economic organization was perhaps the most remarkable feature of the Inca regime. Its basis was the communal ownership of land by the *ayllu*, or clan, which had doubtless existed among the Andean peoples for many centuries. As in Mexico, each family was allotted an area sufficient for its needs. Other portions were tilled for the benefit of the government and the priesthood, and their product was used if necessary to relieve famine in any part of the empire. The well filled storehouses of the Incas afforded a security against want which might be envied by the people of many modern countries.

Agriculture was the principal occupation, and a great variety of fruits and vegetables were grown in the various climatic zones from the hot valleys east of the mountains to the cold *páramos* near their summits. Potatoes, in the highlands, and maize, at altitudes of less than eleven thousand feet, were the chief crops. In the mountains the scanty area of arable land was increased by well built terraces following the contours of the hillsides. Agricultural implements were crude, but the use of fertilizers, including guano in the coast regions, was understood and practised. In the higher and less fertile parts of the mountain regions the people were herdsmen rather than farmers. The llamas and alpacas were the property of the state and their meat and wool was divided among the inhabitants according to the needs of each household, so that *charqui*, or dried flesh, supplemented agricultural products as a staple article of diet. Wild game was captured only in great, officially organized annual hunts.

The Incas attempted to control the most minute details of the life of their subjects. Theoretically there were officials charged with the supervision of each group of ten families, over whom were others ruling groups of fifty, one hundred, and one thousand. The people were divided into ten classes, according to age, and the character of the work to be done by individuals of each class was fixed by law. Certain inhabitants of each community were selected in turn to serve the state as soldiers, shepherds, miners, artisans, messengers, or laborers on public works and this service was credited to the community as a part of its tribute. Marriage, travel, and costumes were officially regulated. Violations of the laws were severely punished because even trivial offenses were looked upon as a sacrilegious disobedience of the *Sapa Inca's* commands, but crime is said to have been rare.

The imperial government frequently transplanted whole groups of its subjects from one region to another. The inhabitants of a newly conquered district whose loyalty was doubtful were often compelled to exchange homes with people from an older section of the empire. At other times pioneers were sent from over-populated provinces to newly conquered and undeveloped frontier regions. In either case the colonists, or *mitimaes*, were given special privileges and material assistance to mitigate the hardships of the transfer.

Among the most notable of the Incas' achievements were their public works. The irrigation systems that already existed in the coastal valleys were improved and extended. Water was brought in some cases for many miles, through tunnels or channels cut in the mountains or over aqueducts supported by masonry walls, and reservoirs were built to assure a continuous supply. The country thus supported a far larger population than it did after the Spaniards, in their ignorance and improvidence, allowed these works to fall into disrepair. The roads, which connected Cuzco with all parts of the empire, were scarcely less remarkable. They were frequently surfaced either with slabs of stone or a mixture of stone and clay, beaten hard, and the steeper slopes were ascended by steps cut in the rock. The gorges in the mountains, which would otherwise have been almost impassable, were crossed by suspension bridges of osier or maguey fiber. At intervals there were storehouses of grain and other supplies for the use of the army, and at more frequent intervals huts for the accommodation of travelers. Messengers, stationed at posts so near together that it was possible to run from one to another at top speed, enabled the ruler to send orders to any part of his domains, and to be informed within a few days of all important happenings in the outlying provinces.

So elaborate an administrative organization could hardly function without some means for recording and conveying information. The Incas had no system of writing, but they had developed a substitute in the form of the *quipus*, which served to show the quantities of articles of various kinds on hand in the storehouses, the population of each district in the empire, and the amount of tribute rendered by their people.

These quipus were cords on which were made knots of almost infinite multiplicity. For the purposes of reckoning, each form of knot represented a different number, and each string a different subject; to some of the strings, subordinate strings were attached, serving as footnotes, and the strings forming one set of accounts were arranged as a fringe along a master-string. An indication of the nature of the objects enumerated was furnished by the colour of each string, and the combinations of colours and types of knots gave an almost endless variety to the uses to which this method of recording could be put.[1]

A specially trained force of *quipucamoyac* or accountants was entrusted with the keeping of these records. The *quipus* seem to have served even to keep alive the memory of historical events, though their usefulness in this connection was obviously limited.

The cities, and especially the capital, were adorned with public buildings of stone laid in regular tiers and cut and fitted with marvelous exactness. Today, the visitor to Cuzco walks through streets where the Inca masonry still serves as the outside walls of the houses. There were many great palaces, for each ruler built a new residence for himself, leaving that of his predecessor as a sort of shrine, and many buildings erected for religious purposes. The most impressive of these was the *Coricancha*, the great temple. Here, in the sanctuary of the Sun, the mummies of former monarchs sat before the great altar, in a room lavishly decorated with plates of gold. The same building had chapels dedicated to the Moon, the planet Venus, the Lightning, and the Rainbow, besides many apartments for the use of the priests. In the temple precincts, according to Garcilaso de la Vega, a descendant of the Incas who wrote their history after the Spanish conquest,[2]

[There was] a garden of gold and silver. . . . It contained many herbs and flowers of different kinds, many small plants, many large trees, many large

---

[1] Joyce, *South American Archaeology*, pp. 102–103.
[2] *The Royal Commentaries of the Incas*, Part I, Book III, Chapter 24, Markham's translation, Vol. I, pp. 282–3.

and small animals both wild and domestic, and creeping things, such as serpents, lizards, and toads, as well as shells, butterflies, and birds. Each of these things was placed in its natural position. There was also a large field of maize, the grain they call *quinua*, pulses, and fruit trees with their fruit; all made of gold and silver.

Religion, as among the other civilized peoples of America, played an important part in the life of the community and was closely identified with the civil authority. Both the peoples of the sierra and the peoples of the coast worshiped a multitude of local gods, or *huacas*, such as rocks, rivers, natural forces, and animals which the various tribes regarded as their ancestors. Homage was also universally paid to the dead. The Sun, the special *huaca* of the Incas, was the great deity of Cuzco, and its worship was imposed upon the conquered peoples as the empire expanded. The already existing local cults, however, were not in most cases suppressed, and even among the Incas the Sun was by no means the sole deity. Each locality, and even each family, had its *huacas*, and all of the people, from the *Sapa Inca* down, had personal fetishes that were supposed to influence the fortunes of the owner during his life and to be buried with him at death. A higher religious conception was represented by the creator god, Huiracocha or Pachacamac, who was worshiped by the Incas and also by some of the coast people, and whose worship, at least among the Inca nobility, was abstract and spiritual rather than material.

There was a numerous priesthood, headed by the *Villac Umu*, who was always a brother or close relative of the ruling Inca. Under him were other religious functionaries of high rank, for the most part of royal or noble blood, but the minor positions were filled by persons serving only for short periods and thereafter returning to their usual occupations. An important function of the priesthood was to ascertain the will of the deity by omens of various sorts, or by consulting oracles. Sacrificial offerings of llamas, precious metals, and food were made to the Sun and also to other *huacas* and to the spirits of ancestors. Human sacrifices, common in earlier times among the Andean tribes, were to a great extent suppressed by the Incas though it is probable that they were practised on rare and important occasions.

Among the most famous institutions of the empire were the convents of the Virgins of the Sun. In these buildings, hundreds of maidens, selected for their noble birth or their beauty, wove the garments used by the royal family and the priests and made bread, *chicha*, and other articles for religious purposes. They were rigorously secluded from contact with the outside world, under the guardianship of older women, but the more beautiful often left the convents to enter the harem of the ruler or to become the wives of lesser chiefs.

In practical statesmanship and in their genius for organization and administration, the Incas far surpassed any other group of American Indians about whom we have definite knowledge. If their culture was in some other respects inferior to that which the Aztecs and their neighbors had inherited from the earlier inhabitants of the Mexican Valley —for the Mexicans surpassed the Peruvians in architecture and sculpture, in their astronomical knowledge and in possessing a system of writing—it was nevertheless of a high order. Such fragments of their poems and prayers as have come down to us show a well developed capacity for self-expression and a depth of real spiritual feeling. Intellectual progress, however, seems to have been confined almost entirely to the ruling class. The masses of the people, living in rude and comfortless stone huts, were doubtless better fed and better cared for than they had been before the time of the Incas, or than they have been since the Spanish conquest, but they were kept in a state of ignorance and the system under which they lived must have precluded the growth of any spirit of initiative or self-reliance. The tradition of unquestioning obedience to despotic authority made it relatively easy for the Spaniards to conquer and hold Peru after they had once obtained control of the person of the monarch.

The Chibchas

In the highlands north of the Inca empire, in what is now the Republic of Colombia, there were a number of other relatively advanced Indian groups. The most important were the Chibchas, or Muiscas, of the plateau of Bogotá, where there were five independent states ruled by priest-kings. The Chibchas worshiped several deities, including the Sun, the Moon, and Bochica, the legendary teacher of the arts of civilization. Their culture was much like that of the other Andean peoples, but they did not have the llama or the alpaca, which played so important a part in the economy of the Indians farther south. They spun and wove cotton, made good pottery, and were especially skilful in working with gold. They lived in towns, but their buildings were of wood rather than stone.

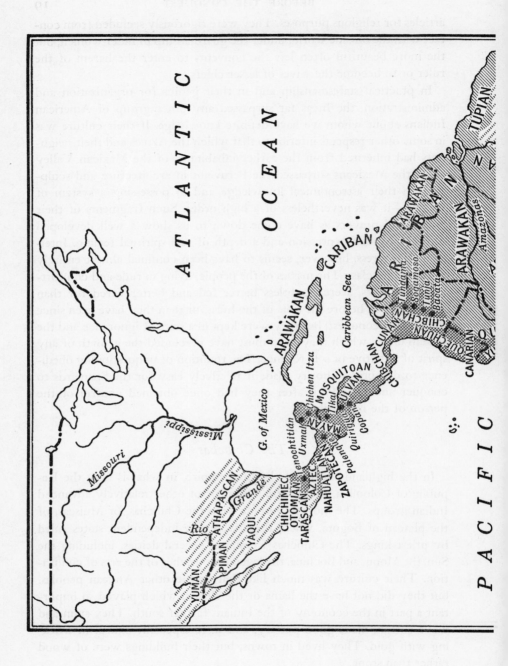

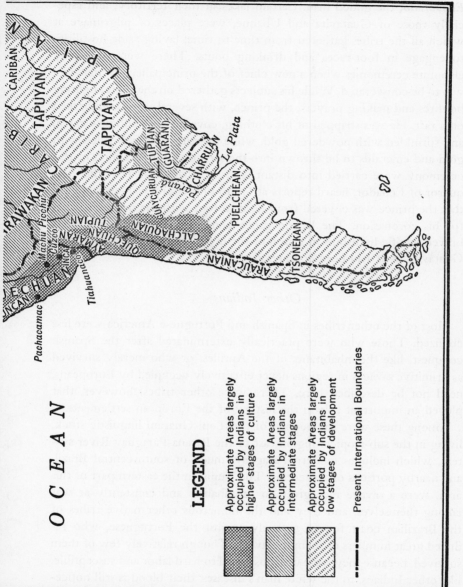

Indian Tribes

One of the customs of the Chibchas gave rise to the famous myth of *El Dorado,* the gilded man. Certain lakes in their territory, and especially those of Guatavita and Ubaque, were places of pilgrimage at which all the tribes gathered from time to time, laying aside hostilities to engage in foot-races and drinking bouts. There were especially elaborate ceremonies when a new chief of the principality of Guatavita was to be consecrated. While his subjects gathered on the shore, lighting bonfires and making prayers, the prince, with several priests, embarked on a raft. He was stripped of his clothing, covered with adhesive earth, and sprinkled with powdered gold, while the raft itself was laden with gold and emeralds to be thrown into the sacred waters. Reports of this ceremony were carried into distant lands, so that Belalcázar, the conqueror of Ecuador, heard reports at Quito of a country so rich in gold that the prince was covered from head to foot with the precious metal for his coronation. The legend grew, and many Spanish expeditions braved terrific hardships in search of the mythical *El Dorado* long after Guatavita itself had been conquered.

Other Indians

Most of the other tribes in Spanish and Portuguese America were less civilized. Those who were practically exterminated after the Spanish conquest, like the inhabitants of the Antilles, or who merely survived as primitive savages in regions never effectively occupied by Europeans, need not be described here. There were other tribes, however, that played an important rôle in the history of the European settlements.

Among these were the peoples of the Tupi-Guaraní linguistic stock, living in the sub-tropical region east of the Paraná-Paraguay River system, which includes modern Paraguay, much of south-central Brazil, and nearby portions of Argentina. The Tupis, in the eastern part of this area, were a savage race given to cannibalism and constantly at war among themselves, and they and the numerous other native tribes of the Brazilian coast fought savagely against the Portuguese, who reduced great numbers of them to slavery. Though relatively few of them survived, because they were unaccustomed to hard labor and susceptible, like other Indians, to the white man's diseases, their blood is still noticeable among the people of several regions in modern Brazil.

More important were the Guaranís, a somewhat more civilized race who lived in semi-permanent communities with large houses of lattice work and straw accommodating twenty or thirty families. They were fairly skilled in making pottery and polished stone implements, and they cultivated the usual Indian crops—corn, beans, and tobacco. At the same time they depended for much of their food on hunting and fishing. Less warlike than their Brazilian relatives, they were easily brought under control by the early Spanish settlers and later by the Jesuit fathers, who established among them the famous Paraguay missions. They were the only Indians east of the Andes who survived to become a considerable element in the population of modern South America. Their descendants, with an admixture of white blood, form the bulk of the inhabitants of Paraguay today and their language is still generally spoken there.

On the grassy pampas of the River Plate region and in the temperate valleys of Central Chile there were Indians of a very different type. Nomads, living by hunting and practising agriculture in a primitive way, they were a warlike people, incorrigibly attached to their personal and tribal independence. Like the Indians of North America, they were pushed back but not conquered by the earlier European settlers. In Argentina they continued to make trouble until they were virtually exterminated by the army in the last quarter of the nineteenth century. In Chile, the tribes north of the Bio Bio River, who had been conquered by the Incas and had adopted a relatively settled way of life, were subdued by the Spaniards after some hard fighting and formed the bulk of the laboring class during the colonial period. The Indians south of the Bio Bio savagely resisted the invaders for more than three hundred years. Like the Pampas tribes, they were finally defeated late in the nineteenth century, and those who survive are living peaceably on reservations today.

Survival of the Indian Race

Much of the culture of the great Indian empires was destroyed by the Conquest, but the majority of the inhabitants of Mexico, Guatemala, Peru, Bolivia, and Ecuador today are either full-blooded Indians who still retain much of their ancient way of life, or people of mixed blood who owe almost as much to their Indian as to their Spanish heritage. Relationships between these three groups, whites, mestizos, and Indians, present many of the most difficult political and social problems that confront these five countries today.

Indians still form an important part of the population of several other American countries. The survival of the Guaraní stock in Paraguay has been mentioned. Many of the people of Colombia are wholly or partly of Indian descent, though most of them now speak Spanish and do not form an important separate community. Somewhat the same situation exists in parts of Venezuela and of Central America, where settled agricultural tribes were also converted into a subject laboring class under Spanish rule. There was a very different situation in regions like the River Plate and southern Chile, where there were only wild nomads. The history of a European community in such a region was certain to be very different from that of a colony in Mexico or Peru. In the one case, it would be almost entirely European in blood. In the other, the white element would be a small ruling class, living on the labor of the conquered race. The striking contrasts that impress the traveler as he goes from one Latin American republic to another today arise largely from differences in the character of the aboriginal population.

2

The Coming of the Spaniards

The Historical Background in Spain

The Spanish peninsula is peopled by the descendants of several dissimilar races. It became a part of the civilized world when the primitive Celtic and Iberian inhabitants were conquered by Rome late in the third century B.C., and was soon one of the richest parts of the Empire. Roman political and social institutions were not entirely destroyed when the peninsula was overrun by Germanic tribes in the fifth century, and the Catholic religion was soon adopted by the Visigothic kings who ruled the greater part of Spain during the next three hundred years.

Early in the eighth century the country was again conquered, this time by the Saracens from North Africa. The new invaders brought with them an advanced culture that made Spain the most civilized portion of medieval Europe and profoundly influenced its later history. The original inhabitants, on the whole, were well governed and fairly treated. There was little attempt to convert them by force to Islam, though many of them embraced that faith to escape the taxes imposed on non-believers, or, in the case of slaves, to obtain freedom from their Christian masters. The tolerant policy of the Moorish rulers also embraced the Jews, and large numbers of these came to Spain to add yet another to the many racial stocks in the peninsula.

The Moslems had hardly consolidated their power before the long wars of the reconquest began. After the Saracen advance into France was turned back by Charles Martel at Poitiers in 732, the Frankish kings helped to preserve Christian rule in Aragon and Catalonia at the base of the Pyrenees. Farther west, in the mountains of Asturias, there were other independent Christian communities that later grew into the kingdoms of Leon and Castile. All of these little states gradually extended their domains. The Moors early abandoned much of the bleak plateau of northern Spain, and their hold on the more attractive regions in the south was often made precarious by factional strife between the Arabs and the North African Berbers or between ambitious local potentates. The Christians also fought among themselves as often as against the infidels, but they were occasionally able to combine their forces, and in 1212 they decisively defeated the Moors in the battle of Las Navas de Tolosa. During the next half century all of southern Spain was re-conquered except the little kingdom of Granada, which remained under Moorish rule until 1492.

For two hundred years after the break-up of the Moorish empire there were five separate kingdoms in the Spanish peninsula. Castile and Leon, united under one crown after 1230, had the largest territory and the most numerous population. The realms of the Kings of Aragon, who had acquired Catalonia in the twelfth century and the Moorish kingdom of Valencia in the thirteenth, lay east of Castile along the Mediterranean coast. To the west was Portugal, which had become independent in the twelfth century; to the south Granada; and in the northeast the little kingdom of Navarre. These states were constantly at war with one another or torn by internal struggles. In Castile especially there were but few intervals of peace in the strife between rival claimants to the throne and between the Crown and the great nobles—a state of affairs that left little opportunity for intellectual or economic advance. Aragon, with more stable political institutions, fared better, and Catalan merchants developed an important commerce throughout the Mediterranean region.

It was the marriage of Ferdinand of Aragon and Isabella of Castile and Leon in 1469 that made it possible for Spain to become a great nation. The union of the heirs to the thrones of the two principal Spanish states came at a time when much of the peninsula was in a state of anarchy. Isabella obtained recognition as Queen of Castile and Leon only after a long struggle, but once established on her throne, in 1474, she showed an ability and statesmanship that her predecessors had lacked. The unruly nobles were brought under control and compelled to cease their private wars, while brigandage and disorder were checked by the organization of an effective police force. When Ferdinand succeeded his father as King of Aragon in 1479, the two realms were united under one effective government, though they retained their separate constitutions. The new monarchs' first great enterprise, after the establishment of order at home, was the conquest of Granada, which was accomplished in 1492 after ten years of warfare. It was only a few months after the fall of the Moorish capital that the sovereigns entered into an agreement with Christopher Columbus for a voyage into the western ocean.

The discovery of America thus came just at the time when the wars of the reconquest ended, and when much of the crusading spirit that had been aroused during the campaign against Granada could be transferred to the enterprise of converting the heathen of the New World. The history of Spain in the centuries before the discovery helps to explain the character of the Spaniards who came to America. The earliest colonists were largely from the hitherto turbulent realms of the Crown of Castile, to which the Indies particularly belonged. Generations of almost constant fighting had developed in them the audacity and indomitable courage which made possible the achievements of the conquistadores; but they had also brought out other traits of character less desirable among permanent settlers in a new country. Among these was a deep-seated aversion to manual labor, either in tilling the soil or in manufacturing. In Castile and Leon climatic and topographical conditions had made stock-raising more attractive than agriculture, and in the more fertile southern provinces the presence of a subject Moorish peasantry had discouraged the conquering race from engaging in farming. The Moors were also more skilful as artisans, and manufacturing was left in their hands. Partly at least because work in the fields or in the shop was regarded as degrading by the Christian Spaniards,[1]

. . . there was an enormous preponderance of personal service in the industrial organism, and much of this was purely for ostentation. Nowhere in the world were there so many nobles, so many officers, civil and military, so many lawyers and clerks, priests and monks, so many students and school boys, with their servants. But as truly, nowhere in the world were there so many beggars and vagabonds.

The lesser nobility, the *caballeros* or *hidalgos*, were an especially numerous class. During the wars of the reconquest, any Castilian who maintained a horse and weapons in a city in newly conquered territory, without engaging in trade, was regarded as a member of this class with extensive privileges, including exemption from general taxation. All of

[1] Roscher, *The Spanish Colonial System* (translated by E. G. Bourne), p. 4.

his sons, legitimate and illegitimate, inherited his status.[1] There was thus a great class of fighting men who were little suited for other occupations when Ferdinand and Isabella established internal peace in Spain; and it was they who made the Spanish armies a formidable factor in the European wars of the sixteenth century and who filled the ranks of the expeditions to America.

The Discovery of America

The discovery of America was but one event in a great era of exploration which began long before 1492, and in which Portugal, rather than Castile, at first played the leading rôle. The development of the art of navigation which made Columbus' voyages possible was largely the work of a Portuguese prince, Henry the Navigator (1394–1460), who had devoted his life to the extension of geographical knowledge and the improvement of seamanship. Expeditions which he sponsored explored much of the African coast and paved the way for Bartholomeu Dias' discovery of the Cape of Good Hope in 1486 and Vasco da Gama's voyage to India in 1497–99. The Spanish voyages into the western ocean were at first little more than an effort to emulate these enterprises of a rival court. Commerce with the Orient was the goal in both cases, and while the Portuguese were still endeavoring to reach the East by sailing around Africa, Columbus persuaded Ferdinand and Isabella to attempt to attain the same result by an expedition westward across the Atlantic.

Columbus had himself been in the service of the King of Portugal, and had married a near relative of one of Prince Henry's captains. He had attempted to interest the Portuguese court in his project and it was after his failure at Lisbon that he began his long, uphill struggle to obtain support from the Spanish monarchs. The story of his efforts is a familiar one and need not be retold here. He finally signed an agreement with Ferdinand and Isabella which assured the needed financial support and granted him the position of Viceroy and the hereditary rank of Admiral in any new lands that he might obtain for the Crown.

Columbus' three little ships sailed from Palos on August 3, 1492, and from the Canary Islands on September 6. On October 12 the expedition reached one of the smaller islands of the Bahamas, probably that now called San Salvador, and the admiral took formal possession of it in the name of the King and Queen. Understanding from the gestures of the natives that a larger island, rich in gold, lay farther south,

[1] Cheyney, *European Background of American History*, p. 108.

he went on to the coast of Cuba, and then eastward to an island which he named Española, because its mountains reminded him of Spain. Here the Indians were friendly, and had considerable quantities of gold, which came, they said, from mines farther east. He was sailing along the coast in this direction when his flagship, the Santa María, ran aground and was wrecked. This compelled him to leave forty of his men on shore in a fort which he named La Navidad.

The admiral returned to Spain, where his exaggerated description of the riches that he had found created a sensation. Ferdinand and Isabella at once took steps to obtain recognition of their sovereignty in the new lands. A papal bull issued in 1455 had confirmed Portugal's exclusive dominion "through all Guinea and beyond toward that Southern shore," [1] and it was feared that this vague grant, which had been formally recognized by Spain, might be interpreted to include the islands that Columbus had reached. The Pope, therefore, was persuaded to lay down a line one hundred leagues west of the Azores and the Cape Verde Islands, beyond which lands not already in the possession of any Christian prince were to belong to the Crown of Castile. This was unsatisfactory to the King of Portugal, and the Treaty of Tordesillas, signed in 1494, finally provided that the "line of demarcation" should run from pole to pole 370 leagues west of the Cape Verdes. Not until six years later was it discovered that a part of South America lay east of this new line—a fact that gave Portugal her claim to Brazil.

The Spanish monarchs meanwhile made hurried preparations to establish a permanent colony in the New World. On September 25, 1493, Columbus sailed from Cadiz with seventeen ships and a large company of artisans, farmers, and missionaries, as well as seamen and soldiers. No women were taken along, but the fleet carried everything else necessary for a permanent settlement: domestic animals, seeds, fruit trees, and tools. When the expedition reached La Navidad, Columbus was horrified to find only the ruins of his fort. The Indians, at first so friendly, had been enraged at the abusive conduct of the Spaniards and had murdered them to a man.

A new settlement, called Isabela, was established on the coast farther to the east, but things went badly from the start. The admiral, as a foreigner, was unpopular with his followers, and the Spanish soldiers resented his insistence that they as well as the paid laborers should take

---

[1] Davenport, *European Treaties bearing on the History of the United States and its Dependencies to 1648*, p. 24.

part in the work of building the town. Disease and the effects of unaccustomed exertion in a hot climate thinned the colonists' ranks. The Indians were soon driven into open hostility by the settlers' demands for food and the abuse of their women, and were only defeated after several months of hard fighting. Notwithstanding these difficulties, Columbus found time to explore the south coast of Cuba and to discover Jamaica, but in 1496 he was compelled to return to Spain to defend himself against charges brought against him by discontented colonists. He was so far successful that he was again permitted to set sail for his colony in 1498.

On this third voyage the admiral followed a new route in the hope of finding richer lands to the south of those already discovered. He reached the Island of Trinidad and soon afterward the nearby mainland, where he found natives more civilized than those of Española, wearing golden ornaments and strings of pearls. Impressed by the Indians' appearance, by the pleasant climate, and by the beauty of the landscape, the admiral concluded that he had reached the very border of the terrestrial paradise itself, for this was reported to be in Asia, beyond the realm of Cathay. After exploring the coast for some distance to the west, he turned north to Española. There he found that his brother Bartholomew, left in charge in his absence, had moved with most of the colonists to the south shore of the island and had established the City of Santo Domingo, the first permanent settlement in America. The troubles with the Indians had continued, and some of the Spaniards, under one Roldán, had revolted and established a separate camp in the interior. Columbus succeeded in making an agreement with the malcontents, but not in allaying the bitter feeling caused by the severity with which his brother had attempted to rule the colony—a bitterness which was aggravated by the colonists' sufferings from want and disease.

Reports of these occurrences made a painful impression on the King and Queen. Isabella, at least, also disapproved of Columbus' sending a cargo of Indians to Spain for sale as slaves. The slave trade had long been the chief factor in the development of Portugal's profitable African commerce, and it was not unnatural that Columbus should turn to this source of potential wealth when he was disappointed in his hopes of finding substantial amounts of gold or other valuable products in the lands which he had discovered. But Isabella from the outset adopted a more enlightened view of her obligations toward the inhabitants of her new possessions. Her disapproval of Columbus' venture was the first of a long series of efforts by the Spanish crown—efforts which as we shall see were not very successful—to protect the Indians from the rapacity of the Spanish conquerors.

The monarchs were finally convinced that Columbus was unfit to act as governor of the new colony, and in 1500 Francisco de Bobadilla was sent to Española to take his place. The admiral and his brother Bartholomew were shipped back to Spain in irons after a one-sided investigation. They were soon released, but Columbus was never restored to the authority which had been promised to him for life. During his fourth and last voyage to America, upon which he embarked in 1502, he was not even permitted to land at Santo Domingo. He explored a long section of the Central American coast, suffering much from storms and other disasters, and returned to Spain broken in health, to die at Valladolid on May 20, 1506.

Since access to the rich markets of the Orient seemed more important than the possession of lands occupied only by primitive savages, exploration of the American coast during the first quarter century after the discovery was directed chiefly toward the search for a route past the new continent to Asia. Several other mariners had made important voyages before Columbus' death. In 1497 and 1498 John Cabot, an Italian sailing under a patent from the King of England, visited the North American coast. In Spain, Columbus' claim to a monopoly of the right of exploration in the Indies was respected until 1499, when both Alonso Niño and Alonso de Ojeda made voyages to the north coast of South America. Niño returned with a cargo of pearls and dye-wood; and Ojeda, who gave Venezuela its name because an Indian village built on piles in the Gulf of Maracaibo reminded him of Venice, also seems to have been fairly successful. In 1500 Vicente Yáñez Pinzón reached the Brazilian coast, discovered the mouth of the Amazon, and followed the shore north and west for some 2,000 miles. Only three months after Pinzón, the Portuguese navigator Pedralvares Cabral also landed in Brazil while on a voyage from Lisbon to India. There were other expeditions of less note, and in 1504, when Columbus returned from his fourth voyage, it was possible for geographers to draw a fairly accurate map of the coast line from Cape Gracias a Dios in Central America to the easternmost point of Brazil.

It is one of the great injustices of history that the American continents were named not for their discoverer but for another Italian mariner who achieved fame more by accident than by desert. Amerigo Vespucci had taken part in some of the early voyages to the New World, and letters that he wrote describing them had been printed and widely read throughout Europe. In 1507, a German professor of geography reprinted one of these, and proposed that the land that had been discovered in the South Atlantic should be named "America." This suggestion was gradually accepted in other European countries, but in Spain the new possessions continued to be called "The Indies."

Santo Domingo and the Beginnings of the Encomienda System

For some years after 1504 the search for a strait lagged and Spanish activity in the New World centered in the Caribbean. Santo Domingo was still the chief settlement. The colony's white population numbered only 300 when Columbus' none too successful management of its affairs ended, but Governor Ovando, who came to the island in 1502, brought with him 2,500 new settlers. Although many of these died of hardship and disease, further immigration increased the number of Spanish inhabitants to 12,000 by 1506. After 1508 the colonists gradually spread into the neighboring islands of Cuba, Jamaica, and Puerto Rico. Gold, hides, and sugar were exported to Spain in increasing quantities, and somewhat later, when expeditions to the mainland were undertaken, the breeding of horses for their use became profitable.

As the plantations expanded there was a more and more urgent demand for native laborers. After the Indians revolted in 1495, Columbus subjected them to a heavy tribute, payable either in gold or in work. In 1499, to placate the discontent that had found expression in Roldán's revolt, the admiral did what Spanish kings had often done after the conquest of territory from the Moors, and granted many of his followers tracts of land with the right to use the labor of the Indians who were already cultivating them. Thenceforth the Indians were exploited more and more ruthlessly. Reports of the cruelties to which they were subjected caused much concern to the Queen.

Isabella wished to protect the natives, but she realized that the colony could not prosper, or even exist, without their labor. Both the climate and inherited prejudices made it impossible for the Spaniards to cultivate their plantations themselves. It seemed reasonable that the Indians should do manual labor, in return for wages, and their reluctance to give up their own simple life was regarded only as evidence of their indolence. Furthermore, the Queen desired their conversion to Christianity, which would be difficult if they were permitted to flee from contact with the Spaniards, as many of them were doing. Ovando, who had at first been instructed to leave the Indians free to go where they wished, was therefore authorized in 1503 to gather them in villages near the white settlements. Each village was to be placed under the protection of a Spanish colonist, who was to see that the Indians were instructed in the Christian faith, and was to be recompensed by the tribute that they were required to pay. The Indians might also be compelled to work for their protector, though as free men and for fair wages. Thus originated the *encomienda* system, which was extended to Mexico and Peru when those countries were conquered and became one of the most important institutions of Spain's American colonies.

Among the primitive people of the Greater Antilles, the *encomienda* lent itself to shocking abuses. The *encomenderos* paid little attention to their obligations although they exploited their charges to the utmost. Overwork and mistreatment, combined with the new diseases brought by the white men, practically wiped out the Indians of Santo Domingo and Cuba within a generation. As the local labor supply diminished, it was replenished by raids in other parts of the West Indies and on the mainland. The victims of these did not even enjoy the doubtful benefits of the *encomienda*, for the Crown had been persuaded to authorize the reduction to slavery of Indians guilty of rebellion or cannibalism, and this afforded a pretext for the capture of thousands of inoffensive savages in regions not yet occupied. People torn from their homes in this way died off even faster than the local Indians, and it was not long before hardly a trace of native blood remained in the island colonies.

The Discovery of the Pacific

In 1509 an effort was made to establish permanent settlements on the mainland. Alonso de Ojeda was given permission to colonize and govern the coast from Cape de la Vela to the Gulf of Urabá, while Diego de Nicuesa received a similar grant from the Gulf of Urabá to Cape Gracias a Dios. Both leaders met with terrific obstacles. Ojeda, finding his efforts to obtain a foothold on the coast defeated by the savage Indians, left the sixty remaining members of his original force of 300 in a fort near the Gulf of Urabá and returned to Santo Domingo in an unsuccessful effort to obtain help and supplies. Shipwrecked on the voyage, he died soon afterward in poverty without returning to his province. Nicuesa established a settlement which he called Nombre de Dios, near what is now the Caribbean end of the Panama Canal, but hunger and disease reduced the number of his followers from 700 to sixty or seventy. When he learned that the survivors of Ojeda's expedition had moved across the Gulf of Urabá into his territory, he attempted to assert his authority over them. This was a mistake, for the colonists compelled him to put to sea in a worm-eaten vessel which never was heard from again.

The transfer of Ojeda's colony to Santa María la Antigua de Darién, as the new settlement was called, had been the work of Vasco Núñez de Balboa, an adventurer who had escaped from his creditors at Santo Domingo by having himself nailed in a cask and loaded on one of Ojeda's ships. Balboa's energy and natural gift for leadership had led the discouraged colonists to follow him rather than the lawyer Enciso, whom Ojeda had left as his representative. The result showed the wisdom of their choice, for by their new leader's diplomacy the Spaniards were able to obtain food and a small amount of gold from the nearby Indian tribes. They also learned of a great sea, lying beyond the mountains, on the shores of which there were said to be kingdoms far richer in the precious metals than any they had yet seen. On September 25, 1513, after an arduous journey of twenty-four days through the tropical jungle, Balboa saw the Pacific from the top of a hill, and four days later he walked into the waters of the Gulf of San Miguel and took possession of the ocean in the name of the King of Spain.

Balboa's exploit caused the King to excuse his usurpation of leadership and to grant him the title of "Adelantado of the South Sea," but before the report of the expedition reached Spain the King had already appointed Pedrarias Dávila Governor of the Darién colony. Pedrarias was a narrow-minded and vindictive but energetic official, already past his seventy-second birthday but destined to play an important part in the history of Central America until his death eighteen years later. He was jealous from the start of Balboa's popularity and independent spirit, and in 1519 he had his rival beheaded, on apparently trumped-up charges of plotting a revolt. In the same year he moved the seat of government from Santa María across the isthmus to Panama, so as to carry on more effectively the exploration of the coast on that side.

The discovery of the South Sea led to new efforts to find a way past the continent to Asia. The veteran explorer Juan Díaz de Solís, carrying the search for a strait farther south, reached the River Plate in 1516, but was killed by Indians when he attempted to land. In 1520 Ferdinand Magellan, a Portuguese in the service of the King of Spain, sailed down the coast of Patagonia and succeeded with much difficulty in passing through the strait which still bears his name. He found the ocean on the other side unusually calm, and it was he who christened it the Pacific. After exploring part of the Chilean coast, he struck out boldly westward, and finally reached the Philippines. There Magellan himself was killed in a battle with the natives, but some of his followers continued their journey and in 1522 completed the first circumnavigation of the world. The route to the Orient had been found, but it did Spain little good for neither the Strait of Magellan nor the later discovered route around Cape Horn were easily navigated by the clumsy sailing vessels of the sixteenth century.

The Conquest of Mexico

The net result of the first quarter century of Spanish enterprise in America had been disappointing. Little profit was to be hoped for from lands occupied by the primitive Indians along the coast from Central America to the River Plate. It was not until the Spaniards came into contact with the richer and more civilized people of Mexico that the real value of Columbus' discovery began to be appreciated.

The first explorers to visit Mexican territory were the members of a slave-catching expedition from Cuba led by Francisco Hernández de Córdoba, who was badly defeated by the Maya when he attempted to land in Yucatán in 1517. The next year, another expedition under Juan de Grijalba explored the coast as far north as Vera Cruz and returned with a small quantity of gold. The reports of these two captains encouraged Diego Velásquez, the governor of Cuba, to send out a larger force, which he placed under the command of Hernando Cortez.

Cortez had come to Española in 1504, when he was only nineteen, and had played a distinguished part under Velásquez in the conquest of Cuba. He had later quarreled with the governor, and had at one time been imprisoned. Relations between the two men had evidently improved, but when Cortez was about to sail the governor became suspicious of him and ordered him to surrender his command. Cortez refused, and proceeded to recruit men and obtain supplies at the smaller settlements along the Cuban coast in spite of Velásquez' effort to stop him. He was thus practically an outlaw when he finally set out for Yucatán in

February, 1519. His defiance of the King's representative was to affect the whole course of his expedition.

Cortez set sail with eleven ships and about 600 men. He had ten bronze cannon and a few smaller firearms, as well as a number of crossbows, but his most important military assets, as events later proved, were sixteen horses. The terror caused by these strange and apparently supernatural beasts, more perhaps than that inspired by the artillery, repeatedly gave the Spaniards the victory over far larger native armies in the months to come.

At Cozumel Island, where Cortez first landed, he was well received by the natives and was so fortunate as to find a Spaniard named Jerónimo de Aguilar, who had been shipwrecked there eight years before and had learned the Maya language. From Cozumel he went on to Tabasco where the Indians opposed him but were defeated with much slaughter. As a peace offering they gave the Spaniards twenty women, and one of these was able to speak both Maya and Nahua. This was the famous Marina, who later became Cortez' mistress. Through her and through Aguilar the Spanish leader was now able to communicate freely with the inhabitants of the territories that he was about to invade.

On April 22 the Spaniards landed near the site of modern Vera Cruz. Two days later they were greeted by emissaries from Montezuma, the *Tlaca-tecuhtli* of Tenochtitlán. Reports of Grijalba's arrival on the coast in the preceding year, with pictures of the Spaniards and their ships, had already reached the Aztec capital, and they had aroused superstitious fear as well as interest. The Nahua had a legend that Quetzalcoatl, the fair god who was often portrayed with a long beard, would one day return from the East across the sea, and they were by no means sure that the light-skinned, heavily bearded foreigners were merely human beings. They were thus disposed to accord them a respectful if not enthusiastic welcome.

The Spaniards could see that they had to deal with a state far wealthier and more powerful than any thus far discovered in America, and there were many who felt that its conquest would be too difficult and dangerous a task for a few hundred men to undertake. Cortez, however, could not turn back, for his only hope of escaping punishment as a rebel was to win the King's forgiveness by some sensational achievement. His immediate problems were to give an appearance of legality to his actions and to make sure that none of his force could desert him, and he proceeded at once to attain both objectives. First, after giving secret instructions to his own loyal supporters, he announced that the expedition was about to return to Cuba because it had already gone as far as Velásquez' instructions authorized. The men whom he had taken into his confidence at once objected, asserting that they had been promised an opportunity to found a new colony. Cortez ostensibly yielded to their demands and permitted them by formal vote to create the municipality of Villa Rica de la Vera Cruz. After he himself had been elected Captain General he sent messengers to Spain to explain and attempt to justify what had been done. He then cut off all possibility of retreat by secretly ordering that all of his remaining ships be sunk. The most discontented and faint-hearted had now no alternative but to follow him.

In the meantime Cortez had been gathering much useful information about conditions in Mexico. He learned that the Totonacs along the coast were restive under the domination of the Aztec confederacy and he encouraged them to revolt. At the same time he endeavored to assure the Aztec leaders of his good intentions. When the people of a nearby town at his suggestion seized the confederacy's tribute collectors, he saved the prisoners from death and secretly sent two of them back to Montezuma with friendly messages. He had already sent gifts to the Aztec war lord and announced his intention to visit Tenochtitlán, but Montezuma, though he sent magnificent presents in return, had urgently begged him not to undertake so difficult and dangerous a journey.

After four months on the coast the Spaniards started into the interior, leaving a strong garrison at Vera Cruz. They met with no resistance as they ascended into the highlands, and after two weeks of marching they entered the territory of the Tlascalans, one of the few people of Central Mexico whom the Aztecs had never been able to conquer. Here they were attacked by tremendous forces of natives, but the horses and the artillery gave them decisive victories in two hard-fought battles. The Tlascalans then decided to make peace and to join the Spaniards in their march against the tribe's traditional enemies at Tenochtitlán. Their help from that time on was of the greatest importance, and the remembrance of it gave the Tlascalans a privileged position among the Indians of Mexico throughout the colonial period.

With some thousands of his new allies, Cortez now proceeded to Cholula, which was one of the chief cities of the Aztec realm. The Tlascalans had warned him that Montezuma planned to have the Spaniards entrapped and murdered in this city but he refused to show any evidence of fear and the Cholulans welcomed him with protestations of friendship. He soon learned through Marina, however, that the Tlascalans had been well informed, and he promptly forestalled his hosts' treacherous plans by massacring all of the chiefs and some thousands of the other inhabitants. This exhibition of cruelty, following so closely upon the apparently miraculous defeat of the overwhelmingly superior Tlascalan armies, doubtless did much to dissuade the Aztecs from offering further resistance to their unwelcome visitors.

Early in November, 1519, the invaders reached Tenochtitlán, where Montezuma came out in great state to welcome them and to assure them of his friendship. The Spaniards, with their horses and their native allies, took up their residence in one of the buildings on the public square. The Indians brought them gifts and entertained them royally, but their situation, in an island city surrounded by hundreds of thousands of potential enemies, was clearly precarious. As usual Cortez decided on a bold stroke. Taking as a pretext a reported plot against the garrison at Vera Cruz, he visited Montezuma with a strong guard and compelled him to come to live with the Spaniards in their quarters. Cortez rightly conjectured that the inhabitants of the city would be reluctant to attack while he held their ruler as a hostage, and he was able in fact to give orders to the Indians through his unwilling but thoroughly frightened guest. One of his first acts was to have Montezuma send for large quantities of gold and silver, which were promptly divided among the officers and soldiers. The Emperor was treated at times with respect, at times with a brutality calculated to impress on him the danger of resistance. His princely bearing and noble character soon won the sympathy and admiration of his captors.

For a time all went well, though the extreme danger of the invaders' position was always evident. The temper of the Indians grew more and more ugly, especially after Cortez decided that he could no longer postpone an attack on the native religion. The crusading spirit was always a powerful motive with the Spanish expeditions to the New World, second only to the desire for wealth and power, and it was impossible for the conquistadores to imagine the toleration of pagan cults among Indians who came under their control. Cortez had already compelled the Indians near Vera Cruz to accept Christianity, and he had attempted to convert his Tlascalan allies. Here, however, he had met strong opposition, and had compromised by permitting the Tlascalans to combine the Christian religion with their own. At Tenochtitlán, closer acquaintance with the horrible character of the native rites made a compromise impossible, and when all efforts at persuasion failed Cortez proceeded to destroy the Indians' chief idols himself. For the moment the natives did not openly resist, but it was evident that they were horrified and infuriated.

When Cortez had been at Tenochtitlán about six months, a new threat suddenly loomed up. Pánfilo de Narváez, sent by Governor Velásquez, appeared on the coast with a force that outnumbered Cortez' by more than two to one. Between the Aztecs on the one side and this new enemy on the other resistance seemed hopeless, but Cortez left Pedro de Alvarado at Tenochtitlán with part of his men, and boldly went to meet Narváez with the rest. For some days the two Spanish forces camped a short distance from one another. Cortez took advantage of the interval to bribe or cajole many of his opponent's lieutenants, and when the overconfident and careless Narváez was surprised by a night attack and badly defeated, the greater part of his followers returned with Cortez to Tenochtitlán.

There the situation had grown worse. Alvarado, aroused by the Aztecs' continued refusal to abandon their idols, had attacked the participants in one of their religious festivals with great slaughter. The Indians had taken up arms in earnest, and when Cortez arrived the Spanish garrison was besieged in its quarters. Cortez entered the city without resistance but on the following day the Indians made a savage general onslaught. They had elected Montezuma's brother Cuitlahua as *tlaca-tecuhtli*, and when the former ruler appeared on the roof of the barracks in an effort to pacify them he was mortally wounded by a shower of stones. The Spaniards, short of provisions, realized that their only salvation lay in getting out of the city.

On the night of June 30, 1520, still famous as the *noche triste*, the sad night, they made their retreat. They had to cross one of the long causeways, hard pressed from their rear and attacked by fleets of war canoes on their flanks. Crowded in a narrow space and loaded down with spoils which they refused to abandon, they could make little use of their superior weapons. Hundreds of Spaniards and thousands of Tlascalans were cut down. Scores were captured, to be sacrificed later to the Aztec gods. The heaviest losses occurred at the openings in the causeway, where the Indians had raised the drawbridges. Less than half of those who started reached the mainland, and all of the cannon and most of the precious horses were gone. The survivors were again attacked by the Aztecs a few days later, but this time, after a hard fight, they won a sanguinary victory. They then marched to Tlascala, where their faithful allies received them with undiminished friendship.

Cortez still refused to abandon his purpose. After a short rest he proceeded to restore Spanish prestige and the morale of his forces by a series of successful raids against allies of the Aztec confederacy. He also received much needed reinforcements and supplies, for a number of men whom Velásquez had sent to join Narváez were persuaded to join him, and other adventurers, attracted by reports of the wealth of Mexico, were beginning to arrive. One of these was a Negro ill with smallpox. This disease, hitherto unknown among the Indians, soon spread throughout Mexico, carrying off vast numbers of people and undermining the Aztecs' power of resistance. Cuitlahua was among those who died, and his nephew Guatémoc took his place.

By the end of 1520 Cortez was again ready to attack Tenochtitlán. He defeated, or won over by diplomacy, several of the tribes hitherto allied with the Aztecs, and occupied the points where the causeways reached the mainland. More important still, he launched on the lake a fleet of small vessels that had been built at Tlascala and brought in pieces from that city by 8,000 Indian carriers. An incipient revolt in his own forces, inspired by friends of Velásquez, was discovered and suppressed. In May, 1521, he began active operations against the Aztec capital. The causeways and the aqueduct that supplied the city with fresh water were seized and a part of the city itself was occupied. The Indians fought so savagely that progress was slow. On one occasion some fifty Spaniards were captured and sacrificed in plain view of their horrified comrades. The invaders were not to be turned back, however, and the terrific losses inflicted by their firearms and pikes combined with suffering from lack of food and water to bring about the collapse of all resistance on August 13. Hardly more than desolate ruins were left. The Spaniards found disappointingly little treasure, although they cruelly tortured Guatémoc in an effort to compel him to reveal where more was hidden.

Cortez' persistent effort to obtain the approval of the Crown now met with success. He had so far had the worst of the contest between his emissaries and those of Diego Velásquez at the court in Spain. Bishop Fonseca, the official most concerned with affairs in the Indies, had in fact sent an official to Mexico in 1521 to investigate his conduct, but Cortez had refused on specious pretexts to recognize the commissioner's authority and had bribed him to return to Spain. With the fall of Tenochtitlán, the conqueror of Mexico had become so powerful that prudence as well as gratitude counseled a recognition of his services. In 1522, therefore, the Emperor formally appointed him Governor, Captain General, and Chief Justice of the new colony. Cortez was thus free to turn his restless energy to the work of reconstruction and the completion of the conquest. The new city of Mexico rose on the ruins of Tenochtitlán, and the tribes in the neighborhood were rapidly reduced to submission.

In 1523–24 Cortez sent two expeditions into Central America. The first, under Pedro de Alvarado, overcame the Maya tribes in the highlands of Guatemala after some hard fighting. Alvarado later became governor of the colony that he established there. The other, led by Cristóbal de Olid, was less successful. Olid repudiated his allegiance to Cortez and imprisoned Francisco de las Casas, who had been sent by Cortez to reduce him to obedience. He then captured Gil González Dávila, who had landed on the north coast of Honduras with an expedition from Santo Domingo. Las Casas and González, however, escaped and killed Olid just before Cortez himself arrived in Honduras, after a long and difficult overland journey, and was cordially welcomed by all factions.

Cortez was soon compelled to return to Mexico, where things were going badly in his absence. His enemies had again persuaded the Emperor to send an officer to investigate his conduct. Though this investigation produced no result, because both the commissioner and his successor opportunely died, Cortez decided to go to Spain in an attempt to clear himself. There he obtained a title and the grant of great estates in Mexico, but the Emperor had already decided to reduce his authority in the government. An *audiencia*, a commission of five judges, was created in 1527 to take charge of civil affairs, and in 1529 the Emperor appointed Antonio de Mendoza Viceroy of Mexico. Mendoza proved to be one of the ablest administrators in Spanish colonial history, and after his arrival in 1535 Cortez had little further influence in the colony's affairs. He busied himself for some years in attempts to explore the coast northwest of Mexico, but his luck seemed to have deserted him and he finally returned to Spain, where he died in 1547.

Meanwhile, the conquest of Central America had been completed, chiefly by expeditions from Panama. Gil González Dávila had explored Nicaragua in 1522, and two years later Pedrarias, the governor at Panama, sent Francisco Hernández de Córdoba to conquer the country. Hernández de Córdoba defeated the Indians and founded the towns of

León and Granada, but when he attempted to claim the province for himself the aged Pedrarias suddenly appeared on the scene and beheaded him. Soon afterward Pedrarias obtained an appointment as Governor of Nicaragua, having recently been supplanted in his post at Panama. His efforts to establish his control over Honduras as well brought him into conflict with Cortez' representatives, and the situation became more confused when a new governor appeared with a commission from the royal authorities at Santo Domingo. For some years intermittent armed strife between the various factions made the history of Central America a gloomy one.

The Conquest of Peru

Spaniards exploring the Pacific coast below Panama had soon heard vague stories of a great and rich empire far to the south, and in 1524 Francisco Pizarro, an illiterate adventurer who had been prominent in the affairs of the colony on the Isthmus since its first establishment, was given command of an expedition to investigate them. To obtain resources for the enterprise, Pizarro formed a partnership with Diego de Almagro, another adventurer of the same type, and a priest at Panama named Hernando de Luque. Almagro was to help in the work of exploration, whereas Luque, who did not live to see his partners' final triumph, was helpful in raising funds.

Two small ships were obtained and Pizarro set out in one of them in November, 1524. The weather at that season was especially unfavorable and he struggled for ten weeks against head winds and currents without reaching any well-settled region where he could replenish his provisions. He finally had to send the ship back to Panama, while he and the greater part of his men waited on the shore, almost starving on a diet of seaweed and palm nuts. When the ship returned, he went on down the coast, but a costly encounter with savage Indians convinced him that he could accomplish nothing without a larger force and he turned back to Panama. Almagro, who followed with the other ship, also had bad luck, and of 180 men who sailed with the two leaders only some fifty survived.

The partners were nevertheless able, with some difficulty, to raise money and enlist men for a new expedition which left Panama in 1526. This time they reached the more populous districts along the Ecuadorean coast and were so encouraged by what they saw that Pizarro decided to remain on the small island of Gallo, in the Bay of Tumaco, while Almagro returned for reinforcements. When Almagro reached Panama, however, he met with a heart-breaking disappointment. Pedro de los Rios, the new governor, not only refused to permit the recruiting of additional men but sent a ship to bring back those who had remained with Pizarro.

There was a dramatic scene at Gallo when the ship arrived. Pizarro refused to obey the governor's order to return, and sixteen of his companions responded to his eloquent appeal not to abandon the undertaking in which they had already suffered so much. The little group were to suffer still more in the months that ensued, but their associates at Panama finally obtained permission to send a ship to relieve them and to continue, though only for six months, the exploration of the coast.

This was the turning-point in Pizarro's fortunes. In the time that the governor allowed him he reached northern Peru and saw unmistakable evidences of the wealth and the high civilization of the Inca Empire. The natives seemed fairly friendly, and the explorers were able to obtain gold and silver and fine textiles, and even llamas, to convince the incredulous at home of the truth of their story. They also carried off two Peruvians, who were valuable later as interpreters.

There could no longer be any question of the importance of their discoveries, but the partners had exhausted their resources and their credit and the governor was still unfriendly. It was decided, therefore, that Pizarro should go to Spain to seek the support of the Crown. His efforts were successful and a royal capitulation, signed July 26, 1529, authorized him to conquer and settle the coast for a distance of two hundred leagues south from the Gulf of Guayaquil. Pizarro was promised a life appointment as Governor and Captain General of this territory. The Crown provided a substantial sum toward the expenses of the new expedition, freed those settling in Peru from certain taxes for a period of years, and authorized Pizarro to distribute land and *encomiendas* of Indians in the territory that he might conquer.

After enlisting several followers in Spain, including his brothers, Hernando, Gonzalo, and Juan, Pizarro returned to Panama. In January, 1531, he sailed from that port with 180 men and twenty-seven horses, in three ships. Landing in northern Ecuador, he proceeded along the coast, finding much gold and silver and meeting with little resistance. The ships meanwhile were sent back for reinforcements, which arrived in small groups as the march continued. At the populous island of Puna, in the Gulf of Guayaquil, the natives were at first friendly, and the

Spaniards remained among them for some time, resting and gathering information. When the Indians began to show signs of hostility, they were defeated with much slaughter and Pizarro then crossed to the mainland and entered what is now Peru. A city, which he named San Miguel, was founded to serve as a base of operations, and the Indians nearby were divided in *encomiendas* among the fifty-five soldiers who became its first citizens.

The Spaniards could hardly have proceeded so far without encountering serious resistance had it not been for events that had recently occurred in Peru. The Inca Empire had reached the height of its power shortly before they arrived. Huayna Capac, who lived to receive reports of Pizarro's first expeditions along the coast, had completed the conquest of what is now Ecuador and had devoted much of his life to the consolidation of his authority there. He had been much troubled by rebellions in the recently acquired territories, and it was perhaps a feeling that the empire had grown too large to be controlled from Cuzco which led him to arrange for the division of his possessions after his death. Atahualpa, his son by a princess of the royal family of Quito, was given the territory that his mother's ancestors had ruled, and Huascar, the legitimate heir, succeeded to the throne at Cuzco. It was not long before the two brothers quarreled and war began. Huascar was defeated and made prisoner, and many Incas of the blood royal were massacred. When Pizarro arrived, Atahualpa, who had assumed the crimson fringe of the *Sapa Inca*, was not yet firmly established on the throne, and the imperial government's control in outlying, recently conquered districts, like those through which the Spaniards first marched, was doubtless relaxed.

The Spaniards had already heard much of the civil war and had learned that Atahualpa was at Cajamarca, ten or twelve days' journey from San Miguel, with a large army. Pizarro, therefore, resumed his southward march, proceeding slowly from one valley to another along the coast and then over the mountains to meet the Emperor. On the way, he received envoys with gifts and a friendly message from Atahualpa. The storehouses along the Inca road provided ample food and lodging, but the Spaniards suffered much from cold and altitude when they crossed the coastal range and were not a little alarmed lest the troops of the Indians should attack them in the narrow defiles. They finally reached Cajamarca, on November 15, 1532, and took up their quarters in stone buildings surrounding the plaza in the center of the town. With his little force of sixty-two horsemen and 102 foot-soldiers, Pizarro calmly laid his plans for the defeat of an army that numbered, according to his Indian guides, fifty thousand men. The Inca's encampment, two or three miles away, was clearly visible.

Hernando Pizarro and Hernando de Soto, the future discoverer of the Mississippi, were sent to speak with Atahualpa and returned with a promise that the Inca would visit the newcomers on the following day. It was evening before he came, accompanied by a vast force of soldiers. What followed is best told in the words of Pizarro's secretary, Francisco de Xerés: [1]

The Governor ordered all the Spaniards to arm themselves secretly in their lodgings, and to keep the horses saddled and bridled, and under the orders of three captains, but none were to show themselves in the open space. The Captain of the artillery was ordered to have his guns pointed towards the enemy on the plain, and, when the time came, to fire. Men were stationed in the streets leading to the open space, and, taking twenty men with him, the Governor went to his lodging. These had the duty entrusted to them of seizing the person of Atabaliba [Atahualpa], if he should come cautiously with so large a force as was coming; but the Governor ordered that he should be taken alive. All the troops had orders not to leave their quarters, even if the enemy should enter the open space, until they should hear the guns fired off. The sentries were to be on the alert, and, if they saw that the enemy intended treachery, they were to give the signal; and all were to sally out of the lodgings, the cavalry mounted, when they heard the cry of *Santiago*.

. . . .

Soon the van of the enemy began to enter the open space. First came a squadron of Indians dressed in a livery of different colors, like a chess board. They advanced, removing the straws from the ground, and sweeping the road. Next came three squadrons in different dresses, dancing and singing. Then came a number of men with armour, large metal plates, and crowns of gold and silver. Among them was Atabaliba in a litter lined with plumes of macaws' feathers, of many colours, and adorned with plates of gold and silver. Many Indians carried it on their shoulders on high. Next came two other litters and two hammocks, in which were some principal chiefs; and lastly, several squadrons of Indians with crowns of gold and silver.

Father Valverde, the chaplain of the expedition, went forward and spoke briefly to the Inca about the Christian religion, handing him a copy of the Bible. This Atahualpa threw to the ground, with a scornful demand that the Christians return at once the cloths which they had

[1] The quotations are from Sir Clements Markham's translation of Francisco de Xerés' *Narrative of the Conquest of Peru*, in Volume 47 of the Publications of the Hakluyt Society, London, 1872, pp. 51 ff.

taken from the storehouses along the road. When Valverde reported what had happened to Pizarro,

. . . the Governor put on a jacket of cotton, took his sword and dagger, and, with the Spaniards who were with him, entered among the Indians most valiantly; and, with only four men who were able to follow him, he came to the litter where Atabaliba was, and fearlessly seized him by the arm, crying out *Santiago*. Then the guns were fired off, the trumpets were sounded, and the troops, both horse and foot, sallied forth.

Within a few minutes Atahualpa had been captured and some thousands of his followers had been killed.

During the whole time no Indian raised his arms against a Spaniard. So great was the terror of the Indians at seeing the Governor force his way through them, at hearing the fire of the artillery, and beholding the charging of the horses, a thing never before heard of, that they thought more of flying to save their lives than of fighting.

The captive Inca was treated with consideration, eating at Pizarro's table and sleeping in the governor's own room. He soon learned some Spanish, and told his captors much about the affairs of Peru. His authority among his subjects seemed little diminished, and the safe conducts that he gave enabled small groups of Spaniards to visit Cuzco and other parts of the empire without molestation. Atahualpa's first thought was naturally to regain his liberty. To this end he offered as a ransom gold sufficient to fill a room twenty-two feet long and seventeen wide, up to a line eight or nine feet from the floor, and enough silver to fill another smaller room twice over. Pizarro agreed to this proposal, and the Indians during the next few weeks brought great quantities of precious vessels and ornaments from palaces and temples. The full amount was not perhaps completed, but Pizarro accepted it, and a treasure worth at the lowest estimate some millions of dollars was divided among the members of the expedition according to their rank and services. The King's share of one-fifth was set aside as the law required, and another portion was given to Almagro and his followers, who had just arrived from Panama.

The Inca, however, was not released. His faithless captors had decided that his death would be expedient, and he was placed on trial for a long series of offenses ranging from adultery and idolatry to murder and rebellion. Of murder, he was probably guilty, for his brother the ex-Inca Huascar had been drowned, presumably by order of Atahualpa, soon after the latter had fallen into Pizarro's hands. The trial was a mere formality, and the Inca was publicly executed in the plaza of Cajamarca on August 29, 1533.

With his force augmented by the men whom Almagro had brought, Pizarro now undertook the long and difficult march through the mountains to Cuzco. The Spaniards encountered some opposition along the way, but none at the capital itself. There they obtained more treasure, and set up a city government in the name of the King. They also installed as Inca a brother of Huascar named Manco, for a younger brother of Atahualpa, who had been invested with the royal fringe after the latter's execution, had died on the road to Cuzco.

By this time reports of the riches of Peru were reaching the outside world, and arousing the interest of the hordes of adventurers in the older settlements of the Indies who were always on the lookout for an opportunity to improve their lot. The forces of Pizarro and Almagro were constantly augmented by new arrivals and their hold on the conquered territory became gradually stronger. They had been at Cuzco only a few months, however, when they received alarming news. Pedro de Alvarado, the conqueror of Guatemala, had conceived the idea of obtaining for himself the region of Quito, and had landed at the Bay of Caráquez in March, 1534, with five hundred Spaniards and two thousand Indians—an army stronger than any which Pizarro could well hope to send against him. Almagro at once left Cuzco for the north to deal with this invasion of the partners' rights. He found that Quito had already been occupied by Sebastián de Belalcázar, the commander of the garrison at San Miguel. The combined forces of the two leaders were still smaller than Alvarado's, but the latter's men were worn down by hunger and the exposure that they had suffered while crossing the mountains. They showed little wish to fight, especially when they learned how small a quantity of treasure had been found at Quito, and realized how much more attractive their prospects would be if they joined Almagro and Pizarro in the south. Alvarado was rather easily induced to sell out his whole expedition for 100,000 *pesos de oro* and to return to his own domain in Guatemala.

Meanwhile, Hernando Pizarro had reached Spain with the royal share of Atahualpa's ransom and had persuaded the King to extend the limits of his brother's territory to a point seventy leagues farther south. At the same time Almagro was given a domain of his own extending two hundred leagues down the coast beyond Pizarro's grant. The jealousy that had long existed between the two partners was revived by this arrangement, for Cuzco lay near the borderline and was claimed by both. Each was hotly supported by his own followers and actual fighting occurred before an agreement reached in June, 1535, averted further conflict for the time being but left the main question undecided. Soon afterward, Almagro left Cuzco with a strong force to undertake the conquest of Chile, which was indisputably his. Pizarro returned to the coast where he had been engaged since the first of the year in building the new City of the Kings, now called Lima, which was soon to become the chief center of Spanish power in South America.

The dissensions among the conquistadores, and the weakness of the force that remained after Almagro's departure, encouraged the Inca Manco to make a last desperate effort to drive the Spaniards from Peru. The Indians of the whole highland area suddenly rose in arms, and Hernando Pizarro was besieged at Cuzco for several months in 1536. Four relief expeditions which Francisco sent from Lima were defeated with heavy losses, but with the approach of the planting season Manco could no longer hold his forces together. He retired to Ollantaytambo and in 1537 he was defeated by the force which Almagro had just brought back from Chile. This ended the revolt, though Manco escaped into the fastnesses of the eastern slope of the Andes and continued for some years to commit depredations against the Spaniards.

Almagro had returned to begin the first of a series of civil wars in which many of the conquerors of Peru were to lose their lives. He had found nothing in Chile to console him for the loss of his rights in Peru. The journey through the desolate and sparsely inhabited Andean highlands had been a trying one even for men inured to hardships, and the fertile soil and delightful climate of central Chile offered little attraction to adventurers whose appetites had been whetted by the gold and silver of the Incas. Almagro was easily persuaded by his followers to return to reassert his claim to Cuzco. The trip back, through the waterless deserts of the coast, was even more difficult than that through the mountains, but his forces were none the less ready to fight when they reached southern Peru. After defeating Manco they occupied Cuzco, in violation of a truce arranged a short time before, and imprisoned Hernando and Gonzalo Pizarro. Gonzalo soon escaped, but Hernando was not released until his brother Francisco had agreed that Almagro should hold Cuzco until the King decided to whom it belonged. Such agreements meant nothing to men like the conquerors of Peru, and Francisco Pizarro renewed the war as soon as his brother was free. Almagro's forces were defeated in the battle of Las Salinas, near Cuzco, on April 6, 1538, and Almagro himself was captured and put to death.

Pizarro did not long enjoy the fruits of his victory. His harsh treatment of the defeated party kept alive the bitter feeling between the two factions. The "men of Chile," as they were derisively called, were deprived of their estates and their *encomiendas,* and they became desperate when they heard an untrue report that a royal official who was on his way to Peru to look into the recent occurrences had perished in a shipwreck. On June 26, 1541, a group of them killed Francisco Pizarro in his own house and forced the cabildo of Lima to recognize Almagro's young son, Diego, as governor of Peru.

Vaca de Castro, the King's representative, had indeed been shipwrecked, but he reached shore and continued his journey overland. He had been authorized by the King to assume the governorship in case of Pizarro's death, and the Pizarro faction at once recognized his authority. Almagro retired to Cuzco, asserting that the city belonged to him under the Crown's grant to his father, but his forces were defeated in a bloody battle near that city on September 16, 1542, and the young leader and many of his advisers were executed as rebels.

There were further disorders when the Spanish government promulgated the "New Laws of the Indies" [1] a few months later. These laws, which provided for the gradual abolition of *encomiendas* and outlawed other abuses against the Indians, aroused a storm of protest in all the American colonies. In Mexico, the royal officials wisely suspended their operation, but in Peru, a new viceroy, Blasco Núñez Vela, attempted to enforce them. The turbulent and greedy adventurers who had flocked to the country in the hope of sharing the spoils of conquest were little disposed to submit to anything that interfered with the gratification of their ambitions, and the viceroy's ill-judged and tactless actions soon produced a revolt. In October, 1544, Gonzalo Pizarro occupied Lima at the head of a rebel army and forced the *audiencia,* or high court, to recognize him as governor. The viceroy continued the war in northern Peru, but he was killed in January, 1546, in a battle near Quito.

Before Núñez Vela's death, the King ordered a priest named Pedro de la Gasca to go to Lima as president of the *audiencia* to reassert the royal authority. La Gasca had no forces at his disposal, but at Panama

[1] See below, pp. 60–61.

he succeeded in winning over the commander of Gonzalo Pizarro's fleet. He then sent messages promising a free pardon to those who returned to their allegiance and announcing the suspension of the most objectionable provisions of the New Laws, and when he reached Peru the rebel army gradually melted away. Gonzalo Pizarro was captured and executed in April, 1548, and La Gasca remained at the head of the government until he returned to Spain in 1550.

The viceroy of Mexico, Antonio de Mendoza, was appointed to the same office in Peru in 1551, but he died ten months after his arrival and left the government in the hands of the *audiencia*. This body was too weak to control the unruly Spanish settlers, many of whom were discontented because they had not received *encomiendas*. There were further disturbances, and a rebellion under Francisco Hernández Girón, in 1553–54, was not put down until after the royal forces, led by the archbishop and the senior judge of the *audiencia*, had suffered humiliating defeats. The disorder and bloodshed that had characterized Peru since the beginning of the Conquest was finally brought to an end by Andrés Hurtado de Mendoza, the Marquis of Cañete, who took office as viceroy in 1556.

New Granada

The most important region that remained to be conquered after the occupation of Peru was the highlands of New Granada. This was one of the most inaccessible portions of South America, shut off from the outside world by rugged, heavily forested mountain ranges to the west and by hundreds of miles of swamp and jungle in the Magdalena Valley to the north. The coast, on the Caribbean side, had been explored at an early date and had been much frequented by pearl fishers and slave hunters, but the deadly climate and the implacable hostility of the Indians made the region unattractive to colonists.

A few settlements had nevertheless been established. In Venezuela, Cubagua Island, the center of the pearl fisheries, was the scene of much activity until the oyster beds began to give out about 1535. The town of Cumaná, on the mainland, had been founded about 1520. In 1529 the Emperor Charles, who ruled over much of Germany as well as Spain, granted a large section of the Venezuelan coast to the Welsers of Augsburg, and this banking firm sent out a mixed company of German,

Spanish, and Portuguese adventurers to take possession of the territory. These explored much of the hinterland, and one party, as we shall see, reached the Chibcha country in the interior. The colony nevertheless did not thrive. The German leaders' cruel treatment of the Indians aroused much criticism and the company's grant was rescinded in 1546.

Farther west, Santa Marta had been established in 1525 and Cartagena in 1533. In 1535, Pedro Fernández de Lugo, a member of a powerful Spanish family, was made governor of these settlements and came out to the colony with a large following. He at once began to explore the surrounding country, and in April, 1536, the colony's chief magistrate, Gonzalo Jiménez de Quesada, set out to investigate reports of a nation of civilized Indians far in the interior.

Quesada went overland from Santa Marta to the Magdalena River while boats carrying supplies were sent around by sea. From the point where the two groups met, he marched southward through the jungle along the river bank, suffering from heavy rains and the attacks of insects, and often from hunger. Eight months after the expedition left Santa Marta, a large part of his force had perished from starvation, disease, and the attacks of the Indians, and no sign of human habitation had been seen for a month. Quesada's companions wished to return, but he insisted upon pushing on. The boats were sent back down the river with the sick and wounded, and the leader, with 200 picked men and sixty horses, began the tedious and dangerous ascent from the river valley into the mountains, now confronting the new enemies of cold and exposure. It was not long before the party came out upon the broad plateau of Bogotá, where cultivated fields and human habitations told them that they were near their goal.

They had reached the country of the Chibchas, and they were soon attacked by a large army under the Zipa, the ruler of Bogotá. Quesada won an easy victory, for the Indians were terrified by the Spanish cavalry, and then proceeded to Tunja, where the other great Chibcha chief, the Zaque, was likewise defeated and captured. Here the invaders found a great treasure in gold and emeralds. Soon afterward the Indians ceased their resistance and begged for help in repelling an attack by their savage neighbors the Panches, whom they feared more than the Spaniards. A successful campaign against the Panches made Quesada master of the plateau region, but he was not satisfied with the treasure which he had obtained, and the Zipa, who had joined the Spaniards as an ally, was tortured to death in a vain effort to force him to disclose where his wealth was hidden.

In 1538, Quesada founded the city of Santa Fe de Bogotá, where he proposed to leave a part of his forces while he returned to Spain to give an account of his conquest. He was preparing for the journey when he was astonished to learn that another group of white men had appeared on the plateau. This was an expedition from the German colony in Venezuela, led by Nikolaus Federmann, which had reached the highlands by way of the upper tributaries of the Orinoco—an exploit hardly less remarkable than that of Quesada himself. At almost the same time Sebastián de Belalcázar, coming from Quito, appeared on the banks of the upper Magdalena. He had already conquered the important tribes of western Colombia, and he now laid claim to the Chibcha territory as a part of the King's grant to Pizarro. Ordinarily such an encounter between rival explorers would have resulted in bloodshed, but the three leaders finally reached a friendly agreement to lay their case before the King in Spain. They departed for the coast together, leaving a strong force to hold the newly conquered territory.

All of them were disappointed, for the Crown decided to place Bogotá under the governor of Santa Marta. Alonso Luis de Lugo, the son of Fernando, had absconded to Spain with a large sum of money, defrauding both his father and the royal treasury, and he was at court when Quesada and his companions arrived. He had just acquired the right to the governorship of Santa Marta by reason of his father's death, and he enjoyed so much influence at court, through his relationship by marriage with the Emperor's secretary, that he was able not only to obtain immunity for past misdeeds but to deprive the conquerors of New Granada of the fruits of their toil. Belalcázar was somewhat consoled by an appointment as governor of Popayán, but Quesada and Federmann got nothing. Quesada was finally permitted to return to Bogotá in an honorable official position and he died there in 1579.

Early Settlements in the River Plate Region

The River Plate, discovered by Solís in 1516, was further explored by Sebastian Cabot between 1527 and 1530. The first real attempt at permanent occupation was made by Pedro de Mendoza, who left Spain with a large expedition in 1535 and, early in the following year, founded a settlement which he named Nuestra Señora de Buen Ayre. Mendoza's chief purpose was to open up communications with Peru, and an expedition which he sent up the Paraná and Paraguay rivers, under Juan de Ayolas, is said to have reached the Inca territory and to have been returning laden with treasure when it was wiped out by the Indians in the wilderness. This was but one of many misfortunes that beset the new colony. Other expeditions into the interior accomplished little, and Mendoza himself fell ill and died in 1537 while on his way back to Spain. The Spaniards could not conquer the nomadic pampa tribes, whose raids made life in the little settlement almost intolerable.

A part of Ayolas' expedition had stayed in what is now Paraguay, and had fared somewhat better. Partly by diplomacy and partly by force, the Spaniards were able to dominate the peaceable Guaranís and most of them married native women. Domingo Martínez de Irala, the founder of Asunción, had taken as wives the seven daughters of one of the principal Indian chiefs. Far in the interior of the continent, the colony had little contact with Spain, and the colonists claimed the right, under a royal order sent them after Mendoza's death, to choose their own governor in the absence of the King's appointee. Irala was the first person so chosen. The great explorer Alvar Núñez Cabeza de Vaca came out from Spain as governor in 1542, but the colonists deposed him two years later, and Irala was reëlected, to serve until his death in 1556.

The settlement at Asunción gradually expanded. Juan de Garay founded Santa Fe in 1573 and resettled Buenos Aires in 1580, giving the colony a seaport that soon had a larger population than Asunción itself. Even Buenos Aires, however, was a relatively unimportant town until late in the colonial period, because few immigrants would go to a region that had neither precious metals nor useful Indians. The one source of wealth was the great herds of wild and half wild horses and cattle. A number of horses left behind by Mendoza's followers when they abandoned the first settlement at Buenos Aires had multiplied amazingly in the grassy pampas, and the horned cattle imported a little later had been hardly less prolific.

The northwestern and western parts of modern Argentina were settled not from Buenos Aires and Asunción but from Peru and Chile. The northwest, with its relatively advanced Indian population, had been a part of the Inca Empire, and its chief cities, including the important town of Córdoba, were founded by expeditions from Peru.

Mendoza and the nearby towns in the west, on the other hand, were settled from Chile, and long formed a part of that province.

Valdivia in Chile

Chile was conquered by Pizarro's lieutenant Pedro de Valdivia, who left Cuzco early in 1540 with a small force of Spaniards and a thousand Indian auxiliaries. Since Valdivia planned to establish a permanent settlement, he took with him seeds, domestic animals, and agricultural implements. The journey across the deserts of the coast was long and arduous, but the party finally reached the first irrigated valley, where Copiapó now stands, and formally took possession of the country. The Indians were sullen and refused to furnish food, but they offered little resistance, and Valdivia pushed on until he reached the northern end of the great central valley, then as now the most populous and fertile part of Chile. Here, on February 12, 1541, he founded a city which he called Santiago de la Nueva Estremadura—a vain attempt to cause the colony's earlier name, associated as it was with poverty and failure, to be forgotten.

At first the colony did not prosper. A few gold and silver mines were discovered, and an effort was made to raise crops, but the natives were unwilling and intractable laborers. A few months after the colonists had established themselves at Santiago the Indians revolted and burned most of the new city before they were overcome. It was clear that more men and greater resources would be needed to hold the colony and to conquer the fertile regions south of Santiago, and Valdivia determined to return to Peru to obtain recruits and supplies. Since he could not succeed in such a mission without money, he offered to permit those of his followers who had accumulated a little more gold and silver than their comrades to return to Peru with their wealth, and then, when the treasure had been placed on board his ship, quietly slipped away without its owners. He reached Lima just in time to help La Gasca suppress Gonzalo Pizarro's rebellion, and thus not only won the viceroy's favor but gained a prestige which was helpful in obtaining recruits for his own enterprise.

Returning to Chile, Valdivia led a force southward from Santiago as far as the Bio-Bio River, where he founded the city of Concepción in 1550. Here he came into contact with the savage Araucanians, a rude nation of hunters with little organized government outside of the temporary confederacies that they formed for war. These Indians had defied the Incas, and it was to be more than 300 years before they were finally conquered by the Spaniards. Valdivia at first defeated them after severe fighting, and established several forts and towns, including that which still bears his name, in and near their territory. In 1553, however, the Indians rose in rebellion under a young chief named Lautaro, who had for a time been employed by Valdivia as a stable boy. They had learned to seek cover against firearms and to dispose their forces so that the Spanish cavalry was of little use, and when Valdivia marched against them he was captured and killed.

During the next four years, Lautaro destroyed most of the new Spanish settlements. At one time he penetrated almost to Santiago, but it was difficult for him to persuade his unorganized troops to leave their own homes and their scanty crops for a long campaign, and an epidemic of disease reduced the fighting population. Fortunately for the Spaniards, moreover, the Indians in the northern part of the central valley showed no inclination to join the Araucanians. Lautaro was finally defeated and killed, and his followers withdrew beyond the Bio-Bio, which was the frontier between the Indian and the Spanish settlements throughout the colonial period.

Other Explorers

We can hardly leave the story of the Conquest without mentioning a few of the other great feats of exploration that added to the world's knowledge of the new continent in the second quarter of the sixteenth century. The reports of Cortez and Pizarro not only drew great numbers of fortune seekers to the territories that they had conquered, but encouraged many others to fit out expeditions to seek for new Mexicos and Perus in regions hitherto unexplored. Some were partially successful; more, perhaps, came to grief. Only a few can be described here.

One of the most notable was the journey of Alvar Núñez Cabeza de Vaca, who accompanied Cortez' former rival Pánfilo de Narváez on an expedition to Florida in 1528. Most of the party perished when they lost touch with their ships and attempted to return to Mexico in boats that they built themselves, but Cabeza de Vaca and a few other survivors made their way overland to the coast of Texas. There they were captured and held for some years as slaves by the Indians. Cabeza de Vaca and three companions finally escaped. During their capitivity they had acquired a great reputation as healers and sorcerers, and great hordes of Indians followed them as they made their way westward on foot across the continent to the Pacific, a ten-months' journey. They reached Mexico in 1536. Cabeza de Vaca was so far from being discouraged that he later obtained the post of Governor of Paraguay and made other remarkable journeys from the Brazilian coast to Asunción and from Asunción to the borders of Peru.

Cabeza de Vaca's story revived interest in rumors already current about great cities to the north of the country through which he had passed, and in 1540–42 Francisco de Coronado made a long and unprofitable journey through the southwestern part of the United States as far as Kansas in search of them. About the same time, between 1539 and 1542, Pizarro's former lieutenant Hernando de Soto was exploring a great area from South Carolina to Arkansas and discovering the Mississippi River. De Soto died of fever, after three years in the wilderness. The principal result of these two expeditions, perhaps, was to show that there was nothing to attract Spanish settlers in what is now the southern part of the United States.

In South America there were several expeditions into the low-lying, sparsely inhabited region east of the Andes. *El Dorado* was long believed to lie somewhere in the upper part of the Orinoco Valley, and many lives were lost in fruitless exploration of the inhospitable *llanos,* where heavy rains made travel difficult during several months of each year.

One further expedition must be mentioned. In 1539 Gonzalo Pizarro, who was then governor of Quito, set out eastward from that city in search of lands said to be rich in cinnamon and other precious spices. The party met with terrific obstacles in crossing the Andes and descending into the jungles at their base, and they were in desperate straits when they reached one of the larger tributaries of the Amazon. A boat that had been built to carry the sick and the baggage was finally sent ahead down the river in search of food. Pizarro entrusted the command to Francisco de Orellana, who seized the opportunity to win fame for himself by an act of treachery. Leaving the men with Pizarro to shift for themselves, Orellana and his companions went on down the river and then down the much larger stream which they soon reached. Among the Indians with whom they had encounters along the way there were some whose women fought as fiercely as the men, and it was from these that the Amazon received its name. With great good luck

Orellana and his companions finally reached the sea in 1541 and made their way to Spain by way of the West Indies to receive credit for their exploit. Gonzalo Pizarro, with the remnants of his party, did not get back to Quito until 1542.

So brief a sketch, covering as it does only a few of the more important expeditions, can convey but an inadequate idea of the amazing story of the Spanish conquest of America. To have any real conception of the dangers and hardships that the conquistadores encountered, or of the courage and persistence with which they faced them, one must read the accounts of those who actually participated in their expeditions, like the fascinating *True History of the Conquest of New Spain* by Bernal Díaz del Castillo. The physical obstacles—the all but impassable, disease-infested jungles of the lowlands, the waterless deserts of the South American coast, and the precipitous slopes of the Andes —were if anything more formidable than the resistance of overwhelmingly more numerous Indian armies. We cannot but admire the audacity with which little bands of Spaniards boldly embarked upon the conquest of unknown empires, even when we are shocked by their cruelty and treachery to the Indians and to one another. The outstanding qualities of the successful conquistadores were their bravery and their brutality, their crusading zeal and their sordid greed, their ability to command the confidence of their followers, coupled with their ruthless lack of scruple in dealing with rivals.

3

The People of the Spanish Colonies

In the quarter century that followed the conquest of Mexico, most of the vast area that was to be known as Spanish America was conquered or at least explored. There were European settlements throughout the highlands from Mexico to Chile. Most of the towns had but a few score or at most a few hundred white inhabitants, but they were the centers from which large numbers of Indians in the surrounding country were governed and exploited. They grew in size as the settlers raised families and as new immigrants arrived from Spain.

The great majority of the colonists were engaged in stock-raising or in agriculture. When a town was founded, each *vecino*, or citizen, was given a grant of land: a *peonía* adequate for the support of a family if he were an ordinary person, or a *caballería*, a larger tract, if he were of higher rank. Greater estates were obtained by persons who had wealth or influence. Much of the land was used for pasturing horses, cattle, and sheep, which were introduced in the first years of the Conquest and increased with great rapidity. Where farming was carried on, old world crops like wheat, bananas, and sugar cane were grown along with the plants that the Indians had cultivated before the Conquest. Nearly all of the produce was consumed locally or in nearby towns and mining camps. Mining was another occupation that employed large numbers of people, and it was an especially important one because it provided the colonies' principal exports.

Indian Labor

Nearly all of the Spanish settlements were in regions where there were large settled Indian populations. Unlike the British colonists

58

farther north, the Spaniards came to America as conquerors, a ruling class that expected to appropriate the wealth and exploit the labor of the native inhabitants. They were little interested in fertile, temperate areas like the River Plate and what is now the territory of the United States, because the Indians were too few and too savage to be utilized as workers. Even the early settlements in the West Indies were almost abandoned after the extinction of the aborigines there. By far the most important of the Spanish colonies were in the former realms of the Incas and the Aztecs, or in other countries, like Guatemala and New Granada, where the Indians had been relatively civilized.

In all these territories the Indians had been effectively subjugated. Most of them had accepted the outward forms of Christianity. The ruling classes were either destroyed or won over to the new order. There were occasional local revolts, but the Indians never showed themselves capable of any concerted resistance to Spanish rule. The native population seems to have decreased greatly during and after the Conquest, for it was particularly susceptible to some of the diseases that the Spaniards brought, and there must have been much suffering from the dislocation of the old economic and social organization. Some millions of Indians nevertheless remained, and they were an all-important factor in the colonies' economic life. The establishment of a workable relationship between them and the European settlers was one of the most difficult problems that confronted the Spanish government.

In theory, the Crown insisted that the Indians were free men and that they should work voluntarily and for fair wages. The difficulty was to persuade them to work. The idea of wages was foreign to their experience, and money meant little to them because they could satisfy their simple wants by cultivating their own land. Compulsion of some sort was necessary if the settlers were to be supported and if the mines were to be exploited. On the other hand, slavery and the *encomienda* system had practically wiped out the natives of the West Indies, and the Crown wished to preserve the people of the mainland colonies from a similar fate.

Confronted by this dilemma, the Spanish government's policy in the first half of the fifteenth century was a vacillating one. It forbade the enslavement of Indians, but then authorized exceptions in the case of cannibals and rebels. It also permitted the *rescate*, the purchase of slaves from other Indians, until it became clear that this practice gave rise to infinite fraud and abuse. Then by the New Laws of 1542 it forbade slavery altogether, and in the years that followed most of the Indians held in bondage were freed. The practice of reducing war captives to servitude nevertheless continued in some of the frontier regions throughout the colonial period.

The Encomienda

The principal means of exploiting the Indians in the first years after the Conquest was the *encomienda*.[1] This institution survived despite repeated efforts to abolish it. Cortez, who had seen its results in the islands, at first recommended that the *encomienda* should not be established in Mexico, and the royal government gave orders to this effect. Cortez changed his mind, however, when he was confronted with the need to reward his soldiers and persuade them to remain in the newly conquered territory. He granted *encomiendas* to them, and the Emperor reluctantly permitted the grants to stand, though he made another unsuccessful effort to abolish the institution after Cortez was supplanted by the *audiencia*. When Pizarro went to Peru, he was authorized to grant *encomiendas* there, so that the system was firmly implanted in both regions when still another effort to destroy it was made in the New Laws of 1542.

The New Laws were the result of a long and bitter conflict between the vested interests of the colonists and humanitarian elements at court. The Indians' most ardent defender was the Dominican friar Bartolomé de las Casas, who had been an *encomendero* in Española and Cuba until the sufferings of the natives touched his conscience and inspired him to start a lifelong campaign for their relief. Las Casas had gone to Spain in 1515 and had so impressed the regent that he returned to Santo Domingo as Protector of the Indians, with authority to bring about reforms. His efforts were defeated by the opposition of the colonists, and a settlement which he then tried to establish in Venezuela to demonstrate that a colony could succeed without enslaving Indians was a miserable failure. Thereafter he passed six years in a convent in Santo Domingo studying and writing, for he was one of the notable contemporary historians of the Conquest. In 1529 he emerged from his seclusion to continue his crusade in Spain and in various parts of the

[1] See above, p. 33.

Indies, and he finally won what seemed to be a great victory when the New Laws were issued.

These did not abolish the *encomiendas*, but they provided that no new ones should be granted and that those already in existence should revert to the Crown on the death of the holders. All officials, priests, and religious institutions were to give up their *encomiendas* at once—an important provision because many of those whose duty it was to protect the Indians in their legal rights had been personally interested in perpetuating the abuses of the system. Such abuses were henceforth to be punished, and enslavement of natives, on any pretext, was to stop. Indians who ceased to be subject to the *encomenderos* were to pay their tribute to the Crown.

There was consternation in the colonies when the provisions of the New Laws became known. The *encomiendas* were the principal form of wealth, and the holders had in most cases been granted the right to pass them on at least to their children and in many cases to subsequent generations. The former companions of Cortez and Pizarro were little disposed to give up what they had won at the cost of many perils and hardships. Feeling ran so high in Mexico that both the Viceroy Mendoza and a special representative sent to put the reforms in operation recommended that they be not enforced. In Peru, as we have seen, the colonists revolted under the leadership of Gonzalo Pizarro, and the Crown's control was not reëstablished for some years. As the result of these events, the government repealed some of the most important parts of the new code, including the clause prohibiting the granting of new *encomiendas* and the provisions against inheritance.

A majority of the Indians consequently continued for the time being under the "protection" of influential settlers. It was estimated in 1574 that 4,000 out of 32,000 Spanish families in the colonies held *encomiendas*.[1] The rest of the natives, who paid their tributes directly to the Crown, were ruled by officials called *corregidores de indios*. The proportion of Crown Indians increased as time went on, but the *encomienda* did not disappear altogether until the eighteenth century. Fortunately it was far less destructive in the mainland colonies than it had been in the Antilles. This was partly because the Indians were of a different type. In the islands, where the natives' primitive agriculture barely met their own needs for food, tribute could be exacted only

[1] Zavala, *New Viewpoints on the Spanish Colonization of America*, p. 90.

in the form of labor, and the *encomienda* had been a cruel type of slavery. In Mexico and Peru the people produced more and were accustomed to regular work. They had long paid tribute to their own overlords and priests, and some of them were perhaps little if any worse off when the conquistadores took the place of the Aztecs and the Incas. The Crown was also more successful in protecting the Indians on the mainland. Theoretically, the *encomiendas* there gave only the right to collect a fixed amount of tribute, and forbid the exaction of "personal service," so that the *encomendero* could not treat his Indians as slaves. This did not save the Indians from being compelled to work, for him or for other employers, but it saved them from some of the worst abuses of an earlier period. It is true that the prohibition against personal service, like other measures for the protection of the Indians, was not always enforced.

The tribute, which legally was the *encomenderos'* sole source of revenue from their charges, was a head tax upon male Indians of working age. Its amount varied from time to time and from place to place, and was theoretically based on ability to pay and on the amount customarily paid to native rulers before the Conquest. In parts of New Spain, it seems to have been a dollar or less at the beginning of the colonial period and somewhat more than four dollars at the end. In South America it was higher, and reached as much as ten dollars in certain regions. It might mean a week's wages or several months'. The law forbid its being commuted into labor and required that it be paid in money or produce.

The *encomendero* had obligations as well as privileges. According to the Laws of the Indies, "the motive and origin of the *encomiendas* was the spiritual and worldly welfare of the Indians, and their indoctrination and instruction in the articles and precepts of our holy Catholic faith, and that the *encomenderos* should have charge of them and defend their persons and properties, endeavoring to see that they receive no injury." [1] The *encomendero* must take oath to treat his Indians well, and was to be deprived of his position if he did not do so. One of his chief obligations was to maintain horses and weapons, since grants of Indians were made not only to reward the conquerors but to provide them with means to defend the colony. He must live in the province, and he could not sell or transfer his privileges. The man to whom the *encomienda* was granted might pass it on to his immediate heir,

---

[1] *Recopilación de leyes de los reinos de las Indias, Libro VI, Título IX, Ley I.*

or in some cases, especially in Mexico, to the third or fourth generation, but thereafter it lapsed and might be incorporated in the Crown or given to some one else.

It may be doubted whether the earlier abolition of the *encomienda* would have helped the Indians very much. The extinction of the system would have left all of them directly subject to the Crown, as a considerable number always had been, and one reason for not fully enforcing the New Laws of 1542 was probably the realization that control by the *corregidores* was about as bad from the natives' standpoint as control by the *encomenderos*. The Crown Indians paid the same tributes, and the *corregidores*, being appointed only for a short term, were apt to be more grasping and unscrupulous in collecting these than permanent overlords who had come to look on their dependents as valuable property. The *corregidores* also exploited Indian labor, often going into business on their own account or compelling the natives to work for other employers whose only aim was to get the most possible out of them in the short time that they had the Indians at their mercy.

Repartimientos and Peonage

After the outlawing of Indian slavery and of personal service in the *encomiendas*, it seemed necessary to find other means to assure a supply of labor for the mines and farms of the Spanish settlers. The Crown still desired that the Indians should work as free men, for fair wages and for employers of their own choosing, but it had been demonstrated that they would not work without compulsion. It consequently authorized *repartimientos*,[1] or drafts of labor, in places where workers were needed to cultivate the fields, to raise cattle, or to operate mines of gold, silver, mercury or emeralds. Forced labor by the Indians was permitted in these occupations because the work was necessary for the maintenance of the colonies. It was not to be used in other undertakings of a private character. *Repartimientos* were also used for public works, like the building of roads or towns or churches, and for such necessary purposes as service in inns or with wagon and mule trains. Frequently a certain proportion of the Indians in each town were required to present themselves in the market place each Monday morning

[1] *Repartimiento* means a "distribution." There has been much confusion in the use of this term because it was also used to describe the distribution of Indians among the first settlers in *encomiendas* and was later used in connection with forced sales of goods to the Indians by the *corregidores*.

to be hired for the coming week by nearby Spanish landowners and other employers. Wages and conditions of work were regulated by the authorities, and an effort was made to see that all Indians except those in privileged positions took their turn. In Peru, the system of *repartimientos* was called the *mita*, a Quechua word applied to a similar institution used by the Incas. In Mexico it was known as the *cuatequil*.

The law forbade the use of forced labor in the cultivation of coca, grapes, or olives. In certain other occupations, like the grinding of sugar cane, the preparation of indigo, and the extraction of pearls, Indians could not be employed even of their free will. The purpose of these restrictions was to protect the Indians from work that was considered too heavy for them, and to prevent the sending of people from the highlands into the hot country where they would soon die. In some cases, as in the attempt to prohibit Indian labor in textile factories, there was likewise a desire to prevent competition with producers in Spain. The restrictions were not always enforced, because Negro slaves, the only alternative source of labor, were scarce and expensive. Late in the eighteenth century, for example, Indians were still being compelled to work under shocking conditions in textile factories in Peru.

The work which bore most cruelly upon the Indians, and which, especially in South America, gave the *mita* a fearsome reputation, was that in the mines. Not only was this harder and more unhealthful, but it involved taking a large number of Indians far from their homes and forcing them to live under miserable conditions for months at a time. This caused an appalling loss of life, especially in Upper Peru, where many of the mines were in desolate and sparsely populated regions. Where the production of silver and gold was involved, the Crown's avarice seemed stronger than its desire to protect the Indians. It did, however, adopt regulations intended to prevent the complete destruction of the labor supply for the mines. In Peru, for example, only one-seventh of the Indians in a given area might be drafted for mining at one time. Such limitations, however, were hard to enforce when labor was needed. The *mita* continued in Peru until the war for independence, though many free workmen, both Indians and *mestizos* or half-breeds, were working in the mines in the last half of the eighteenth century. In Mexico the situation was better. Only one twenty-fifth of the inhabitants could be taken to the mines at one time, and living conditions were not so bad. Indeed, permanent communities of skilled laborers gradually grew up in the mining country, so that the necessity for re-cruiting forced labor finally disappeared.

Agriculture, also, became less dependent on *repartimientos* in the course of time. Employers preferred workmen who were more will-ing and who were available for longer periods, and at least as early as the seventeenth century many landowners were seeking to persuade Indians to live permanently on their *haciendas*. This was accomplished either by an advance of goods or money, which bound the Indian to work until the debt was paid, or by allowing the worker to use a piece of land in return for which he gave the landlord a stipulated number of days of labor each week. By the eighteenth century, peonage, or debt slavery, was the commonest form of relationship between em-ployer and employee. The change was hardly an improvement from the Indian's standpoint, for it was virtually impossible for him to free himself when he once fell into debt.

Efforts to Protect the Indians

Though the Spanish government refused to permit what was re-peatedly referred to as the Indians' "natural indolence" to stand in the way of its exploitation of the colonies, it made a real effort to promote their welfare and to protect them against the greed of the colonists and of its own officials. The Indians continued to live in separate com-munities, speaking their own languages and retaining much of their ancient culture. In local matters they were governed by native of-ficials who were in many cases their hereditary *caciques* or chiefs. These were a privileged class who represented the community in dealings with the Spaniards and collected the tribute due to the *encomendero* or the King. The Indians were exempted from most of the taxes paid by other classes in the community. The Crown attempted to make sure that each village had enough land for its support, and this was often administered by the local community much as it had been in Mexico and Peru before the Conquest. The royal government was particularly interested in the spiritual welfare of the natives, and priests were main-tained in each village.

Legally, the Indians had the right to move freely from place to place, and even to leave villages that had been granted in *encomiendas*, pro-vided that they paid their share of the tribute up to the time of their departure and did not try to evade payment of tribute or the fulfilment of their religious duties in their new homes.[1] In practice, this right was restricted in many ways, and especially by the Crown's policy of compelling those who lived in scattered groups to come together to found new towns where it would be easier to collect the tribute and to provide for religious instruction. The law provided that these *congregaciones* should be brought about by persuasion rather than force and that every effort should be made to assure the prosperity of the new settlements. Force was nevertheless used, and the arbitrary movement of people from one place to another caused great hardship.

The viceroys and other officials were commanded to treat the Indians with special favor and to punish offenses against them more severely than if they had been committed against Spaniards. A special court was created in Mexico for their protection, and elsewhere the *audiencias* were required to give special consideration to cases where Indians were involved. To prevent their being unfairly exploited the law provided that they could make contracts and sell property only under judicial supervision. No Spaniard, Negro, or mulatto could live in their villages, and no *encomendero* might stay among his Indians more than one night or maintain workshops or farms on their lands.

A whole series of laws prohibited specific abuses. Neither *encomenderos* nor officials might compel Indians to work for them as household servants, or interfere with them in selling their produce. Since Indians under the legal age paid tribute if they were the heads of families, it was found necessary to legislate against the *encomenderos'* practice of compelling children to marry. Indians were not to be kept away from their homes and shut up in workshops, even for debt or crime. Travelers were not to carry off native women nor take food and other articles by force. The use of men as carriers was an especially troublesome question. This had been almost the only means of transport before the Conquest, and it was the only means the Spaniards had before pack animals were introduced and roads were built for them, but it was the occasion of much cruelty and abuse. Laws forbidding the practice could not be enforced, and it was finally necessary for the Crown to content itself with limiting loads and the length of journeys and with restricting the classes of people by whom carriers might be used.

The mere enumeration of the prohibitions against mistreatment of

[1] See Silvio Zavala, *La Libertad de Movimiento de los Indios de la Nueva España,* Mexico, 1948.

the natives, and still more the frequent official admissions that these prohibitions were not effective, indicate that the treatment that the Indians received was often different from that which the Crown desired. As a matter of fact, no other class suffered so much from the corruptness and irresponsible self-seeking which characterized the whole Spanish regime. For every case where they obtained redress for injuries or relief from oppression, there were probably many others where they were helpless against the officials and landowners who joined forces to exploit them. Their own *caciques* and other village officials seem to have been among their worst oppressors, and they suffered even more at the hands of the *corregidores*. In Peru and in some of the other colonies these officials were permitted to sell goods to the Indians, as a means of giving them an incentive to regular work, and they abused the privilege by forcing the natives to buy useless articles, such as spectacles and silk stockings, at exorbitant prices. They not infrequently left the country with great fortunes after a five-year term of office.

The Indians also contributed heavily to the support of the Church, paying fees for baptisms, marriages, and burials and numerous "voluntary" offerings. The provisions of the Laws of the Indies, as well as the reports of Spanish travelers, indicate that the parish priests sometimes joined with other members of the ruling class in exploiting the Indians for their own enrichment. On the other hand, the clergy were the Indians' most active advocates and protectors, and the natives' lot would have been far worse than it was had it not been for the Church's influence.

It would be a mistake to suppose that the Indians were nothing more than a race of overworked slaves. The very fact that they offered so rich a field for exploitation indicates that many of them were relatively prosperous. Their condition varied from province to province, and it was improving somewhat at the end of the colonial period. The *encomiendas* were abolished legally in the eighteenth century, and the *mita* was tending to disappear. Some of the Indians were learning to work for wages, and voluntary labor, while better paid, was more efficient. After Tupac Amaru's revolt in Peru in 1780 [1] forced sales to the Indians were discontinued. On the whole, the natives were probably better protected in their rights, and especially in the possession of their lands, than they were in the first century after the war for independence.

[1] See below, pp. 113–114.

Nevertheless, it was they who did the hard work for all other classes in the community and they received little in return. The distinguished scientist von Humboldt, visiting Mexico at the beginning of the nineteenth century, found them a miserable people, living on the least fertile lands, "indolent by nature and still more because of their situation in the community." We get much the same picture from the accounts of travelers who visited other colonies.

The White Settlers

Living apart from the Indians was the Spanish-speaking community, made up of the white upper class, the *mestizos* or people of mixed blood, and the Negro slaves. The white upper class included the conquistadores and their descendants and the new immigrants who arrived from Spain at the rate of a few thousand each year throughout the colonial period. Theoretically, emigration to America was carefully controlled. Unlike other powers, Spain did not use her overseas possessions as a dumping place for persons who were not wanted at home, and permits to go to America were granted only to those who were considered desirable as settlers. Since nothing must be permitted to endanger the colonists' loyalty or the purity of their religious beliefs, all foreigners were legally excluded, as were persons of doubtful orthodoxy such as the sons and grandsons of Spanish Jews and Moors who had been compelled to accept Christianity as an alternative to exile or death. The laws, it is true, were not always enforced, and many foreigners and "new Christians," found their way first and last to Spanish America. The Portuguese were the most numerous, especially between 1580 and 1640 when Spain and Portugal were united under one crown. Nevertheless, the influence of the non-Spanish element was always relatively small.

Though most of the Spanish settlers got their incomes from farms or mines, few of them lived on their estates. The wars with the Moors, which forced people to gather inside walls for mutual protection, had made the Castilians a race of city dwellers and there was the same need for keeping together for defense against possible Indian revolts in the colonies. Usually, although there were exceptions like Cuzco and Mexico City, the Spaniards built new towns, apart from those of the Indians. These were usually laid out on one uniform plan, with streets running at right angles and blocks so far as possible of the same area.

Most of them presented much the same external appearance. In the center was the plaza, or open park, about which were grouped the church, the *cabildo* or town hall, and the houses of the principal inhabitants. Less wealthy white families lived in the adjoining streets, and the *mestizos* and the poorer people generally, in the outskirts. In a town of any size there were other churches in the various wards, as well as a number of monasteries and convents. The house of a wealthy man often covered a large area. Because of earthquakes, such houses usually had only one or at most two stories, but there were many rooms, grouped about several court yards, and accommodating not only the family with its numerous servants and hangers-on but the horses and other domestic animals. Poorer families lived in less comfort, often crowded into one or two windowless, dirt-floored rooms, though even they usually had a small *patio* which gave access to light and air.

The white population early divided into two distinct groups: the *criollos*, or creoles, who had been born in America, and the *peninsulares*, or immigrants from Spain. The first group was of course far more numerous. Some of the creoles were *encomenderos*, others were engaged in trade or mining, but the majority had farms or cattle ranches. These estates were often very large, and they were frequently entailed to assure the succession of the oldest son in each generation. Some of the wealthier landowners and miners had titles of nobility, which were sold by the Crown as a means of raising money.

Most of the higher officials in the government and the Church, and most of the great merchants, were *peninsulares*. The ranks of the Spanish-born were constantly augmented by adventurers who came to America to seek their fortunes. In the first part of the colonial period, most of the bakers, carpenters, shoemakers, and other artisans seem to have been Spaniards, and the members of these trades were organized into guilds like those in Europe. This situation soon changed, apparently because the members of the dominant race disliked even skilled labor in a community where work was the function of Indians and slaves. The skilled trades thus fell more and more into the hands of *mestizos* and mulattoes.

Between the creoles and the *peninsulares*, there were differences in temperament and a feeling of hostility which was not much mitigated by the fact that the children of peninsular Spaniards, if they stayed in America, became creoles themselves. The mere fact of birth in America made the difference. The creoles were little inclined to industry and it was believed in Spain that the American climate had sapped their energy and moral fiber. Partly for this reason, but more perhaps because the Crown desired to maintain a closer hold on the colonies, they were in practice debarred from the higher positions in the government and the more desirable appointments in the Church. They were likewise at a disadvantage in industry and commerce. The immigrant, however poor or humble, seemed to be favored by his fellow Spaniards as well as by fortune, and often rose to a position where he could marry into the best colonial families, to the disgust of his creole rivals. His success, and his assumption of superiority, were bitterly resented. We shall have occasion to return to this subject later, in connection with the causes of the war for independence.

Mestizos and Mulattoes

Below the whites in the social scale were the people of mixed race who were eventually to be the most numerous group of all. Since few women had come to America with the earlier expeditions, intermarriage with the Indians had been frequent and had been encouraged by the authorities. Less regular unions had been still more common. Some of the *mestizos,* as people of part white, part Indian blood were called, inherited property and the privilege of citizenship in the towns from their white fathers, and became members of the upper class. Others simply remained with their mothers in the Indian communities. The majority formed a group apart, not accepted as equals by the Spaniards but feeling themselves superior to the natives. Like other half-castes, they often seemed to combine the worst qualities of both parents. This was only natural in a group which had little chance to benefit by the traditions and moral standards of either of the parent races and which for the most part grew up under the stigma of illegitimacy. The mulattoes, who began to appear with the introduction of Negro slaves, and the part African, part Indian *zambos* had a still lower social position. All persons of mixed blood were subject to various discriminations. They were particularly forbidden to have any part in the exploitation of the Indians, and in the eighteenth century they were barred by law, though not always in practice, from the universities and hence from the learned professions. The mulattoes and *zambos* were compelled to pay tribute, like Indians or free Negroes, and their women were not permitted to wear gold, pearls, or silk, or to dress like those of the upper class. These provisions were probably not very rigidly enforced, but their existence on the statute book was humiliating and helped to create bad feeling between the different social groups.

A large proportion of the people of mixed blood nevertheless became useful members of the community. They formed the bulk of the artisan class in the cities, and many of them were overseers or foremen at the plantations and mines, or small independent farmers. They also served as mule-drivers and teamsters, and in other occupations one step above ordinary manual labor.

Negro Slaves

From the beginning, many of the colonists had Negro slaves. These were brought in chiefly as laborers in regions where the supply of Indians was inadequate or in industries where Indians could not profitably be employed. Many were also used as household servants or workmen in the larger cities. They were better workers than the Indians, though more expensive. Since they were legally slaves, even the humanitarians saw little objection to employing them and had in fact advocated their use as a means of saving the Indians. Contracts for supplying them to the American settlements were granted from time to time, usually to Portuguese or other foreigners, and it was not long before they formed a large part of the population of the West Indian Islands, the Caribbean coast of Central and South America, and a few other districts where sugar and other plantation crops were raised. The total number, however, was never very great, because the cultivation of plantation crops did not prosper in the Spanish colonies as it did in the British and French West Indies.

In contrast with the callous contempt that marked the creoles' attitude toward the Indians, the treatment of the Negroes was relatively humane. They were regarded as human beings and as Christians rather than as mere chattels, and the Church took an active interest in their spiritual welfare, which helped to make their situation easier. One of the most attractive figures in the colonies' history is San Pedro Claver, a Jesuit father who befriended and baptized many thousands of newly arrived Africans at Cartagena in the seventeenth century. Both the Church and the law encouraged manumission, so that there were soon a considerable number of freedmen. Slavery was of course at best a cruel and degrading institution, but it seems to have been less cruel in the Spanish colonies than in those of France and England, partly because there were relatively fewer Negroes and consequently less fear of slave revolts.

Social and Intellectual Life

Colonial society was thus divided into several sharply defined castes: *peninsulares*, creoles, *mestizos*, mulattoes, *zambos*, Indians, free Negroes, and slaves. The distinction between them rested more on wealth and inherited social position than on blood, for the Spaniards had little real race prejudice. Each class nevertheless was jealous of its prerogatives and looked down on the class below. The policy of the Spanish government, with its grants of special privileges to some and its discriminations against others, seemed deliberately designed to create hatreds and rivalries that would prevent unity in the colonial body politic. One of the practices that the creoles most resented was the sale to persons of mixed blood of the privilege of being regarded as white. Caste divisions were to be one of the factors that made it difficult to establish democratic institutions after independence.

In general, only the members of the white upper class, and only the men within that class, received any education. A few schools for Indian boys were set up immediately after the Conquest, but the effort to train Indians as priests and leaders was soon abandoned and the masses of the natives remained not only illiterate but ignorant of the Spanish language. Very few of the *mestizos* or mulattoes ever learned to read or write. Even the white families had scanty educational opportunities, except in the larger towns where there were primary and secondary schools, most of them for boys, and also universities. Most of the educational institutions were conducted by one or another of the religious orders and all were controlled by the Church. The best schools were those of the Jesuits and the Dominicans.

There were eight major universities and many less important ones in the Spanish colonies. The most important were the Universities of Mexico and San Marcos at Lima, both of them founded soon after the middle of the sixteenth century, and supported partly by grants from the royal treasury and partly by endowments of land and *encomiendas*. Theology, law, medicine, and philosophy were the chief subjects taught. Curricula and teaching methods followed medieval patterns, as they did in European universities of the same period. Most of the students were members of the upper class, but there were fellowships for students who could not pay fees. People of mixed blood, as we have seen, were legally excluded from the universities in the latter part of the colonial period, but the Indians were always theoretically eligible for admission.[1]

Teaching in the universities was of course subject to control by the civil and ecclesiastical authorities, and these same authorities dictated, or tried to dictate, what the colonists should read. Nothing could be printed in America without the permission of the Inquisition, and books banned by that institution could not legally be imported. An early decree forbidding shipment to the Indies of any but religious works was not enforced, but there was always an effort to exclude publications that might endanger religious orthodoxy or political loyalty. Large quantities of books were nevertheless brought in. It is probable that the colonists had access to about the same sort of literature that circulated in Spain itself, though they were cut off from contact with the currents of thought that were changing the outlook of the more progressive European nations. It was not until the eighteenth century that modern philosophical ideas began to affect thought in the universities and a few daring individuals began to risk severe punishment by importing and reading "forbidden" books.

Books were also written in the colonies. In the sixteenth century many Spanish ecclesiastics produced historical and geographical works which are still of great value to scholars. Later a few colonial authors, like the poetess Sister Juana Inés de la Cruz, the versatile writer Carlos de Sigüenza y Góngora, and a little later the dramatist Alarcón, won a distinguished place in Spanish literature. Hundreds of lesser poets produced rather indifferent verse, marked by the artificiality characteristic of Spanish writers of the same period. The same lack of originality was evident in art and architecture, though many fine churches were built both in the cities and in smaller towns.

Such interest as there was in literature and art was confined to relatively few of the larger cities. Elsewhere even primary schools were few in number. The majority of the inhabitants, creoles as well as Indians, lived a life in which intellectual and cultural pursuits had no place, and the atmosphere of the provincial towns, separated from the capitals and seaports by many days or weeks of travel by horseback or ox-cart

[1] For an excellent account of the colonial universities, see John Tate Lanning, *Academic Culture in the Spanish Colonies.*

over the worst of roads, probably changed little from the sixteenth century to the nineteenth. Even the wealthier families lived simply and had few comforts.

Life was not always uneventful. Earthquakes and epidemics were frequent, and so too were violent and sometimes bloody quarrels between governors and bishops or between creoles and Spaniards. Armed rebellions and Indian uprisings were not unknown, and many of the coastal settlements were terrorized by pirate raids in the seventeenth century and by attacks of foreign governments in the eighteenth. The day by day existence of the colonists must nevertheless have been somewhat dull. The women especially led a secluded life in which the principal diversions were the afternoon promenade in the park for the younger set and the *tertulias*, or gatherings of families and their closer friends for conversation in the evening. For the men there were cockfighting and other forms of gambling, as well as the incessant intrigue to curry favor with officials or other powerful persons who might aid in obtaining a *repartimiento* of Indians or some other valuable concession from the government. Quarrels and lawsuits were frequent, and those who were more wealthy or influential were constantly called upon to help or protect less fortunate relatives and friends or give assistance in various ways to the multitude of dependents who attached themselves to each prominent family. Both sexes attended church regularly, and the celebration of religious festivals, with processions and fireworks, afforded one of the community's principal diversions.

4

The Government and the Church

The civil administration and the Church were the two great mutually supporting branches of the governmental system through which Spain ruled her American colonies. To the Spanish kings, political loyalty and religious conformity were almost inseparable concepts. They did irreparable injury to the economic life of the peninsula by expelling the Jews and the Moors to assure the extirpation of heresy, and preservation of religious purity was a cardinal principle of their policy in America. The conversion of the Indians inevitably followed their reduction to obedience, and the Crown relied upon the clergy to inculcate among them and among the creoles the duty of obedience to its autocratic authority.

It was not difficult to establish a system of absolutism in the colonies because the settlers brought with them no very robust tradition of self-government. The *cortes* or parliaments of the Spanish kingdoms had formerly been important institutions, but in the fifteenth century they lost much of their independence because the selection of the *procuradores* or representatives fell more and more under the control of the Crown, and in the sixteenth century they ceased to have any real power. The cities likewise had been deprived of much of the autonomy that they once enjoyed. This was especially true of Castile, where Isabella's centralizing policy had been welcomed as an alternative to the disorder and misgovernment prevalent before her accession. The Catholic Queen and her successors ruled that kingdom practically as absolute monarchs, though the consent of the *cortes* was theoretically required for levying new taxes and the forms of municipal self-government were partially observed. It is important to note that the Indies were regarded as belonging to Castile rather than to Aragon, where the people had retained more of their ancient liberties.

The people of the colonies could not claim even such traditional political privileges as might still exist in Castile, for the Indies were the property not of the nation but of the Crown. No one could go there without the royal permission, and no one could acquire rights there except by grant from the king. The conquistadores had been partners of the king in what were essentially business enterprises, and they and their successors in the government were responsible only to the king. Sometimes, it is true, they were unable to assert their authority and the settlers temporarily took matters in their own hands, but such irregular proceedings never resulted in the colonists' obtaining any recognized right of self government.

From the beginning, the king ruled the Indies through an administrative system quite separate from that of Spain. Juan Rodríguez de Fonseca, a priest who later became Bishop of Burgos, was appointed to make arrangements for Columbus' second voyage in 1493 and except for brief intervals continued to handle American affairs at court until his death in 1524. In that year the organization that he built up was converted into the Council of the Indies. This body thenceforth had full authority, under the king, in all matters relating to the overseas possessions. It drew up laws and gave advice on appointments and questions of major policy. As the organ through which the royal commands were transmitted to the colonies it exercised a close and continuous supervision over the conduct of all officials there, both civil and ecclesiastical. It acted as a court of appeals in cases decided by the colonial judges, and had general supervision over the *Casa de Contratación*, which controlled commerce with the Indies. Similar in its organization and functions to the great councils through which the king governed Spain itself, it had in the sixteenth century a president, a chancellor, eight councilors, and a number of secretaries and other officials. Decisions were taken by vote of the councilors, among whom some at least were usually qualified for their work by previous experience in important official posts in America. The Council was by no means free from the inefficiency, corruption, and favoritism that characterized other branches of the Spanish administration, but it was a hard-working body, in session several hours each day, and the great law code of the colonies, the *Recopilación de leyes de los reinos de las Indias*, is a monument to its industry and its good intentions.

Political Organization in the Colonies

In America, the first representatives of the Crown were the conquistadores. Columbus, Cortez, Pizarro, and a number of other leaders were rewarded for their services by appointments as governors of the territories that they conquered, but few of them long enjoyed the authority which was conferred on them. The very qualities which made their exploits possible caused the Crown to distrust them, and their own conduct frequently increased this distrust. Those who were not killed by other Spaniards or by the Indians were in most cases sooner or later deprived of a part or all of their power.

The machinery through which the colonies were to be governed throughout the colonial period took shape within a few years after the conquest of Mexico. We have seen how the *audiencia*, a royal commission which was primarily a court of justice but also exercised political functions, replaced Cortez in the civil government in 1527. This experiment was a failure, because the judges quarreled among themselves and grossly abused their power for their own benefit, and it soon became clear that a stronger hand was needed to control the turbulent adventurers who made up the white population of the new settlements. The Crown consequently decided to concentrate authority in the hands of one official who would have sufficient power and prestige to inspire fear and command respect, and Antonio de Mendoza was sent to New Spain as Viceroy in 1535. At the same time, the *audiencia* was continued in existence as a check on his authority and as a high court. A second viceroyalty was created in Peru under the New Laws of 1542, but there the civil wars prevented the establishment of orderly government until several years later.

The viceroys were usually great nobles whose loyalty to the Crown could be implicitly trusted. Subject to the supervision of the Council of the Indies it was their duty to enforce the laws and to see that the revenues were collected, that justice was properly administered, and that the Christian faith was preached among the Indians. As captains general, they had command of the military forces. Since they were expected to maintain a court which by its pomp and ceremony would keep alive among the colonists a sense of the greatness of the Spanish monarch, they were paid princely salaries.

The viceroy's term of office was limited to three, or later to five years, though in practice many served for longer periods. At its end, he was subject, like all other officials, to the *residencia*. This was a public investigation of his conduct by a judge especially appointed for the purpose, carried out after the viceroy relinquished his authority but before he left the colony. All who had complaints were free to submit them without fear of retaliation and the viceroy might theoretically be compelled to make reparation for any injustices proved against him. The *residencia* often produced much scandal, and the prospect of it perhaps prevented some abuses, but the impartiality of such an investigation was always open to question in the case of persons so influential at court as most of the viceroys. The principal effect of the system, with the viceroy and with other functionaries, was to discourage individual initiative in cases where action might have been desirable. An official who did only what his specific instructions authorized could not be found guilty of exceeding his power or making mistakes of judgment.

The viceroy as representative of the king had great power and prestige, but his freedom of action was limited by a great mass of detailed instructions and regulations. The king and the Council of the Indies attempted to dictate policy even in matters of minor importance, especially where any expenditure of funds was involved. They also endeavored to make sure that the viceroy did not become too friendly with the people of the community where he served and that he did not use his position to benefit himself and his family. He was not permitted to invite residents of the colony to dine at his table, and he might not bring his married sons and daughters to America with him, or himself engage in any commercial enterprise. These provisions, and many others of similar character, suggest that the temptations against which they were aimed were not always resisted.

Second in importance only to the viceroys were the *audiencias*, which continued to exist at Mexico and Lima and were later established at several other capitals. The *audiencias* were primarily courts of justice, but they also had political duties. At Mexico and Lima they acted as advisory councils to the viceroy, and had the very important right to hear the complaints of persons who considered themselves injured by that official's acts and to inform the king in cases where they considered that the viceroy had exceeded his authority. At these two capitals they usually assumed control of the government in the viceroy's absence. In other provinces they had a similar relationship to the captain general or governor, and at Quito and Charcas it was the president of the *audiencia* who administered political and even military affairs. As courts the *audiencias* decided civil and criminal cases though the parties might appeal to the Council of the Indies in suits where large sums were involved. The individual *oidores*, or judges, were also sent out regularly on inspection trips to watch over the conduct of lesser officials. The viceroys and captains general were the presidents of the *audiencias* in their capitals, but had no authority to interfere with certain phases of their work. The viceroy, for example, did not have a vote in legal cases unless he were himself trained in the law.

The captains general were officials who exercised practically the same functions as the viceroys in less important areas, and especially in regions where the danger of foreign aggression or Indian depredations made the problem of defense important. These officers were nominally subordinate to the viceroys, but in practice they received their instructions directly from Spain because the great distances from one colonial capital to another and the obstacles to intercommunication made decentralization inevitable.

The principal administrative units might thus be under the direct control of a viceroy or a captain general or an *audiencia*, the president of the *audiencia* being in this last case the nominal head of the government. The boundaries and the status of each unit varied from time to time. Until the eighteenth century, when new viceroyalties were set up in New Granada in 1739 and at Buenos Aires in 1776, the viceroy of Peru usually had nominal jurisdiction over all of Spanish South America except Venezuela, whereas the viceroy of New Spain ruled over Mexico, Central America, and Venezuela. In the latter part of the colonial period there were captains general in Guatemala, Cuba, Venezuela, Chile, and Puerto Rico.

The larger areas were divided into smaller districts where the chief royal official might be a governor, a *corregidor*, or an *alcalde mayor*. These were the representatives of the Crown who had the closest contact with the colonists, and their authority covered a wide range of subjects: judicial, financial, military, and ecclesiastical. We have already seen how much power was exercised and abused by the *corregidores* placed in charge of Indian communities.

The collection of revenues and the custody of funds were entrusted to the *oficiales reales*, the "royal officials," who were in some respects independent of the viceroys and directly responsible to the king. Three of these, a factor, an accountant, and a treasurer, were stationed in each important town. The actual collection of taxes was usually farmed out to contractors, but the royal officials received the proceeds, paid salaries and other expenses authorized by law, and remitted any balance to their superiors for shipment to Spain. Funds in their possession were kept in a chest which had three separate locks and could thus be opened only when all of the officials were present. Except in an emergency, even the viceroy could not draw money from the treasury without an order from the king, and it was the duty of the *oficiales reales* to prevent or report unauthorized disbursements. The home government's avid interest in its income from the colonies made the financial administration very important. Besides the royal fifth upon gold and silver and the tribute paid by the Indians, there were various other taxes. The *alcabala,* which was a levy on sales, was the most disliked and the most burdensome for it reached at times 6 per cent of the value of the merchandise, even upon goods which had already paid a still higher tax before exportation from Spain. Customs duties and other charges upon commerce also produced a substantial revenue.

After the end of the sixteenth century practically all of the officials in the colonies except the viceroys obtained their offices simply by purchase from the royal government, which sold appointments to the highest bidder. This was true even of the most responsible positions. The more important were usually sold in Spain, the others in the colonies. The new functionary's office thus represented an investment from which he naturally expected a financial return, but there is little reason to suppose that the result was worse than if appointments had been dictated by favoritism and bribery, which would undoubtedly have been the alternative.

Corruption and Inefficiency

Contemporary standards of official morality made graft and peculation inevitable under any system of appointment. Public office was regarded in Spain, as in many other European countries in the seventeenth and eighteenth centuries, primarily as an opportunity for self-enrichment. The whole character of the colonial system—the arbitrary power exercised by the Crown's representatives, the special privileges granted to favored persons and classes, and especially the restrictions upon trade which made violations of the law extremely profitable—

afforded an irresistible temptation to bribery and extortion. The vice-roys themselves stooped at times to the establishment of commercial monopolies for their personal profit, or accepted money in return for pardoning criminals. Among their subordinates, from the judges of the *audiencia* to the most humble clerk, corruption was universal and in most cases unpunished. The public treasury was defrauded in count-less ways, and justice or more frequently injustice was for sale in the courts. Even private property was not safe from the rapacity of un-scrupulous military or civil officials. We have already seen how the Indians were deprived of the protection which the Crown sought to give them, and we shall see in the next chapter how official connivance with smugglers made ineffective the Spanish government's commercial policy. The laws of the Indies contained many provisions designed to discourage official misconduct, through frequent inspections by mem-bers of the *audiencia* or specially appointed "visitors," and through the *residencias* which all officials had to undergo at the end of their terms, but these were of little value because they were usually carried out by officials who were themselves profiting by the practices that they were supposed to check. There was often a recognized customary price for a favorable report after a *residencia*.

The Spanish colonial administration was not only corrupt, but, judged by modern standards, inefficient. Some of the earlier viceroys, like Mendoza in Mexico and Francisco de Toledo in Peru, were able statesmen, but the majority, especially in the seventeenth century, were men of mediocre ability. The Crown's insistence that even unimportant questions must be decided in Spain discouraged local initiative and made it difficult for the best viceroys to accomplish much constructive work. Such centralization was the more impractical because communi-cations between the colonies and the peninsula were slow and uncertain, especially when Spain's enemies controlled the seas, and communica-tions between one colony and another in America often took many weeks. The lack of close contact between the home government and its representatives, combined with procrastination and red tape in the Council of the Indies, often caused matters requiring prompt decision to be discussed back and forth for years. On the other hand the Crown was compelled to allow the colonial officials some latitude in enforcing royal decrees issued without full knowledge of the facts. The viceroys frequently nullified the king's commands by suspending laws until they could explain why their enforcement seemed undesirable, using the famous formula: "Let it be obeyed but not executed." Subordinate officials similarly evaded compliance with the viceroys' orders. Such practices could not but encourage insubordination and abuses of power.

Exclusion of the Creoles from Public Office

In practice, though the law did not so provide, the higher offices under the Crown were nearly always filled by peninsular Spaniards. Three creole nobles were viceroys of Mexico between 1696 and 1741, but such exceptions to the general rule were rare. Natives of the colonies occasionally served as governors or *corregidores*, but never in their home districts. The officials were thus a class apart, forbidden to form ties that might create any bond of sympathy with the local community. This had unfortunate results. On the one hand it did much to intensify the antagonism between *peninsulares* and creoles. On the other, the creoles' lack of administrative experience had disastrous effects when they attempted to set up independent national governments.

The Cabildo

The only branch of the political administration in which residents of the colonies customarily participated was the government of the cities. Despite the extinction of municipal liberties in Spain, the forms and the traditions of local autonomy had survived, and when the colonists came to America city governments modeled on those of the mother country were the first political institutions that they set up.

The *cabildo*, or *ayuntamiento*, as the municipal corporation was called, consisted of a council of *regidores*, one or more *alcaldes*, or magistrates, elected by this council, and various minor officials. The original *regidores* were usually appointed by the leader who founded the city, although there were cases where they were elected by the *vecinos*, or householders. Their successors were chosen in various ways. In the sixteenth century the outgoing council often elected the new *regidores* at the beginning of each year, acting to a greater or less extent under the influence of the royal governor. A little later posts in the *cabildo*, like other offices, were sold to the highest bidder for the benefit of the royal treasury, and it became customary for a majority of the *regidores* in each *cabildo* to hold office for life or to have an hereditary right to their seats.[1] In a few cities, where municipal offices

[1] Haring, *The Spanish Empire in America*, pp. 165-8.

were less sought after or where the inhabitants were too poor to buy them, the system of election by the outgoing council continued or the posts were filled by appointment. In most cases the municipal officials were creoles, or at least immigrants from Spain who had made their homes in the colonies, and the city governments thus represented local interests and were in some measure responsive to local sentiment, even though they were in no sense democratic institutions.

The *ayuntamiento* shared responsibility with the governor or the *corregidor* for nearly all governmental activities of a purely local nature such as the enforcement of police and sanitary regulations, the cleaning and repairing of the streets, and the maintenance of markets. It regulated wages and the prices of foodstuffs and other necessities and took action to procure adequate supplies when a scarcity threatened. It often had to administer a considerable amount of property, for besides the areas used in common by the inhabitants for pasture and cutting firewood, it was customary for a newly founded city to be given a tract of land which was rented to private individuals as a means of increasing the municipal revenue. Many towns had representatives in Spain to look after their business interests [1] and in the earlier part of the colonial period, before the colonial administration became so highly centralized as it did later, they frequently appointed *procuradores* to confer with those of other towns about matters of common importance.

The *ayuntamiento's* jurisdiction extended not only to the city proper but to all of the territory to the borders of the next municipality—a natural arrangement when the landowners lived for the most part in the towns rather than upon their estates. In some cases the area was a large one. Buenos Aires, to take an extreme example, at one time reached 300 miles westward toward Córdoba, 170 miles northward toward Santa Fe, and an indefinite distance southward into the wild Indian territory and eastward across the River Plate into what is now Uruguay.[2] The municipality was thus a subdivision of the province rather than a city government in the modern sense.

The power actually exercised by the city officials varied. In the larger capitals they were treated with great respect, and membership in the *ayuntamiento* was a distinction for which wealthy citizens were willing to pay a high price; but their authority was completely overshadowed by that of the viceroy or the captain general. In outlying prov-

---

[1] Haring, *Trade and Navigation between Spain and the Indies*, p. 139.
[2] Kirkpatrick, *The Argentine Republic*, p. 19.

inces, as in Buenos Aires before the establishment of a viceroyalty, they had more real autonomy. Even in such places, however, they could not effectively resist the centralizing policy of the Crown, though they were constantly involved in conflicts with other civil and ecclesiastical officials over questions of authority and prerogatives. The control of the sale of offices in most of the *ayuntamientos* by the royal treasury officials was enough in itself to assure their subservience.

The Administration of Justice

There was no sharp division between administrative and judicial function in the Spanish political system. The governors, *corregidores*, and municipal *alcaldes* all acted as judges. Their decisions were usually subject to review by the *audiencia*, which was the highest court in the colonies, and important cases might be appealed to the Council of the Indies or the king himself.

Only a part of the population was subject to the jurisdiction of the ordinary courts. Several privileged classes, including the civil officials, the army, and the Church, enjoyed the privilege of being tried by their own special courts both in civil and in criminal cases. The *fueros*, as these privileges were called, were extended until a traveler in Venezuela at the end of the colonial period reported that there were few white persons of any importance who could not claim one.[1] The military *fuero*, for example, extended to all members of the creole militia, even though they were not in active service, and the church courts claimed jurisdiction over great numbers of persons who were not priests. The system led to many abuses, for the special tribunals were always inclined to favor members of their own order, and evil-doers often sought some minor military or ecclesiastical employment for the sake of the immunity it conferred. The *fueros* were ardently defended, and quarrels over questions of jurisdiction caused scandalous conflicts and not infrequently bloodshed.

The Church

Standing beside the civil administration, and hardly less important as a part of the governmental organization, was the powerful hierarchy

[1] F. Depons, *Voyage à la partie orientale de la Terre-Ferme dans l'Amérique Méridionale*, Vol. II, p. 60.

of the Catholic Church. The whole ecclesiastical organization in the Indies was controlled by the Crown to an extent unusual in other parts of the world. In a bull of 1493 the Pope gave Ferdinand and Isabella the same right to make ecclesiastical appointments in the Indies which he had earlier conferred on Prince Henry the Navigator in Africa, and this right was confirmed and extended in later grants. The Catholic Monarchs were likewise given permission to receive all tithes in the colonies in return for their promise to support the Church there. Taken together, these and other privileges obtained from the Holy See constituted the *patronato*, the right of patronage, which was one of the Spanish kings' most valued and jealously guarded prerogatives.

All members of the clergy were thus dependent upon and responsible to the Crown. Bishops and other high ecclesiastical officials were named directly by the king, whereas less important appointments, such as those of parish priests and curates, were made by the viceroy or his subordinates acting as vice-patrons, though usually from among candidates presented by the bishops after an examination conducted by the church authorities. No priest could go to America without a license from the Council of the Indies, and none could return without express permission from the Crown or the viceroy. The movements of the clergy in the colonies were directed by the authorities, and an order from the king was necessary to build a church or a convent or to establish a mission among the Indians. The Crown's collection of the tithes gave it control of the Church's most important revenue. Under such conditions, the Church became an integral part of the government. Many clerics, in fact, held high positions in the civil administration itself, and in Mexico the archbishop frequently served for a short time as viceroy when the office accidentally became vacant.

Among the white colonists, the overwhelming majority were devout Catholics who accepted without question the spiritual authority of the Church and the control that it exercised in many matters of conduct and personal relations which are not now considered purely spiritual. The confessional alone gave the priesthood an immense power, and a threat of excommunication inspired fear in the most influential officials. The cemeteries were under Church control, as were the parish registers, which were the official record of births, marriages, and deaths. Offenses against religion might be punished by fine or imprisonment and often by more severe penalties.

The influence of the Church was increased by the very real services that it rendered the community. As we have seen, it provided nearly all of the schools in the colonies. It also maintained the hospitals and asylums and took care of the poor. Persons who wished to give or bequeath money for charity invariably entrusted it to a priest or to one of the religious orders.

Although all of its activities were controlled and directed by the Crown, the Church in the colonies was not a unified, centralized organization. The numerous religious orders worked independently of each other and of the bishops, and there was much rivalry between different groups. A long conflict occurred because the friars, after converting the Indians, clung to their positions as parish priests in the native communities despite the efforts of the secular clergy to displace them. There were also jealousies and quarrels between the various religious orders, several of which usually had establishments in each important town.

The various branches of the Church amassed a great amount of wealth. The tithes, a 10 per cent tax on products of the soil, were collected by the Crown, but the greater part of the proceeds was turned over to the ecclesiastical authorities. There were also other fruitful sources of revenue. Especially important were pious gifts and bequests, for few wealthy persons died without seeking to assure the welfare of their souls by leaving something to the Church. Since many of the bequests were in the form of liens on undivided landed estates, and since the monasteries invested a large part of their other funds in mortgages, religious foundations gradually acquired an interest in a large proportion of the agricultural properties and city real estate and came to own great amounts of land themselves. The Crown made repeated efforts to check this process, but with little result. After independence the Church's wealth became an explosive political issue and a source of danger to the Church itself in several of the Latin American republics.

This wealth was very unevenly divided. Some charitable foundations like hospitals and orphanages were heavily endowed and some of the monasteries had large investments and much land which they farmed themselves or rented to other persons. The incomes of several of the bishops and other important church officials were likewise very great, occasionally exceeding those of the viceroys or of any but the wealthiest members of the creole aristocracy. The parish priests on the other hand often had little income beyond the fees and contributions paid by the poverty-stricken Indians and *mestizos* of the rural villages. Since the more important ecclesiastical officials were peninsular Spaniards and the parish priests were usually natives of the colonies, this disparity was one of the many causes of bad feeling between creoles and *peninsulares*. Both groups were represented in the membership of the religious orders, and they sometimes formed factions whose quarrels disturbed the whole community.

The Inquisition

Persons who embraced unorthodox ideas, religious or political, were likely to run foul of the Inquisition, which set up tribunals at Mexico and Lima under a decree of 1569 and at Cartagena in 1610. Fortunately these were not given jurisdiction over the Indians, who were regarded as children in the faith and whose frequent backslidings into heathen practices were punished by the ordinary clergy. In general the Inquisition in the colonies was a less horrifying institution than in Spain. Serious offenses against religion were not common among the white and *mestizo* colonists because immigration was carefully sifted to prevent spiritual contamination and contact with the outside world was slight. It is said that only a hundred heretics were burned at the stake in Mexico and Peru during the whole colonial period,[1] and many of these were captured foreign pirates. The Inquisition nevertheless found much to do with minor heresies and sacrileges and accumulated much wealth. It was especially dreaded because of the secrecy surrounding its procedure. The fines that it collected belonged legally to the king, but few royal officials had the courage to ask an accounting of an organization which could imprison and ruin persons of any rank without answering to any other authority for its conduct, and whose officials and employees were immune from prosecution except in their own courts.

One of the Inquisition's most important activities, particularly in the eighteenth century, was the effort to prevent the spread of heretical or revolutionary ideas. No books could be imported or printed without its permission, and those who read prohibited works were liable to severe punishment. In 1806, when questions arose between Spain and the United States about the boundary of the Louisiana purchase, a friar who had been designated to make a report on the question for the information of the King of Spain found it necessary to consult two

[1] Bourne, *Spain in America*, p. 313.

foreign histories that the Inquisition had banned. He was refused permission to do so, though the Inquisition finally designated its own representatives to examine the books and extract such information as they considered useful.[1] This rigid censorship, which extended to the works of many authors who were being widely read in other parts of the world including Spain itself, was an important factor in the colonies' intellectual backwardness.

The Church and the Indians

The Indians near the larger Spanish settlements were at least outwardly converted at the time of the Conquest, though we may suspect that it was some time before they grasped the meaning of the mass baptism to which they had been subjected. To see that they were instructed in the faith was an important duty of the viceroys, and ostensibly the main purpose of the *encomienda* system; and the law required that all Indians, Negroes, and mulattoes in each community should be assembled daily for religious instruction. Even where the old pagan worship secretly survived, the new gods, whom the Conquest had proved so much more powerful, were accepted also. The Indians were the more inclined to accord respect and obedience to the Church because they found it their most effective protector. The Church thus acquired an immense authority over the natives which was reinforced by the support of the government. It was the principal channel through which the Indians absorbed a little of the civilization of the conquering race. The influence of the priests and friars probably did more than any other factor to keep the masses of the Indian population submissive to the Spanish regime.

One of the Church's most noteworthy undertakings was the missionary work of the religious orders on the frontiers. During and after the period of the Conquest, Jesuits and Dominicans and Franciscans went into the wildest and most remote regions to preach the gospel with the same indomitable courage that inspired other Spanish explorers in the search for wealth and power. Many were killed by the natives or died of hunger and exhaustion, but others won the confidence of the wild tribes, taught them the rudiments of civilization, and brought them into touch with the Spanish community so that the royal authorities could peacefully establish control over them. Somewhat later more

[1] Lea, *The Inquisition in the Spanish Dependencies*, p. 274.

elaborately organized frontier missions, directed and supported by the Crown, became the chief means through which the Spanish dominions were expanded. The friars were protected by military forces, and compulsion as well as persuasion was used to induce the Indians to give up their nomadic life and settle in permanent villages, or *reducciones*, where their economic and spiritual life could be supervised by the missionaries. The converts had little or no private property and worked for the benefit of the community as a whole, under constant supervision and direction. Such power as their own chiefs exercised was subject to the higher authority of the priests. Until they were considered sufficiently civilized to stand on their own feet, they were carefully kept from any contact with the Spanish community and white settlers were excluded from their neighborhood.

The Indians were taught handicrafts and better agricultural methods, and the introduction of new animals and plants helped to do away with the danger of famine which had formerly been ever present. Many thousands in northern Mexico and the interior of South America were saved from extinction by slave-raiders or Spanish troops. In few cases, however, were the converts able to survive as organized communities after the missions were discontinued. In districts where Spanish colonization later took place, those who did not succumb to disease or mistreatment passed under the domination of white landowners or miners. Elsewhere they usually reverted more or less completely to savagery.

The Paraguay Missions

The most famous missions were those of Paraguay. The Jesuits started work among the Guaranís along the upper Paraná River in the latter part of the sixteenth century, and they were especially authorized to Christianize the Indians of that region by a royal order issued in 1608. When their early settlements were destroyed some twenty years later by the raids of slave-hunting Paulistas from Brazil, they moved their converts south into territory which is now partly in southeastern Paraguay, partly in the Argentine province of Misiones, and partly in Brazil. Here they developed a theocratic community which was practically independent of the neighboring Spanish authorities. There were a score of *reducciones*, each under the paternalistic control of two or more missionaries, with a total population of more than 100,000. The life and industry of the Indians was as closely regulated as in other missions, and efficient management made the settlements very prosperous. The creoles of Asunción and other nearby communities were bitterly hostile to the Jesuits, who protected the docile Guaranís from white exploitation and also sold their *yerba mate* and agricultural products in competition with those of the white settlements.

This hostility was frequently the cause of serious disorders in Paraguay. In the middle of the seventeenth century Bishop Cárdenas of Asunción, who was unfriendly to the Jesuits, became the ardent champion of the creoles. While serving temporarily as governor of the province, he attempted to restrict the activities of the missions and then led the creoles in resistance to a new governor who was sent to replace him. He was defeated by an army from the missions, for the Jesuits had been permitted to train and arm their Indians to repel further aggressions from the Paulistas. The mission troops again helped to put down a creole revolt led by José de Antequera, who held control of Paraguay from 1721 until 1731, and another under Fernando Mompó a little later.

The prosperity of the Jesuit missions came to an end when Spain agreed in 1750 to exchange seven missions east of the Uruguay River for the Portuguese town of Colonia, which had long been the center of an obnoxious smuggling trade. The Indians, who had already suffered so much from the Portuguese, rose in revolt. The ensuing "War of the Seven Reductions" was suppressed after a long and costly struggle, and a worse disaster overtook the missions when the Jesuits were expelled from America in 1767. The Indians passed under the control of the civil authorities, aided by friars of other orders, and their population rapidly decreased.

The power and wealth of the Church inevitably attracted many persons who were unworthy to be priests. We find severe criticism of the conduct of some of the clergy both in travelers' accounts and in the official reports of the viceroys. It was charged that parish priests frequently exploited or mistreated the Indians and that their moral conduct left much to be desired. The ecclesiastical courts were accused of lenience and partiality in dealing with clerical offenders. There were also unedifying quarrels within the Church or between church and civil officials, and these sometimes led to noisy scandals and even riots.

On the other hand, the Church rendered great services to the colonial community through its schools and charitable work and through its vast influence for social stability. It gave the colonies their men of letters and many of their ablest government officials. Its financial resources, and the enterprise and organizing ability of some of the religious orders, especially in their missions among the Indians, were important factors in the colonies' economic development. It was the great prestige and influence of the Church, rather than its shortcomings, that made its position a major political issue after independence.

5

Commerce, Smuggling, and Piracy

The commerce of the Spanish colonies was carried on under conditions that did much to discourage their economic development. In the seventeenth and eighteenth centuries, most colonial powers sought to exploit their overseas possessions for their own benefit. Colonies were expected to supply tropical products and raw materials useful to the mother country and to furnish a market for the manufactures of the metropolis. In the Spanish Empire, the application of these principles had unfortunate results, because the mother country's decadent economy could not absorb the commodities that the colonies produced, nor supply the goods that they needed. Spain's military weakness which made it difficult to protect trade, and governmental corruption and incompetence that prevented the adaptation of the commercial system to changing conditions, made matters worse.

Products of the Colonies

From the beginning, the Spanish government's interest in the economy of the colonies centered chiefly in their production of silver and gold. Most economists of the time believed that the acquisition of the precious metals for their own sake was the principal benefit that a nation could obtain from trade. The conquistadores eagerly sought for mines and placer deposits in each country that they invaded, and they worked thousands of Indians to death in the West Indies to obtain rather small quantities of treasure. On the mainland they had better luck. Rich deposits of silver were found in Mexico within a few years after the Conquest and the fabulously profitable mines of Potosí, in the vice-royalty of Peru, were discovered about 1545. The city of Potosí, on the bleak plateau of what is now Bolivia, was for a period the largest in the New World, with all the turbulence and reckless extravagance characteristic of the center of a mining boom. Other provinces also produced much mineral wealth, though none of them compared in this respect with Upper Peru and Mexico. The output of silver was far more important than the output of gold.

By law, all mineral deposits belonged to the Crown, even though the surface of the land had been granted to another owner. The government usually permitted the discoverer or some other private individual to operate the mines, and reserved for itself a royalty which varied from one-tenth to one-fifth of the gross product. It assured the collection of the royalty by making the supply of quicksilver a government monopoly. The amount that the miners paid was based on their consumption of this metal, which was used in extracting silver and gold from the ore, rather than on the production that they themselves reported.[1] The great Huancavelica mine in Peru provided quicksilver for that viceroyalty, while Mexico was usually supplied from Spain.

The Crown showed less interest in other forms of economic enterprise which actually produced more wealth than did mining. By far the greater part of the population was engaged in cattle-raising or agriculture. In the highlands, where the majority of the people lived, the *haciendas* produced food and draft animals for sale in the towns and mining camps. In warmer areas, like the West Indies and the lower valleys of the mainland, there were plantations of sugar, indigo, cacao, and other tropical products, and these commodities were exported in considerable quantities, though they never achieved so much importance as in the British and French West Indies. The planters were handicapped both by the lack of adequate labor, for the Indians were of little use in the hot country and Negro slaves were scarce and expensive, and by the commercial system, which failed to provide adequate transport for perishable tropical products.

The Casa de Contratación

The most striking characteristic of the commercial system was the effort to confine all trade with the Indies to a few narrow channels where it could be closely regulated and more easily protected from foreign enemies. In Spain all phases of commercial intercourse with the colonies

[1] Whitaker, *The Huancavelica Mercury Mine*, p. 6.

were controlled by the *Casa de Contratación* at Seville. This institution was set up in 1503, when the needs of the little settlements in Española were doubtless best served by one central bureau. It continued for nearly three centuries to examine cargo going to or coming from America and to arrange for the sailing of the fleets.[1]

Nothing might be sent to the Indies without the consent of the Casa, nothing might be brought back and landed, either on the account of merchants or of the king himself, without its authorization. Bullion from the colonies consigned to Spanish merchants belonged to them only when the Casa permitted its release. It controlled and regulated the character of ships, crews, and passengers. In short, it saw to the execution of all the laws and ordinances relating to trade and navigation with America.

Sitting as a court, the Casa had jurisdiction over crimes committed on the voyages and in certain classes of civil suits arising in connection with American trade. It also conducted a school of navigation and devoted much attention to map-making and the improvement of nautical instruments, under the general direction of the Pilot Major. The first occupant of this post was Amerigo Vespucci, and the second, Juan Díaz de Solís, the discoverer of the River Plate.

At first, all ships trading with the Indies had to clear from and return to Seville, but this caused much inconvenience because the city was many miles from the sea on the narrow and shallow Guadalquivir River. In 1508, therefore, permission was granted for outgoing vessels to load at San Lucar, at the mouth of the river, or in the nearby harbor of Cadiz, and in 1535 the *Juzgado de Indias*, an agency of the *Casa de Contratación*, was established at Cadiz. Vessels coming from the Indies were still usually required to go to Seville, or at least to send their cargoes and documents to the Casa for examination. There was much jealousy between Seville and Cadiz, and the regulations governing their trade were changed from time to time in favor sometimes of one, sometimes of the other. The merchants at Cadiz usually enjoyed some share in the trade of the colonies even when the fleet sailed from the Guadalquivir, and after 1680, when the silting up of the river made its navigation more and more difficult for the larger ships which were coming into use, Cadiz became the port of arrival and departure for all of the American fleets. The *Casa de Contratación* itself was moved there in 1717.

[1] Haring, *Trade and Navigation between Spain and the Indies*, pp. 33–34. The description of the Spanish commercial system in this chapter is based largely on this book.

Except for occasional special dispensations, Seville and Cadiz were the only ports through which trade between Spain and America could legally be carried on. The Emperor Charles V granted permission in 1529 for ships to sail directly to the Indies from several other Spanish ports, provided they put in at Seville on the return voyage, but this privilege seems to have been little used and was discontinued after a short time. Later efforts of other cities in the kingdom to obtain a share in the American trade were defeated by the influence of the powerful vested interests which grew up at Seville, or were discouraged because the authorities believed that they could cope with smuggling more effectively if shipments were confined to a single channel. As the commerce of the colonies increased, such centralization became more and more harmful to the mother country and to the overseas possessions, especially as internal customs barriers in Spain made it unprofitable for other regions of the peninsula to send goods to or buy goods from the Indies.

The Fleet System

In America likewise trade was restricted to a few ports. This was partly because of the convoy system which the depredations of foreign enemies compelled the government to adopt. French privateers and pirates began to cause trouble early in the sixteenth century, during the wars between the Emperor Charles and Francis I, and in 1522-23 they captured the ships despatched by Cortez with the king's share of the spoils from the capture of Mexico City. The seas became increasingly unsafe as marauders of other nationalities followed their example. It soon became necessary to have merchant vessels sail in groups protected by warships, and after 1550 practically all trade was carried on in this way. Ordinances adopted in 1564 established the fleet system in the form which it was to retain until well into the eighteenth century.

Normally, two fleets sailed for America each year: the "galleons" with cargo for South America, and the Plate Fleet which served New Spain and the Antilles. There were usually from thirty to ninety ships in each in the sixteenth century, but the number decreased later, partly because ships grew larger and partly because the growth of smuggling caused legitimate commerce to decline. The merchantmen were accompanied by several warships, which themselves frequently carried goods for trade. Great convoys of this sort were awkward to handle, and losses by shipwreck were heavy.

All trade with the west coast of South America, which was the wealthiest and most populous part of the Spanish Empire in the earlier part of the colonial period, was carried on by way of the Isthmus of Panama. The galleons made their first stop at Cartagena. There goods were unloaded for New Granada and messengers were sent overland to Lima to give the signal for the departure of the vessels that would carry the products of Peru, Chile, and Quito to Panama. After some weeks of trading the fleet proceeded to Porto Bello, which at the end of the sixteenth century superseded Nombre de Dios as the principal port on the Caribbean side of the Isthmus. Hundreds of officials, merchants, muledrivers, and hangers-on were crowded into this hot little village for forty or fifty days until the textiles and other European goods brought by the galleons had been exchanged for the gold, silver, cacao, and other products of the colonies. With insufficient accommodations and appalling sanitary conditions a large proportion of those attending the fair always succumbed to the diseases which made the Isthmus dreaded by travelers until the twentieth century. Only the expectation of great profits, which increased the burden already imposed upon the consumer by heavy taxation and by the greed of the Seville monopolists, could have induced merchants to engage in a commerce so dangerous to life and health.

From Porto Bello goods must be transported overland to Panama for reshipment to the west coast ports. While the distance across the Isthmus was short, the difficulty and risk were great, for the roads were mere trails through a tropical jungle where impassable mud-holes and swollen rivers took a heavy toll of mules and cargo. In the rainy season, goods were sent by sea from Porto Bello to the mouth of the Chagres, a journey often made dangerous by pirates lurking along the shore, and from there poled up the Chagres River in boats to Venta Cruz, which was but five leagues from Panama. In the dry season the safer overland trail was used. The Panama–Porto Bello and Panama–Venta Cruz trails were paved with stone in the eighteenth century but they were still impassable for anything but pack animals.

Commerce with New Spain and the Antilles was less difficult. The settlements in the islands, as well as those in Honduras and Yucatán, were supplied by small ships which left the Plate Fleet after its arrival in American waters. The main part of the convoy proceeded to Vera Cruz. The Mexican fair was held in the interior at Jalapa, where accommodations were better and the climate more healthful than on the coast, and the transportation of goods from Vera Cruz to Mexico City was far less costly than from Porto Bello to Lima. It is not surprising that the commerce of New Spain became more important than that of Peru in the latter part of the colonial period.

The main purpose of the fleet system was to assure the safe and regular shipment or silver and gold from Peru and Mexico to Spain. Every effort was made to close all avenues through which bullion might be illegally exported. Although the mines were operated by private individuals, all gold and silver must be presented at the royal assay office for the deduction of the "royal fifth" before it might be sold or used in any way. From there it was shipped under close supervision to the *Casa de Contratación*, where the owner could obtain it "only after long and minute formalities." [1] Despite the most elaborate precautions, there was much smuggling. Aside from the desire to evade the payment of the royalty, there was a powerful temptation to resort to clandestine shipments because the government repeatedly seized properly manifested shipments as forced loans.

The Seville Monopoly

All attempts to modify the fleet system were opposed by the powerful vested interests which the system created. One of these was the *Consulado* of Seville, a close corporation of merchants dealing with the colonies organized in 1543. Its main purpose was to decide commercial disputes by a more rapid and satisfactory procedure than that of the *Casa de Contratación*, but it also provided a means by which the exporting houses could combine to exploit the American consumer and to treat with the royal government for special privileges. The *Consulado* was able to obtain many important concessions by payments of money or by its influence with the *Casa de Contratación*, and outside firms found it difficult to trade with the colonies in competition with its members. The regulations of the Casa, in fact, tended to prevent smaller merchants from loading goods on the fleet at all. The Seville houses worked in close coöperation with their correspondents at Mexico and Lima, where the chief importers were also organized in *consulados*. In the South American trade, for example, the exporters at Seville refrained from sending goods on their own account to points beyond Porto Bello, and the Peruvian importers agreed in return not to make

[1] Haring, *Trade and Navigation between Spain and the Indies*, p. 168.

purchases in Spain but to supply their needs by purchases at the fair on the Isthmus. There all prices were determined before trading began by an agreement between representatives of the Spanish merchants on the one hand and the American merchants on the other.[1] Such cooperation made possible great profits for the firms participating in the system, and efforts to change the legislation upon which their virtual monopoly rested met with strong opposition.

Intercolonial Trade

The effort to prevent trade outside of the fleet system led to the imposition of intolerable and unenforceable restrictions upon commerce by other routes. The chief sufferers in this respect were perhaps the settlers in the River Plate region. Although Buenos Aires was 1,000 miles from Upper Peru, the Spanish government feared to open the port for trade lest it become an outlet for illegal shipments of bullion from the mining region and a point of entry for smuggled goods. At first the settlers were permitted to engage in a limited commerce with Brazil and the Guinea Coast of Africa, where their grain and meat products were in great demand, but after 1618 their direct commerce with the outside world was legally restricted to two or three very small vessels sailing each year from Spain. They did engage in smuggling on a great scale, but the growth of the city and the nearby settlements was much retarded until the liberalization of Spain's commercial policy in the eighteenth century.

Trade between New Spain and Peru, the two great centers of Spanish enterprise in America, was also restricted within narrow limits and at times altogether prohibited. In this case the purpose was to prevent goods imported into New Spain from the Philippines from competing with Spanish manufactures in Peru. All intercourse between Spain and the Philippines was carried on through the Mexican port of Acapulco, and though only one vessel sailed each year it was an important part of the colonies' commerce. The Manila galleon brought great quantities of silks and other prized oriental products to Mexico, and they found their way through irregular channels to other centers where the settlers were rich enough to buy them. At the same time great quantities of Mexican silver dollars reached the Orient and

[1] Juan and Ulloa, *Relación histórica del viaje a la América Meridional*, 1748 edition, Vol. I, pp. 140–41.

became the principal form of money there as they did eventually in the British North American colonies.

One result of the Spanish commercial system was that few residents of the colonies could afford to buy imported goods. The fleet system and the restrictions that went with it aggravated the effect of the already formidable natural obstacles to commerce—the long ocean voyage, the difficult transhipment at the Isthmus, and the lack of roads in the interior—and the trade of the colonies was still further burdened by high taxes. Besides the *almojarifazgo*, or customs duties, collected both when the goods left Spain and when they arrived in the colonies, there were the *avería*, a contribution toward the cost of providing the fleets with military protection, the *alcabala*, or sales tax, and a number of lesser imposts. Moreover, the merchants at Seville combined to force prices even higher than they might normally have gone by deliberately undersupplying the colonial markets in order to make larger profits on each shipment. The cost of bringing an article to Chile, for example, was somewhat more than four times its original value in Cadiz. The various taxes were almost as much as the original value, and the freight across the Isthmus, between Porto Bello and Panama, consumed a similar amount. On the other hand, the price paid by the consumer was often ten times that in Cadiz.[1] The expense of shipping goods through legal channels to Buenos Aires, by way of Panama and Upper Peru, must have been very much greater.

Illegal Trade

The situation of the colonists might have been still more difficult had not a great part of their needs been supplied by goods illegally imported. The commercial restrictions were constantly violated by government officials, by foreign traders, and by the very merchants in whose interests they were maintained. Even in the carefully supervised annual fleets, fraud in loading ships and manifesting cargoes seems to have been the rule rather than the exception. As Spain's industries declined, after the latter part of the sixteenth century, articles originally brought from foreign countries made up an increasing proportion of the exports from Seville to America. The shipment of such articles by Spanish firms was permitted, but many merchants of other nationalities, who could not legally take part in the American trade, also found ways

[1] Galdámes, *Jeografía Económica de Chile*, p. 215.

of doing so, sometimes by acting through Spanish firms which merely lent their name to the transaction, and sometimes by loading goods directly from their own vessels in Cadiz Harbor, without the formality of registration. Gold and silver coming from the colonies found their way into foreign hands in the same manner. Official interference was avoided by bribery, or frequently by intimidation, for the Spanish government during the seventeenth century was too weak to risk offending other powers by confiscating the property of their subjects. Louis XIV of France even sent warships to Cadiz on more than one occasion as a warning not to molest French merchants in their illegal operations.

Besides the goods shipped with the fleets, a great quantity of merchandise was brought to the Indies by smugglers. No one in the colonies wished to see the law enforced. The creoles were glad of an opportunity to obtain foreign goods at more reasonable prices and to sell their own products. The merchants found it convenient to employ their capital in illicit operations during the long intervals between fleets, when it would otherwise have lain idle. The officials were almost universally corrupt, and even if a viceroy or governor were himself honest he could not trust his subordinates. Early in the eighteenth century, for example, one of the viceroys of Peru determined to check the illegal importation of goods in the vicinity of Lima. After encountering many obstacles because of the secret efforts of other officials to protect the smugglers, he finally sent a subordinate to investigate the situation at a port where contraband goods were being introduced with the connivance of the local authorities. This man exacted a share in the profits which the smugglers were making and reported that he had found nothing out of the way. A second investigator followed the same course. A third, sent to confiscate a vessel which had just entered port from Mexico, found dissimulation impossible and was compelled to confiscate the ship and order the arrest of the port authorities. When the case came before the *audiencia*, the highest court in America, only a few of the culprits were punished, and they received very light sentences.[1]

The most active smugglers, especially in South America, were the Portuguese. Despite the long distance and the lack of good roads, goods which they brought to the River Plate could be carried across the continent to Upper Peru and could compete there with those imported through legal channels. So important did this trade become that the great merchants of Lima often maintained agents in Brazil to arrange

[1] Juan and Ulloa, *Noticias Secretas de América* (London, 1826 edition), p. 206.

for shipments by the southern route. Between 1580 and 1640, when the two kingdoms were united under the Spanish Crown, a large number of Portuguese settled in the Spanish colonies and took over much of the wholesale and retail trade. Many of these were of Jewish descent, and in 1635 all business in Peru was disrupted when the Inquisition arrested more than eighty persons, including most of the principal merchants of Lima, on charges of reverting to Hebrew religious practices. Eleven of the accused, after long-drawn-out proceedings, were burned at the stake, and many received less severe punishment. This affair did not put an end to smuggling by the Portuguese. After 1680 Colonia do Sacramento, across the River Plate from Buenos Aires, was the great entrepôt for their trade. This establishment was a source of constant annoyance to the Spanish officials, and it was repeatedly seized by expeditions from Buenos Aires during the wars of the eighteenth century, only to be restored to Portugal when peace was made.

In the Caribbean region, the "Spanish Main," smuggling was carried on by adventurers of many nationalities. The pirates who began to appear in West Indian waters early in the sixteenth century often traded with towns in Española and Cuba when they did not have sufficient forces to seize and sack them. They became more active after the settlement of the mainland. Other European governments, jealous of the wealth which Spain was drawing from the Indies, systematically encouraged them, even in time of peace. The most famous of these searovers in the latter part of the sixteenth century were the Englishmen John Hawkins and Francis Drake. Hawkins made several voyages to the Indies after 1562 with cargoes of slaves which he obtained by fair means or foul on the African coast, trading or plundering as the occasion offered. Drake, who was with Hawkins when the two were defeated and nearly captured by the Spanish Plate Fleet at Vera Cruz in 1568, later made several voyages on his own account, seizing Spanish ships and sacking towns along the American coast. One of his most notable exploits was the circumnavigation of the globe between 1577 and 1580. In 1585 he commanded a large expedition which captured both Santo Domingo and Cartagena, and eleven years later he died of fever near Nombre de Dios after an unsuccessful effort to attack Panama. French pirates also continued their activities in the Indies, and the Dutch, while they were still carrying on an uncertain struggle against Spain for their own independence, began a systematic attack on the overseas possessions of the Spanish-Portuguese monarchy.

Dutch traders had early visited the Venezuelan coast in search of salt, which they needed for curing the product of their great North Sea fisheries. Their commercial relations with that region expanded after they conquered the Portuguese posts on the west coast of Africa, for Negro slaves were one of the commodities which were most in demand in the Spanish colonies. They soon controlled the trade in cacao and tobacco from the north coast of South America so completely that nearly all of the chocolate consumed in Spain itself is said to have passed through their hands [1] and the cultivation of tobacco in Venezuela was forbidden by the Spanish government in an effort to check their activities. In 1621 the Dutch West India Company was established in imitation of the East India Company, which had already virtually deprived Portugal of her great trading empire in the Orient. Students of American history are familiar with the story of the West India Company's activities at New Amsterdam, and we shall see in a later chapter how the Company seized and held for several years the most valuable part of Brazil. In the Caribbean it built up a great commerce both with the Spanish settlements and with the colonies which were by this time being established in the islands by other nations. Curaçao, seized from the Spaniards in 1634, and St. Eustatius, a smaller island in the Leeward group east of Puerto Rico, were the principal centers of its activities.

The West India Company, like the East India Company, carried on war on its own account with Spain. In 1628 one of its fleets, under the command of Admiral Piet Heyn, captured the Mexican treasure fleet, with such a quantity of spoil that the Company was able to declare a 50 per cent dividend on its capital stock. Subsequent victories at sea practically destroyed Spain's already decadent naval power, opening the way not only for a great expansion of Dutch commercial activity but also for trading and colonizing activity by subjects of other powers. The Company was ruined after the middle of the seventeenth century by the Portuguese reconquest of its Brazilian and African possessions, but other Dutch traders continued to be active in the Caribbean.

Foreign Colonies in the Caribbean

The Spaniards, absorbed in the exploitation of the rich mainland colonies, made little attempt to occupy the Lesser Antilles and the

[1] Haring, *Trade and Navigation between Spain and the Indies*, p. 119.

Guianas, where such natives as survived after the slave raids of the early sixteenth century were of little value as laborers. These portions of the Spanish Main were freely visited by smugglers and pirates, and it was not long before some of these interlopers perceived the possibility of cultivating tobacco and sugar there. The Dutch had successful plantations in Guiana as early as 1616, and the first permanent English colony was established in Barbados in 1625. A year or two before that English and French settlers occupied St. Christopher, or St. Kitts, but were driven out by Spanish warships in 1629. They soon returned and gradually spread to the neighboring islands: the English to Antigua and Montserrat, and the French to Martinique and Guadeloupe. Subsequent expansion put the whole chain of the Lesser Antilles in non-Spanish hands. The British colonies grew rapidly in population, for they profited from the same conditions in England that were causing emigration to Massachusetts and Virginia in the second quarter of the seventeenth century. The French, though backed by a company sponsored by Cardinal Richelieu, did not become so prosperous until a few years later. A very important element in the success of both groups of settlements was the aid of Dutch traders who financed their crops, purchased their products, and sold them supplies and Negro slaves.

One result of Dutch enterprise was the establishment of the Danish colony which was later to become the Virgin Islands of the United States. In 1671, finding it difficult to carry on trade under their own flag because Holland was at war with France, a group of Dutch traders persuaded King Christian V to establish a Danish West India Company and to occupy St. Thomas, where several Hollanders driven from St. Eustatius by the French had taken refuge. The island soon became an important center for the slave trade, as well as a rendezvous for pirates. Both the Danish and the Dutch possessions in the West Indies profited during the eighteenth century by the fact that they were generally neutral in the wars between other European powers.

The Buccaneers

For a hundred years after the discovery of America Spain insisted on treating foreigners coming to the Indies as trespassers, but by the seventeenth century she was no longer strong enough to maintain her claim to exclusive possession of territory not actually occupied by Spaniards. She was thus compelled, at first tacitly and later explicitly, to recognize the existence of the colonies of other powers in North America and the Caribbean. She was more stubborn in her refusal to accede to French and English demands for a share in the rich trade of her own possessions. Since these powers refused to respect her rights, and she was unable to enforce them, it became customary to regard the Indies as outside the scope of treaties made with the Spanish government. Normal relations might exist within the "Lines of Amity," east of the meridian of the Azores and north of the Tropic of Cancer, but it became a common saying that there was "no peace beyond the line." Other European governments, even in time of peace, openly encouraged their subjects to prey on Spanish trade in the Indies.

The activities of the Providence Company are an example of the sort of enterprise that this situation made possible. Organized in 1629 by a group of Englishmen who were also prominent in the affairs of Virginia and New England, this company occupied Providence Island, off the east coast of Nicaragua, with the avowed purpose of using it as a base for piracy. It also established small settlements on the Central American coast. The Company hoped for a considerable Puritan immigration, but this did not materialize. Chiefly for this reason the venture was a failure and the colony was destroyed by a Spanish expedition in 1641.

Other English and French colonies continued to offer bases and recruiting grounds for the pirates who became more and more numerous after the destruction of Spanish sea power. The great center for this activity was Tortuga, a small island off the north coast of Española which had been occupied some time before 1630 by a heterogeneous group of foreign outcasts and adventurers. The settlers had first been attracted by the good hunting on the nearby coast of Española, where great numbers of cattle and pigs had run wild after the partial abandonment of Santo Domingo by the Spaniards, and one of their main occupations was the supplying of dried meat and other provisions to passing pirates and smugglers. From their practice of curing this meat on a "boucan," or grill over a fire, they came to be called "Buccaneers"—a term which was later applied to all of the seventeenth-century freebooters in the Caribbean. Piracy seems to have been merely a side line with the settlers at Tortuga at first, but they abandoned hunting for the more exciting and profitable "course" as the supply of game decreased. Their settlement, meanwhile, had gone through many vicissitudes. It had been repeatedly destroyed by Spanish raids, and there had been fights between the English and French parties among the buccaneers. After being for a time under the control of the Providence Company, the island was ruled from 1641 to 1654 by a representative of the Governor General of the French West Indies. By the middle of the century its inhabitants were a numerous and unruly population devoted almost entirely to piracy. They merely scattered when a new Spanish expedition occupied the island in 1654, and returned a few months later when the Spanish forces were withdrawn to confront an English expedition that was attacking Santo Domingo.

This expedition had been sent by Cromwell, in time of peace and without warning to Spain, simply to conquer a part of the Spanish Main. Its attempt to take Santo Domingo was a rather disgraceful failure, but the less strongly held island of Jamaica was occupied in 1655 and at once became the most important of the English possessions in the West Indies. In the war that followed this act of aggression, British naval forces under Admiral Blake captured or destroyed the greater part of the Porto Bello fleet off Cadiz in 1656, and destroyed the Mexican fleet at Santa Cruz in the Canaries in the following year, though not until the treasure had been safely hidden on land. Meanwhile the English forces in Jamaica were no less active. Spanish counter-attacks were beaten off, and naval forces plundered several towns on the mainland. Even after the advent of peace in Europe, following the Restoration in England, the English authorities granted commissions to privateers for attacks on Spanish ships and settlements, and many of the buccaneers who had hitherto had their headquarters at Tortuga began to resort to Port Royal. The sea-rovers were at first a welcome addition to the defensive forces of the new colony, and it was hoped that their depredations would compel Spain to grant the commercial privileges that had been the real objective of the West Indian expedition.

The occupation of Jamaica was thus followed by a reign of terror throughout the Spanish Main. "Between the years 1655 and 1671 alone, the corsairs had sacked eighteen cities, four towns, and more than thirty-five villages—Cumaná once, Cumanagote twice, Maracaibo and Gibraltar twice, Rio de la Hacha five times, Santa Marta three times, Tolu eight times, Porto Bello once, Chagre twice, Panama once, Santa Catalina twice, Granada in Nicaragua twice, Campeche three times, St. Jago de Cuba once, and other towns and villages in Cuba and Hispaniola for thirty leagues inland innumerable times." [1] Many settlements in exposed localities were abandoned and many others suffered an injury from which they never recovered. Perhaps the most famous of the buccaneers' exploits was the destruction of Panama City in 1671 by Henry Morgan, who for this and similar achievements was knighted and made Lieutenant Governor of Jamaica.

The buccaneers, however, were not desirable citizens, and the hope that their depredations would force Spain to relax the restrictions on the colonial trade soon proved illusory. The English government consequently entered into a treaty with Spain in 1670 by which it agreed to check their activities in return for the formal recognition of its sovereignty over the English West Indian colonies. For some years after this date piratical undertakings were sometimes secretly encouraged by the authorities at Jamaica, as well as by officials in the North American colonies, but open governmental support gradually ceased.

The freebooters continued to operate from Tortuga and other places in the western part of Española, where there were by this time several settlements of French adventurers. These colonists had shaken off the control that the authorities at Jamaica had tried to exercise, and in 1664 the western end of the island was taken over by the French West India Company. The new governor, Bertrand d'Ogeron, was a man of foresight and ability who devoted himself with some success to the task of converting what had been little more than a nest of pirates into a flourishing agricultural colony. He not only encouraged the establishment of plantations, but imported several shiploads of women from France as wives for the settlers. His regime laid the foundations for the prosperity that later made French Saint Domingue the richest of the West Indian colonies. As the influence of the home government increased, buccaneering was gradually suppressed there also, for French merchants, who contributed so large a proportion of the goods sent from Spain to the Indies, suffered as much as any one else from attacks on Spanish merchant ships.

In the eighteenth century buccaneering was no longer used as an instrument of national policy. Pirates were treated as outlaws by all nations. Some former corsairs took to cutting dyewood in the jungles of the Central American and Mexican coast, establishing small settlements which were later to be the basis for English territorial claims in

[1] Haring, *Buccaneers in the West Indies in the XVII Century*, p. 267.

that region. Others became planters. Sugar and tobacco cultivation was exceedingly profitable in the British and French colonies during the eighteenth century, and Jamaica and Saint Domingue had many great plantations worked by hundreds of Negro slaves. The owners of these had no desire for a continuance of the old unruly conditions. They still carried on a very extensive smuggling trade with the Spanish colonies, but the old idea that there was "no peace beyond the line" was gradually abandoned, and treaties between Spain and other powers applied in Europe and America alike.

By this time it was clear that Spain's commercial policies had had unfortunate results for the mother country and for the colonies. The fleet system had indeed brought the treasure from the Indies safely to Spain on all but a very few occasions through a period of 150 years. On the other hand, the effort to confine trade to a few routes and to exclude foreigners from participation had simply diverted the greater part of the colonies' imports and exports into illegal channels. There were fewer and fewer ships in the fleets, and at times there were periods of several years when there were no fleets at all. Smuggling was prac- tised everywhere. The final decades of the colonial period were to see important changes in the system under which the commerce of the colonies was conducted.

6

The Last Century of Spanish Rule

In the sixteenth and seventeenth centuries conditions in the Spanish colonies reflected the growing weakness of the mother country, where the stirring days of the Conquest were followed by a long period of stagnation and decline. The Emperor Charles V had been perhaps the most powerful ruler in Europe, with extensive territories in the Netherlands, Germany, and Italy. His son Philip II inherited most of these, though without the imperial title, and annexed Portugal by force when the royal line in that country died out. It was evident even before Philip's death, however, that Spain's greatness rested on insecure foundations. Constant wars had drained her wealth and her manpower, and her population had begun to decrease. The seventeenth century was a period of brilliant achievement in literature and art but of retrogression in other respects. Commerce, industry, and agriculture had been severely affected by the expulsion of Jews and Moors who refused to accept Christianity, and even the treasure pouring in from the Indies could not check the country's economic decline. The kingdom's military strength was likewise affected, and a series of disasters beginning with the defeat of the great armada sent against England in 1588 all but destroyed its naval power. Other nations were not slow to take advantage of this state of affairs. In the seventeenth century the Dutch and Portuguese obtained their independence, and the Dutch and English and French attacked the Spanish possessions in America, and set up colonies in defiance of Spain's opposition. Many of these attained a prosperity that was in conspicuous contrast with the backwardness of the older Spanish settlements.

The Spanish colonies in 1700 were under a corrupt, inefficient regime that had changed little since the early part of the sixteenth century.

Their population had gradually increased, and the settlements had expanded into territory formerly held by wild Indians, but their economic development had been retarded by geographical isolation as well as by the restrictions of the Spanish commercial system. Though there was no question of their loyalty, it would clearly be difficult for the royal government to retain its hold on them in the face of increasing pressure from other powers unless it took measures to strengthen its political control and revise its economic policies. Spain did make changes in her colonial legislation after the Bourbon kings came to the throne in 1700.

Commercial Reforms

Among the most important of these were reforms in the commercial system. In the early years of the eighteenth century this system was clearly breaking down. The fleets sailed at longer and longer intervals with fewer ships and smuggling was practised everywhere. Other powers, furthermore, were demanding and obtaining a share in the colonial trade. During the War of the Spanish Succession (1702–1713) when Spain and France were allies, French vessels sailed freely around Cape Horn to Peru and traded with other provinces. At the end of the war, England exacted from Spain the grant of the *asiento,* the contract for supplying slaves to the colonies, and with it the right to send one ship each year to the fair at Porto Bello. The South Sea Company, to which these privileges were ceded, built up a large trade. The *navío de permiso* often brought half as much merchandise to Porto Bello as the entire Spanish fleet, for she was accompanied by tenders which remained below the horizon during the day and replenished her stock of goods at night. The factories, or agencies, which the company established at several ports in connection with the *asiento* also carried on much smuggling. When Spain attempted to check these practices, the British government supported the company and the "War of Jenkins' Ear" resulted in 1739. The company's privileges were not restored when the war ended.

By this time, however, even the powerful merchants of the Seville *consulado* could not prevent changes in the commercial system. The first break in their monopoly came with the establishment of several chartered companies to develop the trade of regions which had hitherto dealt chiefly with smugglers. Most of these were financed in Catalonia or in northern Spain rather than at Seville or Cadiz. They were given special privileges in the trade of one or more provinces, and expected to organize forces to prevent smuggling there. The earliest was the Honduras Company, set up in 1714, and there were others in Venezuela, Habana, and Santo Domingo. The only successful one was the Caracas or Guipuzcoa company, which was given extensive privileges in Venezuela in 1728. This company's oppressive conduct, and its success in checking smuggling, caused much dissatisfaction among the colonists, but it continued to control the trade of the province until 1781.[1]

The merchant fleets were gradually discontinued. After 1740 traffic around Cape Horn to Peru was permitted and the old route across the Isthmus of Panama practically ceased to be used. Thenceforth legitimate trade with all of the colonies except Mexico was carried on in "register ships" sailing alone. Until 1765 these were generally required to sail to and from Cadiz, but in that year several other Spanish ports were given permission to trade directly with the islands of the West Indies. Similar privileges were soon extended to other parts of the Empire, and after the famous free trade ordinance of 1778 the old restrictions applied only to Venezuela, where the Caracas Company was still operating, and to Mexico. In 1789 the Mexican fleets were finally discontinued. All of the colonies were thereafter allowed to trade directly with the principal Spanish ports, and in 1790 the *Casa de Contratación* was abolished. Most of the restrictions on intercolonial trade were also lifted in the decade of the 1770's.

Spain, like other colonial powers, still attempted to forbid commerce between her possessions and other countries. During the eighteenth-century wars, however, the government not only was frequently obliged to make exceptions in favor of friendly powers, but often found it impossible to prevent trade with merchants of hostile powers. When the British occupied Habana in 1762, and again when they seized Montevideo in 1807, hundreds of ships brought in merchandise and carried away the colonies' products. Ordinary smuggling also continued. The commercial ambitions of other nations—England, France, and the United States—were to have an important influence on the course of events when the colonies began their war for independence.

[1] For the history of this company see Roland Hussey, *The Caracas Company*.

Administrative Changes

There were also important changes in the government of the colonies. The administrative system in Spain itself was reorganized by the earlier Bourbon kings, and in 1714 the Council of the Indies and the *Casa de Contratación* were placed under the control of a Ministry of the Indies, through which the royal government attempted to exercise a more immediate supervision over American affairs. Three years later a new viceroyalty was created, with its seat at Bogotá, to govern New Granada, Venezuela, Quito, and Panama. This arrangement was later abandoned for a time, but was made permanent in 1739. In 1776 another viceroy was sent to Buenos Aires, to rule not only the River Plate provinces but also the mining region of Upper Peru.

Meanwhile the Crown endeavored to strengthen the defense of the colonies. Until the eighteenth century there had been few trained troops there. The principal settlements were in places where geographical barriers discouraged foreign attacks, but the seaports, especially in the Spanish Main, had suffered severely at the hands of Spain's enemies. After the Seven Years' War, a standing army and an organized militia were created. Both were officered and manned chiefly by creoles. Men of good family were eager to obtain commissions in these forces, and many of the military leaders who dominated Latin American politics after independence began their careers in this way.

The local administration became more efficient, especially during the reign of Charles III (1759–1788) who was by far the ablest of the Spanish Bourbon kings. Beginning in 1764, the government of a few of the less important American provinces was entrusted to "intendents" who had more authority and responsibility than the old local officials. The arrangement worked well, and between 1782 and 1790 intendents replaced the governors, *corregidores*, and *alcaldes mayores* throughout the colonies. The new officials were usually abler men than their predecessors and governed larger districts, with *subdelegados* under them in charge of smaller areas. They were still responsible to the viceroys, but they were the supreme representatives of the government in their own territory. One of their most important duties, to increase the royal revenues, was not calculated to make them popular with the colonists. In most cases they even deprived the city governments of what little authority and initiative the *cabildos* had formerly had. On the other hand, the disappearance of the *corregidores de Indios* freed the Indians from some of the many forms of oppression that were practised against them.

These administrative changes were of questionable value from the standpoint of the people of the colonies. They came too late to make any great change in the political heritage that was to shape the development of the Spanish American countries after independence. Their general effect, in fact, was to make the government more autocratic than it had been, and to diminish the influence that some of the creoles had enjoyed through their position as great landowners or as members of the *cabildos* under a less centralized regime. Residents of the colonies now had practically no opportunity for political or administrative experience that would help them after independence. Furthermore, many of the worst abuses of the old system persisted. Charles III made some improvement in the government personnel, but the quality of the officials sent to America deteriorated under his incompetent successors.

Expulsion of the Jesuits

Among the important events of Charles III's reign was the expulsion of the Jesuits. The Jesuits were one of the wealthiest and most powerful of the religious orders, not only in the Spanish colonies but throughout Catholic Europe. They maintained a high standard of discipline and personal conduct, but their ultra-conservative views made them many enemies and brought them into conflict in several countries with statesmen who were attempting to bring about political and economic reforms. The order had been suppressed in Portugal in 1759 and in France in 1764. In 1767 Charles expelled it from all of Spain's possessions. His action caused a tremendous sensation in the American colonies. Since there was some reason to fear that the creoles might resist the execution of the royal decree, all members of the order in each district were arrested secretly the same night and shipped immediately to Europe, without regard for the hardship inflicted on the more aged and infirm priests in regions where travel was difficult.

In the long run, the King's action probably weakened Spain's position in the colonies. It is true that the Jesuits were less amenable to royal control than other branches of the Church, because many of them were foreigners and because their highly centralized organization was directed by a general at Rome. There was even a strong suspicion that they had encouraged the Guaraní Indians to revolt when Spain attempted to trade the mission territory for the Portuguese smuggling post at Colonia in 1750.[1] On the other hand, the Jesuits were one of the strongest links in the political-religious system that tied the colonies to Spain. Besides their missionary work, in other provinces as well as Paraguay, they had been the leaders in education and had had a great influence in the spiritual life of the white communities. Their wealth and organizing ability had made them an important element in the colonies' economic life. No other religious order was able to take their place, and most of their missions and schools were carried on less efficiently or abandoned after their expulsion.

The Eighteenth-Century Revolts

Several outbreaks of disorder during the second half of the eighteenth century showed that Spain could ill afford to weaken her system of control in the colonies. Small uprisings among the creoles or the Indians occurred from time to time throughout the colonial period, but most of them had a purely local significance. After 1750 there were a series of revolts and conspiracies that revealed a growing willingness to defy the royal authority. The chief cause was the government's attempt to impose new taxes to provide funds for defense. In 1765, for example, the populace of Quito, angered by the establishment of a liquor monopoly, drove all *peninsulares* from the city and order was restored only by concessions to the insurgents and by the arrival of a strong Spanish garrison. In 1776–77 the imposition of new taxes in New Granada, Peru, and Chile caused riots in several places and gave rise to a rebellious spirit which soon found a more dangerous expression in Peru and New Granada.

In Peru the spectacle of disorders among the upper class was one of the causes of the great Indian uprising that began in 1780. Its leader was José Gabriel Condorcanqui, the hereditary chief of a village near Cuzco, who had been officially recognized as the heir of the Inca royal family and who, unlike many *caciques*, had for years endeavored to obtain fairer treatment for his people. The *mita* and the forced sales of goods by the *corregidores* still caused much hardship to the Indians, and it was against these that the revolt was specifically directed. Assuming the name of Tupac Amaru, Condorcanqui raised a large army

[1] See above, p. 90.

which killed creole landowners and destroyed property in much of Upper Peru. He himself was captured and executed in 1781, but his followers continued the struggle for two years more and there was a frightful loss of life on both sides before the movement was suppressed. It was not entirely fruitless, for some of the worst abuses against the Indians were done away with after peace was restored.

Of quite a different type was the revolt of the *Comuneros* in New Granada in 1781. In several towns of that province the creoles expressed their resentment against the new taxes by seizing control and organizing local governments which they called *comunes*. After some initial successes against the viceroy's troops, the insurgents proclaimed the independence of the colony and took steps to organize a republic. A number of Indians under the leadership of a descendant of one of the Chibcha royal houses joined the movement, while another group, in the province of Pamplona, announced their allegiance to Tupac Amaru. Peace was restored after a few months through the mediation of the clergy, but not until after the *audiencia* had agreed to abolish the fiscal monopolies and to reduce or discontinue certain taxes. This agreement was repudiated after the rebels disbanded and the royal officials received reinforcements. Four of the leaders in the movement were executed.

Francisco de Miranda

The eightenth-century revolts showed the creoles their own strength and made evident the government's weakness and inefficiency, but their outcome also indicated that the great majority of the inhabitants of the colonies were not yet ready to repudiate their allegiance to the King. The strength of the loyalist element was further demonstrated by the failure of two efforts to destroy Spanish power in America in 1806–7.

One of these attempts was the expedition of Francisco de Miranda, the most famous of the "precursors" of Spanish-American independence. Miranda was born in Caracas in 1750. He entered the Spanish military service as a captain at the age of twenty-two, and took part in operations against England in Florida and the Bahamas during the American revolution. In 1782 he was accused of smuggling and other offenses while acting as aide to the Governor of Cuba, and fled from the island when a military court was about to render a verdict against him. Thereafter he traveled in the United States, where he met Alexander Hamilton and Henry Knox, and in many parts of Europe, persistently endeavoring to persuade one or another of the powers to support a revolution in the Spanish colonies. He was given little official encouragement either in the United States or in France, though the revolutionary government at Paris at first seemed disposed to consider his project favorably. For a time he served as a brigadier general in the French army, but in 1793, being unjustly suspected of treason, he was imprisoned for more than a year. In 1798 he went to England.

The British government apparently gave him a small pension, but it was not ready openly to support his plans in America. It perhaps aided him secretly in organizing the expedition of 200 men with which he sailed from New York in February, 1806, and Admiral Cochrane, a British officer who was later to become a prominent figure in the war for independence, helped him when he reached the West Indies. Miranda occupied the town of Coro in Venezuela but he was soon forced to withdraw for lack of local support. There was much discontent in the colony, where ninety persons had been punished by death or imprisonment or exile after the discovery of a conspiracy headed by Manuel Gual and José María España in 1797; but the mass of the people were not ready to revolt and were still less willing to accept British in place of Spanish domination.

Miranda returned to London, where he met with another disappointment. In 1808, after Napoleon had apparently conquered Spain, the British government decided to send an expedition to prevent the French from obtaining control of the colonies. An army under Sir Arthur Wellesley, later the Duke of Wellington, was almost ready to sail when the revolt of the Spanish people caused the force to be sent to their aid instead. Miranda was heartbroken, but he continued to work for Latin American independence.

The British in the River Plate, 1806–1807

In the meantime, in 1806, the British Admiral Sir Home Popham, who had been interested in Miranda's schemes, decided on his own initiative to attack the Spanish possessions in the River Plate. Crossing the Atlantic from the Cape of Good Hope, which he had just conquered from the Dutch, he landed 1,600 men under General Beresford at Buenos Aires. The Viceroy Sobremonte fled to Córdoba, but a force of creoles from Montevideo, commanded by Santiago Liniers, defeated the invaders and forced Beresford to surrender.

Popham was thus forced to withdraw, but the inhabitants of Buenos Aires realized that the British would undoubtedly make some attempt to avenge his defeat. In the expectation of a new attack, they convened a *cabildo abierto,* a large meeting of the city's principal inhabitants which the municipal authorities were traditionally empowered to convoke in time of emergency. This institution was to be used frequently in all parts of the colonies during the next five years. In the viceroy's absence, the *cabildo abierto* made plans for the colony's defense. Liniers, though he was of French birth and had hitherto held only a minor position in the Spanish navy, was elected commander-in-chief, and a force of creole militia was hastily organized. A part of this was the legion of *patricios* under Cornelio Saavedra, which was later to play an important rôle in the movement for independence. The *audiencia* took over the civil administration, and the viceroy, when he returned to the city, was sent to defend Montevideo. He failed to hold this post when a much stronger British force arrived in February, 1807, but when the invaders moved on Buenos Aires in June, Liniers and the creoles put up a desperate fight. The poor management of General Whitelocke, the British commander, placed his army in so dangerous a situation that he was compelled to surrender, thus ending the British invasion. The viceroy was now deposed by another *cabildo abierto* and Liniers took his place.

These events dealt a fatal blow to Spain's authority in the River Plate. After the inhabitants of Buenos Aires had successfully defended themselves without help from the mother country against so formidable an enemy, and especially after they had once been permitted to take the conduct of affairs into their own hands, the restoration of the old autocratic regime was out of the question. The creoles had acquired a confidence in themselves and a sense of their own power which was again to find expression in the events of 1810. Even the restrictions on trade, which had been broken down while the British occupied Montevideo, were never completely reëstablished, and the desire for a continued enjoyment of the benefits of free commerce was one of the causes of the later revolutionary movement.

Why the Colonies Revolted

By this time it was clear to thoughtful observers that Spain would find it difficult as time went on to maintain her autocratic rule over the

American colonies. She had thus far held them not so much by her own strength as by their traditional loyalty—a loyalty fostered by the isolation imposed by geographical and legal barriers to communication with the outside world, by the vast authority of the Church, and by the influence of the great merchants and landowners whose privileges depended upon the maintenance of the existing regime. These conservative forces were still powerful, but they were being undermined by new intellectual currents that appeared during the eighteenth century.

The colonists, at least in some of the larger cities, were acquiring a new outlook and new habits of thought. With the relaxation of restrictions on trade and navigation, they began to have more contact with the outside world. Travel became less difficult and costly, so that some of the wealthier creoles were able to go abroad, and a few foreigners, including a small number of scientists and men of letters, came to America. There ensued an intellectual movement that was none the less notable because it was confined to a few centers. In the universities, the study of the modern philosophers took the place of the old dogmatic system based on Aristotle, and the students were encouraged to think for themselves as they would not hitherto have dreamed of doing. There was a new and lively interest in the natural sciences and other subjects hitherto excluded from the curricula of the educational institutions, and a new enthusiasm for literary pursuits which found expression in the publication of newspapers like the *Mercurio Peruano* of Lima and the *Papel Periódico* of Bogotá.

However zealously the authorities and the Inquisition might endeavor to restrict this activity to scientific and literary channels, it was impossible to prevent people from thinking about political questions also. The creoles who traveled abroad came into contact with the revolutionary ideas prevalent in the outside world, and some of them brought back books such as the works of Rousseau and the French encyclopedists which they circulated secretly among their friends. Among those most active in spreading radical propaganda in this way were José Antonio Rojas, a member of a wealthy Chilean family, and Antonio Nariño of Bogotá, who suffered a long imprisonment for printing and circulating a few copies of a translation of *The Rights of Man*. Forbidden books stimulated the imagination all the more because those found in possession of them were severely punished.

Spanish officials became more and more alarmed by seditious agitation and by the spread of revolutionary ideas. In many places small groups began to dream of independence or actually to conspire to attain it. Their enthusiasm increased after the successful revolt in British North America and still more after the French revolution, for both of these events touched the imagination of thinking people throughout Spanish America. "Since the Peace of Versailles," wrote von Humboldt, "and especially since the year 1789, one often hears a person say proudly 'I am not a Spaniard at all, I am an American,' words which reveal a longstanding resentment." [1]

Foreign revolutionary philosophies were embraced by only a small minority within the upper class, but there was much discontent among all sections of the population. Each class had its own grievances. The Indians were still poverty stricken and exploited, despite the abolition of the *encomienda* and the *mita* at the end of the eighteenth century. The *mestizos* and mulattoes were subject to legal discriminations which were humiliating if not very oppressive in practice. Even the creole aristocracy, with its wealth and privileges, was becoming dissatisfied as increased knowledge of other countries made the colonists more aware of the shortcomings of the Spanish regime. So long as trade was restricted to the ports of the mother country they still had no adequate markets for their products. The reforms in the political administration had not eliminated misgovernment and corruption, and taxation was if anything more burdensome than before because the establishment of a more effective governmental organization had been followed by efforts to obtain greater revenues for the royal treasury. These efforts, as we have seen, led to several revolts, and the cruel and treacherous treatment which was often meted out to the rebels, after they had been persuaded to lay down their arms, made the colonists still more bitter.

More important than any other cause of discontent, however, was the hatred of the creoles for the peninsular Spaniards. As we saw in Chapter 4, the *peninsulares* held practically all official positions except in the municipal governments, and often played a prominent part even in these. They monopolized the more lucrative positions in the Church, while the poorly paid parish priests were generally creoles. Even in commerce they had a distinct advantage over the less energetic and less thrifty natives. Alexander von Humboldt, the most distin-

[1] *Essai Politique sur le Royaume de la Nouvelle Espagne*, Vol. II, p. 3.

guished foreigner who studied conditions in the colonies, wrote at the beginning of the nineteenth century: [1]

The most wretched European, without breeding and without intellectual culture, thinks himself superior to the whites born in the new continent; he knows that, with the aid of his compatriots and favored by the luck quite common in countries where fortunes are made as rapidly as they are lost, he can one day reach positions to which access is almost forbidden to the natives, even those distinguished by their talents, their learning, and their moral qualities.

Little wonder that the creoles felt they were being exploited by an alien ruling class, and that even those who were sentimentally loyal to the King of Spain were eager to oust the king's local representatives and replace them by natives when the opportunity offered.

[1] *Ibid.*, Vol. II, pp. 2–3.

Part II

THE ERA OF INDEPENDENCE

7

The War for Independence

EARLY in 1808 Napoleon installed his brother Joseph Bonaparte as King of Spain, forcing Charles IV and his son Ferdinand to relinquish their rights to the throne. The Spanish people promptly rose in revolt. *Juntas*, or local governing committees, were set up in all parts of the kingdom, and later in 1808 a central *junta* assumed direction of the movement in the name of Ferdinand, who like his father was a prisoner of the French emperor. The Spanish patriots carried on widespread guerrilla warfare, but they could not stop the advance of the better armed and better trained French troops. At the beginning of 1810 the invaders controlled nearly all of the peninsula.

Though the colonists in America sympathized with the patriot movement, the overthrow of the royal government could not but weaken the position of its representatives in America. The latter could expect no effective support from the peninsula, and the quarrels between different branches of the administration, which had always caused trouble, became more acute when there was no one to settle them. Some officials were loyal to Ferdinand; others, like many of their colleagues at home, were suspected of a disposition to recognize Joseph Bonaparte's authority. In such a situation, the creoles' desire for a greater participation in public affairs inevitably found expression. Many natives of the colonies felt that they had as much right as the people of Spain to set up *juntas* to exercise authority in the name of the captive King, and demands that they be permitted to do so were strongly supported by the radicals who secretly desired complete independence. On the other hand, the majority of the officials and peninsular Spaniards, and usually the more conservative part of the creole aristocracy, opposed any departure from the *status quo*.

There were disturbances in several colonies in 1808 and 1809. In 1808 the viceroy of Mexico, hoping to increase his popularity, agreed at the request of the *ayuntamiento* at the capital to give that body, with its creole membership, a share in the general government. This infuriated the *audiencia* and the peninsular Spaniards. The plan failed when the reactionaries kidnapped the viceroy and removed him from office, but the affair left an aftermath of bitterness between the two parties. In Upper Peru, the *cabildo* of Charcas, with the support of several judges of the *audiencia*, deposed the president of that body in May, 1809, and invited other municipalities to join it in establishing *juntas* to govern in the name of Ferdinand. La Paz responded to the appeal, but the movement was suppressed in both cities by forces from Lima and Buenos Aires and those implicated were punished with great cruelty. A similar affair occurred at Quito, where conspirators deposed the president and set up a *junta* which exercised authority until it was suppressed by loyal troops from Guayaquil. In the River Plate it was the ultra-royalist governor of Montevideo, Francisco Xavier de Elío, who organized a *junta* in 1808 to oppose the Viceroy Liniers, whom he distrusted both because the latter was a Frenchman by birth and because of the circumstances under which he had come into power. Three months later, the pro-Spanish party at Buenos Aires attempted to overthrow Liniers, but was defeated by the creole militia. These events intensified the already existing hostility between the people of Montevideo and Buenos Aires, but both recognized the authority of a new viceroy appointed by the central *junta* in Spain, who arrived in July, 1809.

The Revolts of 1810 in South America

In January, 1810, Ferdinand's cause seemed hopeless. Napoleon's forces had overrun almost all of Spain and the patriot *junta* had been forced to flee to Cadiz, where it transferred what authority it still exercised to a "Council of Regency," named by itself. Many of those who had been most loyal to the monarchy began to feel that the colonies must now choose between French domination and independence, and both Spaniards and creoles realized that the supporters of the old regime in America could expect no further support from Spain. Those who wished to establish a new order had the opportunity for which they had been waiting.

The people of Venezuela were the first to act. In April, 1810, when

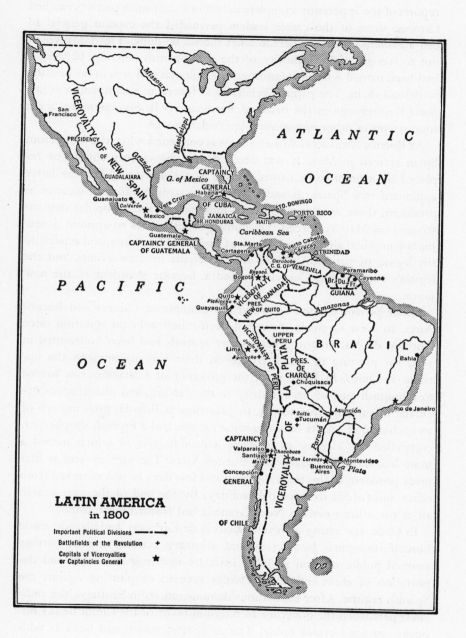

LATIN AMERICA
in 1800

Important Political Divisions — — — —
Battlefields of the Revolution +
Capitals of Viceroyalties
or Captaincies General ★

Labels on map:

San Francisco

VICEROYALTY OF NEW SPAIN

PRESIDENCY OF GUADALAJARA

Rio Grande

Missouri

Mississippi

ATLANTIC OCEAN

CAPTAINCY GENERAL OF CUBA

G. of Mexico

Habana

Vera Cruz

Guanajuato

Calderon

Mexico

Guatemala

CAPTAINCY GENERAL OF GUATEMALA

BR. HONDURAS

JAMAICA

HAITI

STO. DOMINGO

PORTO RICO

Caribbean Sea

Sta. Marta

Cartagena

Puerto Cabello

Caracas

Carabobo

C. G. OF VENEZUELA

TRINIDAD

Paramaribo

Br. Du. Fr.

Cayenne

GUIANA

Bogotá

Boyacá

VICEROYALTY OF NEW GRANADA

Quito

Pichincha

PRES. OF QUITO

Guayaquil

Amazonas

PACIFIC OCEAN

BRAZIL

VICEROYALTY OF LA PLATA

UPPER PERU

Lima

Junin

Ayacucho

VICEROYALTY OF PERU

PRES. OF CHARGAS

Chuquisaca

Bahia

Salta

Tucumán

Asunción

Paraná

Rio de Janeiro

CAPTAINCY

Valparaiso

Santiago

Chacabuco

Maipú

San Lorenzo

Concepción

Buenos Aires

Montevideo

La Plata

VICEROYALTY OF CHILE

GENERAL

125

reports of the apparently complete defeat of the Spanish patriots reached Caracas, some of the creole leaders persuaded the captain general to call a *cabildo abierto* to decide what should be done. This body voted not to recognize the authority of the new Spanish regency, because it had been named without consulting the colonies and was in no position to defend them. The captain general was forced to resign, and a creole *junta* took charge in the name of Ferdinand VII. Similar *juntas* were soon set up in other important Venezuelan towns.

At Buenos Aires a *cabildo abierto* was convened when the news from Spain arrived in May. It was decided that the viceroy should be replaced by a *junta* to be named by the *ayuntamiento*. When the latter appointed two Spaniards and two creoles, with the former viceroy as president, there was an outburst of indignation, and a popular demonstration on May 25 forced the municipal authorities to appoint a new *junta* composed almost exclusively of creoles. The militia, and especially the legion of *patricios*, played an active part in these events, and the legion's commander, Cornelio Saavedra, became president of the new *junta*.

Other provinces soon followed the example of Caracas and Buenos Aires. In New Granada there had been much political agitation since Antonio de Nariño and several other radicals had been imprisoned in 1809 for plotting to attack troops on their way to suppress the uprising at Quito. In May, 1810, the governor of Cartagena was forced to relinquish part of his authority to the *cabildo*, and disturbances occurred in various other towns. In July riots at Bogotá, growing out of an exchange of insults between some creoles and a Spanish shopkeeper, compelled the viceroy to convene a *cabildo abierto* which named a *junta* like those of Caracas and Buenos Aires. The viceroy was at first made president of this body, but within a few days he was removed from office and forced to leave the country. By the end of the year nearly all of the other towns in New Granada had formed local *juntas*.

In Chile, the acting governor, García de Carrasco, had already made himself unpopular by tactless and arbitrary actions, and he further aroused public opinion in July, 1810, by ordering the arrest and deportation of three influential creoles accused of plotting against the Spanish regime. After tumultuous demonstrations in Santiago, the *audiencia* persuaded the governor to resign in favor of the Count de la Conquista, an aged creole noble. The *audiencia*, which had been at odds with Carrasco, hoped that this would placate the populace without further weakening the prestige of the Spanish regime, but the new governor fell more and more under the influence of the creole party. Matters came to a head when it was known that Elío, the governor of Montevideo, had been transferred to Chile. An aroused populace demanded a *cabildo abierto*, and when this met on September 18 it set up a *junta* which at once entered into close relations with that at Buenos Aires.

By the latter part of 1810 the creoles had thus taken matters in their own hands in many of the more important South American provinces. Their actions made it clear that they did not intend that the old regime should return. In nearly every case the *juntas* in the chief cities invited other municipalities to send representatives to discuss a new form of government, and congresses met in response to these invitations in Venezuela, New Granada, and Chile. What the native leaders ostensibly contemplated was the creation of autonomous states under creole control but still nominally subject to the king; but many of them were already planning to seek complete independence, and republican ideas were gradually gaining ground among the people.

The *Junta Central* in Spain and the Regency which succeeded it did what they could to maintain their authority in the colonies and to placate the dissatisfied element there. In January, 1809, in recognition of expressions of sympathy and substantial financial aid from America, the *Junta* declared that the colonies were integral parts of the monarchy and invited each viceroyalty and captain-generalcy to send a delegate to be one of its members. A year later, provision was made for colonial representation in the new Spanish *cortes*, or parliament. In both cases, however, the procedure prescribed would in practice have left the choice of representatives to the royal officials and the number of delegates would have been small compared with those allotted to the Spanish provinces. The creoles thus felt that their claim to equality had received little recognition. Since the colonies legally belonged to the Crown rather than to the Spanish nation, there were many who questioned the authority of a *junta* organized by the Spanish people without effective colonial representation or a regency named by such a *junta*. Colonial resentment increased when it became known that the merchants of Cadiz had been able to procure the revocation in May, 1810 of a decree of the regency that had authorized free trade between American ports and foreign countries. Subsequently, the *cortes* granted the colonists complete political equality with Spaniards and the right to be represented in future *cortes* in the same way as the people of the peninsula, but this action came too late. Even if it had come earlier, it would have meant little to the colonists so long as the government in Spain attempted to maintain in America a regime dominated by *peninsulares*.

The Spanish American revolution, however, was not so much a contest between the colonies and Spain as a civil war in the colonies themselves. Besides the relatively small but very influential group of peninsular Spaniards, there were powerful elements among the creoles which opposed the revolutionary movement because their own material welfare was bound up with the maintenance of the existing regime. Landowners, dependent upon cheap, more or less compulsory labor, were alarmed by the efforts of the radicals to win support from the lower classes. The aristocracy in general saw that it would be difficult to maintain its privileges without outside help, and the creole leaders had to weigh the advantage of throwing off Spanish control against the possibility that they themselves would be supplanted by the *mestizo* military chiefs who began to rise to prominence as the revolt got under way. There were, too, many who had moral scruples against rebellion. Though a number of priests were leaders among the revolutionists, the majority of the higher clergy were peninsular Spaniards, and the Church as an institution threw its vast influence into the scales on the loyalist side. Rebellion, in the minds of a large proportion of the faithful of all classes, was a crime against God as well as against the king.

It was the strength of these loyalist elements which made the struggle so long and uncertain. Except for one brief period after the Bourbon restoration, the supporters of the old regime got relatively little help from Spain. The armed forces in the colonies at the outbreak of the war were composed largely of creole militia, and the royalist commanders continued to recruit men locally throughout the struggle. Many districts both in the north and in the south refused to join the revolutionary movement, at least in its earlier stages, and Peru, which had been the center of Spanish power and special privilege in South America, was a royalist stronghold until the end of the war.

The Two Periods of the War

The story of the war in South America falls into two periods. During the first, the creole regimes in Venezuela, New Granada, Buenos

Aires, and Chile were simply struggling for existence, weakened by rivalries among their leaders, and unable to win decisive victories over the royalists. Many places even in those provinces, and nearly all of the territory now included in Peru, Bolivia, and Ecuador remained under Spanish control. This phase of the contest ended with the reinstatement of the Bourbons at Madrid and the restoration of Spanish authority everywhere except in the River Plate. The second began in 1817 when San Martín crossed the Andes to liberate Chile. Soon after this exploit Bolívar began to reorganize the scattered bands of revolutionists in the Orinoco Valley and to win victories in New Granada and Venezuela. Working independently and coming into contact with one another only when their objective had been almost accomplished, these two great leaders advanced from the south and from the north until the war was finally won in the highlands of Peru.

The War in the North, 1810–1816

Soon after its creation, the *junta* at Caracas sent three commissioners to London to ask recognition and aid from the British government. One of these was Andrés Bello, who was later to become one of the most famous writers and publicists of Spanish America. Another was Simón Bolívar, a wealthy young creole, who had traveled extensively in Europe during the years just before 1810 and had there become imbued with revolutionary ideas. The commissioners failed in their purpose, but in London they met Francisco de Miranda and established contact with the influential group whom he had already interested in the patriot cause. Miranda returned to Venezuela at the end of 1810, and at once became prominent in the congress that met a few months later to consider the adoption of a new form of government. With Bolívar he worked zealously for the abandonment of any pretense of loyalty to Ferdinand VII and for a complete separation from Spain, and his efforts were crowned with success when the congress voted a declaration of independence on July 5, 1811. In December of the same year a constitution was adopted and Venezuela became a federal republic.

The new government was weakened by rivalries between the patriot leaders and the indifference or hostility of a large portion of the inhabitants, and its fate was sealed when a destructive earthquake occurred on March 26, 1812. The priests told the populace that the disaster was a punishment inflicted upon them by Providence for their rebellion. Many abandoned the patriot cause, and Domingo de Monteverde, a Spanish naval officer who had entered the province earlier in the same month with a force of 500 men, made rapid progress against the republican army under Miranda. On July 25, the latter entered into a capitulation which restored Spanish authority in return for a promise that the lives and property of the Venezuelans would be respected. The shameless violation of this agreement, after the rebels had laid down their arms, caused other leaders in the revolutionary party to believe that they had been betrayed, and when Miranda was about to leave the country he was seized by Bolívar and his associates and turned over to the royalists. The great precursor of independence died in a Spanish prison four years later. Bolívar, who was permitted to leave Venezuela under a passport from Monteverde, went to Cartagena to offer his assistance to the revolutionists there.

Cartagena had declared itself an independent republic in November, 1811, and several other provinces in New Granada had followed its example; but local jealousies made it impossible to set up a central government, and the forces of the various towns were fighting among themselves as often as against the royalists who still held Santa Marta in the north and Popayán in the south. When Bolívar arrived at Cartagena, he was given command of a force with which he carried on successful minor operations against the royalists in the Magdalena Valley. Meanwhile the revolted provinces reached an agreement that made some measure of joint action possible, and Antonio Nariño, the President of Cundinamarca, undertook a campaign against Popayán while Bolívar attempted the reconquest of Venezuela. Nariño's campaign, successful at first, ended when he fell by accident into the hands of the enemy in May, 1814. Bolívar was hardly more successful. He overran Venezuela in 1813 and regained control of Caracas, where he was given the title of "Liberator" which was thereafter his proudest possession; but a year later he was driven out of the province by an army that a Spanish adventurer named Boves recruited among the half-savage plainsmen of the Orinoco Valley. During this campaign the leaders on both sides resorted to the ruthless brutality which thenceforth characterized the war in all parts of South America. Bolívar proclaimed a "war to the death," threatening to kill all Spaniards even though they remained neutral, and in February, 1814, he ordered the summary execution of more than 800 prisoners in retaliation for the barbarous cruelties perpetrated by Boves against native patriots.

By this time the overthrow of Napoleon had restored Ferdinand VII to his throne and the Spanish government was in a position to come to the royalists' assistance. In 1815 a force of somewhat more than 10,000 men sailed from Cadiz under the command of General Pablo Morillo. Cartagena was taken after a three months' siege, and the occupation of all New Granada followed. Many of the creole leaders were put to death, and the reconquered towns were treated with a harshness that did nothing to strengthen their loyalty. The revolution in the north collapsed. Bolívar fled to the West Indies, but a few of the other patriots escaped into the *llanos* east of the Andes, where they continued to carry on guerrilla operations.

Failure of the Revolution in Chile

The regime set up by the creole leaders in Chile also had a brief and troubled existence. When the first congress met in July, 1811, its members divided into conservative and radical factions. The conservatives were at first dominant, but in September a young military officer named José Miguel Carrera seized power and reorganized the congress with a radical majority. Later in the same year, Carrera assumed dictatorial powers. He had by this time alienated even the other leaders of his own group, though most of them came to his support when the Viceroy of Peru sent Spanish officers to recruit an army in the still loyal island of Chiloé early in 1813. These royalist forces occupied much of south central Chile during the next twelve months, but the fighting was indecisive and the Treaty of Lircai, in May, 1814, provided for the withdrawal of the Spanish troops in return for the Chileans' promise to continue to recognize the sovereignty of Ferdinand VII.

This agreement was unsatisfactory to both sides. Carrera, who had been captured by the Spaniards during the war, returned to Santiago to protest against it, and again seized control. Bernardo O'Higgins, another leader of the radical wing of the patriot party, organized a counter revolt. Civil war had already begun when word came that the Viceroy of Peru had also disapproved the treaty and was sending another army to Chile. O'Higgins at once placed himself under Carrera's orders, but the patriot forces were defeated at Rancagua on October 2, 1814. The two leaders, with 3,000 men, escaped across the Andes to Mendoza.

The Creole Regime at Buenos Aires

By 1816 the River Plate region was the only important part of Spanish America that had not been reconquered by the royalists. While the patriot movement was rising and falling in the north, a series of weak governments at Buenos Aires were endeavoring, with only partial success, to liberate the rest of the territory of the former viceroyalty. The *junta* set up in May, 1810, sent hastily recruited forces into several of the interior provinces. One which invaded Paraguay was defeated by the people of Asunción who did not wish to be ruled by Buenos Aires, but who quietly removed the Spanish officials and set up an independent government of their own in 1811. Another invaded the *Banda Oriental,* as Uruguay was then called. With the aid of local forces under José Artigas, it laid siege to Montevideo, but suspended hostilities, by agreement with the royalists, when Portuguese forces entered the province from Brazil. A third army took Córdoba, and then went on into Upper Peru. Several royalist commanders, including the former viceroy Liniers, were executed by order of the *junta,* so that war without quarter became the practice in southern South America as in the north. The patriot army reached Lake Titicaca, but was surprised and routed at Huaqui in June, 1811.

In the meantime there had been continual factional disputes at Buenos Aires. Mariano Moreno, the brilliant and enthusiastic secretary of the *junta,* resigned when the *junta,* led by Saavedra, voted to admit to its membership several deputies from the provinces. Moreno died soon afterward, while on his way to Europe on a diplomatic mission, but his followers continued to cause trouble, and in April, 1811, several of them were expelled from the *junta* after a military demonstration by the *Saavedristas.* After the defeat at Huaqui, Saavedra himself was exiled. In September, 1811, the *junta,* which was too large for the effective conduct of business, transferred the executive power to a "triumvirate." This group soon dissolved the parent body and assumed full power, only to be ousted in October, 1812, by a barracks revolt that installed a new triumvirate. Among the leaders in this movement were José de San Martín and Carlos de Alvear, two creole officers formerly in the Spanish army who had recently arrived from Europe to offer their services in the cause of independence.

Military operations continued, with indifferent success. In the north, the royalists had taken the offensive. Manuel Belgrano checked their invasion by defeating them at Tucumán in September, 1812, and at Salta in February, 1813; but he was repulsed when he attempted to invade Upper Peru. In the *Banda Oriental* hostilities against the Spaniards were renewed after British diplomatic pressure persuaded the Prince Regent at Rio de Janeiro to sign an armistice with Buenos Aires in May, 1812. The *junta*'s forces and Artigas again besieged Montevideo, but for several months made little progress.

The second triumvirate ordered the election of a constituent assembly. This met in 1813, with delegates from most of the provinces, and adopted a series of measures that practically terminated the colonial regime in Argentina. The use of the royal coat of arms and the invocation of the King's name in official acts were abolished, entails and titles of nobility were suppressed, and the Indians were exempted from forced labor. All persons brought into the country or born there in the future were declared free, although the existing Negro slaves, of whom there were a considerable number, were not emancipated. Alvear and his associates were very influential in the work of the assembly, and in January, 1814, Alvear's uncle, Gervasio Posadas, was elected to the newly created position of "Supreme Director of the United Provinces of the River Plate."

The assembly did not adopt a constitution or make a specific declaration of independence. Many of the more conservative leaders, though they did not intend to permit the restoration of the old regime, felt that the best solution for the country's problems would be the establishment of a constitutional monarchy. One faction supported the aspirations of Carlota Joaquina, the ambitious and unprincipled sister of Ferdinand VII, who had been carrying on intrigues with creole leaders in the River Plate and Chile for some years. The fact that Carlota was the wife of the Prince Regent of Portugal made her unacceptable, and several persons were executed after the discovery of a plot in her favor at Buenos Aires in 1812; but there was less opposition to other members of the royal family. After the Bourbon restoration, Posadas' government sent representatives to Europe to seek to persuade a Spanish prince to accept the throne, but Ferdinand VII would not permit any of his relatives to consider their proposals.

The desire for a monarchy was strengthened by increasing discouragement over the internal political situation. The government had hitherto been controlled by the *porteños*, or people of Buenos Aires, and this had caused much jealousy in the provinces. When the constituent assembly of 1813 was convened, José Artigas, the great *caudillo* of the *Banda Oriental*, sent the delegates from that region to Buenos Aires with instructions to advocate a "federal" republic in which the provinces would have complete autonomy. The assembly refused to seat them and ordered that new delegates be chosen. Artigas thereupon withdrew his troops from the army that was besieging Montevideo. This was the beginning of a war between "federalists" and "unitarians" which was to keep the "United Provinces" in a state of near anarchy for many years.

Despite Artigas' disaffection, the Buenos Aires army finally took Montevideo in June, 1814. The royalists were thus deprived of their last stronghold in the River Plate. If they had been able to hold the city, it is very possible that the forces which some months later reconquered New Granada might have been sent against Buenos Aires instead. The *porteños*, however, were driven from Montevideo and from the whole *Banda Oriental* by Artigas, in 1815, and federalist *caudillos* in other provinces also revolted. Artigas was soon the head of a loose federation which included Entre Ríos, Santa Fe, Corrientes, and Córdoba as well as his own province. He was for a short time the most powerful figure in the River Plate region, but in 1816 the Portuguese again invaded the *Banda Oriental* and finally conquered the province after four years of fighting. The other federalist leaders turned against him in defeat but they continued their war against Buenos Aires.

The *Porteño* or "unitarian" party continued to hold the capital and some of the interior provinces, but it was weakened by factional quarrels and military reverses. Posadas was soon forced to resign and several short-lived regimes followed. A third attempt to invade Upper Peru failed in 1815, and the royalists might well have conquered northern Argentina had it not been for the heroic resistance of Martín Güemes and his *gaucho* army, which held the frontier until the tide turned in favor of the patriot cause.

Early in 1816 a congress representing the provinces that recognized the authority of the Buenos Aires government met at the northern city of Tucumán. Juan Martín de Pueyrredón was elected Supreme Director of the United Provinces for a three-year term, and on July 9, 1816, the congress adopted a formal declaration of independence. At the same time the delegates renewed the effort to set up a constitutional monarchy. Belgrano, one of the principal *porteño* leaders, proposed the creation of an Inca dynasty, which might be expected to attract the support of the Indians of Peru, and this fantastic plan was seriously discussed. Negotiations were also resumed in Europe, and various candidates, including the future King Louis Philippe of France and Ferdinand VII's nephew the Prince of Lucca, were considered. The efforts to set up a monarchy were to continue, despite popular opposition in Argentina, until the unitarian government was overthrown by the federalists in 1820.[1] They failed, like earlier monarchical projects, because Ferdinand VII refused to give up his own claim to the throne.

Though the federalist-controlled provinces still opposed it, the new Argentine regime had somewhat more prestige and authority than any of its predecessors. Its inauguration made possible the renewal of the war against Spain at a time when continued inaction might have meant the complete defeat of the patriot cause.

San Martín and the Liberation of Chile

The war was renewed through the efforts of one determined leader. José de San Martín was born in 1778 in one of the old Paraguay missions, where his father commanded the Spanish garrison. The family returned to Spain while José was still very young, and the boy entered the royal army at the age of eleven. Twenty-two years later, after serving with distinction in Africa and in Europe, he had reached the rank of lieutenant colonel. Early in 1812 he arrived in Buenos Aires to offer his services to the revolutionary government. He was at once given a commission in the army and soon began to play an influential part in political as well as military affairs. Early in 1813 he distinguished himself by winning a battle at San Lorenzo which drove the royalists out of the littoral provinces. For a short time in 1814, after the failure of the second invasion of Upper Peru, he was made commander-in-chief of the forces in the north, but he soon asked to be relieved of this duty and a few months later obtained the governorship of the province of Cuyo, at the foot of the Andes in western Argentina. He seems already to have had in mind the idea of securing the independence of South America by expelling the Spanish forces from Chile and then making an attack on Peru by sea. For two years he quietly matured his

[1] For this and subsequent events in Argentina, see Chapter 9.

plans and trained his troops, and when his friend Pueyrredón became head of the government he obtained more effective help from the central authorities.

San Martín's passage of the Andes, in January, 1817, is one of the great exploits of military history. The transportation of an army with its supplies and artillery over difficult passes more than two miles above sea-level was in itself a notable feat, made possible only by the care and thoroughness with which the Commander-in-Chief made his preparations and his skill in deceiving the enemy as to his intentions. Within a month he was able to unite his forces in the western valleys, and on February 12 he defeated the royalists at Chacabuco and forced them to evacuate Santiago. The Chileans received him with enthusiasm, for the stupidly repressive policy of the royal officials since 1814 had alienated many who had formerly opposed the patriot cause. After San Martín declined its invitation to assume charge of the government, a *cabildo abierto* at Santiago elected Bernardo O'Higgins as supreme director, and on February 12, 1818, the independence of Chile was formally proclaimed. The viceroy at Lima sent a new army under General Osorio to reconquer the province, and this force defeated the patriots at Cancha Rayada in March, 1818, but three weeks later, on April 5, San Martín won the decisive battle of Maipú. Thereafter small bodies of royalists held out in the south, especially in the island of Chiloé, but the Spaniards did not again threaten central Chile.

San Martín in Peru

The expedition against Peru, San Martín's next objective, would be possible only if the patriots obtained control of the sea. O'Higgins' government therefore set out to create a fleet. Several foreign ships, invited to go to Chile by the patriots' agents abroad, were purchased and put into service under British and North American officers. Among the latter was Captain Charles Whiting Wooster, formerly of the United States Navy, who played an active part in operations that broke the royalist blockade of Valparaiso and finally gave the patriots control of the sea on the South American west coast. Early in 1819 the fleet was placed under the command of Thomas Alexander, Lord Cochrane, a brilliant officer who had been discharged from the British navy after quarreling with his superiors and being convicted, perhaps unjustly, of financial irregularities. Two years later preparations for the expedition northward were completed.

By this time renewed civil war in the River Plate had cut San Martín off from any hope of assistance from Buenos Aires, especially as he refused to obey orders to return to support the government there in its losing struggle against the federalists. On the other hand, he still had his own Army of the Andes, and he had the warm coöperation of the Chilean government under O'Higgins. The prospect for success became brighter when a Spanish army that was about to embark for America mutinied at Cadiz in January, 1820, taking the lead in a revolution that compelled Ferdinand to reëstablish the liberal constitution of 1812. There seemed to be some ground to hope that the new regime in Spain might be willing to accept the independence of the revolted colonies, and it was clear at any rate that the royalist authorities were not likely to receive much help from Spain for the time being.

Escorted by Cochrane's fleet, San Martín sailed from Valparaiso in August, 1820, with somewhat more than four thousand Argentine and Chilean troops. When he landed at Pisco, south of Lima, he found that the viceroy had been instructed by the new Spanish government to endeavor to reach an agreement with him, and an armistice was arranged pending negotiations. The viceroy proposed that the colonists accept the relatively favorable status which the Spanish constitution would have given them, but San Martín insisted on independence, though he was apparently willing to consider the establishment of an American constitutional monarchy under a Spanish prince. The negotiations consequently broke down. They were renewed some months later, after the Viceroy Pezuela had been removed by his own officers and General La Serna had been chosen in his place, but again they failed. Meanwhile there were minor military operations and San Martín occupied points on the coast north of Lima. In July, 1821, La Serna abandoned the capital and marched inland, permitting the invaders to occupy the city without resistance. San Martín proclaimed the independence of Peru on July 28, and assumed dictatorial powers as "Protector" of the new state a few days later. His undertaking had thus far met with success, but the strong royalist forces in the highlands and the pro-Spanish feeling of a large part of the people of the province were still formidable obstacles to its complete achievement. With the forces at his disposal he was in no position to carry the war to a conclusion, and he was compelled to mark time for some months while the now triumphant patriot forces under Bolívar advanced from the north.

Bolívar's Operations in Venezuela, 1816–1819

Though the royal authority was reëstablished in the more settled parts of Venezuela after Bolívar's defeat in 1814, a few small bands kept up a guerrilla warfare in the plains of the Orinoco Valley, coöperating with the New Granadan patriots under Santander who had escaped into the sparsely inhabited *llanos* farther west after the reconquest of Bogotá. Bolívar himself fled to the West Indies. There he obtained help from President Pétion of Haiti, the little state that had freed itself from French rule twelve years before. He led an expedition to the Venezuelan coast in 1816, but dissensions among his followers and their inability to resist the stronger Spanish forces made the venture a failure. He returned to Haiti, where Pétion again helped him, and the end of 1816 found him back in Venezuela, now the recognized leader of the insurgent bands in that province.

During the next two years, while San Martín was freeing Chile from Spanish control, the revolution in Venezuela made little progress. Jealousies and open insubordination made Bolívar's task difficult, and he was compelled at last to shoot Manuel Piar, who had been one of the ablest and most daring of the patriot leaders. Spanish forces that attempted to invade the Orinoco Valley were repulsed, but Bolívar's troops were not strong enough to carry the war into the more populous mountain regions. After a serious defeat at La Puerta in March, 1818, the whole movement seemed certain to end in failure, but Bolívar refused to be discouraged. His army was gradually increasing as the people of the plains rallied to his standard. These wild, ignorant *llaneros* had made up the bulk of the armies that had driven Bolívar from Venezuela in 1814, but they had been alienated from the royalist cause by tactless treatment after Morillo arrived with his Spanish army, and many of them had become revolutionists. Under the leadership of the daring and popular José Páez, they became a formidable cavalry force. At the same time, Bolívar's agents abroad were persuading several hundred British and other foreigners to enlist in his army, and these played an important part in his subsequent campaigns. The Liberator's position was further strengthened when the congress which he convened at Angostura in February, 1819, confirmed his appointment as

Commander-in-Chief of the Army and made him President of the Republic of Venezuela. Meanwhile guerrilla warfare against the Spaniards had continued, and Bolívar was planning a daring new move that was to change the whole situation.

The Liberation of New Granada, Venezuela, and Ecuador

In June, 1819, in the midst of the rainy season, Bolívar made what seemed an almost impossible march into the upper Orinoco Valley to join the New Granadan patriots under Santander. The combined force then crossed the eastern range of the Andes to emerge on the plateau north of Bogotá. Only a daring and resourceful strategist could have conceived such a manoeuvre, and only a commander with Bolívar's qualities of leadership could have executed it. Its success was startling. Though the ill-clad and poorly equipped patriots had suffered terrifically from the cold and from the labor of marching through almost trackless country, they surprised and completely defeated a far superior Spanish force in the battle of Boyacá on August 7, and the victory gave Bolívar control of the most important part of New Granada. With a new base of operations and a new source of recruits and supplies, he was in a position to confront the main royalist army in Venezuela.

For the time being he did not follow up his advantage. Dissensions in the congress at Angostura, where his enemies had obtained the upper hand, compelled him to make the long and dangerous journey back to the provisional capital to restore his authority. Early in 1820, the news of the Spanish revolution arrived and the royalist commander made overtures for a treaty of peace. He offered to leave the patriot leaders in actual control of the provinces that had been liberated provided that the sovereignty of Spain be recognized, but Bolívar, like San Martín, insisted on complete independence. Hostilities were resumed even before the expiration of the six months' armistice which had been agreed upon.

Bolívar now marched eastward through the highlands from New Granada into Venezuela. On June 24, 1821, he won the second of the decisive victories of the war in the north at Carabobo. This practically freed Venezuela from Spanish rule, although Puerto Cabello, the last royalist stronghold in northern South America, was not captured until November, 1823.

The battles of Boyacá and Carabobo made the Republic of Colombia a reality. The existence of this new state, whose territory was to comprise New Granada, Venezuela, and the as yet unconquered Presidency of Quito, had been proclaimed by the congress at Angostura in December, 1819, and Bolívar had been elected its first president. After the battle of Carabobo another congress met at Cúcuta to confirm Bolívar's election and draw up a federal constitution. Bogotá soon afterward became the capital. Great Colombia, as historians now call it, took its place in the family of nations when its government was recognized by the United States in 1822 and by Great Britain in 1824.

With Spanish resistance broken in New Granada and Venezuela, Bolívar was free to turn his attention southward. Early in 1821 he had sent Antonio José de Sucre by sea to Guayaquil, where the creoles had set up an independent government in the previous October. Sucre's first attempt to push into the interior was a costly failure, and Bolívar marched overland to his assistance. He was delayed for some months by the stubborn resistance of the inhabitants of Pasto, who had remained loyal to Spain, and in the meantime, on May 24, 1822, Sucre destroyed the Spanish forces in the region of Quito at the Battle of Pichincha. The Department of the Equator, "El Ecuador," thus became in fact as well as in name a part of Colombia. A few months before, on November 28, 1821, the inhabitants of Panama had thrown off their allegiance to Spain and adhered to the Colombian federation. With the loss of the Isthmus, it became more difficult for Spain to send reinforcements to the royalist commanders still in the field.

The Guayaquil Conference

Peru and Upper Peru were now the only important regions still occupied by Spanish armies. San Martín had made little progress after his occupation of Lima, and his situation was far from encouraging. Many of the people of Lima were still opposed to the revolution, and the military dictatorship which he had been obliged to establish was unpopular. It was impossible to expect large reinforcements from Argentina or Chile. There was much discontent among his own troops, and a quarrel with Lord Cochrane deprived him of the assistance of the Chilean squadron. A serious illness in November, 1821, added to his difficulties. Under the circumstances, he did not feel able to move against the Spaniards in the interior. The latter, as he wrote Bolívar in 1822, had no less than 19,000 veteran troops, whereas the patriot forces could not put more than 8,500 men, mostly raw recruits, in the field at one time.

San Martín hoped to obtain from Bolívar the help which he needed to bring the war to an end. Though he believed that Guayaquil should belong to Peru, he sent troops under General Santa Cruz to assist Sucre in the campaign that led to the battle of Pichincha, and he responded cordially to a letter from Bolívar offering support for a campaign in Peru. On July 26 and 27 of the same year the two leaders met in their famous conference at Guayaquil.

What took place was never fully revealed. San Martín apparently urged that a large Colombian army be sent to Peru and offered to place himself under Bolívar's orders. Bolívar seems to have evaded a direct reply. His motives can only be guessed at. He was probably unwilling to share the glory of freeing Peru with another leader and skeptical of the possibility of whole-hearted coöperation. Furthermore, he disagreed emphatically with San Martín's belief that Peru should become a constitutional monarchy under a European prince, and he perhaps felt that this difference of opinion would lead to future trouble. There was no open break, but San Martín evidently left the conference convinced that Bolívar would not furnish the aid indispensable to the final liberation of Peru under any plan of joint action. With an unselfish patriotism that has few parallels in history, he decided to withdraw from the scene altogether, and when a constituent assembly met at Lima in September he resigned his authority as Protector and left the country.

San Martín went to Chile and thence to Argentina, but in both countries he found that political changes had left him with few friends and no influence. Practically penniless, he sailed for Europe in 1824. Five years later he came back to Buenos Aires but met with so unpleasant a reception that he immediately returned to Europe. He died in obscurity at Boulogne in 1850, and it was not until some years later that his great services to the cause of independence were fully recognized by his compatriots.

The Last Stage of the War in South America

Matters went badly in Peru after San Martín's departure. The constituent assembly entrusted the executive power to a weak *junta*, and in February, 1823, after the defeat of an expedition against the royalists, a military uprising forced the appointment of Colonel José de la Riva Agüero as President of the Republic. Soon afterward Bolívar sent Sucre with a strong force to assist the Peruvians, but internal dissensions continued. An army which Santa Cruz led into Upper Peru in May was almost completely destroyed. Even after Bolívar himself arrived at Callao on September 1 and was given dictatorial powers, the situation did not improve. The Liberator, prostrated by illness, found it difficult to maintain his authority because many people in Lima, and many officers in the Peruvian army, felt that Colombian military rule was hardly less objectionable than that of Spain. The Argentine troops that San Martín had left behind were also dissatisfied, and when they mutinied and permitted the royalists to reoccupy the fortress at Callao in February, 1824, Bolívar had to evacuate Lima and retire to Trujillo.

Within the year, however, the war ended in a complete victory for the patriot forces. Bolívar obtained reinforcements which enabled him to take the offensive. His enemies were weakened by the defection of General Olañeta in Upper Peru, who revolted against the Viceroy La Serna, an appointee of the liberal party, when it was learned that the absolutists had been restored to power in Spain. After Bolívar won an important victory at Junín on August 6, the royalists evacuated Lima. Sucre then took command of the army in the highlands, and on December 9, 1824, won the final great battle of the war at Ayacucho. The viceroy was taken prisoner and the remainder of the Spanish army capitulated. Olañeta attempted to hold out for a short time in Upper Peru, but was abandoned by his troops and killed. Callao, which was still held by the royalists, surrendered on January 22, 1826, after a siege in which the defenders endured ghastly sufferings. Spain had definitely lost South America, although the mother country did not recognize the independence of her former colonies until many years later.

The Independence of Mexico

New Spain was too far away to be directly affected by the war in South America and events there took a different course because the adherents of the established order were more powerful. Mexico City, like Lima, was naturally a royalist stronghold. The military and administrative organization centering around the viceregal court, the creole nobility, the privileged merchants, and above all the hierarchy of the Church were formidable obstacles to the realization of the creoles, aspiration to self-rule. The conservatives were thus able to hold in check, if not to suppress, the revolutionary movement that began in 1810 until they themselves concluded after the liberal revolution in Spain that independence was preferable to a continued connection with the mother country.

The hero of the independence movement in Mexico was Miguel Hidalgo y Costilla, a priest in the small village of Dolores near Querétaro. Hidalgo had already been in trouble with the Inquisition and the Spanish authorities because of his advanced ideas, and had associated with other revolutionary leaders who had been encouraged, like their contemporaries in South America, by the recent events in Spain. On September 16, 1810, he raised the standard of revolt, professing allegiance to Ferdinand VII, but demanding creole supremacy and the abolition of Indian tributes and caste distinctions. *El Grito de Dolores*, the "Cry of Dolores," met with an immediate response among the country people roundabout, and Hidalgo soon commanded a great mob of Indians and *mestizos*, with whose aid he took the provincial capital of Guanajuato. His success, however, was short-lived. Handicapped by incapable leadership and lack of organization, the rebels were no match for the less numerous but better disciplined loyal troops. They were easily defeated early in 1811, and Hidalgo was put to death.

A few scattered bands remained in the field and continued the struggle. They could only engage in guerrilla warfare and were hampered by lack of unified leadership, but they kept alive the spirit of revolt. For a time in 1812 and 1813, the prospect for independence seemed to improve. The proclamation of the Spanish constitution of 1812, with its provisions granting freedom to the press, encouraged revolutionary agitation and made the situation of the royal authorities more difficult. The revolutionists obtained control of much of the region south and west of the capital, and on November 6, 1813, a patriot congress at Chilpancingo issued a formal declaration of independence. Soon afterward the tide turned. José María Morelos, the most prominent of the revolutionary leaders, was captured and executed in 1815, and in the following year Viceroy Apodaca began a vigorous campaign which almost ended the insurrection. Vicente Guerrero and his small band were practically the only rebels remaining in the field by the beginning of 1818.

With the Spanish revolution of 1820 the situation again changed. The Mexican conservatives saw the home government controlled by people whose ideas were as odious as those of the creole insurgents. The radical *cortes*, which a mutinous army compelled Ferdinand VII to convoke, adopted a series of measures which were especially obnoxious to the Church. The Inquisition was abolished, tithes were suppressed, and much ecclesiastical property was sequestrated. Many of the higher clergy felt that independence would be a lesser evil than the execution of such a program, and some of the most prominent officials of the Church entered into a conspiracy to separate the viceroyalty from Spain.

Their chief instrument was Agustín de Iturbide, a creole officer who had some time before retired from the army under a cloud but who now asked and obtained permission to lead a force against Guerrero. Instead of fighting, Iturbide entered into negotiations with the revolutionists, and on February 24, 1821, he met Guerrero at Iguala and signed an agreement under which their forces were to coöperate to bring about independence. The "Plan of Iguala" provided that Mexico should become a constitutional empire ruled either by Ferdinand VII or by some Spanish prince chosen by the Mexican *cortes*. The signers pledged themselves to establish complete independence, to maintain the Catholic Church and the privileges of the clergy, and to bring about the equality of all races before the law. These promises, skilfully designed to attract support from all parties, caused the agreement to be called the "Plan of the Three Guarantees."

The viceroy, who had perhaps had some connection with the clerical plot, took no very active measures against Iturbide, though he refused an invitation to become head of the *junta* which was to rule the country until the new emperor arrived. Because of his vacillation, the faction in the government which opposed independence compelled him to resign in July, but in the meantime more and more of the troops went over to the "Army of the Three Guarantees." When a new viceroy, Juan O'Donojú, arrived at the end of July, the restoration of Spanish authority was clearly impossible; and the Treaty of Córdoba, signed by O'Donojú and Iturbide on August 24, 1821, accepted the chief provisions of the Plan of Iguala. It also provided for the withdrawal of such Spanish forces as remained in Mexico, leaving control in the hands of the creole militia, who already formed the greater part of the army. O'Donojú died soon after taking office as a member of the regency which assumed control of the government. The Crown's repudiation of his actions ended whatever hopes the revolutionary leaders may have entertained of placing a Bourbon prince on the throne, but Mexico had become independent. The story of subsequent events—the meeting of the Mexican congress, the proclamation of Iturbide as Emperor in May, 1822, and the overthrow of his government a year later—will be dealt with in another chapter.

Central America and the West Indies

The loss of South America and Mexico of course affected Spain's position elsewhere in the Western Hemisphere. The five provinces of Central America had remained fairly tranquil until 1821, but it was impossible for Spain to hold them after Mexico and Panama became independent. Even the Spanish officials and the higher clergy realized this, and they joined with the creole leaders at Guatemala on September 15, 1821, in a formal declaration of independence. The Captain General himself became the head of the new government, but he met with opposition in the outlying provinces, and early in 1822 he and his conservative supporters brought about the annexation of all Central America to Iturbide's Mexican Empire. This connection soon ceased, and the Federal Republic of Central America was set up in 1823.

The people of Spanish Santo Domingo also revolted in 1821. They attempted to join the Republic of Colombia, but their territory was immediately overrun by troops from the former French colony of Saint Domingue, where revolted slaves had set up the independent republic of Haiti as early as 1804.

With the loss of Santo Domingo and the cession of the Floridas to the United States, nothing remained of Spain's great American empire but Cuba and Puerto Rico. Both of these islands had enjoyed unprecedented prosperity since the destruction of the plantations in Saint Domingue had made sugar production profitable in other tropical regions, and each had received many immigrants from Spain in the first years of the century. Probably for these reasons there was less enthusiasm for independence among their people than in the colonies on the mainland, and these two West Indian possessions remained in Spanish hands until nearly the end of the nineteenth century.

8

The Problems of the New Republics

Though the last important Spanish forces in South America had been defeated at the battle of Ayacucho, the future of the new republics was still obscure. Few of them had governments that offered any great promise of permanence or stability, and it was by no means certain that they would be left to work out their internal problems without interference from abroad. They were attempting to establish republican institutions at a time when reaction and autocracy were dominant in the Old World and when Spain might well hope for assistance from other European powers in reducing them to subjection. If they were to achieve the purposes for which the revolution had been fought, this danger of foreign intervention must be averted and the equally difficult problem of attaining internal stability must be solved.

Foreign Interest in the Revolution

Fortunately the danger from abroad proved less serious than it appeared. The Spanish American revolutionists had friends as well as enemies in foreign countries. Believers in political liberty were enthusiastic over the establishment of a new group of free republics, and mercantile and shipping interests were eager to share in their trade. Other nations had an exaggerated idea of the wealth of Spanish America and high hopes for the opening of great markets there, once the restrictions of the Spanish colonial system had been broken down. From 1810 on, British, North American, and French vessels appeared in increasing numbers at ports under patriot control, and the creoles had an opportunity to exchange their products for foreign goods under conditions more favorable than any they had hitherto known. The result was a rapid change in customs and standards of living even during the period of the war.

Great Britain, which played the leading rôle in this development, sent not only goods but capital to the new republics. British financial interests had furnished money and arms to the republican armies during the war. After their independence was assured, Mexico, Central America, Colombia, Buenos Aires, and Chile were able to float government loans in the London market, and much money was subscribed for stock in companies formed to take over mines abandoned by Spanish interests. Many of these ventures were wild speculations, and most of them resulted disastrously, but they laid the foundations for a British financial ascendency in Latin America which was to last until the twentieth century. They were also an assurance that the new nations would have British support against any effort to deprive them of their independence.

The United States was interested in Latin American trade, but still more interested in the success of the revolution for political reasons. The natural sympathy for colonists striving for their independence was increased by the desire to be rid of a neighbor whose presence was likely to drag the United States into the complications of European politics. The government at Washington had sent agents on several occasions to maintain informal relations with the revolutionists, and after 1816 Henry Clay, the Speaker of the House of Representatives, ardently advocated the formal recognition of the new republics. The Monroe administration delayed action, chiefly because it desired first to obtain Spain's ratification of the treaty for the cession of Florida, but in 1822 the way was clear and Manuel Torres was formally received as the chargé d'affaires of Colombia. The establishment of diplomatic relations with the other republics followed.

The Monroe Doctrine

Great Britain and the United States were thus opposed to any foreign intervention on behalf of Spain. On the other hand the principal powers of continental Europe, acting together in the Holy Alliance, were opposed on principle to revolution and to democratic ideas and had discussed projects for intervention at several European international congresses. In 1823, when the liberal regime in Spain was destroyed by a French army acting as the agent of the alliance, the danger of similar action in Spanish America seemed to increase. Canning, the British Foreign Secretary, suggested to the American Minister in London that the two governments unite in a declaration against any foreign interference in Spanish America, but President Monroe and his advisers considered it preferable that the United States should act alone.

In a discussion with Russia of the latter's territorial claims in Alaska, the United States had already laid down the principle that the American continents were "henceforth not to be considered as subjects for future colonization by any European powers." In his message to Congress on December 2, 1823, Monroe set forth more fully the doctrine which was thenceforth to bear his name. The political system of the powers of the Holy Alliance, he said, was essentially different from that of America, and the United States would "consider any attempt on their part to extend their system to any portion of this hemisphere as dangerous to our peace and safety." The United States would not interfere with any existing European colony, but it would view as an unfriendly act any European intervention to oppress or control the destiny of the American republics whose independence it had recognized.

We now know that the danger of European intervention had probably disappeared before this message was read. None of the powers of the Holy Alliance was really prepared to send forces to America. The French government, which had intervened in Spain, would have been glad to see republicanism destroyed in the new states but at the same time wished to maintain trade relations with them. It was interested in efforts to establish European monarchies because that would achieve both purposes.[1] In October, 1823, in response to a British inquiry, it disclaimed any intent to interfere between Spain and her former colonies. After this there was little danger that any other power would act. The enunciation of the Monroe Doctrine was nevertheless an event of the greatest importance, for it became and has continued to be the basis for the policy of the United States in the Western Hemisphere.

Bolívar and the Panama Conference

It was well that events abroad dissipated the danger of foreign intervention, for the efforts of the Spanish Americans to combine in the face of a common peril met with little success. Bolívar, the dominant figure in South America, clearly perceived the need for some form

[1] See Dexter Perkins, *The Monroe Doctrine, 1823–1826*, pp. 105 ff.

of confederation against external attack, and Colombia had entered into treaties of alliance with most of the other revolutionary governments while the war was still in progress. In December, 1824, just before the battle of Ayacucho, Bolívar proposed to the other governments that a congress be held at Panama. Since his purpose was not only to bring about an alliance between the former Spanish colonies, but also to find means to assure respect for the principles recently set forth by President Monroe, invitations to attend were extended to the United States, Great Britain, and Brazil. By June, 1826, representatives from Colombia, Peru, Mexico, Central America, and Great Britain, as well as an unofficial delegate from Holland, had gathered on the Isthmus. The governments of Buenos Aires and Paraguay declined the invitation. Brazil accepted but did not attend, and Chile, Bolivia, and the United States were delayed in appointing delegates. At Washington, the delay was caused by a long factional dispute in Congress. When representatives were finally appointed, one of them died en route and the other did not go to Panama, though he later went to Mexico in the hope of attending the proposed second conference there.

The Congress at Panama accomplished little, because national jealousies made any real union impracticable. The Spanish American delegates signed treaties providing for a confederation, for future congresses, and for joint military action under certain conditions, but these were never ratified by any of the states except Colombia. Because of the unhealthful climate at Panama, the Congress adjourned after a few months with the intention of reconvening at Tacubaya near Mexico City. This second meeting never took place. Bolívar was bitterly disappointed, but the failure of his plan for a new international order in the Western Hemisphere was a small matter compared with the other disappointments that he was to suffer during the next five years.

The Bolivarian Republics and the Constitución Vitalicia

The Liberator was still President of Great Colombia, though he had left the administration of affairs there in the hands of the Vice-President, Santander. He was also exercising dictatorial powers in Peru, while Sucre, his most trusted lieutenant, controlled Upper Peru, which was soon to become the Republic of Bolivia. The area where his leadership was accepted included by far the greater part of the wealth and population of Spanish South America, for Argentina and Chile were undevel-

oped and as yet relatively unimportant countries. He was at the height
of his power and prestige, and the future of the newly liberated republics seemed to rest in his hands. In his efforts to establish the new governments on a firm basis, however, he faced obstacles which no one
man could possibly overcome—obstacles which he himself saw more
clearly than most of his contemporaries. The political inexperience of
his fellow citizens, the violent local jealousies that prevented coöperation
between the liberated countries, and opposition to his own excessive
personal ambition were to make the last years of his life an anti-climax
and a failure.

Bolívar had given much thought to the internal political problems
of the new republics, and his conception of the form of government
that they should adopt was embodied in the famous constitution which
he drew up for Bolivia in 1826. This provided for a life president, responsible to no other authority, and empowered to name his own successor. The Vice-President was the responsible head of the administration, subject to impeachment by Congress and the Supreme Court.
The judiciary was completely independent. There was a complicated
procedure for the appointment of local officials, but no provision for
real local self-government. The legislative power was divided between
three chambers: the tribunes, serving four years; the senators, serving
eight years; and the censors, elected for life. Each had the exclusive
right to initiate laws on certain subjects, and the approval of two chambers sufficed to make a law effective. The congress was largely self-
perpetuating, since the chambers filled vacancies in their own membership from lists of three candidates presented by the "electors": a group
chosen every four years by the votes of those citizens who could read
and write. Though there were detailed provisions for the exercise of
the right of ecclesiastical patronage by the government, non-Catholics,
according to Bolívar's draft, were to have freedom of worship. This
provision was too advanced for the members of the Bolivian constituent
assembly, who insisted upon the inclusion of a provision forbidding the
public exercise of any but the Catholic religion.

With all its cumbersome and obviously unworkable features this
so-called *constitución vitalicia* in some respects more nearly responded
to the realities of the political situation of Latin America in 1826 than
did the constitutions modeled upon that of the United States which
several other countries adopted. It at least recognized that the people
of the new republics were not yet ready for democratic institutions,

and that only a strong, permanent executive could give stability to their governments. The regime that it sought to establish would have been fully as representative as the military autocracies that flourished instead in the Bolivarian republics during the next half century. Its chief weakness lay in the fact that it was so obviously designed to perpetuate the Liberator's personal power.

The constitution was adopted in Bolivia in November, 1826. Sucre, who had been ruling there since the end of the war, was persuaded by the inhabitants to become the Republic's first president, but he consented to serve only for two years because he was anxious to return to the fiancée whom he had left at Quito. About the same time a similar constitution was adopted by a plebiscite in Peru, and Bolívar was proclaimed president for life. The Liberator's project for a great "confederation of the Andes," with himself at its head, seemed near attainment.

Disillusionment came almost immediately. There was already much opposition in Lima, where the military chiefs were less devoted to Bolívar than his compatriots in Great Colombia who had served with him throughout the war. The Peruvians had little desire to be ruled by a man whom they regarded as a foreigner. They were also offended by the creation of a separate state in Bolivia, which they regarded as a part of their own territory. When Bolívar was forced to return to Colombia in September, 1826, to deal with a revolt there, his authority in Peru at once began to crumble. General Santa Cruz, who was left in charge at Lima, went forward loyally with the adoption of the *constitución vitalicia* and the presidential election, but the growing resistance of other leaders soon forced him to set the constitution aside and convoke an assembly to frame another. When this body set up a new government under General La Mar in July, 1827, Bolívar made no effort to reassert his authority.

The trouble in Colombia had arisen from a quarrel between General Páez, who had a great following in Venezuela, and the acting president Santander. Bolívar was able to restore order, but even his own compatriots were now less enthusiastic in their loyalty. Though he resumed control of the Colombian government, popular opposition prevented the adoption of the *constitución vitalicia*, and he was compelled to resort to a dictatorship to keep himself in power. The unhappy story of the Liberator's last three years—the expulsion of Sucre from Bolivia in 1828, the ensuing war between Colombia and Peru, and finally the break-up of Great Colombia itself—will be told in later chapters.

The Period of Anarchy

When Bolívar died on his way into exile in 1830, there were many who shared the profound discouragement about the future of the new nations which he expressed in his last days. Throughout the former Spanish colonies the picture was much the same. Mexico was gradually sinking into a state of military anarchy after the overthrow of Iturbide's improvised empire and the adoption of a republican constitution. The Central Americans had been no more successful in their attempt to set up a federal republic. In the River Plate region, civil strife had been almost continuous even during the war with Spain. The hostility of the provinces to Buenos Aires had prevented the establishment of a national government in Argentina, and Uruguay had become an independent state only after a costly war between the Argentine provinces and Brazil. Chile, on the other side of the Andes, had passed through a period of turmoil, and had hardly yet begun to settle down under the autocratic regime of Portales. Chile enjoyed relative peace after 1830, but in nearly all of the other countries disorder and misrule continued for a generation or more to retard internal progress and to invite foreign intervention. The establishment of orderly political institutions was the great problem that the Latin American states must solve if they were to take their place among the progressive communities of the modern world.

Obstacles to Republican Government: Social Inequalities

In most parts of Spanish America, the victorious revolutionists set up republican governments with constitutions like that of the United States. They hardly realized the difficulty of making such governments work in countries where the structure of society was entirely different. In Spanish America the system of caste and special privilege that had been nurtured by the home government as a means of preventing its subjects from uniting against it survived the revolution and made the establishment of political democracy impossible. Subject races, exploited and oppressed by those who had economic and political power, formed the great mass of the population. The revolution made little change for the better in the situation of the Indians. The *encomienda* and the *mita* had disappeared, but debt-slavery and lack of land of his own kept the rural laborer dependent upon the creole proprietors. The Negroes also were still in bondage in most of the countries where they formed any large proportion of the working class, for they were not fully emancipated in Colombia, Venezuela, Ecuador, and Peru until after the middle of the nineteenth century. The *mestizos*, though their condition had probably improved during the revolution, were still for the most part poor and extremely ignorant. Wealth, education, and social position were virtually the monopoly of the creole aristocracy, still predominantly Spanish in descent though many successful soldiers of humble origin and mixed blood joined its ranks during and after the war. It was this class, generally speaking, which dominated political affairs in the new republics. Its power and its relations to other social groups varied somewhat from country to country. Conditions in Peru, for example, were different from those in regions where the Indian population was less numerous, and these differences were to become more important as time went on. But there was no Spanish American republic in the first years of independence where anything like political or social democracy could be said to exist.

Inexperience in Self-Government

The political inexperience of the ruling classes was another great obstacle to republican government. Unlike their neighbors in the British North American colonies, the Spanish Americans had had no training in the management of their own affairs. One of the effects of the colonial system had been to prevent the growth of any spirit of local initiative and to engender a lack of self-confidence. After the revolution there were very few persons who had even a limited experience in public administration, because the creoles had been excluded from any participation in the autocratic regime imposed upon them by the mother country. Even the municipal councils, where they could hold office, were not democratic institutions, for most of the members either bought or inherited their positions. The *cabildos* played an important rôle in the early days of the movement for independence, but their aristocratic traditions made them suspect to the patriot leaders and most of them were soon dissolved or reorganized. Practically all of the machinery of organized government had thus been swept away.

Some of the worst traditions of the old regime survived. The Spanish officials, though subject to elaborate if ineffective supervision in matters in which the Crown was interested, were often arbitrary and greedy tyrants in their dealings with the people under them. Their example, since it represented the only form of government that the colonists knew, was naturally followed by many of their creole successors, despite the efforts of men like Bolívar, San Martín, and Sucre to enforce higher standards of conduct. The whole community had been demoralized by the brutal cruelty of the war, and many of the military chieftains had been accustomed to oppress and rob friends and enemies alike on the pretext of military necessity. They continued after peace was restored to look upon public office chiefly as an opportunity for personal profit.

It was difficult under such conditions to operate a complicated system of government taken over from people of a different race and temperament. The very principles on which the new system rested were unfamiliar. Under the Spanish regime there had been no real separation of powers. Viceroys, *audiencias,* and many local officials had exercised political and military authority, had issued orders that had the force of law, and had acted as judges. It was hard for the Spanish Americans to grasp the concept of a president and congress and judiciary, each acting independently in its own sphere. When authority was further divided between federal and state officials the situation became almost hopeless. There was no accumulated experience or body of precedents to aid in settling disputes about jurisdiction, and few of the political leaders had the forbearance and the spirit of coöperation which such a situation demanded. Furthermore, inexperienced theorists made some of the new constitutions still more unworkable by the addition of clumsy provisions that enabled a small minority to block the election of a president or to paralyze the legislature. There was no way to settle the disputes that arose in such cases, or that constantly occurred between different branches of the government, except by a resort to force.

Impossibility of Holding Elections

Under most of the early constitutions, the upper classes alone were given the franchise. Even they hardly knew how to exercise their civic rights. Often they had no opportunity to do so, for elections were either dispensed with or made a mere farce by military leaders who had fought their way to power and had no intention of relinquishing their authority. Even when the government made a more or less sincere attempt to hold a real election, the result was unsatisfactory. Disputes arose over the qualifications of voters, the counting of the ballots, and the frauds committed by both sides. Since there were no impartial courts to decide such matters, these quarrels led to violence and it was only natural that the intervention of the authorities to restore order should usually benefit the friends of the government. If higher officials honestly attempted to assure fair play, as many of them did, they could not control their subordinates, who had no desire to lose their positions by permitting the party to be defeated. In short, it was impossible for the Spanish Americans to learn overnight to use democratic procedures which had been developed elsewhere as the result of centuries of practice and under conditions far more favorable to success.

It soon became the practice for the party in power to control the electoral process so completely that the victory of the official candidate was a matter of course. By tactics that ranged all the way from petty police persecution to exile or murder, the government made it difficult for its opponents to conduct a campaign against it. On election day they were excluded from the polls by force while the government's supporters voted as often as they chose. If necessary, the ballots were dishonestly counted or the results were arbitrarily changed by the president or congress. Under such circumstances, the opposition frequently did not attempt to contest the election at all. Defeat, even by fraud and violence, hurt the prestige of the leaders in the eyes of their followers. It was hardly worth while to expose the party workers to arrest and mistreatment, or to use funds that might better be saved to buy arms and ammunition.

Since revolutions were usually the only means by which unpopular governments could be changed, they became an accepted and almost a necessary part of the political system. Those in power consequently tended to regard any opposition as an incitement to disorder. For their own protection they imprisoned or exiled leaders whom they regarded as dangerous and kept lesser opponents under constant surveillance. At the first indication of trouble, the government would proclaim a "state of siege," which suspended the citizens' constitutional rights and permitted arbitrary arrests. The lot of members of the party not in power was a hard one. They were the first victims when forced loans were needed for military purposes, and they were persecuted in a great variety of other ways, partly from mere hatred and partly with the deliberate purpose of diminishing their political influence. Political murders, with or without some pretense of following legal forms, were not uncommon. Such treatment often made revolution, with all its dangers, preferable to continued submission, and the result was a vicious circle of revolt to escape from oppression and oppression to prevent revolt.

Military Dominance: The Caudillo

With military force the final arbiter, both in disputes between different branches of the government and in the elections, the leaders of the army became the real rulers of the country. Presidents were set up and deposed and congresses were intimidated or dissolved by barracks revolutions. The losing party, if strong enough, sought to nullify the action of the troops at the capital by taking up arms in other parts of the country. *Golpes de cuartel*, as the barracks revolutions were called, and general civil wars were the two ways in which changes of government were normally brought about during the first half century of independence.

The men who thus came into power were rarely fitted by character or training to cope with the problems which confronted the new governments. In Mexico and Peru the army officers were mostly creoles who had served in the Spanish army or militia and thus had at least some military training, but in the other countries many of them were men who had risen from the ranks during the revolution through qualities which had little relation to their ability as statesmen. In general, they formed a powerful privileged caste, subject to trial only by military courts, and drawing at least a portion of their pay even when not on active service. Except in very rare instances, it was the officers alone who directed the army's political activities. A part of the enlisted men were professional soldiers, but the great majority of the rank and file were ignorant Indians or *mestizos*, ill-paid and ill-treated, who had been recruited by force and were serving only because they did not know how to escape. The standing armies were usually small and always inefficient, but they were influential in time of peace because they were the only organized military force.

When civil war came, improvised forces were hastily recruited by both parties. It was here that the *caudillo* played a leading rôle. The *caudillo* was a leader, a man who could command the personal loyalty of a sufficiently large group of friends and followers to make him an important military or political figure. He represented the inclination to exalt personal leadership which has always been a Spanish trait. He might be either a professional soldier, popular among the subordinate officers or the rank and file of the army, or a landowner backed by the tenants and laborers on his own and neighboring estates, or even a politician whose eloquence or other gifts procured him a following. In the earlier period he was usually a hero of the war for independence. Almost always, whether a professional soldier or not, he held high military rank. If his influence was confined to one locality or to one small group, he was usually himself a follower of some more powerful *caudillo* to whom he was bound by ties of friendship and the expectation of favors to be received. His interest in politics, in most cases, was primarily a selfish one—to obtain power and the perquisites of power. Though almost always an ardent member of one of the great political parties, it was not uncommon to find him shifting his allegiance from one camp to another when such action seemed likely to be profitable.

The *caudillos* drew their followers both from the upper class and from the *mestizo* element. Even the creole landowners seemed more interested in partisan political advantage than in the maintenance of peace, for the theft of a year's corn crop or the loss of some cattle from their carelessly managed *haciendas* was often a less serious misfortune than the defeat of the party to which they belonged. This was especially true in countries where backward economic conditions made office-holding more attractive than productive enterprise. The increasingly numerous *mestizos* had even less interest in stable government. A revolution might mean starvation or death in battle, but it offered a welcome change from the monotony and hardship of daily life and an opportunity for plunder and excitement. Ignorant and excitable, these people of mixed blood were easily stirred up by political agitators and formed the majority of those who served voluntarily in the revolutionary armies. The Indians, who served involuntarily, had little to say about the question one way or the other.

Political Parties

The military *caudillos* who ruled most of the Latin American countries in the period after independence were usually allied with and supported by civilian political groups who regarded them as a dangerous but indispensable instrument for maintaining their own party in power. The civil wars often seemed on the surface to be mere contests for offices and spoils, but they could not have assumed such proportions as they did had it not been for controversies over social and political issues which divided the ruling class, and to some extent the other classes also, into hostile factions.

Usually there were two parties. Whether they called themselves conservatives and liberals, or centralists and federalists, the differences between them were much the same from one country to another. In one camp were many of the landowners and the higher clergy, with their followers among the lower classes, who clung to the surviving features of the colonial social organization, defended the prerogatives of the Church, and distrusted democratic institutions. This group naturally included most of the ex-loyalists, and it was especially strong in cities that had formerly been centers of Spanish power. Primarily interested in the maintenance of the existing order, it tended to favor a strong, centralized government and often supported military leaders of humble origin, like Iturbide in Mexico, Páez in Venezuela, and Flores in Ecuador, when their dictatorships seemed to offer the best means of preserving peace.

Opposed to the conservatives were the advocates of more advanced ideas, including a fraction of the land-owning class and many merchants and professional men, often of mixed blood, who resented the creole aristocracy's claim to social preëminence. Since the Church was on the other side, the liberals were anti-clerical. Frequently they advocated a "federal" or decentralized form of government in order to capitalize upon the jealousy of the provinces toward the capital. The position of the Church and the question of centralization or decentralization in government thus became the two great issues in the political struggles of the first half century of independence.

The Church

Catholicism was the state religion and in most of the republics no other sect was officially tolerated. It is true that the Church had suffered much during the war for independence. Most of the higher clergy had been loyalists and the majority of the bishops had either abandoned or been expelled from their dioceses. Without them the clergy was leaderless, and their number rapidly decreased because it was impossible to consecrate new priests. Within a few years, however, this condition had been corrected. Though the Papacy long refused to recognize the new republican governments, or to admit their claim to the right of patronage, ways were found to fill the vacant sees and appoint new priests.

The Church dominated the minds and consciences of the masses of the people and controlled many aspects of their personal lives as it had during the colonial period. It was thus an invaluable ally of the conservative party. It still virtually monopolized education, though not very successful efforts were made in several countries to establish state schools. The prerogatives of the clergy, with their special courts and exemptions from taxation, had been little affected by the change in government. Priests continued to hold important official positions as they had in colonial days. It was inevitable that the Church should be an object of attack by leaders imbued with nineteenth-century liberal ideas, especially as its wealth was always a temptation to governments chronically in financial straits. Its attempt to defend itself by supporting the conservative party intensified the liberals' anti-clericalism. On the other hand, the liberals' determination to confiscate ecclesiastical property, to abolish the *fueros* or special privileges of the clergy, and to bring education, marriage, and burial under lay control, seemed sacrilegious to the more devout portion of the community. Conflicts over questions of this sort, where irreconcilable and tenaciously held personal convictions were involved, were particularly bitter, and sometimes appalling in their consequences.

Localismo

The question of federalism likewise aroused violent animosities, because it had its origin in the spirit of *localismo*, or narrow local patriotism, which is one of the characteristics of the Spanish race. In each country, the inhabitants of the provinces were jealous of the metropolis and predisposed to revolt against any administration functioning there. It was this separatist spirit that defeated Bolívar's project for a Confederation of the Andes and broke up Great Colombia. It caused the Federal Republic of Central America to dissolve into five little states, and brought years of bloodshed to the River Plate region. *Localismo* was a disturbing influence even in lesser political units, for the smaller towns in each district were jealous of the more important ones and often carried on inherited feuds with each other. In many places, in fact, party divisions became a matter of locality rather than of principle, and a town would be predominantly "conservative" or "liberal" simply because a neighboring town adhered to the opposite faction. Efforts to satisfy the desire for local self-rule by setting up a federal form of government were generally unsuccessful, however, because the administration at the national capital usually interfered continually in state affairs, whatever the constitution might say. Where the state governments did obtain real autonomy, the result was to reduce the central government to impotence, and to increase rather than decrease internal disorder.

Geographical Handicaps

Geographical conditions played a large part in keeping the spirit of *localismo* alive. Mountain ranges and tropical jungles made travel difficult and were formidable obstacles to national unity. Except in a very few places, there were no roads but rough pack trails, and a journey from the national capital to the provincial cities required days or even weeks. A revolution could get well under way before the government heard of it, and the transport of troops to restore order was a slow and dangerous business. The lack of means of communication was also a handicap to economic progress, for mines and plantations could not be developed when their products could not reach a market.

Effects of Civil Wars

In the chapters that follow, a great many civil wars will be mentioned and passed over in one or two brief sentences. It would be impossible to describe each one in detail, but the reader will have but an inadequate picture of the history of Latin America if he does not realize what each of these internal struggles meant to the country where it occurred. Aside from the loss of life, often out of all proportion to the number of troops engaged, there was much suffering among non-combatants. The armies lived off the country, killing cattle and seizing other food wherever they went, and agriculture and industry were paralyzed because able-bodied men who did not join in the fighting went into hiding to avoid recruiting parties. With the roads unsafe for travel, internal trade ceased and imports and exports, upon which the government revenues depended, fell off. The regular forces on both sides looted and committed other outrages, especially in districts where the people were not in sympathy with them, and irregular guerrillas, many of them mere bandits, terrorized regions outside of the zone of major operations. Too often the country found itself at the mercy of the worst elements in the population, under the irresponsible authority of men whose only claim to importance was their ability to command an ignorant and cruel soldiery. After a war, the general demoralization and the hatreds engendered by political executions and other atrocities made it difficult to establish real peace even when one party won a decisive victory.

Internal disorders also embroiled the Latin American states in dangerous international controversies. Europeans and North Americans as well as natives suffered personal injuries and losses of property, and the aftermath of every civil war was a flood of damage claims. Though these were frequently of doubtful validity and usually grossly exaggerated, they were energetically supported by the claimants' governments. In many cases settlements were effected by agreement or arbitration, but in others continued disorder and financial mismanagement made payment impossible. Then foreign powers sent warships, blockaded ports, or even landed troops to force compliance with their demands. Such interventions involved serious dangers, for they might easily lead to a more permanent occupation as one did in Mexico in 1862.

Each of the Spanish American republics in the first years of independence faced the problems described in this chapter. Some were more successful than others in dealing with them, and one of the objects of the chapters that follow will be to show why this was: how some were able to become prosperous and progressive nations while others have been less fortunate. A history of Latin America must emphasize political development because the establishment of stable government was the first requisite for economic and social progress. Without internal peace it was impossible to attract foreign capital for road and railroad building, or to develop natural resources, or to free a part of the revenues of the government for popular education and public-health work. At the same time, stability itself was a result of economic and social progress, and was much more easily attained in countries where rich natural re-

sources were available or where the racial makeup of the population
facilitated the improvement of the situation of the masses of the people.
Each republic had its peculiar problems, and in the course of the nineteenth century what had been one colonial empire developed into a
group of separate nations, each with its own traditions and its own in-
dividuality.

Part III

❦

THE RIVER PLATE AND CHILE

FROM the time when the Spanish Empire broke up into a number of independent states, it is difficult to deal with the history of the area as a whole. There had been differences among the colonies, in the makeup of population and in geographical conditions, and these were accentuated when the outward uniformity of the colonial regime disappeared and each state began to deal with its own peculiar problems. We can discern common factors and trends in the development of Spanish America since 1824, but when we attempt to generalize about these we must note so many exceptions and qualifications that any attempt to write their history without breaking it down into the history of separate states becomes vague and confused.

The countries that advanced most during the first century of independence were those of the South Temperate Zone, a region that had been relatively unimportant in colonial times. The absence of a settled, easily conquered Indian population, which had made this area unattractive to settlers in search of easy wealth, was one of the factors that helped this progress. There was little Indian blood in the people of Argentina and Uruguay, and the native element in central Chile, though much larger, had been to a great extent assimilated. The southern republics thus had a homogeneous population and did not have to contend with problems that confronted countries where the masses were of an alien, subject race, speaking different languages and working under various forms of servitude. They were thus more attractive to a new type of settlers who began to come during the nineteenth century, and European immigration played an important part in their development.

Another important factor was the development of foreign trade. Buenos Aires, Montevideo, and Valparaiso, which had been virtually closed to overseas shipping until nearly the end of the colonial period, became important commercial centers soon after independence. In the last quarter of the nineteenth century exports of meat from Argentina and Uruguay and of nitrate from Chile made the southern region the most prosperous part of Latin America. This prosperity attracted foreign investment and made possible the building of railroads and the still more intensive development of natural resources. It also made for political stability, because people who are making money are rarely disposed to revolt and a government that has ample revenues is usually a strong one.

With a more homogeneous population and higher standards of living, it was easier for the southern countries to develop democratic political institutions. A larger proportion of their people could be reached by education and could learn as time went on to take an intelligent interest in politics. This interest, coupled with a growing desire for internal peace, strengthened a demand for freer elections as a substitute for revolutions. By the end of the first quarter of the nineteenth century, Argentina, Uruguay, and Chile seemed to have achieved truly republican forms of government. There was a retrogression to older political practices during the depression years, but it was short-lived in the case of Uruguay and Chile, and these two countries may be numbered among the world's democracies today.

In Paraguay, the situation is different. The masses of the people are of Indian or mixed blood, and the country has less natural wealth. Two disastrous wars with South American neighbors have retarded political and economic progress. Paraguay is included in this section, however, because it is geographically a part of the River Plate region and because of its very close economic and political relations with Argentina.

9

The Argentine Republic

Argentina in 1810

Argentina, more than a third the size of the continental United States, stretches some 2,300 miles from the tropics in the north to a latitude corresponding to that of Labrador in the south. Except for the Andean foothills in the west and northwest, it is one great unbroken plain. Much of it is unattractive as a home for human beings. The Gran Chaco is a tropical jungle, and much of the west is an arid desert. The vast reaches of Patagonia are of some value for sheep-raising, but they can hardly support any large population. The region which has made Argentina what it is is the *pampa*, the fertile, well-watered central area some six hundred miles square, where the agricultural products of the temperate zone can be produced and where an equable climate permits cattle to graze throughout the year. It is here, north, south, and west of Buenos Aires, that the greater part of the Republic's population is concentrated.

This region attracted few settlers during the colonial period. There was little market for agricultural and pastoral products in Europe, and the primitive and intractable Indians were poor material for the sort of exploitation which enriched the *encomenderos* and the religious orders in Peru and Mexico. Until the last quarter of the eighteenth century it was cut off from the rest of the world by the restrictions of the Spanish commercial system, though the effects of these restrictions were lessened by smuggling. In other ways too, it had been neglected by the Spanish government. This situation was just beginning to change in the generation before independence. Buenos Aires in 1776 became the capital of a viceroyalty that included modern Paraguay, Uruguay, and Bolivia, as well as the present territory of Argentina. Thenceforth the city grew rapidly in population and importance. Its trade received a fresh impetus when many British merchants arrived in the River Plate in the wake of Admiral Popham's squadron in 1806 and remained, with the permission of the local authorities, after the invasion was repulsed. In 1810 the city was thought to have 45,000 inhabitants, but it was still an ill-paved, dirty town, with few decent houses and an inadequate supply of food and water. Even as a seaport, it left much to be desired, for vessels had to anchor several miles out and goods and passengers were carried ashore in lighters and high-wheeled carts.

The provincial towns were described by an English traveler a few years later as mere secluded villages. The more important of them were hundreds of miles from Buenos Aires, in the western part of the country near the foothills of the Andes and in the far northwest on the road to Upper Peru. Outside of these settlements, the same traveler wrote: "although a few individuals are either scattered along the path, which traverses these vast plains, or are living together in small groups, yet the general state of the country is the same as it has been since the first year of its creation." [1]

Gauchos and Indians

These scattered country people were the *gauchos* of the pampas. Around each settlement were great unfenced *estancias*, where from time to time the half-wild cattle were captured and slaughtered. It was the *gauchos* who did this work and gave the herds the small amount of care which they received. Living in crudely built, one-room huts furnished with bullocks' skulls in place of chairs, and subsisting mainly on meat and water, these Argentine cowboys were a lawless lot, much given to personal violence and without great respect for property rights. The majority of them, perhaps, had never visited a town. The isolation in which they lived precluded any influence of church or school, but foreign travelers invariably admired their never failing courtesy and hospitality, their reckless courage, and their marvelous horsemanship. A large proportion of them were of mixed blood, for there was a strong Indian strain among the Argentine people in 1810 and there was also a not inconsiderable number of Negroes.

[1] Head, *Notes on the Pampas*, p. 16.

This scanty population occupied only a relatively small part of modern Argentina. The area of settlement was confined to the vicinity of the towns, and in the central pampa it was barely two days' horseback journey south of Buenos Aires and a much shorter distance north of Santa Fe. Beyond, the land was still held by the Indians. Some of these lived a comparatively civilized life in settled villages and maintained generally friendly relations with their white neighbors; others were predatory nomads. Driving with them large herds of horses, which served not only for remounts but for food, the hostile tribes often traveled hundreds of miles to raid small settlements or *estancias*. The Araucanians from southern Chile were especially active in stealing cattle for sale in the Spanish settlements on the western side of the Andes. Indian depredations grew much worse during the political disorders of the first years of independence, when the authorities were unable to maintain adequate forces along the frontier; and some of the tribes hitherto friendly took up arms because the increased demand for hides for export led the white ranchers to encroach on their land. In the province of Santa Fe their raids were so frequent and so destructive that many formerly prosperous districts were almost completely depopulated.

Obstacles to Unity

Travelers between one town and another were thus continually exposed to attacks by Indians or other robbers. The great distances and the lack of improved roads also discouraged intercourse and trade between the different settlements. Heavier goods were transported across the pampas in carts drawn by several yoke of oxen which usually required seven weeks or more to reach Mendoza from Buenos Aires. Persons with little baggage, however, could make the same journey in a few days, traveling at a break-neck gallop, mounted or in a springless carriage, with frequent changes of horses. Wayfarers slept under the stars or in a comfortless, vermin-infested post-hut, and depended for food on cattle lassoed along the road. It was apparently considered proper to kill these animals if the hide, the only part that had a market value, was left where the owner could recover it.

Aside from difficulties of intercommunication, there were other factors which complicated the task of welding the Argentine provinces into a united nation. The viceroyalty of La Plata had been a political rather than an economic unit. Mendoza and the other western provinces had closer relations with Chile than with Buenos Aires; and the northern provinces had their chief contact with the outside world through Lima. The people of each district were jealous and distrustful of those of other districts, and especially of the creole leaders at Buenos Aires. The spirit of *localismo*, which caused bloodshed in so many parts of Latin America during the first half of the nineteenth century, was intensified in Argentina by real differences in interests and points of view. The anti-clerical policy of the early governments at Buenos Aires seemed outrageous to interior communities like Jujuy, where an American adventurer serving as a colonel in the revolutionary army was imprisoned for three months for inadvertently failing to fall on his knees as the Eucharist was carried through the streets,[1] and the provincial towns resented the fact that the merchants at Buenos Aires controlled their trade and levied a profit on their exports and imports.

Political Affairs, 1816–1828

We saw in Chapter 7 how these local jealousies brought on internal strife between "unitarians" and "federalists" even before the country's independence was secure. The Congress of Tucumán, which declared Argentina's independence on July 9, 1816, represented only provinces where the unitarians were in control, and it lost support in some of these when it moved to Buenos Aires in 1817. The federalists dominated the "littoral" provinces, Entre Ríos, Sante Fe and Corrientes, and local *caudillos* in other districts showed little respect for the government's authority. Pueyrredón, the Supreme Director, did a great service to the cause of independence by his support of San Martín's expedition against Chile, but this did not suffice to placate those who disapproved of the monarchical schemes discussed at Tucumán or of the government's inaction when the Portuguese invaded the *Banda Oriental* in 1816. When the congress in 1819 adopted a constitution providing for a centralized form of government, many of the provincial leaders became more hostile. Pueyrredón, thoroughly discouraged, refused to accept a second term when his first expired in 1819.

In 1820, his successor, General Rondeau, was defeated by the fed-

[1] King, *Twenty-Four Years in the Argentine Republic* (New York edition), pp. 116 ff.

eralists in the battle of Cepeda, and the unitarian regime ceased to exist. The chief federalist leaders, Estanislao López of Sante Fe and Francisco Ramírez of Entre Rios, became for a short time the dominant figures in the political scene. Their continual interference in the affairs of Buenos Aires kept that province in a state of turmoil, with nine changes of government in as many months, until September, 1820, when Martín Rodríguez became governor. A powerful landowner named Juan Manuel de Rosas, who had his own *gaucho* army, helped the new administration to restore order in the province, and López' support was obtained by the delivery of 25,000 head of cattle which Rosas provided from his own *haciendas*. Soon afterward, the combined forces of Buenos Aires and Santa Fe defeated and killed Ramírez. López retired to his own province of Sante Fe, where he ruled for twenty years (1818–1838) and the people of Buenos Aires were left to manage their own affairs.

Most of Argentina outside the province of Buenos Aires was by this time controlled by the leaders of the *montoneras*, undisciplined hordes of *gaucho* cavalry which began to appear on the pampas in the first years of independence. Freedom of trade had brought economic changes which made the *gauchos*' lot harder and which were eventually to compel them to give up altogether their wild, free life on the plains. When the landowners had a better export market for their hides and salt beef, they were less willing to have their cattle killed indiscriminately, and the one food on which the country people depended became difficult to get. This forced the *gauchos* into more regular work for the landowners, and their dependence was increased by the need for protection against the more and more frequent raids of the wild Indians. With their intense love of personal freedom, many preferred to join the first leader who promised a chance for excitement and plunder in a military campaign. Though there were *gauchos* in the armies on both sides, the *montoneras* usually supported the federalists. The men whom they brought to power were sometimes influential landowners or professional soldiers, sometimes ignorant and savage barbarians like Facundo Quiroga, who for some years maintained a reign of terror in La Rioja and several neighboring provinces.

Buenos Aires after 1820 enjoyed some years of relative peace. Rodríguez continued as governor, but the outstanding person in the administration was Bernardino Rivadavia, who had just returned to the country after a long stay in Europe. As minister of state, Rivadavia put into effect a whole series of reforms in the civil government and the courts, and in the economic and ecclesiastical institutions of the province. A university was founded at Buenos Aires, and an effort was made to improve the system of primary instruction. Foreign commerce increased rapidly, and the government's growing prestige abroad enabled it to obtain a $3,000,000 loan in England for port works and for the improvement of the city water supply.

Despite strong centrifugal tendencies, a desire for national unity persisted. The provinces felt a need for coöperation for mutual defense, and the commercial dependence of the other sections upon Buenos Aires made it impossible for them to remain entirely independent. The "quadrilateral treaty" of 1822 united Buenos Aires, Sante Fe, Entre Ríos, and Corrientes in a loose defensive alliance against a feared attack from Brazil, and the other provinces entrusted the conduct of foreign relations to Buenos Aires, so that the United States entered into diplomatic relations with the administration there when it recognized Argentina's independence in the same year. In December, 1824, after General Las Heras succeeded Rodríguez as governor, a congress representing all of the provinces met at Buenos Aires. In February, 1826, this body elected Rivadavia president of the United Provinces, in order to conduct more effectively the war that had just begun with Brazil.

It will be remembered that the Portuguese had conquered the *Banda Oriental* between 1816 and 1820. The territory continued to form a province of Brazil after that country became independent, and many of its leaders took refuge in Buenos Aires. In April, 1825, a small band of these, the famous Thirty-Three, crossed the river and started an insurrection; and a few months later an assembly meeting in the territory which they controlled voted to reunite the province with Argentina. When the congress at Buenos Aires approved their action, Brazil declared war. A hastily organized Argentine squadron under Admiral Brown, an Irish soldier of fortune, defeated the Brazilian fleet in the River Plate, and land forces from Buenos Aires, with smaller contingents from other provinces, won an important victory at Ituzaingó in February, 1827.

The effect of these successes was nullified by renewed quarrels between the federalists and the unitarians. The latter, led by Rivadavia, controlled the Congress, and the constitution which the delegates adopted on July 19, 1826, represented their views and was consequently unacceptable to the provinces. Local *caudillos* like Quiroga and Bustos, the ruler of Córdoba, turned against the new central government, and even at Buenos Aires the feeling against Rivadavia was strong, because the congress at his suggestion had passed a law separating the capital city from the province of the same name and creating a separate federal district. Confronted by such grave difficulties at home, Rivadavia accepted British mediation to bring about peace with Brazil. When the Argentine representative signed a treaty recognizing the *Banda Oriental* as Brazilian territory the unpopularity of the government increased, even though Rivadavia repudiated the agreement and prepared to continue the war. In July, 1827, the President resigned. His successor, Vicente López, stayed in office only long enough to dissolve the congress and restore to the provinces the control of their own affairs.

Manuel Dorrego, who became governor of Buenos Aires Province, resumed peace negotiations with Brazil. Again the British government intervened and thanks to its diplomatic pressure the Emperor Dom Pedro I, in 1828, agreed to a treaty that created the independent republic of Uruguay.

The Advent of Rosas

Dorrego, a federalist, was in office only a few months before he was defeated and shot by unitarian forces returning from the war against Brazil. His friend Juan Manuel de Rosas at once started a counter-revolution. This developed into a general civil war that involved most of Argentina and lasted until José María Paz, the chief unitarian leader, was accidentally captured in May, 1831. When the war ended, federalist *caudillos* resumed their sway in the provinces and there was no attempt to restore a strong central government.

Rosas, who became governor of Buenos Aires in 1829, was a member of an aristocratic family and a successful business man, but he had spent much of his life among the *gauchos* and Indians of the frontier, adopting their ways and winning their enthusiastic admiration by his strength and courage and his brilliant horsemanship. The well-disciplined and devoted army which he maintained on his vast estates in the southern part of Buenos Aires Province had played a part occasionally in the civil wars of the preceding ten years, but had been occupied chiefly in defending his own property and that of his neighbors against the raids of hostile Indians. Even among the Indians, however, he had many devoted friends, and the unitarians frequently accused him of encouraging these allies to make raids on districts where his political leadership was not accepted.

The people of Buenos Aires enjoyed a welcome tranquility during the three years of Rosas' first term and in 1832 the legislature begged him to continue, but he refused. Instead he organized a campaign against the Indians south and west of the city, opening a new stretch of the pampa to white settlement, and increasing his own prestige. Meanwhile, his followers created serious disturbances in the capital, compelling two governors in succession to resign, and in 1834 the legislature again besought him to accept the governorship. In March, 1835, he finally consented after insisting upon a plebiscite in which the voters granted him unlimited dictatorial power.

Within a short time Rosas was the real ruler of all Argentina. Legally he was only the governor of Buenos Aires, but the greater resources and military strength of this province enabled him to dominate the *caudillos* in other regions and to supplant them if necessary with men of his own choice. Rivals were soon eliminated. The most dangerous of these were Quiroga, who dominated most of the western provinces, and López of Santa Fe, whose lieutenants, the Reynafé brothers, controlled Córdoba. In 1835 Quiroga was murdered while passing through Córdoba on a mission that Rosas had persuaded him to undertake. There was more than a suspicion that Rosas had instigated this act, but whatever the truth of the matter, he made it the pretext for overthrowing the Reynafés and putting two of them to death. Córdoba thus fell under the control of one of Rosas' own followers, and López' influence was so impaired that he was thenceforth little more than a lieutenant of Rosas.

Several of the Argentine provinces entered into an offensive and defensive alliance and created a vague sort of union under the federal pact of 1831, and Buenos Aires continued to represent the others in the conduct of foreign affairs. Theoretically each province continued to be independent in other respects but in fact Argentina became unified as it had not been under any preceding government. Buenos Aires came more and more to be the political and commercial capital, and a national point of view took the place of the intense provincialism of the earlier period. Rosas' lieutenants were brutal petty despots, but they suppressed banditry and made the roads safe for travel. Comparative security encouraged agriculture and stock-raising, and foreign capital began to come into the country.

Rosas was popular among the common people of Buenos Aires, and many of the property owners and merchants, after the heavy losses they had suffered from civil strife, were glad to accept a ruler who could maintain order. At the same time he had many enemies, and in dealing with these his regime was an intolerant and sanguinary dictatorship. The official motto: "Long live the Argentine Confederation; death to the savage unitarians," appeared in all public documents. A great number of citizens were executed for participating in revolutionary conspiracies, and many others were killed or mistreated merely because they fell under suspicion. An unofficial band of cut-throats, called the *Mazorca*, and an extensive spy system helped to maintain a demoralizing reign of terror. Opponents who escaped by flight lost all of their property and it was alleged that many were compelled to leave the country by threats and mistreatment simply to make possible the confiscation of their estates. Rosas' system was perhaps no more atrocious than many others which have flourished in the Western Hemisphere, but it attracted much attention abroad and gave him an unenviable distinction as the classical example of Latin American tyranny.

Rosas was constantly embroiled in conflicts with other governments. In 1837–38, he was at war with Santa Cruz, the ruler of Bolivia and Peru, and a little later he was involved in desultory hostilities with Paraguay. Much more important was his intervention in Uruguay. Rivera, the first president of that republic, had angered Rosas by granting asylum to a number of Argentine political exiles, and in 1836 when Rivera revolted against his successor, Oribe, Rosas came to the latter's support. This was the beginning of a long struggle which was soon complicated by a conflict with France.

The Franco-British Intervention

For several years there had been a dispute with France over a law requiring all foreigners in Buenos Aires to serve in the provincial militia. There had also been trouble over pecuniary claims. Rosas arrogantly refused to settle these questions, and in 1838 the French government, partly for internal political reasons, decided to take a more aggressive course. It first established a blockade of Buenos Aires. When this produced no result pressure was applied in the shape of aid to Rosas' enemies. Oribe was driven out of Montevideo and a joint French-Uruguayan expedition seized Martín García Island which commanded river navigation on the Paraná. The trade of Buenos Aires was severely affected, but Rosas refused to yield. French efforts to overthrow him by supporting a unitarian revolution were a miserable failure and merely resulted in wholesale killings of persons suspected of disaffection in Buenos Aires. By 1840, political developments at home and in the Near East made the French government ready to withdraw from an adventure which was clearly unprofitable, and a treaty was signed under which the French claims were to be arbitrated and the blockade withdrawn.

Rosas promptly violated one provision of this treaty by renewing his aid to Oribe. This brought on fresh trouble with France and also with the British government, which objected to the protracted civil war in Uruguay because it affected commerce. In 1845 both powers blockaded Buenos Aires and landed forces at Montevideo to assist Rivera. An Argentine squadron under Admiral Brown was captured, and a British expedition was sent up the Paraná River to aid the unitarians who had obtained control of Corrientes. Despite all this activity the joint intervention was ineffective. Rosas was defiant and his successful resistance to two great foreign powers increased his prestige in Argentina. Pressure from the numerous British merchants in Argentina and renewed friction between England and France made the British government reluctant to continue the blockade indefinitely, and in spite of Rosas' rejection of all conciliatory proposals it withdrew its forces in July, 1847. France was compelled to do likewise a year later.

The Fall of Rosas

The *Riveristas*, however, soon found new allies whose help was more effective than that of the European navies. The powerful governor of Entre Ríos, Justo José de Urquiza, had been restive for some time. He had protested in vain against Rosas' commercial policy which hurt the trade of the other provinces; and he had quarreled with the governor of Santa Fe, who was completely under Rosas' influence. When he prepared for an open break, he was supported by the government of Brazil, which wished to prevent the Argentine dictator's imminent triumph in Uruguay. In 1851 he declared that the Province of

Entre Ríos had withdrawn the authority conferred on Rosas under the Federal Pact of 1831 and led an army into Uruguay.

Oribe was quickly compelled to come to terms with the government at Montevideo, and contingents from Uruguay and Brazil, with a number of exiles from Buenos Aires, joined Urquiza's forces. When the dictator's troops were defeated at Monte Caseros on February 3, 1852, the whole regime collapsed. Rosas resigned and fled with his daughter Manuela to England, where he lived in poverty until his death twenty-five years later.

The Constitution of 1853

Urquiza, as a matter of course, became the new ruler of Argentina. The provincial government that he set up at Buenos Aires under Dr. Vicente López y Planes joined with Entre Ríos, Corrientes, and Santa Fe in conferring upon him the direction of foreign affairs, and on May 31, 1852, a meeting attended by all the provincial governors signed the agreement of San Nicolás, which gave him control of all military forces and authorized him to use a portion of the customs receipts at Buenos Aires pending the holding of a constitutional convention.

The convention met a few months later at Santa Fe, and on May 1, 1853, the delegates signed the constitution of the Argentine Republic. The delegates were much influenced by the views of the Argentine jurist J. B. Alberdi, who had just published a book that examined the reasons for the failure to attain stability under previous constitutions and reached the conclusion that what the country needed was a federal government in which the central authorities would have sufficient power to maintain order and national unity without suffocating the desire for autonomy in the provinces. The result of their work was consequently a document much like the constitution of the United States. It went into effect at once in all the provinces except Buenos Aires and on March 5, 1854, General Urquiza was inaugurated as President of the Republic.

The Separation and Reunion of Buenos Aires, 1852–1862

The Province of Buenos Aires held aloof from the new government. Urquiza, after his long association with Rosas, had few friends among the former political exiles who now controlled affairs at the former capital, and who feared that the ruler of Entre Ríos would simply establish a new dictatorship in place of the old. This group included several notable figures: the future presidents Mitre and Sarmiento; Valentín Alsina, who had carried on an effective newspaper campaign against Rosas at Montevideo; and Dalmacio Vélez Sársfield, later the author of the Argentine civil code. Neither they nor the faction that had formerly supported Rosas had any desire to submit to a ruler from another province, and they revolted against Urquiza's leadership soon after the battle of Monte Caseros. In June, 1852, the Buenos Aires legislature forced the new provincial governor to resign and refused to approve the agreement of San Nicolás. Urquiza dissolved the legislature and installed a regime under his own control, but this was overthrown on September 11 by a revolutionary movement under Valentín Alsina. A new effort to reduce the city to obedience failed when the foreign officer who commanded Urquiza's squadron was bribed to betray him. Buenos Aires did not send delegates to the constitutional convention and the spirit of separatism became stronger when it was learned that that body had passed a law providing that the city should be separated from the province and placed under direct control of the federal government. The law did not go into effect because Buenos Aires did not ratify the constitution.

For nine years, the Argentine Republic, with its capital at Paraná in Entre Ríos, and the Province of Buenos Aires were separate independent states. Both made progress during this period. Much attention was devoted to education, and foreign trade increased. One of Urquiza's most important acts was the signature of treaties in 1853 with Great Britain, France, and the United States by which the Paraná and Uruguay Rivers were opened to international commerce. The 1850's also saw the beginning of the great influx of immigrants which was soon to transform the nation's social and economic life. Several thousand British arrived to take up sheep raising, and agricultural colonies were established by Swiss and other Europeans in Santa Fe and Entre Ríos. The introduction of wheat growing in these colonies was one of the important events in Argentina's economic history.

It was nevertheless impossible for the two states to continue indefinitely as separate political units. Though Urquiza gave up the attempt to control Buenos Aires, and friendly relations were temporarily established, new causes of conflict soon appeared. In 1856 the government at Paraná imposed discriminatory duties on foreign goods transshipped at Buenos Aires, hoping in this way to increase foreign trade at Rosario. Three years later Urquiza's enemy Alsina, who had recently become governor of Buenos Aires, decreed retaliatory measures. This led to war, and on October 23, 1859, Urquiza defeated the Buenos Aires army under General Mitre at Cepeda. Soon afterward Buenos Aires agreed to enter the Federation on the understanding that certain changes be made in the constitution. The capital remained for the time being at Paraná.

A new conflict occurred when the federal congress refused to admit delegates from Buenos Aires on the ground that they had not been elected under the federal constitution. The *porteños* decided to secede from the federation and both sides prepared for war. Urquiza, who had been succeeded as president in March, 1860, by Santiago Derqui, took command of the federal army. Hostility that soon developed between him and Derqui was a help to the *porteños,* and at the battle of Pavón, on September 17, 1861, he was defeated by Bartolomé Mitre, the new governor of Buenos Aires. The latter now assumed provisional control of the federal government, and in October, 1862, he was elected President of the Republic for a six-year term.

The Presidency of Mitre

Mitre was one of the greatest of a group of able presidents under whose leadership Argentina made rapid progress during the last half of the nineteenth century. Though only forty-one at the time of his election, he had already had a notable career. For several years, beginning when he was barely seventeen, he had taken part in the defense of Montevideo against Rosas. Later he fought in civil wars in Bolivia and directed newspapers there and in Chile, returning to Argentina in time to command an artillery force at Monte Caseros. He was the most influential leader of the party that upheld the autonomy of Buenos Aires against Urquiza and the Confederation, but he welcomed national unity on terms that seemed to safeguard the interests of Buenos Aires. He was not only a statesman and soldier, but a prolific poet, a journalist, and an historian. *La Nación* of Buenos Aires, which he founded, is an important newspaper today, and his books on San Martín and Belgrano are still used by students of South American history.

As President, Mitre was compelled to deal with several difficult problems. One was a dispute over the location of the federal capital. Mitre proposed that the entire province of Buenos Aires become a federal district under the central government's direct control, but this was opposed by the provincial legislature, and as a compromise the national government was finally permitted to reside temporarily in Buenos Aires without interfering with the autonomy of the provincial government. Another problem was the maintenance of order. There were troublesome minor revolutionary movements in the interior, and in 1863–64, *montoneras* under a chief named Peñaloza, commonly called "El Chacho," terrorized a great area in the north and west. It was only gradually that the more distant provinces felt the full effect of the creation of a strong national government, but by the end of Mitre's term the union had been established on a firm and lasting basis.

The most serious test of the new government's stability was the war with Paraguay, between 1865 and 1870, which will be described more fully in Chapter 11. Argentina was drawn into this conflict when Francisco Solano López' troops marched through Corrientes to attack Brazil, and Mitre himself for a time commanded the allied Argentine-Brazilian-Uruguayan armies. As the war dragged on with few successes to offset the great expense and the heavy allied losses, there was much discontent and the President had to suppress two small revolts in the interior. In 1868 he turned over the conduct of the Paraguayan operations to the Brazilian Marshal Caxias and returned to Buenos Aires for the final months of his presidential term.

Sarmiento and Avellaneda

With the election of 1868, the control of the government passed out of the hands of the *porteño* group. Mitre did not attempt to impose a candidate of his own, and an epidemic of cholera which drove many people from the capital made it difficult for the leaders at Buenos Aires to oppose successfully the candidate supported by the governors of several other provinces. The new President was Domingo Faustino Sarmiento, who, like Mitre, had spent much of his life abroad as a political exile. Sarmiento's greatest achievement was in the field of public instruction. He had himself taught school for several years at different stages of his career and had had charge of public instruction in Buenos Aires during the period when the province was an independent state. During the last years of Mitre's administration he had been Minister at Washington, where he devoted much time to a study of the educational institutions which he regarded as the basis of North American prosperity. He became a friend and admirer of Horace Mann and was much influenced by the latter's ideas. As President, he undertook a comprehensive reform of the whole Argentine educational system, and as a first step founded several normal schools and engaged a group of teachers from the United States to work in them.

Though Sarmiento had lived for some years at the national capital, he was a native of San Juan, and he owed his election to a combination of the other provinces against Buenos Aires. The *porteños* had little participation in his administration, and the "Córdoba League," as the provincial party was called, was in a position to control the next presidential election in 1874. Sarmiento himself attempted to maintain a scrupulous neutrality, but he could not prevent the use of oppression and fraud by his subordinates, and Nicolás Avellaneda of Tucumán defeated Mitre, who was again the *porteño* candidate. Mitre revolted, but the uprising was suppressed after a short campaign. The very lenient treatment accorded to the vanquished party was in marked contrast to the bloody scenes which had characterized unsuccessful revolts in the preceding generation.

Avellaneda had been Sarmiento's minister of public instruction and he continued the educational work of his predecessor as well as the other enlightened policies which were steadily increasing the prestige of the federal government at home and abroad. The most important accomplishment of his administration was the conquest of the rich pampa south and west of Buenos Aires, hitherto held by wild Indians whose raids made life and property unsafe even in the vicinity of the white settlements. General Roca, the minister of war, led troops into this territory in 1878–79 and systematically exterminated the savages. His operations opened up a vast tract of fertile land for stockraising and agriculture. Unfortunately most of the land was sold in large tracts to speculators or influential politicians instead of being made available to the immigrants who were now arriving in evergreater numbers from Europe.

The Creation of the Federal District

The status of the national capital, still unsettled, was a constant danger to the Republic's tranquility. Buenos Aires was still the most important province, and its people bitterly resented being deprived of the controlling voice in national affairs which they had in the first years of the union. The attempt to have federal and provincial authorities live side by side in the same city led to much friction, and there was always the possibility that an uprising in the capital might overthrow an administration controlled by political groups from other parts of the Republic. To strengthen the federal government's position, the leaders of the Córdoba group revived the proposal to convert the city of Buenos Aires into a federal district, a suggestion which infuriated the *porteños*. It became the chief issue in the presidential campaign of 1880, in which General Roca, with the support of all of the provinces except Buenos Aires and Corrientes, was the official candidate.

Since Roca's victory was a foregone conclusion unless the *porteños* resorted to force, Governor Tejedor of Buenos Aires, who was the opposing candidate, began to recruit and drill troops. Open warfare began in June, 1880. The federal government withdrew to Belgrano, in the suburbs, but after a sharp conflict its forces compelled the leaders in the city to surrender. The municipality of Buenos Aires was now separated from the province and made a federal district, in which only the central government exercised any authority. The province later set up a new capital at La Plata, but although it continued to be one of the most important sections of the Republic, it could no longer hope, after its dismemberment, to dominate the nation's affairs. A political issue that had caused trouble from the first years of independence thus virtually disappeared.

The Beginning of Modern Argentina

In 1880 Argentina was a backward country as compared with some of its South American neighbors. There was more security for life and property than there had been twenty years earlier, but travelers still compared the Republic unfavorably in this respect with Brazil. Though the central government's authority had increased, many of the provinces were still ruled by irresponsible *caudillos* or unprogressive land-owning oligarchies. There was not even a national currency, so that a person going from one province to another must change his money as though he were entering a foreign country. In the interior, local disturbances, as well as the more important national civil wars, had made some sections poorer if anything than before 1810. Even in more prosperous regions little land was under cultivation and cattle were raised mainly for their hides and to make *tasajo*, or jerked beef.

The country was nevertheless beginning the astonishingly rapid economic development that was to continue through the next generation. The livestock industry especially was being transformed in response to the increasing European demand for meat products. The establishment of a more stable government gave the landowners a greater sense of security and they began as early as 1870 to import fine cattle from abroad and to make great changes in the administration of the *estancias*.[1]

Water was provided for the flocks and herds; ranges fenced; breeding regulated; pure-bred stock introduced by the thousands; measures taken to control the ravages of the tick; slaughtering and chilling plants constructed and, most significant of all, alfalfa ranges established on most every *estancia*.

After Roca exterminated the pampas Indians in 1878–79, the area available for cattle-raising was greatly increased and Patagonia was made safer for white occupation, so that sheep-raising became an important business there. The introduction of refrigerator ships in 1877 opened new possibilities. Frozen beef, and later chilled beef, took the place of *tasajo*, and sheep were raised for their meat as well as their wool.

A substantial beginning had also been made in railroad construction. Starting in 1863, the North American promoter William Wheelwright, working with British capital, built a line from Rosario to Córdoba, and this was later extended to Tucumán. There were shorter lines elsewhere, especially in the Province of Buenos Aires, so that the country had a total of 1,500 miles of railway in 1880. The promoters were in most cases given grants of land along the right of way, much of which they sold in small holdings to foreign immigrants. The newcomers devoted themselves mainly to tilling the soil, an occupation always uncongenial to the *gaucho;* and about 1880 the Republic began, for the first time, to export wheat instead of importing it for local consumption.

Progress was much more rapid after 1880. Roca greatly strengthened the power of the central government by a firm but at the same time

[1] Jones, *South America*, p. 312.

conciliatory policy. In the six years of his administration railway mileage more than doubled, the tonnage of ships calling at Argentine ports increased threefold, and immigration, encouraged by peaceful conditions and reports of the country's prosperity, reached figures hitherto unknown. Land values went up rapidly and many of the *estancieros* found themselves wealthy. The Province of Buenos Aires, which occupied the more fertile portion of the pampa and which had successfully asserted a claim to the best part of the lands recently conquered from the Indians, profited far more by this development than did the interior provinces.

Juárez Celmán and the Revolt of 1890

This phenomenal prosperity continued into the first years of the term of Dr. Miguel Juárez Celmán, who succeeded Roca in 1886, but it was soon followed by a reaction. Reckless speculation had created unsound business conditions and the policy of the government, under the new administration, made matters worse. The new President was a brother-in-law of Roca, but the latter's influence was soon superseded by that of provincial politicians of the Córdoba League, many of whom were incompetent and corrupt. There was an orgy of graft and extravagance, made possible partly by borrowing abroad and partly by large issues of unsecured paper money, and when business conditions began to grow worse the Republic's credit was seriously affected. The financial crisis brought on political troubles.

The Córdoba group were unpopular in Buenos Aires, and the administration's opponents were encouraged by support from foreign commercial and financial interests, which were by this time very powerful in Argentina. A political party called the *Unión Cívica* gained more and more adherents in the capital, despite active persecution by the police. In July, 1890, it joined with a part of the army in a revolt at Buenos Aires and there were two days of fighting in the city streets. The movement was suppressed, but the government was so shaken that Juárez Celmán was compelled to resign in favor of Vice-President Carlos Pellegrini. During the two years that ensued before another election, the country passed through a severe commercial depression, which might have been still more serious had it not been for Pellegrini's efforts to reform the government's finances and preserve its credit.

The Unión Cívica Radical

During the movement against Juárez Celmán, a new political element had come into prominence. The membership of the *Unión Cívica* included not only members of the old *porteño* party and other conservative citizens who desired simply to put an end to the corrupt practices of the group in power, but also a number of more radical leaders who sought to take the government entirely out of the hands of the aristocratic groups which had hitherto controlled political life. The chief of these was Leandro N. Alem, an ardent democrat who had a strong following among the populace of Buenos Aires. Alem led the revolt in 1890, when more moderate members of the *Unión Cívica* wished to confine the party's activity to peaceful protests. In the following year he parted company with these moderate elements and continued his agitation for far-reaching political reforms as the head of the *Unión Cívica Radical*. The "radical" party was thenceforth a powerful factor in Argentine politics.

Argentina was still far from being a democracy. As in other Latin American countries, elections were regularly controlled by the party in power through the use of force or fraud, and each president since the time of Sarmiento had dictated the choice of his successor as a matter of course. The ignorance and indifference of the common people made it easy to exclude them from any share in the country's political life, especially during a period when general prosperity inclined all classes to accept the established order rather than risk the destructive effects of civil war. At the same time, the economic progress of the last years of the nineteenth century had brought into existence forces which made impossible the indefinite continuance of the old political regime. As the immigrants from Italy and Spain became assimilated, their children, who were loyal Argentines, added an intelligent and politically conscious element to the electorate. They and the native middle class which was arising in the larger cities were beginning to demand a more influential rôle in public affairs. The old political groups still dominated the government through their control of the electoral machinery, but the agitation for a change became more and more insistent.

By this time the old party divisions coming down from the days of "federalists" and "unitarians" had lost much of their significance. The provinces were no longer serious rivals of the federal government. Railroad construction, which brought all inhabited portions of the republic within easy reach of the capital, had unified the country economically and socially. It was easy to send troops promptly to any area where disaffection appeared. Though the provisions of the Argentine constitution governing relations between the central government and the provinces were very similar to those of the Constitution of the United States, they were applied in practice in a very different spirit, and the federal authorities repeatedly intervened in local affairs simply to remove administrations that were politically obnoxious to them and that were in a position, through the control of elections, to embarrass the party in power at Buenos Aires. The influence of the central government was also increased by its greatly superior financial resources which enabled it to carry out local public works that local authorities were too poor to undertake.

Political Events, 1892–1910

A new alignment was evident in the presidential campaign of 1892. Mitre and Roca, who had long been political rivals, joined with President Pellegrini to bring about the election of Luis Sáenz Peña. The *acuerdo,* as this coalition was called, was violently opposed by the radicals, but the government declared martial law and arrested Alem and his more prominent followers. The new president found his task a hard one. The economic depression had severely affected the country and there was much discontent. A radical revolt in 1893 was suppressed by the army under the leadership of Roca, but in January, 1895, continued political difficulties led Sáenz Peña to turn over his office to Vice-President José Evaristo Uriburu. Roca and Mitre continued to support the administration, and Roca, as the official candidate, was elected to the presidency in 1898.

Many Argentines felt that there should be a military leader like Roca at the head of the government because the country seemed on the verge of war with Chile. There had long been a controversy over the boundary between the two republics. In 1881, with the aid of the United States, they had agreed that the island of Tierra del Fuego should be divided between them, and that the boundary north of the 52nd parallel should run "where the highest peaks of the Andes divide the watershed." Subsequently, however, it was discovered that the watershed actually was some miles east of the highest peaks. This led to another bitter dispute. Fortunately, a peaceful agreement was reached during Roca's administration. The boundary in the north, in the *Puno de Atacama*, was fixed in 1899 by an arbitral commission headed by W. I. Buchanan, the American Minister at Buenos Aires, and the rest of the line was adjusted three years later, after another period of acute tension, by the arbitration of the King of England. In 1904 the establishment of a lasting peace between the two countries was signalized by the erection of the great statue of the Christ of the Andes in the Uspallata Pass. In the meantime another boundary dispute, with Brazil over the eastern part of the Misiones Territory, had been settled by an arbitral award handed down by President Grover Cleveland in 1895.

Manuel Quintana, the administration candidate, was elected President in 1904, but died in 1906 and was succeeded by the Vice-President, José Figueroa Alcorta. The country's prosperity continued, but political conditions were somewhat more disturbed than while Roca's firm hand guided the ship of state. Both the radicals and other political factions endeavored to embarrass the government and Figueroa Alcorta found it necessary to disperse a hostile congress by force early in 1908 —an affair which demonstrated the difference between the working of republican institutions in Argentina and in the United States. He also intervened in several provinces to strengthen the federal administration's political control. At the same time, in an effort to reach an understanding with the radicals, he held a number of conferences with Hipólito Irigoyen, who became the leader of that party after Alem committed suicide in 1896.

The radicals had never ceased their agitation for changes in electoral practices that would assure the free exercise of the suffrage. Though they were one of the strongest political groups, they consistently refused to present candidates in the elections. From time to time they staged revolts. These were easily suppressed because the general public was little inclined to tolerate disturbances that would interfere with the country's rapidly increasing prosperity, but it was becoming more and more evident that something must soon be done to meet the radicals' demands.

Electoral Reform

Electoral reform was accomplished in the administration of Roque Sáenz Peña, who succeeded Figueroa Alcorta in 1910. The new president was an idealist who had already had a romantic career. As a youth he had served as a volunteer in the Peruvian army during the war against Chile. In 1892 he had been a candidate for the presidency, but had withdrawn when his own father was nominated by the *acuerdo*. He had a distinguished record of public service in other positions at home and abroad, and his experience in other countries helped to convince him of the necessity to create real democratic institutions in Argentina. In the full knowledge that the change would end the domination of his own class, he pushed through the congress the electoral law of 1912, which established for the first time the secret ballot and effectively provided for freedom of the suffrage. All citizens were to be allowed to vote, and minorities were given proportional representation.

Progressive electoral laws have often been enacted in Latin American countries without actually changing the character of the electoral process because neither the authorities nor the people were prepared to make democratic institutions a reality. In Argentina, the reform came in response to a widespread and insistent demand and the new law was enforced by a president who sincerely wished to make its provisions effective. In the congressional elections of 1912, more than 640,000 citizens cast votes. The radical party participated, and several of its candidates were successful. The significance of the change was not diminished by the fact that the democratic ideal was still far from attainment: that bribery to some extent took the place of coercion as a means of obtaining votes, and that more than a third of the people were still illiterate.

Sáenz Peña, who had been ill for some time, died in August, 1914, and was succeeded by Vice-President Victorino de la Plaza, whose main concern during his short term of office was the economic dislocation caused by the European war. The sudden falling off in foreign trade and in the government's revenues caused grave difficulties for a time, but by 1916 sales of meat and wheat to the allies had brought about a new period of prosperity.

Hipólito Irigoyen

In the presidential election of 1916, the radical party, with Hipólito Irigoyen as its candidate, was victorious by a narrow margin. The overturn brought into office a new group of men who had little experience either in administrative positions or in congress. Many of the radical leaders were members of old and distinguished families, but the rank and file represented the middle class which had hitherto been excluded from political life. Irigoyen himself was a remarkable character. He had been active in politics for more than forty years, and for the past twenty-five had carried on a constant agitation, sometimes violent, sometimes peaceful, for more democratic methods of government. He had made some money in cattle-raising, and when he held public office, in his earlier years as a teacher in the state schools and later as president, he is said to have given all his salary to charity. Though he almost never made a speech he had a tremendous following among the common people. When elected president he rode to his inauguration in a street-car, and he continued to live in a modest flat, always accessible to the humblest visitors.

The radical party, despite its name, did not attempt to make any great changes, though some progressive labor legislation was adopted. Irigoyen kept the conduct of affairs in his own hands even more than his predecessors had. His ministers enjoyed little or no authority, and such autonomous government as there was in the provinces was under-mined by intervention to place the radical party in control of their affairs. The chief event of the administration was the European war, in which Argentina remained neutral and profited greatly from the high prices commanded by her products.

Marcelo de Alvear, another radical, was elected to succeed Irigoyen in 1922. The country continued at peace, but the new president was much embarrassed, especially in his relations with Congress, by a split in his own party growing out of his attempt to assert his independence of Irigoyen's leadership. The ex-president's unconditional adherents, known as the *personalistas*, were overwhelmingly in the majority; and when Irigoyen announced his candidacy for a second term in 1928 he was easily elected, without making an active campaign and in spite of the unfriendliness of the administration in office.

The Revolution of 1930

By this time the radical chieftain was an old man, and defects as an administrator which had already been evident during his first term made his second period in office a dismal failure. Though it was no longer possible for him to attend personally to every detail, he still refused to delegate authority. Government business of every kind was paralyzed. Important offices remained unfilled, and the mercantile community suffered from the treasury's failure to pay bills. The world depression, which greatly reduced exports, intensified discontent in all classes of the community. The result was the revolution of September 6, 1930, when the military forces, with the support of many civilian political leaders, removed the president from office and proclaimed a provisional government under General José Uriburu. Irigoyen was arrested and remained in confinement for more than a year.

The conservatives, allied with the *anti-personalista* radicals, thus came into power almost without bloodshed. The *personalistas*, who continued to form the radical party proper, nevertheless still had a great popular following, and in April, 1931, they won a provincial election in Buenos Aires. This caused the government to postpone national elections for several months while it intervened in twelve of the fourteen provinces to place its own adherents in control. A small radical revolt in Corrientes in July afforded an excuse for exiling Alvear, now reconciled with the *personalistas* and recognized as their leader. The Radicals made another mistake in September when they nominated Alvear for the presidency. He was clearly ineligible, because the constitution prohibited the reëlection of an ex-president until six years had elapsed after the end of his term, and the government declared the nomination void. When the national election was held in November, there was a spirited contest between other political groups, but the radicals did not participate.

Political Events, 1932–1942

The victor, who was inaugurated as president in February, 1932, was Agustín Justo, an *anti-personalista* who had been a cabinet minister under Alvear. The outlook for the new administration was unpromising. The depression was at its worst and the radicals, confident that they had the support of a majority of the people, were uncompromising in their opposition. Their conspiracies and revolts made it necessary to keep the country under a state of siege during much of 1933 and 1934. Even the aged Irigoyen was rearrested but was released after two months, a very ill man. When he died in July, 1933, a tremendous popular demonstration showed that the events of his last administration had not lessened the people's affection for him. The radicals were still clearly the strongest of the political parties, but they refused until 1935 to take part in national elections. Despite these difficulties, the economic situation gradually improved. The government's finances were reorganized and Argentina was one of the few Latin American countries that continued service on its foreign debts. Exports increased, and by 1935 the country was again fairly prosperous.

Roberto Ortíz, another *anti-personalista*, was the official candidate in 1937. He defeated Alvear, who was again nominated by the radicals, in an election where there were many complaints of intimidation and fraud. Ortíz was supported by the same coalition of *anti-personalistas* and conservatives that had backed Justo, but in 1940 he broke with the national democrats, the conservative party, and reunited the greater part of the radicals under his own leadership. Radical gains in the congressional election of the same year strengthened his position, but the situation suddenly changed in July, 1940, when Ortíz fell ill and was compelled to turn over the government to the conservative Vice-President, Ramón Castillo.

Castillo faced a hostile congress, and his policy toward the European war was unpopular with one large fraction of public opinion. Though ostensibly neutral, his government favored the Axis in many ways, and Argentina's attitude at the Rio de Janeiro conference in January, 1942, prevented the passage of a resolution calling for the immediate severance of relations with Germany and Japan by all the American Republics.[1] For some time it was hoped that Ortíz might recover sufficiently to resume his duties, but he died in June, 1942. Ex-President Justo, another outstanding leader of the group that supported the democracies, died in January, 1943. Thereafter it was clear that it would be difficult to defeat Robustiano Patrón Costas, the conservative candidate, in the presidential election scheduled for September. The radicals and the socialists attempted to join forces against him, but interparty jealousies made their coöperation ineffective.

Patrón Costas, however, had little support even among the conservative group, and in June, 1943, the army forestalled his election by ousting Castillo and setting up a provisional government under General Arturo Rawson. Many expected that the new administration would adopt a policy more favorable to the democracies, but the real purpose of the revolt became evident after Rawson was replaced by General Pedro Ramírez, Castillo's Minister of War, who was known to be pro-

[1] See below, p. 564.

Axis. Congress had already been dissolved, and the calling off of the presidential election made it clear that the country was to be ruled indefinitely by a military dictatorship. Castillo's "neutrality" policy was continued with little change. Ostensibly, the government continued to coöperate with the other American republics in measures for common defense, but it permitted Argentine territory to become a base for espionage and sabotage and even connived with German agents in attempts to bring about revolutions in other American states. One of these, in Bolivia, succeeded.[1]

Ramírez found himself in an embarrassing position when an Argentine consular officer named Hellmuth was arrested by the British at Trinidad and disclosed that he had been sent by the President to seek to obtain arms from Germany. At the same time, the refusal of the other American states to recognize the new government in Bolivia emphasized Argentina's increasing isolation, and increased popular discontent with the government's policies. Ramírez consequently yielded to pressure and broke off relations with the Axis powers on January 26, 1944. This action, however, brought about little change in the government's attitude, and on February 24, when Ramírez was forced to turn over the presidency to General Edelmiro Farrell, the pro-German element regained the ascendency.

The Rise of Perón

The most powerful member of Farrell's government was Colonel Juan Domingo Perón, the leader of a nationalistic military clique that called itself the *Grupo Oficiales Unidos* (GOU). As head of the labor department under Ramírez, Perón had already begun to build up a strong personal following among the laboring class by promises of higher wages and other favors. After the February revolution his influence steadily increased. In October, 1945, a group of army officers staged a *coup d'état* and forced Farrell to confine Perón on Martín García Island, but eight days later he was back in Buenos Aires. Disagreements and irresolution had prevented the democratic parties from taking advantage of their opportunity, and a great demonstration of "*descamisados*," or "shirtless ones," discouraged any effort to prevent his return. From this time on, his dominant influence in the Farrell government was unquestioned.

[1] See below, p. 335.

The United States and most of the other American governments refused to recognize the Farrell regime when it came into power, because they objected to its pro-Axis policies. This diplomatic isolation made Argentina's position increasingly uncomfortable as the end of the war approached. When the inter-American conference at Mexico, in March, 1945, suggested that Argentina might return to the American family of nations if the government would subscribe to the measures that the conference had approved, the invitation was accepted. This involved, among other things, a commitment to take part in the war effort, and on March 27 Argentina declared war on Germany and Japan. Recognition by the United States and the other American republics soon followed. Unfortunately, however, the Farrell government showed little disposition to implement its declaration of war by effective action against Nazi firms and individuals in Argentina. This, combined with the American Ambassador's openly expressed disapproval of the regime's undemocratic internal policies, again strained relations with the United States during the remainder of 1945.

Perón was naturally the official candidate in the presidential election held in February, 1946. Several opposition parties, after long disputes, nominated José P. Tamborini, who had been Minister of the Interior under Alvear. There was violence during the campaign, but the election itself was apparently reasonably free. Perón won by 1,479,000 to 1,210,000. Some votes were probably influenced when the State Department at Washington, twelve days before the election, issued a "blue book" based on captured German documents which showed how deeply Perón and other Argentine officials had been involved in intrigues with Axis representatives during the war. It was a devastating indictment of the government's policies, both foreign and domestic, but its publication may have swung to Perón the votes of many persons who resented outside interference in the country's affairs.

After the new president was inaugurated in June, 1946, it became clear that he planned to control the country's political and economic life more completely than any of his predecessors. Elections continued to be held, and opposing parties polled about one-third of the popular vote and had a substantial number of deputies in Congress; but they had no influence with the *Peronista* majority. Opposition in other quarters was eliminated. In September, 1946, four of the five members of the Supreme Court were impeached on the ground that they had recognized *de facto* governments in 1930 and 1943, a charge that seemed particularly cynical in view of Perón's own connection with the 1943 revolt. The universities, formerly autonomous, were brought under government control and hundreds of professors were removed. Most of the opposition press was throttled. The government apparently hesitated to close *La Prensa* and *La Nación*, which had been two of the world's greatest newspapers, but it undermined their independence by restricting the supply of newsprint and by other forms of persecution. In March, 1949, a convention voted a new constitution which increased the President's powers and removed the prohibition against reëlection for two successive terms. The probability of Perón's reelection in 1952 was increased by a law passed in 1949 that restricted the organization of new political parties and forbade coalitions among existing parties. Another law authorized the imprisonment of any one who insulted a public official, even though the truth of the accusations might be proved.

Diplomatic tension between Argentina and the United States, which had reached a high point when Perón was elected, diminished in the years that followed. After long negotiations in 1947, the Argentine government took measures against German firms and individuals that met some of the criticism directed against it in the "blue book." Since that time normal relations have existed between the two republics.

Perón inherited a great backlog of dollar and sterling exchange resulting from the excess of exports during the war. The active demand for Argentine products in the first two years of his term further increased the government's resources, for the *IAPI*, the official trade promotion agency, bought meat and grain at low prices from the producers and sold them abroad at inflated ones. The government thus had a great amount of money at its disposal. It was able to retire the foreign bonded debt, and to make loans totaling hundreds of millions of dollars to European and Latin American countries, chiefly to finance exports. The British railroads, which formed the largest part of the Argentine railway network, were bought for $600,000,000. This transaction was part of an ambitious program of nationalization, which embraced other forms of transportation and also the country's banking and insurance systems. Expenditure on such a scale could hardly be continued indefinitely, and by 1949 the wartime backlog was practically exhausted and falling prices for Argentine products were confronting the government with difficult problems.

One of these was the problem of finding means to continue the benefits to labor that were an important part of the government's policy. Perón continued to have the support of the army, but his power rested chiefly on the enthusiastic loyalty of the poorest classes in the cities, who gained by the government's advanced social legislation and especially by the President's policy of compelling employers to raise wages and grant other concessions to labor. Though the formerly strong Argentine labor unions had been brought under government control, and leaders who attempted to maintain their independence had been eliminated, it seemed probable that the maintenance of the workers' support would be difficult if economic conditions grew unsettled.

Contemporary Argentina

Though current economic and political conditions may be unsatisfactory, Argentina is basically one of the richest and most progressive of the American republics. The fertility and equable climate of the pampas, which have made so much of her territory ideal for cattle-raising and agriculture; the ease with which railroads and roads could be built between the chief centers of population; and the homogeneity of her people have all contributed to her prosperity. The country is the world's greatest exporter of beef, corn, and flax, and one of the greatest exporters of wheat, and a high per capita trade gives it a commercial importance out of all proportion to its population.

The population of 16,000,000 is less than that of Brazil or Mexico, but the general level of education and well-being is far higher than in those countries. Government reports state that over 90 per cent of the children of elementary-school age are enrolled in schools, and a high standard has been established in the educational institutions of all grades. Except in the west and northwest, the people are overwhelmingly of European descent.

Immigration has played a large part in the growth of the population, for it is estimated that 3,500,000 people came to Argentina as permanent residents between 1810 and 1930. In 1937, nearly 20 per cent of the country's inhabitants were still of foreign birth. Italians and Spaniards, both easily assimilated, have always formed by far the greater part of the new arrivals. Unfortunately many of the immigrants have congregated in the larger cities, living in crowded and unsanitary tenements, and those who have gone into the rural districts have become laborers or tenant farmers rather than landowners. The wealthy Argentine families have been reluctant to break up their great estates even when they could not themselves utilize the land to best advantage. The Republic's social problems nevertheless seem far less difficult of solution than those of its neighbors which have large Indian populations.

10

Uruguay

The Banda Oriental before 1810

The *Banda Oriental*, the gently rolling country east of the River Uruguay, was the last important region of South America to be occupied by settlers of European descent. Until late in the colonial period it was held by the war-like, semi-nomadic Charruas, a people very similar to the tribes of the Argentine pampas and like them inveterate enemies of the white man. Expeditions from the Spanish settlements around Buenos Aires frequently hunted wild cattle there in the seventeenth and eighteenth centuries, but the first European settlement was Colonia, which the Portuguese established in 1680 as a base for the smuggling trade. Montevideo was founded in 1726 by the Governor of Buenos Aires, as an outpost to prevent further penetration from Brazil. As late as 1751 the town had less than 1,000 inhabitants, but the presence of a fort and garrison made it possible for colonists to settle in the country roundabout and the interior was gradually occupied by creole cattle ranchers and their half-wild *gaucho* employees. The Indians were pushed back and finally exterminated, leaving little trace of their blood in the people who took their place. After the Portuguese were expelled from Colonia in 1777, the entire region came under the control of Spain. It was a part of the Viceroyalty of Buenos Aires, and its history both before and after independence was much influenced by the course of events on the other side of the River Plate.

The *Orientales*, as we have seen, played a leading part in the recapture of Buenos Aires from the British in 1806. In the following year Montevideo and other points along the coast were occupied for seven months by Sir Samuel Auchmuty's forces. Several hundred English merchants followed close on the heels of the army, and *La Estrella del Sur*, a newspaper issued by the invaders as a vehicle for propaganda against Spain, spread ideas which profoundly influenced the thought of the hitherto isolated creole community. Nevertheless Montevideo later became the chief center of resistance to independence in the River Plate region. Spanish influence was strong there because it was still primarily a military post and because localistic jealousy made the creoles unwilling to follow the leadership of Buenos Aires.

Artigas

The revolutionary spirit was stronger in other parts of the *Banda Oriental*, where the movement for independence was led by José Artigas, the national hero of Uruguay. Artigas had served for many years as captain in a cavalry force organized by the Spanish authorities to maintain a semblance of order among the turbulent people of the interior, and had taken a distinguished part in the resistance to the British invasion. After the revolution in Buenos Aires he offered his services to the patriot *junta*, and when Belgrano marched against the Spanish force at Montevideo in 1811 Artigas preceded him, recruiting forces among the *gauchos* and bandits of the interior and winning a victory at Las Piedras which opened the way to Montevideo.

Before the city could be taken, the invasion of the *Banda Oriental* by troops from Brazil caused the royalists and the patriots to suspend hostilities in the face of an enemy more bitterly hated by both. The Argentine army was withdrawn, and Artigas retreated to Ayuí, on the west bank of the Uruguay River, taking with him, by persuasion or by force, almost the whole population of the districts where his leadership was recognized. For several months his followers and their families lived in a temporary camp with trees and oxcarts as their only shelter. They followed Artigas back into the *Banda Oriental* after British diplomatic intervention persuaded the Portuguese to withdraw, and by the end of 1812 they were again coöperating with forces from Buenos Aires against the loyalists. After the combined armies defeated the Spanish forces at El Cerrito, they laid siege to Montevideo.

The events that followed the break between Artigas and the Buenos Aires *junta*, the subsequent war between unitarians and federalists throughout the River Plate region, and the establishment of Artigas' control over much of what is now the Argentine Republic, have already been described. The new Portuguese invasion of the *Banda Oriental* in 1816 made the struggle a three-cornered one, and Artigas was defeated by the Portuguese at Tacuarembó in January, 1820, at the very time when other federalist leaders were winning decisive successes against the unitarians. After this battle many of his Uruguayan supporters went over to the Portuguese. Even his allies in the littoral provinces turned against him, and Artigas took refuge in Paraguay, where he lived as a simple farmer until his death in 1850. The *Banda Oriental* became a province of Portugal, and after 1822 of the new Empire of Brazil.

Independence

The *Orientales* were little disposed to submit to foreign rule, and there was an immediate response when thirty-three Uruguayan exiles crossed the River Plate from Argentina and raised the standard of revolt in 1825. Fructuoso Rivera, a former lieutenant of Artigas who had held an important command under the Brazilian regime, joined the movement, and the invaders soon controlled enough territory to convene a representative assembly. This voted for a union with the Argentine Federation and chose Juan Antonio Lavalleja as governor of the province. The ensuing war between Argentina and Brazil was ended, as we have seen, by the mediation of England. In the treaty of peace in 1828 both neighbors agreed to relinquish control over the *Banda Oriental* and to respect its independence.

The total population of the new "República Oriental del Uruguay" was probably less than 75,000, of whom about one-fifth lived in Montevideo. The cattle which were the country's chief wealth had been greatly reduced by long years of warfare, and the only exports were small quantities of hides and jerked beef. Few of the citizens had even the rudiments of an education. Darwin, in 1832, found that the people of Colonia were proud of their representatives in congress because all could at least sign their names, and he tells of falling in with a mail carrier whose route included several of the more important towns of the Republic but whose whole load consisted of two letters.[1] The establishment of a stable government, based on the republican con-

---

[1] Darwin, *Journal of Researches into the Geology and Natural History of the Various Countries Visited during the Voyage of H.M.S. Beagle Around the World* (Everyman's edition), pp. 136-7.

stitution that the representatives of the people adopted in 1830, would clearly be a difficult task.

Blancos and Colorados

Trouble began with the choice of the first president. Rivera, who was inspector general of the army, had defied Lavalleja's authority even during the war with Brazil. When the time arrived to choose a new governor in Lavalleja's place, the assembly sought to avoid further friction by appointing General Rondeau, but he found his situation intolerable and resigned. Lavalleja was then reappointed to serve until the new constitution should come into force, but Rivera, through the army, was able to control the ensuing election, and he became Uruguay's first president in 1830.

Rivera suppressed several uprisings and conspiracies led by Lavalleja, and was able to remain in office during his four year term. In 1835 he passed on the presidency to his associate Manuel Oribe, but he retained control of the army. He soon quarreled with Oribe, and in the civil war that followed Oribe was supported by Lavalleja and also by the Argentine dictator Rosas, who was angered because Rivera had given asylum to exiles from Buenos Aires. Rivera, on the other hand, made common cause with the Argentine unitarians. It was in this conflict that the contending factions adopted the colors which were thenceforth to distinguish the two historic political parties of Uruguay: Oribe's followers became the *blancos*, or whites, and Rivera's the *colorados*, or reds. The *colorados*, with the aid of the French forces that were blockading Buenos Aires, got the upper hand in 1838, and Rivera again became president.

The "Great War"

When the French withdrew from the River Plate in 1840, Rosas helped the *blancos* to resume the war. After some years of fighting, partly in Uruguay and partly in the Argentine littoral provinces, the *colorado* army was destroyed at Arroyo Grande in Entre Ríos in 1842. This made it possible for Oribe to occupy most of Uruguay.

The *colorados* still held Montevideo, and they continued to hold it during a nine years' siege which is one of the famous events of Uruguay's history. As the struggle went on it became one between the people of the country districts and those of the capital, rather than a mere contest for power between Oribe and Rivera. Rivera in fact was finally removed from command and sent into exile in 1846, but the townspeople continued to hold out. Foreign residents were especially active in the defense, for there had been a wave of French, Italian, and Spanish immigration in the six or seven years immediately preceding the siege, and a large part of the capital's population was by this time of foreign extraction. Much of the fighting, on the *colorado* side, was done by a legion of 3,000 French Basques and by a smaller contingent of Italians under Giuseppe Garibaldi, who was later to become a national hero in his own country. What really made the city's prolonged resistance possible, however, was the aid of the Anglo-French squadron blockading Buenos Aires.

When Britain and France tired of their unsuccessful effort to bring Rosas to terms and abandoned the blockade in 1849, the defending forces at Montevideo were compelled to agree to an armistice. This was virtually a surrender, but before its terms could be fully carried out, Urquiza revolted against Rosas in Entre Ríos and Brazil intervened in the conflict. When Urquiza invaded Uruguay, the greater part of Oribe's troops deserted. The two parties then agreed to a settlement by which both were to be represented in a new Uruguayan congress and a citizen acceptable to both was to become president. In 1852 a small force of Uruguayan troops joined the allied army that defeated Rosas at Monte Caseros.

Montevideo suffered surprisingly little from the long siege. Its inhabitants continued their normal social life and the theaters were open and well patronized. The investing army made few assaults in force, and there were long periods when active military operations virtually ceased. Communication by land with the interior was by no means entirely cut off, and the Anglo-French squadrons gave the city free access to the sea. During the blockade of Buenos Aires, in fact, Montevideo became the commercial center of the River Plate, and its merchants enjoyed unusual prosperity. But for the rest of the nation, the "Great War," as it is called in Uruguay, had been a calamity. Farmers and cattle-raisers suffered much from military operations and from banditry, and the products of regions controlled by Oribe could not be shipped out through the Anglo-French blockade. For more than ten years no funds had been available for education or public works. More serious still were some of the after effects: the predominance of military leaders in the Republic's affairs and the hatreds engendered during the struggle. For many years internal strife and governmental weakness continued to expose the country to foreign interference which made it more difficult for the Uruguayan people to work out their own problems.

Brazilian and Argentine Intervention

In the treaties of alliance under which the two governments had joined in the war against Rosas, Brazil had promised to give the new regime at Montevideo both financial and military support. The Imperial government had also taken advantage of the situation to arrange a boundary settlement favorable to Brazil's claims, and a dispute over the ratification of this agreement led to the overthrow in 1853 of President Giró, who had been elected in the preceding year by an almost unanimous vote of the bipartisan congress. Colonel Venancio Flores, a *colorado*, became president, but in 1855 he was overthrown by a revolt of his own party and in the following year a *blanco* administration came into power under Gabriel Antonio Pereyra. These changes occurred in spite of the presence of a Brazilian army of 4,000 men which had been sent to maintain order in Uruguay, and there was a strong suspicion that they were brought about by Brazilian intrigues.

Pereyra survived his term of office, despite a revolt which received assistance from Buenos Aires, and was succeeded in 1860 by another *blanco*, Bernardo P. Berro. In 1863, Flores and other *colorado* leaders invaded the country with the support of the government in Argentina, which was grateful to them for their services in the *porteño* military forces in the wars that ended with Mitre's rise to power. They were also aided by Brazil, which was displeased with the treatment of its subjects by the *blanco* government. When a Brazilian force was sent to aid the revolutionists, Francisco Solano López, the ruler of Paraguay, intervened on behalf of the *blancos*. Argentina's refusal to permit the passage of troops across her territory prevented him from giving effective help, and the *blancos* were compelled in February, 1865, to agree to a settlement that made Flores Provisional President. Meanwhile López had attacked both Argentina and Brazil, and during the next four years Uruguay was involved as an ally of these countries in the Paraguayan war.

At Montevideo, Flores exercised dictatorial powers for three years in spite of strong opposition from his own party as well as from the *blancos.* When he was assassinated on February 19, 1868, the Minister of War, General Lorenzo Batlle, became President. Plots and military mutinies within the *colorado* ranks continued, and in 1870 there was a *blanco* revolt under Timoteo Aparicio. This civil war lasted until 1872, when peace was established through the mediation of Argentina by a compact which gave the revolutionists control of the police in four departments of the Republic and $500,000 in cash.

Political and Economic Progress

This arrangement set the precedent for a series of deals in which offices and money were used to placate the *blancos* and dissuade them from revolt. The *blancos,* since the "Great War," were preëminently the rural party, and the great landowners who led them were less disposed to object to the control of the national government by the politicians in Montevideo if they themselves were permitted to rule their own districts. Such compromises were less costly than armed conflict, and they tended gradually to allay the enmity between the two parties and to make possible the establishment of a more stable government. For a generation to come political disputes were settled by force rather than by the ballot, but revolutions became less frequent and less destructive.

This improvement in political conditions was in part the result of social and economic changes somewhat similar to those which were taking place in Argentina. As in that country, the *gauchos,* who had made up the armies led by *caudillos* like Rivera and Lavalleja, were gradually disappearing as the increasing European demand for meat and other pastoral products led property owners to abandon the old careless methods of stock-raising. The character of the population was changing in other ways also, for 170,000 foreigners entered the country between 1861 and 1874.[1] The total population, which had fallen from an estimated 200,000 in 1840 to 132,000 in 1852, had grown to 420,000 in 1872, with a quarter of the total in the city of Montevideo. Foreign commerce had developed proportionately. The great Liebig plant for the preparation of preserved meats and meat extract had been established at Fray Bentos in 1861, and the first railroad had been begun

[1] These figures are from Acevedo, *Manual de Historia Uruguaya,* p. 146. It is impossible to ascertain the net increase from immigration because the number of foreigners who returned to Europe during the same period is not known.

in 1867. Landowners and merchants, as in Argentina, were becoming more interested in developing their properties and businesses than in politics, and consequently less tolerant of revolutionary disturbances. The governments that ruled Uruguay during the next twenty years were more dictatorial in their methods than their predecessors, and there was less rather than more freedom of the press and of political activity, but the relative absence of disorder made it possible for the country to continue this material progress and paved the way for the later development of democratic institutions.

"The Era of Professional Soldiers"

An Uruguayan historian characterizes the political change which took place at this time as the end of the age of the *caudillos* and the beginning of the era of the "professional soldiers." [1] With the improvement in weapons and military techniques, the standing army had become more powerful and those who controlled it had a distinct advantage in any conflict with old-style political leaders at the head of improvised forces recruited among their friends and partisans. The first of the "professional soldiers" was Colonel Lorenzo Latorre who became the real ruler of the country in 1875, when the army overthrew Batlle's successor, Dr. José Ellauri. Latorre at first permitted the congress to elect Pedro Varela as president, but he frankly assumed power as dictator in 1876 when Varela attempted to throw off his tutelage.

Latorre maintained order and did something to correct the hitherto chaotic condition of the government's finances. The most important accomplishment of his administration was the reform of the educational system, under the leadership of José Pedro Varela. Uruguay, like her neighbors, had been backward in this respect, for the average attendance in the public schools in 1877 was only about 12,000.[2] The increase in the number of schools and students, and even more the improvement in the quality of instruction, were important factors in the transformation of the Republic from a backward community, torn by continual factional strife, into a prosperous and progressive nation. Latorre's regime in fact saw a marked increase of interest in intellectual activities of all sorts, for his repression of political activity tended to divert the energies of the former ruling class into other lines. He was nevertheless

[1] Acevedo, *op. cit.*, p. 125.
[2] *Ibid.*, p. 223.

able to remain in power only by a reign of terror. His chief opponents were openly murdered or simply disappeared, and their less important followers were imprisoned. In 1880, discouraged by popular opposition and signs of disaffection in the army, and finding himself in financial difficulties despite his careful management of the national treasury, he resigned. He was "disillusioned," he stated in a manifesto, "to the point of thinking that ours is an ungovernable country."

The control of the government passed into the hands of Colonel Máximo Santos, the Minister of War, although the new ruler did not have himself elected president until 1882. Santos was as dictatorial as his predecessor and his arbitrary treatment of private individuals caused several revolutionary movements within the country and brought on serious complications with foreign governments. He was finally compelled in 1886 to offer the opposition leaders participation in his cabinet and, soon afterward, to resign, as his predecessor had done. Again the Minister of War, this time General Máximo Tajes, took over the direction of affairs and was elected president.

Political Events, 1886–1903

Latorre and Santos had been supported by the *colorado* military leaders and also by some of the *blanco* chieftains, who still controlled the four departments given to them under the peace agreement of 1872. Other influential groups in both parties had opposed their regimes. Tajes sought the coöperation of these dissatisfied elements, and at the same time diminished the political influence of the army by disbanding some of the regiments which had been most prone to engage in conspiracies and revolts. His tactful policy made possible a period of peace which lasted through the term of Dr. Herrera y Obes, who was the *colorado* official candidate in 1890. The choice of a civilian marked the end of "the era of professional soldiers."

Another *colorado*, Juan Idiarte Borda, was elected president in 1894. In 1897 the "nationalists," as the *blancos* now called themselves, revolted, and during this civil war Idiarte Borda was assassinated. Peace was restored when the revolutionists were promised the control of six departments—nearly a third of the country—and were given a cash payment of $200,000 for the "expenses of pacification."

The agreement also provided for a thoroughgoing reform in the electoral laws. Hitherto opponents of the government had hardly even attempted to vote. The new law provided for control of the voting by representatives of both parties and assured minority representation in congress. Thenceforth elections tended more and more to take the place of civil war as a means of settling political disputes, even though the elimination of fraud and coercion proved to be a difficult matter. The inherent advantages enjoyed by the party in power through its control of the police and the office-holders still constituted an obstacle to the success of an opposition candidate.

Batlle y Ordóñez

Juan Cuestas, who took charge of the government after Idiarte Borda's death, was constitutional President from 1899 until 1903, when he was succeeded by José Batlle y Ordóñez, the principal chief of the *colorado* party. Batlle dominated Uruguayan political life for several years. He was President from 1903 to 1907 and from 1911 to 1915, and his close political associate Claudio Wílliman served the intervening term. His influence was also great in the administration of Feliciano Viera, who was elected in 1915.

During the period of Batlle's leadership great changes took place in the Republic's political and economic life. The *blancos*, alleging that the President had violated the agreement signed in 1897, revolted in 1904. After several months of fighting and much loss of life, they accepted a general amnesty, a payment of $100,000, and a promise of constitutional and electoral reform, but they were deprived of the control that they had hitherto exercised in a large part of the Republic's territory. The position of the central government was thus greatly strengthened. Its stability was not again seriously threatened by general revolts of the old type, and the small uprisings that occurred from time to time were easily put down because they received little popular support. The incentive to revolt became less after the turn of the century because elections were better conducted and the lot of the opposition party improved in other respects. The press enjoyed almost complete freedom and opponents of the government were not exiled or imprisoned for political activity.

Batlle sponsored an ambitious program of social and economic reform. As one of the earliest advocates of the economic nationalism that has since become a powerful force in Latin America, he sought to break down the power of foreign capital in Uruguay and to improve the lot of the native laborer by a series of measures which seemed more radical in the early 1900's than they would today. The Bank of the Republic, established by the government in 1896, greatly expanded its operations, and in 1912 the government bought control of the Mortgage Bank of Uruguay. Through these two institutions the government sought to encourage small savings, provided rural credit, encouraged construction, and helped small farmers, steadily extending its control over the Republic's financial and economic life as time went on. In 1911 the government set up a State Insurance Bank to compete with foreign companies and gradually to take over a monopoly of certain lines of insurance, and in 1912 the production of electric light and power was made a state monopoly. Batlle also attempted to create a national system of railways and highways to diminish the power of the foreign-owned lines, but in this he was less successful.

In the field of labor legislation Batlle's proposals met with more opposition. An eight-hour day, with a forty-eight-hour week, was made compulsory in all industrial establishments in 1915, but the law was difficult to enforce. Further reforms were blocked for the time being by conservative opposition to the growing influence of the Montevideo labor unions, but after the end of Batlle's second term, and while his influence was still powerful, old-age and retirement pensions, compulsory workmen's compensation insurance, and minimum wages for rural laborers were established.[1]

The Constitution of 1917

Meanwhile there had been much discussion of proposals for constitutional reform. Many leaders in both parties wished to see a decrease in the autocratic power of the president and a fairer opportunity for all political groups to participate in public affairs. There had been much controversy, however, as to the character of the changes which should be made. Batlle advocated the establishment of a "collegiate executive" of nine citizens to take the place of the president. The nationalists, as the blancos now called themselves, wished to retain a president but to make the cabinet responsible to congress under a parliamentary form

[1] S. Hanson, Utopia in Uruguay, is the best account of these economic and social reforms.

of government. On the other hand a strong faction among the *colorados*, who later came to be known as the *Riveristas*, opposed any radical change in the existing system. When the constitutional convention of 1917 was elected, the nationalists won more seats than the *Batllistas* and the dissident *colorados* held the balance of power.

The result was a compromise that led to an interesting political experiment. The Republic continued to have a president, who had control over foreign affairs, national defense, and the maintenance of order; but the other duties of the executive—the preparation of the budget, the direction of education, public works, public-health activities, and other administrative functions—were entrusted to a popularly elected National Council of Administration. This was composed of nine members, each serving for six years, and one of the three members chosen biennially was always to be an adherent of the minority party. The president was elected by direct vote of the people, rather than by the congress as under the earlier constitution. The principle of proportional representation was applied in the congress and in the local elective bodies as well as in the National Council of Administration. The secret ballot was introduced, voting became compulsory, and the government was decentralized to some extent by providing for popularly elected local assemblies and administrative councils.

This constitution was in force from 1919 to 1933. Dr. Baltasar Brum, who had achieved much prestige as foreign minister under President Viera, succeeded the latter in 1919, and was followed by José Serrato (1923–27) and Juan Campisteguy (1927–31). Uruguay, like Argentina and Chile, seemed to have passed beyond the era of revolutionary disturbances. Though the *Batllista* wing of the still divided *colorado* party continued to control the administration by a very small margin of votes, the elections were conducted under conditions that gave little real cause for complaint and the number of citizens voting increased from 46,000 in 1905 to 318,000 in 1930. The opposition always had a substantial representation in the administrative council and in the congress. The government's business enterprises were on the whole well managed, and their number increased. A national meat-packing plant was established in 1928 in an effort to assure better prices to producers of livestock, and a government corporation called the *Ancap*, set up in 1931, took over the monopoly of the manufacture and sale of alcohol and went into competition with private companies in the sale of petroleum products.

The Revolution of 1933

The divided authority created by the constitution of 1917 was a handicap to effective governmental action when the world depression caused suffering and discontent in Uruguay as it did in other countries. President Gabriel Terra, who was elected in 1931 as the *Batllista* candidate, quarreled with the National Council of Administration and obtained support from the *Riveristas* and a portion of the nationalists in a movement to abolish it. On March 30, 1933, after the Council and the Congress refused to approve certain measures that the President had taken on the preceding day, both bodies were dissolved by force and Terra assumed dictatorial power.

A convention that met a year later framed a new constitution abolishing the administrative council but requiring that the minority party have half of the membership of the senate and three out of the nine positions in the president's cabinet. The same convention elected Terra as President for a new four-year term. Though the conservative property-owning classes had more influence in the new regime than they had enjoyed while the *Batllistas* were in power, Terra did not abandon his predecessors' social and economic reforms, and if anything the government moved farther in the direction of state socialism. On the other hand, his political policy was more repressive than any which Uruguay had known since the beginning of the century. The publication of opposition newspapers was prohibited and individual liberty was restricted in other respects, especially after the suppression of a small revolt in 1935.

Nevertheless the presidential election of 1938, at the end of Terra's term, was held under fairly normal conditions. The unusually large popular vote of 357,000 was rather evenly divided between three candidates, two of them *colorados* and the third a nationalist. Under Uruguay's peculiar electoral system, all ballots cast for any of a party's candidates are credited to the one who receives the largest vote, and this gave the victory to the leading *colorado*, General Alfredo Baldomir. With his inauguration, normal republican government was restored.

Recent Events

The Second World War caused political complications in Uruguay as it did in Argentina. From the start the government supported the democracies and coöperated effectively with the United States. In May, 1940, it discovered that Germans in the Republic were plotting to seize military control, and suppressed the plot by prompt action. During the crisis, the United States rushed two cruisers to Montevideo as an evidence of moral support, and Brazil aided the government with military supplies. In the summer of 1941 Uruguay proposed to the other nations of the Hemisphere that an American country at war with a non-American power should not be treated as a belligerent—a principle that was generally adopted by the American republics after Japan attacked the United States. The government's policy was savagely opposed by the Herrera wing of the nationalist party, which was openly supported by Argentina; and the fact that the nationalists had three members of the cabinet and half of the senate under the 1934 constitution made it possible for them to obstruct many measures which the administration wished to take.

To eliminate this obstruction, President Baldomir arbitrarily dissolved the congress in February, 1942, and ruled with the aid of an appointed Council of State during the next twelve months. In the meantime the constitution was amended and a new president and congress were elected by popular vote. Baldomir's successor was another *colorado*, Juan José Amézaga (1943–47) who continued Uruguay's policy of coöperation with the democratic powers during the war. The *Herreristas*, supported by both political and economic pressure from Argentina, continued to make trouble for the government, but lend-lease from the United States and loans from the Export-Import Bank helped to strengthen the government's position. Uruguay formally declared war on the Axis powers on February 21, 1945.

Tomás Berreta, a *Batllista colorado*, defeated the perennial nationalist candidate, Luis Alberto de Herrera, in the election of 1946, but by a smaller margin than in the preceding election. He was inaugurated in March, 1947, but died five months later, and the Vice-President, Luis Batlle Berres, became President for the remainder of the term which will expire in 1951.

All of the recent governments have continued the economic and social policies that were inaugurated by Batlle y Ordóñez. Though foreign investments have been better treated than in some other Latin American countries, the government has steadily extended its control of the country's industry and commerce. In 1948 it bought all of the British railways in the country. Despite the government's efforts, however, the country's economic potentialities are still largely undeveloped. Relatively little of the land has been brought under cultivation, and sheep- and cattle-raising have continued to be the chief industries. Wages in the rural areas are still very low, and in many other respects these districts have lagged behind Montevideo, which dominates the country's political and economic life. The social legislation of recent years has primarily benefited the urban worker, and the better conditions of life in the capital have caused a continual drift of population from country to city, so that Montevideo today contains about a third of the Republic's 2,300,000 inhabitants.

11

Paraguay

Paraguay Before 1810

The survivors of Mendoza's ill-fated expedition to the River Plate, who settled at Asunción in 1541, found the Guaranís of the interior less intractable than the fierce Indians of the pampas. The Paraguayan tribes lived in settled villages, practising agriculture in a crude way as a supplement to hunting and fishing, but they had no government beyond that of the *caciques* and village councils in each small community. They were easily conquered and most of those on the east bank of the Paraguay, in the immediate vicinity of Asunción, were apportioned among the settlers in *encomiendas*. Since there were relatively few Spaniards, and no mines or other enterprises in which the intensive use of forced labor was profitable, the Indians seem to have been less cruelly exploited than in some other parts of the continent. Great numbers of them, in fact, were protected from abuse at the hands of the creoles because they were gathered in the Jesuit missions to the southeast. A large proportion survived, and *Guaraní*, rather than Spanish, is generally spoken in rural Paraguay today. Even the upper class was largely of mixed blood, because few women came to Asunción from Spain.

It required more than two weeks for a hardy traveler, on horseback, to reach Asunción from Buenos Aires, which was itself an out-of-the-way place during the colonial period. Sailing vessels, the only means of transporting goods, required three months for the voyage upstream on the Paraná and Paraguay Rivers. Economic development was further retarded by the competition of the Jesuit missions and by internal commotions, for which popular hatred of the Jesuits was at least partly responsible. Until 1779, when coined money is said to have been first introduced by the tobacco monopoly, all trade was by barter and even postage was paid in *yerba mate,* cotton, or tobacco.[1] *Yerba mate,* or Paraguay tea, which was consumed in great quantities in the other River Plate provinces, was the chief export during the colonial period.

At the beginning of the nineteenth century the population was probably between 100,000 and 200,000. Asunción, with some 10,000 inhabitants, was little more than a large village. Such few schools as existed were of the most elementary sort, and there were said to be only two natives of the country who had had the advantage of an education outside of Paraguay. The colony was consequently almost untouched by the intellectual revival that changed the outlook of the creoles in many other parts of Spanish America in the latter part of the eighteenth century, or by the revolutionary propaganda that had been one of its consequences.

Independence

There was thus little enthusiasm in Paraguay when the creoles at Buenos Aires overthrew the viceregal government in May, 1810. An assembly of the principal inhabitants of Asunción, convened by the governor, decided to recognize the authority of the regency at Cadiz rather than that of the *porteño junta;* and traditional dislike of Buenos Aires made it easy to raise an army to repulse Belgrano when he attempted to invade Paraguay some months later. Nevertheless Belgrano, who remained in the country for a time after his capitulation, made friends with the creole officers who commanded the Paraguayan troops, and through his efforts a revolutionary party rapidly grew up. In May, 1811, a military revolt forced the governor to transfer power to a *junta* composed of himself, another Spanish officer, and the influential creole Dr. Gaspar Rodríguez de Francia. A month later the governor's intrigues with emissaries of the Portuguese Princess Carlota caused a second uprising by which he and the pro-Spanish *cabildo* were deprived of all authority. A congress met to appoint a new *junta* of five, including Francia and Fulgencio Yegros, one of the commanders of the troops that had defeated Belgrano. There was by this time a growing sentiment for union with Buenos Aires, but Francia, who from the first assumed the leadership in the new government, astutely blocked all efforts to bring it about. In October, 1811, the representa-

[1] Félix de Azara, *Geografía Física y Esférica de las Provincias del Paraguay y Misiones Guaraníes,* p. 431.

tives of the *porteño junta* signed a treaty virtually recognizing Paraguay's independence.

Francia

Francia is said to have been the son of a Spanish army officer and a creole lady of distinguished family.[1] In his youth he studied theology at the University of Córdoba, which was the chief center of learning in eastern South America. After his return to Asunción he practised law and eagerly read such philosophical and scientific books as he was able to obtain. His reputation for learning gave him a tremendous prestige among his fellow-countrymen, and he further increased his influence by his conspicuous honesty and by the fearlessness and disinterestedness with which he maintained the rights of poor and friendless litigants in his practice of law. He had held various positions in the municipal government at Asunción. Unsociable and with little personal charm or capacity for friendship, he was nevertheless a shrewd politician in a community where politics was a new and untried art.

The extent of Francia's influence became evident when disputes within the *junta* led him to resign. The remaining members found it increasingly difficult to maintain their authority, and in November, 1812, he was persuaded to return, on condition that one-half of the army be placed under his orders. Thenceforth, the control of affairs passed more and more into his hands. A new congress, composed like its predecessors of members invited by the government rather than elected by the voters, met in 1813. The deputies, 1,000 in number, showed more desire to return promptly to their villages than to discuss affairs of state, and without loss of time they approved a constitution drafted by Francia and adopted a formal declaration of independence.

The constitution provided for two consuls, elected for one year. These were to take turns of four months as nominal head of the government, but each was to have personal control of half of the army throughout the year. Francia and Yegros were elected to these positions, and Francia took pains to make sure that it would be his turn to rule when the time to choose new consuls arrived. He was thus able to have himself made dictator for a five-year term when the congress met in October, 1814, and another congress, in 1816, made him dictator for life.

---

[1] For a review of the evidence on this point, about which there have been many conflicting statements, see Blas Garay, *La Revolución de la Independencia del Paraguay* (Madrid, 1897), Appendix B.

From that time until his death "El Supremo," as he required his people
to call him, exercised an unquestioned and unlimited authority, with
no concessions even to the forms of republican government.

For a quarter century, Paraguay was almost completely cut off from
intercourse with the outside world, for Francia was determined to keep
the country from being contaminated by the disorder that reigned in
the rest of the River Plate area. Efforts of other governments to establish diplomatic relations were rebuffed and representatives of foreign
powers were rarely permitted to visit Asunción. Ordinary travelers
were equally suspect. A group of British and other foreigners who had
been held in Paraguay for varying periods were rescued by diplomatic
intervention in 1825, and M. Bonpland, a French naturalist who had
been kidnapped while experimenting with the cultivation of *yerba
mate* in the nearby Argentine province of Corrientes, was finally released after being compelled to live for nine years in a small Paraguayan
village; but almost no one else was permitted to enter or leave the interior of the Republic.

Some imports were of course necessary, if only to supply the government's troops with munitions. Foreign vessels were therefore occasionally permitted to come as far as Pilar, the first port on the Paraguay River, and merchants from Brazil were encouraged to visit Itapúa,
now called Encarnación, on the Paraná. Much of the trade was carried
on for the account of the government itself and the rest under its close
supervision. The amount was always small, for conditions along the
lower Paraná, where local *caudillos* were likely to confiscate any ship
passing the ports under their control, would in any event have discouraged traffic on the river. The Paraguayans were therefore compelled to develop local manufactures, though of a very crude sort, and
to increase their production of foodstuffs, instead of cultivating *mate*
for the Buenos Aires market.

Francia took no advice and had no collaborators. He himself decided
every detail of policy and closely supervised every branch of official
activity. The clergy were made subservient to his authority when the
Spanish bishop was replaced by a vicar general named by the dictator.
No one ventured to criticize. Unfortunate citizens who were even suspected of disaffection were imprisoned without a hearing, and a number of potential opponents, including most of the leaders who had been
prominent in the revolutionary movement before 1814, were put to
death. Although Francia was not a particularly bloodthirsty ruler com-

pared with some of his contemporaries, his gloomy and unapproachable seclusion and the calculated cruelty by which he sought to inspire terror made his regime seem more despotic than others which caused an infinitely greater amount of human suffering. Paraguay was at least governed with comparative efficiency and complete honesty, for the dictator had no interest in money for himself and severely punished graft among his subordinates, and it enjoyed peace and a primitive plenty at a time when neighboring regions were being laid waste by civil war.

Carlos Antonio López

Francia maintained his amazing ascendency over the minds and bodies of the Paraguayans until his death at an advanced age on September 20, 1840. As there was no provision for the choice of his successor, the commanders of the troops at Asunción joined with the *cabildo* in establishing a military *junta* to govern the country pending the election of a congress. In the confused period that followed, while barracks revolts set up and overturned new *juntas,* a civilian named Carlos Antonio López gradually emerged as the most influential political leader. He was one of two consuls elected for a three-year term by a congress that met in 1841, and in 1844 he became president. A constitution adopted in the same year gave him practically unlimited power, subject only to the control of congresses meeting at five-year intervals.

López, a self-trained lawyer, was one of the few educated Paraguayans who had not incurred Francia's suspicious enmity. He had prudently remained in obscurity until 1840, but when the dictator died he soon acquired much influence with the ignorant and politically inexperienced military leaders who attempted to take over the control of affairs. Paraguay made some progress under his leadership. The system of taxation and the judiciary were reorganized, and the first newspaper, a government organ, began publication in 1845. The country gradually emerged from the isolation that Francia had imposed. Rosas, who still professed to regard Paraguay as a rebellious member of the Argentine Confederation, for some years obstructed intercourse with the outside world by way of the Paraná, but after his fall the river was opened to commerce. In 1853 Paraguay was formally recognized by the United States and several European powers. Foreign trade gradually increased, though it was still subject to burdensome restrictions and the most important products, like *yerba mate*, lumber, and hides, were controlled by government monopolies. Regular steamship service was established between Asunción and Buenos Aires and the construction of a railway line was begun at Asunción.

Closer contact with the outside world had some disadvantages, for disputes over the treatment of the foreigners who began to visit the country led to a number of unpleasant diplomatic incidents with France, England, and the United States. When Paraguayan forts fired on the U.S.S. *Water Witch* in 1855, killing several members of her crew, a serious conflict was averted only by the mediation of President Urquiza of Argentina.

López showed somewhat more respect for constitutional forms than Francia, and was less cruel in his treatment of suspected enemies, but he permitted no more freedom of political discussion. All persons of any importance were subject to a constant and humiliating surveillance, and no one openly opposed the President's evident intention to remain in power for life and to secure the succession for his son Francisco. The latter was legally ineligible, both because of his youth and because he was an officer in the army, but constitutional amendments eliminated these difficulties and gave the President the right secretly to designate the person to take office in case of his death. The younger López thus took over the government when his father died in 1862, and a hand-picked congress, overawed by a display of military force, promptly confirmed him in his position.

Francisco Solano López and the Paraguayan War

Francisco Solano López had been brought up in the enjoyment of irresponsible power. The old President had been notoriously slow to check the lawless and licentious conduct of his sons, and Francisco, as the oldest, had been trained from early youth to regard himself as the future ruler of Paraguay. His chief ambition, apparently, was to achieve fame as a soldier. When only nineteen he had been given nominal command of an army during the intermittent conflict with Rosas. Seven years later, while in Europe as his father's Minister Plenipotentiary, he visited the allied camps in the Crimea and came home fired with the idea of making Paraguay a great military power. He also brought with him an Irish mistress, Madame Lynch, to whose influence the Paraguayans later attributed some of his most reckless acts. Partly at least because of his insistence, much of the nation's resources had been devoted to building up the army and accumulating stores of war supplies, and skilled foreign workmen had been employed in the construction of an iron foundry, a powder factory, and an arsenal to make the country partly self-sufficient in the production of munitions. In 1862 the country had a larger standing army than any of its neighbors. There was some justification for these preparations in the fact that Paraguay had boundary disputes with both Brazil and Argentina, but there is little reason to suppose that war with those countries would have occurred if Francisco López had not deliberately provoked it.

When Argentina and Brazil helped Venancio Flores in his revolt against the *blanco* government in Uruguay in 1863, and especially when Brazil actually sent troops into the *Banda Oriental*, López protested against what he regarded as a threat to the balance of power in the River Plate. On November 12, 1864, he declared war on Brazil. Since the trackless country along the frontier between that country and Paraguay was unsuitable for military operations, he demanded permission to send troops across the Argentine territory of Misiones, but this, like a similar request from Brazil, was refused. He then attacked Argentina and invaded the province of Corrientes.

López seems to have hoped for aid from Governor Urquiza of Entre Ríos, whose party had so recently been defeated at Pavón, and to have hoped that a slave revolt would occur when his forces entered Brazil. In both cases his expectations were disappointed, and it was soon clear that his folly and ignorance had involved his people in a hopeless struggle against a group of enemies so superior in manpower and resources that even his better-trained army gave him only a temporary advantage. Argentina, Brazil, and the *colorado* government of Uruguay signed a treaty of alliance against him in May, 1865. In September their forces captured a Paraguayan army that had crossed Misiones and invaded Rio Grande do Sul, and seven months later they were ready to invade Paraguay itself.

During the next two years the allies made little progress. Their fleet, under the Brazilian Admiral Tamandaré, won an overwhelming naval superiority on the Paraguay River by its victory at Riachuelo in June, 1865, but neither it nor the land forces commanded by President Mitre were able to force their way past the strong Paraguayan forts at Humaitá. Long delays were caused by indecision and inefficiency and by a revolt led by Urquiza, which compelled Mitre to return to Buenos Aires. Uruguay's help became negligible after General Flores was assassinated. The Paraguayan forces, however, were weakened by many months of desperate fighting, and in 1868, after the allied fleet had forced its way past Humaitá, López was compelled to withdraw to new positions farther up the river. These also were taken after a hard struggle, and on December 31 the allies occupied Asunción. There was another long delay before the new allied commander, the Brazilian Emperor's son-in-law the Count d'Eu, was ready to pursue López still farther north. By this time the Paraguayans could offer little resistance. López fled into the forests of the north, where he fell into the hands of the Brazilians on March 1, 1870, and was killed as he resisted capture. Madame Lynch, who had remained with him to the end, returned to Europe.

The results of the war were appalling. The Paraguayan people had fought with desperate bravery to repel the foreign invaders, and nearly every male in the country, including young boys and old men, had stayed with the colors to the bitter end. Many thousands had been killed in battle, and a far greater number had died of disease or starvation. Out of a population of probably somewhat over half a million in 1865, only 221,079 were counted by the census in 1871, and all but 28,746 of these were women and children. Agriculture had been neglected, and nearly all of the cattle had been killed for food. The upper class had suffered even more severely than the peasants, for López had treated the leading families of Asunción with insane cruelty during the first years of the war, and had executed hundreds of people, including his own brothers and brothers-in-law and a number of foreigners, on suspicion of conspiracy against his government. Many others, including the wives and families of those who incurred his displeasure, died from torture or harsh treatment.

The Period of Recovery

In 1869, when it was clear that the war was nearly over, the allied commander at Asunción permitted a *junta* of three Paraguayans to set up a provisional civil administration and call together a constitutional convention. A republican government was established, on paper, and Cirilo Rivarola was elected President of the Republic. Lack of real power, desperate poverty, and the occupation of the country until 1876 by Brazilian troops made the new administration's position difficult. Both Brazil and Argentina demanded large war indemnities and proceeded to settle in their own favor long-standing boundary disputes, so that Paraguay lost a considerable area in the north to Brazil and the territory of Misiones, where the Jesuits had once had their principal missions, to Argentina. Argentina also claimed a large part of what is now the Paraguayan Chaco, but the ownership of this area was submitted to arbitration and an award handed down by President Hayes at Washington in 1878 was in the main favorable to Paraguay.

Though it was impossible to hold real elections, and the government relied for support on the police and the small, poorly trained army, no postwar president was able to establish a powerful regime like that of Francia and the two López. Rivarola, after a conflict with the congress, was forced to resign in 1871. Juan Bautista Gill, elected in 1874, was assassinated by personal enemies in the third year of his term, and the next constitutional president, Cándido Bareiro, was forced to resign in 1880 under pressure from the military leaders. The most influential of these was General Bernardino Caballero, the founder of the *colorado* party which had assumed power at the end of the war. This *caudillo* became provisional President in 1880 and was elected constitutional President for a four-year term in 1882. He continued to be powerful during the administrations of Patricio Escobar (1886–90) and Juan Gualberto González (1890–94), and toward the end of the latter's term he again overthrew the government and placed his associate, Juan Bautista Eguzquiza, in the presidency. The latter served until 1898 and was succeeded by Emilio Aceval. In 1902, Caballero and Escobar staged a military *coup*, overthrew Aceval, and placed Colonel Juan A. Escurra in the presidency.

These frequent palace revolutions had relatively little effect on the tranquility of the country. The factions that struggled for power were composed of relatively small groups of politicians and army officers, without any substantial following among the masses of the people. There were thus no general civil wars to delay the slow and painful process of recovery to which the surviving Paraguayans were courageously addressing themselves. Though few men had come back from the war, the women cultivated the fields and internal commerce slowly revived. Foreigners began to invest capital in stock-raising and the exploitation of forest products like *yerba mate* and *quebracho*, and a considerable influx of Italians and other Europeans helped to fill the gaps in the upper class left by López' insensate executions. By the end of the century, Paraguay had recovered from the worst effects of the war.

Political Events, 1904–1932

The *colorados*, or republicans, who had been in power since the end of the war, lost control of the government in 1904 when Escurra was ousted by a popular revolt. The advent of their rivals, the liberals, made little difference in political conditions. A succession of presidents held office for periods of a year or two, only to be driven out by dissensions within their own party. In the twenty years from 1904 to 1924 only one chief executive, Eduardo Schaerer (1912–16), succeeded in remaining in office throughout his constitutional term. Dr. Schaerer's administration was notable for the completion of the railroad from Asunción to Encarnación on the Paraná, where it connects by ferry with the Argentine line to Buenos Aires. After 1924 there was a period of relative tranquility during the administrations of Eligio Ayala (1925–28) and José Guggiari (1928–32). Under Guggiari's successor, Eusebio Ayala, internal political events were pushed into the background by another foreign war.

The Chaco War

The Gran Chaco, an almost uninhabited region of more than 100,000 square miles west of the Paraguay River, had long been in dispute between Paraguay and Bolivia. Though most of the territory was of no value for agriculture or stock-raising, both countries stubbornly maintained their claim to it and several efforts to bring them to an agreement, either for arbitration or for a compromise boundary line, failed. Both pushed farther and farther into the disputed territory with chains of small forts, which were soon dangerously close to one another. In December, 1928, the Paraguayans destroyed a Bolivian post at Vanguardia. Prompt action by a Pan American conference on conciliation and arbitration, that happened to be meeting at Washington, delayed the outbreak of hostilities for the time being, but in June, 1932, new clashes occurred in the Chaco, and the fighting soon developed into a full-fledged war. Appeals for peace from all of the other American republics and from the President of the Council of the League of Nations went unheeded.

The fighting continued for three years. Bolivia had a larger and better-equipped army, but the hot climate of the Chaco caused terrible suffering among the Indians from the high plateau. Paraguay's untrained and ill-equipped recruits were at least accustomed to the tropical climate and the earlier fighting was in regions far from any Bolivian town but relatively near the settled part of Paraguay. After some initial reverses, therefore, the Paraguayans at the end of 1933 began an offensive that gradually pushed the Bolivians back across the Chaco and almost out of the territory in dispute. In the first months of 1935 they occupied part of the oil-bearing region of eastern Bolivia, but here they were too far from their own bases and were soon forced back by counter-attacks.

Both the League of Nations and the other American states persistently endeavored to stop the war, and in June, 1935, with military operations at a stalemate, the United States and several of the South American governments were finally able to bring about a truce. The armies on both sides were disbanded, but the conclusion of a treaty of peace was delayed for more than three years by the intransigeance of both belligerents. When the treaty was finally signed, on July 21, 1938, it gave most of the Chaco to Paraguay, but gave Bolivia access to the upper Paraguay River and provided that she should have the use of Puerto Casado in the Paraguayan Chaco as a free port.

The war had been costly to both belligerents. One hundred thousand men are said to have died in the course of the fighting. In Paraguay, the maintenance of the army, and later the demoralization inseparable from its demobilization, severely affected production and exports. By the end of the war, the already depreciated paper currency had lost five-sixths of its value. Living costs had risen rapidly, government salaries were far in arrears, and there was a moratorium on debts.

Recent Events

President Ayala was overthrown in February, 1936, by Colonel Rafael Franco, who had been one of the heroes of the war. Franco sought the support of the labor element, the university students, and the returning soldiery for a program of extreme economic nationalism and state socialism, but he could not maintain harmony among these different groups and his economic experiments met with little success. In August, 1937, he was forced to resign, but his adherents, the *febreristas*, continued to figure in Paraguayan politics as a new party.

Félix Paíva, a liberal, served as provisional president for two years, and in 1939 another liberal, General José Félix Estigarribia, was elected constitutional president. Estigarribia had been commander-in-chief of the army in the Chaco, and it was hoped that his prestige and popularity might enable him to end the disorders that had plagued the country since the end of the war. Unfortunately, his efforts to gain the coöperation of other political groups had met with little success when he was killed in an airplane accident in September, 1940. General Higinio Morínigo, the Minister of War, became provisional president.

Morínigo soon made it clear that he intended to rule as a military dictator. He imprisoned or exiled many of the civilian politicians, and in 1943 he held an election with himself as the only candidate. There were several plots and revolts, and some politically inspired labor disturbances, but the support of the army enabled him to remain in power. Though Paraguay was especially vulnerable to economic and political pressure from Argentina, he broke diplomatic relations with the Axis powers in January, 1942. Lend-lease assistance and loans from the Export-Import Bank, and also a substantial loan from Brazil, helped him to maintain a policy of coöperation with the democracies. A part of the army, however, sympathized with the military clique at Buenos Aires and caused the President some embarrassment. The army lost some of its influence in July, 1946, when Morínigo permitted several of the civilian political parties to resume activity and appointed a cabinet in which the *colorados* and the *febreristas* were represented. This cabinet, however, resigned in January, 1947, and two months later the *febreristas*, with some communist support, started a civil war. The fighting continued until August, but the government was finally victorious.

A presidential election was held at the end of Morínigo's term in 1948. With the leaders of the recent revolt and many other politicians still in exile, the *colorados*, who now dominated the administration, were the only party in a position to participate. Even they were sharply divided, and the nomination of Morínigo's finance minister, Natalicio González, was forced on the party convention by high-handed methods. After the election, there was still some uncertainty about the President's willingness to step down; and in June, 1948, he was ousted by a military *coup*, and a provisional administration took over until González' inauguration in August.

This was the first of a series of governmental changes caused by continued factional quarrels within the *colorado* party. González suppressed an uprising in the army in October, 1948, but in January, 1949, he was removed, without fighting, by members of his own cabinet. General Raimundo Rolón, his successor, was ousted by a similar movement in February, and Felipe Molas López, who became provisional President and was then elected constitutional President, was forced to resign in September in favor of the veteran statesman Federico Chaves. Chaves was formally elected President in July, 1950.

Though the railroad and the airplane have improved communications with the outside world, Paraguay is still an isolated and backward country. With 1,225,000 inhabitants, it is the least populous of the South American republics. Only a small fraction of its arable land is under cultivation, and its exports—chiefly cotton, *quebracho* extract, hides, and *yerba mate*, amount to but a few dollars per capita. There has been little foreign investment and there are few important agricultural or industrial enterprises. The upper class, since 1870 largely of foreign descent, are politicians, professional men and merchants rather than great landowners. In the country districts, standards of living are low, especially among the Indians and *mestizos* who are the great majority of the Republic's inhabitants. Peonage, or debt slavery, is said to be common. On the other hand the average Paraguayan tenant farmer seems to have enough land to feed himself and his family. The country's social problems are less formidable than those of some of the other predominantly Indian republics, and Paraguay might well have a bright future if she could achieve a stable and efficient government.

12

Chile

Chile is a narrow, mountainous strip stretching more than 2,500 miles along the west side of the continent between the summits of the Andes and the Pacific. Only the central portion of this territory was occupied by people of European descent at the beginning of the nineteenth century. From La Serena north there was a rainless desert, rich in mineral resources which were almost untouched. South of the Bio-Bio River one of the best portions of the country was still held by the savage Araucanians, who had carried on intermittent warfare with the Spanish troops and settlers throughout the colonial period. There were some small Spanish settlements south of the Indian country, around Valdivia and in Chiloé, but beyond these the heavily wooded, excessively rainy mountains were practically uninhabited. The mass of the Chilean people lived in the temperate, fertile Central Valley between Santiago and Concepción.

Chilean Society in 1810

The population at the time of independence was probably between half and three quarters of a million. The colony had attracted few Spanish immigrants, for no important mines had been found there, and geographical isolation, as well as the constant Indian wars, had retarded its development. Cattle-raising was still the chief occupation, though some wheat was grown for export to Peru. There were almost no improved roads, and the towns were small. In the southern part of the Central Valley farms and settlements were still raided from time to time by the Araucanians.

The Indians north of the Bio-Bio, who had been partly civilized by the Incas and lived a more settled life than the wild tribes beyond the river, were more easily conquered by Valdivia and his followers. The first settlers reduced them to servitude under the *encomienda* system, and added to the supply of native labor by wars or raids on the frontier. The capture of slaves to work on the *haciendas*, or even for sale in Peru, was the real motive for many of the expeditions against the Araucanians, and one of the reasons for their inveterate hostility toward the Spaniards. The native population, never very numerous as compared with that in Peru or Colombia, was less able to withstand the effects of contact with the white man than the more advanced peoples of those countries, and by 1789, when the last *encomiendas* were abolished, few pure-blooded Indians remained north of the Bio-Bio. On the other hand, there was a large *mestizo* population whose descendants form the mass of the Chilean people today.

Most of these *mestizos* were *inquilinos*, or tenant farmers, who worked for the creole landowners in payment for the small plots of ground that they were allowed to cultivate. Their condition was hardly better than that of the Indians in other countries, for their wages, when they received any, were extremely low and they were bound to their employer's service by a system of peonage. Though they were miserably poor and underfed, custom and necessity led them to accept their lot as a matter of course and most of them were personally devoted to their *patrones*. Each *hacendado* ruled like a feudal lord on his own estates, settling disputes and punishing minor crimes without the intervention of the public authorities.

The landowning aristocracy was a compact, class-conscious group, which was to dominate public affairs in Chile for more than a century after independence. Some of its members were descendants of the first settlers; others of more recent arrivals. During the eighteenth century there had been a number of immigrants from the Basque provinces and other parts of northern Spain, and the Republic's historians attribute to this thrifty, industrious element many of the qualities that characterize Chilean society today. The landowners seemed to take more interest in the management of their properties than in most of the Spanish colonies, and until late in the colonial period many of them actually lived on their *haciendas*. There was thus little of the hostility between city and country which helped to make the early history of the River Plate republics so turbulent. Local jealousies, though by no means absent, were also less important as a political factor because the great estates were concentrated in a relatively small area and the Province of Santiago was far more populous than the regions to the north and south.

O'Higgins

There was nevertheless much political strife in the first years of independence. Bernardo O'Higgins, who had been installed as *Director Supremo* after San Martín's victory at Chacabuco, remained in power from 1817 until 1823. His chief opponents were the still strong Carrera faction. Juan José and Luis Carrera were executed at Mendoza in 1818 by local authorities friendly to O'Higgins, but José Miguel, the most influential of the three brothers, continued his efforts to overthrow the government until he himself was put to death in Argentina in 1821. The loss of their leaders did not make the other members of the party less unfriendly to the government, and as time went on the Director's popularity with other groups was undermined by opposition to his policies.

O'Higgins, who had lived in Europe, realized better than most of his compatriots how backward Chilean society was. He promoted education and attempted, against increasing opposition from the clergy and the aristocracy, to change local institutions and customs that he deemed unsuitable in a democracy. At the same time he governed as a military dictator, sharing his authority only with a Senate of five members appointed by himself. Though there was an increasingly strong demand for a more representative government, no congress was convened until 1822, and when one finally did meet in that year the Director selected its members and the assembly adopted a constitution that was clearly intended to extend his dictatorship for a further period of ten years. Meanwhile there was much discontent over the high taxes imposed to meet the cost of the war in Peru, and San Martín's inactivity in that country and his quarrel with Admiral Cochrane further hurt the prestige of his friends in Chile. Late in 1822 the government's own troops at Concepción revolted under the leadership of General Ramón Freire. The military forces in other parts of the country joined the movement and in January, 1823, a *cabildo abierto*, attended by the principal people of Santiago, demanded and obtained the Director's resignation.

Liberalism and Federalism

Freire, who was chosen as Supreme Director, was a better soldier than a statesman. Though his popularity, both with the army and the civilian population, made him the chief figure in Chilean politics during the next six years, the very qualities that inspired confidence—his moderation in dealing with political opponents and his freedom from selfish ambition—hampered him in meeting an increasingly difficult situation. The constitution adopted in 1823, which restricted the authority of the executive and placed the real power in the hands of congress, was so obviously unworkable that Freire was soon compelled to suspend it and to assume dictatorial powers with the consent of the congressional leaders themselves. Efforts to frame a new constitution were frustrated by partisan squabbles, and Freire finally became discouraged and resigned in 1826. The principal achievement of his troubled term in office was the conquest of the island of Chiloé, which had remained under Spanish control until this time.

The new constituent assembly that now met was controlled by advocates of "federalism" led by José Miguel Infante. As in the River Plate, there were many persons who thought that governmental decentralization would make for democracy—an idea that was welcomed by the great landowners because it would give them more independence in their own domains. When the assembly met, Infante and his followers proceeded to put their ideas into execution. Hastily drawn and ill-considered laws divided the Republic into eight provinces and provided for the selection of all provincial and local authorities, including parish priests, by popular election. The only result was factional strife and confusion. Disputes over boundaries, quarrels between rival towns, and the utter inability of the inexperienced local political leaders to cope with the problems which suddenly confronted them soon discredited the new system. The country was drifting into anarchy when Freire reluctantly agreed to accept the office of President in January, 1827. He soon resigned again and was succeeded by the Vice-President, Francisco Antonio Pinto.

A new constitution restored some of the authority of the central government, but the administration was beset by financial difficulties and had to contend with frequent mutinies in the army. Party strife also became increasingly violent. The old personal factions, the *O'Hig-*

ginistas and the *Carreristas*, had given place after 1823 to new political groups: the conservatives, popularly known as *pelucones*, and the liberals, or *pipiolos*. The latter supported Pinto and were able to bring about his reëlection in 1829, but a dispute over the vice-presidency, for which no candidate received a majority, brought on a civil war. The government fell when the conservatives under General Joaquín Prieto defeated its forces on April 17, 1830, at the bloody battle of Lircai.

Portales

The outstanding figure in the regime that thus came into power was Diego Portales, a business man who had only recently begun to take an interest in politics. Portales' firm had undertaken in 1824 to provide funds for the service of the government's foreign debt, in return for a lease of the fiscal monopoly of tobacco and certain other commodities, but the venture had been a failure and the settlement of accounts with the treasury had involved him in a series of disputes with the liberal officials and led him to throw his support to the conservatives. By 1829 he was the recognized leader of the opposition.

In the new provisional government he assumed control of practically all branches of the administration. The army was purged of officers who were not in sympathy with the dominant party, and its power for mischief was decreased by strengthening the civil militia. Prompt and ruthless punishment of criminals did much to check the banditry which had grown to be an intolerable curse in the country districts. Government expenses were reduced, the customs service was reorganized to produce more revenue, and political disturbances were suppressed with a heavy hand. The freedom of the press which had existed under the liberal regime became a thing of the past.

Refusing to be a candidate himself, Portales was largely responsible for the election of General Prieto as President of the Republic in 1831. Thereafter he devoted himself to his private business for some years, except for a brief period when he served as Governor of Valparaiso. His influence in the administration, however, was hardly less than if he had held office; and the autocratic, highly centralized government which existed in Chile during the next thirty years was the result of his passion for order and his determination to make the authority of the state respected. His political views were reflected in the Constitution of 1833, which was to remain in force for nearly a century. The president, chosen by indirect election for a five-year term, controlled all branches of the administration, and was given broad powers, especially in dealing with political disorder. At the same time the judiciary was strengthened and its independence safeguarded. All vestiges of the federal system disappeared, for provincial and local affairs were placed in the hands of agents of the central government, though the municipal councils continued to be elective. Catholicism was made the state religion, and the public exercise of any other was forbidden.

Under the liberal regime a real effort had been made to hold fair elections, though the ignorance and political inexperience of the masses of the people and the dependence of the *inquilinos* on the great landowners made it inevitable that fraud and force should usually dictate the outcome. After 1833, the official candidates were nearly always elected as a matter of course. Literacy and property qualifications restricted the suffrage to an insignificant fraction of the population, and the government's authority and prestige, backed if necessary by the use of force, made successful opposition almost impossible. The government was not, however, a mere military despotism, for legal forms were generally observed and the courts and the congress enjoyed a measure of independence. It derived its real strength from the support of the Church and the majority of the aristocracy, who were by this time ready to sacrifice some of their liberty if they could obtain relief from the disturbed conditions which had marked the past six years of political experimentation.

As the end of Prieto's first term approached, a few conservatives who objected to Portales' high-handed methods joined with the liberals in advocating the presidential candidacy of Manuel Renjifo, the Minister of Finance. Portales at once emerged from his retirement, became Minister of War, and proceeded to exercise dictatorial power. Prieto was soon afterward reëlected without difficulty. The chief event of his second term was a war with the Peruvian-Bolivian Confederation under Santa Cruz.

Relations with Peru, embittered by the growing commercial rivalry between Valparaiso and Callao and by disputes over the repayment of money spent by Chile in assisting Peru to obtain her independence from Spain, had become worse after the union of Peru with Bolivia, which the Chileans regarded as a threat to the balance of power on the west coast. Hostilities began when Santa Cruz aided an unsuccessful invasion of Chile by revolutionists under General Freire, and Portales retaliated by sending an expedition to seize the Peruvian fleet at Callao. A few weeks later, in November, 1836, war was formally declared. Neither the conflict itself nor the repressive policies that Portales adopted to stifle opposition were popular in Chile, and on June 6, 1837, the great minister was murdered by mutinous troops near Valparaiso. His death caused a revulsion of feeling which did much to unite the Chilean people behind their government; and though the first expedition sent to Peru was defeated, a second one, under General Manuel Bulnes, destroyed Santa Cruz' forces at Yungay on January 20, 1839, and put an end to the Confederation.

The Administration of Bulnes and Montt

General Bulnes' military exploits made him the logical candidate for the presidency in 1841, since Prieto could not constitutionally be reëlected. He, too, held office, for two consecutive five-year terms, and his administration was a period of notable progress, material and intellectual. Copper, coal, and silver mines, including especially the rich silver deposits discovered at Chañarcillo in 1832, were increasing the nation's wealth, and foreign trade continued the rapid development begun when the restrictions of the old Spanish commercial system were removed. Valparaiso, with its state-owned warehouses where goods might be stored pending reshipment to other ports, had become the great entrepôt of the South Pacific, the chief port of call for ships rounding Cape Horn and a base of supplies for North American whalers. A more stable government helped commerce, and Chilean agriculture began to thrive when the discovery of gold in California opened a profitable market for wheat and other products there. William Wheelwright, the North American who was later to build the first Argentine railroad, took a leading part in many important enterprises in Chile in this period: railroad building, the establishment of an electric telegraph system, and the introduction of gas-lighting and better water supplies in the towns. Through his efforts, the first steamship line from Europe to Chile began service in 1840.

The Chilean aristocracy had hitherto shown little interest in literary pursuits, or indeed in any but the most rudimentary education; but the first years of Bulnes' administration saw the beginning of an intellectual movement which was soon to have an important effect upon the Republic's political life. The inspiration came from a group of distinguished foreigners, like Andrés Bello, the great Venezuelan, and Domingo Faustino Sarmiento, the future president of Argentina, who by their writing and their teaching aroused the younger generation of Chileans to an interest in literature and a receptiveness to new ideas. Bello was the first rector of the University of Chile, opened in 1843, and Sarmiento the first director of the normal school established at about the same time in an effort to raise the lamentably low level of instruction in the primary schools. Much was accomplished in this direction, though education continued to be the privilege of the upper and middle classes and more than six-sevenths of the Republic's inhabitants were still illiterate in 1854.

A direct result of this intellectual movement was the rise of a new liberal party which sought to make the government more responsive to control by the voters. Inspired by the European revolutions of 1848, this group became especially active toward the close of Bulnes' second term. The *Sociedad de la Igualdad*, organized by Francisco Bilbao, even promoted political demonstrations among the workmen of Santiago. The government resorted to its usual weapons—the declaration of a state of siege, the muzzling of the press, and the deportation of the chief liberal leaders—and when an uprising occurred in Santiago in April, 1851, it was suppressed with a heavy loss of life. After Manuel Montt, the administration candidate, was elected president, his defeated rival General José María de la Cruz led a new revolt. This was not suppressed until 2,000 Chileans had been killed and 1,500 wounded in the desperately fought battle of Loncomilla.

Montt, unlike his predecessors, was neither a professional soldier nor a great landowner. The son of a poor family, he had been educated on a scholarship in the National Institute and had later taught and served as rector there. While still a young man he had attracted the attention of Portales, who drew him into the government service. In 1840, at the age of thirty-one, he had become Minister of the Interior. His chief interest was in public instruction, and the number of government schools was greatly increased during his two terms as president. Railroad and highway construction was also pushed forward and the colonization of the region around Valdivia and Osorno, south of the Araucanian country, was encouraged. Many German immigrants settled in this region and their descendants form a substantial part of its population today.

Some phases of Montt's policy were highly objectionable to a portion of the aristocracy. The abolition of the law of primogeniture, by which he hoped to bring about the gradual division of the great entailed estates, was approved by Congress in the face of opposition by many of the landowners, and a conflict with the Church increased his difficulties. The Church, both during the colonial period and after independence, had been far more influential in Chile than in the River Plate region, and it had been a powerful ally of the conservative government since 1830. As in other Latin American countries, however, it had refused to admit that the Republic had inherited the control over the ecclesiastical administration which the Papacy had granted to the King of Spain. Disputes over the right of patronage had embarrassed each of Montt's predecessors. The Church had also clung to many of the special privileges that it had enjoyed under the Spanish regime, and its attitude grew more aggressive under the energetic leadership of Rafael Valdivieso, who became Archbishop of Santiago in 1848. A particularly violent controversy involving the jurisdiction of the ecclesiastical courts occurred in 1856. Thereafter the pro-clerical party opposed the President, joining forces, strangely enough, with the more radical liberal leaders. The moderate wings of both parties supported the administration.

The chief purpose of the anti-government coalition was to prevent the election of Antonio Varas as Montt's successor. Varas, who was also a former schoolteacher and a self-made man, was a lifelong friend of the President, and it had been clear for some time that he would be the official candidate in 1861. The belief that he would continue the authoritarian tradition of Portales, combined with his known anti-clericalism, made him objectionable to liberals and conservatives alike. In 1859, seeing that there was little hope of defeating him at the polls, the coalition resorted to civil war. Its forces were defeated after a short campaign, but Varas withdrew his candidacy in the interest of harmony and José Joaquín Pérez, an administration liberal, was elected with the support of all factions.

The Beginnings of Party Government

Pérez's ten years in office were tranquil ones, except for a brief period in 1865–66 when Chile, as an ally of Peru and Bolivia, became involved in an inconclusive war with Spain.[1] During this conflict,

[1] See below, p. 312.

Spanish forces blockaded the coast and bombarded Valparaiso, but hostilities soon ended with the withdrawal of the enemy squadron. There was no internal disorder. As in Argentina, the prosperity that the country had begun to enjoy led the upper classes to oppose any movement which seemed likely to disturb the peace.

As commerce and mining developed, successful business men began to exercise more influence in public affairs. They usually allied themselves politically with the more liberal groups in the land-owning class, and their influence was one of the factors that gradually brought about a change in the character of the Chilean government. Between 1830 and 1861 real political parties hardly existed. The government expected support because it was the government, and was inclined to regard any opposition as seditious. After 1861, when it became customary for the president to count upon a political group or a combination of political groups for support in the congress, the parties acquired more strength and a more permanent organization. Pérez, for example, after an unsuccessful attempt to govern with a cabinet representing all shades of opinion, fell back upon the same liberal-conservative coalition that had opposed Montt. Under his successor, Federico Errázuriz Zañartu, the coalition broke up, and the liberals, though by this time divided into several more or less unfriendly factions, were able to carry out some of the reforms that they had been advocating for the past twenty years. A constitutional amendment adopted in 1871 prohibited the election of a president for two successive periods, and further amendments now diminished the authority of the executive and increased that of congress, paving the way for the ascendency that the legislative branch was to exercise at a later date. The press was given more freedom and there was an effort to improve the electoral procedure. The anti-clerical tendencies of the liberal party, which had been held in check so long as its various factions were coöperating with conservative groups for selfish political ends, also found expression. The measures actually adopted, restricting the jurisdiction of the church courts and setting aside portions of the cemeteries for the burial of non-Catholics, did not go very far, but they aroused violent opposition among the clergy and misgiving among the more devout supporters of the government.

Toward the end of Errázuriz' term, and during that of Aníbal Pinto (1876–81), Chile felt severely the effects of the world depression of the '70's. Many mining companies failed, and the service of the foreign debt, increased by new loans contracted during the recent period of prosperity, became difficult. In 1878 the government was compelled to relieve the banks of their obligation to convert their notes into coin upon demand. Thus began the paper-money regime which was to be a feature of Chile's economy for many years to come.

The War of the Pacific

In the midst of this financial crisis the country became involved in a foreign war. For some time Chilean companies backed by British capital had been working the guano and nitrate deposits along the desert coast of Tarapacá and Atacama, and their activities had led to disputes with Peru and Bolivia, which owned these provinces. The boundary between Chile and Bolivia, like many others in South America, had never been definitely determined. Disputes over the region around Antofagasta almost led to war in 1865, but a treaty signed in 1866 fixed the boundary at 24° south latitude. The two countries agreed to share the exploitation of guano and mineral deposits between 23° and 25° and to divide the export taxes on products from that area. This treaty was replaced in 1874 by one in which Chile gave Bolivia full control over the region north of 24°, where the principal nitrate deposits were, in return for Bolivia's promise not to increase taxes on the Chilean producers for a period of twenty-five years. Peru and Bolivia, in the meantime, had entered into a secret alliance in 1873, and in 1875 Peru expropriated the Chilean nitrate properties without any adequate arrangement for compensation. In 1878 the Bolivian government imposed a new tax on the exportation of nitrate from Atacama, and when the Anglo-Chilean company which was the chief producer in the region refused to pay the tax its property was seized by the Bolivian authorities. Chile retaliated by occupying Antofagasta in February, 1879. Two months later Chile declared war against Peru, which refused to abrogate the alliance of 1873.

The War of the Pacific, which thus began, was to have far-reaching effects on each of the three participants. The outcome at first seemed doubtful. The combined population of the allies far exceeded that of Chile, but Chile had a better trained and equipped army, and a navy, increased by recent acquisitions, which was twice as powerful as Peru's. The control of the sea was of the utmost importance because it was exceedingly difficult to move troops along the desert coast of the nitrate region. Land operations thus awaited the outcome of the contest between the two navies. One of Peru's two ironclads was destroyed in the hard-fought battle of Iquique on May 21, 1879, but the other, the *Huáscar*, commanded by Admiral Grau, defied the whole Chilean navy for several months. When it was finally captured on October 8, in the battle of Angamos, a Chilean army went north by sea to occupy Tarapacá. The Peruvian forces, after some fighting, retreated along the base of the Andes to Arica, and on May 26, 1880, the armies of the northern allies were defeated at Tacna. This put Bolivia out of the war, and Peru's last hope of checking the Chilean advance vanished when a small force defending the Morro of Arica was destroyed in a surprise attack on June 7. The Chilean navy began a ruthless destruction of towns and plantations along the Peruvian coast, and Callao was blockaded.

Nevertheless, neither Peru nor Bolivia would accede to Chile's demand for the cession of the nitrate provinces when the government of the United States attempted to bring the belligerents to an agreement in October, 1880. The Chilean army consequently occupied Lima early in 1881 after a short but violent conflict. Peru was powerless to offer further resistance.

It was more than two years before a Peruvian government agreed to make peace. When the Treaty of Ancón was finally signed on October 20, 1883, Peru gave up Tarapacá and agreed that Chile should occupy the provinces of Tacna and Arica for ten years. After that a plebiscite was to determine their final disposition, and the country which won them was to pay the other $10,000,000. The failure of the two powers to agree on conditions for holding this plebiscite made the Tacna-Arica question an obstacle to good relations between them during the ensuing forty-five years. A truce with Bolivia was signed in 1884, leaving Chile in possession of Antofagasta and the rest of the Bolivian seacoast, but no formal treaty was concluded until 1904.

After the War

Chile emerged from the war one of the richest and most powerful of the South American republics. Her foreign trade, already large, was tremendously increased. Her new provinces contained great deposits of copper and other minerals as well as nitrate, and the development of their resources, as well as the new market which they offered for agricultural products from the south, made the country more prosperous than ever before. The export taxes on nitrate alone gave the

PERU

Puno
Arequipa
Mollendo
Moquegua
Tarata
TACNA
Tacna
Arica
ARICA
R. Camarones
TARAPACÁ
Iquique
Tocopilla
R. Loa
Mejillones
Antofagasta
ATACAMA
Paposo
Taltal
Chañaral
Caldera
Copiapó

PACIFIC OCEAN

CHILE

Lago Titicaca
R. Beni
R. Mamore
★ La Paz
R. Desaguadero
Cochabamba
BOLIVIA
Oruro
Lago Poopó
R. Guapay
Potosí
Uyuni

ARGENTINA

Bermejo

Boundary between
Chile and Peru
after War of Pacific

Boundary between
Chile and Peru
fixed by Treaty 1929

Boundary between
Peru and Bolivia
before War of Pacific

Boundary between
Chile and Bolivia before
War of Pacific

*SHADED AREAS SHOW TERRITORY
ACQUIRED BY CHILE AFTER
THE WAR OF THE PACIFIC*

SCALE OF MILES
0   50   100   200

Territory under Dispute in the War of the Pacific

government a large part of its revenue. It was chiefly the mercantile and landowning classes, however, which benefited, for the *inquilino* laborers of the interior continued to work for a bare subsistence. Their wages, paid in depreciating paper money, increased little while prices were soaring, and the miners and landowners opposed any change in a currency system that enabled them to obtain labor more and more cheaply while they sold their products abroad for gold.

Domingo Santa María, another liberal, succeeded President Pinto in 1881. Santa María not only had to conclude the war with Peru but to put down an Indian uprising in the south. The Araucanians had made trouble during the civil wars of 1851 and 1859, when the insurgents enlisted their help, and in 1861 the government began a systematic military occupation of their territory. There was a new revolt in 1868, which lasted three years, and another in 1880 after troops were withdrawn from the frontier for service in Peru. At the end of the war, a strong force was sent into the Indians' territory. Several new towns were established and the few Araucanians who remained at the end of the military operations were confined to reservations, where some thousands of them still live.

Another difficult problem arose when the venerable Archbishop Valdivieso died in 1878. The Pope refused to accept a priest of pronounced liberal views who was proposed by the Chilean government as his successor. This revived the old dispute about the *patronato*, and in the controversy that ensued the Santa María administration handed the apostolic delegate his passports. The liberal majority in Congress then passed laws freeing public cemeteries from Church control, making civil marriage compulsory, and providing that the official registry of births, marriages, and deaths should be maintained by the civil authorities rather than by the parish priests. The clergy retaliated by refusing to participate in burials in public cemeteries, and the government forbade burials in places under ecclesiastical control. The conservatives, and the more devout portion of the people generally, supported the Church, and feeling ran so high that an outbreak of violence seemed imminent.

Balmaceda and the Civil War

The situation was still acute when José Manuel Balmaceda, the Minister of the Interior, was elected to succeed Santa María in 1886.

Young, handsome, and a brilliant orator, the new president was one of the most popular leaders in the liberal party, and it seemed possible that his administration might be a successful one. Though he was considered strongly anti-clerical, he reached a compromise with the Church about the appointment of a new archbishop and thus placated the conservatives. He was also able for a time to unite the various liberal groups which between them had a large majority in the congress. The government's revenues were greater than ever before, and the administration increased its popularity by inaugurating an ambitious program of public works.

The mutually hostile factions in the liberal party, however, could not long be made to work together. Balmaceda alienated some of them in attempting to retain the support of others, and dissensions increased as the time for a new presidential election approached.

Despite a growing demand for better elections and a number of attempts to improve electoral practices, the victory of any candidate supported by the president and his cabinet was a foregone conclusion. Consequently, when it seemed probable that Balmaceda would favor Enrique Sanfuentes, the Minister of Public Works, the latter's opponents endeavored to deprive him of effective official support by forcing changes in the cabinet. It had by this time become the accepted practice for the president to select his ministers in such a manner as to command the support of a parliamentary majority. Formerly the prestige of the chief executive had made this a relatively easy matter, but since 1871 the power of congress had been gradually increasing and recently enacted laws forbidding congressmen to hold other official positions had deprived the president of one of his chief means of influencing the parliamentary leaders. It was still an open question whether the executive or the legislative branch would dominate if there were a conflict between them, and it was this question which Balmaceda's opponents now forced to an issue.

Balmaceda denied the right of Congress to force him to change his cabinet, but he nevertheless made an effort to restore harmony. Sanfuentes, who had just been appointed Minister of the Interior, withdrew his presidential candidacy. When Congress suspended action on the tax laws and the budget, which had to be enacted each year, the President gave in further and appointed a neutral cabinet. The tax laws were then passed, but the budget had not yet been approved when friction within the administration led the new ministers to resign. A cabinet made up of Balmaceda's personal followers took office, and the congress again suspended action on the appropriations. When it adjourned without approving them, Balmaceda, confronted by a situation where there was no legal authorization for any disbursement of government funds, announced that the budget for the preceding year would remain in force.

This frankly unconstitutional procedure precipitated the most costly civil war in Chile's history. On January 7, 1891, a majority of the members of Congress issued a statement declaring the President removed from office. They were supported by the navy, but the army remained loyal to Balmaceda. Again it was the control of the sea which decided the issue, for the insurgents seized the nitrate provinces, where they could not be attacked by land, and used the proceeds of the export taxes to equip an army of their own. In August their forces defeated those of the government in two important battles near Valparaiso, and Balmaceda turned over the executive power to General Baquedano. Three weeks later he committed suicide in the Argentine legation, where he had been given asylum. The war had cost some ten thousand lives and many millions of dollars, and both Santiago and Valparaiso had been looted by mobs before the new authorities could restore order.

Several incidents during the revolution led the insurgents to accuse the United States of partiality to Balmaceda, and their resentment increased when the American Minister gave asylum to several members of the defeated party after the war. In the midst of the controversy caused by the Minister's action, in October, 1891, a mob at Valparaiso killed two sailors from the U.S.S. *Baltimore* and injured five others. The ship's commanding officer reported that the sailors had given no provocation and that the police of Valparaiso had been partly responsible for what occurred. Chile at first refused the American government's demand for reparation, and a situation already bad became worse when a cable from the foreign office at Santiago, couched in offensive terms, was made public by the Chilean Minister at Washington. The Chilean government's own investigation convinced it that the American sailors had been at fault and that the Valparaiso police had conducted themselves properly, but it yielded to the demands of the United States when President Harrison asked authority from Congress to use force if necessary to obtain satisfaction. The incident was closed by the payment of an indemnity of $75,000, but it left an aftermath of bitterness in Chile which long clouded the relations between the two countries.

The Era of Parliamentary Government

The revolution of 1891 ended for the time being the preponderance of the executive in the Chilean government. The president, in fact if not by law, was thenceforth compelled to govern through ministers acceptable to majorities in both houses of congress. He could no longer control elections because the conduct of the voting was entrusted to autonomous, popularly elected communal governments that had taken over much of the authority in purely local affairs hitherto exercised by presidential appointees. Since these bodies were controlled by the great landowners, it was they who in fact selected the members of congress in each locality.

The masses of the people had little more voice in political affairs than before. The great majority were still excluded from the suffrage by literacy qualifications, and there were few members of the laboring class who would have ventured to question the authority of the dominant aristocracy. Under the new system, the use of force and intimidation in elections became less common but bribery increased. So serious did this evil become that instances are recorded where the indignant citizens rose *en masse* and stoned the houses of party leaders because agreements between rival factions made an electoral contest unnecessary and thus deprived the voters of what they regarded as a normal source of income.[1]

The parliamentary system, as it existed in Chile during the next thirty-five years, was not a success. There were a number of parties, held together chiefly by tradition or personal ties rather than by a common program. Majorities in congress had to be obtained by forming combinations of hostile factions which coöperated only so long as it suited their individual interests and which were prone to desert the government when minor disputes arose. Cabinets thus came and went with a rapidity which made impossible any continuity or real efficiency in administration, and which might have been disastrous had it not been for the stability of the general social structure and the prosperity which the country enjoyed until after the end of the European war.

The civil war and the world crisis of the early '90's were only temporary setbacks to Chile's economic development. By the end of the

[1] Galdames, *Estudio de la Historia de Chile,* 7th edition, p. 447.

century, foreign trade was again increasing at a phenomenal rate. The export taxes on nitrate gave the government an ample revenue which made for political stability, though at the same time it encouraged extravagance and corruption. Another source of wealth opened up when the great copper mines of El Teniente and Chuquicamata, developed by American capital, began production in 1911 and 1915. The laboring classes, however, shared only to a limited degree in this prosperity. The depreciation of the paper currency kept real wages low, and the ruling class showed little interest in social problems which became increasingly serious as the number of workers in mining and industry increased. Strikes and riots, which occurred with some frequency in the larger cities during the first decade of the twentieth century, were put down by military force, though sometimes not until after much property had been destroyed. Discontent among the urban laborers, however, did not seem a particularly serious threat to the stability of the government so long as the great mass of the *inquilinos* in the country districts were not affected.

The president, from 1891 to 1920, was little more than a figurehead. Jorge Montt, who had commanded the navy during the civil war, assumed the office in 1891. He was succeeded in 1896 by Federico Errázuriz Echáurren, elected by a conservative-liberal coalition after a close contest in which the former partisans of Balmaceda supported the opposition candidate. The chief event of Errázuriz's administration was the boundary controversy with Argentina, already discussed in Chapter 9. This involved the government in heavy expenditures for military preparations and caused disturbances in the commercial and financial world. Because of these expenditures the paper currency, which had been stabilized by a law enacted in 1895, was again made inconvertible, ostensibly at least as a war measure, but greatly to the satisfaction of the classes that profited by its depreciation. There was a revival of prosperity, culminating in a period of wild speculation, under Jerman Riesco, the next president, who was elected as the candidate of the Liberal Alliance in 1901. In 1906, however, the country suffered one of the worst disasters in its history when an earthquake destroyed most of Valparaiso and much of Santiago with the loss of 3,000 lives in the former city.

The defects of the parliamentary form of government were by this time evident. Seventeen different ministries held office during Riesco's administration [1] while the Congress wasted its time in political squabbles to the exclusion of constructive legislation. When Pedro Montt, the son of the man who had ruled Chile from 1851 to 1861, was elected to the presidency in 1906 as the candidate of the conservatives, the *Balmacedistas,* and some of the other liberals, his supporters hoped that he would be able to reassert the authority of the executive power, but they were disappointed because the leaders in congress showed no disposition to give up practices that increased their own influence. Montt died in 1910, just as Chile was preparing to celebrate the centenary of independence, and his successor, Ramón Barros Luco, was elected by agreement between the chief political parties. Neither Barros Luco nor his successor, Juan Luis Sanfuentes, elected after a close contest in 1915, attempted to challenge the supremacy of congress. During their administrations the world war at first caused a serious dislocation of commerce and then brought a great wave of prosperity, with high prices for nitrate and copper. Chile remained neutral throughout the conflict.

Political Changes, 1918–1926

Throughout the first century of independence Chile's government was dominated by a few hundred landowning families. Under their leadership the Republic enjoyed a longer period of relatively stable government and good administration than any other in South America. Even the defects of the parliamentary system did not seriously affect its internal tranquility. Nevertheless increasingly influential groups were dissatisfied with the existing political situation. With the development of mining and manufacturing and the growth of large cities, there had arisen a class of merchants, manufacturers, and professional men who had little connection with the old aristocracy. There was also a host of graduates from the free public schools and the universities who could find little opportunity for employment in the already overcrowded professions. Many of these had taken an active part in politics as party workers, and had held positions in the government; but they were hostile as a class to a political system that limited their opportunities for advancement.

The situation was in many ways similar to that which led to the victory of the radical party in Argentina in 1916, but in Chile it was

[1] Amunátegui, *Historia de Chile,* Vol. II, p. 161.

fraught with more serious implications because of the discontent among the laboring class. Thousands of laborers had left the *haciendas* for employment in the mines or in the cities where their wages were higher than those of the *inquilinos*, but where they lived in crowded and unsanitary hovels, an easy prey to disease and alcoholism. The government had done little for them, and only a few employers, like the American copper companies, showed an interest in improving their condition. Radical agitators, native and foreign, thus found a fertile field in which to sow disruptive ideas, and the increasingly frequent industrial strikes were often accompanied by violence and bloodshed. The laboring class had neither the leaders nor the organization to enable it to assume control of the government, but its vociferous support was an important factor in the election of Arturo Alessandri as president in 1920.

Alessandri came into prominence as a popular leader in 1915, when he ran for senator in Tarapaca. In his appeal for the votes of the laborers in the nitrate fields, he advocated labor legislation and social reforms with an eloquence which won him the enthusiastic support of the working class throughout the Republic. When the congressional elections of 1918 brought into the legislative body a large number of new members whose views were similar to his own, he became for a time the head of the cabinet under President Sanfuentes. In the 1920 campaign, he frankly appealed to the middle classes and the labor organizations for support against the aristocracy. Nearly all the old political groups joined in the *Unión Nacional* to oppose him, with Luis Barros Borgoño as their candidate, and a bitter contest ensued. There was talk of civil war when disputed elections in several districts cast doubt on the final result, but the Congress avoided serious trouble by referring the disputes to a "tribunal of honor" in which the two parties were equally represented. The result was Alessandri's election by a margin of one electoral vote.

Alessandri's supporters, the Liberal Alliance, obtained control of the Chamber of Deputies, but the conservatives retained a majority in the Senate which forced one cabinet after another to resign. The President's projects for social and political reforms were blocked and there was a long controversy before the Congress ratified the Washington protocol of 1922, by which Chile and Peru agreed to submit the Tacna-Arica question to arbitration by the President of the United States. Meanwhile increasing artificial nitrate production in foreign countries was threatening the country's chief industry and chief source of public revenue, and many thousands of unemployed laborers from the nitrate fields were crowding into Santiago and Valparaiso. Alessandri's position became constantly more difficult. It should have improved after the Liberal Alliance obtained control of both houses of congress in 1924, but the new legislative body showed itself no more competent to accomplish anything of importance than its predecessor.

A crisis arose in September, 1924, when the new chambers voted that their members should receive salaries. They had hitherto been unpaid, for seats in congress were an honor for which the aristocracy were willing to spend large sums; and the fact that the new measure was necessary if men who were not rich were to have an opportunity to serve honorably in the legislature did not seem to justify its taking precedence over more urgent business. The younger officers of the army, whose own pay was two months in arrears, vociferously expressed their disapproval, and on September 4, with at least the passive support of their superiors, their representatives visited the President and compelled him to appoint a new cabinet composed of military leaders. The Congress, intimidated by the threat of force, promptly passed a large number of labor laws and other reforms. Alessandri found his own position untenable and on September 10 he fled across the Andes to Argentina. A *junta de gobierno* composed of two generals and an admiral assumed control.

The *junta* soon showed reactionary tendencies which alarmed the younger military men who had led the revolt but whose political views were more like those of Alessandri than those of the conservatives. On January 23, 1925, therefore, a group of junior officers seized the *Moneda*, the presidential palace, and invited Alessandri to return to complete his legal term of office. The President received an enthusiastic reception when he reached Santiago.

During the next few months a new constitution was drawn up and ratified by a plebiscite. Congress lost its power to interfere with the executive branch of the government. Its members could no longer hold office in the cabinet, and the ministers were made independent of congressional approval. The requirement that tax laws and laws fixing the strength of the military establishment be voted annually was abolished, and the budget was to become effective in the form proposed by the president if the legislature failed to act upon it within a given time. The constitution also provided for the complete separation of

Church and State, for the election of the president by direct vote, and for important reforms in the judiciary. These changes, which again made the president the real head of the executive department, did away with some of the worst features of the parliamentary system as it had operated since 1891. The multiplicity of parties continued, and later presidents were often compelled to make changes in their cabinets to hold the support of a congressional majority, but they were no longer so completely at the mercy of the party leaders.

It was some years, however, before Chile again enjoyed orderly constitutional government. Soon after Alessandri was reinstated, a conflict provoked by the presidential ambitions of the Minister of War, Colonel Carlos Ibáñez, forced him to resign. Strong opposition from the civilian political leaders dissuaded Ibáñez from insisting on his own candidacy in the ensuing election, but he continued as Minister of War in the administration of Emilio Figueroa Larrain, who became President in December, 1925, with the support of most of the important parties. His power steadily increased, and he became President in May, 1927, when Figueroa was forced to resign.

Ibáñez

The new regime was more nearly a dictatorship than any that had existed in Chile since 1861, but many citizens who were alarmed by the threat of class warfare were willing to support a strong government, even at the cost of political liberty. Such opposition as there was found little opportunity for expression. The press was muzzled, and many of the President's enemies were sent into exile. The Congress itself generally acted in accord with the President's wishes, and in the election of 1930 the official candidates for senator and deputy were returned without opposition as the result of an inter-party agreement.

The most notable event of Ibáñez' administration was the final settlement of the Tacna-Arica question, which had embittered Chile's relations with Peru since the War of the Pacific. The plebiscite that was to have decided the final disposition of these provinces had never been held because the two governments could not agree on the conditions which should govern it. When the question was submitted to arbitration under the protocol signed at Washington in 1922, the President of the United States decided that the plebiscite should be held, and appointed first General Pershing and then General Lassiter as president of a commission to supervise it. These American officers refused to continue with their task because they felt that the conduct of the Chilean authorities in the two provinces made a fair vote impossible. The plebiscite was abandoned, but an agreement for the division of the territory was reached in 1929 through the mediation of the United States. Chile kept Arica, and Peru received Tacna with an indemnity of six million dollars. Friendly relations were thus established between the two republics for the first time in half a century.

At home, Ibáñez attempted to carry further the program of social reform that Alessandri had advocated. Advanced labor laws were enacted and a modest agrarian program was started. Primary instruction, which had been made obligatory by law in 1920, was extended and improved in quality, so that the number of illiterates over seven years of age decreased from 37 out of each 100 in 1920 to 25 in 1930.[1] At the same time the government financed an ambitious program of public works by loans contracted in the United States and Europe. The inflow of new money, combined with measures for the stabilization of the currency, did much to raise wages and living standards, and a general prosperity was one element in the government's strength.

Depression and Disorder, 1931–1932

Ibáñez' regime collapsed when this prosperity ended. The depression of the early 1930's affected Chile with peculiar severity. The government's revenues, derived chiefly from import and export duties, fell off sharply with the decline of trade. The inflow of foreign capital ceased and thousands of men employed on the public works program lost their jobs. Other thousands were thrown out of work at the mines, as nitrate, iodine, and copper, the three commodities that made up four-fifths of the country's exports, became almost unsalable. The situation of the nitrate industry was especially discouraging because of the competition of synthetic nitrogen. Unimportant before the European war, the extraction of nitrogen from the atmosphere had increased until by 1926 it supplied the major part of the world's requirements, and foreign governments were protecting and subsidizing the new industry in an effort to assure an adequate domestic supply for military purposes. Ibáñez, with the aid of North American capital, endeavored to meet this competition by combining the Chilean producers in one great

[1] *Sinópsis geográfica-estadística de la República de Chile*, 1933, p. 87.

company and substituting new scientific methods of treating the ore for the old wasteful and expensive Shanks process; but the *Cosach*, as the new company was called, suffered heavy losses when the depression came.

As conditions grew worse, opposition to the government increased. The movement which overthrew Ibáñez was an emphatic demonstration of popular discontent rather than an armed revolt. It began with rioting by the university students in Santiago in the latter part of July, 1931. A day or two later, the lawyers, engineers, and school-teachers, and even the physicians, went on strike, and soon afterward the labor unions, which had hitherto supported the government, joined in the demand for a change. On July 26, Ibáñez resigned. Three months later Juan Estéban Montero, with the support of the conservative political parties, defeated Alessandri in a presidential election.

There was little hope for the new administration. Industry and commerce were still paralyzed and the government's finances were completely disorganized. For the first time since the days of Portales, Chile defaulted on the service of the foreign debt. The Chilean peso was depreciating until by September, 1932, it was worth less than a sixth of its former value. Unemployment caused much suffering. Worse still was the breakdown of discipline in the army. After the influential position which they had held under Ibáñez, many of the officers, especially if they held advanced political views, were reluctant to resign themselves to control by a civilian adminstration representing the old aristocracy.

Aided by a part of the army, a group of left-wing leaders overthrew Montero in June, 1932. Dr. Carlos Dávila became provisional President, but in September, after it had become clear that his government would not be able to carry out the social reforms that it had promised, there was another successful military revolt. By this time there was a growing reaction against the near anarchy that had prevailed since June, and more normal conditions were restored when Arturo Alessandri was elected constitutional President in October.

Alessandri's Second Administration

Alessandri was supported, rather unenthusiastically, by a majority of the old ruling class because they feared him less than they feared his principal opponent, the socialist Marmaduke Grove. He thus took office in December, 1932, under conditions very different from those at the beginning of his first term. The right-wing parties had majorities in both houses of Congress, and for some time the President openly accepted the backing of the *milicia republicana*, a private army organized by influential civilians in 1932 to oppose the revolutionary activities of the radical elements in the regular army and to protect the established order against the growing danger from the communists and other extremists. He was able to suppress a number of disturbances fomented by the extremists, and conditions became somewhat more stable as the worst effects of the depression disappeared.

Even with the gradual revival of prosperity, grave economic and social problems remained. The nitrate industry had not recovered. Chile had supplied 55 per cent of the world's nitrogen in 1913, 23 per cent in 1929, 4 per cent in 1933, and only 8 per cent in 1938.[1] Other export industries were not flourishing. The peso recovered only a part of its value and imports still had to be restricted. The rapid growth of local manufacturing only partially offset the effect on local standards of living, and labor suffered especially because wages had not increased as the value of the peso fell. Discontent among the lower classes remained a serious political problem.

Alessandri succeeded in pushing through some measures for the improvement of the condition of the laborers and the *inquilinos*, but his efforts were hampered by conservative opposition. He received more support in measures directed against foreign capital. The *Cosach*, sponsored by North American interests, was dissolved early in his term. The nitrate companies resumed operations as separate concerns, but they were compelled to sell their product through a government agency which retained 25 per cent of the profits in lieu of the former export tax. The American-owned Chile Electric Company was compelled to accept an increased measure of government control. A plan of settlement bitterly criticized by foreign interests was forced upon the holders of the Republic's external bonds. These and many similar measures were a response to a widespread feeling of popular hostility to foreign "economic imperialism" which found expression in other Latin American countries as well as Chile during and after the depression.

Political agitation revived as the election of 1938 approached. In

[1] U.S. Tariff Commission, *Foreign Trade of Latin America* (1940), Part III, Vol. II, p. 286.

1936 the left-wing parties formed a "popular front," which included not only the communists and socialists but also bourgeois political elements like the radical party, to which Alessandri himself had formerly belonged. This group supported a veteran radical leader, Pedro Aguirre Cerda, as their candidate for the presidency, while the conservative parties put forward Gustavo Ross, a liberal, who had been Alessandri's Minister of Finance. Ex-President Carlos Ibáñez was nominated by the Chilean nazi party, a group which advocated fascist ideas but disclaimed any connection with European fascism. He withdrew his candidacy, however, after some of his supporters attempted a *coup d'état* and were slaughtered by the police. The nazis then supported the popular front. Aguirre Cerda defeated Ross by 220,000 to 213,000 votes and was inaugurated in December, 1938.

Recent Events

A month later, a terrific earthquake, centering in the region of Chillán, killed more than 25,000 people and destroyed vast amounts of property. The government was still struggling with the task of relief and reconstruction when the outbreak of war in Europe brought new problems. The internal political situation also became more complicated when quarrels between the socialists and the communists caused the socialists to withdraw from the popular front in 1941. Nevertheless, when Aguirre Cerda died a few months later, Juan Antonio Ríos, the left-wing candidate for the presidency, defeated ex-President Ibáñez, who was put forward by the conservatives.

Partly because of a desire to remain on good terms with Argentina, and partly from fear of a possible Japanese attack on her coast, Chile refused to break relations with the Axis powers immediately after Pearl Harbor when all of the other Latin American countries except Argentina did so. This caused some resentment in Washington, but in January, 1943, the Ríos administration changed its policy and coöperated in the war effort. It took measures against the German and Japanese agents in Chile and obtained lend-lease and other aid from the United States. It declared war on Japan in April, 1945.

Ríos' death in June, 1946, made a new presidential election necessary. Since no candidate received a majority of the popular vote, the choice went to Congress, where some of the conservative groups joined in the selection of Gabriel González Videla, who had been the candidate of the radicals, the communists, and a part of the socialists. In recognition of this support, the new President appointed three liberals as well as three communists to his first cabinet. Such diverse elements could hardly work together, and in April, 1947, the liberals resigned and the President formed a new cabinet from which the communists also were excluded.

The communists, who controlled most of the stronger labor unions, retaliated by organizing a series of dangerous and costly strikes. The worst of these, in the coal mines near Concepción in October, 1947, was finally suppressed by the army. The government charged that these strikes had been fomented by Soviet agents, and it consequently expelled the Jugoslav Chargé d'Affaires and broke off relations with Russia and Czechoslovakia. At the same time many communist officials were removed and some hundreds of the party's leaders were arrested. In July, 1948, the Congress outlawed the party and forbade its members to vote or hold office.

The communists continued to be a formidable political force, though they were compelled to work underground, and the government also faced opposition from the extreme right. In November, 1948, ex-President Ibáñez and a former governor of Santiago were arrested on charges of plotting a revolt. The military prosecutor accused the Argentine consul general and the first secretary of the Argentine embassy of encouraging the plot and the first secretary was declared *persona non grata*.

Though Chile has only about 5,500,000 people, a large per capita foreign trade makes her one of the most important South American countries. She still exports much nitrate, and in recent years she has become the world's second largest producer of copper. Both industries, however, face a difficult situation at the present time. Synthetic production abroad has destroyed Chile's former monopoly in nitrate and has made the future of the industry uncertain. Copper also faces the problem of over-production and meets increasing competition from African mines with lower labor costs. This deterioration in the Republic's position as a supplier of raw materials has been somewhat offset by a great increase in local manufactures, which now supply many articles formerly purchased abroad. The government, through the Chilean Development Corporation, has done much to encourage the growth of industry.

The Republic has serious social problems. Most of the land is still held in large estates. The situation of the *inquilinos* who work on them has improved somewhat, but not very much. The workers in mining and industry, with their low living standards, are still a prey to disease and alcoholism. The poverty of the laboring classes helps to explain the strength that the communist party has attained in recent years.

Part IV

~~~

BRAZIL

W<small>E</small> have thus far been dealing with countries that formed part of the Spanish Empire. We shall now turn to another area, occupying nearly half of South America, which was colonized by Portugal. The history of Brazil may profitably be taken up at this point, both because it is linked in many ways with that of the River Plate countries, and because Brazil, like Argentina and Chile, achieved a fairly stable government and a position of importance in world trade before most of the other Latin American republics.

The institutions and the culture that the Portuguese took with them to America were in many ways like those of the Spanish colonies. Portugal was a part of the Iberian peninsula, and it was an accident that she remained independent when the rest of Spain was being united. The two countries were in fact ruled by the same kings between 1580 and 1640. At the same time there were important differences. Portugal was a smaller and weaker nation than Spain, with not much more than one million inhabitants at the beginning of the sixteenth century. While Spain was conquering the rest of South America, her scanty resources were fully occupied in acquiring a trading empire in the Far East, and Brazil, with no rich native communities like Mexico and Peru, seemed relatively unimportant. The home government's interest increased as time went on, but it was never able to establish a centralized, paternalistic regime like that of Spain or to help the colonists very effectively in their long struggles against foreign aggression. The exploration and

251

occupation of the interior of the continent, carried on in Spanish America by a combination of military and missionary activity directed by the Crown, was left in Brazil to local enterprise. The memory of frequent revolts against the royal authority, of conflicts with the French and the Dutch, and of the exploits of the Paulista *bandeirantes* gave the Brazilians something very like a national tradition before the country became independent.

Other factors, historical and psychological, helped to make the country different from the Spanish American republics. One was the attitude toward religion. The Portuguese had less of the crusading spirit that played so great a rôle in the Spanish conquest. This was evident in their treatment of the Indians and in a less energetic effort to exclude suspected heretics from the colony. The Church never became so powerful or so wealthy as in the Spanish colonies, and its position has not been an important political issue since independence. Some of the other differences are harder to define. The Brazilian seems somewhat more tolerant, in other matters besides religion, and has less of the sensitive pride that often complicates political relations among people of Spanish descent. The spirit of *localismo* is less evident, though by no means absent. If it had been as strong as in Spanish America, it would hardly have been possible for the Brazilian settlements, strung thinly along 4,800 miles of coast, to emerge as a united nation.

13

Colonial Brazil

Portugal acquired a right to a large part of South America under the Treaty of Tordesillas of 1494, and her claim was reinforced when Cabral visited the coast of Brazil in 1500. Other explorers soon followed, but for some years the Portuguese government made little effort to occupy the territory which it had obtained more by accident, apparently, than by design. The Brazilian coast, inhabited by primitive savages, had little attraction for a people who had just found the way to India and the Spice Islands.

The region did offer one valuable commodity: the brazil-wood from which the country soon took its name. This dye-wood was in great demand in Europe, and Portuguese and other mariners frequently visited the coast to obtain it from the Indians, who were taught to cut it and to barter it for tools and trinkets. By 1530 a number of Europeans were living among the natives. Some were shipwrecked or marooned sailors; others were convicts or daring adventurers who had been put ashore in the hope that those not eaten by the Indians would learn their languages and thus become useful as interpreters. There had been a small Portuguese agricultural settlement in Pernambuco as early as 1516, but this was destroyed by a French raid in 1530.

French shipmasters, half trader and half pirate, were at least as active in the brazil-wood trade as were the Portuguese, and their intrusions finally compelled the government at Lisbon to send Martim Affonso de Souza to establish a permanent colony in the territory in 1530. Souza's original destination was the River Plate, which was thought or at least alleged to be east of the line of demarcation, but bad weather turned his ships back and he finally landed near the site of modern Santos. There a Portuguese named João Ramalho, who had been shipwrecked on the coast twenty years earlier, helped him to found São Vicente, the first permanent European settlement in Brazil. Ramalho himself had been living at Piratininga in the nearby highlands, and another small group of colonists joined him there, forming a half-Portuguese, half-Indian community from which the great city of São Paulo later developed.

The First Settlements

Meanwhile, King João III decided to attempt to colonize the whole coast. Brazil was divided into twelve "captaincies," extending in most cases fifty leagues along the shore and indefinitely into the interior, and each was granted to a "donatory" who was to settle and exploit it for his own account. These "donatories" were feudal lords, empowered to charter cities, to apportion land among the colonists, and to administer justice, though they might not inflict the death penalty on persons of gentle blood. Their privileges, both economic and political, were hereditary. For itself the Crown reserved little more than the right to receive the greater part of the customs duties, the royal fifth on minerals, and the tithes, leaving the proceeds of other taxes to the proprietor.

Only a few of the grantees had the enterprise or the resources needed for the establishment of successful colonies. Some of them did not seriously attempt to exercise their rights. Others tried but failed. Of the six settlements which endured, three, at Victoria, Porto Seguro, and Ilheos, barely managed to survive the internal dissensions and the constant Indian attacks of their early years. On the other hand, São Vicente, which was granted to Martim Affonso de Souza, gradually increased in population and the nearby colony of Santo Amaro, founded by Martim Affonso's brother Pero Lopes, shared its modest prosperity. A new settlement in Pernambuco was more successful, chiefly because Duarte Coelho, the energetic proprietor, himself assumed the direction of affairs instead of leaving them, as most of the other donatories did, in the hands of unscrupulous or incompetent agents. Within a few years the mills of this colony were furnishing an important part of the world's sugar supply, and Olinda, its capital, was the chief city in Brazil. A strong hand like Duarte Coelho's was needed in the new colonies. A large proportion of the first inhabitants were convicts, banished to America as a punishment, and the task of governing them would have been difficult even if the small and widely scattered Portuguese settlements had not constantly been exposed to hostile attacks.

The chief danger came from the Indians. The tribes of Brazil were far less civilized than those whom the Spaniards had encountered in Mexico and the Andean countries, though somewhat more advanced than those of the pampas. The coast and much of the interior was occupied by peoples of the Tupi stock, related to the Guaranís of Paraguay, living in small, semi-nomadic groups, and constantly at war with one another. Nearly all of them were cannibals. Many of the native chiefs allied themselves with the French, who were still active along the coast and who furnished the savages with firearms and other weapons. Others were glad to accept the help of the Portuguese against their enemies and in return to assist the colonists in establishing their homes and plantations; but these, too, frequently became hostile as the colonists encroached more and more on their lands. Furthermore, the colonists had already begun to rely on the labor of Indian slaves captured in war or purchased from other natives, and even the friendly Indians were frequently reduced to servitude on one pretext or another.

When it became evident that the scattered, badly administered settlements faced destruction unless the Crown could come to their aid, the King decided to appoint a governor general who would take over the political and military authority that the donatories had hitherto exercised. Thomé de Souza, an illegitimate scion of a noble family who had distinguished himself as a soldier and administrator in other Portuguese colonies, was consequently sent to Brazil in 1549 with 600 soldiers, 400 convicts, and a number of married couples. There were also six Jesuits, whose work was to have consequences of the utmost importance. The sparsely settled region of the Bay of Todos os Santos was purchased from the heirs of the original donatory as the site of a new capital, and the city of São Salvador, better known in English as Bahia, was founded there. Like Martim Affonso, the new governor general was greatly aided by a Portuguese who had already been living among the Indians for many years—the famous Diogo Álvares, or Caramurú. Within a short time Bahia was a flourishing village of one hundred houses, surrounded by gardens and new sugar plantations. Meanwhile, Souza had sent representatives to establish his authority and to improve the administration of justice and the collection of the royal revenues in the other captaincies.

The Jesuits, under the leadership of Manoel da Nobrega, lost no time in starting their work both among the Portuguese and among the Indians. They were shocked by the low state of religion in the settlements. Most of the colonists were a godless lot and the clergy were few in number and in many cases were living in a way that reflected no credit on their calling. The Jesuits endeavored to improve matters, and on their recommendation a bishopric was created in Brazil in 1551. Nobrega and his followers also established several schools, not only for Portuguese children but for the increasingly numerous *mamelucos*, or persons of mixed blood. One of these institutions was founded on the plains near Piratininga by José de Anchieta, who was not yet twenty when he arrived in 1553 to begin the career which made him one of the most famous members of the order. This "College of São Paulo" soon became the center of a community that took the same name, for the settlers in the neighborhood were persuaded by the fathers to move from João Ramalho's original village to the lands around the new institution.

It was as missionaries that the Jesuits did their greatest work. Visiting the Indians of all the colonies along the coast, they learned their languages and gradually won their affection. The task of conversion grew easier as the savages began to realize that they could rely on their new friends to protect them against abuse by the other Portuguese. By a combination of persuasion and force many of them were gathered in villages where they were taught better methods of agriculture and otherwise encouraged to lead a more civilized life. The Jesuits' activities made it more difficult to obtain Indian slaves and consequently aroused much opposition among the Portuguese colonists, but they were effectively supported during these first years both by the Crown and by Thomé de Souza. Nobrega and Anchieta, in fact, soon enjoyed an authority hardly inferior to that of the governor himself.

Duarte da Costa succeeded Thomé de Souza as governor in 1553. He at once began to quarrel with the other authorities at Bahia and especially with the bishop, and when the latter sailed for Lisbon to defend himself at court he was shipwrecked and eaten by the Indians. This sacrilege, which horrified even the none too devout Brazilians, was followed by worse disasters. Encouraged by the spectacle of the settlers fighting among themselves, the natives revolted all along the coast. Even Pernambuco, which had a weaker government after Duarte Coelho's death in 1554, was seriously menaced. The Indian attacks were fomented by French and other foreign interlopers, and while they were at their height it was learned that French enterprise had taken a still more dangerous form with the establishment of a strong colony in the hitherto unoccupied bay of Rio de Janeiro.

The leader in this was Nicolas Durand de Villegagnon, a distinguished naval officer who had the support of the King of France and also of the powerful Admiral Coligny. Coligny hoped that the settlement would serve as a refuge for Huguenots, many of whom had joined the expedition, but he lost interest when Villegagnon quarreled with his Protestant followers and sent home the two ministers whom Calvin himself had appointed to accompany the expedition. The colony nevertheless maintained itself for several years, cultivating friendly relations and trade with the Indians. In 1560, Mem de Sá, the third governor of Brazil, finally attacked it. Father Nobrega, who accompanied the expedition, raised a force of Indians friendly to the Portuguese, and the French were easily dislodged from the fort that they had built on an island at the mouth of the bay. Many of them were captured but others took refuge among their native allies on the mainland.

Hostile Indians, meanwhile, continued their raids on the Portuguese settlements all along the coast from Bahia to São Vicente. Communication between the colonies was interrupted and many of the weaker settlements were all but destroyed. São Paulo was attacked by a great force, but was successfully defended by the converted Indians under the Jesuits' leadership. When the situation seemed desperate, Nobrega and Anchieta undertook to visit the principal hostile chiefs in an effort to make peace, and Anchieta remained for five months as a hostage among the natives, repeatedly facing what seemed almost certain death. The two Jesuits' heroism and persistence finally made possible a treaty which ended the immediate danger to the colonies. The French were driven out of the district around Rio de Janeiro in 1567, a year after the governor's nephew, Eustacio de Sá, had founded there the city which was later to become the capital of Brazil.

Though both Indians and interlopers continued to cause trouble, the Brazilian settlements advanced rapidly during the latter part of the sixteenth century, and particularly under the able rule of Mem de Sá. In 1549, there were only some 5,000 colonists, including both white immigrants and Negro slaves. Forty years later there were perhaps eight times that number. Bahia and Pernambuco were by far the most important of the captaincies, with many sugar plantations and a flourishing trade in cotton and brazil-wood. Their capitals were little more than villages but many of the planters who lived in them were quite wealthy. Elsewhere along the coast the Portuguese communities were less prosperous, and the life of many of the settlers was hardly less primitive than that of their Indian neighbors. The great majority, in fact, were living with Indian women, giving rise to a population of mixed blood to which a strong Negro strain was soon to be added.

Indian Slavery—The Paulistas

During the first century of the colonies' existence it was the Indians who furnished the principal labor supply. Accustomed as they were to the profitable African slave trade, the Portuguese looked upon the natives simply as a part of the exploitable wealth of their new possessions. Slave hunting was carried on even when it endangered the very existence of the new settlements, for the first thought of the immigrant was to obtain possession of a few Indians to hunt and till the ground for him. The larger numbers needed for the sugar plantations had been procured in various ways. Many Indians were simply kidnapped, or induced to sell themselves or their children into servitude for a term of years, often probably without realizing what they were doing. Others were purchased from tribes which had captured them in war, or taken by the Portuguese themselves in suppressing "rebellions." In their endeavor to increase the supply of captives, the settlers often sought pretexts to attack the natives and systematically encouraged feuds between them. Constant fighting, combined with pestilences brought by the white men, rapidly destroyed the natives on the coast, and within a century after the Portuguese arrived it was necessary to go farther and farther into the interior to obtain slaves.

The Jesuits exerted all of their influence to put a stop to these abuses, and their efforts to protect the natives led to a long and bitter conflict. Under pressure from both sides, the Portuguese government, like that of Spain, followed a vacillating policy. It attempted to confine the taking of slaves to officially authorized wars, and to prevent frauds by requiring that all slaves be registered. The *rezgate*, or purchase of Indians from other Indians, was at one time forbidden but later permitted under restrictions. A law was even issued in 1609, while Portugal was subject to the King of Spain, declaring all Indian slaves free, but protests from the colonists caused this to be modified before any effort to enforce it was made. In northern Brazil, as we shall see, the Indian question gave much trouble during the second half of the seventeenth century. It was not until the middle of the eighteenth century, when the native population had been greatly reduced, that Indian slavery was legally prohibited.

The hardy, energetic inhabitants of São Paulo, themselves of mixed blood, were the chief purveyors of Indian laborers to the sugar plantations of the other settlements. Since the natives of the nearby plateau were mostly under the protection of the Jesuit missions, the Paulistas began soon after 1600 to make raids farther into the interior to obtain slaves, at first for their own farms and later for sale elsewhere. Accompanied by their families and their domestic animals, their *bandeiras* or expeditions were often buried in the wilderness for years at a time, stopping now and then to sow a crop when their food supply ran low. On their return they brought back droves of Indians and distributed them among the sugar plantations along the coast. We saw in Chapter 4 how they destroyed the Jesuit missions in Guayrá, and forced the fathers to remove what was left of their flocks to southeastern Paraguay. In many other sections the native population was practically wiped out. The Jesuits asserted, probably with some exaggeration, that 300,000 natives were enslaved by the Paulistas between 1614 and 1639. On the other hand, the *bandeirantes* did their country a great service by exploring and occupying the interior of the continent. It was because of their enterprise that great areas which might otherwise have been claimed by Spain, lying west of the line of demarcation, are a part of Brazil today.

Negro Slavery

Indian labor was at best unsatisfactory, and as the settlements became wealthier the planters began to show a preference for Negroes as field hands and workers in the sugar mills. A Negro cost seventy-five dollars or more, whereas an Indian could be bought in some places for as little as five dollars, but the Africans were more tractable and less likely to run away, as well as far better able to endure regular sustained labor. Their importation was encouraged by the Portuguese government, which controlled the chief depots of the slave trade on the African coast. Their number increased in the latter part of the sixteenth century, and as time went on they practically supplanted the Indians as a laboring class in the older settlements. Though the death rate among new arrivals was exceedingly high, they were on the whole well treated compared with the Indians. As in Spain's colonies, both the law and local custom encouraged emancipation, so that free Negroes, as well as mulattoes, soon became numerous. Many slaves escaped into the wild country back from the coast and established free communities, called *quilombos*, which occasionally gave the colonists some trouble. The most famous of these was Palmares, in Alagoas, which was estimated to have twenty thousand inhabitants after the wars with the Dutch, and which was finally destroyed in 1697 after ten years of fighting.

Brazil under Spain, and the Dutch Wars

When Philip II of Spain successfully asserted his claim to the throne of Portugal in 1580, he became the sovereign of Brazil also. The Spanish monarchs governed the colony through Portuguese officials and under Portuguese laws, without attempting to make it an integral part of their existing empire in America, so that the effect on Brazilian institutions was not very great; but the union did expose the Brazilian settlements to new external dangers. Portugal, in her growing weakness, had endeavored to remain at peace by a policy of conciliation, often even paying compensation to interlopers whose ships were seized by her forces or making trade concessions to induce governments like the English and the French to restrain their subjects from buccaneering. Spain, on the other hand, was constantly at war. At the same time she was too weak on the sea, especially after the destruction of the "invincible armada," to protect her trans-Atlantic possessions. Brazil felt this weakness even more than Spain's own colonies, because Pernambuco and Bahia were more exposed to pirate attacks than the chief cities of Mexico and Peru. In the last decade of the sixteenth century, the Englishmen Cavendish and Lancaster sacked several of the settlements, while smugglers from several European nations intensified their activities and incited the Indians to revolt.

To check this renewed foreign aggression, the authorities in Brazil decided to occupy the hitherto neglected region north of Pernambuco. In the first years of the seventeenth century, settlements were established in Parahyba and Ceará, and in 1614 Jerónymo de Albuquerque drove out a group of French colonists who had built a fort in what is now Maranhão. Since it was difficult to govern the northern region from Bahia because the trade winds and the equatorial current made it hard for sailing vessels to weather Cape San Roque from the west, a separate "State of Maranhão" was set up in 1621. A number of industrious families from the Azores were brought in as colonists, and the new settlements were soon quite prosperous.

It was especially unfortunate for Brazil that union with Spain involved Portugal in the war between Spain and the Dutch. Merchants in the low countries, many of them persons of Portuguese-Jewish descent who had business relations with "new Christians" in Brazil, played an important part in the colony's commerce and were the chief distributors of Brazilian sugar in Europe. When they could no longer trade legitimately, they turned to smuggling and piracy. Many Portuguese Jews living in Holland became stockholders in the Dutch West India Company, which was incorporated in 1621 to attack the Spanish-Portuguese monopoly in America.

The Company's first Brazilian venture was an expedition against Bahia in 1624. The city was easily taken, because the royal authorities had made no real provision for its defense, but it was recaptured by a Spanish fleet a year later. Other raids on Brazilian ports followed and in 1630, when the West India Company's treasury had been replenished by Piet Heyn's capture of the Plate Fleet from Mexico, a force of nearly eight thousand men, with supplies of all sorts for the establishment of a permanent colony, was sent against Pernambuco. Again the Portuguese were unprepared, and Olinda and Recife, the chief towns of the province, were occupied with little difficulty. In the country districts the inhabitants offered more resistance, and patriot forces operating from a hamlet called the Arraial do Bom Jesus carried on guerrilla warfare for two years, with little help from the peninsula or from the royal officials elsewhere in Brazil. Finally one of their leaders, a halfbreed named Calabar, deserted to the enemy, and several Indian tribes which had hitherto resisted the invaders followed his example. After this the Dutch rapidly extended their control over an area that contained the majority of the population and the greater part of the wealth of Brazil, extending along the coast from the province of Maranhão in the north to the river São Francisco in the south.

In 1637, the West India Company sent Jan Mauritz, count of Nassau, to take over the government of the conquered territory. Nassau was a statesman of vision and liberal ideas, with a keen interest in art and science. He completely reorganized the administration of the colony and encouraged trade by removing burdensome restrictions. His policy of religious toleration won the coöperation of many of the native inhabitants, who were further conciliated by being given a share in the government, and attracted to Pernambuco large numbers of Portuguese Jews, whose wealth and business ability helped to make the district more prosperous than ever before. Many of these newcomers bought the confiscated plantations of Brazilians who refused to submit to Dutch rule. With the inflow of capital and more freedom of trade sugar production greatly increased. The commerce in slaves, both Negro and Indian, also took on a new importance, especially after the West India Company occupied some of the principal Portuguese possessions on the coast of Africa. Nassau, nevertheless, met with much opposition from his own people, for the Calvinist ministers who came out with the invaders opposed his tolerant conduct and the directors of the West India Company were by no means convinced that his liberal policy was calculated to produce the largest dividends. He was consequently removed in 1644.

Even after Portugal revolted against Spain and became an ally of Holland, the States General continued to support the aggression of the West India Company in Brazil. The government at Lisbon was too weak and too much in need of Dutch help at home to resist, and it did not dare to aid the colonists openly when the Brazilians themselves resumed the war after Nassau's removal. Nevertheless the people of Maranhão were able to expel the Dutch from their province in 1644. The next year there was an insurrection in Pernambuco, led by João Fernandes Vieira, a rich merchant who had fought against the Dutch until the fall of the Arraial do Bom Jesus, but had later become one of Nassau's chief advisers. The war dragged on with varying fortunes for eight years. Though the Dutch were too busy with enemies in Europe to send large forces across the Atlantic, the Brazilians, in spite of victories in the field, were unable to take the enemy stronghold at Recife. Gradually the Portuguese government, which had secretly encouraged the revolt, grew somewhat bolder, and in 1649 it created the *Companhia Geral do Commercio do Brasil*, for the dual purpose of establishing a convoy system to protect Brazilian trade and assisting in the recovery of the invaded provinces. In 1654 the Company's fleet supported the colonists in a successful attack on Recife and the war was brought to

an end. It was not until 1661, however, that the Dutch formally abandoned their claim to Brazil in return for money indemnities and trade
privileges.

Progress and Territorial Expansion, 1654–1700

The protracted struggle against the Dutch had caused much destruction of life and property in northern Brazil, but it had hardly affected
the provinces that remained under Portuguese control. After the war
there was a period of rapid development, and so many immigrants
came from Portugal that the home government was concerned lest its
European territory be depopulated. The growing importance of the
settlements was recognized by the establishment of bishoprics at
Maranhão, Rio de Janeiro, and Pernambuco, while the See of Bahia
became an archbishopric. The rapid increase in wealth and perhaps also
the stimulating effect of contact with the Dutch were bringing about
a change in the intellectual and social life of the colonies. Education
had hitherto been neglected, except for the primary schools under the
Jesuits and the courses given rather irregularly for the training of priests,
but in the latter part of the seventeenth century a number of young
Brazilians went to Portugal to study at the University of Coimbra.

On the plateau of São Paulo, where sugar cane did not flourish as
it did on the coast, the inhabitants continued to lead their rude, wild
life. *Bandeiras* were still exploring the far interior and during the period
of the Dutch war the Paulistas began the conquest and settlement of the
provinces southward along the coast, adding to Brazilian territory a
fertile area with a temperate climate which is one of the important
portions of the country today. After they had penetrated into Rio
Grande do Sul, with its wealth of wild cattle, Portugal attempted to
assure her possession of the entire region as far as the River Plate by
establishing a military post at Colonia do Sacramento in 1680. The garrison was at once attacked and expelled by forces from Buenos Aires,
just across the river, but Portugal protested to Spain and an agreement
was reached through the mediation of England, France, and the Pope
by which the place was returned to Portugal pending an investigation
to determine the exact location of the boundary fixed by the treaty of
Tordesillas. The line in reality passed far to the east of the River Plate,
but though Colonia was repeatedly captured by the Spanish in time of

war, it was as often returned when peace was made and remained in Portuguese hands for nearly a century. The post did not give Portugal the hoped-for control of the rich country north of the River Plate estuary, which was gradually occupied during the eighteenth century by Spanish settlements, but it was important as a base for the smuggling trade with Peru.

The northern state of Maranhão also grew more prosperous in the second half of the seventeenth century in spite of a series of disturbances provoked by the efforts of the Jesuits to protect the Indians. The planters in this region still depended chiefly on native rather than Negro labor. Many of them had obtained control of villages of peaceful natives under conditions not unlike the Spanish *encomienda* in its worst days. Others had enslaved Indians by purchase or fraud or had taken them in forays on the wild tribes. There was constant warfare on the borders of the settlements, and the same abuses flourished that had been practised a little earlier in the south.

The most determined defender of the Indians was Father Antonio Vieira, the Superior of the Jesuit order, who was one of the most distinguished Portuguese writers and statesmen of his time. In 1655 Vieira obtained from the Crown full authority to control Indian relations in Brazil, and he proceeded energetically to free those who were illegally in bondage in Maranhão and to establish missions where the natives would be protected from the colonists. His activities aroused violent opposition, and in 1661 the settlers at Pará seized him and shipped him off to Lisbon. Soon afterward, he fell from favor at court, but in 1680 he was able to persuade the King to enact a law forbidding the enslavement of Indians in Maranhão. Two years later, in order to encourage the importation of Negroes, a chartered company was granted a monopoly of the chief branches of trade in the northern provinces. These measures brought on another revolt, under the leadership of one Manoel Beckman, who seized control of the district around São Luiz and expelled both the Jesuits and the representatives of the Maranhão Company. The movement soon collapsed, as such movements usually did in colonial Brazil, because many of the participants lost interest after the first outburst of indignation. Beckman was executed, and the Jesuits were reinstated. On the other hand, the privileges of the commercial company were restricted, and the laws for the protection of the Indians were not enforced.

Discovery of Gold and Diamonds, 1695–1729

There was tremendous excitement in 1695 when two Paulista explorers discovered rich gold deposits in what is now the State of Minas Geraes. The new source of wealth was all the more welcome because the sugar industry, which had created many great fortunes in Brazil, was beginning to feel the effects of competition from the newer English and French plantations in the West Indies. Many thousands of persons abandoned the older settlements, taking their slaves with them, and other thousands came from Portugal. These immigrants from Europe—the *Emboabas*, as the Brazilians called them—were soon engaged in a bloody contest with the Paulistas who considered the mines theirs by right of discovery. The newcomers were better led and better organized, and their chief, Nunes Viana, was for a time virtually the ruler of the mining district. Even the governor was at first refused permission to enter the district, and it was some time before the royal officials were able to assert their authority and to restore a semblance of order.

The Paulistas were somewhat consoled for their defeat in Minas Geraes when they discovered other rich gold mines in Matto Grosso in 1719 and in Goyaz in 1725. Still more important was the finding of diamonds in 1729 in the gold washings along some of the tributaries of the São Francisco River. The influx of population into the mining regions continued on a scale that seemed to threaten the depopulation of the agricultural districts of the coast, and great cities arose where there had been no inhabitants a few years before.

As in the Spanish colonies, the law required that one-fifth of all gold and silver extracted be paid to the king, but it was so difficult to collect these royalties in the early days of the gold rush that the Crown agreed to accept a relatively small lump-sum payment from the miners' organization. Later, the regular tax on gold was imposed for a time, but in 1735 it was replaced by a head tax on slaves employed in the mines. This was less easily evaded, but it encouraged wasteful methods of exploitation, so that many of the richer placer deposits were exhausted before the end of the eighteenth century. The collection of the royalty on diamonds was still more difficult because the precious stones were so easily concealed. A head tax on slaves was therefore imposed in the diamond washings also, and this was gradually increased to an exorbitant amount in an effort to check the sharp drop in prices that had occurred when Brazilian stones began to flood the world's markets. In 1771 the government itself took over the control of production and excluded from the diamond district practically every one but its own officials and workmen.

The Government of Brazil, 1649–1750

Compared with the elaborate if not always efficient political machinery of the Spanish colonies, the government of colonial Brazil was a haphazard affair. In Portugal, the king was an absolute monarch. He was assisted by various boards such as the Privy Council, the Inspectors of Finance, and the *Mesa da Consciencia e Ordens*, in charge of ecclesiastical matters; but there was little plan or coördination in the governmental structure. Confusion inevitably resulted when the authority of each board in its own sphere was simply extended to colonial matters. There was no central organization responsible for affairs in Brazil until the period of Spanish domination. A Council of India, later called the Council of Ultramar, was set up in 1604, but it never attained the prestige and authority of its counterpart at Madrid. Its powers were restricted, especially in financial matters, and the king and other high officials frequently disregarded it.

There was also little effective centralization of authority in Brazil. The Crown's representative at Bahia, whose title varied but who was usually a governor general between 1601 and 1714 and a viceroy thereafter, was nominally the head of the colonial administration, but inadequate means of communication made it difficult for him to exercise authority in the other captaincies. This was especially true of the northern provinces, and these, as we have seen, were made a separate "state" after 1621. Even in places like São Paulo and Rio de Janeiro the local governors usually received their orders directly from Lisbon and dealt with their own problems with little reference to their nominal superior at Bahia. In the absence of any effective control from outside, they tended to be corrupt and oppressive, and they often monopolized the most lucrative branches of commerce for their personal benefit. Their authority, however, was frequently defied by the lawless colonists or by the local clergy. The Crown never supported its representatives in Brazil with any adequate force of regular troops, and the undisciplined local militia might take either side when dissensions arose. Several instances have already been noted where unpopular measures, like laws for the protection of the Indians, had to be abandoned because of local resistance.

Thomé de Souza, when he went to Brazil in 1549, took with him a *provedor mór*, or superintendent of finances, and an *ouvidor geral*, or chief judge. The departments headed by these two officers continued to be the most important branches of the civil administration. The principal revenues of the Crown were the customs duties, the product of royal monopolies like the trade in brazil-wood, the royal fifth on metals and precious stones, and the tithes, which were paid to the civil authorities as they were in the Spanish colonies, although the proceeds were supposedly destined for the support of the Church. Though the actual collection of the taxes was usually farmed out to contractors, leading to many abuses, the burden of taxation does not seem to have been intolerable. The heirs of the original donatories were entitled to receive certain dues from the colonists, even after they had been deprived of political authority, but these privileges were gradually extinguished by purchase or confiscation in the eighteenth century.

The administration of justice was one of the weakest points of the colonial administration. Only minor offenses and disputes were tried by municipal judges named by the local authorities or by *ouvidores*, sent out from Lisbon. Even the *ouvidor geral*, for a long time the highest judicial authority in the colony, did not have final jurisdiction in civil suits when the amount involved exceeded about $300, and he could not inflict the death penalty or other severe punishment except on persons of the lowest rank. All important cases must therefore go to Lisbon for trial, an arrangement which involved intolerable inconvenience and caused many crimes to go unpunished. In 1588 the Crown tried to establish a court of more ample jurisdiction, but the galleon carrying the judges failed to reach Bahia, apparently simply because of poor seamanship, and returned to Lisbon more than a year later. A *Relação*, or high court of justice, was finally set up in Bahia in 1609, but it was abolished in 1626 to save money for the war against the Dutch and was not reëstablished until 1652. It seems to have been a doubtful blessing even to the people of Bahia, for many lawyers came to Brazil with it and litigation greatly increased. The inhabitants of some of the other captaincies found it less convenient to have important cases tried in Bahia than in Portugal, where many of the richer colonists had agents and business connections.

Official corruption and inefficiency were at least as prevalent as in the Spanish possessions. The governors and other officials were in fact apparently permitted to augment their salary by private business ventures until 1673, when a royal order forbade them to engage in trade, to establish monopolies for their own profit, or to bid for tax collection contracts. There were many frauds in connection with the royal revenue and the judges were notoriously venal. Many officials were also ignorant and incompetent, for the general level of education among the upper classes and the standards in the public service in Portugal were inferior to those in Spain. The very weakness of the governmental organization, however, was perhaps a benefit, for local initiative was given freer play than in most of the Spanish colonies.

Theoretically natives of the colony were eligible to any office, and a royal order issued late in the seventeenth century, which was perhaps not much observed in practice, provided that they be given preference in making appointments to positions in Brazil. The more lucrative and important posts, however, usually went to Portuguese who had influence at court, and others, especially in the courts of justice, required a training at the University of Coimbra, which few Brazilians could obtain. Offices were filled by royal appointment rather than by sale, and it was sometimes difficult, at least during the first century of the colonial period, to persuade or compel Portuguese officials to accept posts in Brazil.

Each city with its surrounding territory had its own *Senado da Camara*, or municipal council. In most cases *vereadores*, or aldermen, were chosen theoretically either by the principal inhabitants or by their own predecessors. In practice the elections were frequently controlled by the governors, and after 1696 the members of the council were simply appointed in some of the most important cities. Nevertheless, the *Senado da Camara*, usually composed of influential native landowners, was a very important branch of the government, especially during the first two centuries of the colonial period. From motives of economy, the Crown entrusted to these bodies many functions which might more appropriately have been performed by royal officials, and in the absence of any institution like the *audiencia* of the Spanish colonies they alone provided continuity in the administrative organization. Their influence was increased by the fact that the governors and other representatives of the Crown usually served only three years and were consequently dependent upon the councilors for advice and information. When there was a vacancy in the governor's office, the *Senado da Camara* often chose a temporary incumbent or itself assumed control. In many cases it defied the governor's authority to the point of open rebellion, and *procuradores,* or representatives of the towns, were frequently sent to Lisbon to petition the king for legislation desired by the colonists or to complain of the conduct of obnoxious officials.

The Church

The Church was less influential than in Spanish America. It was equally subject to the royal authority, for the king, in his capacity as Grand Master of the Order of Christ, had full control of the patronage, but the Portuguese monarchs showed less concern for the spiritual welfare of their colonies. Many suspected heretics were sent to Brazil as settlers, and even non-Catholic foreigners were not completely excluded from residence and trade. Backsliding "new Christians" or other heretics were occasionally burned in Brazil or sent to Portugal for trial, but no council of the Inquisition was established in the colony.

The Jesuit order was the richest and most powerful branch of the Church. Its most important work was the conversion and protection of the Indians. There were thousands of these in the mission villages, and the fathers sometimes took the lead in making war on heathen tribes to increase the number of their neophytes. Unlike the principal missions in the Spanish colonies many of these villages were founded near the Portuguese settlements, and their inhabitants traded with the Europeans or worked for them under the supervision of the priests. The Jesuits were supported by the Crown, and sometimes by the officials in Brazil, but they were constantly in conflict with the settlers and the municipal councils over the Indian question, and they consequently had less influence with the people of European descent than in the Spanish colonies.

Some of the other religious orders had large plantations and other property, but the Church as a whole was poor. Even the principal bishops had revenues that seem insignificant compared with those of prelates in the Spanish colonies, and the salaries of the parish priests' were too small to be attractive to men of ability or high social position. Nevertheless, religious observances and the celebration of church festivals occupied much of the colonists' time, and such education as their children received was obtained from the Jesuits or other members of the clergy. There were already sixty-two churches and three monasteries in the Bahia district in 1581.[1]

Commercial Policy

Portugal's commercial policy was directed chiefly toward increasing the government's revenues and obtaining benefits for privileged interests in the mother country. Royal monopolies controlled the trade in brazil-wood and to a less extent the trade in tobacco. The cultivation of grapes, olives, and mulberries, which might have competed with industries in the mother country, was forbidden, and all sugar must be sent to Portugal to be refined. The making of salt, which could easily be obtained by evaporating sea water, was prohibited in 1690 for the benefit of a contractor who was given the exclusive privilege of exporting that commodity from Portugal to Brazil. There were many other vexatious regulations and restrictions of similar character, and even those adopted for the purpose of stimulating production in the colony were too often harmful rather than helpful. Fortunately for the Brazilians such legislation was frequently not enforced.

In some respects, however, Portuguese policy was at first comparatively liberal. Before 1649, any Portuguese ship was free to go to Brazilian ports, and even foreigners were permitted to engage in commerce and agriculture until after the union with Spain in 1580, though they were subject to taxes and restrictions from which Portuguese traders were exempt. Dutch firms carried on much trade with Pernambuco and had factories and plantations in São Vicente and São Paulo. These connections were broken off when the Spanish kings enforced a more exclusive system, and the result was an increase of smuggling and piracy which finally made it necessary for the Portuguese government, like the Spanish, to adopt a convoy system.

We have already seen how the *Companhia Geral do Commercio do Brasil* was established in 1649 for the double purpose of protecting trade and aiding in the expulsion of the Dutch. The Company's capital was obtained partly by promising that money invested in it by "new Christians" would be exempt from seizure by the Inquisition. It undertook to send two well-armed fleets to America yearly, and these were to have a monopoly of the transportation of goods between Portugal and Brazil. At first it enjoyed a monopoly for the sale of the most im-

[1] Southey, *History of Brazil*, Vol. I, p. 318.

portant staple imports—codfish, wheat flour, oil, and wine—but this was discontinued because of loud complaints from the colonists. The Company rendered a useful service in its first years, but its privileges soon made it unpopular. It came more and more under the control of the royal government, and was dissolved in 1720. The fleet system, however, was continued. The Maranhão Company, also mentioned previously, was no more successful. It was badly managed and continued to be extremely unpopular after the suppression of Beckman's revolt.

The effort to exclude other powers from Brazilian trade broke down for a time after the separation from Spain, because Portugal was too weak to refuse the demands of the Dutch and English governments for commercial privileges. These concessions, however, were gradually made worthless by a systematic discrimination against foreigners, and in the early part of the eighteenth century Brazil was as effectively closed to non-Portuguese commerce as were the Spanish possessions. The Dutch were no longer strong enough to exact special treatment, and England, which had by this time become Portugal's ally and protector, had less need to trade directly with Brazil because the Methuen Treaty of 1703 gave her virtual control of the commerce of the mother country itself. Goods and even ships that came to Brazil were made in England and sent out for the account of English merchants, and a large part of the colony's exports went to pay for them.

Foreign Aggression and Internal Disorder, 1700–1750

It was the protection afforded by the British alliance that enabled Portugal to hold what was left of her once great colonial empire. She was by this time one of the weakest of the European kingdoms. The revenues that she received from Brazil were far less than they might have been if the newly discovered mines had been more efficiently administered, and little or none of this income was spent to promote the welfare of Brazil or even to defend the colony against foreign enemies. The result of this neglect was evident during the War of the Spanish Succession, when French expeditions twice attacked Rio de Janeiro. The first one, in 1710, was driven off by the inhabitants after several public buildings had been burned, but the second a year later took and sacked the town.

The colonial government's incompetence was also manifested by events that occurred at about the same time in Pernambuco. Olinda, the capital of this province and the home of the more important native families, had been built by Duarte Coelho on high ground at some distance from the place where ships customarily anchored, and many merchants had therefore established themselves at Recife, the "reef," which was more convenient to the port. Though this settlement had grown rapidly during and after the Dutch wars, it remained a part of the municipality of Olinda and its inhabitants, most of them Portuguese immigrants, were excluded from any share in the local government. The *Mascates*, or peddlers, as the Brazilians derisively called these newcomers, had therefore persuaded the Crown in 1710 to make Recife a separate city. This led to violent quarrels. When the governor attempted to arrest some of the more obstreperous native leaders, the people of Olinda expelled him from the province, and both sides took up arms. There was a year of savage fighting before a new governor restored order by promising amnesty to both parties. Recife, generally called Pernambuco by English-speaking people, continued to grow in importance, and has now far out-stripped its one-time rival.

The Reforms of the Marquis of Pombal

Between 1750 and 1777, the decline of Portugal was temporarily arrested under the vigorous administration of the Marquis of Pombal, the great minister of King José I. In the colonial sphere the most important change was the unification of Brazil, including Maranhão, under a viceroy who had real authority over the provincial governors. If this measure had not been adopted, there might well be several nations of Portuguese origin in America today instead of one. The capital of the colony was moved in 1763 to Rio de Janeiro which was by that time the chief city and the port through which the product of the gold and diamond mines reached the outside world. The administration of the finances and of justice were improved, and official corruption was to some extent reduced. Pombal also promoted efficiency by ending the practice of appointing governors and other officials for terms of only three years, a limitation that had often deprived the Crown of the services of competent men just when they were becoming most useful.

The Marquis was less successful in his commercial policy. In an effort to retain for Portugal part of the profits that British merchants were making from the colonial trade, he created two privileged companies, one in Pará and Maranhão and the other in Pernambuco and

Parahyba. The former seems to have encouraged the economic development of the northern provinces, but the Pernambuco Company was oppressive and unpopular, and both were dissolved when Pombal fell from power in 1777. On the other hand, the abolition of the fleet system in 1765 was a long step toward a greater freedom of trade. Another step that benefited the colonies was the final extinction, by purchase or confiscation, of the proprietary rights of the sixteenth-century donatories.

The Indians were legally freed from all forms of tutelage in Maranhão in 1755 and in the rest of Brazil in 1758. This reform was directed especially against the Jesuits, who were Pombal's most influential enemies in Portugal. The Prime Minister had been especially indignant when the Jesuits' converts in Paraguay forcibly resisted the execution of the treaty of 1750 by which Portugal was to have received the mission territory east of the Uruguay River. The dissolution of the Brazilian missions made the feud still more bitter, and in 1759 Pombal persuaded the King to banish the Jesuits altogether, both from Portugal and from her colonies. This action was followed by similar measures against the Jesuits in Spain and other European countries. The Indians from this time on theoretically enjoyed the same rights as the Crown's other subjects, but the change in their legal status by no means ended their exploitation. Early in the nineteenth century, in fact, after the royal family had come to Brazil, a decree was issued permitting the practical enslavement for a term of years of Indians who revolted against the Portuguese authorities. This opened the door for widespread abuses, especially as many of the Indians hitherto leading a peaceful life in the Jesuit missions had reverted to savagery and had occasionally committed depredations against the Portuguese settlements. The number of Indians in Brazil, however, was by this time insignificant as compared with the other elements in the population, and during the nineteenth century the aboriginal stock almost disappeared in the more settled parts of the country.

At the End of the Colonial Period

As the end of the colonial period approached, Brazil's population was probably from 3,000,000 to 3,500,000, of whom two-fifths were Negro slaves. Rio de Janeiro, with a population of more than 100,000, was second only to Mexico among the cities of the Western Hemisphere. The gold mines had lost much of their importance, but sugar was again a profitable crop, especially after the rich plantations of French St. Domingue were destroyed by a slave revolt. Intellectually, however, Brazil was still more backward than the Spanish American possessions, for there was not a single printing press in the country and the government made the importation of any but religious books almost impossible. For nearly a century, since a policy of rigid exclusion had succeeded to the comparative liberality of earlier times, the colonists had had little contact with foreigners. In the mines and on the sugar plantations the most primitive methods and techniques were still practised, and there were few of the inhabitants who had any conception of the material advances that had been made during the past century in other parts of the world.

An increasing number of the richer Brazilians, however, were going abroad to study at Coimbra and other European centers of learning, and some of them came home with new ideas and points of view. There were signs of an intellectual awakening like that which was taking place at Mexico City and Bogotá. Several Brazilians achieved distinctions as writers or scientists during the latter part of the eighteenth century. Especially notable was the appearance at Ouro Preto, the capital of the mining district, of a group of young poets, some of whom, like Claudio Manoel da Costa, Gonzaga, and Alvarenga Peixoto, were "counted among the most illustrious of the Portuguese tongue." [1]

Several of the Minas poets were involved in the famous conspiracy of 1789, which was a movement for independence. The leaders in this were a small group of theorists who were inspired by French and North American revolutionary ideas, but they were supported by some of the miners in the province who resented an attempt by the government to collect a large amount of back royalties on their operations. Unfortunately for the conspirators, their plans were betrayed before they were ready for action and the whole movement came to nothing. The principal leader, a young army officer best known by his nickname of Tiradentes, was executed and several of the other participants were exiled to Africa.

The Minas conspiracy, unimportant in itself, was new evidence of the same spirit which had found expression in Beckman's revolt and the war against the *Mascates* in Pernambuco. The Brazilians, with their long tradition of resistance to despotic authority and with the spirit of

[1] M. Oliveira Lima, *Formation Historique de la Nationalité Brésilienne*, p. 123.

self-confidence which they had never lost since the time when they expelled the Dutch from their territory, were clearly not likely to remain indefinitely subject to a mother country which they were rapidly outstripping in wealth and population. Early in the nineteenth century a series of fortuitous events were to give them their independence without the long struggle that was required for the emancipation of their Spanish American neighbors.

14

Brazil—The Empire and the Republic

The Royal Family in Brazil

When Napoleon's army invaded Portugal in 1807, Prince Regent João and his court escaped to Brazil under convoy of British warships. His arrival at Rio de Janeiro early in 1808 made that city the temporary capital of the Portuguese Empire. The advantages of the change were soon apparent, for a military school, a medical school, and a national bank were established, a newspaper was published, and the royal library of 60,000 volumes was thrown open to the public. Many foreigners began to visit Brazil, and the Prince Regent invited several French artists and scientists to make their home there. Rio de Janeiro and other ports were opened to the trade of all friendly nations, and goods of foreign manufacture began to replace the home-made articles which even wealthy families had hitherto been compelled to use. The lion's share of the new trade went to British merchants, who were given tariff preferences in a treaty signed in 1810.

The presence of the royal family averted any strong movement for Brazilian independence during the period when other South American nations were revolting against Spain. The Prince Regent, who became King João VI on the death of his insane mother in 1816, was easy-going to the point of irresponsibility, but he had many statesmanlike qualities. Compared with the colonial regime, his government was enlightened and progressive, and his popularity was increased by an aggressive foreign policy. While his notoriously unfaithful wife Carlota Joaquina was intriguing to obtain a throne for herself in the revolted Spanish colonies, his own forces occupied French Guiana in the north and the *Banda Oriental* in the south. The former province was given up under pressure from the powers at the Congress of Vienna, but the latter, conquered between 1816 and 1820, continued to be a province of Brazil until 1828.

The presence of the court entailed some disadvantages. The Brazilians now had to support not only the royal family but great numbers of the exiled nobility and thousands of Portuguese hangers-on, and the arrogance of the newcomers intensified the already existing hostility between natives and Portuguese. In Rio de Janeiro, pride at being the capital and a lavish distribution of honors and titles did much to offset these causes of irritation, but elsewhere there was more discontent. In Pernambuco, where there had always been a strong spirit of local patriotism, a group that sought to set up a republic worked secretly for three years before the discovery of their plans forced them into open revolt in 1817. The movement met with little support outside of the province, and it lost many of its adherents in Pernambuco when the republican leaders advocated radical ideas that alarmed the land-owning class. It was soon suppressed and many of the participants were executed.

João became deeply attached to his new home and refused to return to Europe after Napoleon was overthrown. His continued absence, and the commercial stagnation that followed the abolition of the colonial trade monopoly, caused much dissatisfaction in Portugal. At the same time liberal propaganda had affected the army there as it had in Spain. In 1820, after the Spanish revolution, a similar movement took place in Lisbon and Oporto, and rebellious army leaders convoked a Cortes to frame a constitution. The revolutionists had many supporters in Brazil, especially among the officers of the "auxiliary division" which had been brought from Europe after the Pernambuco revolt, and on February 26, 1821, a military demonstration forced the King to promise to accept whatever constitution the Cortes might adopt and to appoint a ministry satisfactory to the leaders of the troops.

Many Brazilians at first sympathized with the liberal movement but their enthusiasm diminished as the real aims of the Portuguese revolutionists became apparent. One of the early acts of the Cortes was to publish a manifesto attributing all of the misfortunes of the kingdom to the absence of the Court and the opening of Brazilian ports to the commerce of other nations. This became known in Brazil a few days after the demonstration of February 26, and the native leaders' alarm was intensified when the King reluctantly yielded to the pressure of his Portuguese advisers and announced his intention of returning to Lisbon.

On April 20, 1821, apparently hoping to obtain support in reversing this decision, João called a meeting of the parish electors who had been chosen in Rio de Janeiro as one of the first steps in the complicated process of selecting deputies to the Cortes. The electors not only insisted that the King remain, but also obtained from him a decree promising to put into effect at once a constitution like that of Spain. This document, as several historians have remarked, had probably never been read either by the King or by the electors, but the latter thought that its adoption would forestall the formulation by the Cortes of a constitution containing provisions harmful to Brazil. The King's action had barely been made known, however, when the Portuguese troops brutally attacked and dispersed the electors' meeting, and João was compelled to abrogate his decree. On April 26 he embarked for Portugal. His son, Pedro, who was suspected of having instigated the action of the Portuguese faction because he wished to be left to rule Brazil himself, was made Regent. Before sailing, João told Pedro that Brazil might soon become an independent nation and exhorted him to seize the Crown if this should occur.

Independence

João's parting counsel showed a clear perception of the political forces that were at work both in Portugal and in Brazil. The Cortes at Lisbon, obsessed with a desire to restore the old colonial relationship, was as blind to realities as the Spanish Cortes had been ten years before. The young regent gave every evidence of a sincere desire to discharge his duties as his father's representative, but in April, 1821, the Cortes destroyed his authority in the greater part of Brazil by inviting the people of each district to form provincial *juntas* corresponding directly with itself. The refusal of these bodies to remit the public revenues to Rio de Janeiro crippled the treasury, and matters became worse when the incompetently and dishonestly managed national bank was compelled to suspend specie payments. On September 29, the Cortes decreed the abolition of the principal administrative and judicial tribunals that had been established at Rio de Janeiro during the residence of the Court. At the same time, it ordered Pedro himself to return to Portugal, traveling first through England, France, and Spain "to complete his political education." Later it voted to appoint a governor in each province who should receive his orders directly from Lisbon, and decided to send additional troops to Brazil to enforce these decrees.

In Brazil these proceedings aroused increasing indignation. For the first time, political affairs were being discussed freely and publicly, especially in the numerous newspapers that had sprung up since the advent of constitutional government, and the native leaders, who were determined to prevent what they called "recolonization," decided that separation from Portugal was the only alternative. Among these were not only the liberals but also many conservatives who distrusted the radicalism of the Cortes and feared that Pedro's leaving Brazil would result in anarchy. The clergy, most of whom were Brazilians, also supported the movement. The desire to obtain the help of these royalist groups, and the feeling that the maintenance of the dynasty offered the only hope of curbing the separatist tendencies that were already manifesting themselves in the provinces, led even those who would have preferred a republic to center their efforts on persuading the Prince to take the lead in making Brazil independent. They were encouraged to hope for success because Pedro, like many of the radical leaders, was a Mason.

The Portuguese party was still strong. Several thousand nobles and merchants had left since the King's departure, but the troops of the "auxiliary division" were still stationed at Rio de Janeiro and Bahia. A part of the well-disciplined army trained by British officers during the peninsular war, these forces had an influence out of all proportion to their numerical strength. At Bahia, the commander, supported by the Portuguese merchants resident in the city, openly refused to recognize Pedro's authority. At Rio de Janeiro a demonstration staged by the garrison in June, 1821, compelled Pedro to swear allegiance to the constitutional regime in Portugal and to dismiss his chief minister, who had aroused the officers' distrust.

The advocates of independence nevertheless soon gained the upper hand. When the Cortes ordered Pedro to return to Europe the provincial *junta* of São Paulo presented an eloquent memorial urging him to defy the Cortes, and another of like tenor bearing 8,000 signatures was laid before the Prince by the president of the municipal council of Rio de Janeiro. Impressed by this evidence of popular support, Pedro publicly declared on January 9, 1822, that he would remain in Brazil. The Portuguese troops were intimidated by the resolute attitude of a great concourse of townspeople and were finally prevailed upon to embark for Portugal after receiving their pay for three months in advance. A few weeks later, when a Portuguese fleet came to carry Pedro back to Lisbon, it was not permitted to enter the harbor until the commander had agreed to comply with Pedro's orders.

A new ministry was appointed at Rio de Janeiro and José Bonifacio de Andrada, the president of the provincial *junta* at São Paulo, became Pedro's chief adviser. José Bonifacio [1] was perhaps the most notable Brazilian of his time. Born at Santos in 1763, he had attended the University of Coimbra and had traveled in several European countries studying mineralogy and metallurgy with the great authorities of the day. He afterward held important official positions at Lisbon and fought at the head of a group of students against the French when they invaded Portugal in 1807. In 1819, he returned to Brazil. With the aid of his two brothers, Martim Francisco and Antonio Carlos, he soon became the chief political leader in São Paulo. He was now to play a leading rôle in the political affairs of Brazil during one of the critical periods of the country's history.

Pedro's refusal to obey the Cortes' command to leave Brazil made a final break merely a question of time. Though his authority was respected only in the southern provinces—Rio de Janeiro, Minas Geraes, São Paulo, and Rio Grande do Sul—and none of the others responded when the new ministry convened a council of *procuradores*, or representatives of the people, in February, 1822, he assumed the title of Perpetual Protector and Defender of Brazil on May 13, and, on June 3, issued a call for a constituent assembly. On September 7, 1822, while Pedro was visiting the Province of São Paulo, he received despatches which convinced him that the moment for a final decision had arrived. Drawing his sword, he dramatically cried "Independence or Death"— the *Grito de Ypiranga* which has ever since been commemorated as the Brazilian declaration of independence. His action was enthusiastically acclaimed in São Paulo and Rio de Janeiro, and on October 12 Pedro was solemnly proclaimed constitutional Emperor of Brazil. Portuguese residents were given the alternative of accepting the new regime or leaving the country.

Under the energetic leadership of José Bonifacio, the imperial government rapidly extended its control over the provinces still in the

---

[1] In Brazil Christian names, without the family name, are often used in speaking of well-known persons.

hands of the Portuguese. Lord Cochrane, who had left Peru after his quarrel with San Martín, was employed to organize a navy, and other officers and seamen were brought out from England under contract. In July, 1823, forces sent by land and sea forced the Portuguese to evacuate Bahia, and by September the provinces north of Cape San Roque, which had been in a state of near anarchy since 1820, submitted to Cochrane's fleet. The Portuguese commander at Montevideo soon afterward surrendered. The Cortes was no longer in a position to support its adherents, for it had itself been swept away by a counter revolution.

The Reign of Pedro I

The Andrada cabinet was less successful in dealing with internal questions. José Bonifacio was tactless and arbitrary in his treatment of political opponents, and was accused of using his position to persecute personal enemies. His attacks on the freedom of the press, and the establishment of an extensive system of political espionage, increased his unpopularity. Even the Masonic lodges, in which the Andradas had hitherto been prominent, were closed when their members ventured to criticize the government's actions. The Emperor, who was himself perhaps somewhat jealous of his minister's great prestige and authority, was finally persuaded to dismiss him in July, 1823. The Andradas at once aligned themselves with the liberal opposition in the Constituent Assembly. This body, which had been in session since April, had already shown a disposition to oppose Pedro's views, and its antagonism to the Crown now became more evident. On November 12 Pedro dissolved it by armed force and deported the three Andrada brothers to France.

Pedro now entrusted the task of framing the constitution to a commission of ten members named by himself. The new code, which was to remain in force until the advent of the Republic in 1889, guaranteed personal liberty and freedom of the press, and abolished all privileges of rank and caste. There was to be a chamber of deputies elected for four years, and a senate chosen by the Emperor from lists submitted by the electoral colleges and holding office for life. A measure of self-government was granted to the provinces and municipalities. On the whole the constitution was a liberal one by comparison with those of other monarchical states and also by comparison with that which had been under consideration by the recently disbanded Assembly. It was formally sworn to by the Emperor on March 25, 1824, after it had been submitted to the municipal councils throughout the country for approval.

The dissolution of the Constituent Assembly caused renewed agitation in Pernambuco, and in 1824 the liberals there proclaimed the establishment of a republic called the "Confederation of the Equator." This was to have included all northern Brazil, but the movement received little support in the neighboring provinces. A reaction soon occurred in Pernambuco itself, and after Pedro's forces occupied Recife, with the aid of Cochrane's fleet, other places that had revolted were soon reduced. This campaign marked the end of Cochrane's career in South America. He had had a dispute with his employers over the disposition of prizes taken in his earlier operations, and he now proceeded to settle his account with the imperial government by seizing Maranhão, where he took about $100,000 from the custom-house. He then sailed away to England on one of Pedro's vessels.

The revolt of the Spanish-speaking inhabitants of the *Banda Oriental*, which began in April, 1825, was a more serious affair, for it involved Brazil in a war with Argentina that dragged on for three years before it was finally ended by British mediation. The conflict reflected little credit on the incompetently led imperial army and navy. Aside from the permanent loss of the Cisplatine province, its chief result so far as Brazil was concerned was the impoverishment of the treasury and a decrease in the prestige of the imperial government.

The outcome of the war was one of a number of factors which by 1828 had destroyed Pedro's one-time popularity. The chief cause of discontent was the feeling that his government had never been truly Brazilian. The Emperor was still surrounded by Portuguese advisers and army officers, who had remained in Brazil from personal loyalty or from other motives, and the few natives whom he took into his confidence were for the most part conservatives and ultra-royalist members of the newly created nobility who had little political following. There had been much criticism of an agreement negotiated through British mediation in 1825 by which Pedro assumed part of the Portuguese debt in return for the mother country's recognition of Brazil's independence, and the Brazilians had disliked his preoccupation with efforts to have his daughter Maria da Gloria recognized as Queen of Portugal after João's death in 1826. To make matters worse, Pedro's personal conduct was undignified to the point of vulgarity. Even the far from puritanical Brazilians were shocked by his treatment of his wife and the influence which his mistress, the Marchioness of Santos, was permitted to exercise in public affairs. All of these matters were discussed passionately and often scurrilously in the newspapers, for the government had by this time relaxed its restrictions on the press. By far the most important of the opposition papers was the *Aurora Fluminense*, founded in 1827 by Evaristo Ferreira da Veiga, who was one of the leaders in the liberal movement.

Despite the constitution, Pedro continued to rule almost as though he were an absolute monarch. The first meeting of the legislative chambers was delayed on various pretexts until 1826, and though regular sessions were held thereafter the views of the people's representatives received little consideration. The deputies were at first too much in awe of the imperial authority to assert their prerogatives effectively, but they grew bolder as the government's difficulties increased and the majority was openly critical and unfriendly in the sessions of 1827, 1828, and 1829.

When the term of the first deputies expired and a new Chamber met in May, 1830, it was clear that a crisis was at hand. The greater number of the new members were frankly hostile to the Emperor and his advisers, for the technique of controlled elections, by which the government in later times always obtained a majority, had not yet been developed. Pedro made some concessions that merely encouraged his adversaries, and the news of the July revolution in Paris helped to arouse the liberals' enthusiasm. There was an outburst of popular indignation when a radical Italian journalist named Badaró was murdered at São Paulo in November, supposedly by order of the imperial judge. The Emperor made a belated effort to placate public opinion by appointing a cabinet of native Brazilians, and then in April, 1831, committed the final error of replacing these ministers by members of his own immediate circle. A mob gathered to demand that the former cabinet be reinstated, and many of the troops whose officers had been won over by the radical leaders joined in the movement. Pedro at first refused to yield, but on the early morning of April 7 he suddenly signed an abdication in favor of his five-year-old son, Pedro de Alcantara, and named José Bonifacio de Andrada as his children's guardian. Immediately afterward he embarked for Europe on a British warship. Those members of the parliament who happened to be in the capital elected a regency of three members to rule in the name of the new Emperor during his minority.

The Regency

The leaders who assumed control faced a formidable task, made harder by political inexperience, local jealousies, and the tradition of corrupt and despotic administration. The inhabitants of the Empire were scattered over an area far greater than that of any of the other South American countries, and there were several of the provincial cities that were almost as important as the capital. The people were perhaps even less prepared for constitutional government than their Spanish-speaking neighbors. Few even among the upper class had more than the barest rudiments of an education. Half of the population were Negroes, for the most part slaves, and a large proportion of the other half were persons of mixed blood who had until very recently been treated by the law as an inferior caste, subject to various political and social restrictions. In the larger cities, the visits of foreigners and the increase of commercial contacts with the outside world were already modifying colonial customs and points of view, but in the country the change was less apparent. The owners of the great plantations were often petty despots. Not only their own slaves but also the free people of the neighborhood looked to them for support and protection, and it was from among them that the government usually appointed the *capitão mór*, who was its representative in each rural district. It was this class which exercised the preponderant influence in political affairs in the nation as a whole.

The nine years that followed the revolution of 1831 were a period of factional strife at Rio de Janeiro and disorder in the provinces. The first Regency was supported by the moderate liberals, and especially by Evaristo da Veiga's "Society for the Defense of Liberty and National Independence," which organized behind the government the native commercial and landholding interests. It was opposed on the one hand by the *exaltados*, or radical federalists and republicans, and on the other by the still powerful Portuguese element allied with many conservative Brazilians, like José Bonifacio de Andrada, who sought the restoration of Pedro I. Both of these groups made repeated attempts to overthrow the new regime. Revolts at the capital were suppressed by the firm hand of Father Feijó, who was Minister of Justice during the first year of the Regency and who became sole Regent, superseding the commission of three, in 1835; but there was much strife between ambitious local military leaders in Pernambuco, Pará, and Maranhão. The numerous advocates of local autonomy were somewhat placated in 1834 by a constitutional amendment permitting the election of provincial legislative assemblies, but this did not prevent one of the worst local civil wars in Brazil's history, the "Guerra dos Farrapos" in Rio Grande do Sul, which began in 1835.

Feijó's inflexible disposition and somewhat radical ideas alienated many of the moderate liberals, and the new conservative party, which was organized under the lead of Bernardo Pereira de Vasconcellos, attracted the support of most of Pedro I's partisans after the ex-Emperor died in 1834. The liberals who continued to support the Regent were joined by many of the *exaltados,* but these lost much of their following as the public grew tired of continued political disorder. The government's inability to restore peace in the provinces, and especially in Rio Grande do Sul, made Feijó's position untenable, and when his opponents obtained a parliamentary majority in 1837 he quietly turned over the Regency to the conservative leader Araujo Lima.

The new government was hardly more successful than its predecessor. The war continued in the south, while fresh revolts occurred at Bahia and Maranhão. Araujo Lima's reactionary policy, and especially the restriction of the limited autonomy granted to the provinces in 1834, increased the feeling of discontent, and early in 1840 the liberal leaders began a campaign to have the fourteen-year-old Emperor declared old enough to rule. Their immediate purpose was to do away with the conservative regency, but they were supported by many influential people who hoped that the factional struggle for control of the government would lose its violent character when the nation had a ruler independent of either political party. Under the leadership of the two surviving Andradas, for José Bonifacio had died in 1838, the movement soon had the support of a majority in the Chamber of Deputies. The Regent at first temporized, and then attempted to adjourn the Parliament. This was the signal for a bloodless revolution. The two Chambers met in defiance of the Regent's order, obtained the Emperor's consent, and on July 23, 1840 proclaimed him of age to rule in his own name.

The Reign of Pedro II

Under the new Emperor, Brazil was to enjoy nearly half a century of internal peace and material progress. Despite his youth, Pedro II soon showed a surprising capacity to give the country precisely the kind of government that its political and social development seemed to demand. Educated by conscientious tutors under a strict regime that left him little opportunity for contact with the court influences which had shaped his father's character, he grew up to be serious minded, irreproachable in his private life, and indefatigable in the performance of what he considered his duty. He was keenly interested in art, science, and literature, well-informed though not profound or brilliant, an able and intelligent ruler if not a great statesman. His subjects loved him for his simplicity and his democratic ways even when they regarded his weaknesses with tolerant amusement or criticized his official acts with all the freedom permitted by a broad-minded and tolerant policy toward the press.

Though the new regime was warmly welcomed by the great majority of the people, it was several years before the political disturbances inherited from the Regency were suppressed. Factional rivalry was still virulent. The Andradas, who had formed a ministry after their victory in 1840, soon disagreed with the Emperor, and when a new conservative cabinet dissolved the liberal-controlled Chamber of Deputies revolts broke out in São Paulo and Minas Geraes. They were suppressed by General Luiz Alves de Lima e Silva, later known as the Duke of Caxias, and in 1845, by a succession of military victories followed by the promise of a general armistice, Caxias also ended the ten-year war in Rio Grande do Sul.

At the capital, the liberals returned to power in 1844, but were again forced to give way to the conservatives in 1848. This was the occasion for the last serious disturbance of Dom Pedro's reign, the "*praieira*" revolt in Pernambuco. The liberal officials in that province had made political rivalries more acute than usual during their recent tenure of power by openly encouraging a campaign of terrorism against resident Portuguese merchants, and they now attempted to prevent the conservatives from assuming control of local affairs. The revolt was suppressed after a few months of fighting. A newly established coastwise steamship service which carried troops rapidly to disaffected areas facilitated the task of restoring order.

The Emperor had by this time begun to exercise the great personal influence which kept party strife within bounds during the remainder of his reign. There were no important differences in political aims between the liberals and the conservatives and neither group had a very large popular following. For several years in the 1850's affairs were conducted by "cabinets of conciliation" representing both parties. Later Pedro usually called on one group or the other to assume the responsibility of administration, but the fall of a cabinet meant little more than a change in personnel and involved no disturbance of public order. The Emperor was the real head of the government, making the most important decisions and carefully supervising his ministers' work. It was he rather than the voters who decided which party should be in power. The ministers were drawn from the group that had a majority in the Chamber, but it was a simple matter to dissolve this body and obtain a new one with a majority favorable to the other party when the Emperor felt that the time for a political change had arrived. Elections were no more free than in other South American countries, but Dom Pedro endeavored to rule in harmony with public opinion, and his government perhaps approached the ideal of a constitutional monarchy as nearly as the political education of the Brazilians permitted. His influence and his untiring attention to the work of administration made the government more efficient and less corrupt than its predecessors, at least so far as the higher officials were concerned, and the Senate, whose members were carefully selected by the Emperor from lists presented by the provincial electors, became a highly respected body, though an exceedingly conservative one. Among the lower ranks of office holders the bad practices inherited from the colonial period seem to have persisted to a greater degree.

The most troublesome question that confronted the Empire after the establishment of internal peace was the continued existence of the African slave trade. In 1826 Pedro I was compelled by pressure from Great Britain and as a condition for the recognition of Brazilian independence to agree by treaty to stop this traffic. It was consequently made illegal in 1830, but North American and Portuguese vessels continued to import many thousands of Negroes annually with the connivance of the authorities. Many planters felt that their labor supply could not be maintained if the law were enforced, for the Negro population in Brazil had never held its own by natural increase. The continued existence of the trade was a constant source of friction with

Great Britain, and in 1845, when Brazil attempted to terminate the treaty of 1826, the British parliament passed the Aberdeen Act, which permitted the condemnation of slave ships by British admiralty courts rather than by the joint commissions that had acted under the treaty. Five years later it authorized its cruisers to seize such ships even in Brazilian territorial waters. After this act of aggression Dom Pedro insisted upon the passage of the Queiroz Law of 1850 by which the trade was effectively suppressed.

The result was an increase of white immigration, especially to the southern provinces. Rio de Janeiro, Minas Geraes, and São Paulo were henceforth more important than the older settlements in the north, where the cultivation of sugar, tobacco, and cotton was no longer so profitable as in the first years after independence. Coffee had become the Empire's chief export, and it was in this period that Brazil began to supply more of this commodity to the world's market than all other countries combined. With internal peace and a growing foreign trade both population and national wealth increased rapidly, despite the foreign wars that occupied much of the government's attention in the years between 1850 and 1870.

These wars have been mentioned in earlier chapters. Brazil's intervention in Uruguay, which culminated in the overthrow of Rosas in 1852, cost the Empire little and gave it for the time being a preponderant influence in eastern South America. Another intervention in Uruguay twelve years later, however, brought on the long conflict against López of Paraguay, in which the imperial army lost 33,000 men and the government spent several hundred million dollars. At its close, in 1870, Brazil was exhausted morally and economically, but the Emperor's prestige, somewhat shaken by reverses in the earlier part of the war, was restored by final victory.

Why the Empire Fell

A traveler who visited South America in 1881 was much impressed by the contrast between Brazil and other countries on the east coast of South America. Despite the continued existence of slavery and the mixture of races among its people, the Empire seemed "really civilized," with a government that appeared to be securely established and far better able to maintain order than those of the River Plate republics.[1]

1 Knight, *Cruise of the Falcon*, p. 333.

To such an observer, the monarchy must have seemed responsible for much of the difference. It would have been difficult to suppose that the Emperor would soon be overthrown, for no contemporary ruler was apparently more beloved by his own people or more highly regarded in foreign countries.

Several factors were nevertheless working to weaken Dom Pedro's position. Many business men were dissatisfied with what they considered his failure to grasp the importance of the new economic problems created by the growth of population and trade, and many political leaders criticized his government as undemocratic and ultra-conservative. Before 1870, a reorganized and more aggressive liberal party began to demand electoral reforms and to work for the abolition of slavery, objectives with which the Emperor had much sympathy but which he did not consider immediately attainable. While opposition was thus growing among the progressive elements, many conservatives were becoming lukewarm, if not hostile. Among these were the more devout Catholics. Dom Pedro was extremely tolerant in religious matters, but at the same time he firmly maintained the government's authority over the Church. Ecclesiastical questions gave little trouble until after a conflict between some of the clergy and the Freemasons—brought on by Pope Pius IX's condemnation of the Masonic order—aroused much public excitement in the early 1870's. When the bishops of Pará and Pernambuco ordered the *irmandades,* or lay religious fraternities, to expel all Masons from their membership, and sought to force compliance by laying interdicts, the government intervened and the two bishops were imprisoned for disobedience in 1874. This caused a great scandal; and the release of the bishops a few months later in response to the pressure of public opinion did not help the Emperor's prestige.

Much more important was the controversy over slavery. Slavery had been done away with in nearly all other civilized countries and there was a strong abolition movement in Brazil. In 1871 the government had forced through parliament the Rio Branco law which declared all children born thereafter legally free, though requiring them to work for their mothers' owners until the age of twenty-one. This satisfied the advocates of emancipation for the time being, but after 1878 there was a vigorous campaign for complete abolition, led by Joaquim Nabuco. In 1884 the provinces of Ceará and Amazonas freed slaves in their territory by local action, and in 1885 the imperial parliament freed all slaves over sixty years of age. Thousands more were emancipated by the voluntary action of their masters so that whereas a quarter or more of the inhabitants of Brazil had been in servitude in 1865, there were approximately 700,000 in a population of 15,000,000 in 1888. Many of these were becoming unruly. In São Paulo great numbers simply abandoned the plantations, assisted and protected by emancipation sympathizers, and the army refused to help the civil police to capture them.

Dom Pedro disliked slavery and he suffered keenly from the criticism directed against Brazil in foreign countries, but he had not been inclined to force any sudden and radical solution of the problem because of the economic interests involved. His daughter Isabel was less cautious and more ardent in her zeal for emancipation. In 1888, when the Princess was acting as Regent while her father was making one of his occasional visits to Europe, a bill freeing all slaves was proposed by the Crown and passed by a large majority in both chambers. Since there was no provision for compensation, the owners were deprived at one stroke of property worth hundreds of millions of dollars. The "Golden Law," as the Brazilians in their enthusiasm called the measure, caused a bitter feeling among the landowning class which more than offset its popularity among the masses of the people.

There was thus a growing discontent among the very groups to which the dynasty might normally have looked for support, and a growing feeling that the institutions under which Brazil had enjoyed so long a period of peaceful progress had outlived their usefulness. The desire for a change was increased by the unpopularity of Isabel, who was Dom Pedro's prospective successor, and by the dislike of the Brazilians for her French husband, the Count d'Eu. There were relatively few Brazilians who advocated a revolution during the Emperor's lifetime, for he was still personally popular, but an increasing number looked forward to the establishment of a republic after his death. Since 1870, a small but vociferous republican party had carried on propaganda with little interference from the imperial authorities. This group acquired some importance in São Paulo and Minas Geraes, and Dom Pedro's rapidly failing health encouraged it to intensify its activities. In 1889 the avowed republicans were probably a small minority, but there was a strong desire among the educated classes generally for political reforms of some sort.

Though the Emperor was welcomed as affectionately as usual when he returned from Europe, he could not but realize the strength of this feeling. He had said that he would not resist if his people desired to abolish the monarchy, but he sought to avert the threatened revolution by making concessions. The Viscount of Ouro Preto, who became Prime Minister in June, 1889, proposed a series of constitutional changes, among them the granting of autonomy to the provinces, the extension of the suffrage, and the abolition of life tenure in the Senate. His program was defeated in Parliament, and though a new election, controlled by the customary methods, gave the cabinet a majority, the government's position was much weakened.

The immediate cause of the Empire's fall, however, was not civilian discontent but the so-called "military question." For several years there had been increasing evidence of insubordination in the army. Officers had repeatedly violated a regulation prohibiting them from breaking into print on controversial subjects without permission from the Minister of War, and the government's timid and ineffective attempts to restrain them had simply made the offenders more arrogant. At the same time much republican propaganda had been spread among the younger officers by the teachings of Benjamin Constant Botelho de Magelhães, a popular professor in the military school at Rio de Janeiro. On November 15, 1889, when the Ouro Preto cabinet attempted to send some of the more disaffected regiments into distant provinces and to offset the influence of the professional soldiers by strengthening the national guard, a portion of the garrison at Rio de Janeiro, led by General Deodoro da Fonseca, seized control of the city. There was almost no bloodshed, because the Adjutant General, Floriano Peixoto, refused to obey the Cabinet's order to resist.

The army leaders originally planned merely to overthrow the Cabinet without displacing the Emperor, but Benjamin Constant and other radical leaders persuaded Deodoro to abolish the monarchy altogether. The Emperor was deposed and sent into exile. A Federal Republic, the United States of Brazil, was proclaimed, and Deodoro became the head of the "provisional government by the army and the navy, in the name of the nation."

Military Governments, 1889–1894

The establishment of the Republic was the work of a small fraction of the army with little support or opposition from the mass of the Brazilian people. Though Deodoro's first cabinet included such civilian leaders as Ruy Barbosa and the future president, Campos Salles, his regime was little more than a military dictatorship. Freedom of the press disappeared and elections were controlled by those in power. The provisional government nevertheless addressed itself energetically to the complete reorganization of the national and local administration and carried out a number of reforms, among them the complete separation of Church and State. When a constituent assembly met in November, 1890, it drew up a constitution much like that of the United States, except that the federal government was given power to enact general criminal, civil, and commercial codes and the states were permitted to levy taxes on exports. The same convention elected Deodoro first president of the Republic.

Deodoro was an able soldier, with a reputation for personal honesty, but he showed little skill in dealing with political questions. There was much opposition to his autocratic methods, and he met with a growing resistance in the Assembly, which had now become the first federal Congress. The President finally dissolved the Congress, illegally and by military force, and announced that he was assuming dictatorial powers to frustrate a plot for the restoration of the monarchy. This provoked a revolutionary outbreak in Rio Grande do Sul, and there were lesser disturbances in several other provinces. In November, 1891, when the navy turned its guns on Rio de Janeiro and demanded his resignation, Deodoro quietly turned over his office to the Vice-President, General Floriano Peixoto.

Peixoto had the army behind him and was able by persuasion or coercion to command the support of a majority in the Congress, but his regime was not popular with the mercantile class and other conservative groups, who felt that the sole result of the revolt of 1891 had been to exchange one military dictatorship for another. The navy, officered by men from the aristocratic class and jealous of the army's preponderance in the government, was especially disaffected. Under the leadership of Admiral Custodio de Mello, who had also led the uprising two years before, the entire fleet revolted in September, 1893. The insurgents controlled the harbor of Rio de Janeiro for six months, but the determined attitude of the commanders of several North American and European warships prevented them from bombarding the city or blockading the port. Admiral de Mello consequently left Rio de Janeiro with a part of his forces to coöperate with a revolutionary movement led by Gumercindo Saraiva in Rio Grande do Sul.

The insurgents obtained control of much of southern Brazil, but they failed to follow up their successes with a movement on the capital. Admiral Saldanha da Gama, who had been left in command of the insurgents there, had meanwhile made it known that he favored the reestablishment of the monarchy, and his attitude cost the rebels many supporters even though there was little evidence that the other leaders had the same purpose. In March, 1894, when several new warships purchased abroad by the government arrived off the harbor, the movement collapsed. A large number of those implicated in the revolt were put to death by the federal authorities.

Republican Governments, 1894–1914

The presidential election of 1894 was held while the revolt was still in progress, with Prudente de Moraes, one of the original republican leaders from São Paulo, as the official and consequently the successful candidate. Peixoto, to his credit, made no attempt to remain in power himself or to perpetuate the control of the army; and the inauguration of an able civilian president gave the republican regime a stability that it had not thus far had. Nevertheless, the new President had to deal with many troublesome questions. Financial problems inherited from his predecessors became all but insoluble as the effects of the world depression of the '90's made themselves felt, and there were several unsuccessful uprisings in the army, which resented its loss of political power. Some of the participants in the recent revolt continued guerrilla warfare in Rio Grande do Sul until August, 1895. In 1896 a group of religious fanatics in the back country of Bahia, led by one Antonio Maciel, generally called Antonio Conselheiro, came into conflict with the authorities and order was not restored until several federal expeditionary forces had been ingloriously defeated and a great amount of money had been wasted. In 1897 a conspiracy to assassinate the President himself, instigated by military officers and rival politicians, resulted in the death of the Minister of War.

In spite of these difficulties, Prudente de Moraes maintained the prestige of the federal government, and his successors had less trouble with internal disorder. By 1898 economic conditions were improving. Dr. Manoel Ferras de Campos Salles, who became President in that year, was able to put the finances in relatively good order, for the first time in the Republic's history. Under his successor, Dr. Francisco de Paula Rodrigues Alves (1902–1906) a costly program of municipal improvements enhanced the great natural beauty of Rio de Janeiro, and a campaign against yellow fever, directed by the Brazilian physician Oswaldo Cruz, made the capital a safer place to live. During the same period the Baron of Rio Branco began his long and brilliant service as Minister of Foreign Affairs, in the course of which he settled by arbitration or friendly agreement nearly all of the boundary disputes that were a potential source of trouble between Brazil and other South American republics. Continued prosperity during the administration of Affonso Augusto Moreira Penna, who was elected to the presidency in 1906, made it possible to stabilize the fluctuating and depreciated paper currency which had been a handicap to commerce since the days of the Empire.

Throughout this period the republican party, the only political group with a permanent organization, controlled the administration. The party was directed by a relatively small number of leaders in the states of São Paulo and Minas Geraes, most of them members of the same land-owning aristocracy that had supplied the statesmen and politicians of the Empire. The first three civilian presidents were from São Paulo, which had been the original center of the republican movement, while Penna was a native of Minas Geraes.

The smaller states, less advanced politically and economically, had relatively little influence. Their local administrations were dominated by the group in control at the capital and the federal government did not hesitate to intervene in their affairs when such action seemed necessary for political reasons. Elections were no more free than in the days of the Empire.

There were many political leaders in the other states who resented this state of affairs and there was much discontent in the army, which had never resigned itself entirely to the loss of the power that it enjoyed before 1894. The opponents of the São Paulo–Minas Geraes coalition obtained control temporarily after Affonso Penna died in 1909 and the Vice-President, Nilo Peçanha, took his place. Through the machinations of Pinheiro Machado, the political boss of Rio Grande do Sul, a congressional caucus chose Marshall Hermes da Fonseca, a nephew of Deodoro and a native of Rio Grande do Sul, as the official candidate. Those who opposed a return of military domination supported the eminent jurist Ruy Barbosa, but official pressure decided the election as it always did. Hermes da Fonseca's administration was corrupt and inefficient, and there were several small uprisings in the navy and among other discontented groups, but he served out his term from 1910 to 1914. The São Paulo–Minas Geraes coalition returned to power in 1914, when Wenceslau Braz Pereira Gomes of Minas Geraes was chosen by the administration as the next president.

Coffee, Rubber, and Immigration

As in most of the Latin American countries, political events in Brazil in the last years of the nineteenth and the first years of the twentieth century were of less interest than the economic progress which was rapidly giving the Western Hemisphere a new importance in world affairs. Coffee and rubber were doing for Brazil in these years what meat and grain were doing for Argentina, and a great wave of immigration was having the same effect as in the River Plate countries. The arrival of some three million European laborers, most of them from Italy, Portugal, and Spain, more than offset any bad economic effect from the abolition of slavery, for the newcomers were far more useful, especially on the coffee plantations, than slave labor had been. Like the earlier immigrants, most of them came to São Paulo and the less developed regions farther south.

Coffee was still the most important export, and Brazil was by this time furnishing three-fourths of the total world supply of this commodity. During the last decade of the nineteenth century coffee production outran consumption and prices fell. To check the decline, the State of São Paulo prohibited planting of new trees for a period of ten years after 1902. In 1906, with the coöperation of the federal government and with financial help from London and New York bankers, the State undertook the first of a series of experiments in "valorization," buying up a large amount of coffee which was withheld from the market until prices improved. The success of this scheme and of a similar operation during the European war led in 1922 to the adoption of a permanent plan of control which has continued in one form or another to the present time.

Rubber, in the first decade of the century, was an almost equally important export. For generations the greater part of the world's supply had been obtained from the wild trees of the Amazon valley, and with the development of the bicycle and the automobile the demand rapidly increased. Many thousands of laborers from the drought-ridden state of Ceará and other nearby districts were employed in gathering it. Manáos, a riverport 1,000 miles from the sea, became a large city. After 1912, however, the plantations of the Far East, with their cheap labor, began to produce great quantities of rubber, and the Brazilian product, gathered under great difficulties from scattered trees in the tropical jungle, ceased to be an important item in world trade.

A large amount of sugar, consumed chiefly in Brazil itself, was still raised in Pernambuco, and the cultivation of cacao and tobacco was important in Bahia. These older communities, however, had advanced far less rapidly than those of the south. Their population was still predominantly of Negro blood and their hotter climate made them less attractive to immigrants. They had shared to a relatively small extent in the new railroad mileage that had been built since the fall of the Empire. The south had definitely become the most important section of the Republic. Minas Geraes and São Paulo had populations larger than those of most of the independent Latin American countries, and Rio Grande do Sul, with its growing cattle industry, had more influence in Brazilian affairs than Pernambuco.

Political Events, 1914–1930

The First World War affected Brazil as it did her neighbors. When it started, imports and exports fell off sharply and with them the government's revenues. The conversion office was closed and new paper money was issued to meet current expenditures. The export trade, however, soon revived and the inconveniences caused by the dislocation of ocean transport and the shortage of goods were offset by an increased demand for products like cotton and sugar. Since Brazil declared war on Germany in 1917, her government was represented at the Peace Conference and she became one of the first members of the Council of the League of Nations. She left the League in 1926, however, when the other powers refused to make her position in the Council a permanent one.

Ex-President Rodrigues Alves was elected to succeed Wenceslau Braz in 1918, but he died at the beginning of his term and Epitacio da Silva Pessoa of Parahyba, who had distinguished himself as the head of the Brazilian delegation at Versailles, was chosen in his place. The new administration embarked upon an ambitious program of public works, financed in part by foreign borrowing. This involved the government in difficulties when depression followed the brief post-war boom. There was a sharp contest in the election of 1922. Ex-President Nilo Peçanha was the opposition candidate, put forward by the same political-military group that had been in power between 1910 and 1914, and when he was defeated by Arthur da Silva Bernardes, who had the support of the administration, there was some talk of revolution. Small uprisings did occur in the army as the result of a conspiracy headed by Hermes da Fonseca, but they were suppressed before Bernardes' inauguration. A much more serious revolt took place in July, 1924, when a portion of the army seized the city of São Paulo and held it for three weeks before loyal troops were able to gain the upper hand. Other disturbances frequently compelled the government to establish martial law in one region or another during the remainder of Dr. Bernardes' term, but after Dr. Washington Luis Pereira de Souza became President in 1926 coffee prices were higher, business conditions improved, and the political situation was more tranquil.

The Collapse of Coffee Valorization and the Revolution of 1930

Unfortunately the prosperity of the coffee industry was partly factitious. During the post-war depression, the federal government again attempted to stabilize the market, and in 1922 an Institute for the Permanent Defense of Coffee was established. Two years later this national organization turned the problem over to a state institute in São Paulo, which worked with the coöperation of similar bodies in other Brazilian states. In order to maintain prices, the amounts exported each month were limited by compelling growers to ship their production to warehouses in the interior, from which it was forwarded to the ports in amounts determined in accordance with the condition of the market. Loans were made to the planters on coffee that had not yet been sold, and production was not restricted. On the contrary it tended to increase because prices were artificially maintained at a high level and direct purchases were made by the coffee institute when the market needed support.

Two very large crops in succession, in 1927–28 and 1928–29, finally brought into being a tremendous oversupply at a time when increasing tightness in the world's money markets made it difficult to continue the foreign borrowing by which the system of valorization had been maintained. In October, 1929, the world price of coffee suddenly collapsed, bringing ruin to planters and merchants and gravely affecting the government's financial situation. The catastrophe had serious political repercussions, because the plan of valorization was the work of the same group of political leaders in São Paulo who controlled the federal administration under Washington Luis.

Washington Luis made matters worse when he put forward another Paulista, Julio Prestes, as the official candidate in the election in 1930. This was a violation of the arrangement by which the dominant political groups in São Paulo and Minas Geraes had maintained their supremacy in federal affairs and had taken turns in presenting candidates for the presidency, and the leaders in Minas Geraes consequently threw their support to Getulio Vargas, the Governor of Rio Grande do Sul. The party in power, however, controlled the administrations and the electoral machinery in nearly all of the other states, and was consequently victorious by a popular vote of 1,089,000 to 735,000.

The losers seemed inclined at first to accept the result peaceably, but their attitude changed when several of their party who had apparently been elected to Congress were counted out by the board that canvassed the returns, and when the federal authorities intervened in Parahyba to set up a state administration controlled by their own partisans. On October 3, 1930, revolts began simultaneously in Rio Grande do Sul, Minas Geraes, and Parahyba. A civil war involving much of the Republic's territory seemed imminent. Before very much fighting had actually occurred, however, a group of military leaders seized control at Rio de Janeiro and São Paulo, establishing a provisional *junta* which some days later recognized Getulio Vargas as Provisional President.

Getulio Vargas

Dr. Vargas ruled Brazil during the next fifteen years. When he first assumed control, all federal, state, and local legislative bodies were dissolved and the constitutional guarantees were suspended. The arbitrary conduct of the young military officers who served as interventors in most of the states aroused much dissatisfaction even in the Provisional President's own party. In May, 1932, however, public opinion was somewhat mollified by an announcement that a constituent assembly would be convened, and the people of São Paulo received little help from other states when they made a desperate effort to recover their ascendency in the federal government by armed revolt the following July. Fortunately, the war was a short one, and the insurgents surrendered early in October. Though the chief leaders were exiled, the defeated party was treated with a moderation that did much to facilitate a return to normal conditions.

The constituent assembly met in November, 1933, after an election in which the secret ballot was used for the first time in Brazil's history. The administration apparently made an effort to assure freedom and fair play, and opposition parties were well represented, though the majority of the delegates were supporters of the government. The new constitution, promulgated on July 16, 1934, differed in several respects from that of 1891, especially in its provisions for advanced social legislation and in the restrictions that it imposed on participation by foreigners in business and in the learned professions.

The assembly elected Dr. Vargas president for the term 1934–38, and in the months that followed the state governments were reorganized and the constitutional order was generally restored. The economic situation improved, but political conditions were still unsettled. Besides the old factions centering around leaders in the various states, two extremist parties, the communists and the fascistic *integralistas*, had made their appearance. The communists were accused of inciting a radical revolt in the army and navy, which was put down with much bloodshed in November, 1935. Thereafter the party was driven underground, and its leader, Luiz Carlos Prestes, was sentenced to a long term in jail. The *integralistas*, on the other hand, coöperated for some time with the Vargas administration.

In 1937 political agitation increased with the approach of the time for the election of a new president. The most prominent candidate was Salles Oliveira, a former governor of São Paulo, but he was not acceptable to Dr. Vargas and his chances were diminished when his most powerful ally, Governor Flores da Cunha of Rio Grande do Sul, was driven from power by a federal intervention. Under the constitution, Dr. Vargas could not be reëlected to succeed himself, but on November 10, 1937, he settled the problem by setting aside the constitution and proclaiming a new one that extended his term for six years. The new fundamental law gave the executive very extraordinary powers. Its most remarkable provision, perhaps, was that it should not go into effect until the President should see fit to submit it for popular approval in a plebiscite. In the meantime, under its emergency provisions, the President was to legislate by decree and to take such actions as he saw fit to maintain order. Since the plebiscite was never held, Vargas was the absolute ruler of Brazil until he left office in 1945.

Unlike most Latin American dictatorships, the *Estado Novo*, as the new regime called itself, made little pretense of being republican in form. For a time, some of the President's advisers seemed inclined to adopt the ideas and methods of European totalitarianism, but Vargas himself was too shrewd a politician to espouse a philosophy that was repugnant to most of his fellow citizens. The native fascists, the *integralistas*, who had supported him in the *coup d'état*, were given little part in the new government; and when they attempted to kill the President and seize power in May, 1938, several hundred were imprisoned. Thereafter neither they nor the communists gave the regime much trouble. All other political parties were dissolved by order of the government, and the freedom of the press was greatly restricted.

The establishment of the dictatorship met with surprisingly little opposition. Vargas was popular personally and he was able to obtain the coöperation of many other influential leaders. The common people felt that an effort was at last being made to improve their situation, for the new constitution contained several provisions intended to benefit the working man. The propertied classes were glad to have a strong government, especially in view of the increasingly threatening international situation.

The rise of fascism in Europe was a greater danger to Brazil than to most of the other American republics. In the southern states of Rio Grande do Sul, Santa Catarina, and Paraná, there were perhaps a million people of German descent who, unlike the Italian and Spanish immigrants, had retained their own language and to some extent their loyalty to the mother country. Nazi propaganda, backed by economic coercion, had been alarmingly successful among these people and by the end of 1937 there was a strong potential fifth column throughout the region. In April, 1938, Vargas issued a decree-law forbidding foreigners to engage in any sort of political activity. The need for this was emphasized when officials of the German legation at Rio de Janeiro were implicated in the *integralista* revolt a month later and the German minister was declared *persona non grata*. Later decrees forbade the maintenance of schools by foreign minorities and sought in other ways to compel the rapid assimilation of the German population.[1]

The outbreak of the World War in 1939 seriously dislocated commerce and industry. The loss of European coffee markets was a severe blow, only partially cushioned by the signature of the Inter-American Coffee Agreement.[2] On the other hand, shipments of many other products to the United States were increased as the war went on, until coffee in 1940 accounted for less than one-third of the total exports. An extensive program of road and railroad building helped to improve conditions, and a loan was obtained from the United States Export-Import Bank for the erection of a steel mill to utilize the country's rich iron deposits. Brazil's strategic raw materials, such as manganese and quartz crystals, were of great value in the allied war effort.

Brazil, like most of the other Latin American countries, broke off relations with the Axis powers immediately after Pearl Harbor, and on August 22, 1942, the government declared war on Italy and Germany. Brazilian troops were actually sent to the front in Italy, and the navy and air force carried on anti-submarine operations off the South American coast. The airfields in the Republic's territory were extremely important to the United States in maintaining communication across the South Atlantic to Africa.

Recent Events

Vargas refused to consider the holding of elections while the war was in progress, but he promised that constitutional government would be restored with the return of peace. In February, 1945, however, the pressure of public opinion compelled him to relax the ban on political activity and to agree to call a presidential election. There were two principal candidates: General Eurico Gaspar Dutra, the Minister of War, and General Eduardo Gomes, who had the support of some of the more liberal elements. Dutra was supposedly the government's candidate, but there were many who doubted whether Vargas would actually step down when the time came and this skepticism increased

[1] For the best account of the Vargas regime, see Karl Loewenstein, *Brazil Under Vargas.*

[2] See below, p. 562.

when Vargas apparently accepted the support of the communist leader Luiz Carlos Prestes, who was released from jail in April with other political prisoners. A repetition of what had happened in 1937 was prevented when the army forced Vargas to resign in October, 1945, and the Chief Justice of the Supreme Court took over as provisional president. General Dutra was elected to the presidency five weeks later, and was inaugurated on January 31, 1946. There was little complaint about the fairness of the voting, in which more than five million citizens participated.

A new constitution, adopted in 1946, restored a normal republican form of government, with a five-year term for the President and Vice-President. The states regained the autonomy that had been taken away under the highly centralized *estado novo*. One provision authorized the suppression of undemocratic political parties or associations.

This was directed against the communists, who polled more than half a million votes in December, 1945, and who showed even more strength in congressional and local elections held early in 1947. In May, 1947, by a 3-2 vote, the Supreme Electoral Tribunal declared the party outlawed, and the government at once seized all of its offices and took over the direction of the Brazilian Workers Confederation, which had been under communist control. In October, after the Moscow press had published articles which insulted President Dutra, Brazil broke off diplomatic relations with Soviet Russia. The communists nevertheless continued to participate in political affairs, and in November, 1947, their leader, Prestes, and ex-President Vargas campaigned side by side against the government-supported candidates in local elections in São Paulo. Some of them also continued to serve in Congress, until that body expelled Prestes from the Senate and fifteen deputies from the lower house in January, 1948.

Brazil is the largest of the South American republics, with a population of more than 47,000,000 and a territory greater than that of the continental United States. Her rapid economic progress, which began under the Empire, has continued to the present time. Coffee is still the principal export, and Brazil is still the chief source of the world's supply, but the excessive dependence on this one crop, which was a danger fifteen years ago, has recently been decreased by the large-scale production of cotton and several other agricultural products. There has also been a remarkable development of manufacturing, especially in São Paulo, which is now the greatest industrial center in South America.

The country's wealth, however, is very unevenly divided. The southern states, with their good farm land, are far more prosperous than the tropical North. Even in the South, however, standards of living are low among the masses of the people, and malnutrition, bad housing, disease, and illiteracy are obstacles to the development of political democracy and an encouragement to the growth of communism. A severe post-war inflation has helped to make conditions worse.

Among the country's most pressing needs is an improvement in transportation. Most of the population is still spread in a thin ribbon of settlement along the coast, just as it was in colonial times. Much of the interior, it is true, is not particularly attractive for human habitation. The Amazon Valley can hardly support a large population in the foreseeable future, because the soil, from which most of the natural plant food has been leached by excessive rainfall, is generally unsuitable for agriculture. Farther south the *sertao*, the great inland plateau, has an inadequate rainfall and only a scanty population, engaged chiefly in stockraising. But it is said that only 10 to 20 per cent of the country's total area, a far smaller proportion than in any of the world's other major political divisions, is entirely unusable,[1] and there are great regions of the interior where farming can be profitable and where settlement has been retarded by lack of roads or railroads.

[1] James, *South America*, pp. 387–8.

Part V

❦

THE REPUBLICS OF THE CENTRAL ANDES

IN Chapter 1 we spoke of the divergence in political and social development which must result from dissimilarities in the character
of the aboriginal Indian populations of the various countries of Latin
America. The most striking illustration of this divergence is the contrast between the republics of the South Temperate Zone and those
of the Central Andes: Peru, Bolivia, and Ecuador. The Andean region
was the home of populous, civilized native communities before the
Conquest. Today it has a small upper class of Spanish descent, and a
much larger group of mixed race; but the majority of the people, taking the region as a whole, are Indians. Most of them live in their own
communities, and speak *Quechua* or *Aymara* rather than Spanish.

The *encomienda* and the *mita* have long since disappeared, but custom and economic necessity still compel the Indians to work for the
white families and the Church, who own most of the better land. Some
receive an infinitesimal wage, others give several days of labor each
week in return for the plot of ground on which they produce their
own food. Peonage, or debt slavery, survives in many places, despite
laws forbidding it. In some regions, Indian families are required as a
part of their customary payments to the landlord to furnish a certain
number of *pongos*, or household servants, to work either at the *hacienda* or in the landlord's city house—an arrangement reminiscent of
the "personal service" which the Spanish government vainly attempted
to abolish in the sixteenth century.

The ignorance and poverty which help to keep the Indian in subjection to his landlord have also exposed him to exploitation at the hands of officials, priests, and private individuals, and a local expression, *gamonalismo*, is used to describe the manifold forms of extortion that are practised against him. In one respect, at least, the Indians' situation seems to have become worse since independence, for many of the *ayllus* or village communities which possessed lands under royal grants during the colonial period have lost a part or all of them through fraud or violence in the past century. The development of republican institutions was inevitably more difficult in countries where so large a part of the population was not only ignorant and poverty-stricken but also cut off by prejudice and language barriers from contact with other groups.

The geography of the Andean countries is another obstacle to political and economic progress.[1] High mountain ranges cut off the coast from the interior and isolate the valleys and plateaus where most of the people live. Until the advent of the airplane, journeys from one section to another were a matter of many days or even weeks. From the time of independence, the spirit of *localismo* and the ambitions of local *caudillos* have been a menace to peace and order. The high cost of road and railroad building has also discouraged economic development.

[1] The geography of the region is briefly described on p. 12.

15

Peru

First Years of Independence

There were 1,249,723 inhabitants in what is now Peru according to a census taken in 1795.[1] Lima had been the great center of Spanish power in America earlier in the colonial period, but the establishment of separate viceroyalties in New Granada and the River Plate, the changes in commercial legislation, and the decreasing production of the mines had diminished the relative importance of the city and the province of which it was the capital. The country had nevertheless been the chief stronghold of the loyalists during the war for independence. The creole nobility and other privileged classes had little sympathy for the revolution, and the Indians, though they fought as unwilling conscripts on both sides, were on the whole more inclined to support the royal authority. The patriot party was too weak to win independence without outside help, which came first from Chile and then from Colombia. It lacked effective leadership and popular support when it was compelled to assume the responsibility for organizing a national government.

We have seen how Bolívar, who was ruling Peru at the end of the war, failed in his attempt to make the Republic a part of his great Confederation of the Andes. The Liberator's authority crumbled when he left the country in September, 1826, and General Santa Cruz, his lieutenant, was soon forced by pressure from other military leaders to set aside the *constitución vitalicia* and to convene a constituent assembly. When this met in June, 1827, its leading spirit was the veteran patriot Luna Pizarro, a priest who had been one of the earliest advocates

---

[1] Basadre, *Historia de la República del Peru*, p. 13.

of Peruvian independence but who had opposed both San Martín and Bolívar. Through his influence, General José de la Mar was elected President of the Republic, while Santa Cruz accepted a diplomatic appointment abroad.

Military Dominance, 1827–1835

La Mar was the first of a long series of soldier-presidents. The control of the government after Bolívar's departure naturally fell into the hands of military leaders because years of constant warfare had accustomed all classes to regard armed force as the only basis of authority and because there was no other group sufficiently powerful to dispute their predominance. The creole aristocracy had never had any political influence and had been discredited by the adherence of most of the great families to the royalist cause. Even the civilian leaders who participated in the revolution, and who were active in politics as "liberals" after independence, had little popular following. Some of them, like Luna Pizarro, were influential as advisers or aides to the military *caudillos*, but they could not obtain power for themselves. For some forty years after independence, Peru's political life was dominated by the "marshals of Ayacucho"—the group of officers who had risen to prominence during the revolution. Most of them, including Santa Cruz, La Mar, Gamarra, Orbegoso, and Castilla, had served in the Spanish army during the earlier years of the war, but had joined San Martín in 1820–21. They were professional soldiers rather than political leaders, and they represented the force of the troops under their command rather than any section of public opinion. It was their rivalries and jealousies which caused Charles Darwin to observe in 1835 that "no state in South America, since the declaration of independence, has suffered more from anarchy than Peru." [1]

A conflict with Colombia made matters worse. Bolívar had to acquiesce in Peru's withdrawal from his confederation, but his lieutenants held Guayaquil, which was claimed by Peru, and also Bolivia, which many of the leaders at Lima regarded as a part of their country. The war began when Agustín Gamarra, the military commander at Cuzco,

[1] *Journal of Researches into the Geology and Natural History of the Various Countries Visited During the Voyage of H.M.S. Beagle Around the World* (Everyman's edition), p. 352.

invaded Bolívia on his own initiative in 1828 and overthrew Sucre's government. Sucre avenged himself a few months later by defeating the Peruvian army in Ecuador. Neither country was in a position to carry the conflict further, for Bolívar's regime in Colombia was breaking down and there were internal dissensions in Peru.

Gamarra revolted against La Mar in 1829, and was President until 1833, despite several efforts to turn him out. There was one especially sensational affair at Lima when one of his lieutenants who tried to seize power during the President's absence from the city was driven from the country by Gamarra's energetic wife. There was further trouble with Bolivia, where Santa Cruz had become President and was intriguing with dissatisfied elements in Peru, but Chilean mediation prevented an outbreak of war. Gamarra nevertheless completed his constitutional term. His government was not so despotic as some of the other regimes that flourished at the same time in Latin America. Political opponents, though frequently imprisoned or exiled, enjoyed some freedom of expression in the congress and in the press, and elections were less effectively controlled than in more recent times.

In 1833, in fact, the President was unable to bring about the election of General Bermúdez, whom he had chosen as his successor. No candidate received a majority of the popular vote and the constituent assembly, acting under the leadership of Luna Pizarro, chose General Luis José Orbegoso as Provisional President.

Orbegoso was a creole of Spanish descent, more in sympathy with the aims of the civilian liberal group than were *mestizo caudillos* like Gamarra and Santa Cruz. It was hoped that his election would diminish the influence of the army in the government. He had been in office only a few days when the troops at Lima under Gamarra's leadership attempted to depose him and would have done so if the inhabitants of the city had not rallied to his support. Unfortunately his popularity vanished as it became evident that he was ineffective and incompetent. Early in 1835, the army again revolted under the leadership of Felipe Santiago de Salaverry, a daring young *caudillo* who had earlier led several uprisings against Gamarra. Orbegoso sought aid from Santa Cruz, and the Bolivian President responded by invading Peru. In the fighting that ensued Salaverry was defeated and put to death by Santa Cruz' order, despite the fact that he had surrendered upon the promise that his life would be spared.

Santa Cruz' Confederation

Santa Cruz was now able to realize what had long been his major ambition. Peru was divided into two republics with Orbegoso as President in the north and General Ramón Herrera in the south, and these states were united with Bolivia in a confederation of which Santa Cruz became the "Protector." The new regime was virtually a monarchy, for the ruler was to hold office for life and his position was to be hereditary. The change was not unpopular in Peru, for Santa Cruz' efficient administration in Bolivia had impressed the propertied classes and the Inca blood which he inherited through his mother gave him prestige among the Indians of both countries. The confederation had been in existence only a few months, however, when it was attacked by foreign enemies from two sides. An army sent by Rosas of Argentina was easily defeated, but the war with Chile, already discussed in Chapter 12, ended with Santa Cruz' defeat at Yungay in January, 1839. The confederation was dissolved and Gamarra, who had returned with the Chilean army, again became President of Peru.

Ramón Castilla

The next five years were a period of great disorder. Santa Cruz' adherents were still powerful in Bolivia and their leader from his exile in Guayaquil endeavored to foment revolts in Peru. When Gamarra invaded Bolivia he was killed in the battle of Ingavi in 1841. Then a series of short-lived military regimes held power until Ramón Castilla, a professional soldier who had participated in most of the civil wars since independence, emerged as master of the situation in July, 1844.

Castilla's advent to power marked a turning point in the history of Peru. Until 1844, military anarchy had prevented progress. Many of the customs and institutions of the colonial period had survived. Negroes were still in slavery, though San Martín and later law-givers had decreed the freedom of children born after the revolution, and the Indians paid tribute as in the days of the viceroys. The colonial aristocracy were impoverished by thirty years of civil war, but they still had their social preëminence and their great entailed estates. Even in manners and dress, the people were only just beginning to feel the influence of nineteenth-century Europe. In some respects, indeed, the country was more backward than in Spanish times. In 1835 Darwin had found Lima "in a wretched state of decay," with nearly unpaved streets heaped everywhere with filth.

Much of this changed during the next two decades. Castilla's rather tolerant policy helped to disarm factional bitterness, and after 1845 the country enjoyed several years of relative tranquility. One reason for the government's strength was the wealth which began to flow in from increased sales of guano to foreign countries. The great deposits of bird manure on the islands along the coast, though used from early times by the Indians, received little attention after the Conquest until an increased demand for fertilizers abroad made it profitable to exploit them. As the best deposits were the property of the nation, the new industry gave the government a tremendously increased income. The foreign debt, in default since the first years of independence, was refunded and it was possible for the first time to undertake the construction of much needed public works. Many great private fortunes were also built up, for contracts for exporting guano were often granted on terms that were more favorable to the contractor than to the government. At the same time, Wheelwright's new steamship line, starting service about 1840, aided commerce in general and encouraged travel to the United States and Europe.

One result of closer contact with the outside world was a resurgence of the civilian liberal party. As in Chile, the activity of this group was in part a reflection of the European revolutionary movement of 1848. The liberals were defeated at the polls in 1851, when Castilla brought about the election of General José Rufino Echenique as his successor, but in 1854 Castilla himself joined forces with them in a revolt caused by Echenique's corruption and extravagance. During the war the liberals persuaded Castilla to issue a decree freeing the Indians from tribute, and another abolishing Negro slavery but promising the owners an indemnity of $300 for each of the 25,000 slaves to be emancipated. A year later, after Castilla had again become President, a liberal majority in the constitutional convention made one of the few attacks that have been made in Peru upon the privileged position of the Church. The clergy were subjected to the jurisdiction of the civil courts and the tithes and certain other ecclesiastical duties were abolished. Soon afterward, however, the liberals fell out with Castilla, and the party went into opposition when the constitutional convention was disbanded by the army in 1857.

Public order was disturbed anew in 1857 when Vivanco, an old rival of Castilla, revolted at Arequipa and was defeated only after an eight months' siege had caused much suffering among that city's inhabitants. In 1859, a boundary dispute with Ecuador led Peru to send a military expedition to Guayaquil, but the differences between the two governments were adjusted by treaty before bloodshed occurred. Neither of these affairs seriously affected the country's economic life and Castilla's third and final term as president from 1858 to 1862 was generally tranquil.

The War with Spain

Grand Marshal Miguel de San Román was elected without opposition to succeed Castilla in 1862, but he died a few months after his inauguration. The Vice-President, General Juan Antonio Pezet, had not been in office long when relations with Spain, already strained by disputes over pecuniary claims and by the Peruvian government's outspoken disapproval of the interventions in Mexico and the Dominican Republic, were made worse by the "Talambo affair." A group of Basque immigrants, who had complained of mistreatment at the hands of the wealthy planters who had brought them to Peru, were brutally attacked by native laborers. No real effort was made to bring the offenders to justice, and when a Spanish "Royal Commissioner" was sent to Lima to demand satisfaction, the government refused to deal with him because it considered his title offensive. In April, 1864, a Spanish fleet seized the Chincha Islands, which were the site of some of the richest guano deposits. Pezet, who had no naval forces strong enough to resist this aggression, finally signed a treaty providing for the return of the islands upon payment of an indemnity to Spain. This act of surrender so outraged public opinion that he was overthrown in 1865 by a revolution under General Mariano Ignacio Prado.

Prado's revolt had at least the moral support of Chile, which itself declared war on Spain in September, 1865. In December, Chile and Peru signed an offensive and defensive alliance to which Ecuador and Bolivia later adhered. The war was short and inconclusive. Valparaiso was bombarded in March, 1866, and an attack on Callao on May 2 was repulsed. Soon afterward the invading fleet withdrew from American waters. In 1871 a truce was arranged through the mediation of the United States, and in 1879 a treaty of peace was signed.

After the war internal dissensions again made their appearance. Castilla took up arms in 1867, and the revolution finally succeeded although Castilla himself died during the campaign. In 1868, the victorious party installed Colonel José Balta as President.

The Climax of the Guano Era

The steadily increasing prosperity of the past quarter century reached its climax during Balta's administration. Revenues from guano exports furnished nearly three times as much income to the government as all other sources combined. They were used as a basis for large foreign loans to make possible an ambitious program of public works in which several railroads, built under the direction of the American Henry Meiggs, were the most important feature. The inflow of new capital encouraged reckless expediture and governmental corruption so that even the unprecedented revenues were not sufficient to cover the budget and successive deficits were met by borrowing against future guano shipments.

Agricultural production also expanded. The labor problem, which had become acute on the plantations of the coastal valleys even before slavery was abolished, was partially solved by the importation of Chinese coolies. A law enacted in 1849 granted subsidies to encourage contractors to bring immigrants to the country, but it was abrogated in 1853 after some 4,000 foreigners had been imported, most of them under contracts that compelled them to labor for a long term of years at low wages. Three years later the entry of Chinese, who had formed the majority of those arriving, had been made illegal. This prohibition was raised in 1861, and nearly 85,000 coolies were brought in between that year and 1875 when a treaty with China forbade any but voluntary migration.[1] The material advantages from this traffic were offset by its undesirable features, for the immigrants' condition was hardly better than slavery. The descendants of these Oriental laborers constitute a considerable element in the population of the Peruvian coast today.

The Rise of the Civilista Party

Balta's administration marked the end of another political era. Up to this time most of the presidents had been members of one military

[1] Ugarte, *Bosquejo de la historia económica del Peru*, pp. 60–63.

group, led first by Gamarra and then by his former lieutenant, Castilla. The efforts of the civilian liberals to obtain control had met with little success, for La Mar and Orbegoso, whom they placed in the presidency, were unable to dominate the other army chiefs. Castilla, who worked with them for a few years after 1854, later turned to the more conservative elements for support, and Prado, despite their help in the nationalistic revolution of 1865, did not give them any important share in his government. The conditions that made the army preponderant in politics were nevertheless changing with the increasing importance of trade and the development of a new wealthy class among the planters and merchants, and a political movement directed primarily against the continuance of military rule took shape during Balta's administration. The *partido civil,* though it has been described as "a fusion of a plutocratic class with a part of the hereditary nobility" [1] included also many of the old liberals. The reaction of public opinion against the extravagance and financial mismanagement of Balta's administration brought it many adherents, and in 1872 its candidate, Manuel Pardo, was elected to the presidency in spite of the government's opposition. It was the first time that the official candidate had been defeated since 1833.

Balta accepted the result of the popular vote, but Tomás Gutiérrez, the Minister of War, made a desperate effort to keep the army in power. Balta was arrested, and soon afterward murdered, while the army chiefs sought to set up a military dictatorship. The people of Lima and Callao, however, revolted as they had in 1834, and the usurper and two of his brothers were barbarously put to death within a few days after their *coup d'état.* Soon afterward Pardo assumed the presidency.

Financial Troubles, 1872–1878

Peru's first period of civilian government was not a happy one. Pardo diminished the importance of the army by establishing a national guard, and he encouraged education and attempted to bring about other useful reforms, but he was handicapped by financial difficulties. The government's expenditures, increased by the still uncompleted railroad program, were far in excess of its revenues, and the proceeds of the guano sales were by this time entirely mortgaged to foreign bondholders. The collapse that a reckless fiscal policy made inevitable was hastened by the world depression. In 1875 the banks were compelled

[1] Basadre, *Peru: Problema y Posibilidad,* p. 95.

to suspend specie payments and the government defaulted on its foreign debt. An increasing spirit of disaffection found expression in several small revolts. Financial and commercial conditions continued to grow worse in the first years of the administration of General Prado, the ex-President, whom the *civilista* party placed in office as Pardo's successor in 1876.

The drop in the price of guano, which was a major element in the country's financial difficulties, was caused partly by the competition of nitrate from the Peruvian province of Tarapacá and the Bolivian province of Atacama. The deposits were exploited by private companies in several of which Chilean and other foreign capital was invested. These interests blocked a plan proposed by Pardo in 1873 to establish a sales monopoly in order to protect the guano revenues, and in 1875 the Peruvian government established a monopoly of production and proceeded to expropriate the existing private plants, despite the fact that the state of the treasury made adequate compensation impossible.

The War with Chile

The results of the government's nitrate policy and of the alliance with Bolivia signed in 1873 have been described in Chapter 12. The War of the Pacific found Peru woefully unprepared. The *civilista* administrations had reduced the army in an attempt to reduce its political power and had fallen behind Chile in naval strength. Bolivia could give little or no help. The Chilean advance was held up for some months by Admiral Grau's daring operations at sea, but after the *Huáscar* was sunk the enemy easily overran Tarapacá. In December, 1879, President Prado suddenly embarked for Europe, ostensibly to purchase munitions. Nicolás de Piérola, an audacious political agitator who had been Finance Minister under Balta and had later led several unsuccessful uprisings against the *civilista* regime, seized control of the government but was no more successful than his predecessor in checking the enemy. Tacna and Arica were lost, the effort to end the war through mediation by the United States failed, and Lima itself was occupied by a Chilean army in January, 1881. Piérola withdrew into the interior where he continued for some months to lead an ineffective opposition to the invaders.

At Lima a government headed by Dr. Francisco García Calderón was set up under the protection of the Chilean commander. The new administration, however, refused to accept Chile's demands, partly at least because it hoped for diplomatic support from the United States. After a few months, when the Peruvian generals in the interior had recognized García Calderón's authority and had begun to act in his name, the President was arrested and deported to Chile. The Peruvian leaders kept up their opposition for another year, but at the end of 1882, after Chilean expeditions had dispersed the forces of some of the other chiefs, General Miguel Iglesias assumed the presidency and agreed to the invaders' terms. By the treaty that was signed on October 20, 1883, Peru lost Tarapacá and agreed to a temporary Chilean occupation of Tacna and Arica—a provision which, as we have already seen, was a source of friction for many years. The Chilean army of occupation was withdrawn in 1884, after the treaty had been ratified.

Political Affairs, 1884–1919

The military chiefs who had opposed a surrender revolted after the Chileans left, and General Andrés Avelino Cáceres came into power after several months of hard fighting. During his presidential term, from 1886 to 1890, Peru began to recover slowly from the demoralization and impoverishment caused by the war. The Chileans had levied heavy contributions on the people of the occupied districts and had carried off or wantonly destroyed much valuable property. Many of the rich valleys along the coast had been systematically laid waste. The guano deposits which remained to Peru were now of relatively little value, and such income as they still produced was pledged to foreign creditors.

One of the most urgent problems was the reorganization of the public finances. With annual revenues of less than $6,000,000, hardly a third of what they had been fifteen years earlier, the government could barely meet the most necessary expenses of administration, to say nothing of paying interest on its $150,000,000 foreign debt. After prolonged negotiations, an arrangement with the British bondholders was reached in the Grace contract of 1890. The government was relieved of responsibility for its outstanding bonds and in return ceded the state railways to the bondholders for sixty-six years. It further agreed to pay 80,000 pounds sterling annually for thirty-three years and to give the bondholders a right to extract and export a total amount of 3,000,000 tons of guano.

In 1890 Nicolás de Piérola made a vigorous bid for the presidency at the head of the democratic party, which opposed continued military domination. His campaign was cut short, however, when the government imprisoned him, and the official candidate, Colonel Remigio Morales Bermúdez, was elected. Morales' administration was dominated by the Cáceres group and was also supported by the *civilistas*. The latter, however, refused to back Cáceres when he himself sought reelection in 1894, and joined with the *Pierolistas* in a revolt that was successful after three days of savage fighting in the streets of Lima.

Piérola, who was President from 1895 until 1899, gave Peru an efficient government which hastened the process of recovery. The depreciated and fluctuating currency was stabilized, public works were constructed, and the army was again brought under the government's control. A return of military domination was made more difficult by a law promulgated in 1896 which entrusted the conduct of elections to boards chosen chiefly by the legislative and judicial branches of the government.

Relative freedom in the voting gave an advantage to the *civilista* party, which represented the wealthy classes, because bribery became an important factor as the use of force and intimidation grew less common. Partly for this reason, but more especially because control of the governmental machinery was a still more important factor, the *civilistas* were victorious in the elections of the next twelve years. Their candidate, Eduardo de Romaña, succeeded Piérola in 1899. Though the *Pierolistas* broke with the administration in 1903, another *civilista*, Manuel Candamo, became President in that year. He died after eight months in office, and José Pardo was chosen in a hotly contested election to take his place. Pardo, the son of the first *civilista* president, was an able man who carried out a number of constructive measures and especially attempted to build up the neglected public school system. At the end of his term in 1908 Peru had enjoyed thirteen years of practically unbroken peace and the country was sharing in the prosperity that most of South America was enjoying.

Augusto B. Leguía, a business man who had been Minister of Finance under Candamo and Pardo, was elected as the official candidate in 1908, but he soon broke with his former associates and established a semidictatorial personal regime. A revolt by Piérola's followers was suppressed in 1909 and vigorous measures were taken against other opposing political leaders. Leguía nevertheless failed when he attempted to have his friend Antero Aspíllaga chosen as his successor in 1912. The elections were unusually disorderly, and when Congress met it annulled them and chose the *Pierolista* candidate, Guillermo Billinghurst, as the new chief executive.

Billinghurst had much popular support at the outset of his administration, but he lost most of this during his first year in office. After a quarrel with Congress and an unfortunate effort to compromise the Tacna-Arica dispute with Chile, he was overthrown in February, 1914, by a group of military leaders working in connivance with the *civilistas*. Colonel Oscar Benavides assumed charge of the government temporarily, and in August, 1915, José Pardo was again inaugurated as constitutional President. The high prices of petroleum, copper, sugar, and cotton during the European war made Peru unusually prosperous in his four years in office. The sympathies of the government were openly on the side of the United States after that country entered the conflict, and Pardo severed diplomatic relations with Germany in October, 1917.

The Dictatorship of Leguía

At the end of Pardo's second term, the *civilista* party had been in power, except for short intervals, for nearly a quarter century. In recent years, however, its influence had been undermined by much the same sort of economic and social changes that were weakening the political aristocracies of Argentina and Chile. The Indians still had no part in the nation's political life, but the working people and the lower middle classes in the cities were taking more interest in matters of government, and it was among them that Piérola's "democratic" party, in opposition since 1903, found many of its supporters. There was also an increasing number of business and professional men who had no family or other connections with the *civilista* group and resented its monopoly of political power, and their importance increased during the war years when many new fortunes were created. In 1919 most of these elements opposed to the party in power supported ex-President Leguía, who won the election despite the government's efforts in behalf of its own candidate. Since there was some reason to fear that the Congress might attempt to upset the result when it made the final canvass of the vote, Leguía's followers seized the presidential palace by force and installed their leader in power shortly before the end of Pardo's constitutional term.

This *coup d'état* inaugurated a dictatorship that lasted eleven years. Leguía's popularity, combined with the general prosperity of the 1920's, enabled him to override all opposition. Constitutional changes first extended his term to five years, and then legalized his reëlection in 1924 and 1929. His opponents were powerless in the face of his efficient military and police forces and his active secret service. Those who did attempt to revolt received harsh treatment. In many ways, however, Leguía was an enlightened and progressive ruler. The most important event of his administration was the settlement of the Tacna-Arica controversy which had so long embittered Peru's relations with Chile. At home, something was done to improve the position of the working classes, an educational mission was brought from the United States, and irrigation systems, harbor improvements, and other public works were constructed. Funds were obtained by floating large loans abroad. Unfortunately the inflow of capital and the governmental and private extravagance which it encouraged made the reaction all the more severe when the depression set in.

Sánchez Cerro and the Leticia Incident

Leguía, like Irigoyen and Ibáñez, fell in the wave of revolutions that marked the first years of the depression. On August 22, 1930, the military commander at Arequipa, Colonel Luis M. Sánchez Cerro, rose in revolt. The attitude of the army chiefs and of public opinion at Lima made resistance impossible, and on August 25 Leguía resigned, to spend the last years of his life in prison. Sánchez Cerro became provisional President. Six months later widespread popular opposition and discontent among the troops forced him to resign, but he was the victorious candidate in the election held in October, 1931, and in December he became constitutional President.

The new administration was compelled to suppress revolutionary movements in various parts of the country, but its position was probably strengthened by the conflict with Colombia over the Leticia corridor. This sparsely inhabited area in the upper Amazon valley had been given to Colombia by a treaty between the two countries signed in 1922. The arrangement had been unpopular among the people of the nearby Peruvian territory, and on the night of August 31, 1932, a group of private individuals seized the little village of Leticia and expelled the Colombian officials. The Peruvian government disavowed their action, but later made it clear that it would resist a Colombian force which was sent up the Amazon to reoccupy the territory. There were minor armed clashes in the region in the first months of 1933. The League of Nations, to which both countries belonged, supported Colombia, as did several American powers, but their efforts to bring about a peaceful settlement were thwarted by Sánchez Cerro's attitude.

The assassination of Sánchez Cerro, on April 30, 1933, made a settlement possible. General Oscar Benavides, who was hastily elected to the presidency, entered into informal negotiations with Colombia and in May accepted a new proposal of the League of Nations. The area in dispute was turned over to an international commission, which governed it for a year and then turned it back to Colombia. The controversy caused little loss of life but it involved both governments in heavy expenses for armament at a time when their financial problems were already acute.

Political Affairs Since 1933

Benavides, like his predecessor, was compelled to adopt severe repressive measures against political enemies and to put down several armed revolts. Since the fall of Leguía, the strongest opposition party had been the "Apra" (Asociación Popular Revolucionaria Americana), a radical group which had been organized originally as an international movement against foreign imperialism, political and economic. The Apra's founder, Victor Raúl Haya de la Torre, was one of the candidates in the presidential election of 1931. He had many adherents in Peru, and an outbreak of his followers in the northern highland region was suppressed with some difficulty in March, 1933. Thereafter the party was virtually outlawed and its leaders were imprisoned or exiled, but it continued to make trouble.

Haya de la Torre was not permitted to be a candidate in the presidential election of 1936 because the government maintained that he represented an international organization rather than a Peruvian political party. The apristas consequently voted for Luis Antonio Eguiguren, another radical opposition leader, and their support enabled him to obtain a majority over the official candidate, Jorge Prado. Before the votes were officially counted, however, a constituent assembly annulled the election and extended Benavides' term for three additional years. A revival of business helped to make the general political situation more tranquil, and there was no effective resistance to the government's high-handed action. A number of *apristas* were nevertheless arrested and held in jail for long periods. Benavides exercised dictatorial powers, since the annulment of the elections left the country without a congress, and in 1939 constitutional amendments greatly increasing the authority of future presidents were adopted by plebiscite.

Later in the same year Manuel Prado y Ugarteche was chosen as Benavides' successor, in an election in which the *apristas* were again debarred from participation. Prado was in office throughout the World War. His government broke off relations with the Axis in January, 1942, and its policy of coöperation with the United States met with little opposition from other political groups. An increased demand for the country's copper and other products, combined with substantial financial aid from the United States, helped the economic situation, and there was little political disorder. Congress granted the President extraordinary powers for the duration of the war, and the principal opposition parties, including the *Apra*, were not permitted to carry on even normal political activities.

With the approaching victory of the democracies in Europe, an aroused public opinion began to demand more democratic procedures in many of the Latin American countries, and this demand was supported by the weight of public opinion abroad. This trend affected Peru, and the election of 1945 was one of the freest in the Republic's history. A direct conflict between the *apristas* and the conservative-military group that controlled the government was avoided when both Haya de la Torre and ex-President Benavides withdrew their candidacies. The *apristas* joined with some of the other anti-administration parties in a "national democratic front," and their votes were chiefly responsible for the election of José Luis Bustamante y Rivero, who became President in July, 1945. With a near majority in Congress, they were the most powerful element in the new administration.

The *Apra*, like most native radical parties in Latin America, was hostile to communism. Its attitude toward the United States had changed, and it now advocated coöperation with American capital to develop Peru's natural resources as well as a series of measures for the improvement of social conditions in Peru. Everything that it stood for, however, was opposed by the conservatives, both in Congress and in Bustamante's cabinet, and the President's position was made more and more difficult by the savage conflict between the two groups. Matters became worse in January, 1947, when the *apristas* were accused of

instigating the murder of one of the owners of a newspaper which opposed them, and the party's three representatives in the President's
cabinet resigned. The loss of their support weakened the administration, and when the conservative senators prevented Congress from
functioning, by refusing to attend meetings, the government was all
but paralyzed. Things came to a head after an unsuccessful revolt, said
to have been instigated by the *apristas*, in October, 1948. A part of the
army, accusing Bustamante of leniency to his former allies, overthrew
him on October 29, and General Manuel Odría became provisional
President. There was a general purge of *aprista* office-holders. When an
election was held in July, 1950, no opposition candidacies were permitted
and Odría became President for a six-year term.

Peru Today: The Indian Problem

With 7,000,000 people, Peru today is one of the more important countries in South America. Petroleum in the desert around Piura, cotton
and sugar in the irrigated coastal valleys, and copper from the mines of
Cerro de Pasco have greatly increased the volume of her export trade
since the beginning of the century. Even the depression of the 1930's
proved but a temporary setback, followed by a rapid recovery. The
country has suffered severely from inflation since the end of the war,
but its economic future seems bright. The political outlook is more uncertain. The fact that less than half a million votes have been cast in
recent elections indicates that republican government does not yet rest
on a broad basis of popular support and participation, and the revolution
of 1948 made it clear that democratic procedures have not yet supplanted force as a means of deciding political disputes. It is difficult to
hope that they will do so until there has been a change in the position
of the Indians.

The outlook for the Indians has become a little brighter in recent
years. Peruvian public opinion seems to be awakening to the importance
of the problem, and the *apristas*' advocacy of social reform was one of
the factors that won them many votes. Recent governments have
sought to check the most vicious forms of *gamonalismo*, and the Indians themselves have shown a disposition to stand up for their rights.
Many of them have gone to work in the mines or on the plantations on
the coast where working conditions are freer and wages higher. In the
sierras many of the ancient *ayllus*, or land-owning communities, con-

tinue to exist, despite the efforts made in the early days of the Republic to force the distribution of their lands among the individual members, and their position has been strengthened by the fact that the constitution of 1920 for the first time legally recognized their existence. There is little doubt that the Indian will some time demand relief from exploitation and a larger participation in the country's political life. Peru's future welfare will depend to a great extent upon the ability of her statesmen to solve the Indian problem by evolution rather than by revolution.

16

Bolivia

The Country and the People

There are few sections of South America where civilized communities contend with greater geographical and climatic handicaps than in Bolivia. Only a small part of the Republic's extensive area provides a decent living for human beings. The distinctive geographical feature is a great plateau, 12,000 to 14,000 feet above sea-level and bordered by higher snow-covered peaks. Much of this is too cold and too arid for agriculture, but a considerable number of people live there, some of them working in the mines upon which the nation's economy largely depends and others tending the flocks of llamas and alpacas that graze on the sparse vegetation. There are other centers of population around the edges of this bleak tableland. One is the district near La Paz and Lake Titicaca, where the prehistoric city of Tiahuanaco flourished, and where hardy plants like potatoes and *quinoa* can be cultivated, though with constant danger of crop failure from cold or drought. Others are in the more temperate valleys on the eastern slopes of the plateau, which have small amounts of good agricultural land.

These settled areas are separated from one another, and from the outside world, by great distances over country where travel is difficult. Still more isolated is the country east of the Andes, which comprises two-thirds of the Republic's territory. Much of this is either tropical jungle or hot, low-lying plains, flooded part of the year and drought-stricken at other seasons. One district, around Santa Cruz de la Sierra, has a good climate and is said to be more fertile, but lack of means of communication has retarded its development.

What is now Bolivia had a large Indian population before the Conquest, and its mineral wealth made it one of the most valued Spanish possessions during the colonial period. At the time of independence, however, the output of the once fabulously rich silver mines had virtually ceased, and other forms of mineral wealth which have since become important had not been developed. The population, greatly reduced by the cruelties of the *mita*, had been further diminished after 1809 by fifteen years of particularly cruel civil strife. There were probably somewhat less than 1,000,000 people in the country in 1825.

The majority of these were Indians, either Quechuas like the people of southern Peru or the more sullen and intractable Aymaras. Like their Peruvian neighbors they still spoke only their native dialects and retained many of their primitive customs. Exploited and oppressed by the officials and landowners, undernourished and suffering constantly from the cold, their lot was even harder than that of the natives in other parts of the Andean region. In several places, especially in the more remote and unproductive regions, they had been allowed to retain their ancient communal agricultural system, but elsewhere their lands and much of their livestock had passed into the hands of the descendants of the conquistadores and they themselves had become debt-slaves or tenant farmers, obliged by law or custom to work for the benefit of the landowner. Above the Indians in the social scale, but only slightly less ignorant and primitive in their way of living, were the Spanish-speaking *cholos*, or *mestizos*, some of them farmers, others artisans or small tradesmen in the towns.

Both the Indians and the *cholos* far outnumbered the people of more or less pure Spanish blood, who lived in the small, isolated towns. Though a few of the creoles had studied at the ancient University of Chuquisaca, their general standard of intellectual attainment was low. The meager revenues from their estates, worked by the Indians under *cholo* overseers with little or no attention on the part of the owners, made it possible for them to live in idleness, but with few comforts and fewer diversions. Only a handful had any conception of conditions beyond the mountains and deserts which cut off the plateau from the outside world.

First Years of Independence

Since the provinces of the plateau had been governed from Buenos Aires between 1776 and 1810, and from Lima during the revolution, both the Argentine Confederation and Peru claimed the territory when

Spanish resistance collapsed after the battle of Ayacucho. When Sucre occupied the country, however, he found a strong local sentiment for independence, and an Assembly that he convened voted in August, 1825, to establish a separate republic bearing the name of Bolívar. The Liberator, though he had at first appeared to oppose the independence movement, accepted the Assembly's invitation to draw up a constitution for the new state. The draft that he submitted was accepted but with one important change: the delegates could not agree with Bolívar's rather liberal views about religion and insisted upon an article prohibiting the public exercise of any but the Roman Catholic cult. The other provisions of the *constitución vitalicia* have been described in Chapter 8.

Sucre, though he himself urged the selection of a native Bolivian, was chosen President and reluctantly consented to serve for a period of two years. The Venezuelan general had been the real ruler of the country since the end of the war. His tactful leadership had made the orderly establishment of the new Republic possible, and he had already reorganized the administrative and fiscal system. He had also begun to build up a school system, but the effort to implant the educational methods of ancient Sparta, sponsored by Bolívar's old teacher Simón Rodríguez, does not seem to have been a great success.[1] Sucre had remained in Bolivia, however, only from a sense of duty and he was eager to return to Quito to be married. Never ambitious on his own account, he made no attempt to build up a personal regime as other lieutenants of Bolívar were already doing in Venezuela and Ecuador.

His position grew more difficult after the collapse of the Liberator's authority in Peru. The new rulers of that country intrigued against him and his own soldiers were becoming homesick. Sucre was wounded when some of them mutinied at Chuquisaca in April, 1828, and could offer little resistance when the Peruvian General Gamarra invaded Bolivia. In July he assented to a treaty that required him to leave the country with his Colombian troops. Andrés Santa Cruz, who was at the time in Chile, was chosen by the Congress as his successor.

Santa Cruz, who had already figured prominently in events in Peru, was a *mestizo*, claiming descent on his mother's side from the royal family of the Incas. Born on the shore of Lake Titicaca, he had a great following among the Indians on both sides of the Peru-Bolivian frontier. He fought on the Spanish side during the greater part of the war for independence, as did most of the Peruvian generals, but he joined San

[1] Pinilla, *La Creación de Bolivia*, pp. 269–70.

Martín's army in 1821. Later, as we have already seen, he served under Bolívar, and governed Peru for a short time as the Liberator's lieutenant.

There was much disorder, fomented by Gamarra's intrigues, before Santa Cruz reached Bolivia, and General Velasco, the acting President, was overthrown and then restored by barrack revolts. The hostility of the populace finally forced Gamarra to withdraw his army, and when the President-Elect assumed power in May, 1829, the war between Peru and Colombia had ended for the time being the danger of a new invasion. One of Santa Cruz' first acts was to set aside the Bolivarian constitution. His regime was a dictatorship, but it was nevertheless one of the best governments in Latin America and without question the best government that Bolivia was to have for many years. His able administration and careful financial management won him much support while his sagacious but firm handling of opponents prevented disorder. A large and well-disciplined army further strengthened his hand, and for several years the country enjoyed a measure of prosperity. We have already seen how this state of affairs impressed the propertied classes in Peru and helped to make possible a union of the two countries, with Santa Cruz as "Protector," which was proclaimed in 1836 but was destroyed by Chilean intervention in 1839.

Even before the defeat of Santa Cruz's army at Yungay, his leadership had been repudiated by his subordinates in Bolivia, and he was compelled to dissolve the Confederation and go into exile. General José Miguel de Velasco, who had been Provisional President in 1828–29 and President of the State of Bolivia under the Confederation, became head of the government. Popular, but inept and easy-going, he was soon struggling against revolts fomented by other military leaders. When he was overthrown by partisans of Santa Cruz, in 1841, Gamarra invaded Bolivia to prevent his old enemy's return to power. The Peruvian President supported a revolution under General José Ballivián, but the latter, when he had defeated his opponents, turned against his ally and Gamarra was defeated and killed at the battle of Ingavi.

Under Ballivián the country had six years of relative peace. A new constitution gave the president an eight-year term with practically dictatorial powers. Those who conspired against the government were promptly executed, and Santa Cruz, the chief trouble maker, was finally persuaded to live in Europe on a generous pension. There was an effort, though not a very effective one, to promote road building and education. Not one school had been open in Bolivia in 1841, but some 4,000 pupils, still a pitifully small number, were receiving instruction a few years later.[1] A few foreign scientists and teachers were brought to the country and the first real newspaper was established. The net result of these progressive measures, however, was small, for the country remained almost as isolated and poverty-stricken as before.

The Era of Military Despotism, 1847–1879

Ballivián was overthrown in 1847 by a military mutiny under Colonel Manuel Isidoro Belzu. Velasco again became President, but he had been in office only a few months when Belzu led a new revolt and assumed power himself. Belzu's administration was the first of a series of sanguinary and corrupt despotisms which have few parallels in the history of Latin America. A professional soldier, uneducated and with no conception of the responsibilities attaching to his high office, the new President was typical of the military *caudillos* who were the leading figures in Bolivian politics. Since the overthrow of Sucre, nearly every change of government had been the result of a mutiny in the army and every officer of the higher ranks had come to regard himself as a potential dictator. Personal bravery, lack of scruples, and a readiness to kill an enemy in cold blood were the qualities which seemed to assure success. Civilian leaders, though they held important posts in the cabinet and congress, played a secondary rôle. There were no real political parties, and even the purely personal factions that surrounded each *caudillo* were frequently disrupted by jealousy or treachery. The constant interference of Peru, whether by armed intervention or by intrigue and bribery, made the establishment of stable government more difficult. Trouble makers, both native and foreign, found a fertile field for their activities in the intense spirit of *localismo*, which made rivalries and antipathies between the different towns more important in the eyes of the ruling class than questions of national concern.

Belzu, himself of humble birth, sought popularity by appealing to class hatred. Mobs were encouraged to sack the properties of his opponents among the upper class, and the *cholos* were encouraged to regard themselves as the new rulers of the country. The President became the idol of the *pueblo*, the turbulent artisans of the towns. He was nevertheless continually beset by conspiracies and revolts, which were not discouraged by the brutal punishment of enemies who fell into his

[1] Arguedas, *Historia general de Bolivia*, p. 117.

hands. On one occasion he was nearly killed by would-be assassins, and the Council of Ministers, during his convalescence, shot not only those implicated in the plot but also the President of Congress and other high officials of whom they were jealous for political reasons. In 1855 Belzu wearied of the struggle to remain in power and presented his resignation, informing Congress that "Bolivia has become ungovernable." His son-in-law, Jorge Córdova, a foundling trained in the army, was "elected" to succeed him, but was overthrown in 1857 by José María Linares.

Linares, unlike his predecessors, was a civilian, highly respected for his upright character and his intellectual attainments. He had been acting President for a short time in 1848, and since then had led one revolution after another, sacrificing much of his personal fortune in the effort to restore what he believed to be the constitutional order. Once in power, however, he established a dictatorship little less arbitrary and ruthless than those that had gone before. His energetic but often ill-considered attacks on long-standing political and social abuses made many enemies, and he was finally betrayed by two of his own ministers, who seized power by a *coup d'état* and sent him into exile in 1861.

The next president, General José María de Achá, was chosen in an election more nearly free than any since the time of Sucre. Achá offered cabinet positions to members of all of the larger political factions, and apparently made a real attempt to govern constitutionally, but his tolerant policy merely encouraged intrigue and revolt. Shocking scenes occurred in La Paz, where more than sixty political prisoners, including ex-President Córdova, were massacred to thwart a rumored jail-delivery. The President, like most of the military *caudillos*, was ignorant and incompetent, but he remained in office until the end of 1864 when his close associate, Mariano Melgarejo, ousted him by a barracks revolt.

Melgarejo, starting as a common soldier, had risen to high position in the army, and consequently in the government, chiefly by his audacity and complete lack of scruples. He established his authority only after a sharp struggle with several other leaders, including Belzu. This *caudillo*, still popular with the *cholo* class, defeated the new government's forces and occupied La Paz, but while Belzu was celebrating the victory Melgarejo entered the palace with six men, killed Belzu, and overawed the mob that a moment before had been cheering for his rival. Once in power the new President showed a complete contempt for legal restraints and private rights, cruelly suppressing every evidence of discontent and using the public funds for the gratification of his vices and the enrichment of his friends. During his frequent periods of drunkenness he was capable of atrocities that terrified even his unprincipled associates.

Melgarejo was overthrown in 1871 by another professional soldier named Agustín Morales. Though hardly less ignorant and dissolute than his predecessor, the new President attempted at first to obtain the support of the better elements, and permitted the restoration of a semblance of constitutional government. When he was killed in a brawl with his own nephew in 1872, a rich merchant, Tomás Frías, became Provisional President and held an election in which Adolfo Ballivián was chosen as President. Frías again assumed the presidency shortly before Ballivián's death from illness in 1874. The interval of civilian government was a brief one, and it ended when General Hilarión Daza, the Minister of War, overthrew Frías in 1876.

The War with Chile

The outbreak of the war with Chile, which came in Daza's administration, found Bolivia completely unprepared. The country's rulers, absorbed in a bloody struggle to gain or hold power, had paid little attention to the threatening situation that was developing in the south. There had never been any close connection between the interior and the inaccessible coastal province of Antofagasta, because Arica, in Peru, had been the chief port for such foreign commerce as the Republic had. Ballivián had urged the purchase of arms, but his proposals had been defeated in Congress. The army, though it dominated the country's internal politics, was insignificant compared with that of Chile, and lacked modern weapons and real training. Neither Daza nor his predecessors seem to have realized this, and they recklessly allowed the quarrel with Chile over the taxation of foreign nitrate companies to develop into armed conflict.

The story of the war has been told in Chapter 12. Daza at first took command of the Bolivian army, but his troops revolted in December, 1879, after his treacherous abandonment of his allies in Tarapacá, and an uprising in the interior made General Narciso Campero President of the Republic. In May, 1880, the allied forces under Campero's command were routed at Tacna. So far as Bolivia was concerned the war was over, though Campero endeavored to raise a new force in the interior. Chile took the rich nitrate fields of Antofagasta, and Bolivia became a land-locked country. The Bolivians never reconciled themselves to the loss of their access to the sea, and their resentment continued to be a dangerous element in the international politics of South America even after a formal treaty of peace was signed with Chile in 1904.

Progress after the War

Public opinion was sharply divided over the question of continuing the war or accepting defeat, and the issue gave rise to political parties which for the first time were something more, though not very much more, than mere personal factions. Those who wished to resume the struggle, led by Campero and another war hero, General Camacho, called themselves liberals. Their opponents, though divided into two factions, the "conservatives" and the "democrats," were able to defeat the administration candidate in 1884. Neither obtained a majority of the popular vote, but they combined when Congress met to bring about the election of Gregorio Pacheco, a wealthy miner, as President.

Both economic and political conditions improved after the war. The country was somewhat more prosperous, thanks to a revival of silver production, and it began to have more intercourse with the outside world, especially after the railroad connecting Oruro with Antofagasta was opened in 1892. The government was definitely more stable. Aniceto Arce, who succeeded Pacheco in 1888, and Mariano Baptista, who became President in 1892, were both highly respected leaders of the conservative party. Though the liberals were discontented, such revolts as occurred were unsuccessful, and the recurrent military mutinies of the pre-war period, with the wholesale executions which often followed them, seemed to be a thing of the past. Elections, however, were controlled by the authorities, and opponents of the government were frequently imprisoned or sent into exile.

Severo Fernández Alonso, another conservative, became President in 1896. He was overthrown three years later when a dispute over the location of the national capital caused an outburst of the still violent spirit of *localismo*. Sucre, the ancient Chuquisaca, was constitutionally the seat of the government, as it had been in colonial times, but presidents and congresses usually found it more convenient to carry on the administration from less inaccessible places. Proposals to move the capital had frequently aroused controversy. La Paz was especially insistent upon its claims as the largest and most important town, and when Congress voted to make Sucre the capital permanently members of both parties in the rival city revolted under the leadership of Colonel José Manuel Pando. After several months of fighting, Pando became President, and the government offices were moved to La Paz.

Liberal and Republican Administrations, 1899–1932

The liberals were in power from 1899 until 1920, controlling elections by much the same means as their conservative predecessors. After Pando, the progressive and able Ismael Montes was President from 1904 until 1909 and again from 1913 until 1917, after Eliodoro Villazón served the intervening term. During this time Bolivia enjoyed the longest period of internal peace in her history. Tin production, which became important at the turn of the century, increased until the Republic was producing a quarter of the world's supply, and new copper and lead mines helped to bring about a rapid increase in foreign trade. Railroad construction did much to encourage this economic development, and also to promote internal stability by bringing some of the hitherto isolated, mutually hostile provincial towns within easier reach of the capital. A line from Lake Titicaca to the heights above La Paz, completed in 1903, connected that city with the Peruvian seaport of Mollendo, and other lines were completed in 1913 from La Paz to Arica and from La Paz to Oruro, connecting with the existing railroad to Antofagasta. Branch lines to Potosí and Cochabamba were also built, but great sections of the Republic still remained without adequate means of transportation.

Railroad building was made possible partly by foreign borrowing, to which Bolivia now resorted for the first time, and partly by payments made to Bolivia in connection with the settlement of outstanding diplomatic questions. A dispute with Brazil over the administration of the rich rubber district of Acre on one of the upper tributaries of the Amazon was settled in 1903 by the cession of the territory to Brazil in return for a cash payment of £2,000,000, and in 1904, when a long overdue peace treaty replaced the truce which ended hostilities with Chile in 1884, the Chilean government agreed under one of its provisions to build the railroad from Arica to La Paz.

The liberals did not avoid the disintegrating effects of a long tenure of power, and several of their leaders formed a new opposition group called the republican party. This failed to prevent the election of the administration candidate, José Gutiérrez Guerra, in 1917, but overthrew his government, with the aid of the army and with little bloodshed, in 1920. Thereafter an election in which only republicans voted made Bautista Saavedra President for the term 1921–25. In Saavedra's administration and in that of Hernando Siles, who took office in 1926, bond issues floated in the United States increased the foreign debt from approximately $6,000,000 to more than $60,000,000. Some beneficial results were obtained from this great expenditure, including especially the completion of a connecting link between Bolivia's railway system and that of Argentina; but much of the money went for non-productive purposes, to buy arms and munitions, or simply to meet the chronic deficits in the budget. To obtain the loans the country pledged nearly all of its principal revenues and entrusted the supervision of their collection to a permanent fiscal commission, nominated partly by North American bankers. This arrangement broke down during the depression when the Republic stopped service on its foreign debt.

The depression also caused a political crisis. Siles was overthrown when he attempted to remain in power at the end of his term and Daniel Salamanca, a civilian, was elected President in 1931 by a republican-liberal coalition.

The Chaco War and its Aftermath

Much of the proceeds of the recent foreign loans had been spent in preparing for the war with Paraguay which began in 1932.[1] Bolivia's stubborn refusal to agree to a peaceful settlement in the Chaco was partly an expression of her desire for an outlet to the sea, which had been almost an obsession since the loss of Antofagasta in the War of the Pacific. The Chaco would have given her ports on the Paraguay River. She did obtain a strip of territory on the upper reaches of the river at the end of the conflict, but it was of little practical use.

In every other respect, the war was a disaster. Its cost in human life and money was out of all proportion to the value of the territory in dispute. The Bolivian troops, taken from the cold highlands into the low, hot plains where the fighting took place, suffered much more than did their opponents. The drafting of men into the army caused a shortage of labor that seriously crippled mining and agriculture, and

[1] For the story of the war, see pp. 219-20.

the maintenance of the army severely strained the country's financial resources. Great sums were borrowed from the mining industry and from private individuals, and an excessive inflation of the currency caused hardship to all classes.

Party quarrels continued even during the war, and in November, 1934, when Salamanca went to the Chaco and attempted to dismiss the Commander-in-Chief, General Peñaranda, the army arrested him and the Vice-President, José Luis Tejada Sorzano, seized power at La Paz. After the fighting ended, there was much discontent. A new radical party, composed largely of students and demobilized soldiers, overthrew Tejada Sorzano in May, 1936, and installed the Chief of the General Staff, Colonel David Toro, as the head of what professed to be a socialist regime. Toro involved Bolivia in a dispute with the United States when he expropriated the properties of the Standard Oil Company in March, 1937, and some of his other policies brought on conflicts with powerful Bolivian mining and banking interests. These local interests helped to overthrow him in July, 1937, but his successor, another army officer named German Busch adopted policies that seemed equally dangerous to the business community. When Busch committed suicide, or was murdered, in August, 1939, there was a reaction. The army remained in control for a time, but in March, 1940, with the election of General Enrique Peñaranda as President, the constitutional order was restored with the more conservative political groups in control.

During the Second World War, Bolivia's internal politics became a matter of importance to the outside world. Bolivian tin became indispensable to the allied war effort after Japan conquered Malaya, and the country's other strategic minerals were desperately needed. The Peñaranda government was pro-ally, and in July, 1941, it expelled the German minister after the discovery of a subversive conspiracy in which the German legation was involved. After Pearl Harbor, the government obtained aid from the United States in the form of lend-lease and Export-Import Bank loans and settled the chief source of disagreement between the two countries by paying the Standard Oil Company $1,500,000 for its expropriated properties. The President declared war on the Axis powers in April, 1943, and his action was confirmed by the Congress in November. Meanwhile, however, the government was struggling with increasingly grave internal problems. While some classes in the community were profiting greatly from the increased mineral exports, inflation made worse the already bad situation of the Indians who worked in the mines, and made them susceptible to extremist propaganda. The killing of a number of striking miners at Cataví in December, 1942, caused a painful impression in Bolivia and abroad. This affair strengthened the Leftist Revolutionary Party, the PIR, which opposed the government on one side, while the chauvinistic pro-Axis National Revolutionary Movement, the MNR, worked against it at the other extreme.

In December, 1943, the MNR, with the support of part of the army, overthrew the Peñaranda government. The revolt was planned in Buenos Aires, with the connivance of German agents and high Argentine officials, and the new administration, headed by Lieutenant Colonel Gualberto Villaroel, was consequently refused recognition by the United States and by most of the other American republics. Villaroel, however, insisted that he intended to coöperate with the democracies. To show his good faith, he removed the principal leaders of the MNR from their positions in the government, and expelled 82 Germans and Japanese from Bolivia. These acts helped him to obtain recognition from the other American countries in June, 1944. The MNR nevertheless obtained more seats than any other party in a constituent assembly elected in July, and at the end of the year, when the government's position had been weakened by a formidable though unsuccessful revolt, its leaders came back into the cabinet. It was fortunately too late for them to be of any great help to the Axis.

Brutal treatment of the government's opponents aroused much hatred, and when a successful uprising took place in July, 1946, Villaroel was seized by a mob and hanged from a lamp post in La Paz. A provisional government held free and fairly orderly elections in January, 1947. There were two candidates, each supported by a group of the civilian political parties. The vote was extremely close and there might well have been trouble if Luis Fernando Guachalla, the liberal candidate, had not conceded the victory to his opponent Enrique Herzog, who was inaugurated as President in March, 1947. During the next two years Dr. Herzog had to contend with opposition from the MNR and the allegedly communist PIR and also with dissensions among his supporters in the moderate parties. There was much disorder, some of it political and some caused by continuing unrest among the laborers in the mines. A revolt by the MNR, in August and September, 1949, was suppressed only after heavy fighting in several parts of the Republic. Some time before this started, Dr. Herzog had become incapacitated through illness, and in October, when he resigned, the Congress chose Mamerto Urriolagoitia as his successor.

It will be difficult to establish a stable government in Bolivia until there has been an improvement in the condition of the masses of the people. Despite the wartime prosperity of the tin-mining industry, the miners' wages have remained pitifully low while the cost of living has risen excessively. Other laboring groups, and especially the Indian agricultural workers, are still worse off. One of the chief factors in the country's poverty is the lack of arable land, in the plateau region where the bulk of the inhabitants live, and the inaccessibility of the country east of the Andes, some of which is apparently better suited to agriculture and cattle raising. There is consequently some hope for the future in the road to Santa Cruz de la Sierra which is now being built with money lent to Bolivia by the United States and which should open up that area to settlement.

17

Ecuador

Ecuador in many ways resembles the other Central Andean countries. Perhaps a half of her people are Indians—*quechua*-speaking descendants of civilized tribes that formed part of the Inca Empire, occupying a chain of high valleys between the two ranges of the Andes, and living and working under much the same conditions as the Indians of Peru. In Ecuador, however, the highland region lacks the mineral wealth of the mountains farther south, and its inhabitants, though they supply themselves with most of the products needed to maintain a very simple standard of living, contribute little to foreign trade. Most of the country's exports—cacao, ivory nuts, coffee, rice, Panama hats, and gold—come from the coastal plain along the Pacific, which is wider and has a heavier rainfall than in Peru. The coast has a considerable population of mixed Spanish, Negro, and Indian descent, and Guayaquil, the chief seaport, is the Republic's largest city. Steep, jungle-covered mountains make communication between this region and the interior very difficult, and the separation of the country into two sections, with different interests and different points of view, has encouraged *localismo* and has made it difficult to establish a stable government.

Though the Presidency of Quito had close relations with Peru, it became a part of the Viceroyalty of New Granada in the eighteenth century and was thus claimed as a part of Bolívar's Republic of Colombia when that state was created. Colombian control was assured after Sucre defeated the royalists at Pichincha. Those who preferred independence were helpless in the face of the Liberator's prestige and popularity, especially as the country was occupied by veteran troops from Colombia and Venezuela. In one respect at least the future

337

Republic of Ecuador profited from the union, for the people of Quito without outside help could hardly have resisted Peru's claim to Guayaquil, which was the only seaport accessible to them and which was consequently indispensable to their existence as a separate state.

Flores and Rocafuerte

The military commander in Ecuador in 1830 was General Juan José Flores, a thirty-year-old Venezuelan who joined the patriot forces as a common soldier when little more than a child, and rose to high rank after the war by his courageous and tactful handling of several difficult assignments. Though of obscure origin and with practically no schooling, he married into one of the best families of Quito and made many friends among the creole aristocracy. He thus had some local support to offset the resentment of the *Quiteños* at being ruled by a foreigner with the support of foreign troops. He was apparently loyal to Bolívar so long as the Liberator retained control at Bogotá, but he lost no time in seizing power for himself when it became apparent that Great Colombia was breaking up. At his instigation, the more prominent citizens of Quito met in May, 1830, to declare Ecuador independent, and some months later a constituent assembly elected him President of the Republic.

It was not long before organized opposition appeared. One of the leaders was Colonel Hall, an ardent English liberal who had settled in Quito after serving in the patriot army. Hall encouraged a group of young patriots to start a newspaper called *El Quiteño Libre* in 1833, and when this began to denounce the government as a foreign military despotism and to criticize its corrupt administration of the finances, Flores suppressed the paper and arrested those connected with it. The "nationalists" then revolted, but their military chief, Vicente Rocafuerte, soon fell into the government's hands.

Instead of shooting his captive, Flores won his support by promising him the presidency for the next term. Rocafuerte, who thus became the head of the government in 1835, was a wealthy creole from Guayaquil. He had spent much of his life abroad, first in school, then as an American deputy in the Spanish Cortes, and later as a diplomatic representative of Mexico in England. His writings on political subjects had won him some distinction, and the nationalist group had eagerly accepted his leadership when he returned to his own country. His presidency, however, was little more than a continuation of the preceding regime, because Flores remained in command of the army and frequently interfered in political affairs. The government's energy was absorbed in maintaining order, and its treatment of opponents was so harsh that there were many who welcomed Flores' return to the presidency in 1839. Flores' second administration, however, was more corrupt and arbitrary than Rocafuerte's. He ruled without a congress, after quarreling with the legislative body in 1840; and in 1843 he changed the constitution and brought about his own re-election with increased powers, for a new term of eight years. This caused a break with Rocafuerte, who had expected to be president himself. Further unpopular actions such as the imposition of a general head tax and the granting of freedom of worship to non-Catholics strengthened the opposition; and when a revolution broke out in Guayaquil on March 6, 1845, the government collapsed. Flores accepted $20,000 and a pension in return for his agreement to leave Ecuador for two years.

Foreign Interference and Internal Disorder, 1845–1860

A constituent assembly elected Vicente Ramón Roca, one of the leaders of the revolt, as President. The Republic now had a government controlled by its own citizens, but its political life for some years to come was to be influenced by the interference of more powerful nations. Roca's administration was much disturbed by Flores' efforts to bring about a counter-revolution with the help of Spain. The ex-President apparently obtained the support of the Queen Mother María Cristina by holding out hopes of establishing a Spanish prince as ruler at Quito, and he was able to recruit a large force in Europe. The plan collapsed when the South American ministers at London persuaded the British government to seize three ships that were to have carried the expedition to America, but the threat of a Spanish reconquest of Ecuador greatly alarmed the Republic's neighbors and led to the meeting of an American congress at Lima in 1847 to consider plans for mutual defense.

Under Roca's successors, party strife was frequently aggravated by the interference of Colombia or Peru. Diego Noboa, who was made head of the government by a military *coup* after the Congress failed to elect a president in 1849, nearly brought on a war with Colombia by giving asylum to the Jesuits whom the liberals had just expelled from that country. General José María Urbina, who overthrew Noboa in 1851, forced the Jesuits to leave and adopted a mildly anticlerical policy in other respects. This aroused the enmity of the conservative government of Peru, which helped the ever-active Flores in an unsuccessful counter-revolution.

These events, and especially the repercussions of the bitter Church-State conflict in Colombia, gave a new meaning to the party divisions in Ecuador, where the names conservative and liberal had hitherto been used as convenient labels by the friends and enemies of Flores without signifying any great differences in ideology. Urbina adopted several of the policies espoused by liberals in the neighboring countries. The influence of the Church was still strong enough to prevent any serious attack on its prerogatives, but in 1854 Negro slavery was abolished and a little later Indian tributes were suppressed.

At the end of his term in 1856, Urbina installed General Francisco Robles as his successor, but kept the real power in his own hands through the control of the army. The new President, neither able nor popular, was soon involved in difficulties at home and abroad. The most serious was the old boundary dispute with Peru, which became acute when the Ecuadorean government proposed to discharge a portion of its share of the revolutionary debt of Great Colombia by granting lands in the disputed region to some of the bondholders. Peru finally declared war, blockaded Guayaquil, and encouraged discontented leaders in Ecuador to start revolts so that the country was soon in a state of anarchy. Robles and Urbina were forced to flee. General Franco, the commander at Guayaquil, made a truce with Peru, but he was unable to control the interior, where Gabriel García Moreno, with the help of Flores, finally obtained control after a series of brilliant campaigns. The provisional government set up by these two leaders defeated Franco, and García Moreno became President in 1861.

The Dictatorship of García Moreno

Ecuador had made little progress in forty years of independence. The cities were declining in population and public buildings were falling into decay. There was little foreign commerce. The only road from the interior to the coast was the trail from Quito to Guayaquil, passable only for pack mules, and this was closed to traffic six or eight months each year by the rains. Though slavery and tributes had been abolished, both

Negroes and Indians were still working for insignificant wages under a peonage system established by law, exploited and oppressed as in colonial times by landowners, priests, and officials. The sanguinary struggles between rival military leaders had taken a heavy toll in life and property. Many were beginning to feel that a monarchy under a foreign prince might be better than continued anarchy, and García Moreno himself made unsuccessful efforts to make Ecuador a protectorate of France during the civil war in 1859.[1]

A measure of internal peace was established under a heavy-handed dictatorship after García Moreno assumed the presidency. The new ruler, though he had been the ablest leader of the recent revolt, was not a professional soldier but a lawyer. Since his father was a loyal Spaniard, the family property had been confiscated during the revolution, and García Moreno himself grew up in poverty. A charitable friar took charge of his education, and his intellectual ability, combined with utter fearlessness and indefatigable energy, soon made him one of the leaders of the younger generation. He became active in politics at an early age, first as a "nationalist" against Flores and later as a conservative against Urbina and Robles. For a time, as a political exile, he studied in France. He now came into power with Flores' support, but the old *caudillo* had little influence in his administration. The new President centered all authority in his own hands. Opponents and even peaceful critics were shot or imprisoned without regard to legal forms, and counter-revolutionary movements under Urbina and other liberals were suppressed with ferocious energy. The congress was reduced to obedience when several of its more independent members were sent into exile, and the press was permitted no freedom.

García Moreno dominated Ecuadorean politics for fifteen years. Since the constitution forbade reëlection, he permitted Gerónimo Carrión, the liberal candidate, to become President in 1865 but dictated the appointment of his cabinet and made him little more than a figurehead. In 1867, when Carrión allowed Congress to get out of hand, García Moreno demanded his resignation and installed another liberal, Javier Espinosa, in his place. As the election of 1869 approached, and several presidential candidates appeared, Espinosa attempted to remain neutral and was promptly ousted by the army. A few months later García Moreno again became President under a new constitution which gave

[1] George Frederick Howe, *García Moreno's Efforts to Unite Ecuador and France,* Hispanic American Historical Review, Vol. 16, p. 257.

him a six-year term, eliminated the prohibition against reëlection, and greatly increased his authority.

The clergy gave García Moreno the same sort of support that they had given the Spanish authorities in colonial times. Despite the infiltration of foreign ideas since independence, the Church still had much influence with the masses of the people, and even the liberals had not dared to abrogate the constitutional provision against the public exercise of any but the Catholic religion. Monasteries and other pious foundations owned great amounts of land and had great economic power. García Moreno was himself extremely devout, at least in outward practice, and he systematically built up the Church's influence as a means of maintaining his own power. A concordat promulgated in 1863 gave the ecclesiastical authorities control over the publication and importation of books and supervision of all education. At the same time, the President was relentless, though largely unsuccessful, in his effort to eradicate the abuses that had grown up among the native clergy since the separation from Spain.

In many respects, García Moreno was a statesman of vision and constructive ability, honest in his management of public funds, and an indefatigable worker. He gave much attention to the improvement and beautification of the cities of the Republic and also to popular education, entrusting to the Jesuits the direction of the secondary schools and bringing Christian Brothers from France to take charge of primary instruction. The number of children in school increased three-fold, and the quality of the teaching, hitherto grievously neglected, was improved. Equally important, perhaps, was the building of a cart road from Quito to Guayaquil, which revolutionized transportation between the coast and the interior.

Political Events, 1875–1895

García Moreno was assassinated in 1875 by a group of political conspirators. His war minister, who had perhaps been involved in the plot against him,[1] seized control, but was soon overthrown by other military leaders, and Antonio Borrero, a liberal with many friends among the conservatives, was peacefully elected as President. Borrero attempted to retain the support of both parties by a policy of conciliation, but the liberals turned against him when he refused to call a convention to

[1] Pedro Moncayo, El Ecuador de 1825 a 1875, p. 332 ff.

modify the reactionary constitution that García Moreno had imposed. General José Ignacio de Veintemilla overthrew him in 1876, and during the next seven years, with Veintemilla as President, there was a return to the old evils of military rule and governmental corruption.

In 1883 the civilian elements of both parties joined forces in a successful revolution. The conservatives assumed control under José María Placido Caamaño, who attempted to return to the authoritarian methods of García Moreno and to restore the close alliance with the Church, which had been attacked in its privileges but more alarmed than hurt during the liberal regime. The President's reactionary policy was too much for many members of his own party, and the "progressives," as the more moderate conservatives called themselves, were able to obtain control of the government in the election of 1888. The new President was Antonio Flores, the son of the founder of the Republic and himself for many years a prominent figure in Ecuador's politics. Under his administration the country had four years of tranquility. Private rights and the freedom of the press were respected and an effort was made to introduce greater honesty and efficiency in the government.

Flores' successor, Luis Cordero, another "progressive," showed less ability, and in 1895 he became involved in a noisy scandal. The government of Chile had sold one of its warships, the *Esmeralda*, to Japan for use in the war with China and had attempted to conceal this breach of neutrality by nominally transferring the vessel first to Ecuador. When it became known that Cordero had permitted this misuse of the national flag there was an outburst of indignation, and the liberals seized upon the opportunity to revolt. After some months of fighting, under the leadership of General Eloy Alfaro, the insurgents obtained control of the country.

Alfaro and his Successors, 1895–1920

Alfaro, who was to be the chief figure in the Republic's politics during the next seventeen years, had been active as a conspirator and revolutionist since García Moreno's first administration. In several years of exile at Panama, he had built up a fortune in private business. A close friend of the great Ecuadorean liberal thinker Juan Montalvo, he had a somewhat more definite ideology than many of the earlier leaders, to whom "liberalism" had been little more than a convenient party label. His anticlerical views made him highly objectionable to the more extreme conservatives. The latter were defeated, however, when they attempted a counter-revolution with aid from Colombia, and Alfaro's own moderation, combined with the wise policy of Archbishop González Suárez, prevented the issue of Church and State from becoming acute during his first term as President (1897–1901). The Law of Patronage, enacted in 1899, gave the civil authorities a large measure of control over the Church.

A series of anticlerical measures, including laws authorizing the practice of other cults, permitting civil marriage and divorce, and expropriating much church property, were enacted under Alfaro's successor, General Leonidas Plaza (1901–5), and a new constitution, which contained no provision making Catholicism the state religion, was adopted in 1906. By this time Alfaro was again in power, for he had forcibly ejected Plaza's successor, Lizardo García, within a few months after the latter had taken office. His second term was a period of violent political agitation, and the government adopted harsh measures to suppress conspiracies and incipient revolts. Foreign affairs also were troublesome, and a revival of the boundary dispute threatened for a time to bring on war with Peru. It was nevertheless possible to complete the railroad from Guayaquil to Quito, upon which Alfaro had concentrated much of his energy during his first term. The new line was of the greatest value not only from an economic but from a political standpoint, but the bonds issued to finance it soon went into default, with unfortunate effects upon the country's credit.

Emilio Estrada, "elected, as usual, by the soldiers and public employes,"[1] succeeded to the presidency in 1911. Alfaro attempted at the last minute to prevent the new chief executive from taking office, because of the latter's ill health, but he had by this time many enemies even in his own party and a revolt of the troops and populace at Quito sent him into exile. When Estrada died suddenly four months later, Alfaro made a new bid for power, but was captured by government troops led by his old associate General Plaza. In January, 1912, the ex-President was dragged from his prison at Quito and killed by a mob in the streets. A prominent civilian presidential candidate, Julio Andrade, was also murdered shortly afterward.

For some years after this outbreak of violence, the country had a period of relative tranquility. General Plaza, who again became Presi-

[1] Reyes, *Historia de la República del Ecuador*, p. 272.

dent, had to suppress an uprising by Alfaro's former partisans, and had to contend with the temporary dislocation of trade and finance that came with the outbreak of the European war, but he was able to serve out his term. Under his successor, Alfredo Baquerizo Moreno (1916–20), both economic and political conditions improved. The question of Church and State had by this time lost much of its importance as a political issue, and the government made no effort to influence the selection of a new archbishop when the venerable González Suárez died in 1917.[1]

The most important event of Baquerizo's administration was the sanitation of Guayaquil. The presence of endemic yellow fever and the danger from other tropical diseases had long made shipmasters reluctant to dock at this city, which was the Republic's chief port, and it was clear that a continuance of these conditions would deprive Ecuador of many of the benefits anticipated from the opening of the Panama Canal. The work of sanitation, which included especially the eradication of yellow fever, was carried out with the help of the Rockefeller Foundation.

History Since 1920

José Luis Tamayo, President from 1920 to 1924, was a liberal, like his predecessors, but he appointed many conservatives to positions in the administration. He was opposed, on the other hand, by a growing element in his own party, which believed that the banks, and especially the Banco Comercial y Agrícola of Guayaquil, were exercising an undue influence in the country's politics in order to maintain their privilege of issuing irredeemable paper money. The depreciation of the currency had caused much hardship among the laboring classes because prices had risen whereas wages, especially on the plantations of the interior, had remained almost unchanged. In 1922–23 this situation caused riots both at Guayaquil and in the interior, and many lives were lost in restoring order. The left-wing liberals were so strong by 1924 that the government considered it advisable to permit the election of one of their leaders, Dr. Gonzalo Córdoba, as President but only after exacting promises which left him little freedom of action. This did not satisfy the "liberal-radicals," especially as the new chief executive was soon

[1] Reyes, *op. cit.*, p. 279.

compelled by illness to turn over the presidency to Vice-President Guerrero Martínez; and in July, 1925, with the help of younger officers in the army, they ousted Guerrero Martínez by a *golpe de estado*.

After some months of government by a military *junta*, Dr. Isidro Ayora was made Provisional President in 1926. The new administration, on the advice of Professor Kemmerer of Princeton University, established a central bank with the sole right of note issue and stabilized the currency. The reëstablishment of constitutional government was delayed until these and other reforms were effected, and it was not until 1929 that Ayora was formally elected President by a constituent assembly. Unfortunately the government's financial reforms like similar reforms in other Latin American countries, were made ineffective by the depression.

The depression also caused political unrest, and in 1931 Ayora was forced to resign. During the next four years governments rose and fell with kaleidoscopic rapidity. Disputes with Congress, insubordination in the army, and discontent caused by continued bad economic conditions made it impossible for any president to remain in office more than a few months. Finally, in September, 1935, the army set up a military dictatorship under Federico Páez.

Páez struggled for two years against opposition from many quarters. Several conservative leaders were imprisoned or exiled, and the religious question was revived as a political issue when the government expelled all foreign priests in order to "nationalize" the Church. Radical elements also gave trouble, and a drastic "social security law" was adopted to check their activities. Military revolts occurred from time to time. In 1937 a constituent assembly met to pave the way for a return to constitutional government. Its members had been elected under conditions that gave the opposition parties little chance to participate, but it nevertheless got out of hand, and during the ensuing political crisis the army forced Páez to resign in favor of Alberto Enríquez, the Minister of War.

Enríquez dissolved the assembly and proceeded to promulgate a series of radical economic measures that increased tension between the political parties and alarmed foreign business interests. Among them were a minimum wage law, the confiscation of the properties of an American gold-mining company, the arbitrary revision of other concessions and contracts under which business firms were operating, and the reorganization of the Central Bank. In August, 1938, Enríquez submitted his resignation to a new constituent assembly in which the liberals, conservatives, and socialists were all represented. Three Provisional Presidents held office for short periods before Carlos Arroyo del Rio, a liberal-radical, was elected constitutional President in 1940.

A few months later a flareup of the boundary dispute with Peru developed into a real though undeclared war. The United States, Argentina, and Brazil offered their mediation, but it was some months before they were successful in establishing a neutral zone that stopped the fighting. While the foreign ministers of the American republics were meeting at Rio de Janeiro early in 1942 to consider the situation created by Japan's attack on the United States, Ecuador and Peru were persuaded to agree on a definite boundary. Ecuador had to relinquish her claim to a great area in the upper Amazon basin.

Dissatisfaction with the agreement weakened the position of Arroyo del Rio, who had been troubled by plots and revolts even while the fighting was in progress, but he weathered the storm and coöperated effectively with the United States in the war. Bases in the Galápagos Islands and at Salinas on the mainland did much to facilitate the defense of the Panama Canal. In return, Ecuador received lend-lease and loans from the Export-Import Bank, and a development corporation established with the help of the United States carried on a program of public health work and road building and did much for the rehabilitation of the coastal province of El Oro which had been devastated by Peruvian troops. Unfortunately the expenditure of foreign funds, combined with a great increase in exports of balsa wood, rubber, and other strategic materials, brought on a serious inflation.

In May, 1944, as the time for a new presidential election approached, a revolt in Guayaquil and a general strike in Quito forced Arroyo del Rio to resign. A *junta* representing all of the opposition parties, from the conservatives to the communists, took control and José María Velasco Ibarra was proclaimed President. Velasco Ibarra had been considered a left-wing radical, but he had disagreements with the communists and socialists and after 1945 he worked chiefly with the conservatives. In August, 1947, he was removed by the army in a bloodless *coup* and a series of temporary presidents held office for short periods.

In June, 1948, there was a general election, in which about 240,000 votes were cast. Galo Plaza Lasso, who was supported by a coalition of other parties, defeated the conservative candidate by a narrow margin. The new president, a graduate of Cornell, had been Ambassador to the United States during the war.

Economic and Social Problems Today

Since 1924 no president of Ecuador has been permitted to serve a full constitutional term. Continual strife between the numerous political factions that have existed since the breakup of the old liberal party and the activity of radical groups like the socialists and communists have been partly responsible for this state of affairs, but the underlying cause is probably the general dissatisfaction with economic and social conditions. The Republic has had but a small share in the wealth that increasing foreign commerce has brought to other South American countries and it has been especially unfortunate in the vicissitudes that have befallen its one important export crop, cacao. Ecuador was for many years the chief source of the world's supply of chocolate, and a steady increase in the output of her plantations from the time of García Moreno until 1916 brought the country a modest prosperity which was reflected in the relative stability of the government during much of the period. Since 1916, however, the *monilia* and witches'-broom diseases have wrought havoc with the crop, and recent exports have been less than half the amount shipped abroad during the First World War. The other products of the coast—tagua nuts (for making buttons) and Panama hats, the best of which come from Ecuador—are relatively less important, and the highland region still supplies little for export. Few American countries have a smaller *per capita* foreign trade at the present time.

The lack of adequate means of transportation between the Coast and the Sierra is still an economic and political handicap and has helped to perpetuate the deep-seated jealousy between the two regions. It is not an accident that so many of the country's revolutions have started in Guayaquil, the coastal metropolis. The building of the railroad between that city and Quito, and more recently the construction of automobile roads, have improved matters to some extent, but the highlands of the interior are still one of the most isolated inhabited portions of South America.

The great social problem, however, is the condition of the Indians. As in Peru and Bolivia, the masses of the native race work on the properties of the white upper class. The *huasipungo* in the highlands is still bound to the soil, by custom if not by law, and the number of laborers attached to an *hacienda* is one of the most important elements in its market value. In 1857, when Indian tributes were abolished, the civil code legalized a system of *concertaje*, or debt slavery, which persisted in practice even after imprisonment for debt was legally abolished in 1918 and does not seem to have disappeared entirely today. Standards of living are still low. In 1931, it was reported that the average wage of the free rural laborer was about ten cents and that many victims of the peonage system received little or nothing.[1] Today, with the depreciation of the paper currency, real wages in the highlands are probably even more inadequate.

[1] Sáenz, *El Indio Ecuatoriano*, p. 56.

Part VI

❧

THE NORTH COAST

COLOMBIA and Venezuela are neither predominantly Indian countries like the Central Andean republics, nor predominantly European like Argentina and Uruguay. The descendants of the Chibchas and other tribes that lived in the northern part of South America before the Conquest have for the most part given up their native languages and cultures. They still form a substantial fraction of the population, and the non-European element was increased after the Conquest by a considerable importation of African slaves, but both Indians and Negroes have been assimilated into the Spanish-speaking community and no longer form separate castes, as do the Indians in the Andean countries. People of Spanish descent still own much of the land and direct public affairs, but other groups are by no means excluded from political life. As ardent members of the traditional parties in Colombia or as followers of local *caudillos* in Venezuela they took an active part in the civil wars that retarded progress in both countries in the nineteenth century and participate in the somewhat less violent conflicts of the present day.

The political development of the two countries has been quite different. In Colombia, to a greater extent than in most Latin American countries, political strife has centered around ideas rather than personalities, and conflicts between opposing schools of thought as to forms of government, and more especially as to the relations between Church and State, have been the real cause rather than merely the pretext for civil war. This concern with ideas seems to be one expression of an intense individualism which has affected political institutions in other ways, making for an intolerance of any curb on freedom of expression or political action, and at the same time frequently impairing party cohesion and discipline. It helps to explain why dictatorships of the ordinary Latin American type have been almost unknown in Colombia. In Venezuela, on the other hand, *personalismo* has been the chief factor in political life, and a series of dictators have ruled the country during most of the period since independence. This divergence between two neighboring countries which are otherwise similar in so many ways seems to stem from differences in the character of the people, arising partly perhaps from differences in the character of the Spanish immigration during the colonial period.

18

Colombia

Geographical Problems

Colombia is another country where political and economic development has been influenced by isolation imposed by geography. Nearly all of the principal settlements except the ancient coast towns of Cartagena and Santa Marta are in the inaccessible plateaus and valleys of the Andean highlands. The Andes, at their northern end, form three great ranges, one along the west coast, another between the deep valleys of the Cauca and the Magdalena Rivers, and the third, east of the Magdalena, which extends along the north coast into Venezuela. This eastern range, with the broad plateau of Bogotá, has always been one of the two great centers of population in Colombia. The other is in the central range and the rich Cauca Valley.

Until very recently, communication between these two regions, and between them and the coast, was exceedingly difficult. As late as 1842, there was not even a mule trail, and travelers from the west regularly went over the Quindío pass in the central range on the backs of men, a nine days' trip on a dangerous foot path, and then climbed four days more on horseback from the hot and unhealthful Magdalena Valley to Bogotá, 8,563 feet above sea-level. Between the interior and the ports on the north coast, through which passed such commerce as the country had with Europe and North America, all traffic was by small boats on the Magdalena River. The rapidity of the voyage depended, as it does now, on the depth of the water, which changed from day to day, and on the boatmen's luck in avoiding snags and sandbanks. Land travel through the swamps and forests of the valley was impossible. When General William Henry Harrison went to Colombia as American Minister in 1828 he considered himself fortunate in completing in six weeks the canoe trip from the coast to Honda, where travelers obtained horses for the ascent to Bogotá.[1] Under such conditions there could be little contact with the outside world, and within the Republic the spirit of *localismo* was unusually intense.

Great Colombia

At the beginning of the nineteenth century New Granada proper probably had somewhat more than 1,000,000 people. Except on the coast and in the Cauca Valley, where there were many Negro slaves, the great majority were of Indian blood, but the descendants of the Chibchas and other aboriginal tribes had for the most part adopted the language and religion of their conquerors and did not form a separate community as in Peru or Mexico. In the cities, the principal families were of Spanish descent, and it was they who dominated the country economically and politically.

We saw in Chapter 7 how local jealousies helped to defeat the first movement for independence in New Granada between 1810 and 1816. During the reign of terror after the reconquest, the small bands of patriots who escaped to the *llanos* of the interior coöperated with Bolívar's Venezuelan troops in the guerrilla warfare that kept the movement for independence alive during the next three years. When the Liberator crossed the Andes and won the decisive victory of Boyacá in 1819, New Granada was again free, and Bolívar was naturally elected to the presidency when the Republic of Colombia was created by the Congress of Angostura in the same year. The new state, which historians have called Great Colombia, was to include not only New Granada and Venezuela but also the province of Quito, which was freed from Spanish control three years later. Its government was given a more definite organization by a constituent assembly that met at Cúcuta in 1821, and Bolívar was reëlected, with Francisco de Paula Santander, the New Granadan revolutionary leader, as Vice-President. It was the Vice-President who administered the government at Bogotá during the next five years while Bolívar was busy in Quito and Peru.

Santander had entered the patriot army as a young man at the beginning of the revolution. Though an able and at times a cruel military leader, he was a statesman rather than a soldier by temperament. He

---

[1] Scruggs, *The Colombian and Venezuelan Republics*, p. 45.

gave the new Republic an orderly administration, with congresses functioning regularly and in relative independence. The machinery of government was reorganized and funds for the prosecution of the war were obtained by floating loans in London, creating a debt which was to cause embarrassment in future years. In Bogotá, at least, there was general enthusiasm for republican institutions and a civic spirit which found expression in efforts for change along many lines. English ideas and fashions especially became popular and many of the old colonial customs began to disappear.

Unfortunately this happy state of affairs did not last. Great Colombia was held together only by Bolívar's authority and prestige, and from the beginning the Venezuelans disliked being ruled by the Vice-President and Congress in New Granada. General Páez, the military commander at Caracas, joined with other dissatisfied leaders in 1825 in urging Bolívar to supplant the government by a personal dictatorship, but the Liberator refused to consider their proposal. In the following year, when the Congress ordered Páez to appear before it to answer charges of arbitrary conduct in recruiting troops, the *llanero* leader rebelled against the central government. The quarrel was patched up by Bolívar, who returned from Peru in response to Santander's urgent summons, but Páez retained his position and the prestige of the central government suffered.

Meanwhile news of Bolívar's plans for the perpetuation of his control over Bolivia and Peru under the *constitución vitalicia* reached Bogotá and a violent conflict of opinion arose between advocates and opponents of a similar arrangement for Colombia. Bolívar himself continued ostensibly to support the constitution of Cúcuta, but several municipalities were encouraged by his friends to demand the establishment of a life-presidency, and there was soon a definite break between the Liberator and Santander, who headed the party opposing the scheme. Both the President and the Vice-President had been reëlected in 1826, and Bolívar personally took over the executive power in 1827.

The next three years were the tragic period of the Liberator's career. His popularity declined, and a convention which met at Ocaña in 1828 to attempt to devise a more workable constitution than that of 1821 broke up because a majority of the delegates opposed his proposal for a strong centralized government with a president elected for an eight-year term. Bolívar then suspended the constitution of 1821 and assumed dictatorial power in an effort to curb the disorders that were breaking out in many of the provinces. On September 25, 1828, he barely escaped being assassinated in his house by a well-organized group of conspirators, and fourteen participants in the plot were executed. The war with Peru in 1828–29, and revolts in Popayán and Medellín, made the situation worse. So discouraging did the outlook become that the council of ministers endeavored in 1829 to obtain the support of the English and the French governments for a plan by which Bolívar would rule Colombia in his lifetime but would be succeeded by a European prince. Nothing came of this proposal, which was unpopular in Colombia and was apparently opposed by Bolívar himself.

When Bolívar suspended the constitution of Cúcuta in 1828, he issued a call for a new constituent assembly. Before this met in January, 1830, Páez placed himself at the head of a separatist movement in Venezuela and his example was followed by Juan José Flores whom Bolívar had left in command of the troops at Quito. Venezuela and Ecuador thus became independent republics. At Bogotá Bolívar refused to continue in office and the assembly elected Joaquín Mosquera as President. It voted an expression of gratitude to Bolívar and granted him a life pension of $30,000 annually.

The Liberator, ill and discouraged, left Bogotá in May, 1830, intending to go to Europe. At Cartagena he received the sad news of the murder of General Sucre, who had been his most faithful and perhaps his ablest lieutenant. Before he could sail from the coast his illness became worse, and on December 17, 1830, he died at the *quinta* of San Pedro Alejandrino near Santa Marta.

The Administrations of Santander and Márquez

A few months earlier a movement that had as its ostensible purpose the restoration of Bolívar's authority had overthrown the government at Bogotá. General Rafael Urdaneta assumed control with the support of the local garrison, but revolts throughout the country ousted this purely military regime and a new Congress was elected. In February, 1832, a constitution for "the Republic of New Granada" was adopted, and in the following month Santander, who had been in exile since 1828, was elected to the presidency.

For a time things went well. Despite the dissatisfaction of many of Bolívar's former followers, the new government was popular and the President displayed the same administrative ability that marked his first term. The government's financial difficulties were somewhat relieved by economies and good management and the school system was improved. There was no serious disturbance when a new president was elected in 1837. Santander did not attempt to impose a candidate, and when none received a majority of the popular vote the Congress chose Dr. José Ignacio de Márquez, though he had been supported by political groups unfriendly to the outgoing administration. The country remained tranquil, except for two unimportant military mutinies, through the first two years of the new president's term, for the opposition, led by Santander until his death in 1840, confined itself to constitutional methods. During this period Márquez concluded an agreement with Venezuela and Ecuador for the apportionment of the old Colombian foreign debt, now increased by many years' unpaid interest, and endeavored to reëstablish the country's credit by a partial resumption of payments.

By this time the political leaders were beginning to form the two political parties that have ever since divided the Colombian people. Santander and his followers were "liberals," while the group that supported Márquez, which included many of Bolívar's friends, was the nucleus of the conservative party. Rivalry between the two factions gradually became more bitter, and the difficulty of maintaining order was increased by the strong spirit of *localismo* inevitable in a country where communication between the capital and the outlying provinces was so difficult. The first revolt occurred in July, 1839, in the old royalist stronghold of Pasto, where the populace objected to the government's closing four almost deserted monasteries. Soon after this was suppressed, General José María Obando, who had been the unsuccessful candidate in the election of 1837, led another uprising near Popayán. He too was defeated, but in the meantime several local *caudillos* in other sections started revolts on their own account. While the army was dealing with these, revolutionists attacked Bogotá, but were repulsed by the determined resistance of the townspeople. Fighting continued all over the Republic for two years before the rebels were entirely defeated. A wise moderation in the treatment of the vanquished made the results of the war less appalling than they might otherwise have been, but many thousands of lives had been lost in battle and in a smallpox epidemic which swept through the country in the wake of the armies. Crops and live stock had been destroyed and commerce was at a standstill.

Conservatives and Liberals, 1842–1857

After the civil war of 1840–42 the dominant political group began to develop the characteristic policies of the conservative party. Under the leadership of General Pedro Alcántara Herrán, who was elected President in 1841 while he was still leading the army in the field, there was a reaction from the liberal political philosophy that had prevailed in the time of Santander. A new constitution adopted in 1843 strengthened the authority of the central government at the expense of individual and local liberties, and the freedom of the press was restricted. Closer relations were established with the Church. The Jesuits, excluded from the country since the royal edict of 1767, were invited to return, and the clergy were given a larger part in the educational system. In the schools such studies as Roman law and the humanities were substituted for subjects like constitutional law and parliamentary procedure, which were considered dangerous.[1]

Herrán's successor was General Tomás Cipriano de Mosquera, who was the candidate of the more extreme conservatives, including the army and the Church. During Mosquera's term (1845–49) the liberal party began to recover from the effects of its defeat in 1842, and there was much political agitation in Congress and in the press. The Jesuits especially were the target for violent partisan attacks. The hopes of the opposition were raised by the overthrow of the conservative regimes in Ecuador and Venezuela, and also by a split which developed in the government party at home as the time for new elections approached. As in Chile and Peru, public opinion was stirred by the French revolution of 1848, and many of the younger generation enthusiastically espoused European radical ideas. In the presidential election of 1849, the liberal candidate General José Hilario López received a substantial plurality, though not a majority, and the final choice, as usual, fell to Congress. In that body there was a small conservative majority, but popular demonstrations in and around the church where Congress met so intimidated its members that López was elected after four ballots. The situation was well described by the President of the Chamber, who wrote on his ballot: "I vote for General José Hilario López so that the deputies may not be assassinated."

The new regime embarked on a series of radical reforms. It expelled

[1] Arboleda, *Historia Contemporánea de Colombia,* Vol. II, p. 93.

the Jesuits and adopted other anti-clerical measures, and when the
ecclesiastical authorities protested, it exiled the archbishop and two
bishops. In 1851 it abolished slavery, with compensation to the owners.
The Congress of Cúcuta had provided that children born in bondage
should be free at the age of eighteen, but there were still some 26,000
slaves in the country at the time of the census of 1843. The government
also abolished the death penalty for political offenses and established
freedom of the press.

The government's program intensified the antagonism between the
two parties, and the conservatives revolted in several places in 1851.
They were defeated, but violent political agitation continued. Young
people in both parties, aroused to a new interest in public affairs by the
events of 1848–49, had organized political societies which often engaged
in sanguinary brawls or small uprisings, and sometimes degenerated into
criminal gangs that made life and property unsafe in large sections of
the country. The worst of these were liberal clubs whose members took
advantage of the government's unwillingness to curb its own partisans.
There was, however, a growing division within the dominant party.
The *gólgotas*, the more aristocratic but at the same time the more
radical wing, controlled Congress, while the President was supported
by the *democráticos*, who had many followers among the artisan class.
Each faction had its own clubs, and there were frequent clashes between
them. When López objected to the provisions for freedom of religion
and the press and for universal secret suffrage which the Congress insisted on incorporating in the new constitution of 1853, there was an
open break. This led to a bitter contest in the presidential election of
the same year, even though the conservatives refrained from voting.

The government's candidate, the veteran *caudillo* José María Obando,
was elected, with the support of the army and the *democráticos*. The
gólgotas continued to control Congress, and strife between the two
groups, intensified by class hatred, soon made the new President's position intolerable. In April, 1854, the troops at Bogotá seized control and
offered to make him dictator, but he declined and a military government was set up under General Melo. This in turn was overthrown after
a short but bloody struggle by a coalition of prominent men in both
parties, inspired by the repugnance to dictatorship that has characterized
the Colombians even in the most difficult periods of their history. A
bipartisan government was established under Manuel María Mallarino
to serve the remainder of Obando's term, and in 1857 the conservative

leader Mariano Ospina, who had received 96,000 votes in the popular election as against 82,000 for his liberal opponent and 32,000 for General Mosquera, became President.

The Period of Federalism

Much of the disorder from which Colombia had suffered since 1848 had been caused by local jealousies and by the central government's inability to maintain contact with the outlying provinces. Many leaders in both parties had consequently begun to look on "federalism," an increase in local autonomy, as the only solution for the country's political ills. A long step in this direction had been taken in the constitution of 1853, which gave each of the thirty-five provinces the right to elect its own governor and to control its local affairs. Subsequent laws gradually grouped the provinces into states with still greater powers of self-rule, and a new constitution adopted in 1858 provided for still further decentralization. Ospina found himself powerless to suppress the continual revolts within individual states or the not infrequent wars between states, and his ineffectual attempts to assert the federal government's authority merely made matters worse. At the same time the general removal of liberal office-holders, and the return of the Jesuits, intensified partisan bitterness.

Local revolutions, some liberal and some conservative, directed against the party that happened to be in power in each state, were going on in many parts of the country in 1859, and in 1860 a country-wide civil war began. Ex-President Mosquera, now governor of the state of Cauca, quarreled with the conservatives and joined forces with the liberals under General Obando, and the struggle continued until the end of 1862. Mosquera became the leader of the revolution after Obando's death. His army was finally victorious and among his first acts when he entered Bogotá were a series of harsh measures against the Church which showed, and perhaps were intended to show, how completely he had abandoned his former political associates.

Mosquera had long been known as a brilliant but erratic soldier, unscrupulous, ambitious, and often cruel. Many of the other leaders of the revolution distrusted him, and their fear that he might attempt to remain in power indefinitely colored all of the proceedings of the constituent assembly which met at Río Negro in 1863. He had many partisans among the delegates and it was not possible to prevent his election to the presidency, but his term was made to expire in the following year and it was provided that future presidents should be chosen for two-year periods and should not be eligible for immediate reëlection. The desire to curb his authority, as well as the still strong sentiment for federalism, was evident in provisions that still further restricted the powers of the national executive and increased those of the states. The delegates sought to preclude the possibility of a reaction against the federal system by providing that amendments might be adopted only by unanimous vote of the states in the national Senate.

Mosquera, with his personal following and his prestige in the army, continued to be powerful and was again elected to the presidency in 1866. In the following year, after a violent quarrel with Congress, he attempted to establish a dictatorship but was overthrown and sent into exile. Thereafter the control of the government was in the hands of the former *gólgotas*, who now called themselves "radicals."

The liberal party remained in power for twenty years after 1863 under the Río Negro constitution. Throughout this time the central government had little prestige or effective authority and it would serve no purpose to enumerate the presidents who were either chosen legally for the short two-year term or installed provisionally for still shorter periods after successful revolutions. There was continual disorder and at times virtual anarchy. Civil wars on a national scale were infrequent because subversive movements generally had as their purpose the control of individual states, but more than forty local armed conflicts are said to have occurred during the two decades.[1]

Curiously enough it was during this same period, when political conditions were at their worst, that Colombia became one of the chief intellectual centers of South America. Literary pursuits had received little attention during the earlier years of the Republic, but there had been a revival of interest about 1843. Poets like Gregorio Gutiérrez González (1826–1872), José Eusebio Caro (1817–1853), José Joaquín Ortiz (1814–1892), and Julio Arboleda (1817–1862), helped to justify the *Bogotanos'* description of their city as "the Athens of America." Jorge Isaacs (1837–1895), the author of "María," was a famous novelist as well as a poet, and José Cuervo (1844–1911), who passed most of his life in Paris, was one of the greatest of Spanish philologists.

[1] Henao y Arrubla, *Historia de Colombia*, 5th ed., p. 674.

Rafael Núñez

The division within the liberal party continued, and in 1880 the so-called independents wrested control from the radicals who had dominated the administration since 1866. The independents' leader, Rafael Núñez, was elected President for the term 1880–82, and was again elected in 1884. In that year he was supported not only by the independents but by the conservatives, and it was the latter who saved the government from defeat when the radicals rose against it in 1885. The President, who had at first attempted to govern with a cabinet representing all political groups, was compelled thenceforth to rely on his new allies for support, and the suppression of the revolt marked the beginning of a long period of conservative supremacy.

Núñez was a poet and a writer on public affairs as well as a statesman. He believed that the abandonment of the unsuccessful experiment in federalism and the establishment of a strong centralized government were indispensable if Colombia was to achieve the economic progress which several of the more stable South American countries were already enjoying. He looked upon the influence of the Church as a powerful factor in preserving order, and consequently reverted to an extremely pro-clerical policy. His political ideas were embodied in the new constitution of 1886, which was drawn up by a "national council of delegates" after the Río Negro code had arbitrarily been set aside. The states became departments under governors appointed and removed by the president, and their separate codes of laws were replaced by national codes. The president was elected for six years instead of two, and was given greatly increased powers. The liberty of the press was restricted. The Church, though left free to manage its own internal affairs, was officially protected and given control over the national school system. Núñez continued as President until his death in 1894, but he actually occupied the office only for a few brief periods. At other times he lived in Cartagena, wielding a controlling influence in political affairs but leaving the work of administration to others. Carlos Holguín, a militant conservative, was the active head of the government from 1888 until 1892. He was succeeded by Miguel Caro, who was elected Vice-President in 1892 and became President after Núñez died.

Civil War and Territorial Dismemberment, 1895–1903

The disappearance of the leader whose prestige had been its chief support was a blow to the conservative regime. Before the election of 1892 rivalries between the "historic conservatives" and the "nationalists," among whom were the former independent liberals, had badly split the dominant party. Núñez' influence had procured a victory for the latter, but the opposition liberals were encouraged to a new activity by the divisions among their opponents. The fear that this group would resort to arms led the government to close their newspapers and to exile or imprison many of their leaders. When they did revolt early in 1895 they were rapidly defeated by government forces under General Rafael Reyes, but the end of the war did not restore tranquility.

An agreement between the two conservative factions made possible the election of Manuel Sanclemente and José Manuel Marroquín as President and Vice-President in 1898. Sanclemente, who was an old man in bad health, at first permitted Marroquín to assume the presidency. The new chief executive made a real effort to diminish political tension and placate the opposition. "The evils which threaten Colombia, and which already afflict her," he said in his inaugural address, "are not much less serious than the consequences of a foreign invasion." [1] When he proposed a number of concrete reforms, including an improvement in electoral methods and a greater freedom for the press, the nationalists opposed them and prevailed upon Sanclemente to assume power himself. This revived the old feud within the party and weakened the administration, which further lost prestige when Sanclemente's illness compelled him to leave Bogotá for a lower altitude.

The liberals seized the opportunity to revolt, and in 1899 the Republic was plunged into the longest and most sanguinary civil war in its history. After July, 1900 when the *históricos* removed Sanclemente by a *coup d'état* and installed Marroquín as President, the government gradually got the upper hand, but fighting continued throughout the country until 1902. It has been asserted that 100,000 men were killed in battle, to say nothing of the loss of life from other causes. [2] When the revolutionists finally signed treaties of peace, commerce and industry were paralyzed and the government was practically bankrupt.

[1] Henao y Arrubla, *op. cit.*, p. 754.
[2] *Ibid.*, p. 760.

The paper dollar, already depreciated before the war, was worth one cent in gold.

A year later Colombia suffered another calamity. The secession of Panama, to be discussed in more detail in Chapter 22, was not only a material loss but a blow to the national pride. It intensified the revulsion inspired by the terrific consequences of the recent internal conflict, because thinking people realized that the recurrent civil wars, in which the Isthmus had always been a battleground, had created the conditions which made foreign intervention there possible.

The Conservative Era, 1904–1930

The loss of Panama, in fact, marked a turning point in the Republic's history, the beginning of a long era of internal peace. As in other Latin American countries, the change was partly the result of economic development. The production of coffee, which had been the principal export since the 1880's, was increasing rapidly. Since coffee was grown chiefly on small farms, rather than on large plantations as in Brazil, the industry was creating a substantial class of prosperous peasant proprietors who had everything to gain by the maintenance of peace. Other classes too were becoming more dependent on foreign trade and felt the effects of civil war more than in the days when each region was relatively self-sufficient. There was a growing realization that the country was far behind many of its neighbors in commerce and transportation and in the development of its resources, and that there could be little improvement in these respects until foreign capital should be attracted by more stable political conditions.

Party rivalries by no means disappeared, but their bitterness was somewhat alleviated by new political practices. General Rafael Reyes, who became President in 1904, had been out of the country during the recent war, and had fewer enemies among the defeated party than most of his associates. He was thus in a position to attempt a policy of conciliation, and one of his first acts was to name two prominent liberals to his cabinet. When a number of conservative senators and deputies objected to these appointments, he dissolved Congress and replaced it by a more amenable "national assembly" chosen by the departmental councils. This extra-legal body proceeded to adopt several important amendments to the constitution, among them a provision for proportional representation in Congress and other elective bodies which assured the liberals an opportunity to share in the task of government. The minority was thus encouraged to contest elections instead of devoting its energies to preparing for revolt, and the electoral machinery, though still defective, was gradually improved as the public began to show more interest in exercising its right to vote.

Under Reyes' leadership, the country recovered rapidly from the effects of the war. New roads and railways were built, especially in the highlands and between the plateau of Bogotá and the Magdalena River, and coffee production increased. The currency was reorganized and stabilized. An agreement for the resumption of service on the foreign debt restored the nation's credit and made it possible to obtain loans for public works. The new regime was more autocratic than any that Colombia had had in modern times, but it was for some years accepted with comparatively little opposition by a people weary of disorder and civil strife.

Opposition increased, however, when the National Assembly voted to extend Reyes' term to December 31, 1914, and still more after he negotiated the tripartite treaties of 1909, by which Colombia agreed to recognize the independence of Panama in return for concessions from that country and from the United States. Ratification of these agreements was violently opposed and there were vociferous demands that they be submitted to a constitutional congress rather than to the hand-picked National Assembly. In the face of demonstrations in the capital, which showed that public opinion was strongly aroused, Reyes withdrew the treaties and consented to the election of a congress to meet in February, 1910. This concession hurt the government's prestige without placating its opponents, and in June, 1909, Reyes quietly left the capital and resigned. Many of the laws that he had sponsored were declared void, but a constituent assembly which met in 1910 made permanent the arrangement for minority representation in Congress.

The same assembly elected Carlos Restrepo, a conservative, as President for the term 1910–14. Restrepo was the candidate of the *Unión Republicana*, the bi-partisan coalition which had opposed Reyes, but this broke up before 1914 and the conservatives took control. The liberals, however, still had a substantial representation in Congress, and under Restrepo and his immediate successors, José Vicente Concha (1914–18) and Marco Fidel Suárez (1918–21), liberals served in the cabinet. There was thus some coöperation between the two parties.

At the same time there was more freedom of speech and of the press, and political persecution was unusual. Elections began to approximate a real expression of the wishes of the citizenry, though complaints of high-handed or fraudulent practices in behalf of the official candidates by no means ceased.

Relations with the United States had been clouded since 1903 by the bitter feeling aroused by the Panama affair. The failure of the tripartite treaties of 1909 if anything made the situation worse, but negotiations between the two governments continued. A new treaty, in which the United States expressed "sincere regret" for what had happened and promised to pay an indemnity of $25,000,000, was signed in 1914. Ratification was delayed for several years by opposition in the Senate at Washington to anything in the nature of an apology, and President Suárez, who was more friendly to the United States than his predecessors, finally consented to the elimination of the expression of regret and also rescinded a decree affecting American oil interests in Colombia which had been another obstacle to North American approval. Conservatives as well as liberals violently criticized these concessions, and the political situation became so tense that the President resigned in 1921 in favor of General Jorge Holguín, the first *designado*. The treaties, without the expression of regret, were nevertheless ratified soon afterward.

The election of 1922 was a real contest, for the liberals, who had not usually presented presidential candidates, united in support of General Benjamín Herrera. They were defeated by 413,000 votes to 256,000, and General Pedro Nel Ospina, the conservative choice, was President from 1922 until 1926. Under him, and under his successor Dr. Miguel Abadía Méndez, the country was unusually prosperous. Brazil's coffee valorization helped the Colombian producers by increasing world prices and the product of the newly developed oil fields furnished a new export. Business in general was stimulated by the inflow of capital from abroad. The treaty indemnity from the United States was paid in annual installments of $5,000,000 between 1922 and 1926, and much greater sums of new money were obtained by borrowing in New York. Not only the central government but also several departments and municipalities contracted foreign debts for public works and other purposes, and new road and railroad construction was begun in nearly every section of the country.

The Liberals in Power, 1930–1946

The inflation that accompanied the spending of such great sums made worse the collapse that came with the world depression. Reaction had already set in when it became time to elect a new president in 1930. The conservative regime faced the same situation which caused the overthrow of several other Latin American governments in that year, and the party's chance of success was further diminished by internal feuds. Two factions supported rival candidates for the nomination, and the Archbishop of Bogotá, who usually had a controlling voice in the party's councils, wavered uncertainly between them.

The liberals decided at the last minute to take advantage of the situation. With the support of many conservatives, they nominated Enrique Olaya Herrera, who had served brilliantly as Minister at Washington during the past two administrations, and who now returned to Colombia for a short but effective campaign. Addressing voters in all parts of the country in person or by radio, Dr. Olaya advocated a program of political and social reform which met with an enthusiastic response. He was elected by a large majority and the forty-five years of conservative rule ended.

The orderly manner in which the liberals were permitted to take over the administration and the moderate policy which they pursued after their victory showed how completely political conditions in Colombia had changed. The constitution of 1886 and even the concordat with the Papacy remained in force. There was no serious disturbance of public order, though the economic crisis grew increasingly acute during the first years of the new administration. The effects of the depression were aggravated in 1932 by heavy expenditures on military preparations occasioned by the Leticia controversy with Peru,[1] and the government was compelled to reduce payments on the foreign debt and to float large internal loans. Despite these difficulties, Olaya retained his personal popularity and, thanks in part at least to his able leadership, the country escaped the political vicissitudes that marked the depression period in some of the other republics.

Many conservatives held official positions under the Olaya government, but in 1934 their leaders decided to abstain altogether from the

[1] See above, pp. 319–20.

presidential election, in which they would obviously have little chance for success, and not even to take advantage of the constitutional provisions which would have assured them a number of seats in Congress. The administration that came into power in that year was thus exclusively liberal and the new President, Alfonso López, had no political obligations to elements outside his own party. Abandoning Olaya's conciliatory policy, he put into effect some of the reforms that liberal leaders had long advocated. Constitutional amendments deprived the Church of its control over public instruction and opened the way to a larger measure of government control over foreign and native business enterprises; and negotiations were begun with the Holy See for changes in the concordat in order to make possible the institution of civil marriage, supervision of cemeteries by the government, and other reforms. Efforts were made to expand the public-school system and to provide for much needed public-health work, and 1,000 miles or more of new roads were built. A reform of the tax system, with much increased levies on business and private wealth, helped to provide funds.

Ex-President Olaya was to have been the liberal candidate to succeed López, but his sudden death in 1937 upset the plans of the party leaders and brought on a conflict between the moderate and the radical wings of the party. Though López supported the radicals, Eduardo Santos, a moderate, obtained the liberal nomination in 1938 and was chosen President in an orderly election in which the conservatives again refused to vote. His administration coöperated with the United States in the war, in the face of strong resistance from Laureano Gómez, the conservative leader, who was openly pro-German. The conservatives again participated in elections in 1939, and from that time on they held the balance of power in Congress as between the two liberal factions. In 1942, they supported the moderate liberal candidate instead of nominating one of their own, but the coalition was defeated by ex-President López, who was the candidate of the radical wing.

López' second administration was a period of violent political agitation. His followers failed to obtain a majority in Congress, and his position was further weakened by accusations of improper conduct directed against some of his associates. In November, 1943, he obtained leave of absence and went to the United States to obtain medical treatment for his wife. When he returned, the labor unions and other groups that supported him staged country-wide demonstrations in his honor and the Senate refused his proffered resignation; but in July, 1944, there were several minor revolts and the President himself was kidnapped and held prisoner for a short time by disloyal army officers at Pasto. A state of siege was imposed and Gómez, the conservative leader, was forced to leave the country. Finally, in July, 1945, López resigned and the generally respected liberal leader Alberto Lleras Camargo became provisional President.

Recent Events

The division within the liberal party continued, and in the presidential election of May, 1946, the conservative candidate Mariano Ospina Pérez was victorious, with 523,000 votes, as against 401,000 for Gabriel Turbay, the candidate of the right-wing liberals, and 332,000 for the left-wing candidate Jorge Elíecer Gaitán. The liberals, however, still had a majority in Congress. The new President attempted to govern with a bi-partisan cabinet, but labor troubles and the postwar inflation made his position difficult and political unrest continued. Early in 1948 there were serious disturbances in some of the provinces and the liberals withdrew their ministers from the cabinet. The opposition party became much more aggressive after both liberal factions agreed to support Jorge Gaitán for the presidency in 1950.

On April 9, 1948, while the Ninth Conference of American States was meeting at Bogotá, Gaitán was murdered, apparently by a personal enemy. The left-wing leader had been extremely popular among the laboring class, and within a few minutes angry mobs were killing, looting, and wrecking government buildings. For a time it seemed that the government would fall, but the coöperation of the chief liberal leaders, who agreed to the formation of a coalition cabinet, made it possible to restore order after hours of anarchy. It was officially reported that 1,200 persons were killed in Bogotá and 300 more in similar riots elsewhere,[1] and the material damage ran into hundreds of millions of dollars. The small Colombian communist party had been active in the riots, although it probably had not planned the affair, and Colombia broke off diplomatic relations with Russia some weeks later. The Inter-American Conference continued its sessions, though the building in which it had been meeting was destroyed by the mob.

[1] *The New York Times*, April 22, 1948.

The liberals again withdrew from Ospina's cabinet in May, 1949, and the political situation rapidly grew worse. For several months there were almost daily reports of killings resulting from party rivalries. Ospina's successor was to have been elected in June, 1950, but in September, 1949, the liberal majority in Congress passed over the President's veto a bill advancing the date several months in order to have the election while Congress was in session. This caused further bad feeling. Ospina offered to turn the government over to a bi-partisan commission which would rule the country until 1954, but this proposal was apparently unacceptable to the extreme elements in both parties, and early in November the President imposed a state of siege. Dario Echandía, the liberal candidate, thereupon withdrew, and on November 27 the conservative leader Laureano Gómez was elected without opposition for the presidential term beginning August 7, 1950.

With more than 10,000,000 inhabitants, Colombia now ranks fourth in population among the Latin American republics. It produces more coffee than any other country in the world except Brazil. The development of its economic potentialities, however, is still held back by lack of adequate transportation for which the country's geography is largely responsible. Serious political and social problems also remain to be solved. Though Colombia is one of the four or five Latin American countries that have made the greatest progress toward truly republican government, the events just described show the strength of the explosive tendencies in her political life. The old conservative-liberal rivalries, and even the differences over the position of the Church, are still acute, and in recent years questions of social policy have furnished a new element of discord.

19

Venezuela

Venezuela in 1821

There were probably about 700,000 people in Venezuela at the end of the war for independence. Most of these, like their descendants to-day, lived in the pleasant, temperate valleys of the Andean range which crosses the country from west to east within a few miles of the Caribbean coast. There were also settlements on the coast, and in the hot lowlands around Lake Maracaibo. Another region of some economic importance was the *llanos* or plains of the Orinoco Valley, alternately parched by the sun or drenched by torrential rains, where half-savage *mestizo* cowboys tended cattle belonging to creole families in the highlands. The great area south of the Orinoco was unoccupied and almost unexplored, as it is today.

As in many other Latin American countries, the upper class were the landowners of Spanish descent, who lived in the towns and left the management of their properties to overseers. Most of the labor on the farms, especially in the neighborhood of Caracas, was done by Negro slaves. The majority of the country's inhabitants were of colored blood, for except in the western part of the highlands, few Indians had survived. The Venezuelan provinces had never been particularly prosperous. At the beginning of the nineteenth century there were no roads over which even an ox-cart could travel between the chief agricultural regions and the seaports, and travelers reported that there were no wheeled vehicles even in Caracas. Schools were few in number and poor in quality, and there had been no printing press in the country until Miranda brought one with his filibustering expedition of 1806.[1]

[1] González Guinán, *Historia de Venezuela*, Vol. II, p. 31.

During the war for independence, Venezuela probably suffered more than any other South American country. Twice freed and twice reconquered before the final patriot victory at Carabobo, the people of the highlands experienced both the horrors of Bolívar's "war to the death" and the brutality of the Spanish reaction. In the *llanos* many years of guerrilla warfare all but wiped out the cattle industry. A large proportion of the able-bodied men were compelled to abandon agriculture and stock-raising to take part in the conflict, and several thousand left the country to accompany Bolívar in his campaigns for the liberation of New Granada, Ecuador, and Peru. Many of these did not return at the end of the war, for Venezuelan leaders like Sucre, Flores, and Bolívar himself remained abroad as rulers of other South American countries, relying largely upon their Venezuelan troops for support.

In Venezuela itself the military caste, looking to the public treasury for support and insisting upon the maintenance of its special privileges, dominated the country's political life for many years after independence. Local *caudillos* in each district either exercised power as representatives of the central government or conspired to revolt against it. They were intolerant of civilian control and had little respect for any law save that of force. The parties that they headed were built around personalities and held together chiefly by a desire for office or a thirst for revenge for past persecutions. Questions of principle played a secondary rôle, though certain issues, like federalism, were sometimes used as a means of winning popular support. Even the problem of Church and State, so productive of strife in Colombia, was of secondary importance in Venezuela because the Church had lost much of its prestige and authority by the end of the war for independence. Such conditions are peculiarly favorable to the growth of dictatorships, and the Republic was ruled throughout the first century of its history by a series of "strong men."

Páez

The first of these was the *llanero* general, José Antonio Páez, whom Bolívar had left in command of the military forces in Venezuela after the battle of Carabobo. A daring and brilliant soldier, with little education but a great capacity for leadership, Páez maintained his preeminence as much by his prestige and popularity as by force. From

1821 until 1829 he ruled Venezuela as Bolívar's lieutenant. His revolt in 1826 [1] failed because the Liberator's influence was still too strong, but he came out of the affair with enhanced authority. He encouraged the separatist tendencies which became stronger as Bolívar's popularity declined; and in 1829, when the people of each locality were invited to express their opinion as to changes which should be made in the Colombian constitution, the majority of the towns in Venezuela declared for complete independence under his leadership. Early in 1830, Páez set up a provisional government and summoned a convention to draft a constitution. Secession was accomplished practically without bloodshed because the authorities at Bogotá were powerless to resist, but there was a rather formidable though unsuccessful revolt in Venezuela itself early in 1831 under the leadership of General José Tadeo Monagas.

This revolt represented various elements of discord which continued to make trouble. One was the jealousy of Páez' military rivals, many of whom remained loyal to Bolívar and opposed the movement for secession. Another was the ever-present jealousy of the provincial towns toward Caracas which found expression in the demand for federalism—the slogan of many revolts in years to come. A third cause of dissension was the opposition of the clergy to the new constitution because it did away with some of the special privileges of the Church and contained no special provisions safeguarding the Catholic faith.

Páez' first term as constitutional President (1831–35) was nevertheless fairly peaceful. The country enjoyed a more truly republican government than it was to know for a century to come. Both congress and the press were relatively independent and elections were actively contested with but little official interference. Páez' successor, Dr. José Vargas, was less fortunate. Vargas was a civilian who had been supported by the richer landowners and merchants in an effort to diminish the power of the military caste, but he soon found himself unable to cope with the responsibilities that he had very unwillingly assumed. Within a few months he had been driven from office by an uprising in the army. Páez, who had retired quietly to his farm, hastily recruited a new force which restored the constitutional order, but he did not approve Vargas' action in shooting or exiling several of the rebel leaders, and further friction between the two men compelled

[1] See above, p. 151.

Vargas to resign in 1836. The government was administered by vice-presidents more amenable to Páez' influence until 1839, when Páez himself again became President. He was succeeded in 1843 by his close associate, General Carlos Soublette.

There was by this time a rising opposition to Páez' long-continued predominance. In 1840, Antonio Leocadio Guzmán, formerly one of the *caudillo's* chief advisers, had organized the liberal party to avenge himself for the loss of his position in the government. Hard times helped him to build up a following, and he attracted support from various dissatisfied elements including especially the friends of the still exiled participants in the revolts of 1831 and 1835. Though over-whelmingly defeated in the election of 1842, the liberals became stronger during Soublette's term and the conservatives, or followers of Páez, won the vice-presidential election of 1844 and the presidential election of 1846–47 only by using force and fraud to an extent that had not formerly been necessary. The contest between the two parties, though almost entirely a matter of personality rather than of principles, aroused a new interest in political affairs, and the landowning aristocracy, hitherto glad to follow Páez' leadership in the interests of peace, divided into hostile factions.

The Monagas Brothers

In 1846, each party split its vote among several presidential candidates and the final decision, in the absence of a majority, went to Congress. The victor was General José Tadeo Monagas, the chief *caudillo* in the eastern provinces, whom Páez had supported in the final days of the campaign despite the fact that Monagas had once been his most formidable opponent. The new President soon showed that he did not intend to be a figurehead like his predecessors. After coöperating with Páez for some months, he broke with the conservatives and turned to the liberals for support. When the Congress attempted to impeach him in 1848, a mob invaded its meeting place and killed three of the deputies. This outrage, and the celebration of its anniversary as an official holiday, increased the bitterness between the two parties, but Páez was defeated and exiled when he revolted.

Monagas had his brother, José Gregorio Monagas, elected as President for the period 1851–55, despite opposition from both parties. Serious disturbances resulted, especially in 1853 and 1854, and it was in the hope of diverting attention from the political situation that the President forced through Congress in 1854 a law for the complete abolition of slavery with compensation to the owners. There were still some 13,000 slaves and 27,000 *manumisos*, or persons born of slave mothers and bound to serve their masters until the age of twenty-five. In the same year José Tadeo Monagas was elected to the presidency for a second term. The government had now become a dictatorship, with elections a mere form and with increasing restrictions on the freedom of the press. In 1857, after making the necessary changes in the constitution, Monagas had himself elected for a new term of six years.

Civil War and Federalism, 1858–1872

A year later the government was overthrown by a revolt of members of both parties. The titular leader, General Julián Castro, was one of Monagas' own military commanders who was promised the presidency because his aid was necessary to success. He had little personal following, and his government lasted barely twelve months before the conservative leaders to whom he entrusted the control of the army arrested and imprisoned him. The liberals were already in revolt under the leadership of General Juan C. Falcón, and the veteran Páez, despite much opposition within his own party, returned from exile to take command of the conservative army. In 1861 Páez proclaimed himself dictator, but a series of liberal victories forced him to agree to a treaty of peace in 1863 by which Falcón assumed the presidency. Páez again went to the United States and died there ten years later at the age of eighty-three.

Since the liberals at the beginning of the war had proclaimed their adherence to "federalism," the states now set up autonomous governments, and in 1864 a federal constitution was adopted. The result was as unfortunate as in Colombia. There were constant disorders within the states and quarrels between them, as well as less frequent uprisings against the central government. Falcón was popular, but he was a poor administrator, and his dislike of official life at Caracas led him to entrust the actual exercise of power to others during much of his term.

A "blue" revolution, so called from the color that its army adopted, put José Tadeo Monagas in the presidency in 1868, but he died after a few months and his son José Ruperto succeeded him. The liberals, now called the "yellow" party, soon revolted. In April, 1870, they took Caracas. The war continued in other sections for two years more, but the "blues" were finally beaten. After fourteen years of almost continual strife the country was more than ready for a period of peace. It was to enjoy this under the rule of Antonio Guzmán Blanco.

Guzmán Blanco

Guzmán Blanco, the son of Antonio Leocadio Guzmán, had been Falcón's ablest lieutenant in the five years' war. As acting president during two of the several periods when Falcón withdrew temporarily from office, he had shown marked capacity as an administrator. By 1870 he had become the leader of the liberal party. Within a short time after the "yellow" victory he built up a more absolute power than any former ruler of the Republic had enjoyed. The states, retaining their prerogatives on paper, were ruled in fact by puppets entirely subservient to his will, and all branches of the national government were controlled in the same way. Opposition, or even criticism, was sternly punished. At the same time roads and railroads were built, ports were improved, and the larger cities were modernized and beautified. No earlier ruler had done so much to promote material progress. None, on the other hand, had gone to such lengths of self-glorification. The President caused statues of himself to be erected everywhere, and it was indiscreet to make a speech or publish a book that did not render a tribute of adulation to "The Illustrious American, Regenerator of Venezuela." His administration was efficient, and the situation of the national treasury was far better than under his predecessors; but at the same time the dictator and his relatives accumulated great private fortunes. The country in general benefited from the establishment of peace and submitted to his firm rule for many years with relatively little evidence of discontent.

At the beginning of Guzmán Blanco's regime there was a new conflict with the Church. The Archbishop of Caracas had been expelled from the country in 1870 because he made difficulties about celebrating a Te Deum in honor of one of the "yellow" victories. In the years that followed the few remaining convents were closed, the seminary at Caracas was suppressed, civil marriage was authorized, and the cemeteries were placed under lay control. On one occasion the dictator even threatened to establish a national church independent of Rome, but his attitude became less hostile after the offending archbishop resigned.

After seven years in office, first as provisional and then as constitutional president, Guzmán Blanco brought about the election of his friend Francisco Linares Alcántara as his successor. The dictator himself went to Europe, but Linares' death and a revolt that followed forced him to resume control of the government. He was again President from 1879 until 1884. In 1881 he brought about the adoption of a new constitution, ostensibly modeled on that of Switzerland, that provided that the chief executive should be chosen for a two-year term and should not be eligible for reëlection, and after 1884 he spent much of his time in Paris, sending his orders by mail and cable to lieutenants who successively occupied the presidency.

The great popularity that Guzmán Blanco enjoyed in 1870 had vanished by 1888, and Dr. Rojas Paúl, who was elected President by order of the dictator in that year, was enthusiastically supported by public opinion when he began to show an unexpected independence. Guzmán Blanco's wishes were flouted, first by the disapproval of concessions that he had granted in Paris and then by bringing to Venezuela the body of his old enemy, General Páez, for burial in the national pantheon. Other exiles were allowed to return and the press was permitted to discuss political questions. The authorities endeavored to avoid an open break with the dictator, but the populace tumultuously prevented the celebration of his Saint's Day and the anniversaries of his victories, which had hitherto been national holidays, and in October, 1889, his numerous statues were destroyed by simultaneous mob action in all sections of the Republic. Thereafter Guzmán Blanco wisely remained abroad, though he made futile attempts to foment a counter-revolution.

Crespo's Administration and the Guiana Boundary Dispute

Dr. Andueza Palacio, who succeeded Rojas Paúl in 1890, was overthrown two years later by General Joaquín Crespo. The latter, a professional soldier from the *llanos*, gave the country a period of comparative peace from 1894 to 1898. His administration was notable chiefly for the sensational controversy over the boundary between Venezuela and British Guiana. The question was an old one, but it had recently become acute with the discovery of gold in the disputed territory. The British government refused to arbitrate it unless a large area was recognized in advance as a part of the Guiana colony. The United States intervened in this discussion because it considered that any European occupation of territory legally belonging to Venezuela would be a violation of the Monroe Doctrine; and in July, 1895, Secretary of State Olney demanded an arbitration in a note to the British government which contained a statement that "the United States is practically sovereign on this continent, and its fiat is law upon the subjects to which it confines its inter-position." When the British government made a tardy and unsatisfactory reply, President Cleveland proposed to Congress the appointment of a commission to investigate the dispute. He indicated that the United States, after thus satisfying itself as to the rightful boundary, would forcibly resist the occupation by a European power of territory belonging to Venezuela. This arrogant stand might have brought the United States and Great Britain very close to war, but the government at London was occupied with more important problems elsewhere and soon agreed to an arbitration with Venezuela. An award handed down in 1899 decided the controversy without granting the extreme demands of either party.

Cipriano Castro

Crespo peacefully turned over his office to General Ignacio Andrade in 1898, but was killed soon afterward leading the government forces against one of several revolutions which again plunged the country into anarchy. Even when an agreement between the various military leaders placed General Cipriano Castro in the presidency in 1899, new revolts occurred and it was not until 1903 that something approaching order was established. Castro, an unscrupulous and greedy politician, supported chiefly by the army and by associates who profited from his corrupt financial practices, remained in power as dictator until 1908.

Castro is best remembered for his offensive treatment of foreign powers. Controversies with other nations over debts and claims had embarrassed the Venezuelan government since the days of Páez, and the recent civil wars had caused new injuries to foreign life and property for which Castro arrogantly refused to make compensation. At the end of 1902, therefore, British, German, and Italian naval forces blockaded the Venezuelan coast, seized four gunboats, and bombarded Puerto Cabello. Since the governments concerned had previously assured the United States that no seizure of territory was contemplated,

President Roosevelt did not consider it proper to object to their action, but he exerted his good offices to persuade all concerned to agree to an arbitration of claims and the blockade was raised early in 1903. The incident had an important influence, as we shall see later, upon the general Caribbean policy of the United States. Apparently it had less effect on Castro, for new violations of foreign rights kept his administration in hot water in later years.

Juan Vicente Gómez

Castro's chief aid was Juan Vicente Gómez, who had been one of the ablest military leaders in the civil wars between 1899 and 1903, and had continued to be powerful despite Castro's growing jealousy. Late in 1908, when the President was compelled to go abroad for medical treatment, Gómez was left in charge. He at once made himself master of the situation and the ex-President was defeated when he attempted to return at the head of a filibustering expedition.

During the next twenty-seven years Gómez ruled Venezuela with a heavy hand. He was not president continuously, but he retained command of the army and with it a complete control of the government during the periods when he allowed straw men like Dr. Márquez Bustillos, from 1914 to 1922, and Dr. Juan Bautista Pérez, from 1929 to 1931, to exercise the executive power. He also dominated the governments of the states, finally amending the constitution to give himself the right to appoint their presidents by decree. The methods by which his authority was maintained were those characteristic of tropical American dictatorships. Opponents were treated with severity and often, it is said, with fiendish cruelty. The press was compelled to praise the ruler and his policies, and an elaborate spy system made criticism dangerous. The army, well trained and equipped with modern weapons, prevented resistance by a people who were entirely deprived of firearms. All traces of the old political parties disappeared and revolutionary movements, after the first years, were few and unimportant.

Gómez had little or no education, but his energy and acumen had made him a prosperous cattle man before his entry into politics. As dictator he showed himself a keen judge of men, and he was able to obtain the coöperation of many of the country's best minds. His administration was lawless and corrupt but the country derived some material benefit from it. While the dictator and many of his relatives were growing rich by graft or extortion, roads were improved, something was done for education, and the entire foreign debt was paid off. The amazing growth of the petroleum industry made the government rich during the last decades of the Gómez regime. Anglo-Dutch, and later North American companies began to exploit the rich oil deposits around Lake Maracaibo immediately after the First World War, and within ten years Venezuela had become one of the great sources of the world's supply.

Recent Governments

When Gómez died, at the age of eighty, in December, 1935, the cabinet chose General Eleázar López Contreras, the Minister of War, as Provisional President. The new administration, to the surprise of many observers, was able to survive the violent popular reaction that followed the removal of the dictator's iron control. Much of the property of Gómez and his relatives was destroyed or looted by mobs, and sanguinary riots occurred in Caracas; but the removal of several high officials hated for their connection with the Gómez regime prevented more serious outbreaks. The army supported the new order, as did also many influential groups which were primarily interested in the maintenance of peace. Some of the most objectionable features of the Gómez regime were done away with, and free elections for a new Congress were promised. Meanwhile the old handpicked Gómez Congress chose López Contreras as constitutional President.

Continuing prosperity made the new government's task easier, but there was opposition from liberal and radical groups and in 1937 the opposition parties won an unexpected victory in the congressional elections. López Contreras thereupon arrested several of the newly elected deputies and senators, accusing them of being communists, and a little later expelled from the country a large number of leftist leaders. Thereafter the government encountered less opposition, and it was able in 1941 to obtain a large majority in the congress which, under the constitution, was to elect the next president. López Contreras did not attempt to succeed himself, and in the same year General Isaías Medina, a veteran soldier who had until recently been minister of war, was installed as President.

Venezuela's support of the democracies in the World War was particularly important because of her oil production, and the government's policy of coöperation strengthened its position. As the end of Medina's term approached, however, the political situation became increasingly uncertain. The *Acción Democrática,* a radical party, had developed much strength, but it had no chance to win because the next president would be named not by the people but by Congress. It seemed probable that the choice would fall either on López Contreras, who had broken with Medina but was also opposed by the liberal groups, or on the President's candidate Ángel Biaggini, who had few supporters outside of official circles. Many of the younger officers in the army, however, were dissatisfied with the leadership of the group of generals who had been in control since the days of Gómez, and in October, 1945, some of them overthrew Medina and installed a provisional government headed by Rómulo Betancourt, the leader of the *Acción Democrática.*

A popularly elected assembly drew up a more democratic constitution, and in December, 1947, the distinguished novelist Rómulo Gallegos was elected President of the Republic. The new regime seemed to have much popular support. It had little chance, however, to develop the liberal program that its leaders advocated because the army staged a new revolt in November, 1948, and installed a military *junta* headed by Lieutenant Colonel Carlos Delgado Chalbaud.

Venezuela's chief economic and social problems today arise not from poverty but from an excess of wealth. The Republic's vast oil production, which is exceeded only by that of the United States and possibly by that of Russia, has probably given it a higher per capita income than any other Latin American country, but the benefits go to a relatively small part of the population. While the workers in the oil industry enjoy high wages, other groups suffer from a fantastically high cost of living, and a shortage of labor for agriculture compels the country to import much of its food. Fortunately for Venezuela, however, the oil industry has developed under concessions that assure the government a considerable share in its profits, and there has been some attempt under recent administrations to use this income in a way that will benefit the community as a whole. Their efforts have been seconded by Mr. Rockefeller's International Basic Economy Corporation. In 1948 this company's Venezuelan subsidiary, partly financed by the oil companies, inaugurated an ambitious program designed to increase local food supplies and to cut down the cost of distribution.

Part VII

༄

MEXICO

THE history of the countries north of the Isthmus of Panama is more intimately connected with our own than is the history of the South American republics. This is especially true of Mexico, the only Latin American state with which we have a land frontier. The course of events in Mexico has repeatedly been affected by influences emanating from the United States, and relations with Mexico have frequently been an issue in our domestic politics.

This is not the only reason why the history of Mexico is especially interesting to the North American student. With a population larger than that of any other Latin American state except Brazil, our southern neighbor is one of the most important nations of the hemisphere. Furthermore, its troubled history illustrates with peculiar vividness the character of the political and social problems that have complicated the development of many of the other countries of Spanish origin: the difficulty of establishing stable republican institutions, the conflict between Church and State, and above all the social tensions arising from the presence of an unassimilated, exploited Indian population. The Mexicans have made a real effort in recent years to solve some of these problems, and their experience, whether of success or of failure, is important to any one who wishes to understand the problems of the other countries where somewhat similar conditions exist.

creased by separation from Spain. Since it refused to admit that the new American states had inherited the right of patronage, it was no longer amenable to political control. At the same time it jealously maintained its *fueros* or special privileges—its exemption from taxes and the right to have its own courts. It was supported by other groups which had had a favored position under the colonial regime, such as the principal merchants of Mexico City, both Spanish and creole, and the owners of the great entailed estates.

On the other side were the same elements that formed the liberal party in other Latin American countries: intellectuals of the upper class who advocated liberal ideas for their own sake; middle-class professional men and small merchants, often of *mestizo* origin; and leaders in other parts of the country who felt that the provinces were being exploited commercially and politically by powerful groups in Mexico City and who were eager to obtain more control over their own local affairs. At first federalism was the chief political issue, as it was in so many of the other Spanish American countries during the 1820's. Later, when the federalists and liberals found that the Church was their most formidable opponent, they centered their efforts on destroying that organization's political influence.

The struggle between these political groups is the central theme of Mexico's history, but neither of them ever really controlled the government for any length of time. Conflicts between them were always decided by the intervention of professional soldiers who were in most cases more interested in obtaining power and the emoluments of office for themselves than in questions of principle. Even in recent times, most of the presidents of the Republic have been generals.

In the first years of independence the military forces had deteriorated in discipline and efficiency, but they were still better organized than any other group that aspired to power. The officers were for the most part men trained in the Spanish army or militia who had participated in the sudden change of front that made independence possible. After helping to set up and then overthrow the imperial government of Iturbide, they were disposed to seek advancement and personal profit through further ventures of the same sort. Few of them had much interest in the social and political issues that divided the civilian community, but they were always ready to espouse the cause of one party or the other in order to further their own ambitions. The army, to quote an American diplomat, became "the greatest nuisance, and the most insuperable barrier to the prosperity and progress of Mexico." [1] It consumed an inordinate proportion of the public revenue, despite the fact that the common soldiers—unfortunate Indians or *mestizos* recruited by force—received but a small part of their nominal pay; and its *fuero*, or exemption from the jurisdiction of the civil courts, gave its members a privileged position which was frequently abused.

The Rise and Fall of Iturbide

The army and most of the civilian political groups worked together in the last stage of the movement for independence. Both the conservative supporters of Iturbide and the hitherto unsuccessful revolutionists under Guerrero agreed on the "Three Guarantees" of the Plan of Iguala: the defense of the Church and its privileges, the maintenance of Mexican independence, and the establishment of racial equality. Though many of the revolutionists were republicans, they acquiesced in the plan for a constitutional monarchy under a Bourbon prince, which appealed to the conservatives as the surest means of maintaining the integrity of the old regime. By the treaty of Córdoba, signed August 24, 1821, the Viceroy O'Donojú consented to this arrangement, but it was agreed that another person might be made emperor of Mexico if no Spanish prince were available. A regency headed by Iturbide and composed chiefly of conservatives assumed charge of the government pending the choice of the new monarch.

When the *Cortes* in Spain rejected the Treaty of Córdoba and the hope of obtaining a Bourbon prince vanished, it soon became clear that Iturbide had designs on the throne himself. The majority of the constituent assembly, which met in February, 1822, opposed his ambition, for a number of the delegates were republicans and many conservatives who had desired a Bourbon monarchy had no desire to be ruled by a man whom they distrusted and disliked as a social inferior. On the other hand Iturbide had the army behind him and also a great following among the people of Mexico City, and in May a street demonstration by the soldiers and populace, accompanied by forceful measures against some of the more recalcitrant deputies, compelled the reluctant assembly to elect him Emperor.

Agustín I held his throne only a few months. The assembly, which

[1] W. Thompson, *Recollections of Mexico*, p. 168.

had been intimidated but not cowed, continued to oppose him and in October, 1822, he dissolved it. By this time he had lost much of his popularity even among the soldiers. When Antonio López de Santa Anna raised the standard of revolt at Vera Cruz in December, he was joined not only by many of the old revolutionary leaders like Victoria, Guerrero, and Bravo, but also by a large part of the army. The Emperor was unable to resist, and abdicated on February 19, 1823. He was permitted to go into exile, but when he attempted to return to Mexico seventeen months later he was captured and shot.

The Inauguration of Republican Government

The assembly, which had been reconvened by Iturbide in a last-minute effort at conciliation, appointed a triumvirate to exercise the executive power and ordered that a new congress be chosen to formulate a republican constitution. In the election there was a spirited contest between the advocates and the opponents of federalism. The federalists won a majority of the seats, and the new constitution which was proclaimed in October, 1824, provided for a government very similar to that of the United States. On October 10 Guadelupe Victoria was inaugurated as first President of the Republic and Nicolás Bravo as Vice-President.

The new chief executive, whose real name was Manuel Félix Fernández, had assumed his somewhat fantastic pseudonym during the war for independence. He had been one of the heroes of the struggle during the dark days before the Plan of Iguala. Popular, honest, and tolerant, though not of outstanding ability, he assumed office under favorable auspices, with a cabinet in which both federalists and centralists were represented. He had, however, to contend with the fundamental divergence of views between the various political factions and the selfish personal ambitions of their leaders. At the beginning of his administration the central government had little authority in the states and rival factions frequently waged civil wars which endangered the stability of the national regime. Commerce and mining had suffered much during the long years of disorder since 1810, and the government's finances were in bad shape. Silver production was only about a quarter of what it had been at the beginning of the century, but it increased somewhat when British interests took over many of the mines during an outburst of speculative enthusiasm that brought much new capital into the Spanish American countries after 1825. Conditions gradually improved, and Victoria's administration, despite a conservative revolt led by Vice President Bravo in 1828, was on the whole more tranquil than any that Mexico was to have for many years to come. One of the President's important achievements was the expulsion in November, 1825, of the Spanish garrison that still held the Castle of San Juan de Ulua at Vera Cruz.

Though the conflicts between monarchists and republicans and between centralists and federalists left the upper class divided into several hostile factions, there were as yet no well-organized parties. The most active political groups during Victoria's administration were the rival Masonic lodges. The Scottish rite Masons, or *escoceses*, had probably been established in Mexico as early as 1806 and had received many recruits from the officers of the Spanish forces sent to combat the revolutionists in 1811.[1] They had been prominent in the movement to oust Iturbide. Many of them were centralists in the election of 1823, and the federalists consequently organized the York rite, or *yorquino* lodges, in 1825. In this action they were encouraged and advised by the first American minister to Mexico, the active but not always judicious Joel Poinsett, whose dislike of the rather conservative *escoceses* was intensified by a belief that they were under the influence of his rival the British minister. President Victoria and many of his collaborators were members of the new organization.

The conservative opposition, centering in the Scottish rite lodges, grew stronger as Victoria's effort to govern with the aid of all parties proved a failure. Poinsett was violently criticised for his interference in the country's internal politics, and when the conservatives revolted in 1828 one of their demands was for his expulsion. The influence of the Scottish rite lodges was destroyed when the revolt failed and many of their leaders were exiled. The *yorquinos*, split into hostile groups, also ceased to be an important political force a year or two later.

The *yorquinos* split on the question of the presidential succession. Victoria's candidate, Gómez Pedraza, was supported by one faction and by many of the *escoceses*. Vicente Guerrero, who was the grand master of the York rite lodges, was backed by the more radical element, including Poinsett. The hero of the revolution had a great popular following, and there were loud complaints of fraud and official interference when the electoral votes, cast by the state legislatures, gave Gómez

[1] Callcott, *Church and State in Mexico*, p. 37.

Pedraza a small majority. The defeated party promptly obtained the support of Santa Anna and other military leaders in a revolt that gave them control of the government early in 1829. The Republic's electoral machinery had broken down in its first important test, and political parties in Mexico were thenceforth to rely upon force rather than upon the will of the voters as the surest means to attain and hold power.

Santa Anna and his Contemporaries, 1829-1846

The revolt of 1828 again brought into prominence the military leader who was to dominate Mexican politics during the next twenty-five years. Antonio López de Santa Anna, as an officer in the Spanish army, had served with distinction against the revolution until the Plan of Iguala. Thereafter, as we have seen, he had helped to overthrow Iturbide. Crafty and unscrupulous, with few convictions and little administrative ability, he derived his influence from a popularity among the troops which survived misfortunes that would completely have discredited another leader. He enjoyed power, but not the responsibility of exercising it, and he often permitted others to assume the presidency while he retained military control. His political views were flexible. In his earlier years he was usually on the side of the liberals, but he became the champion of the conservatives and helped to maintain the supremacy of the aristocracy and the Church when that course seemed more likely to forward his own ambitions.

Santa Anna was responsible for a series of revolts that brought the country to a condition approaching anarchy in the years following 1829. He soon turned against Guerrero, who proved weak and incompetent, and whose mixed blood and radical views made him disliked by the aristocracy. The President was compelled to abandon the capital, after some fighting, and the Vice-President, Anastasio Bustamante, took office early in 1830 with conservative support. Guerrero attempted to continue the struggle but was treacherously captured and executed—an act which aroused indignation among the liberals and helped to bring on a new revolt in 1832. Again Santa Anna was the leader, this time supporting Gómez Pedraza, who still claimed that he had been elected as constitutional president in 1828. The latter was installed in office for the few remaining months of the four-year term, and for the new period, starting in 1833, Santa Anna himself was elected, with a liberal vice-president and an overwhelmingly liberal congress.

By this time there was a clear-cut division between the two political parties that were to wage a savage struggle during the next thirty-four years. The conservatives, or centralists, who had been divided and disorganized after the failure of the effort to establish a monarchy, became more aggressive after 1828, and the Church also increased its political activity. The Church's power decreased temporarily after the fall of Iturbide, because disputes over the right of patronage made it impossible to fill the places of the Spanish bishops who left the country or died; but after 1831 Bustamante made concessions which permitted the filling of the vacant sees and the clergy regained much lost ground. Their growing influence alarmed the liberals, or federalists, and when this party came into power in 1833 it at once launched an attack on the Church.

Vice-President Valentín Gómez Farías, who was an ardent liberal, took charge of the government for long periods in the first year of the new administration, while Santa Anna either led the troops against revolting conservatives or enjoyed life at his country estate. Under his leadership, the Congress enacted a series of anti-clerical laws. Indian missions and their property were brought under government control; the Church was deprived of its monopoly over education; the government ceased to use its authority to compel the payment of tithes or the fulfillment of monastic vows; and the right to exercise the *patronato* was reasserted. Each of these measures was violently opposed by the clergy and the conservatives, who revolted in the summer of 1833 but were defeated after several months of fighting. Santa Anna supported the constitutional regime at this time, but when it became apparent that the liberals had lost the support of public opinion by going too fast and too far he threw in his lot with the forces of reaction. Resuming the presidency in April, 1834, he dissolved the Congress, removed liberal state governors, and arbitrarily abrogated many of the recently enacted laws. Gómez Farías was forced to flee the country.

A new congress, dominated by the conservatives, met in 1835. The federal form of government was abolished and the constitution of 1824 was replaced by the so-called "Seven Laws" of 1836. These provided that the president should be elected for an eight-year term, but hedged him about with restrictions that showed the civilian politicians' distrust of Santa Anna, among them being a provision for a *"poder conservador"* to maintain the equilibrium between the executive, the legislative, and the judiciary. The new fundamental law seems to have been satisfactory to no one; but even a much more workable form of government would hardly have received a fair trial in the midst of the internal and external difficulties that beset the Republic during the next few years.

The worst of these was the revolt in Texas. Before the end of the Spanish regime the viceroy had given Moses Austin permission to establish a colony of Roman Catholics in Texas. This grant was confirmed by Iturbide, and later by the republican government, when Stephen Austin took up the enterprise after his father's death. Similar grants were made to other persons, and several thousand North Americans settled in the region during the 1820's. Their presence soon became a source of concern, especially in view of the United States Government's openly expressed desire to acquire the territory. Mexican efforts to restrict immigration and to bring the colonists under more effective control increased the tension between the newcomers and the authorities, and an attempt to prohibit slavery in the territory produced no result. The colonists were especially resentful when Texas was united with Coahuila as one state in 1830. Encouraged by the continual party strife in Mexico, they revolted in 1835, and in April, 1836, they defeated the Mexican forces at San Jacinto and captured Santa Anna himself. A treaty which they made with their prisoner was repudiated by the government at Mexico City, but the latter was in no position to carry on further military operations and Texas became an independent republic.

Despite these events, the conservatives remained in control at Mexico City and their position was somewhat strengthened when both Spain and the Papacy recognized Mexico's independence in 1837. Nevertheless Anastasio Bustamante, who became President in 1837, had to contend with continued internal disorder, and aggression from abroad soon made matters worse. Many foreigners had been injured in one way or another during the continual strife of the past fifteen years. Their governments had insistently pressed demands for compensation, but with little result, and in 1838 France sent a fleet to Vera Cruz and summarily demanded payment of claims amounting to $600,000. It will be remembered that the French government was at this same time endeavoring to restore its waning prestige at home by aggressive action against Rosas in the River Plate. When Bustamante rejected the demand, Vera Cruz was occupied and other ports were blockaded. This "Pastry War," so called because one of the French claims was that of a baker whose shop had been sacked, was finally ended through British mediation, when Mexico agreed to pay the sum demanded.

Santa Anna commanded the Mexican forces in their unsuccessful resistance at Vera Cruz, and a fortunate wound, which compelled the amputation of one leg, restored his popularity. Very soon he was again plotting to resume power. For a time he supported Bustamante in suppressing the persistent revolts of the federalists, but in 1841, under the "Plan of Tacubaya" he again seized control of the government. He had by this time definitely aligned himself with the centralist party, and a new constituent assembly was dissolved when it showed federalist tendencies. In its place a handpicked assembly of notables drew up a new constitution, the *Bases Orgánicas* of 1843, which was no more liberal than the "Seven Laws" but did away with some of their more impractical features. Santa Anna was elected President in 1844, but he continued, as on other occasions, to spend much time on his country estate while Valentín Canalizo, as acting President, struggled with federalist disaffection and a rising opposition in Congress. The government fell before the end of the year and José Joaquín Herrera was installed as provisional President. He in turn was overthrown late in 1845 by General Mariano Paredes, who had revolted against Santa Anna in 1844 but now reappeared as the leader of a conservative reaction.

The War with the United States

The ostensible purpose of Paredes' revolt was to set up a government that would take a firm stand against the United States. Relations between the two countries, long clouded by Mexican suspicion of American territorial ambitions and made worse by blundering diplomacy and disputes over claims, had been especially strained since the revolt of Texas. Mexico resented the recognition of Texan independence by the United States in 1837, and a number of incidents increased the hostile feeling on both sides. When Texas was annexed to the United States by joint resolution of Congress in March, 1845, a conflict became all but inevitable, for the Mexican government had announced as early as 1843 that such an act would be regarded as a declaration of war. First Herrera and then Paredes refused to receive an American commissioner sent to attempt a peaceful settlement. In February, 1846, General Zachary

Taylor was ordered to move into territory between the Nueces River and the Rio Grande which, the Mexicans claimed, had never formed a part of Texas. In April hostilities began. The untrained and poorly equipped Mexican troops were defeated in several battles, and before the end of 1846 Taylor occupied much of northern Mexico and other American forces took possession of New Mexico and California.

At the capital the government was weakened by the chronic lack of funds and by internal dissension. Paredes' popularity declined, especially after his chief adviser, the centralist leader Lucas Alamán, openly advocated the establishment of a monarchy. This was an idea that many of the reactionary conservatives had never given up, but the proposal aroused the opposition of all the republican elements. The controversy that ensued gave Santa Anna the opportunity for which he had been waiting. This time he sought the support of the federalists, though he worked chiefly, as always, through his friends in the army. In 1846 there were uprisings in his favor in different sections of the country, and in August General Salas "pronounced" for him at Mexico City and overthrew the Paredes regime. Santa Anna himself landed at Vera Cruz a few days later. He was allowed to pass through the American blockading squadron because President Polk was given to understand that he would accept American proposals for peace if he were allowed to resume power, but once in Mexico he took command of the army and prepared to resist the invaders. He was no more successful than his predecessor, and in February, 1847, he was defeated by Taylor in the important battle of Buena Vista near Saltillo.

Meanwhile his associates at Mexico City were making efforts to strengthen the national defense. In their desperate need for money they turned their attention to the Church, which had retained much of its wealth while the commercial stagnation and disorder of the past quarter century were causing most of the great private fortunes of an earlier period to dwindle away. In January, 1847, the Congress authorized the government to raise $15,000,000 by mortgaging or selling church property, an act which aroused a storm of opposition from the clergy and their supporters. Santa Anna, though elected to the presidency, had characteristically refrained from taking office in order that Gómez Farías, who was again Vice-President, might assume the responsibility for a policy certain to be dangerous politically; and when it became evident that public opinion would not support the government's action, he returned to Mexico City, compromised with the Church for a payment of $2,000,000, and eliminated Gómez Farías by causing the office of vice-president to be abolished.

Since Taylor's victories in the north had not brought Mexico to terms, another American army under General Winfield Scott landed in March, 1847, at Vera Cruz. By September, after much fighting, it had occupied Mexico City, and on February 2, 1848, representatives of the two nations signed the Treaty of Guadelupe Hidalgo. Texas, New Mexico, and California became a part of the United States, which paid $15,000,000 by way of compensation. In July the American army was withdrawn.

Political and Religious Conflict, 1848–1860

Santa Anna was compelled to relinquish his authority after the loss of Mexico City. First Manuel de la Peña, the president of the supreme court, then General Anaya, and then De la Peña again, occupied the presidency while peace negotiations were going on. In June, 1848, General José Joaquín Herrera became President by election, serving under the federalist constitution of 1824 which Santa Anna had reëstablished. A moderate liberal, supported by the influential elements that had advocated the conclusion of peace with the United States, Herrera earnestly endeavored to repair the damage wrought by the war. He had assumed office with great reluctance, for the difficulties which he faced seemed well-nigh insuperable. The finances, as usual, were in a bad state, and foreign claims continued to cause trouble. During the war the already weak prestige of the central government in the more remote sections of the country still further diminished, and the wild Indians in several regions were committing depredations against towns and *haciendas*. A race war in Yucatán, where the Mayas took up arms against the officials and *hacendados* who had oppressed them since the Spanish conquest, caused heavy losses of life and property for several years. At the same time, both the extreme conservatives led by Paredes and the *"santanistas"* staged unsuccessful revolts. Nevertheless Herrera served out his legal term and passed on the presidency in 1851 to his constitutionally elected successor, General Mariano Arista.

Arista, without his predecessor's ability and prestige, was less fortunate. There were controversies in some of the states over the religious question, which Herrera had kept in the background, and there was much discontent in the army because the number of officers and men had been reduced to save money. Even the liberals gave the administration little support. Revolts and disorders gradually made its position untenable, and in January, 1853, Arista resigned.

A few weeks later Santa Anna returned from exile to assume the presidency. With conservative support, he set aside the constitution, dissolved the national congress and the state legislatures, and finally in December, 1853, proclaimed himself dictator for an indefinite term with power to name his own successor. This arrogant assumption of supreme power, climaxed by the unpopular sale to the United States of the Mesilla Valley, "The Gadsden Purchase," soon brought on a reaction. Early in 1854, General Juan Álvarez and Colonel Ignacio Comonfort started a revolt in the State of Guerrero under the Plan of Ayutla, appealing to the liberals for support. Indecisive fighting went on for more than a year until Santa Anna, deserted by many of his followers, decided to take refuge abroad. His flight permitted the insurgents to take over the government without much opposition and marked the end of his active influence in Mexican politics.

The revolution of Ayutla marked the beginning of a new phase in the struggle between the powerful classes that had hitherto dominated Mexico's political life and the more democratic elements that were now demanding a voice in the government. The chief issue was the relationship between Church and State. The Church had continued to be active in politics, partly because it constantly had to defend its property against needy federal and state governments, but the liberals, after their unfortunate experience in 1833–34, had shown little disposition to attack it during the brief periods when they were in power. The revolution now brought into office a group of leaders who were determined to assume a more aggressive policy.

The most important of these was the full-blooded Indian, Benito Juárez. Born of poor parents in a small Zapotec village near Oaxaca, Juárez entered the service of a white family in that city while still a child and so aroused the interest of his employer that he was given unusual opportunities to obtain an education. Though at first destined for the priesthood, he soon left the seminary to take up the study of law, and in 1829, at the age of twenty-three, he entered local politics as a member of a *yorquino* lodge. From then on he was an active liberal, first in his own state of Oaxaca and then at Mexico City. As a representative of the middle-class element which was challenging the political preeminence of the old creole families, he was to be the chief figure in Mexico's political life during the next quarter century, as Santa Anna had been in the preceding period.

Juárez was a member of the cabinet under General Álvarez, whom the revolutionists installed as provisional President, and was the author of a law promulgated in November, 1855, which limited the jurisdiction of both the ecclesiastical and the military courts. This was an attack on one of the most cherished *fueros*, or special privileges, of the clergy and the professional officer caste in the army. Since most of the leaders of the army had supported Santa Anna it was natural that the liberals should try to curb its privileges and diminish its capacity for mischief, but the *Ley Juárez* was also bitterly resented by the portion of the military forces that was supporting the new government. The storm that it aroused was one of the reasons why General Álvarez, an honest but not very competent provincial *caudillo*, was forced to turn over the presidency to Comonfort in December, 1855.

Comonfort was more moderate in his liberalism, but his associates continued to push the reform program. In June, 1856, the Congress enacted the *Ley Lerdo*, drafted by Miguel Lerdo de Tejada, which required the Church to sell all real estate not actually used for religious purposes, and in April, 1857, the *Ley Iglesias* deprived the Church of its control over cemeteries. Another law compelled the clergy to perform services gratuitously for impoverished parishioners. Meanwhile the new constitution of 1857 had been drawn up, and the principles of the *Ley Juárez* and the *Ley Lerdo* had been incorporated in it, together with other provisions for which the liberals had contended: a federal form of government, manhood suffrage, and freedom of speech, of teaching, and of the press.

The Church furiously opposed the whole reform program. Revolts inspired by the clergy at Puebla and elsewhere were suppressed but unrest continued. The Archbishop of Mexico excommunicated all persons taking oath to support the new constitution, and the Pope approved his stand. The liberal party itself was still divided and those who approved the new laws were probably a minority of the nation as a whole. A reaction was inevitable. The conservatives had their opportunity when Comonfort quarreled with the majority in the Congress. The President at first accepted the aid of a group of conservative army officers in abolishing the new constitution and assuming dictatorial powers, but was soon afterward deserted by his new friends and compelled to leave the country. Félix Zuloaga, the chief of the army, was installed as provisional President early in 1858, while Juárez, claiming the presidency as Comonfort's constitutional successor, placed himself at the head of a liberal counter-revolt.

For the next three years the "War of the Reform" deluged Mexico in blood. Juárez, defeated in the interior north and west of Mexico City, fled by way of the west coast and Panama to Vera Cruz, where he established his capital. Thenceforth the fortunes of war favored first one side and then the other. Zuloaga resigned late in 1858 and was replaced by the brilliant young General Miguel Miramón. After the inexcusable murder of a number of prisoners by the conservative General Márquez in 1859, captured officers were regularly executed by both sides. The bitterness between the two parties increased when Juárez issued decrees confiscating all ecclesiastical property except church buildings, suppressing monasteries, and instituting civil marriage in districts under liberal control. While the conservatives had the sympathy of several European powers, Juárez was supported by the United States, and an attack on Vera Cruz was frustrated in 1860 by the intervention of American warships. By the end of that year the conservatives had been decisively defeated and the liberals had taken possession of Mexico City. A few months later, after an election, Juárez took office as constitutional President.

The French Intervention

The conservatives continued guerrilla warfare in the interior, and while Juárez was still struggling to establish order a new danger appeared from abroad. During the long civil war, military requisitions, destruction of property, forced loans, and outrages against individuals had greatly increased the already large amount of foreign claims. The treasury had no money even for the service of the bonded debt, and when the Congress voted to suspend all debt payments for two years Great Britain, France, and Spain signed an agreement for a joint intervention to obtain reparation for injuries to their citizens and to compel Mexico to meet her financial obligations. The United States was invited to take part, but declined.

The three-power treaty of October 31, 1861, ostensibly barred any interference in Mexico's internal political affairs, but it was evident from the first that at least two of the signatories had other purposes in mind than the mere protection of their citizens' financial interests. The Spanish government had openly supported the conservatives during the War of Reform and its ambassador had been expelled from Mexico after the liberal victory. For three years Spain had been toying with the idea of restoring its control over what had once been its richest colony. Napoleon III, on the other hand, had ambitions of his own. Encouraged by the Civil War in the United States, which made North American interference unlikely, he had been intriguing with some of the Mexican conservatives to set up a foreign monarchy under French protection, and Maximilian of Hapsburg, the brother of Emperor Franz Joseph of Austria, had already been chosen as its head. These two powers were thus working at cross purposes with each other and with Great Britain, which was interested solely in the collection of claims. Although British participation in the intervention was confined to naval action, both France and Spain sent considerable bodies of troops.

A Spanish fleet seized Vera Cruz in December, 1861, and French and British forces arrived soon afterward. Juárez entered into negotiations and agreed that the allied forces might march inland from the fever-infested coast while the discussions continued. In the ensuing conferences, the French commissioner took a position that made any peaceful settlement impossible. His most indefensible demand, perhaps, was for full payment of the Jecker claim, based on a $16,800,000 bond issue agreed to by Miramón shortly before his government collapsed. Only a small portion of the proceeds of the loan had ever reached Mexico, and the French action in espousing the claim was the more scandalous because Jecker himself was a Swiss citizen at the time the loan was made and had only recently acquired French nationality under suspicious circumstances. The British and Spanish representatives were unwilling to support such a demand, and their increasing realization of the divergence of views between the three allies led them to withdraw with their forces, leaving France to continue the intervention alone.

Napoleon's real purpose now became evident. General Juan Almonte, one of the leaders of the group that sought foreign intervention, was permitted to proclaim himself President of the Republic under the protection of the French troops, and the latter marched inland toward Mexico City, despite their earlier promise to withdraw to the coast if negotiations failed. At Puebla, however, they were defeated with heavy losses by a Mexican army under General Zaragoza, in a battle which made May 5 one of the great anniversaries in Mexican history. The invaders' advance was held up for nearly a year—a delay which in the long run proved fatal to their designs.

Resistance became more difficult after General Forey arrived with 30,000 fresh troops, and the French occupied Mexico City in June, 1863. An "Assembly of Notables," convoked by the invaders, voted on July 8 to establish an hereditary monarchy and to offer the crown to Maximilian or to some other Catholic prince proposed by Napoleon III. In the meantime a regency headed by Almonte nominally assumed the executive power, though those parts of the country occupied by the invaders were in reality under French military rule. Juárez and his associates continued to fight in the interior and for a time held a large part of the country.

After insisting that the invitation of the Assembly of Notables be ratified by a plebiscite, which of course was a farce, Maximilian accepted the throne on April 10, 1864. At the same time he signed a convention with Napoleon by which the latter promised military support during the first years of the new regime, to be paid for by the Mexican treasury, and obtained a loan on exorbitant terms with the aid of English bankers. Encouraged by these arrangements, he and his wife, the Belgian princess Carlota, entered Mexico City on June 12, 1864.

The new Emperor, still in his thirty-second year, was an affable, well-educated prince, who had served as Commander-in-Chief of the Austrian navy and as Governor-General of Lombardy-Venice. In the latter post he had shown a mildly liberal disposition which enhanced his prestige in Europe but made him less rather than better fitted for the enterprise he was now undertaking. Such support as he had in Mexico came from the conservatives, who were already disillusioned because the French commander had refused to restore the property that the Church had had to sell under the *Ley Lerdo*. He further alienated the more extreme members of this party when he not only refused to restore the Church to the position that it had held before the revolution of Ayutla, but attempted to establish a free press and to obtain liberal support by an offer of amnesty. The conservative leaders were also jealous of the continued dominance of French officers in military affairs, and the situation was not improved by the organization of an imperial force of Austrian and Belgian volunteers. The liberals, on the other hand, showed little interest in Maximilian's efforts to conciliate them, even though some prominent members of the party, to the disgust of their opponents, were given important posts in the government. Their resistance stiffened when Maximilian changed his policy and ordered that those who opposed the government should be treated as bandits, so that internal strife continued with all the savagery which had marked the war of the reform.

For a time the French armies were generally successful. Juárez was forced back until he was compelled to establish his capital at El Paso on the Texas frontier, and Porfirio Díaz, who had held most of the country south of the capital, surrendered at Oaxaca in February, 1865. By this time, however, the Civil War in the United States, which had compelled that country to maintain an outward neutrality, was approaching an end, and the government at Washington made it clear that it would not permit the French protectorate to continue. Confronted by the threat of American intervention, and influenced also by the situation in Europe, Napoleon III decided early in 1866 to withdraw his troops from the adventure within the next two years. Thenceforth the defense of the imperial interests was left more and more to Mexican troops, and the tide of battle turned in favor of the liberals. Maximilian's pleas for continued French aid fell on deaf ears. He was disposed to abdicate, but the extreme conservatives persuaded him to make a final stand with their support and in February, 1867, he went to Querétaro at the head of his army. He was besieged there by overwhelming superior liberal forces, but he resisted until the city was taken through treachery on May 14. A month later he was condemned to death and shot, in spite of the remonstrances of foreign diplomatic representatives.

The Liberals in Power, 1867–1877

The liberal party had won a decisive victory after thirteen years of almost continuous and unprecedentedly savage civil war. The conservatives were not only defeated, but discredited by their connection with the hated foreign intervention. Juárez, who had continued to claim the presidency though his legal term had long since expired, was the hero of the hour, and he was elected again in 1867. The reforms for which he had fought seemed now to be securely established, and he endeavored, with only moderate success, to revive commerce and restore tranquility. The country was by no means at peace, for guerrilla bands were still operating in out of the way sections and rival leaders were fighting for control in several states, but Juárez' own position was not seriously challenged until he brought about his reëlection in 1871.

The principal opposition to Juárez' continuance in power came from Porfirio Díaz, who had escaped from prison after his surrender to the French and played a distinguished part in the events of the closing months of the war. Díaz had been a candidate for the presidency in 1867, and when he was again unsuccessful in 1871 he led a revolt. He was defeated, but many of his partisans were still under arms when Juárez died suddenly on July 18, 1872, and Sebastián Lerdo de Tejada, the President of the Supreme Court, took his place. Díaz accepted the new regime and the country was relatively peaceful during the next three years. In 1874, several of the radical anti-ecclesiastical measures promulgated by Juárez during the War of the Reform, were formally incorporated in the constitution.

The Díaz Regime

Lerdo, though popular at the beginning of his term, was unable to hold the support of the mutually jealous factions within the liberal party; and when he sought reëlection Díaz ousted him in 1876 and became constitutional President in May, 1877. Several revolts by Lerdo's followers were suppressed and order was gradually established. At the end of his term, since a man who had made no reëlection his battle cry in two revolutions could hardly be a candidate for reëlection himself, Díaz placed his friend General Manuel González at the head of the government. From Díaz' point of view the choice was a good one, for the new President was able to repress opposition but made himself so unpopular by unwise and corrupt financial measures that he could not have opposed Díaz' return to power if he had wished to. The latter assumed the presidency in 1884, to begin the longest unbroken period of personal rule in the history of Spanish America.

Porfirio Díaz was born in Oaxaca in 1830. His father, a minor employee in a commercial house, was white or nearly white; his mother half Indian. Despite the family's poverty, he received some education, studying at one time for the Church and later for the law. He began his active participation in politics, as a liberal, during the revolution of Ayutla. Later he served as Governor of Tehuantepec, which he held for the *juaristas* during the War of Reform, and was one of the outstanding heroes of the struggle against the Empire. His political astuteness, combined with a ruthless energy and firmness of purpose, made him the perfect type of successful *caudillo*. He owed his long tenure of power partly to these qualities and partly to the rapidly increasing prosperity that Mexico enjoyed under his rule. As in other Latin American countries, political rivalries became less acute as the ruling class turned their attention to new opportunities created by the growth of foreign commerce and the development of the country's natural resources.

Díaz gave positions in his government to rivals in the liberal party and to many former conservatives, including some who had coöperated with Maximilian. The Church, still influential despite its losses, became more friendly when he showed a willingness to relax the enforcement of the laws of reform, and it gradually recovered some of its property and much of its importance as a social force. Party enmities lost much of their virulence, and those who sought governmental favors found it more profitable, and far safer, to court the dictator than to organize a revolution. The revolts that occurred were quickly crushed and their leaders killed. In 1879, nine persons accused of conspiracy were executed without trial at Vera Cruz. Such acts of cruelty might merely have provoked further outbreaks under other circumstances, but they were effective in discouraging disorder when the great majority of thinking people were sick of civil war. The disappearance of armed political opposition was followed by the elimination of banditry, long the curse of the Mexican countryside. A well-trained rural police, recruited largely from former professional revolutionists and highwaymen, made life and property, at least for the upper classes and foreigners, safer than in many parts of the United States and Europe.

For the first time the government of Mexico became a real personal dictatorship. Hitherto the local *caudillos* who controlled the state governments had had much independent power. The dominant party in Mexico City had naturally sought to assure the control of the states by its own partisans, by armed intervention if necessary, but it had often been compelled to compromise with the local leaders and to purchase rather than to command their support. It was the state governors who had in practice controlled the electoral machinery—a fact which explains the occurrence of disputed elections in a country where there was never any real freedom of suffrage. Under Díaz this situation changed. The power of local *caudillos* was systematically undermined and finally destroyed, and the state governors became mere subordinates of the president, named and removed at his pleasure. Elections, as in the past, were a mere form so far as the voters were concerned, but the outcome was now dictated from Mexico City. There was thus no longer any opposition group in Congress. The press, which had enjoyed some freedom under Juárez and Lerdo, was brought into line by a combination of repressive measures and bribery.

Díaz carefully prevented any other member of his government from building up a prestige that might threaten his own power. By promptly relegating to obscurity any lieutenant who became too influential, and by fomenting jealousies and rivalries in his official family, as well as by exiling or terrorizing potential opponents, Díaz made sure that there was no one in Mexico who could successfully aspire to replace him in the government. The only group that seemingly attempted to influence his policies were the so-called *cientificos*, originally a loose association of young deputies who attempted rather ineffectively to bring about political reforms while outwardly supporting the administration and enjoying many favors at its hands. Their importance as a political factor does not appear to have been great, but one of their leaders, José Limantour, was Minister of Finance for a long period, and in this capacity was largely responsible for the dictatorship's most important achievements.

The Republic's finances, when Díaz succeeded González in 1884, were in the chaotic condition that had been normal since independence. Expenditures far exceeded receipts, salaries were unpaid, and the foreign debt was in default. By economy and better administration, matters were soon much improved. After Limantour became Minister of Finance in 1893 a series of brilliantly successful financial reforms were carried out. The old burdensome taxes inherited from the Spanish regime, and especially the internal customs duties, were abolished or modified. The budget showed a surplus, for practically the first time in the country's history, and the currency was placed on a gold basis. Mexico's credit became so well established that it was possible to issue bonds abroad with a coupon rate of 4 per cent—a rate which no other Latin American country had hitherto been able to approach. With the aid of borrowed money the government was able to purchase a controlling interest in the majority of the country's railway lines after 1904.

One of the reasons for the general prosperity that made these achievements possible was a great influx of foreign capital. Because of this, mining developed rapidly, until Mexico was again the world's chief silver producer and was second only to the United States in the production of copper. Railroad building also made remarkable progress, until there were nearly 25,000 kilometers of railways in the Republic in 1911, as compared with 691 kilometers in 1876.[1] Industrial plants of many kinds, most of them it is true leading an artificial existence behind high customs barriers, were established in the principal cities. The country's foreign commerce increased five-fold, and the petroleum industry, just becoming established at the end of the Díaz regime, gave promise of far greater exports in the future. Most of the new undertakings were financed and managed by foreigners, but the benefits of material progress accrued also to many thousands of Mexicans and the Republic appeared to foreign observers to be one of the most fortunate of the American republics when the centenary of the *grito de Dolores* was celebrated in 1910.

Beneath the surface, however, there was much discontent. The monopoly of public office by Díaz and the clique that surrounded him irritated other people who had political ambitions. A more acute feeling of unrest was growing among the common people. On the great plantations, the Indian and *mestizo* laborers were still subject to a peonage system which had kept their wages practically unchanged for a century while increases in prices depressed their already low standard of living. More and more of the country people had become debt-slaves during the past fifty years because the *haciendas* had been steadily expanding at the expense of the small landholders and the village communities. As in Peru and Bolivia, but probably to an even greater extent, the Indian had been systematically despoiled by those who had wealth or political power. The constitution of 1857, which required the division of village communal holdings as well as the sale of church property, had facilitated this process; and other laws of the Díaz period, providing ostensibly for the surveying of the national domain, had permitted favored individuals to build up vast estates on lands which theoretically belonged to the nation but which in fact were often the property of the Indians. The peasants, whose lot had thus become harder than ever at a time when the rest of the country was enjoying an unheard-of prosperity, were consequently ripe for revolt as soon as the dictator's grip should weaken. Their desperate determination to recover their lands made the agrarian question the most pressing political problem in Mexico under the revolutionary governments which followed Díaz.

Since much of the land had passed into the hands of foreigners, discontent among the peasants tended to take on an anti-foreign charac-

[1] Rabasa, *L'Evolution Historique du Mexique*, p. 165.

ter. This was also true of the less acute but still active discontent among the laborers in mining and industry. The employer, in most cases a North American or a European, was usually supported by the army and police in dealing with labor agitators or strikes, and he often profited by tariff protection and other special privileges. Díaz sought to encourage the investment of capital as a means of developing the country, but many of his fellow citizens were dismayed to see the control of the Republic's economic life and natural resources pass out of Mexican hands. A change in this situation became another of the chief objectives of the political groups that were soon to come into power.

After 1884, Díaz was reëlected as a matter of course at the end of each successive term. The constitutional prohibition, which he had felt compelled to respect in 1880, was modified to permit one reëlection in 1888 and was completely removed a few years later. In 1904 the presidential term was extended to six years. At the same time, as a concession to public opinion, the aging ruler consented to the establishment of the office of Vice-President, but he selected for the position Ramón Corral, who had no popular following or personal prestige. It was clear that he intended to remain in office for life. Though his mental and physical powers were obviously declining after the turn of the century, and the generally friendly attitude of the ruling classes was giving way to indifference or hostility, no real political opposition appeared until 1910, when the whole regime collapsed with surprising suddenness.

21

Mexico Since 1910

The misery of the landless peasantry, the dislike of foreign economic domination, and an increasing discontent among the new class of industrial laborers found expression after 1910 in a long-drawn-out revolt against all that the Díaz regime stood for: a revolt which at first seemed purposeless and hardly different from earlier struggles for power among ambitious military leaders, but which gradually took the form of a real social revolution. During the past forty years the agrarian program, the expropriation of large amounts of foreign property, and the rising power of the labor unions have transformed the Republic's economic life. The revolutionary period is one of the most interesting, not only in Mexico's history but in that of all Latin America, because the problems with which the Mexicans have been attempting to deal exist and urgently demand a solution in many of the other republics of the continent.

The End of the Díaz Regime

As Díaz approached the end of his sixth consecutive term, Mexico appeared to be one of the wealthiest and most stable of the American republics. To all outward appearance the President was at the height of his prestige, even though it was obvious that a ruler who was about to celebrate his eightieth birthday could not continue indefinitely at the head of the government. For a generation no important political group had dared to challenge his authority. Discontent, though widespread and, as subsequent events showed, deep-seated and bitter among the poorer classes, had found little chance for expression.

The election of 1910 might have been as uneventful as its predecessors had it not been for the interview which Díaz permitted an American writer named Creelman to publish in *Pearson's Magazine* in March, 1908. Mexico, the President said, was now ripe for democracy and he would welcome the establishment of an opposition party and the holding of a free election. This statement, evidently intended only for foreign consumption, caused a sensation in Mexico. After its publication the government could not well prevent an unwontedly free discussion of political affairs in the Mexican press. Few ventured openly to oppose the President's reëlection, but a movement was soon under way to make Díaz' prominent supporter, General Bernardo Reyes, vice-president instead of Corral, the official candidate. When Reyes was sent off on a mission to Europe, many of his supporters backed Francisco Madero, who had the temerity to accept an opposition nomination for the presidency. Though Madero was arrested and later forced to flee to the United States, his campaign, following that of Reyes, afforded an opportunity for political agitation, and the President's failure to show his accustomed vigor in suppressing any sign of discontent or resistance did much to hurt his prestige.

After Díaz and Corral were reëlected, Madero, from his refuge in Texas, issued a call for a revolt to begin on November 20, 1910. The movement had no effective organization or leadership, but there were small local rebellions in many parts of the country and it soon became evident that the government did not have the will or the power to suppress them. There was surprisingly little real fighting. After the rebels' first important success, the capture of Ciudad Juárez on the American border in May, 1911, Díaz agreed to turn the government over to Francisco de la Barra, the Minister of Foreign Affairs, with a cabinet named by the revolutionists. Díaz left Mexico and in November, after an election, Madero became President.

Madero and Huerta

Madero was a member of a wealthy landowning family in the north of Mexico. He had no previous administrative or military experience. As the man who had dared to become a presidential candidate when the rest of the nation was still in awe of the dictator, he had naturally become the titular head of the revolution, but he had taken little part in actual military operations. Unfortunately he had few qualifications for his new office. Apparently he had no conception of the catastrophic political forces that his revolt had unleashed, though a rather vague promise in his revolutionary program to restore the land to the dispossessed peasantry seems to have brought his movement much support among the lower classes. His administration was little less conservative than that of Díaz, but he lacked completely the political skill and the ruthless energy which had kept his predecessor in power. Partisans of the Díaz regime or dissatisfied leaders in the revolutionary party staged several small revolts and Emiliano Zapata and his followers began a long, desperate struggle to regain land for the peasants in the State of Morelos. The propertied classes, dismayed by the government's inability to maintain order, began to wish for a return of the strong hand of the old regime.

It was the army, still commanded by officers who had served the dictatorship, that finally overthrew Madero. Félix Díaz, the dictator's nephew, and General Bernardo Reyes had been imprisoned in the capital for participating in earlier revolts. On February 9, 1913, they were released by mutinous troops who seized control of several strong points in the city. Reyes was killed in the ensuing fighting, but for ten days Félix Díaz and the forces at the presidential palace carried on an artillery duel in the heart of the capital. The destruction of noncombatant lives and property seemed the more shocking when it transpired that the commander of Madero's troops, Victoriano Huerta, was in league with the rebels, and was simply awaiting a favorable opportunity to betray those of his comrades who were still loyal. On February 18 Huerta imprisoned Madero and the Vice-President, Pino Suárez. After some discussion, in which members of the diplomatic corps participated, the President and Vice-President reluctantly agreed to resign in return for a promise that they would be permitted to leave the country.

Huerta, with the approval of Congress, at once assumed the presidency. A few days later Madero and Pino Suárez were murdered by the officials who had them in custody. Though this and several other equally brutal acts foreshadowed the character of the new administration, it received support from conservative elements in Mexico and from foreign interests which hoped for a restoration of a strong government on the Díaz model. Within a few months it had been recognized by all of the principal powers of Europe. It was not, however, recognized by the United States, and in Mexico the administration was soon contending with new armed revolts which again endangered foreign as well as native life and property.

President Wilson refused to countenance what he considered an inexcusable usurpation of power. Recalling the American Ambassador, who had been openly sympathetic with the Huerta regime, he sent Mr. John Lind as his personal representative to propose the establishment of a constitutional government by means of an election in which Huerta would not be a candidate. Huerta not only rejected this suggestion, but showed his disregard for legality by suspending the constitution, dissolving the congress, and imprisoning several of its members. Wilson thereupon announced that nothing done by the dictator would be regarded as legal, and endeavored to persuade foreign governments to withdraw all diplomatic support from his regime. In February, 1914, the embargo on the shipment of arms to Mexico, which had been imposed in 1912, was lifted in order to help the "constitutionalists" under Venustiano Carranza, who by this time controlled much of the north.

On April 9, 1914, an incident at Tampico afforded the occasion for a more effective intervention. A boat's crew from the U.S.S. *Dolphin*, landing for supplies, were arrested by Mexican forces and held for more than an hour before higher officials ordered their release and offered an apology. Huerta himself expressed regret, but when Admiral Mayo demanded a salute to the American flag he refused to comply except under conditions which were deemed unacceptable. On April 20 Wilson laid the matter before Congress and asked approval for the use of armed force to compel Huerta to recognize "the rights and dignity of the United States." Before Congress had time to act, however, word arrived that a German steamer was about to land arms for Huerta at Vera Cruz, and on April 21 American forces occupied that port after severe fighting with Mexican troops. Huerta considered this an act of war and dismissed the American chargé d'affaires. Even Carranza, who stood to gain most from the action of the United States, protested and demanded that the American forces be withdrawn.

A real war might have ensued if Argentina, Brazil, and Chile had not offered their mediation, which was promptly accepted. A conference which met at Niagara Falls in May attempted to work out a plan for a government acceptable to all parties, but its efforts were frustrated by the intransigeance of the rapidly advancing revolutionists. Carranza, who did not participate officially in the conference, would not even agree to an armistice, and the United States sympathized with him in his insistence that the civil war could be ended only by a constitutionalist victory. Meanwhile the position of Huerta steadily became more desperate, and on July 15, 1914, he resigned in favor of Francisco Carbajal, the President of the Supreme Court. A month later, when the constitutionalist army occupied Mexico City, Carranza formally assumed the "Executive Authority of the Mexican Republic."

Carranza and Villa

Unfortunately, Huerta's fall did not end the civil war. The twelve months that followed were one of the most chaotic periods in Mexico's history. Francisco Villa, who had won several important battles for Carranza, had already become restive under the "First Chief's" leadership, and in September, 1914, he revolted and joined forces with Emiliano Zapata, who was still carrying on his own revolt in Morelos. Under the influence of the two leaders, a convention of generals designated Eulalio Gutiérrez as provisional President, and Carranza was forced to withdraw to Vera Cruz, which had just been evacuated by the American forces. Gutiérrez in turn quarreled with the other generals, and was succeeded as titular head of the "convention government" by Roque González Garza and then by Lagos Cházaro. Mexico City was taken and retaken by the contending factions, and the large foreign population there, as well as the Mexican residents, suffered from food shortages and disease and from the tyranny of irresponsible military leaders. In some districts of the interior conditions were even worse. Foreign mining and oil interests complained loudly of lack of protection and many North Americans and Europeans were mistreated or killed. It became more and more difficult for the United States Government to maintain its policy of "watchful waiting."

In June, 1915, President Wilson publicly called on the Mexican factions to come to an agreement, saying that the United States would otherwise lend "active moral support" to some leader who could restore order. Somewhat later several of the other American republics joined with the United States in proposing the establishment of a provisional government and the holding of elections. Villa agreed, but Carranza, whose troops were by this time getting the upper hand, was as uncoöperative as always. Nevertheless the governments which had made the proposal decided in October to recognize Carranza, and the United States imposed an embargo on the shipment of arms to other factions which materially aided the constitutionalist regime in establishing its control over the greater part of Mexico.

Peace did not come at once. Zapata's followers in Morelos did not lay down their arms until after their leader was killed by treachery in 1919. Villa, defeated in battle, continued to operate near the American frontier and showed his resentment at the recognition of Carranza by atrocities against Americans and other foreigners. On March 9, 1916, he attacked Columbus, New Mexico, killing sixteen Americans and burning a part of the town. This compelled the United States to act, and a force under General Pershing was sent into Mexico to capture the bandit leader. The expedition failed, partly because Carranza refused to coöperate and in fact assumed a definitely hostile attitude. Pershing's force was withdrawn in February, 1917, when it became clear that war with Germany was imminent.

Carranza's unfriendliness to the United States, which had been evidenced even when he was profiting from North American diplomatic support, did not abate during the World War. His government was neutral but distinctly uncoöperative. There is no evidence, however, that he took seriously the famous Zimmermann note, delivered by the German minister in Mexico, which proposed that he enter the war on the German side in order to regain California and New Mexico.

The Constitution of 1917

By this time the Carranza government had made some progress in restoring order in the interior, and a constitutional convention representing the various factions which supported it had met at Querétaro. The result of this body's labors was the constitution of 1917, which embodied most of the principles that have since inspired the policy of the revolutionary movement. It had become clear by 1917 that the fall of the Díaz regime and subsequent events had aroused hopes and aspirations which must be satisfied before any government could hope to command lasting popular support. Many of the military chieftains were determined to destroy the oppressive features of the old regime, and even those who, like Carranza, were chiefly interested in obtaining power for themselves had made promises of reform which could not be ignored.

The land question was especially urgent. In the general disorder of the past few years, the peasants had seized and divided the large estates in many sections of the country and had fought savagely under leaders like Zapata to destroy the power of the landlords in other districts. Madero and several of the later revolutionists had promised agrarian reform, more often perhaps in the hope of attracting followers than from conviction, and in 1915 Carranza issued a decree providing for the restoration of lands unjustly taken from the villages and for the granting of lands to villages which owned none. Article 27 of the new constitution adopted this decree as the basis for a radical program of agrarian reform. It declared null and void the legal proceedings by which many of the villages had been deprived of their communal lands since 1856, and provided that villages which could not establish a legal right to lands should receive them by "dotation." The nation assumed the obligation to divide large estates for this purpose.

By Article 27 the Republic also claimed the ownership of all minerals and subsoil deposits—a provision which particularly affected the growing foreign oil industry. Minerals in the Spanish colonies had always belonged to the government, whoever the owner of the surface might be, but in Mexico a series of laws during the Díaz regime had apparently changed this rule with respect to hydrocarbons such as coal and petroleum, and had made it possible to acquire the ownership of subsoil deposits by buying the land under which they lay. The oil companies had acquired most of their properties in this manner. Their interests were consequently jeopardized, and their situation was made still worse by another clause of the same article which provided that foreigners, if they were to own land or obtain concessions for the development of natural resources, must agree to forego the protection of their own governments.

Another important part of the new constitution was Article 123, which contained a long series of provisions, culled from the most advanced legislation of other countries, dealing with labor and social welfare. Among other innovations it authorized the government to establish an eight-hour day, restrictions on the labor of women and children, minimum wages, a right to share in profits, and compensation for accidents and industrial diseases. The laborers' right to organize and to strike was established and provision was made for the arbitration of disputes. These provisions affected only the relatively small industrial laboring class in the cities and the mines, but their importance increased as new industries were established. A clause that abolished peonage, or debt-slavery, benefited an immensely greater number, for it did away with a device by which the masses of the rural population had been kept in servitude to the landowners since the seventeenth century.

In other articles, the Church was treated even more harshly than in the "Laws of Reform." It was forbidden to conduct primary schools; the state legislatures were authorized to limit the number of priests in each district; and the title to all church property was vested in the nation. Most of these provisions, however, were not immediately enforced.

Many other portions of the new code were too revolutionary to be put into effect at once. They represented, perhaps, the aspirations of the more radical members of the convention rather than the views of Carranza and his chief supporters. Nevertheless, they were a promise to the landless peon and the working man, and much of the program was carried out more or less effectively by later governments.

At the same time they were a threat to foreign interests and a new disturbing factor in the Republic's already strained relations with the United States. Though President Wilson perceived more clearly than most foreign statesmen that the revolutionary movement was fundamentally a struggle to establish more tolerable conditions of life for the poorer classes, and consequently persisted in his policy of non-intervention despite terrific pressure at home and almost intolerable provocation in Mexico, the American government could not be indifferent to provisions that threatened severe injury to legally acquired American property rights. Carranza, both before and after the recognition of his government, assured the United States that private property of foreigners would be respected, but he soon gave evidence of an intention to apply Article 27 of the new constitution in a way hardly consistent with these pledges. A tax decree issued in February, 1918, which required the oil companies to recognize the Mexican government's ownership of the petroleum in the subsoil, gave rise to a diplomatic controversy which had not been settled when Carranza's government fell.

Obregón and the Question of Recognition

Carranza's successor was to be elected in the summer of 1920. General Álvaro Obregón, the government's chief military leader, was apparently the strongest candidate, and when the President attempted to bring about the election of his friend Ignacio Bonillas, Obregón's friends revolted in April, 1920. Carranza, abandoned by most of his followers, was murdered, and Obregón was elected President.

The change of government by revolution again raised the question of recognition by foreign powers. The United States, in view of the oil controversy, was not disposed to resume diplomatic relations without some definite assurance of protection to American interests, and Secretary Hughes proposed a treaty which would prevent the confiscatory application of Article 27 of the new constitution. To this Obregón would not agree. Recognition was consequently withheld until 1923, when the chief difficulties between the two governments were adjusted, temporarily at least, by a joint commission which met in Mexico City. It was arranged that all pending claims, including those of American citizens for losses suffered during the disturbances since 1910, should be arbitrated. The United States reluctantly consented to permit its citizens to be paid in bonds instead of cash, within certain limitations, for property taken in connection with the agrarian program which the new administration was beginning to carry out. With respect to the oil controversy, the commissioners achieved a working arrangement rather than an agreement on the fundamental question of the legal ownership of petroleum deposits. The Mexican Supreme Court, in the case of the Texas Company, had decided that Article 27 did not deprive the owner of the surface of his right to the oil in the ground, provided that he had shown by some "positive act" an intent to exploit this oil, and this principle, expanded to apply also to lands which the foreign companies had bought for future use, was finally accepted, though with reservations, by the American government.

Recognition was thus obtained. Its practical value became apparent when Adolfo de la Huerta, formerly a member of Obregón's cabinet but now an opposition candidate for the presidency, started a revolt in the latter part of 1923. The movement was a formidable one, supported by a large part of the army as well as by the still powerful conservative groups, including the clergy and the great landowners. It was soon suppressed, however, by the energetic action of General Calles, greatly aided by arms purchased from the government of the United States.

Calles and his Successors, 1924–1935

Plutarco Elías Calles was the official candidate and consequently the successful candidate for the presidency in 1924. Long a prominent leader in the revolutionary party, and a close personal friend of Obregón, he had shown marked administrative ability as a member of the latter's cabinet. As head of the government he made a real effort to carry

out a part of the program of economic and social reform embodied in
the 1917 constitution. His predecessors had made little progress in this
direction, partly because of internal political difficulties and partly because of the opposition of the United States and other foreign governments. Calles apparently felt strong enough to disregard both of these
obstacles. A new land law injected fresh vigor into the agrarian program, and another act limited the right of foreigners to inherit agricultural land. A petroleum law, which violated the agreement of 1923,
revived the controversy with the oil companies. These measures, combined with Mexico's opposition to the policy of the United States in
Nicaragua,[1] brought on a crisis in the Republic's relations with its northern neighbor.

In this situation Calles was suddenly confronted by a flare-up of the
religious question. Up to this time the government had shown little
disposition to provoke a new conflict with the Church. A number of
minor incidents had kept alive the antagonism between the Catholic
hierarchy and the leaders of the revolutionary party, but the anti-
clerical articles of the 1917 constitution, like many of its other provisions, had not been implemented by regulatory laws. On April 21, 1926,
however, the bishops of Mexico issued a statement declaring that the
Church refused to recognize these articles and would combat them.
The government retaliated by a series of decrees and laws putting the
constitutional provisions into effect. Catholic schools and convents
were closed and all priests were required to register with the government. The Church refused to comply, and a league of Catholic laymen
announced a campaign to paralyze the economic life of the nation by
restricting purchases to the barest necessities. In many sections of the
country small armed bands rose in rebellion, and there was much loss
of life before order was restored in July, 1927. The Knights of Columbus and other Catholic organizations in the United States gave the
Church much moral support in the conflict, and the *Cristeros,* as the
rebels were called, were undoubtedly encouraged by a belief that the
numerous controversies between the United States and the Calles government would weaken the latter's position.

Fortunately more friendly relations between the two countries were
restored after 1927, when Mr. Dwight Morrow was appointed American Ambassador. The most objectionable provision of the petroleum
law, the requirement that oil companies apply for fifty-year conces-

[1] See below, p. 475.

sions to confirm their acquired rights, was declared unconstitutional by the Mexican Supreme Court; and an amended law, giving them concessions unlimited as to time, was enacted early in 1928. Administrative regulations which Calles issued soon afterward ended this phase of the oil controversy, and a more conciliatory attitude on both sides facilitated the handling of American claims and other pending questions. Even the religious question became temporarily less acute as the result of a compromise worked out through Mr. Morrow's informal good offices.

Obregón was elected to succeed Calles in 1928, but when he was assassinated by a religious fanatic some months before the end of the presidential term Emilio Portes Gil was installed as Provisional President by Congress. Calles refused to continue in office, but he retained the leadership of the National Revolutionary Party and his influence dominated the government during the next six years. He took command of the army when a group of dissatisfied generals revolted in March, 1929, and quickly suppressed the uprising. Later in the same year he brought about the election of Pascual Ortiz Rubio to serve during the rest of Obregón's unexpired term, which had been fixed at six years by a constitutional amendment. He was apparently dissatisfied with the new President's conduct, and in September, 1932, Ortiz Rubio was compelled to resign and Abelardo Rodríguez was chosen to succeed him.

The policy of the government in this period was relatively conservative. The Mexican leaders apparently sought to avoid new complications with foreign powers, and some of the revolutionary chieftains, as they grew older and acquired greater personal wealth, seemed less interested in social and economic reform. There was, however, a new conflict with the Church. A great demonstration at the shrine of the Virgin of Guadelupe, in December, 1931, revived the antagonism between the Church and the government, and in the months that followed the federal authorities limited the number of priests in the capital city and the territories to one for every 50,000 people. Many of the states took similar or even more drastic action. Feeling ran especially high after the government amended the constitution in 1934 to require that all education should be "socialistic" in character, and for a time civil war again seemed imminent.

An important faction in the revolutionary party opposed the growing conservatism of Calles and his associates, and in 1934 this group was able to persuade the older leaders to put forward Lázaro Cárdenas as the official candidate for the presidency. After his election the new chief executive showed an unexpected independence, and in 1935, when Calles criticized the administration for encouraging a wave of strikes fomented by radical labor elements, Cárdenas reorganized his cabinet, forced changes in the government of several states, and made it clear that he would accept no dictation. Calles went to the United States. He returned to Mexico at the end of 1935, but was forcibly deported a few months later.

Cárdenas and the Agrarian Reform

Under Cárdenas, the distribution of land was resumed on a large scale. Much had already been accomplished in this direction, especially during the administrations of Calles and Portes Gil, and by the end of 1933 nearly 19,000,000 acres had been definitely allotted to villages containing three quarters of a million heads of families.[1] For the most part this had been accomplished by "dotation," or grants of land from expropriated large estates, rather than by the restitution to the villages of lands unjustly taken. The government theoretically proposed to compensate the original owners of the land thus distributed, but payments had been made in only a few cases, and then usually in bonds which had little market value. The *ejido*, as the tract granted to each village was called, was usually in part pasture or woodland, for the common use of the inhabitants, and in part crop land which was divided among the heads of families under restrictions designed to prevent them from selling or mortgaging their holdings. The government for a time endeavored to introduce collective farming in the *ejidos* but met with little success.

Obstacles of many sorts had hampered the successful execution of the agrarian program. The examination and disposition of so many thousands of cases was a difficult matter, especially as it was complicated by governmental red tape, friction between federal and state authorities, factional politics, and official corruption. There was tenacious opposition from other conservative groups as well as the landlords, and also from foreign governments which objected to the seizure of their nationals' property without compensation. Even the villages which received land did not always seem to benefit, for the plot given to each

[1] Simpson, *The Ejido*, pp. 170–71.

family was often too small for its support and the lack of tools and machinery prevented efficient cultivation. The government endeavored to provide capital for the new landowners through the establishment of an agricultural bank and the encouragement of coöperatives, but lack of money and administrative difficulties made its efforts only partly successful.

These obstacles were not overcome by the Cárdenas administration, but the government proceeded aggressively to carry on the distribution of land in spite of them. Local conservative opposition, which had often taken the form of violence and intimidation, was discouraged by systematically arming the peasants to enable them to defend themselves and incidentally to support the administration in case of need. Foreign diplomatic opposition was less effective after the adoption of the "Good Neighbor" policy by the United States, especially as the two governments reached an agreement in 1938 for the eventual compensation of Americans who had lost their land. By 1940 it was said that between 60,000,000 and 70,000,000 acres of land had been distributed among nearly 2,000,000 heads of families since 1915.[1]

Increasing Power of Organized Labor

The provisions of the Constitution of 1917, though too advanced to be immediately enforced, had made possible a substantial improvement in the situation of the laboring classes. Peasants who had not received land under the agrarian program had benefited by the government's fairly successful efforts to abolish peonage and to check exploitation by company stores. Industrial workers had been encouraged to organize, and union leaders had played an increasingly prominent rôle in politics. The *Confederación Regional Obrera Mexicana*, the C.R.O.M., which was a national federation embracing most of the larger unions, helped Obregón to overthrow Carranza in 1920, and its leader, Luis Morones, was a powerful figure in the Obregón administration. In the years that followed many of the benefits promised by the constitution were actually attained. In 1931 a general federal labor law established a system of collective labor contracts, enforceable by boards of conciliation and arbitration, which greatly strengthened the position of the worker as against the employer. The law also provided for the fixing of minimum wages in the various sections of the country, and specific minimum

[1] *Seis Años de Gobierno al Servicio de México, 1934-1940*, p. 330.

wages were in fact established in the federal district and in many of the states in 1934.

Meanwhile there had been internal dissensions in the labor movement, and the influence of Morones had declined. A more radical group supported Cárdenas for the presidency, and after the formation in 1936 of the *Confederación de Trabajadores de Mexico*, the C.T.M., Vicente Lombardo Toledano was the most powerful of the country's labor leaders. Lombardo Toledano, who had been a teacher and a writer, was an avowed Marxist, and his evident purpose was to substitute labor management for capitalist control throughout Mexican industry.

In carrying out this program, he had effective support from President Cárdenas. The national railways, in which the government had had a majority stock interest since the time of Díaz, were expropriated in 1937 and turned over to the railroad workers' union for operation in 1938. Other less important concerns were expropriated in much the same manner, and in some cases where strikes or other labor trouble made operation of an enterprise unprofitable, the government forbade the closing of the plant and exerted pressure on the owners to surrender it to the workers. Foreign interests suffered especially, because the elimination of foreign economic control was as important a part of the revolutionary policy as the improvement of the condition of the workers. In 1940 Lombardo Toledano claimed that syndicates of the C.T.M. were managing street railways, buses, and other municipal services, several sugar mills and textile factories, and all of the Mexican ships carrying on commerce in the Gulf of Mexico, as well as the railroads.[1] The program of socialization might have gone still farther had it not been for practical difficulties. Inefficient management, lack of discipline, and inability to obtain capital made operation by the workers' coöperatives unsatisfactory, and the railways, especially, were in a deplorable state by the end of Cárdenas' term.

The Expropriation of the Oil Companies

One of the most important events of the Cárdenas administration was the expropriation of the North American and British oil companies. These still represented one of the largest foreign investments in the Republic, though the production of the Mexican fields was relatively

[1] Lombardo Toledano in *Annals of the American Academy of Political and Social Science*, Vol. 208, pp. 52–53 (May, 1940).

far less important than it had been. The agreement between President Calles and Ambassador Morrow settled the dispute about subsoil rights, but frequent demands for higher wages and the increasingly aggressive spirit of the labor unions made the situation of the foreign companies more and more difficult. In May, 1937, the workers struck to obtain a large further wage increase and demanded at the same time a measure of participation in the management of the industry. Work was resumed after the dispute was submitted to the Federal Board of Conciliation and Arbitration, but in December that office handed down an award which the companies considered confiscatory. When they refused to accept it, President Cárdenas on March 18, 1938, issued a decree expropriating the property of all the larger foreign-owned concerns. The administration of the nationalized industry was entrusted to an official organization in which the labor unions had a considerable voice.

Since there was little probability that Mexico could or would make any adequate payment for the seized properties, the expropriation brought a vigorous protest from the United States and led to a break in diplomatic relations with Great Britain. The government at Washington, which had been buying newly mined Mexican silver at prices far above its market value, ceased to do so. This severely affected the country's economy, and at the same time the export of oil became difficult because the companies that had formerly operated in Mexico controlled most of the world's tanker tonnage. Some shipments were made to Germany and Italy, but these ceased with the outbreak of war in Europe. In the oil fields, production fell off and costs increased under the new management. The government, however, was enthusiastically supported by public opinion, and these economic difficulties did not seriously weaken its position.

The Election of 1940

The official candidate for the presidency in 1940 was General Manuel Ávila Camacho, who had been Secretary of War in Cárdenas' cabinet. His chief rival, General Juan Andreu Almazán, was also a member of the revolutionary party. Almazán received much conservative support, as well as some backing from labor unions that had had disagreements with Cárdenas. The government did not prevent its opponents from carrying on an active campaign, but on election day many of the usual abuses appeared and there were disputes and minor disturbances at the polls. Though some observers thought that Almazán had received a majority of the votes, the official count gave an overwhelming victory to Ávila Camacho. There was much talk of revolution, but Almazán formally withdrew from the contest when the United States Government announced that it had named Mr. Wallace, the Vice-President-Elect, as special Ambassador at Ávila Camacho's inauguration.

Mexico and the Second World War

The United States' action was doubtless inspired by a desire to avoid a revolution at a time when it was essential for all of the American governments to work together for hemisphere defense. Mexican public opinion was emphatically on the side of the democracies, and the labor unions, despite the communist leanings of some of their leaders, had taken a strong stand against the Axis during the period when Russia was coöperating with Germany. Relations with the United States, during Ávila Camacho's administration, became more friendly than they had been for many years. American forces were permitted to use Mexican airfields and other military facilities in transporting planes to Panama, and the United States was assured of a preferential position in obtaining the important strategic raw materials that Mexico produced. In November, 1941, a series of agreements provided for the settlement of the oil controversy, the payment of other outstanding claims, the resumption of silver purchases, and substantial loans to Mexico from the Export-Import Bank. It was arranged that the indemnity to the American oil companies should be decided by experts representing the two governments, and in 1942 the companies were awarded $23,995,991. This was far less than they had claimed but the award ended the controversy.

Mexico was one of the first American states to break diplomatic relations with the Axis after Pearl Harbor, and on June 1, 1942, the Republic declared war and began to take part in anti-submarine operations in the Gulf of Mexico. Three years later an air squadron was sent to the Far East, making Mexico one of the two Latin American countries that actually sent troops to the fighting front.[1] Meanwhile, by agreement between the two governments, more than 100,000 Mexicans entered the United States to work on the railroads and in the harvests. There was a close coöperation in many other aspects of the war effort.

[1] The other was Brazil.

Recent Events

In the presidential election of 1946, Miguel Alemán, with the support of the C.T.M. and other important groups in the revolutionary party, easily defeated Ezequiel Padilla, who had been Secretary of Foreign Relations during the war years. The new administration had to deal with the same difficult problems of inflation and readjustment that plagued other Latin American countries in the post-war period. It had hardly taken office, furthermore, when it was confronted by an outbreak of hoof and mouth disease that threatened untold loss to the Mexican livestock industry. A long campaign, in which the United States furnished technical help and many millions of dollars in financial aid, seemed to have checked the spread of the disease by the end of 1949.

The last two administrations, though more conservative than some of their predecessors, and especially more tolerant in their treatment of the Church, have continued to adhere to the revolutionary program embodied in the Constitution of 1917. The agrarian reform, the most important feature of the program, has gone forward, but much more slowly than in Cárdenas' time. The chief problem is still to give the new landowners the training and the financial help that they must have if they are to be prosperous farmers. To date the reform seems to have decreased rather than increased production, which is a serious matter in a country where the population is increasing rapidly and the food supply has long been inadequate. It has also discouraged the investment of capital in agriculture, and thus retarded the development of the country's resources. On the other hand there can be little question but that thousands of Indians in the central region and thousands of *mestizo* peons in the North are happier, more self-respecting citizens than when they were working as debt-slaves on the old *haciendas*.

Closely connected with the agrarian problem is the problem of education. Between 1920 and 1925, when José Vasconcelos was Secretary of Public Instruction, the government inaugurated a program under which schools were established in thousands of rural communities where the people had hitherto been almost completely illiterate. There was a special effort, especially in the first years, to improve the status of the hitherto despised and neglected Indian, and to preserve rather than destroy the best elements of the aboriginal culture. Adults as well as children were taught to read and write, and were also taught improved agricultural methods and simple trades. The bitter conflict with the Church, in the 1920's and early 1930's, was a serious obstacle to the success of the program, and the government's poverty and the lack of trained teachers greatly limited the number of schools that could be established. The problem was more difficult because so large a part of the rural population lives in small, isolated communities speaking a great number of different Indian languages. Nevertheless much has been accomplished, and the percentage of literacy has unquestionably increased greatly since 1910.

There has perhaps been less progress toward political democracy. The government's authority still rests more on armed force than on respect for law and for the expressed will of the voters. At each succeeding election the party in power has used long-familiar methods to obtain the victory for the official candidate, and the opposition has had no chance to win except by armed revolt. On the other hand, the "revolutionary party," which has frequently been reorganized and renamed and which now calls itself *"partido revolucionario institucional,"* has usually had strong popular support. In general it has represented the army, the principal labor unions, the large and influential class of government office holders, and the more politically conscious groups among the peasants. Its adherence to the principle of "no reëlection" has made it difficult for any one man to entrench himself in power. If it has not as yet been able to give Mexico the sort of democracy to which the country's liberal leaders have always aspired—and this will be difficult until the political education of the masses of the people has progressed much farther—it has nevertheless greatly increased the number of people who participate in political decisions and has brought appreciably nearer the time when real elections can be held.

Relations between Mexico and the United States are of the greatest importance to both countries. As we have seen, the two governments have coöperated closely in many fields of activity in recent years. There is still, unfortunately, a less friendly feeling among some elements of the Mexican people. Some of the extreme conservatives, influenced by sympathy with the Spanish *falange,* were pro-Axis during the war. Their chief political organization, the *sinarquista* party, which has violently opposed the religious policy of the Mexican government, was outlawed in January, 1949, but presumably continues to work underground. At the other political extreme are the groups under the influence of Moscow. The Mexican communist party is very small, but the

Soviets have had an important ally in the person of Vicente Lombardo Toledano, the founder of the Mexican Labor Confederation and also the head of the communist-dominated Latin American Labor Confederation, the C.T.A.L. Lombardo Toledano was for a time one of the most powerful figures in the group that governed Mexico, but his influence declined after the C.T.M. repudiated his leadership in 1947.

Propaganda against the United States finds a readier reception because of other factors that affect the attitude of many persons who have no sympathy either with *sinarquismo* or communism. The memory of past conflicts is fresher in Mexico than it is with us and the fear of American imperialism has not entirely died. The thoughtless and ill-mannered conduct of some American visitors to Mexico, and more especially the discriminatory treatment to which Mexican visitors are sometimes subjected in the United States, cause much resentment.

Part VIII

◦◦◦

THE CARIBBEAN REGION

THE history of the Central American and West Indian republics, like that of Mexico, has been much influenced by their relations with the United States. Their proximity to our own territory, and especially their location with respect to the strategically and commercially important transisthmian transit routes, made it essential to the safety of the United States that they should not fall under the control of any other foreign power. In the nineteenth century, however, several other powers also had interests in the Caribbean region. Great Britain, Spain, France, the Netherlands, and Denmark had colonies there, and Great Britain, at least, was as unwilling as the United States that any other great power should dominate the projected transisthmian canal. International rivalry for the control of the canal routes and their approaches frequently affected the course of internal politics in the countries of the region. In the twentieth century, after the United States began to build the canal at Panama, it was more important than ever that no other power should obtain a foothold in the Caribbean.

The Canal, by enabling the battle fleet to move rapidly from coast to coast, practically doubled the efficiency of our navy, but it could be used safely only so long as its approaches were kept clear of potential enemies. The existing European colonies were no longer a cause for concern, because they had lost much of their economic importance and were in friendly hands, but the situation would be different if any foreign power should undertake to obtain new possessions, and thus make the Caribbean the scene of a contest for territory and spheres of influence like the contests that were going on at the end of the nineteenth century in Africa and the Far East. Rightly or wrongly, many American statesmen of the period before the First World War believed that Germany and perhaps other powers had their eyes on the Caribbean as a field for imperial adventures and would not be indisposed to challenge the Monroe Doctrine should a favorable opportunity arise.

Internal disorder and financial mismanagement had already exposed Latin American countries to aggression on many occasions. Mexico had suffered twice from foreign invasions to collect claims, and Honduras and Nicaragua had nearly lost portions of their territory because they were too weak to resist British encroachments on the Mosquito Coast. Other countries had frequently been compelled by force to adjust pecuniary claims or to pay indemnities for the mistreatment of foreigners, and foreign troops had repeatedly been landed to protect lives and property in times of civil disturbance. Such occurrences had been especially common in the Caribbean, because the countries of that region were the smallest and weakest—and some of them were among the most turbulent—of the American republics. It was always possible that a European intervention of this sort might be made the pretext for a more permanent occupation.

In the early 1900's the right of a nation to intervene in the affairs of a weaker state to protect the lives and property of its own nationals was too firmly established in current international practice to be easily challenged. The Caribbean countries would apparently be safe from aggression only when the conditions that continually invited aggression were rectified. The Hague Court's decision in the Venezuela case in 1904 seemed likely in fact to encourage the practice of intervention.[1] It was to meet this situation that President Roosevelt enunciated his so-called corollary to the Monroe Doctrine: that the United States, if it wished to prevent European interference in the Western Hemisphere, must help its neighbors to do away with the political instability and financial mismanagement that made such interference justifiable. This became the basis of American policy in the Caribbean during the first two decades of the twentieth century. The underlying principle of the corollary had already found expression in the Platt Amendment, which gave the United States the right to intervene to maintain a government adequate to protect life, property, and individual liberty in Cuba. It was to be

[1] See above, pp. 378–9 and below, p. 540.

invoked by later administrations to justify military interventions and other interference in the internal affairs of several Caribbean countries.

American policy in the Caribbean after the turn of the century sought primarily to prevent European intervention there, but it was influenced also by other considerations. One was the growth of our own economic interests in the Caribbean. During the first years of the twentieth century American capital was invested in sugar companies in Cuba, in banana farms in Central America, in mines, and in railroads. Increasing numbers of American citizens were employed in the management of these enterprises. Except in Cuba, the amount of money involved was not particularly important, but controversies over the rights of American companies were troublesome and warships were frequently sent to protect resident Americans in time of civil disturbances.

Hardly less important was the question of public health. During the nineteenth century epidemics of yellow fever, brought in from Cuba and other Caribbean countries, had repeatedly caused a heavy loss of life at American Gulf ports and even at times in Philadelphia and New York. With increasing contact the danger became greater. It was also imperative to protect the Canal Zone against infection from nearby countries. The United States consequently insisted upon measures to improve sanitary conditions in Panama and in Cuba, and at a later date the Public-Health Service was one of the most important Treaty Services in Haiti. A greater number of people benefited from the magnificent work done throughout tropical America by the International Health Division of the Rockefeller Foundation, which coöperated with several Latin American states in campaigns against yellow fever, hookworm, and other menaces to health.

The so-called intervention policy caused much bad feeling in the Caribbean countries and in the rest of Latin America, and it was repudiated by public opinion in the United States. It was gradually modified in the 1920's, and after 1933 it was formally abandoned. These developments will be dealt with in later chapters.

22

Panama and the Canal

Early Interest in a Canal

The first proposal for a waterway between the Caribbean Sea and the Pacific was made soon after the discovery of the Central American Isthmus. The idea met with little favor in Spain, where the land barrier was looked upon as the best protection of the rich colonies on the South American west coast, but it was revived after independence. Several projects for construction were brought forward during the first half of the nineteenth century. None of these passed the stage of discussion, but after the acquisition of California by the United States the idea took on a new importance. Despite the hardships involved and the appalling death rate from yellow fever and malaria, many travelers went from the eastern seaboard to the gold fields by way of Panama or Nicaragua before the opening of the transcontinental railway, and there was a revived interest in projects for a canal that would avoid the expense and danger of transhipment at the Isthmus.

The Panama and Nicaragua routes were the most feasible of several that were advocated. At Panama, where the traffic between Spain and Peru crossed in colonial times, the Isthmus reaches its narrowest point, and the mountainous backbone of the continent sinks to an altitude of a few hundred feet. In Nicaragua the divide is still lower and the San Juan River and the great lake provide a natural waterway for small vessels from the Caribbean to a point within a few miles of the Pacific. Both routes involved tremendous engineering problems, the magnitude of which was hardly realized until construction actually began.

Both routes were in countries that could not possibly build the canal themselves. It was clear that it would have to be built, and presumably

431

controlled, by foreign enterprise, and the question of who would control it was important not only to the United States but to other powers. Great Britain, as the principal maritime and commercial nation, had a very special interest in an enterprise that would provide a new trade route to South America and the Orient as well as to California, and after the war between the United States and Mexico British efforts to obtain control of the Nicaragua route led to a long-drawn-out diplomatic conflict.[1] One result of this was the Clayton-Bulwer Treaty of 1850, in which Great Britain and the United States agreed that neither would seek to control any canal that might be built.

The government of New Granada, or Colombia, to which the Isthmus of Panama belonged, also realized the dangers involved in international rivalries over the canal routes, and in 1846, after vainly attempting to obtain similar agreements with other countries, it signed a treaty with the United States by which that government guaranteed the neutrality of the Isthmus and New Granada's sovereignty there. In return the United States was granted the right of free transit by any existing or future means of transport. This was not an exclusive privilege, but it gave the United States a special position on the Isthmus, especially as the Colombian government in subsequent years frequently asked American intervention to keep the transit routes open in time of civil war. During the period when the transit route was being used by travelers going to California, and especially after an American company completed the railroad across the Isthmus in 1855, American influence on the Isthmus increased.

The French Canal Company

Nevertheless the first real effort to build a canal at Panama was made by a French company that obtained a concession from Colombia in 1878 and started work in 1880. Ferdinand de Lesseps, the builder of the Suez Canal, was the leading spirit in the enterprise, and a large capital was obtained by popular subscription. The undertaking was regarded with little favor in the United States. President Hayes informed Congress in 1880 that "the policy of this country is a canal under American control," but opposition diminished when American capital and a few important American politicians were given an interest in the company.

The company originally planned to build a waterway at sea-level, but

[1] See below, pp. 452-3.

it found that this would involve far more work and expense than the engineers had estimated, and a lock canal was decided upon instead. Even so the company's resources, depleted by extravagance and gross mismanagement, were unequal to the task, and the terrific loss of life among its employees from yellow fever and other diseases made the continuance of the work almost impossible. Though a substantial amount of excavation was accomplished, De Lesseps' company failed under scandalous circumstances in 1888, and the new company which took over its rights and property had too little capital to carry on work of any importance.

The American Government Undertakes the Task

The collapse of the French effort, and the failure of a North American company which was incorporated by act of Congress in 1889 to build a canal in Nicaragua, made it evident that the canal could not be built by private enterprise. By 1898, when the need for the waterway was impressed upon the American public as never before by the anxious weeks of waiting while the battleship *Oregon* rounded South America to join the fleet at the outbreak of the Spanish American War, it was clear that the American government itself would have to do the work.

The Clayton-Bulwer Treaty, which was an obstacle to the construction and operation of a canal by the United States, was abrogated by the Hay-Pauncefote Treaty signed with Great Britain in 1901. Meanwhile a commission created by Congress carefully examined both the Nicaragua and the Panama routes and recommended that the latter be adopted if the French company would sell its rights for $40,000,000 and if a satisfactory arrangement could be made with Colombia. The Spooner Act of June 28, 1902, authorized the President to undertake the work of construction, and an agreement was reached with the French company. With the way thus prepared, the Hay-Herrán Treaty was signed with Colombia in January, 1903. By this, Colombia would have authorized the French company to sell its rights to the United States and would have granted to the United States the use of a zone ten kilometers wide for the construction of a canal. Colombia was to receive $10,000,000 and in addition an annuity of $250,000 starting nine years after the ratification of the treaty. The Congress at Bogotá, however, refused to approve this agreement, apparently because it hoped that a delay might enable Colombia to obtain more favorable terms from the French company or from the United States. The result was the independence of Panama.

The Panama Revolution

The Isthmus of Panama from the beginning had owed such prosperity as it enjoyed to the transit route that crossed its territory. Its importance had declined in the latter part of the colonial period when the galleons no longer came to the great fair at Porto Bello. It revived somewhat in the days of the gold rush to California, but the opening of transcontinental lines in the north again left the Isthmus in a backwater so far as international trade was concerned. The Panamanians enjoyed another short period of prosperity while the French company was at work, and they looked forward eagerly to the resumption of construction by the United States.

There was therefore much disappointment when the rejection of the Hay-Herrán Treaty made it seem probable that the American government might again turn its attention to the Nicaraguan route. Well-informed people were not surprised when a group of revolutionists, with the support of the commander of the Colombian garrison, seized control of Panama City on November 3, 1903, and declared the independence of the Republic of Panama. The movement was promoted and financed by Philippe Bunau-Varilla, an engineer connected with the French Canal Company, who had persuaded the revolutionists that they could count on the support of the United States.

It was never proved that the United States Government instigated the revolt, but its conduct unquestionably prevented Colombia from suppressing it. Just before the outbreak the U.S.S. *Nashville* had been sent to Colón. This was not an unusual step, for the United States, acting under the treaty of 1846, had often landed armed forces to protect the transit route during the civil wars in Colombia. On this occasion, however, the commander of the *Nashville*, under instructions from Washington, prevented a Colombian force from crossing the Isthmus to put down the revolt, and four days later the government of Panama was formally recognized by the United States. On November 18, a treaty signed at Washington guaranteed the independence of the new Republic and put an end to any possibility of Colombia's restoring her authority over the Isthmus.

The events just described were the subject of much controversy.

President Roosevelt's action was defended on the ground that the construction of the canal was an urgent necessity, that it was being prevented by the obstructive conduct of Colombia, and that the people of Panama had a right to revolt against an action which "threatened their most vital interests with destruction and the interests of the whole world with grave injury."[1] It was asserted that the course followed by the United States was justified by the provisions of the treaty of 1846, the main purpose of which was the construction of a canal. On the other hand, the American Government's acts were severely criticized both in Latin America and the United States, and they seemed difficult to justify in view of the American guarantee of Colombia's sovereignty over the Isthmus. We have already seen how a $25,000,000 indemnity was finally paid to Colombia in recognition of the injury that she had suffered.

The Canal Treaty

The treaty of November 18, besides guaranteeing the independence of Panama, provided for the construction of a canal by the United States. Negotiated by M. Bunau-Varilla, who had been appointed the new Republic's minister at Washington, it granted more extensive privileges than Colombia had been willing to concede. The United States was given the perpetual "use, occupation, and control" of a zone ten miles wide, and the right to take such additional lands as might be needed for the construction, maintenance, operation, sanitation, and protection of the canal. The cities of Panama and Colón, at either end of the canal route, were not included in the Zone, but the United States was to have the right to intervene if necessary to maintain public order in them. Panama, in return, received $10,000,000, with the promise of an additional payment of $250,000 annually to begin nine years after the treaty went into effect.

The situation of the new Republic of Panama was a peculiar one. Its territory extended some 200 miles on either side of the transit route, but the region to the east was still held by unconquered Indian tribes, and that to the west was undeveloped and thinly populated. Economic and political life centered in two cities, Panama and Colón, which were separated only by imaginary lines from North American towns in the Zone. Until a corridor connecting Panama with the Republic's terri-

[1] Secretary Hay to the Colombian Minister, *Foreign Relations of the United States*, 1903, p. 302.

tory to the east was created in 1914, both of the cities were entirely surrounded by the area controlled by the United States. Their prosperity depended almost entirely on the canal. On the other hand, Panaman coöperation, especially in such matters as sanitation and military defense, was essential to the operation of the canal. Relations with the United States were bound to be extremely close, and many delicate questions, often involving vital interests of both countries, were certain to arise.

The First Years of the Republic

A *junta* named by the municipality of Panama City took over the government at the time of the revolution, and in January, 1904, a convention met to frame a constitution. One provision of this authorized the United States to intervene in any part of the Republic if necessary to maintain order. The convention chose Dr. Manuel Amador Guerrero, the leader of the revolution, as President of the Republic. His administration was at first supported by a coalition of the two political parties that Panama had inherited from Colombia, but the liberals soon became dissatisfied and induced the commander of the army to threaten a *coup d'état*. Disorder was only prevented by the intervention of the American Minister, and the army was soon afterward disbanded and replaced by a civilian police. The influence of the United States also helped to prevent outbreaks when municipal and congressional elections were held in 1906.

Meanwhile work on the canal had begun. The most urgent problem at the outset was the conquest of yellow fever and malaria, which had been major causes of the French company's failure. Since this could not be accomplished without strict sanitary controls in Panama City and Colón, the treaty of 1903 had given the United States a virtually unlimited authority with respect to public-health measures in these municipalities, and early in 1905 the Panaman government turned over to the Zone authorities the administration of sanitary regulations in both cities. Under the direction of Dr. William C. Gorgas of the United States Army, yellow fever was promptly eradicated. Malaria, a hardly less formidable enemy to human welfare, was brought under control in the areas near the settlements. For the first time in its history, the Isthmus became a safe place to live.

Another question involving the rights of the United States under the canal treaty was not so easily settled. In June, 1904, President Roosevelt formally opened the Canal Zone to commerce and established custom-houses and postoffices there. There was a storm of protest in Panama, for it was clear that the merchants of the Republic would be deprived of much business and the government would lose much of its revenues if commerce were allowed in the Zone. The Panaman government took the position that the treaty gave the United States only such rights in the Zone as it needed for the "construction, maintenance, operation, sanitation, and protection" of the canal, and insisted, as it always did, upon a narrow interpretation of these rights. The United States, on the other hand, pointed out that Article III of the treaty gave it "all the rights, power and authority within the zone . . . which the United States would possess and exercise if it were the sovereign of the territory." Nevertheless, it disclaimed any desire to inflict unnecessary hardship on Panama, and when Secretary of War Taft visited the Isthmus in the fall of 1904 a compromise was arranged. Thereafter imports into the Zone were limited in general to goods for the use of the United States and its employees or for sale to vessels passing through the canal, and the general public was not permitted to trade at the commissaries which the American authorities established. This arrangement was satisfactory in principle to both governments, but it did not prevent disputes over the operation of the commissaries from embittering their relations at frequent intervals in succeeding years.

Work on the canal began rather slowly, but after 1907 it was pushed forward more energetically under the direction of Colonel George W. Goethals. Some thousands of North Americans and a much larger number of Negro laborers from the British and French West Indies were brought to the Isthmus to work on the project. Large communities grew up at either end of the waterway, close to Panama City and Colón, with schools and club-houses and commissaries maintained by the United States Government. Many other North Americans and several thousand colored West Indians settled in the territory of the Republic. The Panaman cities flourished on the great sums of money spent in the Isthmus during the construction period and on the tourist trade after the canal was opened to commerce in 1914.

The canal itself is one of the great achievements of modern engineering. At either end, three locks raise ships to Gatun Lake, an artificial body of water created by damming the Chagres River at Gatun and flooding 164 square miles in the center of the Zone. South of the lake, vessels pass through a cut, 300 feet deep, from which tremendous quantities of earth were removed before troublesome landslides were brought under control. The transit, from Cristóbal on the Caribbean to Balboa on the Pacific, requires about six hours. The waterway at once became one of the world's principal trade routes. It benefited especially the countries of the west coast of South and Central America, which now had readier access to the eastern United States and Europe with more frequent and adequate steamship services. It also became an important link in the domestic communication system of the United States, for it was cheaper to send many commodities by sea via Panama than overland by rail. Equally significant, from the standpoint of the United States, was the usefulness of the canal from a military point of view.

Internal Politics, 1906–1924

The people of Panama had little experience with self-government during their connection with Colombia, and the extraordinary geographical and economic situation created by the canal was hardly conducive to orderly political development. In the first years of independence there was much factional strife among the small groups of politically minded persons in Panama City and Colón and on several occasions disorder that would have interfered with work on the canal was only averted by the influence of the United States. The American government was at first rather reluctant to interfere in Panaman internal affairs. When new members of Congress were to be chosen in 1906, it informed the Panaman leaders that it did not undertake to guarantee the holding of free elections; but it was soon compelled to change its attitude and to threaten to intervene if peace were disturbed. Its representatives then helped to bring about an agreement between the contending parties.

In the presidential election of 1908, when a coalition of liberals and conservatives opposed President Amador's choice of Ricardo Arias as his successor, both parties asked that an American commission be appointed to hear electoral complaints. The Amador government, however, joined in this request reluctantly, in response to diplomatic pressure, and before the election Arias withdrew his candidacy. José Domingo de Obaldía consequently became president in 1908. He died in 1910 and was succeeded by Pablo Arosemena. There was a new threat of disorder as the election of 1912 approached. The liberals, now in opposition, had a majority in Congress and could thus name the electoral boards. On the other hand Arosemena and the conservatives could count on the police. Under these circumstances both sides appealed for American supervision, and a committee of American officials, with more than two hundred assistants, took charge of the election. Before the voting the administration party withdrew from the contest, claiming that it had not received fair treatment, and Dr. Belisario Porras, the leader of the liberal party, became President.

Dr. Porras dominated Panaman politics during the next twelve years. He declined to accept American supervision of the election of 1916, and the opposition consequently refused to participate. His follower, Ramón Valdés, became President, but died two years later. Thereafter Porras was again elected acting President, but only after a violent controversy during which American troops took over the policing of Panama City and Colón.

The United States intervened on this occasion, not only to prevent political disorders but for other reasons. It had long been dissatisfied with conditions in the Panaman police force. There had been a series of clashes between police and American soldiers or sailors, some of which had ended in fatalities, and in 1916 the American legation had compelled the Panaman government to take away the rifles with which the police had hitherto been armed. During the European war, when a large number of troops were stationed in the Canal Zone, the failure to control drug-selling and other undesirable activities had been a further cause for complaint. These conditions were now remedied, and an American instructor already in the employ of the Panaman government was given authority to effect a thorough-going reform of the police force. At the same time the United States insisted on reforms in the government's financial administration, and an American "Fiscal Agent," nominated by the United States, served for some years as a sort of financial adviser and comptroller.

Dr. Porras resigned shortly before the end of his term in order to be eligible as a candidate in the election of 1920. He was reëlected without difficulty, after the United States had refused to interfere, and served until 1924. The chief event of this administration was a short war with Costa Rica. The boundary between Panama and Costa Rica had long been in dispute, and in 1914 Panama had refused to accept an arbitral decision by Chief Justice White of the United States Supreme Court and had continued to hold the Coto region on the Pacific coast which Mr. White had awarded to Costa Rica. After long negotiations in which the United States urged Panama to accept the award, Costa Rica invaded Coto in 1921. Her forces were defeated by an improvised army composed chiefly of Panama City policemen, and at this point hostilities were checked by the diplomatic intervention of the United States. Some months later, acting under the authority which it claimed as the guarantor of Panama's independence, the United States insisted that Costa Rica be permitted to occupy the Coto region without resistance. This action caused much bitterness against the United States, but Panama's relations with Costa Rica soon improved, and the boundary question was finally settled by a treaty signed in 1941.

Relations with the United States, 1924–1936

Rodolfo Chiari, a political associate of Dr. Porras, became President in 1924. At the outset of his administration he was confronted with the problem of negotiating a new treaty with the United States. The Taft Agreement of 1904, which was intended only as a *modus vivendi* during the period while the canal was under construction, was abrogated by the United States on June 1, 1924. This raised again the whole question of commercial operations in the Canal Zone. This and several other problems that had arisen in the relations between the two governments since 1903 were dealt with in a treaty signed in 1926, but when this was submitted to the Panaman Congress, ex-President Porras, who had quarreled with Chiari, brought about its defeat. Negotiations for a new agreement began soon afterward, but it was several years before one was signed. In the meantime, however, the United States of its own accord continued to exclude private business from the Canal Zone and to confine sales at the commissaries to persons connected with the canal or ships passing through.

During the 1920's changes that were taking place in the general Caribbean policy of the United States were reflected in a growing disinclination to interfere in internal affairs in Panama. Elections were conducted without American supervision after 1918, and the powers of the American Inspector General of Police and the Fiscal Agent were gradually curtailed after 1922. Except for one brief period in 1925, American troops were not again called on to maintain order in Panaman territory.

By this time party lines had broken down and politics had become almost entirely a matter of personalities and desire for office. Since the manner in which elections were conducted made it difficult if not impossible for an opposition candidate to win, a small group had been able to perpetuate itself in power, and there was increasing corruption and inefficiency. Discontent with this situation, aggravated by the effects of the world depression, was especially evident during the administration of Florencio Harmodio Arosemena, who succeeded Chiari in 1928. On January 2, 1931, a group of the President's opponents suddenly seized control of Panama City. There was some fighting, in which several policemen were killed, but the United States did not intervene. After the revolt had succeeded, however, the American Minister used his good offices to bring about a settlement which had the outward appearance of constitutionality, and the United States continued normal diplomatic relations with the new provisional regime headed by Dr. Ricardo Alfaro. In 1932 Harmodio Arias, one of the leaders of the revolution, was elected President.

A new treaty with the United States, which made important concessions to Panama's national pride and material interests, was signed on March 2, 1936. The United States abrogated its formal guarantee of Panaman independence and gave up its right to intervene to maintain order in Panama City and Colón. It also accepted important limitations on its freedom of action in the Canal Zone, in which only employees of the United States and persons connected with the operation of the canal were henceforth to be permitted to live. It gave up the right to take additional land outside of the Zone for canal purposes, and ceded to Panama a corridor connecting the city of Colón with the rest of the Republic's territory. A dispute that had arisen when the United States devalued the dollar and attempted to pay the canal annuity in the new currency was settled by an agreement that the annuity should be the equivalent in gold of the former payment.

One of the more important provisions of the new treaty was Article X which provided that in case of war or threat of aggression the two governments would act to protect their common interests and would consult regarding any measures that either government considered necessary, if these measures affected the territory of the other. Under the old treaty, the United States had claimed the right to use Panaman territory for military purposes in any way that seemed necessary, and a reluctance to give up full freedom of action in defending the canal led the United States Senate to delay its approval. By an exchange of notes in February, 1939, however, Panama agreed that manoeuvres of American troops in territory adjacent to the Zone were an essential measure of preparedness, and that in an emergency the United States might take action to defend the canal in advance of consultation between the two governments. This clarified the situation, and in July, 1939, the treaty was ratified and went into effect.

Recent Political Events

The election at which Harmodio Arias' successor was chosen in 1936 was one of the most closely contested in the history of the Republic. The official candidate, Juan Demóstenes Arosemena, was declared ineligible for technical reasons by the National Elections Jury, but the President insisted upon Arosemena's right to run and after the voting removed one member of the jury to procure a majority which would declare him elected. On the face of the returns, Arosemena received a small majority over his principal opponent, Domingo Díaz, but the latter's supporters loudly impugned the fairness of the final count.

Arosemena died in December, 1939, and Dr. Augusto Boyd served out the few remaining months of the presidential term. In the election of 1940 Dr. Arnulfo Arias, Harmodio Arias' brother, was the government candidate. His opponent, Dr. Ricardo Alfaro, withdrew from the race in May after several of his supporters had been arrested and others had been compelled to flee into the Canal Zone. A few months after Arias took office a constitutional change extending his term to six years gave color to charges that he was setting up a dictatorship with fascist tendencies. The suspicion that he inclined toward totalitarianism increased in October, 1941, when he forbade the arming of Panaman merchant ships. This was an act of some importance, because a large number of vessels owned by companies in the United States had been registered under the Panaman flag and several had been sunk in the war zone.

On the day after this decree was issued, Arias secretly flew to Habana, where, as he later said, he wished to consult an oculist. His cabinet, discovering that he had left the country without obtaining the necessary permission from Congress, promptly declared that he had forfeited the presidency and installed Ricardo Adolfo de la Guardia in his place. The change took place without disorder, and the new administration made it clear that it proposed to coöperate with the United States in questions of hemisphere defense. An agreement signed in 1942 gave the United States the use of a number of military bases in the Republic's territory, in return for the transfer to Panama of the water and sewer systems and much valuable real estate in Panama City and Colón. In January, 1943, De la Guardia's term of office was extended for two additional years.

During these two years Arias' followers provoked occasional minor disturbances, and at the end of 1944 opposition in the Congress caused De la Guardia to dissolve that body and suspend the constitution. Several opposition deputies who fled to the Canal Zone attempted to set up a new government but met with no success. The pro-administration parties controlled a constituent assembly that met in June, 1945, and elected Enrique Jiménez as Provisional President.

One of the most difficult problems that confronted Jiménez was the negotiation of an agreement with the United States to govern the status of several military bases that the American government desired to retain for the defense of the Canal. American forces had occupied more than 130 defense sites of various kinds during the war, but had evacuated most of them by the middle of 1947. In December, 1947, an agreement signed after prolonged negotiations gave the United States a ten-year lease on the important Rio Hato air base and a five-year lease on thirteen less important sites, but the Panaman Congress, influenced by turbulent anti-American demonstrations, unanimously refused its approval. The United States at once abandoned all of the military installations outside of the Canal Zone.

The first regular presidential elections in eight years were held on May 9, 1948. The voting was orderly, and the former President Arnulfo Arias, supported by extreme nationalist and anti-United States elements, seemed at first to have a small majority. Three months later, however, when the National Elections Jury completed its canvass, the liberal, pro-administration candidate Domingo Díaz Arosemena was proclaimed the victor. President Díaz was inaugurated on October 1, 1948, but he died the following August.

Daniel Chanis, who took his place, attempted in November, 1949, to remove the chief of police, Colonel José Remón, who was accused of maintaining several profitable rackets in Panama City. The police at once forced Chanis to resign and installed Roberto Chiari in his place.

When the National Assembly and the Supreme Court both upheld Chanis, Colonel Remón arranged to have the National Elections Jury recount the votes cast in 1948, with the result that Arnulfo Arias was proclaimed the duly elected President. The United States expressed disapproval of the violent manner in which the change of government had been effected, but it recognized the new administration after consulting with the other American Republics.

23

Central America Before 1900

The Country and the People

The five Central American provinces, today the Republics of Guatemala, El Salvador, Honduras, Nicaragua, and Costa Rica, were ruled in colonial times by a Captain General at Guatemala City, with governors under him in each province. Their principal settlements, in the volcanic region on the western side of the Isthmus, were cut off from the east coast by high mountains and tropical jungle; and though the San Juan River gave access to the interior in Nicaragua, its dangerous bar and troublesome rapids diminished its value as a trade route. On the Pacific side there were few good ports, and these were rarely visited by ships. The provinces thus had little contact with the outside world, and most of their towns were small and unprogressive. Nevertheless, the region was densely populated at the end of the colonial period as compared with many other sections of Spanish America. With an area less than half that of Venezuela or New Granada, it probably had somewhat over a million inhabitants, of whom the majority were in Guatemala.

There were important differences in the character of the population in the various provinces. These differences still exist, and they must be borne in mind if we are to understand the history of the Central American republics as independent nations. In Guatemala the majority of the people are pure-blooded Indians of Maya stock, descended from a race that gave prehistoric America one of its highest civilizations, but now an ignorant and oppressed laboring class, speaking native dialects and completely excluded from the political and intellectual life of the conquering race. The country's economic and social conditions are thus much like those of Central Mexico or Peru, and we should not expect to see any rapid progress toward democracy. On the other hand, the willingness of the white ruling class to support strong governments resting on military force, in order to maintain their own dominance over the Indians, gave the government a relative stability. In El Salvador, Honduras, and Nicaragua the aboriginal population, less advanced and less numerous before the Conquest, was more completely assimilated and the masses of the people, as well as many of the principal families, are of mixed blood. In Honduras and Nicaragua especially, the land-owning aristocracy has been less powerful and the common people have taken more interest in politics. A larger proportion of them have participated in the civil wars, and the damage done by internal strife has been correspondingly greater. In Costa Rica, on the other hand, there were still fewer Indians, and only an insignificant number survived the first years of Spanish domination. The lack of a native labor supply made the colony unattractive to immigrants, but those who did come were hardy farmers whose descendants today are an industrious people more completely European in blood than those of any other Latin American country except Uruguay. In such a community the development of real republican government was possible.

Central American Independence

The Central American provinces were at first little affected by the movement for independence in the other colonies. There were a few small revolutionary disturbances between 1811 and 1814, but the inhabitants as a whole seemed content to maintain the connection with Spain. The creole leaders who felt otherwise had little following. After 1820, however, freedom of speech and press under the new Spanish constitution gave the more radical element an opportunity to advocate changes in the colonial political and social organization. This alarmed the conservatives and the clergy, who were already shocked by the conduct of the liberal government in Spain, and made them less averse to breaking away from the mother country if they could thereby retain their own prerogatives. Iturbide's revolt in Mexico set the example and precipitated their action. Their movement met with little resistance because the acting Captain General, Gabino Gaínza, proved willing to work with the advocates of independence in return for their promise to make him head of the new government.

On September 15, 1821, an assembly of royal officials, high ecclesiastical officers, and prominent creoles met in Guatemala City to declare the independence of Central America. Gaínza retained his position but shared power with a *junta consultiva* of influential citizens. Both the conservatives and the more radical revolutionary leaders took part in the proceedings, but it was not long before the existence of the new regime was threatened by internal disputes. The liberals objected to the predominance of the conservatives in the *junta* and to the latter's efforts to control the election of the Congress that was to decide upon a permanent form of government. The conservatives were divided among themselves, and the Spanish governors of Honduras and Nicaragua, who were unfriendly to Gaínza, soon threw off his authority and announced their adherence to Iturbide's Plan of Iguala.

The idea of annexation to Mexico was taken up by other conservatives, and especially by those who opposed the establishment of a republic, and in November Iturbide announced his intention of sending troops to support his partisans. The latter, thus encouraged, hastily obtained approval of their scheme by a majority of the municipal councils throughout the five provinces, and on January 5, 1822, the union with Mexico was proclaimed. General Filísola, who was sent by Iturbide to take charge of the government, was well received in Guatemala. He encountered more resistance in El Salvador, where republican sentiment was especially strong, and where the Congress, in the hope of obtaining outside help, voted to ask that the province be admitted as a state into the North American Union. Before this request could reach Washington, however, the city of San Salvador was occupied by the imperial troops. The union of Central America with Mexico lasted a little more than a year, for Filísola relinquished his authority when Iturbide fell in February, 1823.

The Federal Republic

A Central American Congress which Filísola convoked named a triumvirate to take charge of the administration. While this *junta*, weakened by quarrels among themselves and handicapped by lack of money, strove to maintain some semblance of organized government, the Congress drew up a federal constitution. There were to be a president and a congress at Guatemala City, with state governments in each of the provinces. A limited suffrage and a cumbersome indirect system of voting assured the maintenance of power in the hands of the wealthier and better educated class. Catholicism was made the state religion and the public exercise of all others was prohibited. Negro slavery, never a very important institution in Central America, was abolished.

In 1825 Manuel José Arce became President of the Republic. Arce was a liberal, but he soon quarreled with the liberal majority in the legislative body and was driven to seek conservative support. His term of office was a stormy one. It proved impossible for the federal and state authorities to exist side by side in harmony in Guatemala City, and minor quarrels over questions of jurisdiction culminated in the forcible ousting of the liberal state governor and his replacement by a conservative. Meanwhile the Congress was paralyzed by party strife, and the federal authorities were reduced to impotence by disorders in the states. The people of the city of San Salvador, angered by their failure to obtain the creation of a new diocese in their state, and led by Father Delgado, the disappointed aspirant to the bishopric, rose in revolt in 1827. They were joined by disaffected groups in other states, and there ensued two years of general civil war which finally ended in the government's defeat. The leader of the victorious liberal army was Francisco Morazán, a native of Honduras, who was barely thirty years old.

Morazán was elected to the presidency of Central America in 1830. His party obtained control of all the state governments, but within a few months the conservatives resumed the civil war. Revolts were suppressed in Guatemala and Honduras, but only after severe fighting. There was also renewed friction between the federal and the state authorities in Guatemala City, and when Morazán decided to move his headquarters to San Salvador, where the liberal party was stronger, he met with armed resistance from the state government there. He nevertheless made San Salvador the capital of the Republic in 1834. Soon afterward he was reëlected as President, but his prestige was waning and the Federal Republic itself was disintegrating. In 1838 the national Congress dissolved and declared the states free to adopt any form of government that they desired. In 1840, after more than a year of renewed civil war, Morazán was defeated by the forces of Nicaragua, Honduras, and Guatemala, and went into exile.

The Aftermath of the Federation

The attempt to unite Central America under one government had thus failed. The people of the Isthmus were no better prepared to make a success of democratic institutions than their neighbors in Mexico, and the ignorance and indifference of the voters and the political inexperience of the leaders made it especially difficult for them to operate the complicated machinery of a federal system. The government's task had been complicated by the long distances from one province to another and by the lack of roads, which made communication and travel slow and uncertain. More serious still was the intensity of the localistic spirit, which made the people of the provincial towns and villages jealous of the national capital and caused dissensions within the states.

Attempts to reunite Central America after Morazán's downfall were uniformly unsuccessful. In Guatemala, many of the great families and the clergy preferred a local government under their own control to the uncertainties of a revived federation. In Costa Rica there was an equally strong separatist feeling. Geographical isolation had enabled the Costa Ricans to avoid participation in the civil wars which destroyed the federal republic, and they had no desire to become involved in new complications. In El Salvador, Honduras, and Nicaragua, on the other hand, unionist sentiment was stronger, and these states repeatedly endeavored to set up a new federal government, even though only the three of them participated in it. In 1842 they did establish a loose confederation, which broke up two years later when they started fighting among themselves. In 1849 they made another attempt, inspired by the desire for mutual defense against the British encroachments on the Mosquito Coast, which will be described below. The central council which they set up had little power, and when an effort was made to strengthen it in 1852 the whole project failed. Thereafter interest in the union seemed to decline, but it revived from time to time in later years.

Unfortunately the political enmities formed during the federal period persisted after the union was dissolved, and liberals and conservatives in each country continued to support their former associates in the others and to aid them in time of civil strife. International wars frequently occurred simply because neighboring states were ruled by administrations of different political complexions, for each government was tempted to aid revolutionary movements against the other if only to forestall similar action by its neighbor. The weaker states naturally suffered most from this practice. For many years after the breakdown of the federation, the political history of El Salvador, Honduras, and Nicaragua was little more than a confused story of internal and interstate conflicts, provoked in most cases by the interference of Guatemala.

Rafael Carrera

In Guatemala, more than in the other countries, the political parties were divided on real issues. Lines were drawn much as they were in Mexico, with the clergy, the remnants of the colonial nobility, and many of the great landowners and rich merchants on the conservative side, and creole and *mestizo* professional men and other groups who had a less privileged position in colonial times forming the liberal party. The hostility between the two groups became acute during the last years of the federal republic. The liberals, when they came into power with Morazán, suppressed the monastic orders and pushed through other anti-clerical measures, which aroused bitter opposition. The Guatemalans, like their neighbors in Mexico, were not ready for such radical reforms, and the liberal leaders soon found themselves facing resistance not only from the aristocracy but from the Indian and *mestizo* country people, among whom the priests still retained much of their influence.

The conservatives had their opportunity when an epidemic of cholera broke out in 1837. By spreading a story that the government was poisoning the wells to destroy the natives and make way for Protestant immigrants from England, they provoked a popular uprising in the isolated mountain region east of Guatemala City, and the movement soon spread to other sections. Its leader was an illiterate youth named Rafael Carrera who built up a great following among his fellow Indians and became the chief general on the conservative side in the civil wars that caused the disintegration of the federal government. The liberals, weakened by their own factional quarrels, were finally driven out of Guatemala City, and when they attempted to set up the separate state of Los Altos in the western part of the country they were defeated there. By 1840 the conservatives were in full control. Their leaders, however, found themselves at the mercy of the chieftain of the half-savage horde that had won the victory for them, and though others occupied the presidency, Carrera remained at the head of the army and was the real ruler of the country. In 1844 he took the presidency himself. He met with some difficulties at first, and political opposition forced him to relinquish power for brief periods, but by 1852 his authority was firmly established. In 1854 he made himself President for life, and ruled as dictator until his death in 1865.

Carrera gave Guatemala a welcome period of relative tranquility. His power rested chiefly on the blind devotion of the Indian masses and the loyalty of a well-paid army, but he was also supported by native and foreign property owners who desired the maintenance of peace, and by the Church, which again became a powerful political force. The liberals' anti-clerical legislation was naturally repealed, and the Jesuits and other religious orders were invited to return.

Guatemala's neighbors enjoyed less internal peace, and their difficulties were made worse by Carrera's continual interference in their internal affairs. In 1840 a Guatemalan army defeated the liberal regime that had supported Morazán in El Salvador, and placed that country under the *de facto* control of a military leader named Francisco Malespín. In the same way, a conservative government was set up in Honduras. Personal quarrels, however, prevented any lasting coöperation between the rulers of the three states, and in 1844–45 all of them, and Nicaragua as well, were involved in a general war which was both an international conflict and an internal struggle in each state. In El Salvador, the liberals came into control for a brief period, were overthrown in 1851 by Carrera, and then returned to power in 1860 under the popular and able Gerardo Barrios. In 1863 a new Guatemalan intervention replaced Barrios by Francisco Dueñas. In Honduras the story was much the same; Francisco Ferrera, an ally of Carrera, dominated the government through his control of the army until 1852. In that year Trinidad Cabañas, a liberal, became President. In 1855 Cabañas was overthrown by Carrera and was succeeded by General Santos Guardiola. The latter was assassinated in 1862, and a year later the liberals, who had regained power, were driven out by Guatemalan and Nicaraguan intervention.

Anglo-American Rivalry in Nicaragua

Nicaragua was involved in many of the conflicts between her northern neighbors and suffered constantly from internal strife, made more virulent by the inveterate enmity between the two chief cities, León and Granada. León was the liberal center, Granada the conservative, and all differences of policy or principle were lost sight of in what became simply a regional feud. There were level-headed leaders in both cities who endeavored to bring about harmony, but their efforts were frustrated by popular hatreds and by the machinations of military leaders who profited from the continuance of disorder. The heads of the army, rather than the numerous "Chiefs of State" who succeeded one another for two-year terms, were the real rulers of the country. Casto Fonseca, a liberal, was *comandante de armas* until 1845, when the conservatives, with their allies from Honduras and El Salvador, barbarously sacked León and killed many of its inhabitants.

During the next twelve years, Nicaragua was the victim of aggression from outside of Central America. It will be remembered that one of the two practicable transisthmian canal routes lay within her territory, and that Great Britain and the United States were both interested in controlling these routes. The British had had a foothold in Central America since the seventeenth century, when buccaneers from Jamaica frequently cut dye-woods on the mainland at times when piracy was unprofitable or too dangerous and established small settlements which the Spaniards were never able completely to destroy. Belize, or British Honduras, became a British colony after the independence of Central America, and in the 1830's the Mosquitos, a primitive race of mixed Indian and Negro blood living in northeastern Nicaragua and eastern Honduras, were taken under British protection. During the same period the Bay Islands, off the coast of Honduras, were occupied. This gradual encroachment met with little resistance, but in 1848, British forces, acting in the name of the Mosquito King, provoked a diplomatic crisis by seizing San Juan del Norte at the mouth of the San Juan River.

San Juan del Norte, or Greytown, had never been considered a part of the Mosquito protectorate, and the obvious purpose of the seizure was to obtain control of the eastern end of the prospective canal route. The United States, more than ever interested in the canal project since the acquisition of California, made a vigorous protest. In the ensuing negotiations it became clear that each government was actuated primarily by fear of the other's intentions. It was consequently possible to reach an agreement, in the Clayton-Bulwer Treaty of 1850, that neither would "obtain or maintain" any exclusive control over the proposed waterway, and that neither would occupy any part of Central America or seek any special privileges for its nationals in connection with the canal which were not also offered to the people of the other country. The British soon afterward evacuated San Juan del Norte. There were disputes about the application of the treaty to some of the other British-held territories, but they were gradually settled after further negotiations. The Bay Islands, which had been proclaimed a British colony in 1852, were returned to Honduras in 1859, and the Mosquito protectorate was relinquished in 1860, under a treaty with Nicaragua which stipulated that the Indians should govern themselves in a reservation that did not include the territory at the mouth of the San Juan River.

San Juan del Norte became the eastern terminus of a transisthmian passenger service established by the Accessory Transit Company for the benefit of travelers between New York and California. Large numbers of persons used the small steamers that the company operated on the San Juan River and Lake Nicaragua and the carriages that covered the short distance between the lake and the Pacific, for crossing the Isthmus, either in Nicaragua or in Panama, was on the whole less dangerous and difficult than going overland through the United States. This American concern soon became involved in a sensational series of events in Nicaragua.

William Walker and the Filibusters

After the conservative victory in 1845, the capital of Nicaragua was moved to Masaya and then to Managua, both of them small towns near Granada, but a few years later the new *comandante de armas*, Trinidad Muñoz, betrayed his conservative supporters and reëstablished the capital at León. When the conservatives regained power in 1851, with help from Honduras and Costa Rica, they first vainly attempted to set up a coalition government, and then subjected the liberals to a repressive regime which goaded the people of León into revolt in 1854. Carrera intervened on the conservative side, and the liberals turned for help to a band of "filibusters" recruited in the United States by one William Walker.

Walker came to Nicaragua in June, 1855, with fifty-eight men. In October he seized Granada by a surprise attack, and the conservative leaders, though their army was undefeated, made peace in order to save their families from mistreatment. A conservative became President, but Walker was made commander of the army. Disbanding the native troops, he soon made it clear that he proposed to rule the country with his "American Phalanx"; and in 1856, after the leaders of both parties had started a revolt against him, he had himself "elected" President of Nicaragua. By this time hundreds of adventurers were coming to Nicaragua to join his forces. His activities aroused much interest in the United States, both because they seemed likely to defeat British efforts to obtain control of the canal route, and because many persons in the South hoped that he would eventually bring Nicaragua into the Union as a new slave state.

Walker's most useful ally was the Accessory Transit Company. He made a mistake, however, when he supported a group within this company that was trying to wrest control from its former president, Cornelius Vanderbilt; and when he canceled the company's concession and granted a new one to his friends, Vanderbilt quickly avenged himself. By this time armies from all of the other Central American states as well as forces representing both parties in Nicaragua were marching against the intruders. While Walker was preparing to make a stand against these enemies in western Nicaragua, Vanderbilt's steamers on the San Juan River and the great lake helped a Costa Rican force to cut off his communications with New York. The filibusters held out against overwhelming odds for several months, but they lost heavily from disease and desertion, and on May 1, 1857, Walker surrendered to the commander of an American warship. Twice in the next three years he attempted to return to Central America with filibustering expeditions, but his career ended when he was captured and executed in northern Honduras in 1860.

In Nicaragua both parties were under arms at the end of the war and it seemed probable that the disappearance of the common enemy would be followed by a new struggle between them. They reached an agreement, however, when Costa Rica attempted to take advantage of the situation to retain possession of territory that Nicaragua claimed along the San Juan River; and Máximo Jerez, the leader of the liberals, consented to the establishment of a conservative government under Tomás Martínez. This was the beginning of a long period of relative peace under the control of the conservative party.

Costa Rica, 1821–1870

Though they took an active part in the war against Walker, the people of Costa Rica were usually able to remain aloof from the political struggles that kept the neighboring countries in a state of turmoil. Most of the Costa Ricans lived in or near four little towns, all within a few miles of one another on a pleasant plateau in the interior. Descended from sturdy North Spanish peasants who had come to the colony because they were not afraid to work with their hands, the majority were small farmers, ignorant and conservative but industrious and self-respecting. There were few wealthy landowners, and at the other end of the scale few Indians or Negroes.

Even in the first years of independence, the Costa Ricans suffered less from internal political strife than did their neighbors. There were brief struggles between the various towns, arising from disputes over the location of the capital, and there were periodic revolts and *coups d'état* provoked by factional rivalry, but they caused relatively little bloodshed or destruction of property. Political affairs were dominated by a few prominent families, among whom the Montealegres and the Moras, heads of rival groups, were the most important. Juan Mora was the first President, serving from 1825 until 1833.

Braulio Carrillo was President from 1835 to 1837 and from 1838 until 1842. It was he who first promoted the cultivation of coffee, which soon became the country's chief export. He also strengthened the peasant class by encouraging the subdivision of the common lands formerly held by the towns. He was an able administrator, but his dictatorial methods, and especially his attempt to make himself president for life, made him unpopular. His own troops deserted him when Francisco Morazán landed in Costa Rica to start a revolution in 1842.

Morazán still aspired to restore the federal republic of which he had so recently been the head, but when he began to raise money and recruit men for an attack on the other states the Costa Ricans turned against him and put him to death. There followed seven years of factional quarreling and frequent governmental changes. The government became more stable under the firm hand of Juan Rafael Mora, who became President in 1849 and who distinguished himself in the war against the filibusters in Nicaragua. When Mora was overthrown and shot, after ten years in office, the old rivalry between his family and the Montealegres again threatened to cause a civil war, but a compromise was reached and the country was fairly peaceful under the administrations of Jesús Jiménez (1863–66) and José María Castro (1866–68). The army, under two leaders named Blanco and Salazar, exercised much influence in the government during this period.

The Liberal Regime in Guatemala

The long period of conservative domination in Northern Central America came to an end when Vicente Cerna, who had become President of Guatemala after Carrera's death in 1865, was overthrown by the liberals in 1871. Miguel García Granados became President, but his authority was overshadowed by that of the most prominent leader in the recent revolt, Justo Rufino Barrios. Under the latter's influence, the Jesuits and some of the higher church authorities were expelled from the country and the property of the monastic orders was confiscated. In 1873 Barrios became President, to rule as a dictator until his death twelve years later. With the enthusiastic support of a strong popular following, he ruthlessly crushed all opposition and permanently destroyed the political influence of the Church and the conservative aristocracy. He helped to maintain liberal governments in power in Honduras and Salvador, and continued to interfere in the internal affairs of those countries whenever their rulers attempted to resist his domination.

Barrios' great ambition was to reunite Central America under his own leadership. In his efforts to achieve this, he met with opposition even in the neighboring countries whose governments owed their existence to his support. Resistance was especially strong in El Salvador, where there was a deep-seated traditional jealousy of Guatemala; and in 1885 Barrios was killed at the battle of Chalchuapa while leading his army in an attack on that country.

The liberal regime was by this time so firmly established in Guatemala that even the death of its leader did not upset it. As in many other Latin American countries during this period, the development of agriculture and foreign trade made for political stability. Coffee-growing had become an important industry, in which foreign as well as native capital was invested, and the planters exercised a powerful influence to prevent civil strife which would interfere with the harvesting of their crops. Manuel Lisandro Barillas, one of the *designados*, succeeded Barrios and was able to make himself President for the next term. In 1892 a comparatively free election placed José María Reyna Barrios, a nephew of Justo Rufino, at the head of the government. When he was assassinated in 1898, the first *designado*, Manuel Estrada Cabrera, assumed power. This was the beginning of a cruel and unprogressive dictatorship which was to last until 1920.

El Salvador and Honduras

El Salvador also was enjoying prosperity with a rapid increase in coffee production and was moving slowly toward more stable political conditions. After 1885 the country suffered relatively little from outside interference in its political affairs. Rafael Zaldívar, who had been one of Justo Rufino Barrios' closest allies before they separated over the question of the Union, was overthrown soon after the battle of Chalchuapa, and was succeeded by Francisco Menéndez. When the latter died in 1890, the two Ezeta brothers seized control and maintained a rather barbarous military despotism until they were ousted in 1894. Under Rafael Gutiérrez, the next President, El Salvador joined with Honduras and Nicaragua in an attempt to set up a "Greater Republic of Central America." A treaty signed in 1895 provided for a "diet" which was to conduct the three states' foreign relations and draft a federal constitution. In 1898, a federal council met at Amapala, Honduras, to assume the general government. At this point, however, the opponents of the union revolted in El Salvador and General Tomás Regalado became President.

Honduras, with less land suitable for coffee-growing and few other natural resources, was less prosperous. The other governments continued to interfere in her political affairs. Guatemalan intervention put Ponciano Leiva in the presidency in 1873, forced him out in 1876, and in 1883 forced the resignation of his successor, Marco Aurelio Soto. Luis Bográn was President from 1883 until 1891. Thereafter presidents followed one another in quick succession until 1894, when Policarpo Bonilla, an ardent liberal, came into office with the aid of President Zelaya of Nicaragua. Bonilla was followed by another liberal, General Terencio Sierra, in 1899.

Nicaragua

The Granada conservatives, who came into power after the war with the filibusters, ruled Nicaragua until 1893 and gave the country the longest period of relative peace and good government that it has ever enjoyed. The Granada aristocracy was a homogeneous, well-organized group, whose leaders succeeded one another in the presidency by agreement and followed a conciliatory policy toward the liberals. The country made some material progress, though its natural wealth was far less than that of Guatemala or El Salvador. As time went on, however, the prolonged domination of one small group was increasingly distasteful to the people of León and to the country at large. The first serious dissension within the oligarchy was the signal for a successful liberal revolt, headed by a young leader from Managua named José Santos Zelaya, who set up a personal dictatorship that was to last sixteen years.

Costa Rica

The liberal victories in the four northern countries had their counterpart in Costa Rica in 1870, when an army officer named Tomás Guardia overthrew the government, exiled the leaders of the two political groups that had hitherto competed for control, and set up a regime in which the Moras and the Montealegres had no part. Guardia dominated affairs, though not always as President, until his death in 1882, and was succeeded in power first by his close friend Próspero Fernández and three years later by the latter's son-in-law, Bernardo Soto. Soto's administration was especially notable for the establishment of free compulsory education in the principal towns and villages of the Republic, under the direction of his minister Mauro Fernández.

In 1889 an aroused public opinion compelled Soto to permit the holding of a real election, probably the first in the history of Central America, in which the opposition candidate, José Joaquín Rodríguez, was chosen as President. Despite its origin, the new administration, supported by the Church, was practically a dictatorship, and Rodríguez' successor, Rafael Yglesias, was put in office for two terms (1894–1902) by the electoral methods formerly in vogue. Yglesias, however, was an able ruler, and the country owed much to his progressive policy. When he left office, Costa Rica, despite its small area and scanty population, was a well-governed and peaceful community, where an increasingly intelligent public opinion would very soon demand a government republican in fact as well as in form.

Central America at the Turn of the Century

Elsewhere in Central America the prospect was not so bright. Coffee had brought prosperity to the upper class in Guatemala, but the Indians, who formed the great mass of the population, were on the whole worse off than when Thomas Gage gave so sad an account of their condition in the seventeenth century. As coffee planting developed, much of their land was taken, often by force or fraud, and Justo Rufino Barrios and his successors sought to help the new industry by extending and making more effective the systems of forced labor which had always existed. As in colonial times, Indian villages were compelled to furnish groups of laborers, called "mandamientos," when local planters needed them. Still worse, from the Indians' point of view, was the peonage system, enforced by law, under which laborers were tricked or forced into debt, and then compelled to work for wages which in 1916 were equivalent to from five to eight cents per day in United States currency.

In El Salvador, Honduras, and Nicaragua, the *mestizo* laboring class was better off, but wages and standards of living were low and tropical diseases made miserable the lives of a large part of the population. In El Salvador, as in Guatemala, the rapid increase in coffee production had benefited principally the landowning aristocracy. In Nicaragua there had been less agricultural development; in Honduras almost none. In all three countries disorder and governmental poverty made it difficult to establish schools or to take other measures to improve the lot of the common people. The great majority were probably little better qualified to be citizens of free republics than they had been in 1821. Despite the trend toward greater stability in the last years of the century, changes of government by revolution or *coup d'état* were still the rule rather than the exception, and constant interference by the various states in one another's internal affairs brought on frequent international conflicts.

24

Central America and the United States
1900–1950

Increasing Contact with the Outside World

The Central American states still had relatively little contact with the outside world in the closing decades of the nineteenth century. Their commerce was too unimportant to arouse the interest of other nations, and political disorder and lack of transportation discouraged the investment of foreign capital. Though most of their principal towns were by this time connected by railroad with the Pacific coast, inadequate and irregular steamer service made them difficult of access. Comparatively few of their people were able to travel or study abroad, and few foreigners came to Central America.

After 1900 this situation began to change, partly because of the growth of the banana industry. Minor C. Keith, a North American, began to plant bananas in Costa Rica in 1872 to provide paying freight for a railroad that he was building from the east coast to San José, and when the line finally reached the capital in 1890 the export of bananas from Port Limon, its eastern terminus, had already become an important business. Keith later established plantations in Colombia and Panama, and in 1899 he joined with other banana interests in creating the United Fruit Company. This great concern extended its operations to Guatemala in 1906 and soon afterward to Honduras, where two other American firms also had plantations. Wherever they operated, the fruit companies established lines of fast steamers that carried passengers as well as fruit, and built railroads to bring bananas to the ports. In Guatemala and El Salvador, as well as in Costa Rica, these lines were extended into the interior. Guatemala City was connected with Puerto Barrios on the Caribbean in 1908 and service between San Salvador and Puerto Barrios was opened in 1929.

The banana industry brought great tracts of hitherto uninhabited jungle under cultivation, and bananas became the principal export, after coffee, in the trade of the Isthmus. The plantations at first were operated largely with imported Negro labor from the West Indies; but as time went on they employed many natives of the country at relatively high wages. On the other hand the fruit companies naturally dominated the economic life of the districts where they operated, and sometimes became involved in local politics. The United Fruit Company, which was by far the most important, was accused in its early days of ruthlessly eliminating competitors and oppressing the small growers who had no other buyer for their fruit.

The centers of production in the banana industry shifted from time to time because disease usually invaded the plantations after some years of cultivation, destroying much of the value of the great investment in farms, railroads, and port facilities. Thus Costa Rica, the most important Central American banana area before the First World War, gave place to Honduras, which exported 31,000,000 stems in 1932 but now ships half of that amount. The production of bananas for export was at first confined to the hitherto neglected and almost uninhabited lowlands along the Caribbean coast, but more recently plantations have been established on the Pacific side of the Isthmus.

Communications with the outside world were further improved with the opening of the Panama Canal in 1914, for an increasing number of steamers, including passenger vessels bound for San Francisco or New York, began to call at the west coast ports to land goods or pick up coffee. About the same time the automobile came into more general use and the building of improved highways brought places like Tegucigalpa, the capital of Honduras, and Quezaltenango, the second city of Guatemala, within fairly easy reach of the coast. The automobile opened up many sections of Central America where goods had formerly been transported on muleback or on the backs of men.

Political Conditions

At the turn of the century the majority of the Central American states seemed to have achieved a measure of political stability. In Guatemala and El Salvador, the two richest and most populous countries, the old party lines had broken down and the landowning classes were inclined to frown on efforts to provoke civil war because it hurt their interests. The governments still rested primarily on military force, but their position had been strengthened by increasing prosperity.

Manuel Estrada Cabrera was President of Guatemala from 1898 until 1920. An astute and unprincipled politician, without personal popularity, and apparently with no aspiration beyond merely staying in office, his regime was a despotism maintained by a reign of terror. All classes were demoralized by an omnipresent spy system and elections were the merest farce. Little or nothing was accomplished in the way of public works or social welfare, but the maintenance of order and the government's support of the increasingly oppressive peonage system made the regime acceptable to native and foreign property interests.

The government of El Salvador was somewhat more efficient and progressive, but hardly more democratic. Though each president usually surrendered his office at the end of his term, it was almost always to a successor of his own choice. Regalado, the leader of the revolution that broke up the union with Honduras and Nicaragua in 1898, was President until 1903, and was followed by Pedro José Escalón (1903–7), Fernando Figueroa (1907–11), and Manuel Enrique Araujo (1911–13). Araujo was assassinated, and Carlos Meléndez, the Vice-President, succeeded him. This was the beginning of a long period of rule by one family, for Carlos Meléndez was reëlected in 1915, his brother, Jorge Meléndez, became President in 1919, and his brother-in-law, Alfonso Quiñónez, followed in 1923. During this period there were no important revolts and the country made substantial material progress. Roads were built, the schools were improved, and the coffee industry flourished.

In Costa Rica, where the people were predominantly of Spanish descent and coffee had brought prosperity to thousands of small landowners rather than merely to a few wealthy families, political conditions were different. Ascensión Esquivel was made President by an agreement between the political parties in 1902, but his successors, Cleto González Víquez (1906–10) and Ricardo Jiménez (1910–14), were chosen at free elections. Both were able statesmen who governed by law rather than by force. There was complete liberty of the press, and no persecution of political enemies. With internal tranquility and orderly administration, the country enjoyed as truly republican institutions as any in the American continent, and the Costa Ricans proudly boasted that they had more school teachers than soldiers.

Nicaragua and Honduras had less land suitable for coffee-growing and were consequently less prosperous. In both countries the revolutionary tradition was still strong. In Nicaragua especially, the traditional rivalry between León and Granada continued unabated. A citizen was born a liberal or a conservative and regarded all members of the opposite group as enemies. The liberals had come into office in 1893 after the long era of conservative rule. José Santos Zelaya, who had become President in that year, was a native of Managua, and at first did not have the full support of the leaders at León, but he skilfully played off one group against another and even obtained some conservative support. Within a few years his despotic and corrupt dictatorship was firmly established. The more militant conservative leaders revolted time after time but were always defeated. By the turn of the century, Zelaya was challenging Estrada Cabrera's position as the dominant figure in Central American politics.

Honduras, which was certain to be a victim in a struggle between these two leaders, was the poorest and most backward of the five states. Her stronger neighbors had continually intervened in her affairs and civil wars instigated or aided from abroad had kept party hostility alive. A liberal, Terencio Sierra, was president at the turn of the century, but the conservatives came to power after a revolt led by Manuel Bonilla in 1903.

The Washington Conference of 1907

With the adoption of the Roosevelt corollary to the Monroe Doctrine the United States began to take an increased interest in Central American problems. Despite the progress of the past quarter century, political conditions in the Isthmus were far from satisfactory. In each country except Costa Rica enemies of the regime in power were eagerly awaiting an opportunity to overthrow it. Without free elections they could only hope to do so by armed revolt. Since the customary method of starting a revolution was to obtain arms and a base for operations in some neighboring country, each government felt unsafe so long as neighboring governments were in unfriendly hands, and was thus inclined to give encouragement or open aid to exiles from neighboring states to make its own position more secure. This practice not only fomented internal strife but caused frequent international wars. Failure to protect foreign lives and property during these disorders frequently caused complications with European powers, and unpaid debts and claims were a further source of trouble.

In 1906 Regalado, the Minister of War of El Salvador, provoked a war between that country and Guatemala by giving aid to a revolution against Estrada Cabrera. Honduras was drawn in on the side of El Salvador, but the fighting was soon stopped by the joint mediation of the United States and Mexico. A few months later a general Central American conference met at San José, Costa Rica, to adopt treaties that would prevent similar affairs in the future. This meeting, however, accomplished little because Zelaya not only refused to attend but attacked Honduras and installed his friend Miguel Dávila as President there. The Nicaraguan dictator then attempted to foment a revolution in El Salvador, apparently hoping to pave the way for a new union of Central America under his own leadership. When Guatemala prepared to resist his plans a general war was imminent. Again the United States and Mexico offered their mediation, and this time Zelaya was compelled by diplomatic pressure to agree to send representatives to Washington to discuss the settlement of all outstanding Central American problems.

The Washington Conference of 1907, at which all five republics were represented, adopted a series of important treaties. It was agreed that all international disputes in Central America should be submitted in the future to a permanent court consisting of one judge from each state. Honduras, up to that time a battleground for her stronger neighbors, was to be neutralized. The five governments promised to restrict the activities of political refugees from other states and to refrain from any encouragement to revolutionary movements. A number of conventions looking toward a closer coöperation in different economic and cultural fields were adopted. Some of these had little practical result, but they were an expression of the desire of the Central American statesmen to pave the way for the eventual reconstitution of the union.

The new treaties might have assured peace if the signatory governments had acted in good faith, but neither Zelaya nor Estrada Cabrera respected them. Zelaya continued to aid revolutionary attempts in El Salvador until United States naval forces were ordered to intercept his filibustering expeditions. On the other hand, both El Salvador and Guatemala were accused of aiding a revolution against Zelaya's ally, the President of Honduras, and this affair would have brought on a war involving all four countries if the United States and Mexico had not made strong representations. The matter was referred to the newly established Central American court, which absolved Guatemala and Honduras from the charges against them. Unfortunately it seemed clear that political considerations rather than the weight of the evidence had influenced the votes of several judges and the court lost much prestige as a result.

The First American Intervention in Nicaragua

Relations between the United States and Nicaragua were by this time thoroughly bad, for there had been disputes over claims and other matters as well as friction arising from Zelaya's violations of the 1907 treaties. The authorities at Washington were thus predisposed to sympathize with a revolution that started on the east coast of Nicaragua in 1909, and they openly took sides when the government's forces executed two American soldiers of fortune who were in the revolutionists' employ. Secretary Knox told the Nicaraguan chargé d'affaires that the Zelaya regime was "a blot upon the history of Nicaragua" and expressed the conviction that the revolution represented "the ideals and the will of a majority of the Nicaraguan people." Diplomatic relations were broken off, and were not resumed even after Zelaya resigned the presidency in favor of Dr. José Madriz, a generally respected liberal from León. When the revolutionists were defeated in the interior and driven back to their original base at Bluefields, the American naval commander refused to permit the government forces to attack them there, on the ground that fighting in the town would destroy the property of Americans and other foreigners. Soon afterward, in August, 1910, Madriz' regime collapsed, chiefly because its supporters felt that the attitude of the United States made their cause hopeless.

The victorious revolutionists set up a government at Managua, but it was soon clear that their regime was not likely to survive without outside help. It was headed by General Juan J. Estrada, formerly Zelaya's governor at Bluefields, who had been promised the provisional presidency as an inducement to join the revolution with the troops under his command. One of his principal advisers was another liberal, General José María Moncada, who had been a personal enemy of Zelaya. The other leaders of the revolution, and the overwhelming majority of the victorious army, were conservatives. Their most popular chieftain was General Emiliano Chamorro, the hero of many past revolts, but there were rival factions headed by General Luis Mena and by Adolfo Díaz. The group in power was thus weakened by internal dissensions and mutual distrust, while the liberals were still strong numerically and united in their desire to regain control. It was only through the good offices of the representative of the United States, Thomas C. Dawson, that the revolutionary leaders were persuaded to accept a program under which Estrada became President and Díaz Vice-President for a two-year term. At the same time they agreed that the pressing question of foreign claims should be dealt with by a commission in which the United States should participate and that a foreign loan, secured by a customs collectorship, should be obtained to relieve the desperate financial situation.

A treaty providing for the customs collectorship was signed on June 6, 1911. It was never ratified, because the United States Senate withheld its approval, but while it was still pending two New York banking firms which had obtained the contract for the proposed bond issue made a small short-term loan to meet Nicaragua's most pressing needs. To secure this, they established a customs collectorship under an American citizen named by them and approved by the Department of State. They also helped Nicaragua to establish a national bank and to reform the depreciated paper currency, and acted as agents of the Republic in making an agreement to resume service at a reduced rate of interest on a loan which Zelaya had obtained in 1909 from a British syndicate. The American bankers were thus deeply involved in the situation when the failure of the treaty made the proposed larger loan impossible. Nicaragua could not repay the advances already made, and in fact required several further small advances during the next two years. The customs collectorship was continued, and in 1913 the bankers bought a 51 per cent interest in the National Bank and in the national railroad, both of which they were already managing.

Meanwhile, factional rivalries made the political situation worse. A constituent assembly was elected, but Estrada dissolved it when he found that it was controlled by the adherents of Chamorro. The latter went into exile, but when a new assembly was elected it was dominated by friends of Mena, who was Minister of War. On May 9, 1911, Mena forced Estrada and his chief minister, Moncada, to resign and made Díaz President. Mena remained as Minister of War, but in 1912, when he had the constituent assembly elect him President for the term beginning in 1913, Díaz removed him and placed Chamorro at the head of the army. Most of the government's forces followed Mena in a revolt in which the liberals also joined, and the government would have been overthrown if the United States had not intervened at Díaz' request and suppressed the movement by force. Seven American soldiers were killed in the fighting.

For thirteen years after this a legation guard of about a hundred American marines was stationed at Managua. This small force was regarded in Nicaragua as a symbol of the determination of the United States to uphold the existing government, and its presence enabled the conservative party to remain in power despite growing opposition. Adolfo Díaz was reëlected as President, and was succeeded by Emiliano Chamorro in 1917, after the American Minister informed the liberal candidate that he would not be recognized if elected. Diego Manuel Chamorro, a relative of Emiliano, became President in 1921.

The United States sought by its intervention in Nicaragua not only to promote peace within the Republic and in Central America as a whole, but to improve the disorganized condition of the government's finances and thus to remove one possible cause of intervention by other foreign nations. Despite the failure of the loan treaty, upon which the whole program had rested, something was accomplished. An efficient customs service was created, the fluctuating and rapidly depreciating paper currency was stabilized, and service on the British debt, in default after the revolution, was resumed. The government nevertheless was constantly in financial difficulties, and payments for supplies and salaries were greatly in arrears. When the European war temporarily dislocated the country's commerce in 1914, both the New York bankers and the English bondholders were compelled to agree to a suspension of payments due them, and even the new currency system seemed about to break down.

Partly with the idea of affording some financial relief to the Nicaraguan government, the United States entered into the Bryan-Chamorro Treaty of 1914, which provided for the payment of $3,000,000 to Nicaragua in return for the exclusive right to construct a transisthmian canal in her territory. The United States was also to obtain naval bases in the Gulf of Fonseca and on the Corn Islands in the Caribbean Sea. This agreement brought angry protests from Costa Rica and El Salvador. Costa Rica maintained that she had a right to be consulted before Nicaragua made any grant for canal purposes in the San Juan River, and pointed out that this right had been specifically affirmed by President Cleveland when he arbitrated a boundary dispute between Nicaragua and Costa Rica in 1888. El Salvador claimed that a naval base in the Gulf of Fonseca would imperil Nicaragua's neighbors and also that the waters of the Gulf belonged jointly to the three states which bordered upon it. After futile protests to Nicaragua and to the United States, these two countries brought suits against Nicaragua in the Central American Court of Justice. Both obtained decisions condemning Nicaragua's action in entering into the treaty, but not declaring the treaty itself invalid.

The United States and Nicaragua refused to recognize the Court's right to pass judgment in the matter, and Nicaragua soon afterward denounced the convention under which the Court operated. An important part of the peace machinery set up by the 1907 treaties thus disappeared. The Court had accomplished little of value in ten years of existence, but it was unfortunate that the United States should have been partly responsible for its demise. The naval bases contemplated by the Bryan-Chamorro Treaty were never established, and there is no immediate prospect that the Canal will be built.

The $3,000,000 was paid to Nicaragua, but only after a long dispute as to the way in which it would be used. The bankers, relying on promises by Nicaragua, maintained that their claims and those of the British bondholders should be paid first, but the Department of State insisted that other American creditors should have equal consideration. A compromise was finally reached in the Financial Plan of 1917, which limited the Nicaraguan Government's current expenditures to a fixed sum each month and made the balance of its revenues available for the payment of debts. The operation of this plan, and of a similar plan adopted in 1920, was supervised by a High Commissioner, appointed by the Secretary of State at Washington, so that for some years there was a considerable measure of American control over Nicaragua's finances. Under both plans large sums were available for debt payment, and by 1924 the government had discharged its debts to the American bankers and repurchased the latter's stock in the National Bank and the national railroad. Even after the bankers had no further financial interest in Nicaragua, however, they continued for several years, at the government's request, to manage both of these companies.

Dollar Diplomacy in Other Central American States

The same motives that inspired its action in Nicaragua led the government of the United States to interest itself in the affairs of other Central American countries. The Taft administration, believing that financial mismanagement was the chief cause of instability and the most likely pretext for European intervention in the Caribbean, was especially interested in the establishment of some form of control over revenues and the refunding of the existing foreign debts, which were in default in every Central American state except El Salvador.

The United States had endeavored to promote a reorganization of Honduras' finances at the same time it was drawing up the unsuccessful loan treaty with Nicaragua. Honduras' foreign debt, originating in bond issues floated under scandalous circumstances in London between 1867 and 1870, had long been in default, and by 1909, with the accumulation of interest, had reached an amount which the country could never be expected to pay. After long negotiations, the bondholders agreed to accept somewhat less than four cents on the dollar from funds to be provided from an American loan secured by a customs collectorship. The plan had to be abandoned, however, when neither the Honduran Congress nor the Senate at Washington would approve the treaty with the United States under which the customs collectorship was to be established. Years later, in 1926, the British bondholders agreed to accept thirty annual remittances of £40,000 each in full payment of a nominal debt of approximately £30,000,000.

While the Nicaragua and Honduras treaties were under consideration, Secretary of State Knox expressed a willingness to help bring about financial reforms in all of the Central American states, but his proffers of assistance met with no very warm reception. Costa Rica forestalled possible interference by reaching an agreement with her European creditors in 1911. In Guatemala, Estrada Cabrera, who had been especially shameless in his treatment of foreign creditors, entered into negotiations with an American banking syndicate which proposed a refunding plan, but all of the State Department's efforts to bring about an agreement were futile. The wily dictator avoided any definite action until 1913. Then, when the British Government sent a warship to Puerto Barrios, he simply resumed payments on the existing debt.

El Salvador at this time had no serious disputes with foreign creditors.

In 1922, however, in order to obtain a loan for public works, the government agreed to permit the supervision of its customs administration by American bankers, with a proviso that the actual collection of the customs revenues should be taken over in case of default by an official nominated by the bankers with the approval of the Secretary of State of the United States. All disputes under the contract were to be referred to a member of the United States federal judiciary. These provisions, however, were not made effective when El Salvador defaulted in 1932.

The Non-Recognition Policy and the Tinoco Affair in Costa Rica

The United States was somewhat more successful in its efforts to promote political stability. The overthrow of Zelaya had been a warning to other potential trouble makers, and energetic diplomatic representations usually sufficed to prevent flagrant violations of the Washington treaties in the years that followed. Discontented elements were thus cut off from outside aid, and outbreaks within a country were frequently discouraged by the prompt appearance of an American warship at the nearest port. For a time, revolutions almost seemed to have become a thing of the past. Estrada Cabrera remained in undisputed control in Guatemala, while small groups of political leaders passed on the presidency from one to another in Nicaragua and El Salvador. In Honduras the conservatives ousted Zelaya's friend Dávila in 1910, and remained in control until 1919, first under Manuel Bonilla and after 1915 under Francisco Bertrand. In all of the republics except Costa Rica elections continued to be little more than a farce, and the policy of the United States tended to strengthen the position of any regime that outwardly observed constitutional forms. This was especially true after President Wilson enunciated his policy of refusing to recognize governments coming into power by force in Latin America.

The first test of the non-recognition policy in Central America came, strangely enough, in Costa Rica. In the election held in that country in 1914 no candidate received a majority of the popular vote, and Alfredo González was made President by the Congress under circumstances which cast some doubt on the validity of his tenure. González made many enemies by his advocacy of heavy taxes on wealth, and in January, 1917, he was overthrown by a *coup d'état* led by Federico Tinoco, the Minister of War, who promptly had himself elected President. Nearly all of the country's political groups were prepared to coöperate with the new administration, but the United States publicly denounced Tinoco and warned American citizens against business dealings with him. This attitude encouraged the opposition, though the United States did not countenance open revolutionary movements, and Tinoco remained in power for two years only by dictatorial methods. In 1919 he was overthrown by a revolution headed by Julio Acosta, who was later elected President. Costa Rica thereupon resumed her normal orderly political life.

Political Events, 1919–23

The Tinoco affair and a revolution by which the liberals returned to power in Honduras in 1919 disturbed the relative tranquility that the Isthmus had been enjoying. A still more important new element entered the picture when Estrada Cabrera was overthrown in Guatemala. Partly because the United States made clear its disapproval of repressive measures, the old dictator had failed to break up an opposition party that had been organized in 1919, ostensibly to work for a Central American Union. The movement rapidly gained strength, and by April, 1920, it had so affected the President's prestige that the Congress ventured to impeach him and to elect Carlos Herrera, a wealthy business man, as President. There was some fighting, because a part of the army remained loyal, but order was restored when Estrada Cabrera capitulated. He was imprisoned for some months, but later released and permitted to live quietly in Guatemala until his death in 1924.

There were still many persons who looked upon the reëstablishment of a federal republic as the highest aspiration of Central American statesmanship, and the victory of the unionist party in Guatemala made it seem possible that this ideal might now be attained. In December, 1920, a conference met at San José, Costa Rica, to draw up a treaty of union. A quarrel over the validity of the Bryan-Chamorro Treaty caused Nicaragua to withdraw from the meeting, but the other four states signed an agreement. Though Costa Rica, traditionally reluctant to become involved in her neighbors' political affairs, failed to ratify this, Guatemala, Honduras, and El Salvador went ahead with the plan and set up a provisional federal council at Tegucigalpa in June, 1921. Before this body had begun to exercise any real authority, however, a *coup d'état* in Guatemala on December 6, 1921, drove the unionist party from power and killed the whole project.

By 1922 there was political unrest and a revival of international tensions throughout the Isthmus. Relations between the new regime at Tegucigalpa and the somewhat weak government of Diego Manuel Chamorro in Nicaragua were especially bad, and each was accusing the other of encouraging revolutionary activity on the frontier. There was also bad feeling between the Guatemalan government and the other partners in the abortive union. The 1907 treaties, which had been relied upon to prevent international friction of this sort, seemed to have lost much of their efficacy.

The United States consequently invited the five republics to a conference at Washington at which a new set of Central American treaties were signed early in 1923. These were in general similar to the treaties of 1907, except that a new form of court, consisting of a panel of Central American and foreign judges from which the parties to a dispute could select a tribunal in each case which arose, took the place of the five permanent, politically appointed judges of the old court. The pledges to settle all disputes by peaceful means and not to give aid or permit aid to be given to revolutionists conspiring against the government of another Central American country were reiterated, and machinery for enforcing these pledges was provided in the form of international commissions of inquiry to investigate disputes over questions of fact. The United States became a party to the convention that provided for these commissions.

The new treaties also contained in more explicit form a provision which had appeared in the 1907 treaties but which had had little application in practice. The five countries agreed not to recognize a government coming into power in a Central American country by revolution or *coup d'état* against a recognized government, so long as the freely elected representatives of the people had not constitutionally reorganized the country, and even after such reorganization not to recognize a new government headed by one of the leaders in the revolutionary movement or by any one who had held certain high offices in the preceding government. Revolutions were thus to be made unattractive by preventing those who organized them from enjoying the fruits of victory. The significance of the provision was greatly enhanced when the United States announced that it would follow the same principle in its own policy in Central America.

The non-recognition provision received its first application after a protracted and destructive civil war in Honduras which overthrew President López Gutiérrez and brought the conservatives back into power in 1924. The fighting was ended and a provisional government established through the mediation of the United States. The chief leader of the conservatives, General Tiburcio Carías, had been the party's candidate in the election of 1923, and now expected to become President as a matter of course when new elections were held; but he was compelled to withdraw when the United States declared that he would not be recognized if elected. Dr. Paz Barahona, another conservative but a civilian, became President instead.

The Second Intervention in Nicaragua

Another application of the non-recognition principle, in 1926, helped to involve the United States in one of the most unfortunate episodes of its Caribbean policy. Nicaragua was still ruled by the conservative party, which had been able to remain in power because its opponents believed that the continued presence of the legation guard meant that it had the support of the United States. This situation had long since become an embarrassment to the American government, but the Department of State hesitated to withdraw the guard and thus almost certainly precipitate a civil war. Instead, it pressed the Nicaraguan government to hold a free election. Its efforts met with little success in 1920, but after taking office President Diego Manuel Chamorro employed an American expert, Dr. Harold W. Dodds, to draw up a new electoral law and assist in its application. In November, 1923, the Nicaraguan government was informed that the United States intended to withdraw the legation guard upon the installation of a new administration at Managua in January, 1925. Secretary Hughes pointed out that the new government should be in a strong position if it were the result of a really free election, and he offered the assistance of American experts not only in holding the election but also in training an efficient constabulary to maintain order after the marines were withdrawn.

While this note was in the mail, President Diego Chamorro died and was succeeded by the Vice-President, Bartolomé Martínez. When

Martínez showed a desire to be the conservative candidate in the approaching election, he was opposed by Emiliano Chamorro, who was still the chief figure in the party, and he therefore turned to the liberals and formed an alliance with them. He was forced to relinquish his own presidential aspirations when the United States pointed out that he could not legally be elected under the Nicaraguan constitution, but he threw his support to a coalition that nominated Carlos Solórzano, a conservative, as president, and Dr. Juan Bautista Sacasa, a liberal, as vice-president. When the date of the election approached, he declined to accept any further assistance from the American experts who had helped earlier with the registration of voters. No one was surprised when the government candidate defeated Chamorro, the conservative nominee, by a substantial majority.

When Solórzano took office, in January, 1925, he asked that the legation guard remain at Managua pending the organization of the proposed constabulary. His government showed little zeal in creating the new police force, however, and in August, 1925, the American marines left the country. Disturbances began almost immediately. The new President had little ability or political following, and his administration was weakened from the start by distrust and rivalry between the conservatives and liberals among whom the principal offices were divided. In August, 1925, two liberals withdrew from the cabinet after a military demonstration led by the President's brother-in-law, and in October the conservatives obtained full control by a *coup d'état* engineered by General Chamorro. The latter now sought to make himself president without open departure from legal forms. First the Vice-President, Dr. Sacasa, was forced to flee the country, and then the Congress, from which several supporters of the coalition had been expelled, named Chamorro first *designado*. He thus assumed the executive power early in 1926 when Solórzano was "given" a leave of absence.

Both the United States and the other Central American governments refused to recognize the new regime, for the case fell clearly within the provisions of the 1923 treaty. The liberals almost immediately started a revolt on the east coast, and this gradually developed into one of the most bitterly fought civil wars in the Republic's troubled history. The United States vainly endeavored to bring about an agreement between the contending factions. It finally persuaded Chamorro to withdraw from the presidency so that a government with some claim to constitutionality might be established; and in November, 1926, the Congress, reorganized to include most of the members expelled by Chamorro, chose Adolfo Díaz as President. The United States recognized him, but the liberals continued the war. Dr. Sacasa, the Vice-President, returned to Nicaragua in December, 1926, and set up a government on the east coast. When his regime was recognized by Mexico and began to receive arms from that country, the situation became worse, for the United States, which had been greatly concerned at President Calles' attitude toward American interests, had no wish to see the Mexican revolutionary philosophy spread through Central America.

American marines had already landed at several places on the east coast to protect Americans and other foreigners, and in January, 1927, the legation guard was reëstablished at Managua. By March 15 the American forces in the country amounted to 2,000 men. After Díaz was recognized, the American government sold him arms and helped him to obtain a loan from New York bankers. With this help he was able to maintain himself in the west, but it was increasingly clear that he was not strong enough to carry the war to the revolutionists on the east coast. Meanwhile much of the country was in a state of anarchy, and marauding brigands made the situation of non-combatants intolerable even outside the zones of military operations.

The war seemed thus to be developing into a stalemate, and in April, 1927, President Coolidge sent Mr. Henry L. Stimson to Nicaragua to insist on a settlement. After brief negotiations, both sides agreed to surrender their arms to the American forces in return for a promise that the United States would supervise a free election in 1928. To assure fair play, a constabulary was to be trained by American officers, and until this was ready for service the American marines were to maintain order. Díaz continued as President, but liberals were restored to many of the positions which they had held in the coalition government before Chamorro's *coup d'état*.

In the negotiations that led to this settlement the liberals were represented by General José María Moncada, the principal leader of the revolutionary army. Sacasa and his civilian advisers were inclined to object to the arrangement, but they made no effort to prolong the war. The greater part of the forces on both sides cheerfully surrendered their weapons, and a few recalcitrants were forcibly disarmed. The population as a whole was relieved and pleased that the war had ended. It seemed probable that the program of pacification would be carried through without great difficulty. Matters took on a different aspect, however, when Augusto César Sandino suddenly attacked and very nearly overwhelmed a garrison of American marines and Nicaraguan constabulary at Ocotal in July.

Sandino, one of Moncada's lesser generals, had broken his agreement to disband his forces and had escaped with them into the sparsely inhabited northern provinces. He never had more than a few hundred men under arms, but the mountainous, heavily forested terrain encouraged guerrilla warfare and made it difficult for the American marines to catch and destroy his forces. As he attracted more and more attention by ambushing small patrols or raiding unprotected towns and plantations, he won much sympathy in Latin America and among anti-imperialists in the United States. His movement thus took on a significance far beyond its actual military importance. It did more to create Latin American ill-will than any other episode in our foreign policy since the "taking" of Panama.

Sandino's operations had less effect in Nicaragua itself. Peace was restored in the more important sections of the country, and the new constabulary, the *Guardia Nacional*, became a fairly efficient body under its American officers. The presidential election, supervised by General Frank R. McCoy, was held late in 1928 under conditions satisfactory to both parties. General Moncada was the liberal candidate, and Señor Adolfo Benard was nominated by the conservatives after the United States had pointed out that the Nicaraguan constitution would make General Chamorro's election illegal. Moncada won, and was peacefully inaugurated on January 1, 1929.

Shortly before the election both candidates agreed that the winner would ask for American supervision of the election of 1932, hoping in this way to diminish the possibility of renewed party strife in the meantime. Moncada not only honored this agreement but also arranged to have American officers conduct the congressional election in 1930. In both cases the liberals won, despite some dissension within the party. The President who took office in January, 1933, was Dr. Juan Bautista Sacasa, the titular leader of the revolt of 1926–7.

Sandino had continued to make trouble. In 1931, when an earthquake destroyed Managua and killed nearly 1,000 people, he took advantage of the general confusion to sack Cabo Gracias on the east coast, murdering nine North Americans and a number of other civilians. In January, 1933, however, the last of the American marines were withdrawn from Nicaragua and the objective for which the rebels had ostensibly been fighting was accomplished. At the same time Sandino was confronted by an agreement between the liberals and conservatives to coöperate energetically against him, and in February, 1933, he made peace with the Nicaraguan government.

Political Events in the Other Republics, 1923–1933

Elsewhere in the Isthmus, the decade that followed the Washington Conference of 1922–3 was relatively peaceful. The moral support given to constituted governments by the United States discouraged revolutions, and loans floated in the American market helped to make possible railroad and road construction and extensive municipal improvements in Guatemala, El Salvador, and Costa Rica. Even Honduras, at that time the world's greatest producer of bananas, enjoyed a relative prosperity.

Internal political conditions still varied greatly from country to country. Costa Rica resumed her orderly political life, and the highly respected ex-President Ricardo Jiménez succeeded Julio Acosta in 1924. Another of the country's great elder statesmen, Cleto González Víquez, was elected in 1928 and Jiménez was reëlected in 1932. At that time one of the defeated candidates attempted a revolt, but surrendered after three days of fighting in the capital.

In Honduras there had been two free elections, in each of which the opposition candidate had been victorious. As the result of these, Vicente Mejía Colindres succeeded Paz Barahona in 1929, and General Tiburcio Carías, the conservative leader, became President in 1933.

In El Salvador there had been increasing dissatisfaction with the continued dominance of the Meléndez-Quiñónez family. Pío Romero Bosque, who was made President by Alfonso Quiñónez in 1927, repudiated his predecessor's leadership and held a relatively free election at the end of his term in 1931. Arturo Araujo became President, but he was removed a few months later by General Maximiliano Martínez, his Minister of War. The other Central American countries and the United States refused to recognize Martínez, because he was ineligible under the 1923 treaty, but he remained in power, after suppressing with much unnecessary bloodshed what was described as a "communist" revolt.

The government of Guatemala was still a military dictatorship. Lázaro Chacón became President after the sudden death of Orellana in 1926. There was some disorder when Chacón was incapacitated by illness in

1930, but the United States seems to have intervened diplomatically to insist on the observance of constitutional forms. In 1931, General Jorge Ubico became President.

Central America and the Good Neighbor Policy

The policy of the United States since the Washington Conference of 1907 had done much to promote peace in Central America. International wars had become a thing of the past and the refusal to recognize revolutionary governments had discouraged internal disorders. In 1933 governments which were the result of real elections were in power in at least three of the five republics. On the other hand, some of the American government's actions had aroused much bad feeling. Foreign interference was unpalatable even when it took place at the request of local leaders, and the Nicaraguan affair, especially, aroused fear and distrust of the United States in the other Central American countries. At the same time, interventionist policies were increasingly unpopular in the United States. As a matter of fact, the trend of American policy was away from interference in the Caribbean even before the Nicaraguan civil war, and this trend was accentuated after 1929. After 1933 the Good Neighbor Policy precluded the use of non-recognition or other forms of pressure to promote democratic procedures.

During the later 1930's all of the Central American republics except Costa Rica were ruled by dictators. Martínez remained in power in El Salvador and obtained recognition from his neighbors and from the United States in 1934. Ubico, who was President of Guatemala until 1944, was an able and in many ways a progressive ruler but he sternly repressed all signs of opposition. Carías, in Honduras, soon established a dictatorship, though he had attained his position by a free election. He had to suppress several liberal revolts, but he was able to do away with the constitutional prohibition against reëlection and to remain in office until 1948.

In Nicaragua, the prospect for peace seemed fairly bright when the American marines left in 1933. The two great political parties had not only coöperated in bringing Sandino to terms but had worked out agreements intended to provide guarantees of electoral freedom and minority representation in congress and in other government offices. Before the necessary constitutional amendments could be adopted, however, unforeseen developments caused the plan to miscarry.

Sandino had been permitted to maintain a small private army in the North, and had begun to carry on radical propaganda in the interior, capitalizing on the prestige that he had built up during his resistance to the United States. His activities were particularly offensive to the leaders of the *Guardia Nacional*, who had resented the lenient treatment accorded him by the armistice, and on February 21, 1934, members of this force killed him and his brother just after Augusto Sandino had dined with President Sacasa. The President attempted to have the murderers punished but failed because the *guardia* commander, General Anastacio Somoza, assumed responsibility for their act. It became clear that the constabulary, created to support the constitutional government, had become the government's master. Somoza, in fact, soon indicated that he intended to be the next President. The fact that he was Sacasa's nephew made him constitutionally ineligible, but he solved this difficulty by engineering a revolt that forced Sacasa to resign, and a provisional chief executive was installed by the Congress. Somoza then became the candidate of the Moncada wing of the liberal party while other liberal leaders joined with the conservatives in nominating Leonardo Argüello for President and Emiliano Chamorro for Vice-President. In the election, held while Argüello and Chamorro as well as Sacasa were in exile, Somoza was credited with 117,000 votes, against 1,000 for the opposition ticket. In 1939 at the end of his first term a constituent assembly did away with the constitutional prohibition against reëlection, and voted to continue Somoza in office until 1947.

Costa Rica was the only Central American state where republican institutions worked fairly well during the period between 1933 and the end of the Second World War. León Cortés succeeded Ricardo Jiménez in 1936, and Rafael Angel Calderón Guardia became President in 1940. There was some violence in connection with the election of 1944, and much criticism of the way in which it was conducted, but Teodoro Picado, the official candidate, took office without serious difficulty.

Recent Events

The dictators in the four northern countries profited from the help that the United States gave its Latin American allies during the war. All of the Central American governments declared war immediately after Pearl Harbor and coöperated in measures for the defense of the Panama Canal. The United States spent much money on road building, air bases, and projects for developing the production of rubber and other strategic raw materials. An effort was made to open the Pan American Highway for overland traffic to the Canal Zone, but this project was still far from complete at the end of the war. North American expenditures gave the governments larger financial resources and offset the dislocation of normal trade, though they also contributed to an inflation that caused trouble when the war was over.

Martínez nevertheless fell from power in El Salvador in 1944. In April of that year, just after a constituent assembly had extended his term for another five years, there was a military uprising in which a large area in the heart of the capital city was destroyed by airplane bombing and fire. This movement was suppressed, but a month later a general strike forced the President to resign. General Menéndez, who succeeded him, was ousted by Colonel Aguirre in October. Aguirre suppressed a revolt by a civilian liberal group, but he was denied recognition by the other American republics. In January, 1945, Salvador Castaneda Castro, the official candidate, was elected President, after two opposition candidates withdrew from the contest claiming that they had not received fair treatment. During most of Castaneda's term, the country was under a "state of siege," with constitutional guarantees suspended. He was ousted by the army in December, 1948, when it became apparent that he was manoeuvring to have the approaching presidential elections postponed, and a military *junta* took charge. In March, 1950, the head of the *junta*, Major Oscar Osorio, was elected President.

The fall of Martínez encouraged opposition groups in Guatemala. A series of strikes and minor disorders, in which the university students took a leading part, made the President's position untenable, and on July 1, 1944, he turned over the executive power to a *junta* selected by the general staff of the army. This left his friends in control, but in October the Provisional President, General Ponce, was ousted by some of the younger army officers working with civilian liberals. In November Juan José Arévalo received an overwhelming majority in a free election.

Arévalo, a school teacher who had been living during the past ten years in Argentina and was little known in Guatemala, was the candidate of an advanced liberal group that included most of the university students. As President, he sponsored reforms in education and brought about the enactment of advanced labor and social security laws. These affected chiefly the industrial workers in the towns and the employees on the great banana farms of the United Fruit Company, but the position of the Indians was also improved. Under Ubico, the peonage statute had been replaced by a law that compelled each Indian to work a certain number of days in the year, but with somewhat more freedom in choosing employers and bargaining for wages. This "vagrancy" law was repealed by the Arévalo administration, and the Indian, theoretically at least, became a free man. His wages, though still pitifully small, seem to have increased considerably in recent years. Guatemala also began to enjoy freer political institutions, and opposition parties not only participated in elections but sometimes won them. Nevertheless, the government was compelled to suppress many subversive plots and small revolts between 1945 and 1950.

In Honduras Carías announced in 1948 that he would withdraw voluntarily from the presidency at the end of his term. The liberals, who had failed repeatedly to oust him by armed uprisings, nominated the veteran revolutionist Angel Zúñiga Huete as their candidate to succeed him, but before the election they withdrew from the contest, claiming that the government had interfered improperly with their campaign. Consequently, the official candidate, Juan Manuel Gálvez, Carías' Minister of War, was inaugurated as President on January 1, 1949.

Somoza continued to be the *de facto* ruler of Nicaragua. Early in 1947 he permitted the liberal leader Leonardo Argüello to be elected President, but he retained the command of the *Guardia Nacional*. He was thus able to remove Argüello, when the latter after less than four weeks showed an unexpected independence. A constituent assembly chose Victor Manuel Román y Reyes as President. These changes, clearly designed to maintain Somoza's own control over the country, were viewed with disapproval by the other American governments, and most of them refused for several months to recognize the new administration. When Román y Reyes died in May, 1950, Somoza was again elected President.

The worst disorders of the post-war period occurred in Costa Rica. As the end of Picado's term approached there was a strong demand for measures that would prevent a recurrence of the frauds alleged to have been practised in 1944. After a series of strikes and riots, the administration agreed to electoral reforms. When the voting took place in February, 1948, the opposition candidate, Otilio Ulate, obtained a substantial majority over ex-President Calderón Guardia, who had been supported by the government and by Manuel Mora the communist leader. The defeated parties, however, claimed that there had been large-scale frauds, and the Congress, where they had a majority, annulled the election. When Ulate's supporters revolted they had to fight both the government's forces and the communists, who for a time held one of the barracks and the airfield at San José. The revolutionists nevertheless took the capital after about six weeks of fighting. On May 8, 1948, a *junta* headed by the military leader of the revolt, José Figueres, took charge of the government. A constituent assembly elected in December validated Ulate's election but he did not take office until November 8, 1949.

The internal unrest that has plagued all of the Central American states since the end of the war has been aggravated by international tensions. A part of the army that won the civil war in Costa Rica was the so-called "Caribbean legion." This was apparently a group of exiles from various countries that had been organized to attempt the overthrow of dictatorial governments, not only in Central America but in the West Indies, and which was alleged to have the sympathy of "democratic" governments like those in Guatemala and Cuba. The legion's activities were naturally objectionable to Somoza, and he had sent aid to Picado, despite a strong protest from the United States. In December, 1948, supporters of the defeated party, led by ex-President Calderón Guardia, invaded Costa Rica from Nicaragua, and the Costa Rican government appealed to the Council of the Organization of American States. The Council, after an investigation, blamed both parties: Nicaragua for permitting the invasion to occur and Costa Rica for harboring the Caribbean legion. Both countries were asked to abide strictly by the principle of nonintervention, and on February 21, 1949, they signed a treaty of friendship that apparently ended the dispute. The affair marked an epoch in inter-American relations, not only because the dispute was the first to come before the newly established Organization, but also because it suggested that the responsibility which the United States had formerly felt for maintaining peace in Central America would now be shared by all of the nations of the Hemisphere.

25

Cuba

Cuba in the 19th Century

Cuba and the smaller island of Puerto Rico were the only Spanish possessions in America that did not become independent in the first quarter of the nineteenth century. Apparently their people had less desire to break away from the mother country than had the people of Venezuela or the River Plate, even though they complained of many of the same abuses that inspired the revolts elsewhere. One reason, especially in the case of Cuba, was the prosperity that they were enjoying. The British occupation of Habana in 1762, during the Seven Years' War, had opened that port to foreign ships, and a sudden outburst of commercial activity revealed for the first time the colony's potential wealth. After the British withdrew, restrictions on trade with Spain were somewhat relaxed, and at times during the Napoleonic wars foreign vessels were freely admitted to Cuban ports. After 1818 commerce with other countries was generally authorized, though on less favorable terms than commerce with Spain. Meanwhile, beginning in the last years of the eighteenth century, there had been a phenomenal increase in production. After the slave revolt in French Saint Domingue, and the destruction of the rich sugar and coffee plantations of that colony, the cultivation of both of these crops in Cuba became much more profitable. Many refugees from Saint Domingue and many immigrants from Spain came to the island, and the importation of slaves rapidly increased.

The new settlers from Spain were little inclined to revolt, and after the revolution on the mainland started, the loyal population was increased by a further influx of refugees from the colonies there. Creoles who advocated independence consequently made little headway. After 1820 they formed a number of secret revolutionary societies, of which one called "The Suns and Rays of Bolívar" was the most important, but their feeble conspiracies were easily suppressed. The colony's insular position made it practically immune from attack by the patriot armies on the mainland. There was a proposal, in 1825, to free it with help from Colombia and Mexico, but this was discouraged by the United States, partly, perhaps, because North American statesmen hoped to acquire Cuba for themselves, and partly because they feared that a breakdown of Spanish authority might lead to a slave revolt like that in Saint Domingue. This same fear made many conservative Cubans averse to any change.

Growing Opposition to Spanish Rule

Disaffection increased as time went on. Spain's colonial policy changed little after the loss of her mainland possessions, and the island remained under an arbitrary and frequently corrupt regime in which native Cubans had little part. Trade was still subject to burdensome restrictions, and taxation was heavy and unevenly distributed. Continual internal troubles in Spain prevented any intelligent consideration of the problems of her overseas possessions, and even when political reforms were adopted in the mother country they were not extended to the colonies. Worse still, the prosperity of the early nineteenth century did not continue. Coffee production suddenly declined after 1835 because of foreign competition. Sugar growing continued to expand, but the subsidizing of beet raising in Europe diminished the planters' profits.

Nevertheless, it was a long time before any serious revolutionary movement developed. In the first half of the nineteenth century the chief danger to Spain's possession of Cuba came from other powers, and loss of the island to France or England or the United States was probably averted only by the determination of each government that neither of the others should acquire it. To the United States, the fate of Cuba, from which a powerful enemy might control both entrances to the Gulf of Mexico, was vitally important for strategic reasons. Successive generations of American statesmen had hoped that the island would sooner or later become American territory, and in the South especially there was an active desire to add a new and rich slave state to the Union. In 1848 an offer to buy Cuba was summarily rejected by Spain. In the next three years filibustering attacks aroused the same interest and sympathy in the South that later supported Walker's venture in Nicaragua.

The most noted leader of these attacks was Narciso López, a Venezuelan who as a boy had fought first for the patriots and then for the loyalists in his own country. After living several years in Cuba he organized a revolutionary conspiracy there in 1848. When it failed he escaped to the United States and recruited a force of North Americans. The federal authorities checked his first attempt to leave American waters, but in 1850 he eluded them and landed with a small army at Cárdenas, only to be defeated and forced to flee. When he returned to the United States he was prosecuted in the courts, but public sentiment in his favor made it impossible to obtain a conviction, and a year later he sailed for Cuba with a new force. This time he and fifty of his companions were captured and executed.

The López affair nearly brought on a conflict between Spain and the United States and seemed likely for a time to cause complications with other powers. Great Britain and France threatened to send naval forces to protect Cuba. In 1852 they suggested an arrangement by which they would join with the United States in guaranteeing Spain's possession of the island, but the United States refused to sign such a treaty. In 1854 the American ministers to England, France, and Spain met at Ostend in Belgium and let it become known that they were advising the Secretary of State that the United States would be justified under certain conditions in seizing Cuba if Spain refused to sell the island. This "manifesto" was criticised in the United States as well as in Europe. Fortunately the Pierce administration repudiated the policy which it suggested, and as the slavery crisis in the United States grew more acute, interest in Cuban affairs declined.

In 1868, at a time when there was a revolution in Spain itself, a group of Cuban patriots made the first formidable bid for independence. The war that they started dragged on for ten years. Continuing internal troubles in Spain made it difficult for the royal government to suppress the revolt, but there was a strong loyal element in Cuba itself, and the insurgents, despite local successes, were unable to win a decisive victory. Their own dissensions weakened them. In 1873, Carlos Manuel de Céspedes, who had been chosen as Provisional President of the Republic of Cuba, was deposed from leadership, to be captured and executed by the Spaniards a few months later. The war caused much loss of life and much destruction of property, and public opinion in other countries was shocked by reports of atrocities committed. In 1871, for example, the Spanish forces executed eight Cuban students for a trivial offense which they apparently did not commit. In 1873, they shot more than fifty members of the crew of the blockade runner *Virginius*. The majority of these were British or American, and the number killed would have been much greater if the captain of a British cruiser had not intervened by force to stop the executions. This episode might have caused a serious conflict had it not been demonstrated that the *Virginius* was illegally flying the American flag. As it was, Spain paid an indemnity to the families of those killed.

The "*Virginius* affair" was only one of a number of incidents involving injury or death to American citizens and loss of American property, and there was some agitation in the United States for intervention to end the civil war. The American government offered its mediation, with no success, and later discussed with the British government the possibility of further interference. By 1875, however, the reëstablishment of peace in Spain made it possible to send more troops to Cuba, and Máximo Gómez, one of the chief insurgent leaders, was decisively defeated at Puerto Principe. Thereafter the revolution lost much of its strength and early in 1878 most of the leaders agreed to the Treaty of Zanjón, under which they laid down their arms in return for an amnesty and a promise of political reforms.

The Cubans found that this promise meant little, and they had other causes for discontent in the years that followed the war. Taxes continued high, for the expense of the war was added to the already heavy Cuban debt. Much property belonging to insurgent sympathizers had been confiscated during the war and had passed into the hands of peninsular Spaniards. The changes which were being forced on the sugar industry by increasing foreign competition, and especially the concentration of production in larger units financed by Spanish or other foreign capital, also ruined many formerly prosperous creole families.

One conservative creole group which had hitherto been especially interested in the maintenance of the status quo was seriously affected by the abolition of slavery. The importation of slaves, which first assumed large proportions at the end of the eighteenth century, continued through the first half of the nineteenth, despite the legal prohibition of the trade in 1820, and the Negro population eventually outnumbered the white. The liberals in Cuba opposed slavery, and during the ten years' war the revolutionists promised general emancipation after independence was established. Many Negroes obtained their freedom by serving in the army on one side or the other and in 1870, partly in response to pressure from the United States and partly as a conciliatory gesture to the Cubans, the Spanish government decreed the liberty of all children born thenceforth of slave mothers. In 1880 another law provided for gradual emancipation, and in 1886 slavery was totally abolished.

Nevertheless, the island as a whole prospered during the fifteen years after the "Great War," and the chief cause of the revolt which finally brought about independence seems to have been the sudden disappearance of this prosperity. In 1890 the United States placed sugar on the free list, and a reciprocity treaty with Spain a year later assured the Cuban planters the full benefit of this change. They promptly increased their crop by more than 50 per cent, so that it exceeded 1,000,000 tons in 1894, but in that year the Wilson tariff suddenly restored the American duty. At the same time sugar prices, like other prices, were falling rapidly as a result of the world depression and Cuba began to suffer severely from poverty and unemployment. The bad economic situation nullified Spain's belated attempt to placate political discontent in Cuba by a grant of partial home rule early in 1895, for a new revolution broke out before it was possible to put the measure in execution.

The War for Independence

The leading spirit in the revolt was José Martí, who had worked for Cuban independence since the ten years' war, organizing Cuban exiles in the United States and other countries and making plans for the movement which now began. Martí was killed in the first weeks of fighting, but the veteran patriot Máximo Gómez carried on as commander in the field. Tomás Estrada Palma, who had been President of the revolutionary government during a part of the ten years' war, worked for the success of the movement as head of a *junta* in New York and did much to pave the way for the later intervention of the United States.

In Cuba the revolutionists systematically paralyzed the island's economic life and murdered those who did not coöperate with them. On the other side, the Spanish commander, General Weyler, attempted to control the situation by "reconcentrating" the country people in garrisoned towns, where many died of disease and starvation. The fighting thus caused much destruction of property and terrific suffering among non-combatants.

For three years the United States maintained a policy of strict neutrality. Both President Cleveland and President McKinley repeatedly endeavored to persuade Spain to grant the Cubans concessions that would induce them to make peace, and in 1897, when the liberals came into power at Madrid, it seemed possible that a settlement might be reached. General Weyler was recalled, his reconcentration policy was ostensibly, though not actually, abandoned, and the Cubans were offered a large measure of self government. Unfortunately the hatred between the insurgents and the numerous Cubans still loyal to Spain was so bitter that neither group would consider a compromise, and the effort to set up an autonomous Cuban government was a failure. The war dragged on. Its horrors were avidly played up by the "yellow press" in the United States, so that sympathy for the insurgents ran high and there was a rising popular demand for intervention.

The climax came when the U.S.S. *Maine* blew up in Habana harbor in February, 1898, with the loss of 260 men. The cause of the explosion was never ascertained, but the United States alleged that the Spanish authorities had failed to provide the protection due to a warship of a friendly power. The American government demanded reparation and further demanded the abandonment of the reconcentration policy and the granting of an immediate armistice to the rebels, to permit peace negotiations through the mediation of the United States. Spain ultimately acceded to most of these demands but her action came too late. President McKinley, who had hoped for a peaceful solution, could no longer withstand the pressure of Congress and public opinion, and on April 11, 1898, he asked Congress for authority to intervene by force to terminate the Cuban war.

A joint resolution of Congress, approved April 20, declared that "the people of the Island of Cuba are, and of right ought to be, free and independent." It demanded that Spain withdraw from the island, authorized the President to use force against her if necessary, and disclaimed for the United States any intention to exercise sovereignty over the island except for its pacification. Diplomatic relations were broken off and war began.

The Military Government and the Platt Amendment

Less than four months later the Spanish government agreed to a preliminary peace protocol by which it surrendered all claims to Cuba. In the negotiations that followed it endeavored, without success, to have either the United States or the future government of Cuba assume responsibility for the large Cuban debt. It also expressed great concern for the interests of loyal Spanish citizens in the Island, and the United States, to prevent a breakdown in the negotiations, finally agreed to advise any future Cuban government to assume the obligation to protect foreign lives and property—a promise that was later cited as a reason for insisting on the Platt Amendment. The Treaty of Paris, formally ending the war between Spain and the United States, was signed December 10, 1898.

The United States Army set up a military government in Cuba after the Spanish troops withdrew. The never very important Cuban revolutionary government was disregarded, and the patriot army, after some difficulty, was persuaded to disband after receiving $3,000,000 from the United States Treasury. The first task of the American authorities was the restoration of order and the relief of the starving civilian population. After this was accomplished, General Leonard Wood, who became Military Governor in December, 1899, reorganized all branches of the civil administration, set up a school system, and inaugurated a program of sanitation. It was during this period that a commission headed by Dr. Walter Reed demonstrated the truth of a theory which had already been set forth by the Cuban physician Dr. Charles Finlay: that yellow fever was carried by the *stegomyia* mosquito. This discovery for the first time made possible the control of that dreaded disease.

The most important purpose of the occupation was to pave the way for the establishment of an independent Cuban government. There were some North Americans who advocated holding on to the island, and Spain in the peace negotiations had suggested that it be annexed to the United States, but the American government insisted on carrying out the promise embodied in the Joint Resolution of April 20th. To this end, a census was taken, an electoral law was drawn up, and municipal officials were chosen by the voters. The United States felt, however, that its own political and strategic interests, as well as the obligations toward Spain assumed in the Treaty of Paris, required the establishment of a special relationship between itself and the new Cuban government, and General Wood presented his government's views to the Cuban Constitutional Convention that met in November, 1900. In March, 1901, the United States Congress adopted the so-called Platt Amendment to the military appropriation bill for the coming year. This provided that the

United States should not withdraw from Cuba until certain provisions were incorporated in the Republic's constitution and in a permanent treaty with the United States. These provisions, as they appeared in the treaty of May 22, 1903, were as follows:

ARTICLE I

The Government of Cuba shall never enter into any treaty or other compact with any foreign power or powers which will impair or tend to impair the independence of Cuba, nor in any manner authorize or permit any foreign power or powers to obtain by colonization or for military or naval purposes, or otherwise, lodgment in or control over any portion of said island.

ARTICLE II

The Government of Cuba shall not assume or contract any public debt to pay the interest upon which, and to make reasonable sinking-fund provision for the ultimate discharge of which, the ordinary revenues of the Island of Cuba, after defraying the current expenses of the Government, shall be inadequate.

ARTICLE III

The Government of Cuba consents that the United States may exercise the right to intervene for the preservation of Cuban independence, the maintenance of a government adequate for the protection of life, property, and individual liberty, and for discharging the obligations with respect to Cuba imposed by the Treaty of Paris on the United States, now to be assumed and undertaken by the Government of Cuba.

ARTICLE IV

All acts of the United States in Cuba during its military occupancy thereof are ratified and validated, and all lawful rights acquired thereunder shall be maintained and protected.

ARTICLE V

The Government of Cuba will execute, and, as far as necessary, extend the plans already devised, or other plans to be mutually agreed upon, for the sanitation of the cities of the island, to the end that a recurrence of epidemic and infectious diseases may be prevented, thereby assuring protection to the people and commerce of Cuba, as well as to the commerce of the Southern ports of the United States and the people residing therein.

ARTICLE VI

The Island of Pines shall be omitted from the boundaries of Cuba specified in the Constitution, the title thereto being left to future adjustment by treaty.

ARTICLE VII

To enable the United States to maintain the independence of Cuba, and to protect the people thereof, as well as for its own defense, the Government of Cuba will sell or lease to the United States lands necessary for coaling or naval stations, at certain specified points, to be agreed upon with the President of the United States.

The Cubans objected strenuously to what seemed to them a serious restriction on the new Republic's independence, and the opposition in the constitutional convention was only partly allayed by assurances that the third clause of the amendment would not be "synonymous with intermeddling or interference with the affairs of the Cuban Government." The act of Congress left no alternative, however, and on June 12, 1901, the convention accepted the Platt Amendment as an annex to the new constitution.

The Establishment of the Republic

Tomás Estrada Palma was elected President of Cuba in December, 1901, and on May 20, 1902, the military government transferred to him the government of the island. One of his first duties was to settle several pending questions with the United States. In addition to the Permanent Treaty embodying the Platt Amendment, which governed their political relations until 1934, the two governments negotiated an agreement giving the United States the naval station that it still maintains at Guantánamo, and the right, never exercised and later relinquished, to establish another at Bahía Honda. Another treaty, not ratified by the United States until 1925, recognized Cuba's sovereignty over the Isle of Pines. Still more important was the Reciprocity Treaty of December 11, 1902, which gave Cuban products entering the United States a 20 per cent customs preferential as against those of any other nation, a concession that greatly encouraged the Cuban sugar industry.

Cuba's foreign trade, from the beginning, was greater than that of many of the older and more populous Latin American republics. Large investments of foreign capital had developed and were continuing to develop its natural resources. The great majority of the people were nevertheless illiterate and poverty-stricken. Though the proportion of white blood had been increasing through immigration, a substantial part of the inhabitants were still descendants of a race that had been in slavery until ten years before the war for independence.

The Second Intervention

It became evident before the end of Estrada Palma's term that these conditions would make it difficult to operate republican institutions successfully. The President was generally respected and conspicuously honest, but he was not a forceful leader or an experienced executive. He at first attempted to conduct his administration on a non-partisan basis, but factional quarrels made this difficult and a desire to obtain the enactment of urgently needed laws led him finally to seek support from the "moderate" or conservative group in Congress as against the "liberals" who became the opposition. This did little good, so far as legislation was concerned, but it enabled the moderates to control preparations for the presidential elections of December, 1905, with Estrada Palma as their candidate. The liberals refused to take part in the election because they foresaw that they would be beaten, but in August, 1906, some months after Estrada Palma's second inauguration, they started a revolt which rapidly spread through the island.

Estrada Palma, who had made no effort to build up a strong army, promptly appealed to the United States for help. President Roosevelt expressed great reluctance to intervene, but he sent Secretary of War Taft and Assistant Secretary of State Bacon to Cuba to give such aid as they could, and upon their arrival the belligerents agreed to a truce. The American commissioners' investigation convinced them that the recent elections had been vitiated by violence and fraud. They proposed that the President should remain in office, but that all of the other recently chosen officials should resign so that their places might be filled by new elections held under fairer conditions. The liberals seemed inclined to accept this proposal, but the government rejected it. The moderates, in fact, were determined to compel the United States to intervene. First the cabinet and then the President and Vice-President resigned, and their partisans made it impossible to obtain a quorum in Congress. Cuba was left without a government, and on September 29, 1906, Secretary Taft proclaimed the establishment of a provisional regime under his own direction.

The sole purpose of the provisional government was to restore order and hold elections, but this required more than two years. After the delicate task of disarming and disbanding the military forces of both parties had been completed, a census was taken and an advisory commission headed by Colonel Enoch H. Crowder drafted laws covering elections, municipal and provincial government, the civil service, the judiciary, and other matters which should long since have been dealt with by the Cuban Congress. The commission's work met with general approval and was of real permanent value, but the provisional government was less fortunate in dealing with some of its other problems. Charles E. Magoon, who succeeded Taft as Provisional Governor in October, 1906, had a number of American assistants, but the administration as a whole was still in the hands of the "moderate" officials who had served under Estrada Palma. This created a bad situation, which was little improved when the Governor, in accord with a promise made by his predecessor, filled vacancies as they arose with liberals recommended by a party committee. Playing politics did not make for efficiency or honesty in the administration as a whole, and the Governor was accused of permitting improper and extravagant expenditures, of pardoning great numbers of criminals for political reasons, and of undue generosity in awarding concessions and contracts. Competent American historians have exonerated Magoon of the more serious of these charges, but the fact that they were made, and that many Cubans believed them, had an unfortunate effect on subsequent Cuban-American relations.

The provincial and municipal elections in August, 1908, and the national election held three months later were supervised by a board headed by Colonel Crowder. The conservative party, organized by some of the former "moderate" leaders, put forward General Mario García Menocal as its candidate for the presidency. The liberals were divided into two factions, headed by General José Miguel Gómez and Alfredo Zayas, but after their opponents won some unexpected successes in the local elections, they combined forces. Gómez defeated Menocal by a substantial majority and was inaugurated as President on January 28, 1909.

The Era of the "Preventive Policy"

Under the new administration, Cuban political life took on some of the characteristics that were to distinguish it for a long period. Gómez differed from Estrada Palma in many ways. He was popular, astute, and unscrupulous, especially where money was involved, and he retained his followers' loyalty not only by his personal magnetism but by permitting them to profit by their party connections. There were many times after 1907 when Cuban politics seemed little more than a systematic effort to exploit the treasury for the benefit of the professional political class.

This situation was not peculiar to Cuba, but graft was possible there on a relatively larger scale because of the island's great wealth. By 1907 the sugar industry was reaping the full benefit of reciprocity with the

United States, and trade was rapidly increasing. The Cuban government's income was correspondingly large. At a time when Mexico's revenues, in the prosperous years of the Díaz regime, were approximately $3.25 per capita, and Colombia's less than $3.75, Cuba, where geographical conditions favored economical administration and facilitated the construction of roads and public works, was collecting $14 or more per capita. Many of the higher officials, including especially members of Congress, had excessive salaries and allowances, and thousands of persons were carried on the payroll who did no work whatever for the government. The country's prosperity also opened up opportunities for illicit profit in the granting of all sorts of concessions, and the Gómez administration was involved in several highly questionable deals with foreign interests, some of them involving millions of dollars.

The United States made ineffective efforts to prevent some of these transactions, for President Taft and Secretary of State Knox believed that a timely discouragement of policies that might lead a Caribbean government to insolvency and political disorder was better than armed intervention after a breakdown had occurred. This so-called "preventive policy" also led to interference in other matters. In 1913 the American legation successfully opposed the enactment of an "amnesty" bill which would have freed common criminals as well as political offenders, and on two occasions it felt compelled to make threats of intervention to discourage armed revolt.

The first of these was in 1911–12 when an organization of veterans of the war of independence began to agitate for the removal of all office holders who had been on the Spanish side in that struggle. The movement attracted support from many who were dissatisfied with Gómez' political and financial policies, and for a time civil war seemed possible. A warning from the United States, however, united both factions in opposition to outside interference, and the veterans and the President signed an agreement which ended the episode. The Negro revolt of 1912, instigated by colored politicians who claimed that their race had not received its fair share of government offices, was a more serious affair. There was some fighting and some destruction of Cuban and foreign property. The United States landed a force of marines and threatened further action, but order was fortunately restored within a few weeks.

When internal divisions had threatened to defeat the liberals in the election of 1908, Gómez, in order to obtain Zayas' support, had apparently promised that the latter should be the party's candidate in 1912.

There was continued friction between the two leaders, however, and there was more than a suspicion that Gómez, despite his denials, was seeking reëlection for himself. Zayas obtained the liberal nomination, in spite of the President's opposition, but the administration's unfriendly attitude made it impossible for him to win the election and the conservative candidate, General Mario García Menocal, became President on May 20, 1913.

Menocal and the Revolution of 1917

Menocal had been educated in the United States and had worked for several years as a young man with American engineers in the Nicaraguan canal company. He had served brilliantly in the war for independence, rising from the ranks to a major generalcy, and had later been the successful manager of a great sugar plantation. Independently wealthy, he had no need to indulge in dishonest practices for his own benefit. His first term was a period of increasing prosperity, for the war abroad cut off European supplies of beet sugar and encouraged a rapid increase in Cuban cane production. Nevertheless, the President did not achieve any great popularity, and as the election of 1916 approached it became evident that his candidacy for reëlection would meet with obstacles.

Menocal, like Gómez, had pledged himself not to seek a second term, but he seems to have changed his mind under pressure from friends and family. He obtained the conservative nomination only with difficulty and by the use of questionable methods, and his chances for reëlection were not improved when the liberals succeeded in composing their factional difficulties and united in supporting Alfredo Zayas. In the campaign that followed, and during the voting, workers on both sides endeavored to influence the outcome by violence and fraud. The number of votes cast greatly exceeded any possible estimate of the number of qualified electors. The liberals were not at too great a disadvantage because they controlled the police in several provinces and municipalities and because Menocal did not attempt to make full use of the government's power, and on the face of the earlier returns the opposition seemed to have won. At this point, however, the government began to intercept and apparently to alter the reports coming in from the provinces. The liberals protested and were upheld by the Central Electoral Board and the Supreme Court, which awarded them the majority in two of the most important provinces. This seemed to make a liberal victory certain unless the government obtained a phenomenal majority in the new elections that were ordered in certain districts of two other provinces.

In February, 1917, before the new elections could be held, the liberals revolted, with ex-President Gómez as their leader. They were convinced that the government intended to steal the election, and hoped apparently to bring about a repetition of the events of 1906. In this they were disappointed. A small force of American marines was landed in Oriente Province and kept there until after the close of the European war, but only to protect foreign life and property. Instead of intervening, the United States issued public statements severely condemning the uprising, and its attitude was an important factor in the collapse of the revolt after a few weeks of fighting. Meanwhile the elections were completed and Menocal began his second term as President.

The "Dance of the Millions" and The Crowder Mission

On April 7, before the revolt was completely suppressed, Cuba followed the example of the United States in declaring war on Germany. The Republic's chief contribution to the allied cause was a further increase in the production of sugar and the sale of the 1917–18 and 1918–19 crops to an international committee at fixed prices, high enough to assure substantial profits to the growers but probably not so high as those they might have obtained in free trading. The expansion of the industry was aided by large investments of private American capital and by a $15,000,000 loan from the United States Treasury, and all classes enjoyed undreamed-of prosperity.

This prosperity attained its peak after the war when the governmental control of sugar sales ceased. For a brief period prices skyrocketed to unbelievable levels, until an all-time high of 22.5 cents per pound, at Cuban ports, was reached in May, 1920. Every one felt rich, and there was a period of governmental and private extravagance that has since been called "the dance of the millions." Then, suddenly and with little warning, came the inevitable collapse. In December, 1920, the price of sugar had declined to four cents. Prices of other merchandise had also fallen with the depression in other parts of the world, and importers and merchants as well as planters were hard hit. The banks, which had made excessive loans on the basis of high prices, were in even worse shape. To prevent complete collapse the government was compelled in October, 1920, to proclaim a moratorium, which was continued from month to month during the first part of 1921.

With matters in this state, the time arrived for a new presidential election. In 1919, at the suggestion of the United States Government, both parties had invited General Enoch H. Crowder to come to Cuba to draw up a new electoral law, and the United States had made it clear that it would use its influence to prevent a repetition of what happened in 1916. It even sent a number of observers to watch the conduct of the election, but these had no real authority and they were powerless to prevent the violent and fraudulent practices which no mere changes in the law could abolish. The result was an apparent victory by a narrow margin for Alfredo Zayas, who had become Menocal's candidate after Zayas' followers, now called the "Popular Party," had joined the conservatives to oppose the liberals under José Miguel Gómez. The liberals, who participated in the election only because the United States urged them to, promptly demanded new elections in a great number of districts. The conservatives obstructed the consideration of their appeals by the electoral boards and the courts, and there was every prospect that an armed revolt would make the country's plight even worse than it was.

In an effort to clear up a situation which might well have led to another armed intervention, the President of the United States sent General Crowder to Cuba as his personal representative in January, 1921. In response to Crowder's urging, the electoral machinery began to work and the two presidential candidates reached an agreement which should have assured fair play in the new elections that were ordered in about 20 per cent of the voting districts. At the last moment, however, the liberals refused to participate and asked that a new general election be held under American control. The United States could not comply with this request, and Zayas was consequently inaugurated as President of Cuba in May, 1921.

General Crowder also devoted himself energetically to Cuba's economic problems. At his suggestion, the moratorium was gradually lifted and business began to revive, but it was not possible to prevent the failure of every bank in the island except the branches of two foreign institutions. This made worse the government's already bad financial situation. Menocal's second administration had been more extravagant and corrupt than any of its predecessors, and governmental expenditures had exceeded even the very large revenues of the war period. There was thus a considerable floating debt, which increased as income fell off without a corresponding reduction in expenditures.

General Crowder persuaded Zayas to make great reductions in the budget and helped him to get a small emergency loan which met the government's most pressing needs. It was obvious that only a much larger loan could put the government on its feet, but the United States refused to approve this pending assurances that Zayas would remedy some of the bad practices which had grown up under his predecessors. General Crowder demanded a long series of reforms, including the restriction of expenditures, the cancellation of illegal or improper contracts, and especially the reorganization of the national lottery, from which a great number of favored politicians were making illicit profits. After several months of negotiation, many of the measures that he advocated were adopted, and the President, as an evidence of good faith, appointed a cabinet that seemed to give assurance that the proposed reforms would be effective. In November, 1922, therefore, the United States gave its approval of the proposed $50,000,000 loan. Two months later General Crowder's mission as personal representative of the President terminated, though he remained in Cuba as American Ambassador.

Zayas' interest in reform ceased when the money from the loan had been received. With loud assertions that Cuba would no longer tolerate foreign interference in her internal affairs, he dismissed the "honest cabinet" and proceeded to undo most of its work. As the government's revenues gradually increased economy was forgotten and the government was no less extravagant and corrupt than former administrations. Discontent with its policies found expression in a small revolt started by the "Veterans' and Patriots' Association" in 1924, but this was easily suppressed.

The Machado Administration, 1925–1933

In 1924 ex-President Menocal defeated Zayas for the conservative nomination and the President avenged himself by supporting Gerardo Machado, the liberal candidate. The latter won easily, in an apparently fair election, and took office in May, 1925. Machado was a veteran of the war for independence and had been a successful business man. During his first term things went fairly well. The sugar industry was already feeling the effects of world overproduction, but the flotation of large foreign loans for public works and the growth of the tourist trade, resulting partly from prohibition in the United States, helped to hide the fundamental unsoundness of the economic situation.

By a skilful distribution of offices and other favors, Machado persuaded all three party machines, the liberal, the conservative, and the popular, to nominate him for reëlection in 1928. Changes in the electoral law which perpetuated the control of each party by a small group of men, and the large "slush fund" provided by the national lottery, helped to prevent any effective opposition. The lottery was still one of the great causes of corruption in Cuban politics, for the tickets were regularly sold on the streets for much more than their face value and the extra money went not to the government, which owned the enterprise, but to "collectors" who had the privilege of distributing stated quantities of tickets. It has been estimated that nearly a third of the $31,000,000 that the people of Cuba spent annually on the lottery represented illegal profits of this sort.[1] Before the election, a constitutional amendment provided that the presidential term should be six instead of four years.

These proceedings aroused much antagonism, and discontent increased as Cuba felt more and more severely the effects of the depression. Machado made matters worse by his increasingly dictatorial policy. He had trouble especially with the students of the University of Habana, who noisily opposed his reëlection and continued their agitation during the next four years, even after many of them had been killed or imprisoned and the University had been closed. Other opposition groups became more active. After the army easily supressed a small revolt in 1931, the discontented elements began a campaign of terrorism and sabotage which led to still more harshly repressive measures by the police. Murders and bombings and cruel official reprisals received much publicity in the United States and brought about a growing demand for interference, voiced frequently by the same people who had criticized intervention in other Caribbean countries.

In June, 1933, most of the underground revolutionary groups agreed to accept the mediation of the American Ambassador, Mr. Sumner Welles, in an effort to restore order. They insisted, however, that Machado leave office, which he refused to do. Negotiations dragged on for some weeks until a general strike, which paralyzed commercial activity in Habana, and a bloody clash between the populace and the police brought matters to a head. On August 11, the army, which had

[1] Chapman, *History of the Cuban Republic*, pp. 555–6.

been Machado's mainstay, demanded his resignation. The next day he left the country.

Revolutionary Governments, 1933–34

Machado's constitutional successor was Dr. Carlos Manuel de Céspedes. De Céspedes was a former ambassador at Washington, not hitherto very active in politics but generally respected and apparently acceptable to several of the opposition political groups. Most of these were represented in his cabinet and it was hoped that he would be able with the moral support of the United States to restore normal political conditions. It would have been difficult, however, for any government to restore peace while conditions were what they were in the sugar industry.

The output of the Cuban sugar *centrales,* about one million long tons in the first years of independence and four million during the First World War, had reached five million long tons by 1929. Too much production deprived Cuba of the benefit of the preferential duty under the reciprocity treaty of 1903, because competition among her producers tended to bring the price in the United States down to that prevailing in the world market. The world market, meanwhile, was depressed by expanding production in other countries, and during the depression years great stocks accumulated for which there was no demand. Many Cuban mills were forced to suspend or curtail operations, or at least to cut wages. The government made several efforts from 1925 on to reduce production in the island and to reach agreements with other producing countries to fix quotas in the world market, but none of these were notably successful.

The discontent aroused by these conditions was directed largely against the foreign financial interests that controlled not only the sugar industry but also the railroads, the banks, and much of the country's commerce. Of these, North American interests were by far the most important. American investments in Cuba were estimated at from one to one and a half billions of dollars in 1928—an amount greater than that invested by United States citizens in any other foreign country except Canada and Germany. More than a third of the crop had been ground at American-owned mills before the First World War, and many additional properties were taken over by New York banks during the economic collapse of 1920–21. In 1934 it was estimated that North

American mills produced 68.1 per cent of the annual output.[1] The actual growing of the cane remained to a greater extent in Cuban hands, but the *colonos,* as the farmers who produced it were called, had to sell their crops to the nearest *central* and were further dependent on the *central* for loans with which to carry on their operations. Foreign domination of the Republic's economic life was thus an important political issue, especially as Machado was accused of having unduly favored foreign interests. The principal revolutionary groups not only sought to destroy the evils of the traditional political system but also to do away with "economic imperialism."

These groups turned against de Céspedes when it became clear that he would not support their ideas. Other factions, like the conservative followers of Menocal and especially the university students, opposed him from the start. The students had continued to act as a political group although the university had been closed for several years and many of them were now mature men.

On September 5 the students and a group of non-commissioned officers in the army staged a successful revolt. The military leader was Sergeant Fulgencio Batista, who persuaded the enlisted men to mutiny against their officers and to seize control of the forts and barracks. Dr. Ramón Grau San Martín, a former dean of the medical school in the University, was made Provisional President a few days later. The new chief executive was popular with the younger revolutionary element, but he had little administrative experience and his government was weakened from the start by dissension among his student supporters. Furthermore, the economic situation was growing worse. Great numbers of men were out of work: a worse catastrophe in Cuba than in most tropical countries because so much of the arable land was planted to sugar cane that the island depended largely on imported food, which unemployed men were unable to buy. The distress of people who were close to actual starvation offered a fertile field for communist and other agitators, who promised the redistribution of wealth and the confiscation of the foreign-owned sugar estates.

For a time, the country seemed threatened by anarchy. The United States withheld its recognition of the new administration and sent a number of warships to Cuban ports to protect American citizens—a step which was clearly necessary in view of the dangerous attitude of the workmen on sugar estates in many parts of the interior. On October

[1] Commission on Cuban Affairs, *Problems of the New Cuba,* p. 227.

2, Habana's largest hotel was the scene of a pitched battle between the soldiers and five hundred of their former officers who had established themselves there. Even after Batista, now holding the rank of Colonel, began to restore the army's discipline and efficiency it was increasingly difficult to maintain order. Terrorist outrages, attempted revolts, a default on the foreign debt, and strikes which threatened to tie up vital public services destroyed confidence both in Cuba and abroad, and as the cane-grinding season approached it became evident that few of the mills would be able to operate unless conditions changed.

Confronted by this threat of complete economic disaster, Dr. Grau San Martín resigned on January 15, 1934. After a short interval, Colonel Carlos Mendieta, one of the few older political leaders who had consistently opposed Machado, became Provisional President. The United States' refusal to recognize Grau San Martín, on the ground that his regime had no substantial political support, unquestionably helped to bring about this change of government. When Mendieta came into office, as the result of an agreement between the army and most of the less radical political groups, his government was recognized within a few days. The moral support of the United States, further evidenced by a $10,000,000 credit for the purchase of food, did much to strengthen his position.

During the next few months other measures placed both economic and political relations between the two countries on a new basis. One of these was the signature on May 29, 1934, of a treaty abrogating the Platt Amendment. The United States retained the naval station at Guantánamo, but gave up any formal right to intervene in Cuba's internal affairs. The provisions of the Amendment had not been invoked for some years, but its abrogation ended a situation which was galling to Cuban pride and which was a potential danger to the country's independence. It could not alter the fact that geography and economic ties made Cuba's welfare dependent on the policies that the United States government might adopt.

A realization of the responsibility involved in this relationship inspired several other measures which greatly improved Cuba's economic situation. In March, 1934, President Roosevelt set up the Second Export-Import Bank, with a capital of $2,750,000, specifically to encourage trade between Cuba and the United States. Later, under the Sugar Stabilization Act of 1934, the Republic was granted a quota of nearly 2,000,000 short tons in the American market, with a reduction in duty which assured an opportunity to sell at least a part of the crop at fair prices. The revival of business was further aided by a Cuban-American trade agreement, signed in August, 1934, which granted tariff concessions to many other Cuban products.

Events Since 1934

Political conditions improved more slowly. Besides the remnants of the older political groups, several new factions which had helped to overthrow Machado were ambitious for power. Some of these opposed Mendieta from the start and others, like the A.B.C., which had been the strongest of the secret anti-Machado organizations, fell away as the result of quarrels within the government. All were jockeying for advantage in the elections which would set up a permanent constitutional government, and many of them again began to resort to the terrorist tactics which they had learned during the period of the dictatorship. The situation grew especially bad early in 1935, when there were a series of tumultuous strikes and revolutionary outbreaks. Colonel Batista, however, was building the army into a more powerful force than it had ever been before, and he finally abandoned his hitherto rather tolerant policy and took severe measures against some of the disorderly elements. These restored peace but left the country under military control.

Factional disagreements compelled the postponement of presidential elections until early in 1936. Meanwhile Mendieta had resigned in December, 1935, and had been succeeded by José Barnett. The more conservative factions, after much manoeuvring, finally grouped themselves behind two principal candidates: Dr. Miguel Mariano Gómez, the son of José Miguel Gómez, and ex-President Menocal. The radical elements, driven underground by the army, were temporarily out of the picture. Gómez won by a large majority, and the coalition that supported him obtained ninety of 162 seats in the lower house of Congress and all of the seats in the Senate. Menocal, however, was won over to the support of the new regime by a constitutional amendment which increased the number of senators from twenty-four to thirty-six and enabled him to appoint his friends to the new positions. Gómez thus took office with the support of practically all of the old-line political elements.

The new president's authority was overshadowed by that of Colonel Batista, who was gradually extending his control over civilian as well as military affairs. While the civilian politicians quarreled over jobs and personal political interests, the army, which was now consuming a very large proportion of the government's revenues, steadily increased its sphere of activity. In the summer of 1936 Batista announced a plan for a great system of primary schools under army control, and a few months later he came to an open break with Gómez when he asked Congress to impose a new tax for their support. In December, 1936, Congress passed the tax measure over the President's veto, and then impeached and removed Gómez himself. Federico Laredo Bru was elected in his place.

The coalition which had backed the administration at the beginning of 1936 had by this time broken up. Gómez, Menocal, and Grau San Martín, now the principal radical leader, refused to permit their followers to participate in the congressional election of 1938, and their attitude made necessary several postponements of the projected election for an assembly to revise the constitution. This was finally held, however, in November, 1939. Not only the recognized political parties, but the hitherto outlawed revolutionary and terrorist groups were allowed to vote, and the fairness of the election was indicated by the fact that the opposition factions won forty-one out of the seventy-six seats. After the assembly met, however, a deal between Batista and Menocal, who controlled one of the largest blocks of delegates, gave the two leaders control of the proceedings.

This same coalition enabled Colonel Batista to defeat Grau San Martín in the presidential election held in July, 1940. He thus became the titular as well as the real head of the government, serving under the new constitution which was proclaimed in the following October. His government was one of the first to declare war on Japan and Germany after Pearl Harbor. During the war years the bulk of the sugar crop was sold to the government of the United States, and price controls prevented anything like the wild speculation that had led to disaster in 1920. The island suffered somewhat from shipping shortages and from inflation, but on the whole was distinctly prosperous.

Batista not only refused to be a candidate to succeed himself in 1944, but held an election that was generally conceded to be one of the fairest in Cuba's history. The parties that supported his regime had some difficulty in picking a candidate, but finally selected Carlos Saladrigas. The opposition groups nominated ex-President Ramón Grau San Martín, who was elected by a large majority.

During the next four years there were many minor political disturbances and strikes, but economic conditions were generally good. The President was unable to hold together the coalition that elected him, and for a time seemed to be supported only by his own "revolutionary" party, the *auténticos,* and by the communists. He broke with the latter, however, when he helped the non-communist group to obtain control of the Cuban labor confederation in 1947, and the more radical elements consequently lined up against the administration in the presidential election of 1948. The administration candidate, Carlos Prío Socarrás, nevertheless defeated his three opponents and was inaugurated for the term 1948–52.

26

Haiti

Saint Domingue under French Rule

The western end of Hispaniola is one of the most mountainous parts of the West Indies. Three great ranges, their slopes in many places too steep or too stony for cultivation, traverse the country from east to west, leaving only a few areas of flat land along the coast and in the river valleys between them. Even in the plains there are large sections where the rainfall, cut off by the mountains, is inadequate or irregular. Where agriculture can be carried on, however, the soil is rich and the climate, though hot, is not unpleasant.

The French settlers, who occupied the country in the days of the buccaneers, turned their attention to planting as piracy was gradually suppressed. The colony flourished during the eighteenth century, and by 1789 Saint Domingue was supplying much of the world's sugar and most of the world's coffee.[1] Despite its small area, it was by far the most valuable of France's overseas possessions, with exports which exceeded in value those of the United States. The richest district was the Province of the North, and especially the plain behind Cap François, now called Cape Haitian, which was the principal city. The Province of the West, including the Artibonite Valley and the Cul de Sac near Port au Prince, had been settled more recently, but had made rapid progress with the construction of extensive irrigation works. So also had the isolated southern peninsula, the Province of the South.

The wealth of the colony was divided among a very few people. Some 450,000 out of a total population of 520,000 were slaves, whose

[1] Von Humboldt, *Essai Politique sur le Royaume de la Nouvelle Espagne*, Vol. III, p. 193, footnote.

lot was if anything harder than that of the plantation laborers in the other West Indian colonies because the overwhelming preponderance of the blacks made constant vigilance and strict control imperative. Some 27,500 more were colored freedmen, some of them black, the majority of mixed blood. Many of the mulattoes, especially in the newer regions of the west and south, had been educated in France and owned property and slaves, but they were all subject by law and custom to humiliating regulations and discriminations, rigidly enforced by the whites who hated and feared their growing influence. The 39,000 whites [1] were themselves divided into mutually hostile groups: officials sent out from France, wealthy creole planters, and *petits blancs* or poor whites.

The Revolution

The revolution in France in 1789 weakened the home government's authority which had hitherto kept these class and race hatreds under restraint. The creoles seized control through assemblies that they elected in each province, and dissensions between planters and poor whites and between royalists and democrats kept the country in turmoil. Matters became worse when the mulattoes, with the support of sympathizers in the National Assembly in Paris, began to demand political and social equality. A freedmen's revolt in the north, led by Vincent Ogé, was cruelly suppressed in 1790; but in 1791 the mulattoes of the Artibonite Valley and the Cul de Sac joined with the still numerous royalist faction among the whites in a more serious outbreak.

At almost the same time a worse catastrophe overwhelmed the rich northern plain. On the night of August 22, 1791, there was a sudden uprising of the Negro slaves. The whites on the plantations were massacred, and dwellings and sugar mills were destroyed in an outburst of savage fury. Thereafter the Negro hordes held the rural districts in the north, while mulattoes and whites waged a confused struggle for dominance around Port au Prince. Only in the southern peninsula did the planters retain control.

Meanwhile the National Assembly in France was following a vacillating policy which made matters worse rather than better. Three

[1] These are the figures given by Moreau de St. Méry whose *Description Topographique, Physique, Politique et Historique de la Partie Française de Saint-Domingue* is the best description of the colony before the revolution.

commissioners sent to Saint Domingue in 1791 failed to restore peace. After the radicals came into power at Paris the position of the planters seemed hopeless. The National Assembly ordered that mulattoes and free Negroes should have the same political rights as whites, and in 1792 a new commission was sent to the colony with 6,000 troops. Its most active member, Sonthonax, first alienated all classes of the white population by consorting with the mulattoes, and then lost the support of that group by his open sympathy with the blacks. In June, 1793, when the whites at Cap François resisted his authority, he permitted the rebel Negroes of the northern plain to loot and burn the city. A few months later he and his colleagues proclaimed the abolition of slavery—an act which made both the whites and the mulattoes more desperate than ever without stopping the Negro revolt.

Toussaint Louverture

By this time France was at war with England and Spain. English troops, at the invitation of the white planters in the south, occupied Port au Prince and other points on the coast in 1793 and 1794, and Spanish troops overran the north, obtaining help from several of the Negro chieftains. What is now Haiti might well have become a British or Spanish colony had it not been for Toussaint Louverture.

François Dominique Toussaint, who later took the surname "Louverture," was a full-blooded Negro born in Saint Domingue. Serving his master as a coachman, he seems to have picked up a little knowledge of reading and writing, a rare accomplishment among the slaves. He was one of the principal leaders among the revolted Negroes, and the 4,000 men under his command were the best-trained black troops in the island. He joined the Spanish army in 1793. A year later, when it seemed that the British invasion might restore slavery and the plantation system, he decided to throw his support to France. His desertion forced the Spanish to withdraw, and he soon became the ruler of the northern part of the colony. Meanwhile the mulatto General André Rigaud had obtained control of most of the southern peninsula, and the British, with their ranks depleted by yellow fever, found it more and more difficult to maintain their position at Port au Prince. They finally signed an agreement with Toussaint in 1798 under which they withdrew their forces from the island.

A sanguinary struggle ensued between blacks and mulattoes. Toussaint put down mulatto uprisings in the north and then attacked Rigaud. He had by this time entered into commercial agreements with Great Britain and the United States, and warships of both of these powers helped him to defeat his rival. By 1800 he had control of the south, and his lieutenant, Dessalines, followed up the victory by systematically murdering some 10,000 persons of mixed blood. Toussaint next proceeded to conquer the Spanish end of the island, which had been ceded to France by the Treaty of Basel in 1795 but had not yet been actually transferred. Early in 1801 he was master of all Hispaniola.

While still maintaining an outward allegiance to France, Toussaint now assumed the title of Governor General for life, with power to name his own successor. Many white proprietors were encouraged to resume possession of their estates, upon which the former slaves were compelled to work under military control, and other properties were cultivated for the benefit of the new government and its officials. For a brief period the colony was again fairly prosperous.

The French government, beset by enemies in Europe, had been in no position since 1793 to reassert its authority in Saint Domingue, and the emissaries whom it did send to the island were intimidated or outwitted by the resourceful Toussaint. With the peace of Amiens, however, the situation changed and in December, 1801, Napoleon's brother-in-law, General Leclerc, sailed from France with 20,000 veteran troops. Leclerc's instructions were to pursue a conciliatory policy until he felt strong enough to remove the black generals and exile them to France, but he met with more resistance than was anticipated. Henri Christophe, Toussaint's lieutenant at Cap François, burned that city before abandoning it. In the interior the Negroes carried on a guerrilla warfare which culminated in the epic defense of the fortress of Crête-à-Pierrot, which the French took only after heavy losses. Toussaint and his followers finally submitted in April and May, 1802, but were able to stipulate that they should retain their rank and their commands in the army.

The End of French Rule

Leclerc had barely achieved this rather doubtful victory when an epidemic of yellow fever attacked his European troops. Within a few months his army had been virtually destroyed, and reinforcements sent

from France suffered the same fate. Stupid acts of the French authorities
had meanwhile united the Haitians against them. The mulattoes were
infuriated by the restoration of the discriminations against their class,
and the Negroes by the restoration of slavery in the nearby islands of
Guadeloupe and Martinique and the abrogation of prohibitions against
the slave trade in the French colonies generally. Toussaint had been
treacherously arrested and sent to France soon after his capitulation,
to die in prison a year later, but several of his former lieutenants were
still in command of trained troops. When the mulatto leader Clervaux
deserted the French army and took to the hills in October, 1802, Dessalines and Christophe, the principal black generals, followed his example.

By this time only a fraction of the French troops were alive and fit
for duty, but their health improved somewhat with the coming of the
dry season. General Rochambeau, who took command after Leclerc
died of the fever in November, was able to take the offensive. The
struggle was now a war of extermination, and each side vied with the
other in wholesale atrocities. The outcome was still in doubt when the
renewal of hostilities between France and England in May, 1803, and
the restoration of the British blockade made the position of the French
army hopeless. In November Rochambeau surrendered to a British
admiral. On January 1, 1804, Jean Jacques Dessalines, the leader of
the rebel army, proclaimed the independence of Haiti, the first free
nation in Latin America. The territory of the new Republic included
only the western end of Hispaniola, as French forces, and later Spanish
forces, remained in control in the east.

Dessalines, Christophe, and Pétion

Dessalines at first took the title of Governor General, but in September, 1804, in imitation of Napoleon, he had himself proclaimed Emperor.
The former slave of a free Negro, entirely without education, the new
ruler's chief qualifications for office were the courage and ferocity
which had won him his position in the army. His administration was a
military despotism, acquiesced in because both blacks and mulattoes
feared a new French invasion. All functions of the government, and
even the direction of agriculture—somewhat revived as in the days of
Toussaint by means of forced labor—were concentrated in the hands

of the army chieftains. The Frenchmen who remained in the island, with the exception of a few priests, physicians, and skilled artisans, were systematically massacred, but British and American merchants were encouraged to resume trade.

The brutality and corruption of Dessalines' regime caused much discontent, and it was not long before several of his chief lieutenants were conspiring against him. The mulattoes especially were restive under black rule, and when the Emperor arbitrarily deprived many colored planters of their lands a revolt spread through the west and south. Dessalines marched against the rebels, but in October, 1806, he was killed in an ambush in the outskirts of Port au Prince.

Henri Christophe, Dessalines' chief lieutenant, was accepted by both factions as the head of a provisional administration pending the meeting of a constituent assembly. As the principal surviving hero of the war against the French, and the commander of the best military forces, Christophe expected as a matter of course to dominate the assembly, but he had not counted on the ingenuity of the mulatto leaders who now controlled the west and the south. By the simple expedient of creating new parishes, each of which had a right to representation, these obtained a majority in the assembly and proceeded to draw up a new constitution which gave all real authority in the new government to an elected senate. They offered Christophe the presidency, but he refused to accept it and attacked Port au Prince, where the assembly was sitting. He was repulsed, and from 1807 until 1820 the country was divided into the "State of Haiti" under his rule and the "Republic of Haiti" controlled by the mulattoes.

The State of Haiti, which included the north and the Artibonite Valley, was a well organized military dictatorship. Christophe was at first President for life, but in 1811 he made himself King and created a numerous nobility. His reign is perhaps the most picturesque episode in Haiti's eventful history. A native of one of the British West Indies, with some white blood,[1] he had served while still a slave as a waiter in a hotel and as a privateersman, and he is said to have taken part in the French expedition against Savannah during the American Revolution. He spoke English as well as French, and had a predilection for things English. Though uneducated, he was intelligent and showed much administrative ability. He made some effort to establish schools

[1] Mackenzie, *Notes on Haiti*, Vol. I, p. 159.

and other appurtenances of civilization, and foreign merchants were encouraged to visit Haitian ports, though they could trade only with a royal monopoly. Henri's system of government, however, bore heavily on the masses of the inhabitants, and he grew more despotic toward the end of his reign. The building of the great citadel of Laferrière is said to have cost many lives. Public works of this sort, and also the ordinary work in the fields, was carried on under a system little better than slavery, and the peasant masses were cruelly exploited for the benefit of the royal treasury and the military caste. Christophe maintained his power chiefly by the fear that he inspired in his subordinates, and when he had a paralytic stroke in 1820 his followers began to abandon him and he killed himself rather than fall helpless into their hands.

In the south, in the Republic of Haiti, the mulattoes retained control. Alexandre Pétion, elected President early in 1807, was the free-born son of a white Frenchman and a colored woman, better educated than most of his compatriots, and perhaps the most influential member of his caste. He had fled to France after Toussaint's victory over Rigaud, but returned as an officer under Leclerc. When it became clear that the French would restore slavery and the color line, he left them and became one of Dessalines' chief lieutenants in the final struggle for independence. Though chosen under the same constitution that Christophe had rejected, he soon rid himself of the Senate and ruled practically as a dictator. He was reëlected in 1811 and 1815, and became President for life in 1816. His regime was milder but also less efficient than that of Christophe. He did not attempt, and probably did not dare, to subject the peasants to forced labor, and it was perhaps the contrast between their relatively easy existence and the harder lot of their brothers in the north that induced the Negro masses to remain quiet under mulatto domination.

An indecisive war between the two sections began in 1807 and continued for several years. Both Christophe and Pétion supported rebellions in the other's territory, and the situation grew more complicated when Rigaud returned to Haiti in 1810 and set up an independent state in the southern peninsula. Rigaud soon died, however, and his successor, General Borgella, reincorporated the south into the Republic in order to present a common front against a formidable attack launched by Christophe in 1812. The attack was repulsed, and hostilities were thereafter suspended, though without a formal truce.

Boyer

When Pétion died in 1818 the Senate, under pressure from the army, chose Jean Pierre Boyer, the chief of the presidential guard, as his successor. Boyer was a free-born mulatto who had had some education abroad and served for a time in the French army. Able and honest, he proved to be one of Haiti's best presidents. In 1820, when Christophe killed himself, Boyer took advantage of the ensuing confusion to occupy Cape Haitian before the northern generals could concert measures to oppose him, and the two sections were thenceforth united under one government, with the capital at Port au Prince. Two years later, when the inhabitants of Santo Domingo revolted against Spain, Boyer occupied their territory, bringing the whole island under Haitian rule. He maintained his authority with a firm hand for a quarter century, suppressing occasional minor revolts but on the whole giving the country an era of peace which all classes welcomed after thirty years of almost continuous bloodshed.

The mulattoes, who ran the government under Pétion and Boyer, were practically the only people in Haiti who had even a vague understanding of political problems, but their position was a precarious one. Their numbers had been greatly reduced by the wholesale massacres during the revolution, and the Negro peasants, who remembered that the freedmen had also been slave-holders, hated and distrusted them almost as much as they had the whites. The mulattoes, on their side, looked down on the peasants as an inferior race. They even drew a color line socially against the relatively small number of educated Negroes and the black officers in the army, though they found it politically advisable to give many of the higher offices to members of both of these groups. In the north, in fact, the Negro element remained predominant in politics, so that the rivalry between the two races tended to take on a sectional character.

There was a great gulf between the *élite*, as the mulatto aristocracy called itself, and the masses of the people. The members of the *élite* spoke French, and many of them had some education, either in France or at home, which made them familiar with European ideas and ways of living. The culture of the masses, on the other hand, was essentially African. Only one-third of the slaves in the colony in 1789 had been born there.[1] The rest had been imported, most of them as adults, from various sections of the dark continent. Nearly all spoke the creole patois, based on French but African in structure, but they had otherwise learned little from contact with their white masters. The Church, which had little influence among the French planters, had had even less among the slaves, and most of them were votaries of *voudou*, a mixture of African superstitions and Christianity which even today is the religion of the majority of the Haitian peasants.

By 1820 little remained of the rich plantations of the colonial period. Sugar mills and other buildings had been burned or torn down during the first slave revolt, and irrigation systems had been allowed to fall into disrepair. The lands confiscated from French proprietors were generally treated as public domain. Some were given to military officers as a reward for service in the revolution, some recognized as the property of the mulatto sons of former owners, and some rented to persons who attempted to farm them with the labor of the former slaves. The latter were forbidden by law to leave the *habitation* to which they were attached, but this and other provisions of the labor code were less rigidly enforced after 1820 because Boyer, like Pétion, hardly dared to jeopardize his position by oppressing the black masses. Large-scale agriculture was consequently practically abandoned. The peasants grew food for their own use on lands which they rented or occupied as squatters, and coffee, which they could pick from the trees on the abandoned plantations, took the place of sugar as the chief export. The *élite*, more and more divorced from any connection with agriculture, devoted themselves principally to politics. They had little interest in the welfare of the black masses or the development of the country, and little money was spent on schools or roads. The public treasury, in their eyes, existed to provide a living for their class.

The prosperity of the French colony was a thing of the past, but the Haitians had their freedom. The peasants no longer worked under the lash, and the *élite* were masters in their own house, free from humiliating discrimination on account of their race. All classes were determined to prevent the return of white domination in any form. African blood or marriage to a Haitian was a requisite for citizenship. White people were looked on with suspicion, and each successive constitution from 1805 until 1918 forbade foreigners to own land. If this attitude discouraged trade and prevented the development of the

[1] Moreau de St. Méry, *op. cit.*, p. 27.

country's resources, it also preserved the country from foreign economic domination.

For many years after 1804, all classes lived in fear of an attack from abroad. The new Republic was an international pariah, for none of the great powers were disposed to enter into normal diplomatic relations with a government which owed its origin to a successful slave revolt. The immediate danger, of course, was from France. Immediately after the Bourbon restoration, Louis XVIII sent unofficial representatives to seek to persuade the Haitians to acknowledge French sovereignty, but they were rebuffed. Later, the Haitian government indicated a willingness to pay an indemnity for the confiscated French properties in return for a recognition of independence, and negotiations were carried on for some years in an effort to reach an agreement on this basis. In 1825, when a French fleet appeared at Port au Prince, Boyer was finally forced to accept an offensively worded royal ordinance which granted independence on condition that French trade be given preferential treatment and that Haiti pay an indemnity of $30,000,000 in five years. Only a small part of this sum was ever remitted, but efforts to meet the payments, and disputes with France because the government was unable to do so, caused trouble for years to come.

1843–1870

Boyer's government was described by a foreign observer as "a sort of republican monarchy, sustained by the bayonet." [1] The Congress, chosen by a very limited franchise and with much official intervention, could only consider laws which the President saw fit to introduce. During its session of 1833, its most important act was to expel two members "for systematically opposing the measures of the executive, and persisting in demanding a statement of the public expenditures." [2] For more than twenty years there was astonishingly little opposition to the President's regime. Toward the end of this period discontent became more apparent. Boyer continued to rely on the assistance of a small group which had dominated affairs since the days of Pétion, and the younger elements of the *élite*, feeling that they were excluded from public office, began to agitate for a change and to demand a more democratic form of government. In 1843 these "liberals" started a

[1] Brown, *The History and Present Condition of St. Domingo*, Vol. II, p. 259.
[2] *Ibid.*, II, p. 260.

revolution in the southern peninsula. The government's forces were defeated and Boyer fled to Jamaica, which was to be the refuge of many defeated Haitian leaders in years to come.

The revolutionists installed Charles Rivière Hérard as President and proceeded to frame a new constitution, which provided that local officials and judges, as well as the president and congress, should be chosen by popular election. This arrangement proved unworkable, and the disputes which arose weakened the prestige of the new regime. At the same time there was discontent in the army, where the older officers disliked having young revolutionary leaders placed in authority over them, and unrest among the peasants, whose hostility to the *élite* had been deliberately fomented by the liberals during their campaign to attain power. The Congress, attempting to assert its new authority, caused further discord. The weakness of the government at Port au Prince gave the Spanish-speaking inhabitants of the eastern end of the island the opportunity for which they had been waiting, and in February, 1844, they declared the independence of the Dominican Republic. Hérard led an army against them, but he had met with little success when a peasant revolt, instigated by the Salomon family, broke out in the southern peninsula. The specter of a new race war terrified the *élite*, and though the insurgents were defeated the incident caused a revulsion against the liberal regime and helped some of Boyer's former associates to overthrow Hérard in May, 1844.

In the hope of strengthening their own position and allaying the growing discontent among the blacks, the group which now came to power decided to make a Negro general President of the Republic. Their first choice was Philippe Guerrier, an illiterate veteran of the war for independence, eighty-seven years old, but still influential among the people of his own race and especially in the north, where there was always hostility to any mulatto regime at Port au Prince. When Guerrier died after a few months in office, he was succeeded by another octogenarian, a brother-in-law of Christophe named Jean-Louis Pierrot, who dismayed his sponsors by suddenly moving the capital to Cape Haitian. He was promptly removed with the help of the army, and still another aged general, Jean Baptiste Riché, became President in 1846.

When Riché died a year later the mulatto statesmen who controlled the government made a mistake. They had some difficulty in agreeing among themselves upon a successor, but finally chose a captain of the palace guard named Soulouque, whose ignorance and stupidity seemed to assure his being a pliant instrument in the hands of his supporters. The new President had never shown an interest in politics, and it was difficult to persuade him that his election was not a joke. Once in office, however, he resented the superior airs of his aristocratic advisers and soon broke with them. When they conspired to regain power, he encouraged the mob in a savage attack on the mulattoes, and great numbers of them were killed or forced to leave the country. Meanwhile he made an effort to reconquer the Dominican Republic, but suddenly abandoned his campaign after some initial successes, and was dissuaded from renewing it by strong diplomatic representations from England, France, and the United States. In 1849 he made himself Emperor of Haiti, and created a peerage which included four princes, fifty-nine dukes, ninety-nine counts, and a host of lesser nobility. During the next ten years Faustin I ruled with a firm hand, constantly growing more cruel in his treatment of the terrified *élite*.

Soulouque was overthrown in 1859 by Fabre Geffrard, the head of his general staff, who started a revolt when he learned that he had fallen under suspicion of disloyalty. The new President, a dark mulatto, attempted to obtain the support of both of the country's racial groups. During his administration, in 1862, the Haitian government was formally recognized by the United States. A still more important event was the conclusion of a concordat with the Holy See in 1860. The Haitian Church had been in a deplorable state, without recognized bishops and served mainly by priests whose antecedents and character would hardly bear investigation, and the establishment of a regular priesthood recruited in France did much to bring the country into closer touch with European civilization. One of the most noteworthy consequences was the establishment of schools by several religious orders. Public instruction had hitherto been grievously neglected, and it had been difficult even for the *élite* to obtain any sort of an education except by going abroad.

Geffrard nevertheless had many enemies. There was strong and successful opposition to his proposal to amend the constitution to permit foreigners to own land, and there were frequent revolts followed by numerous executions. An uprising under Sylvain Salnave was suppressed in 1865 only because British warships bombarded the insurgents in retaliation for an attack on the British consulate at Cape Haitian. This incident hurt the President's prestige and strengthened his adversaries, and another outbreak in 1867 forced Geffrard to resign.

The liberals, who had participated in this revolt, hoped to return to power, but when a constituent assembly met to choose the new president threats of mob violence compelled it to elect Salnave, who was the idol of the troops and the populace. It was soon evident that the new government would be more despotic than its predecessor. Congress was arbitrarily dissolved, and several political opponents were put to death. The liberals organized revolts in several sections of the country, and they were supported by the leaders of the *cacos*, turbulent peasants from the districts along the northern part of the Dominican border who were to play an increasingly important rôle in Haitian politics as time went on. Salnave, on his side, sought help from the *piquets*—country people of the south—and for more than two years the country endured one of the worst civil wars in its history. The final outcome was the overthrow and execution of Salnave and the victory of the liberals.

Liberalism and Reaction, 1870–1908

The liberals were in power during the greater part of the next nine years. Nissage-Saget, whom they made President in 1870, was an elderly gentleman whose faculties are said to have been somewhat impaired by eight years of imprisonment under Soulouque. He was greatly hampered by factious opposition in Congress, fomented by the rival liberal leader Boyer-Bazelais, but he refused to coerce the legislative body, saying, with a rare understanding of constitutional principles, that "each ass should bray in his own pasture." [1] Some of his advisers, however, were less tolerant, and as the end of his term approached they removed him, installed a new and more subservient congress, and brought about the election of Michel Domingue, the commander of the army.

The new President was an African-born Negro, without education, and with an unpleasant reputation for cruelty. In political matters he was under the influence of his better educated but unscrupulous and erratic nephew Septimus Rameau. The murder of several political adversaries and the flotation of a loan in France, on very unfavorable

[1] Dorsainville, *Manuel d'Histoire d'Haiti*, p. 312.

terms, made the administration unpopular, and in 1876, when it was reported that the government was to be removed to Cayes, an infuriated mob killed Rameau and forced Domingue to flee.

Domingue's successor, Boisrond-Canal, was one of the ablest of the liberal leaders. He made a real effort to restore constitutional government, but continued quarrels within the liberal party paralyzed Congress and finally made the President's position so intolerable that he resigned in 1879. His withdrawal left the country in disorder, and a weak provisional government was easily overthrown when Lysius Salomon, the chief adviser of Soulouque, returned from exile to seize power. This marked the end, for a long period, of the political power of the mulatto aristocracy of Port au Prince. Many of the *élite* continued to hold important positions in the government, but the rulers of the country, until the American intervention in 1915, were a series of military leaders, most of them from other sections of the Republic.

Salomon, with his great influence among the peasants of the southern peninsula, had been the most feared opponent of successive Haitian governments since the fall of Faustin I. As leader of the black party, he was disliked and distrusted by the *élite*, but he was as well educated as most Haitians of the upper class and he had shown ability in important governmental positions under Riché and Soulouque. He had lived in Europe, and was married to a white French woman. The understanding of political and economic problems obtained during his long exile showed itself in an energetic and progressive policy when he returned to power in Haiti. He established a national bank, tried to encourage agriculture, and engaged French instructors for the higher schools and for the army. At the same time he was ruthless in his treatment of his liberal opponents and on one occasion he is said to have encouraged the mob to sack the better residential quarters of Port au Prince in retaliation for the *élite's* opposition to his government. The liberals were almost constantly in revolt until the death of Boyer-Bazelais in 1883, but thereafter they ceased to be an important political force.

Salomon was reëlected in 1886, but he was overthrown two years later. After some months of civil war between the north and the south, the northern general Florville Hyppolite became President in 1889. One of the principal events of his administration was a flurry of excitement over an unsuccessful effort by the United States to lease the Mole St. Nicholas, which Hyppolite had apparently promised to cede for a coaling station in return for assistance from the American navy during his struggle for power. During the term of Tiresias Simon Sam, who became President after Hyppolite died suddenly of heart failure in 1896, there was another incident involving a foreign power. This was the "Luders Affair," when two German war vessels appeared at Port au Prince to compel the payment of a large indemnity to a German who had been imprisoned for a short time for resisting the local police.

Antenor Firmin, the most influential member of the cabinet, expected to succeed Sam, but other leaders opposed him. During the civil war that ensued, Firmin's warship, the *Crête-à-Pierrot*, seized a shipment of arms which a German merchant ship was carrying to his adversaries. The German cruiser *Panther* was ordered to capture her, but Admiral Killick, the commander of the *Crête-à-Pierrot*, sent his crew ashore and blew up his ship. This caused Firmin's defeat, and in December, 1902, a victorious army compelled the Congress to elect his rival, a general from the north named Nord Alexis, as President.

Though an uneducated soldier, already more than eighty years old, Nord Alexis was an able ruler. One of his first acts was to prosecute the leading men in the preceding government and several foreign officials of the National Bank for frauds in connection with the consolidation of the floating debt. Simon Sam and several of his ministers were convicted. None of them, however, seem to have been punished, and it is interesting to note that three of those found guilty later served as presidents of the Republic.[1] The National Bank, which had been established under French management in 1881, had been implicated in other scandalous transactions at the expense of the national treasury and its charter was now revoked.

From the accession of Salomon in 1879 until the end of Nord Alexis' administration in 1908 Haiti enjoyed a relatively stable government. High coffee prices made the country prosperous, and ample revenues strengthened the government's position. Unfortunately there was little real progress. A succession of military dictators maintained order, but they did little to relieve the poverty and ignorance of the masses of the people. Public funds were still spent solely for the benefit of the ruling class. Despite increased income the government's finances were in bad shape, for corruption pervaded all departments and continual deficits were met by borrowing or by issues of paper or nickel fiat currency. The fundamental unsoundness of the political structure was to become evident in the next few years.

[1] Davis, *Black Democracy*, p. 138.

The "Ephemeral Governments"

Antoine Simon, a soldier of humble origin, led a revolution that compelled Nord Alexis to flee to Jamaica in 1908. The new President, a southerner, was unpopular in the north and at Port au Prince. He was violently criticized when he contracted a large external loan in 1910, and the ever-present fear of foreign influence was further aroused by contracts with an American promoter for a railroad and for the development of a banana industry. It was not difficult, therefore, for Cincinnatus Leconte to march down from the north and seize Port au Prince with a *caco* army in August, 1911, and the Congress, as usual, did not dare to refuse to elect the leader of the victorious revolutionists as President.

During the next four years Haiti had six presidents, serving for periods which grew shorter and shorter. Leconte, before he had been in office for twelve months, was killed with 300 soldiers of his guard by an explosion in the national palace. Tancrède Auguste, hastily elected by the Congress to succeed him, died after eight months under circumstances which caused some suspicion of poison.[1] He had not been buried when street fighting broke out between rival military leaders who sought to surround the meeting place of Congress to dictate the choice of his successor. The victor, a popular lawyer named Michel Oreste, was in office eight months before a revolt in the north led by Davilmar Théodore forced him to flee to Jamaica. Théodore had not even reached Port au Prince when he was defeated in February, 1914, by Oreste Zamor. In October, Théodore overthrew Zamor, only to be overthrown himself five months later by Vilbrun Guillaume Sam. Each revolution in turn was the work of the *cacos*, who barely installed one man in power and were paid for their services before they sold their support to another. Guillaume Sam's term ended on July 27, 1915, when his *caco* troops deserted him just as they had deserted his predecessors.

On the same night, 167 political suspects, many of them members of prominent families in Port au Prince, were slaughtered in cold blood in prison by Sam's lieutenants. The people of the city learned of the massacre the next day, and an enraged mob of friends and relatives dragged the ex-President from the French legation where he had taken refuge and tore him to pieces in the streets. The capital was still in a

[1] Davis, *op. cit.*, p. 147.

state of anarchy a few hours later when Admiral Caperton entered the harbor with the *U.S.S. Washington* and landed forces to restore order. This was the beginning of an American military occupation that lasted sixteen years.

The American Occupation

Continual disorder and administrative inefficiency had involved Haiti in more and more serious complications with other governments. Between 1911 and 1915, French, German, British and American armed forces had repeatedly been landed to protect foreign life and property, and claims for losses or injuries to foreign nationals, some of them well-founded and some fictitious, had assumed alarming proportions. Certain European governments, moreover, had shown what seemed to the government at Washington an unwholesome interest in Haitian affairs. French cultural influences were predominant among the *élite* and French bankers had supplied the greater part of the loans that constituted the Republic's foreign debt. German merchants, on the other hand, controlled the Republic's trade, and they had been active during the past few years in financing revolutionary movements, buying at a fraction of their face value revolutionary bond issues which were afterward assumed as obligations of the state. Both France and Germany had served notice that they would wish to participate in any foreign financial control which might be established in Haiti, and Germany was believed to desire to obtain control of the Mole St. Nicholas as a coaling station. The outbreak of the World War had of course eliminated any danger of European interference in Haiti for the time being, but the United States wished to guard against the possibility of future interference.

Furthermore, American interests in the island had suffered from the turbulent conditions there and had repeatedly appealed to Washington for diplomatic support. The most important of these interests were the National Railroad Company, which was endeavoring to build a line from Port au Prince to Cape Haitian under government subsidy, and the American shareholders in the National Bank, which had been reëstablished in 1910 with French, German, and American capital. The bank played an especially important rôle in the events which led up to the intervention. Under its charter it was the treasury of the Haitian government, receiving all revenues and paying over to the government's creditors the proceeds of the taxes which were pledged to them

—an arrangement which had assured interest payments on the foreign debt even when political conditions were most disturbed. The bank had also regularly advanced money to the government for current expenses. In 1914, however, it refused to continue these advances and the government retaliated by taking the treasury service out of its hands. This made a default on the foreign debt unavoidable, and for some time before the intervention finally occurred the United States had been endeavoring without success to persuade successive revolutionary governments to accept American financial control.

With its forces in possession of Port au Prince, the American government embarked on a more ambitious program. The Congress, protected by American troops, was persuaded to elect a new president, Sudre Dartiguenave, who gave assurances in advance that he would accede to the wishes of the United States. A treaty was signed on September 16, 1915, under which the United States was to "aid the Haitian Government in the proper and efficient development of its agricultural, mineral and commercial resources and in the establishment of the finances of Haiti on a firm and solid basis." A General Receiver of Customs and a Financial Adviser, both appointed upon the nomination of the President of the United States, were to control the financial administration. A constabulary, officered by Americans similarly appointed, was to assume the maintenance of order, and American engineers were to direct measures for "sanitation and public improvement." In general, the United States was to "lend an efficient aid for the preservation of Haitian Independence and the maintenance of a government adequate for the protection of life, property and individual liberty." The treaty was to be in force for ten years, but in 1917 this period was extended by agreement to twenty years. American marines had meanwhile been landed at several ports, and a technical state of military occupation was established throughout the Republic. The control of the United States was made still more effective by two agreements signed in 1918: one providing that the American legation should be consulted before any project of law was submitted to the legislative body, and the other giving the financial adviser a veto over all expenditures.

The first years of the occupation were troubled ones. There was much friction between the treaty officials and the Haitian government, and a bitter dispute with the Haitian Congress over the adoption of a new constitution, written, in part, by officials at Washington. After President Dartiguenave dissolved the Congress, with the support of the

American-officered constabulary, the constitution was adopted by "plebiscite" in 1918. One of the provisions insisted upon by the United States was a change in the article prohibiting foreign landownership. These events increased the discontent already existing among the *élite*. At the same time the new constabulary officers provoked much hostility among the peasants by blunders and abuses in the enforcement of the *corvée*, the system of compulsory labor on the roads. The result was a revolt of the *cacos* in the north and west, which continued for two years and cost nearly 2,000 lives before it was finally suppressed by American marines.

The painful impression caused by this revolt and the realization that little of real value had thus far been accomplished led to a reorganization of the American treaty organization in 1922. Brigadier General John H. Russell of the United States Marine Corps was appointed High Commissioner, to act as diplomatic representative of the United States and at the same time to supervise and direct the work of the treaty officials. This made possible a unity of direction that had hitherto been lacking. At the same time there was a marked improvement in the relations between the two governments, for Louis Borno, who succeeded Dartiguenave as President in 1922, coöperated effectively with the High Commissioner in carrying out the purposes of the Treaty of 1915.

Much was accomplished during the next seven years. A loan floated in New York in 1922 made possible the refunding of the foreign and internal debts and provided a substantial sum for public works, which was supplemented by increased efficiency in the financial administration. It was consequently possible for the Public Works Service to build roads and trails in all parts of the country and to repair and extend the old French irrigation works. The Public Health Service, under the direction of United States Navy doctors, organized hospitals and rural clinics which brought medical care for the first time within the reach of the great mass of the population. In 1923, a Service of Agriculture and Vocational Instruction was set up under the treaty and a number of small rural farm schools were established. Meanwhile, the constabulary maintained order, and its district commanders, most of them sergeants in the Marine Corps, took the place of the old military commandants as the principal local officials in the rural districts.

The American occupation was nonetheless disliked by the majority of the Haitian *élite*. Though this group had returned to power with the intervention, after the long period of subjection to black military leaders and *caco* chieftains, they felt that they had derived little benefit from the change. In the past the government's revenue had nearly all found its way, through one channel or another, into the pockets of the ruling class. Now it was being spent by foreigners on projects that benefited the masses of the people. The expenditures of the departments under Haitian control had been reduced to a minimum. The occupation was in itself offensive to national pride, and President Borno's policy of co-operation was increasingly unpopular. There was no legal channel, however, through which the opposition could act, because a "transitory" provision of the Constitution of 1918 authorized the president to postpone congressional elections as long as he saw fit, and provided that the legislative power should be exercised in the meantime by a Council of State. It was this body, appointed by Borno himself, which voted him a second four-year term in 1926.

As the end of this term approached, the fear that the President would be elected again, or would place in office one of his friends, brought on a political crisis. In the last months of 1929, a minor dispute in the agricultural school led to a strike of Haitian employees in various government departments, accompanied by violent political demonstrations. For the first time in many years the American marines were compelled to assist in maintaining order. Normal conditions were restored without bloodshed at Port au Prince, but at Cayes, where there was an effort to incite the peasants to revolt, several persons were killed in a clash with a small marine detachment.

Soon after these events, President Hoover appointed a commission headed by Mr. W. Cameron Forbes to consider "when and how we are to withdraw from Haiti" and "what we shall do in the meantime." This body made a brief visit to Haiti early in 1930, and recommended that a civilian minister be appointed to take over the functions of the High Commissioner and to carry out the early "Haitianization" of the treaty services. With General Russell's help, it also worked out an agreement between the contending political factions, by which Eugene Roy, a generally respected banker in Port au Prince, would become President when Borno's term expired in May, with the understanding that he would convene a congress and then resign in order to permit the election of a new chief executive. This plan was duly carried out. The election held in the summer of 1930 was as nearly free and fair as any could be in Haiti, and the Congress, meeting in November, chose Stenio Vincent, a leading opponent of the occupation, as President.

The new American Minister at once began negotiations for the termination of the intervention. The military occupation was formally ended in 1931, and the public-works, public-health, and agricultural services were turned over to Haitian officials at the same time. The "Haitianization" of the constabulary was slower, because it was first necessary to train native officers in the higher ranks, but it was concluded in August, 1934, and all American marines were then withdrawn. The financial administration presented a more difficult problem. The United States felt that both governments had formally obligated themselves to maintain American control over the collection and application of the pledged revenues so long as any bonds of the 1922 loan were outstanding, but the Financial Adviser-General Receiver was nevertheless replaced in 1934 by a "Fiscal Representative" with more restricted powers.

Since 1934

Throughout the "Haitianization" negotiations, President Vincent and his advisers emphasized the importance of maintaining the efficiency of the treaty services, and to a great extent they were left in the hands of capable natives who had served in important positions under the American directors. Haiti, in the years immediately following the withdrawal of the American forces, was thus a very different country from the Haiti of 1915. The constabulary, under its trained officers, was a far more efficient force than the old army, and road building and other improvements carried out during the intervention did much to unify the country and to raise the general standard of living. The people as a whole seemed little inclined to countenance a return of the turbulent conditions of preintervention days.

Nevertheless, serious social and political problems remained unsolved. The peasants were hardly better fitted than before 1915 to take their place as citizens of a free republic. The rural schools established under the treaty had hardly made a dent in their illiteracy or their ignorance of the first principles of farming. Production had increased very little, and only one or two of several agricultural enterprises established by American capital during the occupation had been at all successful. Meanwhile, population had increased even more rapidly than before 1915, partly because of the work of the Public-Health Service. With some three million people crowded into a none-too-fertile area of 10,000 square miles,

Haiti is today one of the most crowded countries of the Western Hemisphere.

President Vincent remained in power after the American withdrawal. In 1934 he arranged to buy the National Bank from the American interests that had acquired its stock in 1920. The plan met with opposition in the Haitian Senate, but a "plebiscite" upheld the President by a majority of 454,357 to 1,172, and eleven senators were thereafter summarily removed from office as being "rebellious against the will of the people." The Bank thus became the property of the government, and in 1941 the United States agreed that it should take over the loan service, under the supervision of American citizens appointed to its board of directors. The office of the Fiscal Representative was thus discontinued.

Another plebiscite in June, 1935, approved a new constitution that extended President Vincent's term to 1941 and provided for the election of future presidents by popular vote instead of by the Congress. This strengthened the executive's position, because a popular election was easier to manipulate. There was little effective opposition to the government during the next six years despite the fact that the vicissitudes of the coffee industry caused an acute economic depression. This was somewhat relieved after 1938, when the J. G. White Corporation of New York undertook a large public works program financed by a loan from the United States Government.

During Vincent's second term Haiti nearly became involved in a war with its neighbor the Dominican Republic. The hostile feeling between the people of the two ends of the island, which had originated in the days of the buccaneers and had been intensified by the Haitian occupation of Santo Domingo between 1822 and 1844, had been kept alive by disputes over the boundary between the two countries. The boundary line was finally fixed by a treaty signed in 1935, but this did not settle the problem presented by the great numbers of Haitians who had infiltrated into the Dominican Republic in recent years to work on the sugar plantations or to farm land along the border as squatters. In 1937 several thousands of these immigrants were suddenly massacred by Dominican troops, and thousands more were driven back across the border. Fortunately the other American republics were able to avert a conflict between the two countries, and the Dominican government agreed to pay Haiti a substantial indemnity.

Many observers had expected M. Vincent to be a candidate for a third term in 1941, but he decided to withdraw from office and Elie Lescot, who had held several important positions in his administration, was chosen to succeed him. Haiti coöperated in the war effort, chiefly by increasing the production of sisal, which helped to relieve the shortage of Manila hemp, and by joining with the United States in an ambitious but unsuccessful effort to produce rubber from the *cryptostegia* vine. The Haitian American Agricultural Development Corporation, known as the *SHADA*, leased over 100,000 acres of land and converted some 40,000 peasant farmers temporarily into day laborers at wages 50 per cent higher than those formerly prevalent. When the experiment was given up as a failure in 1944, it was difficult to replace the farmers on their land, though the United States provided large quantities of seeds and fruit trees for replanting.

Political discontent increased after the National Assembly in 1944 extended Lescot's term until 1951, and there were minor revolutionary activities and repressive measures by the government. In January, 1946, strikes forced the President to resign and three officers of the *Garde* took control. A new congress, elected in May, chose Dumarsais Estimé as President of the republic. This marked the end of thirty years of rule by the mulatto portion of the *élite*. The new administration announced an extensive program of reforms and internal improvements. One of its first achievements was the payment of the balance of the external loan of 1922, a step that made it possible to eliminate the last vestiges of foreign control over the country's financial administration. For some years there were no serious political disorders, although there was a slight flurry in 1949 when President Trujillo permitted an exiled colonel in the *Garde* to use the Dominican radio for violent attacks on President Estimé. The incident was apparently closed when the Council of the Organization of American States expressed the hope that the two countries would improve their relations. In May, 1950, however, when Estimé attempted to amend the constitution to authorize his own reëlection, he was forced to resign and was superseded by a military *junta*.

27

The Dominican Republic

The Spanish colony of Santo Domingo, the first European settlement in the New World, was left with only a scanty population after the extermination of the Indians and the emigration of many white settlers to Mexico and Peru. The island had little importance in the eyes of the Spanish government, and when the buccaneers began to make forays on the north and west coast at the beginning of the seventeenth century, the authorities removed the settlements of that region into the interior instead of attempting to defend them. The resulting establishment of the pirate headquarters at Tortuga, and its development into the French colony of Saint Domingue, has already been described.

During the eighteenth century the growing prosperity of the French end of the island had its effect on the older Spanish settlements. The sugar and coffee plantations offered a market for cattle, and there was a fair amount of trade between the two sections. The landowners in the eastern end began to import considerable numbers of slaves. There was also some white immigration from the Canary Islands, encouraged by the Spanish government as a means of strengthening its hold on the colony. By 1789 the population of the Spanish colony was estimated at 125,000, of whom 15,000 were Negro slaves. It still seemed backward to the inhabitants of French Saint Domingue; and one of the French creoles, influenced no doubt by the inveterate antipathy between the people of the two colonies, described the people of the Spanish section as illiterate, unprogressive, and superstitious.[1] In the rural districts even the wealthier farmers went barefoot and lived in a very primitive way. There were no good roads. On the other hand the Spanish colony did not

[1] Moreau de Saint-Méry, *A Topographical and Political Description of the Spanish Part of Saint Domingo* (Philadelphia, 1798).

have the social and racial problems which were soon to bring so terrible a catastrophe upon its western neighbor. There were no large plantations where heavy and regular labor was required, and the treatment of the slaves, as in other Spanish colonies, was relatively humane. More important still, the great majority of the Negroes were "creoles," who spoke Spanish and practised Catholicism, rather than recent arrivals from Africa. They thus had little in common with the followers of Toussaint Louverture and Dessalines, and were more disposed to join with other classes of the population in resisting Haitian invasion than to support the Negro chieftains in a race war against their former masters.

Haitian, French, and Spanish Rule, 1795–1844

The people of Spanish Santo Domingo were nevertheless severely affected by the cataclysm in the other end of the island. The more conservative creoles were horrified when Spain ceded the colony to revolutionary France in 1795, and many began to emigrate to territory which remained Spanish. A great many other white families left after Toussaint Louverture occupied Santo Domingo and freed the slaves in 1801. Only a part of them returned when Napoleon's expeditionary force occupied both ends of the island in 1802.

The French General Ferrand remained in Santo Domingo after the destruction of Leclerc's army in the west and was able with the help of a French fleet to repulse an invasion by Dessalines and Christophe in 1805. For a time all went well, but when the people of Spain rose against Napoleon, the Dominican creoles followed their example. In 1808–9, with the aid of the British fleet, Juan Sánchez Ramírez led a revolt that reëstablished Spanish rule.

After the restoration of Ferdinand VII the mother country's illiberal policy caused much of the colonists' loyalty to evaporate, and on November 30, 1821, the Spanish authorities at Santo Domingo City were overthrown with little or no bloodshed and an independent government was set up under José Núñez de Cáceres. The creole leaders proclaimed the union of "Spanish Haiti" with Great Colombia, but before they could ask help from Bolívar, Haitian troops under President Boyer were approaching the capital. The Dominicans offered little resistance, and the still strong pro-Spanish faction seems in fact to have welcomed the invaders, who annexed the whole territory to the recently reunited Republic of Haiti.

For twenty-two years after 1822, the people of the eastern end of the island were ruled from Port au Prince. Their lot was an unenviable one. Even though the Haitian constitutional provisions which excluded whites from citizenship and landownership were not fully enforced in Santo Domingo, the creole families found their situation almost intolerable. Many left the island, and those who remained were restive under the rule of people who differed from them in language and culture and whom they regarded as historic enemies. Boyer seems to have made a real effort to conciliate them and to protect them against abuses, but they were inevitably exploited and mistreated in many ways. All classes suffered from the inefficiency of Haitian rule and the total neglect of roads, schools, and other public services, and resented the government's hostile attitude toward the Church, which had been more influential in the east than in the west. They also resented the fact that taxes were levied in the east to help pay the heavy indemnity imposed on Haiti by France in 1825.

There was nevertheless little overt opposition to Haitian rule until the disorders following the overthrow of Boyer in 1843 encouraged the Dominican patriots to act. A secret society called "La Trinitaria" had been organized in 1838 by Juan Pablo Duarte, a young man who had been educated abroad and had only recently returned to Santo Domingo. This group joined in the conspiracy of the Haitian "liberals" against Boyer and helped to make it a success; but when their real purpose became apparent the new Haitian government took measures which forced their leaders to flee into exile. President Hérard, however, soon had his hands full with opposition at home and on February 27, 1844, a group of Duarte's associates seized the forts at Santo Domingo and proclaimed the independence of the Dominican Republic. *Caudillos* in other sections of the former Spanish colony followed their example. Duarte returned from Curaçao to become a member of the *Junta Central* which took charge of the government, and an army was raised to repel the Haitian forces which had already crossed the border. The outcome was still uncertain when a new revolt in Haiti caused the invaders to withdraw.

Santana and Báez, 1844–1859

The Dominican leaders, in the meantime, had already quarreled among themselves, and in June Duarte's followers in the *Junta Central* attempted to dismiss Pedro Santana, the commander of the army, whose dilatory tactics against the Haitians aroused their distrust. Santana promptly marched on the capital, exiled his opponents, and convened a congress which gave him dictatorial powers. He was President until 1848, when he fell ill and the Minister of War, Manuel Jiménez, seized the opportunity to supplant him. A year later, however, a new Haitian invasion forced the government to give Santana command of the army, and after he had repulsed the enemy it was an easy matter to oust Jiménez. Santana permitted his associate Buenaventura Báez to become President, but he retained control of the army and had much influence in the new administration. He again took over the presidency in 1853 when Báez' term expired.

There was much quarreling and some armed strife during the first decade of independence, and the country's new rulers had little chance to organize an efficient government. At best they had scanty resources with which to work. The emigration of a large proportion of the upper classes had deprived the country of many of its natural leaders. The country people, many of them recently freed Negro slaves, were ignorant and poverty-stricken. Even in the towns, illiteracy was general, for there had been very few schools under the Haitian regime, and only five, accommodating forty pupils each, were provided for in the budget as late as 1857. Agriculture, stock-raising, and commerce had greatly declined. The government's revenues, in 1845–46, were estimated at less than $650,000, and of its expenditures, estimated at $1,186,000, $1,000,000 went to the army.[1] Under such conditions it was difficult to look for any substantial material progress.

The Dominicans' chief preoccupation, however, was their fear of a new invasion from Haiti. The weak administrations that succeeded one another at Port au Prince for some years after 1844 were unable to renew the war, but it was clear that the first strong government that appeared there would attempt to reconquer the eastern end of the island. Haiti had a far greater population and greater resources, and the recollection of earlier invasions, with their wholesale massacres and destruction of property, made the renewal of hostilities a terrifying prospect. Many of the Dominican leaders, including Santana, felt that the only alternative to reconquest was the protection of some foreign state. Efforts to persuade one or another of the European powers or the United States to establish a protectorate played an important part in the Republic's history throughout the first thirty years of independence.

[1] 41st Congress, 3rd Session, House Exec. Doc. 42, p. 11.

At first these efforts met with little success. Neither France nor Spain responded favorably to Santana's overtures, and the United States failed even to accord diplomatic recognition to the new Republic. None of the powers was enthusiastic about assuming an unattractive and unprofitable responsibility. At the same time, none of them was willing to see another government obtain control of Samaná Bay, the fine natural harbor in the northeastern corner of the island that commands one of the principal entrances to the Caribbean Sea. When negotiations with one power began to look hopeful, the representatives of the others often engaged in intrigues of the most sordid character to defeat them, and their task was made easier by the fact that many patriotic Dominicans opposed any arrangement that would deprive them of their independence. Furthermore, even leaders who advocated a protectorate when their party was in power opposed it when another party stood to profit by it.

Successive presidents, however, persisted in their attempts to obtain foreign aid. When Faustin Soulouque came into power in Haiti in 1847 and the expected invasion actually took place, first Jiménez and then Báez unsuccessfully begged for help from France and from the United States. Fortunately Soulouque suddenly withdrew his troops of his own accord, and urgent diplomatic representations by Great Britain, France, and the United States forced him to give up for the time being his plans for a new attack. When he did renew the war in 1855 his army was defeated by Santana. This was the last formidable Haitian invasion, but the victory seemed at the time a mere temporary success and it did not diminish the Dominican government's desire for a foreign protectorate.

Before the Haitian attack, Santana's government had signed a treaty of amity and commerce with the United States. The representative of the American government also endeavored to obtain the cession of a naval base at Samaná, but this scheme was blocked by the opposition of the European consuls at Santo Domingo whose intrigues finally forced Santana out of the government. Báez, who had quarreled with his former chief, became President in 1856. The new administration, however, lasted but a short time, for when Báez rewarded the Spanish, French, and English consuls by permitting them to profit with him in scandalous transactions connected with large new issues of paper money, public opinion turned against him. After his foreign supporters quarreled among themselves, and the Spanish chargé d'affaires was recalled, he could no longer maintain himself. The capital was taken by revolutionists in 1858 after a long siege, and Santana returned to the presidency.

Reannexation to Spain

Still convinced of the need for foreign help, and despairing of obtaining effective support from the United States, Santana now entered into negotiations with Spain. The government at Madrid was less reluctant to consider his proposals because the United States, on the verge of civil war, was in no position to uphold the Monroe Doctrine by force. In 1860, at Santana's request, Spanish troops were sent to support his administration, and on March 18, 1861, the Dominican President proclaimed the reannexation of the Republic to the mother country. The authorities at Madrid, after some hesitation, gave their approval and named Santana Captain General of the colony. More Spanish troops arrived, and with them a number of peninsular officials. Those who opposed the surrender of independence staged several small revolts, but they were repressed by Santana with a cruelty which shocked his new associates and caused the first of a series of increasingly serious disagreements.

From the beginning, the reunion was an unhappy one. The Dominicans were disgusted when they saw Spain restoring the same unenlightened centralized regime which had been repudiated by the American colonies a half century earlier, and they resented the replacement of native by foreign officials. The clergy were incensed by efforts of the new Spanish archbishop to reform their conduct and discipline. The attitude of some of the Spanish officials who came from the slave-holding colonies of Cuba and Puerto Rico angered the colored inhabitants, and there was even a fear lest slavery be reëstablished in Santo Domingo.

Santana, who found himself with less and less authority, resigned as Captain General and was given a title of nobility and a pension early in 1862. A year later he took the field against insurgents who revolted in the interior, but met with little success, and in 1864 he died suddenly, perhaps by his own hand. Meanwhile yellow fever, the old enemy of European conquerors in the West Indies, attacked the Spanish army, and the growing Dominican revolt caused further losses and heavy expense. By the end of 1864 the Spanish government was weary of the whole affair, especially as it was clear that the approaching end of the civil war would soon permit the United States to follow up the strong protest against the occupation which it had made in 1861. After unsuccessful attempts to treat with the rebels, therefore, the Spanish forces simply abandoned the island in July, 1865.

Báez and the United States

The provisional government set up by the insurgents was already weakened by quarrels among rival leaders, and General Pimentel, who was its head when the Spaniards withdrew, was overthrown by a revolt at Santo Domingo City. General José María Cabral became President, but could not restore order, and at the end of 1865 Báez returned to power. Though Santana's old rival had lived in Europe during the Spanish occupation and had in fact accepted honors and money from the Spanish government until it was clear that the reconquest would not last, he was still the most influential of the Dominican political leaders, and intrigues which he directed from Curaçao forced the victorious *caudillos* of the war of liberation to consent to his return. His rivals, however, were little disposed to coöperate with him, and the interference of the Haitian government helped to keep the country in a state of disorder. Cabral, with the aid of President Geffrard, forced Báez to flee into exile, and then found his own position weakened by Haitian aid to his enemies after Geffrard was overthrown by Salnave. By January, 1868, the "reds" or *Baecistas* controlled the country, and a few months later their leader was back in the presidency.

Báez revived the idea of a foreign protectorate. Though he had been pro-French and anti-American in his earlier career, he had no choice but to turn to the United States, for no European power was now likely to challenge the Monroe Doctrine. Furthermore, the government at Washington was not averse to assuming new responsibilities in the Caribbean Sea. Secretary of State Seward had visited Santo Domingo in 1866, and in the following year the American government had again proposed to lease or buy Samaná Bay for a coaling station. These negotiations failed because of popular opposition in the Dominican Republic, but they were resumed later in 1867 when the Cabral government was on the point of collapse. Báez continued them, and when President Johnson suggested to Congress the desirability of annexing the Dominican Republic he expressed his full agreement.

Congressional hostility to Johnson made the realization of this project impossible for the time being, but the advocates of annexation resumed their efforts after President Grant's inauguration. The chief movers in the scheme, on the American side, were two adventurers named Cazneau and Fabens, who had obtained various concessions which would increase in value if annexation were effected. Despite their unsavory records and equally questionable methods, these men had apparently gained Seward's confidence, and they were no less successful with the new administration. Grant became much interested in their proposals and in 1869 sent his military secretary, General Orville Babcock, to Santo Domingo to confer with Báez. The result was the signature of two treaties, one providing for the annexation of the Dominican Republic to the United States and the other for a ninety-nine year lease of Samaná Bay. A plebiscite held in February, 1870, ostensibly indicated that the Dominican people approved the proposed agreements by an overwhelming majority.

President Grant and some of his chief advisers were actuated by a real interest in the Dominican Republic and a desire for imperialistic expansion, but their annexation project was discredited when it became evident that other and more sordid influences were also behind it. Cazneau and Fabens had enlisted the support of several influential Americans who were financially interested in the scheme, and Fabens was connected with a London banker named Hartmont, who had agreed to make a loan to the Báez government in 1869. This contract was one of the most improvident transactions in the history of Caribbean finance. The government was to receive £420,000, out of which it was to pay Hartmont a commission of £100,000. In return it was to pay £58,900 annually for twenty-five years, giving the customs receipts at Santo Domingo and Puerto Plata as security and authorizing the bankers to maintain representatives in the custom-houses there. It also gave the bankers a mortgage on the coal mines and forests of the Samaná district, and by a separate concession authorized Hartmont to work the mines for his own profit. Under the loan contract, Hartmont offered £757,700 of the Republic's 6 per cent bonds to the public at 70 per cent of their face value. The arrangement would have been an unconscionable one if it had been carried out in good faith, and when Hartmont failed to comply with his end of the bargain it left the government with a heavy debt for which it had received little in return. The promoters hoped to have their profits made secure by the consummation of the annexation project, but instead the contract was canceled, at the instance of the American government, when they failed to comply with their obligations. The bonds, however, could not be repudiated. They were long in default, but the government was compelled eventually to refund them.

When the Dominican treaties reached the United States Senate there was a bitter fight, with Senator Sumner leading the opposition. A tie vote, far short of the two-thirds necessary for ratification, defeated the proposal in June, 1870. Grant refused to drop the matter, and Congress authorized him to send a commission of inquiry which visited Santo Domingo early in 1871 and returned with a report supporting the administration's policy. By this time, however, the strength of the senatorial opposition and the indifference of public opinion precluded any possibility of favorable action, and the whole matter was dropped.

Strife between "Reds" and "Blues," 1871–1882

American naval forces helped to keep Báez in power during the negotiations, and his position was precarious when they were withdrawn. His opponents, the "blues," received help from Haiti, where Báez' enemy Nissage-Saget was now in power, and where the annexation project had caused much alarm; and he lost support among his own followers when he sought to replenish the treasury by leasing Samaná Bay to a private American company. He was overthrown in 1874 by one of his lieutenants, General Ignacio María González, who was in turn overthrown by a "blue" revolt in 1876.

The contest between "reds" and "blues" kept the country in a state of anarchy during the next three years. The "reds" still followed Báez, whereas the "blues" were led by Gregorio Luperón, a semi-illiterate, very popular Negro chieftain, who was content to let others occupy the presidency while his party was in power. Ulises Espaillat, elected President after the "blue" victory in 1876, was one of the Republic's most respected and enlightened citizens, but his effort to establish better conditions ended after a few months with a successful revolt under González. Before the end of 1876 the latter was in turn overthrown by Báez, only to return to power in 1878, and again to be forced out by the "red" General Guillermo. Luperón regained control in 1879 and after a brief period as Provisional President made his friend Father Meriño head of the government. Order was now restored, though not until two attempts at revolt had been cruelly suppressed, and when Meriño's two-year term expired, his minister of the interior, Ulises Heureaux, was "elected" without difficulty to succeed him.

Heureaux

The man who thus came into the presidency dominated Dominican political life during the next seventeen years. Though he was compelled to permit Luperón's candidate, General Billini, to succeed him in 1884, he soon forced Billini to resign in favor of Vice-President Woss y Gil, and in 1887 he returned to the presidency himself. Two years later he had a constitutional convention extend his term of office until 1893, and from then until the end of his life he was reëlected at regular intervals.

Heureaux was a full-blooded Negro, the illegitimate son of a Haitian and a woman from one of the other West Indian islands, with little education but much native intelligence. He had distinguished himself by his courage and ruthlessness in the war against Spain and the ensuing civil struggles, and he was fairly popular when he first took office. His administration was comparatively liberal at first, but it soon became a cruel and greedy despotism, with all of the demoralizing features inherent in such a system. He won the support of many other political leaders by bribery or intimidation, and there was little internal disorder during his long tenure of power—the first era of peace in the history of the Republic. Agriculture prospered and commerce took on new life. Sugar production, which had begun to increase in importance during the ten years' war in Cuba (1868–78) when several refugees from that island set up mills in Santo Domingo, was still further expanded by North American capital. The country thus felt the effect of the same influences which were making for stability and economic development in other Latin American countries in the closing years of the century.

On the other hand, Heureaux's financial transactions involved the country in grave difficulties. His first foreign loan in 1888 was floated by the Dutch firm of Westendorp. Its primary purpose was to refund the Hartmont bonds, whose holders had been supported by the British government in their demands for repayment, but it also provided a substantial sum for Heureaux's own use. Two years later, another loan was obtained from the same firm, ostensibly for railroad construction. This was a failure, and the Westendorp company, in financial difficulties, turned over its Dominican interests to an American firm, the "San Domingo Improvement Company," in 1892. The outstanding debt, already in default, was scaled down and refunded, and the customs receipts were pledged to the service of a new bond issue. Their collection was entrusted to a "*regie*" directed by the bankers, with a provision that it should be taken over in case of another default by nominees of the British, French, American, Dutch, and Belgian governments.

The Improvement Company thus not only supplied the government with funds but collected the major part of its revenues. It also carried on construction work on the Central Dominican Railway, and in 1895 it took over the control of the National Bank, hitherto owned by a French company. These operations were profitable to the bankers and to Heureaux personally, but successive bond issues were sold on more and more unfavorable terms, and the public debt rapidly increased. In 1897 there was a new default, followed by another adjustment at the bondholders' expense, and by still another default. When further loans became impossible, the government turned to the issue of depreciated currency to obtain funds.

Internal Disorder and Foreign Complications, 1899–1904

Heureaux was assassinated on July 26, 1899, by Ramón Cáceres, one of a group of conspirators which included Horacio Vásquez, Cáceres' cousin, who was a powerful political leader in the Cibao, and Juan Isidro Jiménez, a merchant at Monte Cristi. This group obtained control of the government after a brief civil war, and Jiménez became President. The new administration, virtually penniless, was beset by foreign claims, supported by diplomatic pressure or by warships. It was compelled by public opinion to attempt to dislodge the Improvement Company from its control of the customs and the National Bank, but the attitude of the United States forced it to agree to a compromise which satisfied no one. At the same time the Improvement Company's failure to maintain service on the government's bonds, most of which had been sold in European markets, and the government's own inability to meet bills for supplies and claims for damages, caused trouble with France, Belgium, Germany, Italy, and Spain.

The settlement of these problems was made more difficult by constant internal dissension. The *Horacistas*, as Vásquez' followers were called, overthrew Jiménez in 1902. Vásquez became President, only to be overthrown a year later by former partisans of Heureaux under General Alejandro Woss y Gil. Jiménez supported this revolt, but later in the same year his followers joined with the *Horacistas* in a new one, which was likewise successful. Jiménez expected to become president, and he promptly started an uprising of his own when the *Horacistas* prevailed on the *Jimenista* military leader Carlos Morales to seize power for himself. There were some months of fighting before a truce was arranged through the good offices of an American naval officer.

These financial and political difficulties led a few of the Dominican leaders to turn to the old idea of foreign help. Woss y Gil had tentatively offered Samaná Bay to the United States in 1903, and Morales soon after he came into office advocated placing the custom-houses under North American control. This, he thought, would not only relieve the pressure from other foreign creditors, but would also discourage revolutions, for the first step in a revolt was usually the seizure of a custom-house as a means of obtaining funds. The idea was an unpopular one in Santo Domingo, but it became increasingly clear that foreign intervention of some kind was practically unavoidable. The Republic now owed more than $32,000,000, and the annual fixed charge on the funded debt alone would have consumed $1,700,000 of the government's total estimated revenue of $1,850,000. If the debt service were maintained, there would be no funds for the conduct of the government.

The creditor powers nevertheless insisted on a settlement. In January, 1903, the government was compelled to promise the United States that it would pay $4,500,000 to the Improvement Company in return for the transfer of all the latter's interests in the country; and an arbitral award which fixed the manner of payment authorized a fiscal agent appointed by the United States to take over the collection of customs at several ports in case of default. This conflicted with agreements previously extorted from the Dominican government by several European creditors, under which the revenues from the same ports had been promised to them, and complications became inevitable when the American fiscal agent actually took possession of the Puerto Plata custom-house in October, 1904.

Establishment of the Customs Receivership

Several of the creditor powers were by this time threatening to take action against the Dominican Republic unless a general settlement of claims were brought about. It seemed very probable that one or more of them would actually occupy some of the Dominican ports. Since the recent decision of the Hague Court in a case arising from the Anglo-German blockade of Venezuela [1] had established the principle that nations which used force to collect debts should receive payment ahead of other creditors, it seemed probable that European intervention in Santo Domingo would hurt the American creditors, besides creating possible political dangers. These considerations impelled President Roosevelt to

[1] See above, pp. 378–9.

propose a plan which would protect the interests of all concerned. Morales agreed, and on February 7, 1905, a treaty was signed under which the United States undertook to collect the Dominican customs revenues and to attempt a general arrangement with all of the Republic's creditors.

Opposition in the United States Senate prevented prompt ratification of this pact, but a customs collectorship was nevertheless established in March under a *modus vivendi* or informal agreement. Of the funds received, 55 per cent were held in trust for the creditors for the time being. During the next year, with the help of the United States, Federico Velásquez, the Dominican Minister of Finance, worked out a general settlement by which outstanding obligations were to be scaled down and paid from an American loan of $20,000,000. A new treaty, providing that the customs receivership should continue so long as the bonds were outstanding, was signed February 8, 1907, and was promptly ratified.

A few months earlier, Morales had been forced out, after making an unsuccessful attempt to free himself from the domination of his *Horacista* cabinet. Vice-President Ramón Cáceres succeeded him and was reëlected for a six-year term in 1908. Cáceres was able and popular, and though Vásquez and other leaders of his own party turned against him, he easily suppressed all attempts at revolution. He had effective support from the United States, which did not hesitate to use its treaty right to prevent any interference with the collection of the customs, and his position was stronger because the country enjoyed a considerable measure of prosperity. Thanks to the American loan and a large increase in the customs revenues, the government's creditors were satisfied and money was available for public works and other purposes. For a time it seemed that the Republic's worst problems had been solved.

Renewed Disorder, 1911–1916

On November 19, 1911, Cáceres was murdered by political enemies, just as he himself had killed Heureaux twelve years earlier. The assassins' leader was captured and killed and the commander of the government's troops at Santo Domingo, Colonel Alfredo Victoria, took advantage of the situation to seize power for himself. He was too young to be elected to the presidency, but he forced the Congress to choose his uncle, Eladio Victoria, who was a respectable but ineffective gentleman with little personal following. This disappointed the other political leaders, and several of them promptly started revolts.

For five years the country suffered from almost continuous disorder which finally ended in the catastrophe of American military intervention. Neither the *Horacistas* nor the *Jimenistas* would accept peacefully any government that their party did not control, and the turbulence was increased by the activities of ambitious military leaders who seemed to welcome civil war, even when they were employed by the government, because it gave them greater opportunity for graft. The most prominent of these was Desiderio Arias, a partisan of Jiménez, who was to play a leading part in the events leading to the intervention. The United States exerted every effort to maintain peace, but its interference often seemed to do more harm than good. This was partly because of the ineptitude of its diplomatic representatives. There are few sorrier chapters in the history of American diplomacy than the career of James M. Sullivan, whose service as Minister at Santo Domingo from 1913 to 1915 was a shining example of the viciousness of the practice of treating diplomatic appointments as a reward for political services.

The United States could not remain aloof because it was obligated under the 1907 treaty to protect the customs service. The situation was especially bad along the land frontier, where the uncertainty about the boundary favored the operations of Haitian forces which were unofficially aiding Dominican revolutionists. In an effort to correct this situation, the United States simply fixed a de facto line in September, 1912, and insisted that both governments observe it. At the same time two American commissioners, accompanied by 750 marines, were sent to Santo Domingo to establish peace. At their suggestion, backed by a threat to withhold the customs collections from the government, President Victoria resigned, and the Archbishop of Santo Domingo, Adolfo Nouel, was elected by the Congress as Provisional President.

Monsignor Nouel attempted to keep the support of all parties by dividing the government offices between them, but he found it impossible to satisfy one without arousing the enmity of the others, and even the moral support of the United States was not enough to make his administration a success. In the interests of peace, he yielded more and more to the arrogant demands of Desiderio Arias, until the latter's growing power caused the *Horacistas* to threaten a revolt. The Archbishop then refused to remain longer in an office which he had been reluctant to accept in the first place, and in March, 1913, he resigned and went to Europe. After some weeks of balloting, the Congress elected José Bordas Valdés as Provisional President for a one-year term.

Bordas was an *Horacista*, but he soon quarreled with the other leaders of his party and began to intrigue with Arias and other military leaders in an effort to continue in power. The *Horacistas* revolted, but laid down their arms under pressure from the American Minister in return for a promise that a free election would be held. The United States did rather ineffectively attempt to supervise the election of a constituent assembly later in 1913, but trouble between the President and Congress prevented the holding of a new presidential election, and when Bordas' term ended he simply stayed in office. Meanwhile Arias took to the hills because the President had refused his demands for the vice-presidency and for a cash payment of $300,000. Vásquez soon joined him, and by July, 1914, the country was again in a state of anarchy.

Throughout the disturbances of the past three years the American government had fruitlessly cajoled and threatened and remonstrated with the Dominican leaders. In August, 1914, it came forward with an ultimatum, described as the "Wilson Plan." The contending factions were told to lay down their arms and to choose a provisional president who would hold elections to establish a constitutional government. These would be closely observed by American representatives, and if they proved free and fair the United States would support the new government and would insist that no further revolutions should occur. If they were not satisfactory, a new election would be held. If the leaders failed to agree upon a provisional president, the United States would name one and would place him in office. The plan was to be presented and carried out, without giving "any person or faction" an "opportunity for argument."

Faced with the threat of armed intervention, the Dominican political leaders after some controversy selected Dr. Ramón Báez as Provisional President. Since Báez was a partisan, though not a very active follower, of Jiménez, the latter had an advantage in the elections that were held under the supervision of American observers a few weeks later, and defeated Vásquez by a small majority. The new President took office on December 5, 1914. He had the promise of active North American support, by armed force if necessary, but at the same time he was confronted with demands from Washington to which he could not accede without alienating his followers in the Dominican Republic.

It was clear by this time that the customs collectorship alone did not assure either political or financial stability, and the government of the United States had decided to insist upon a greater measure of control over the Republic's internal affairs as a means of attaining these ends. The heavy expenses occasioned by the disorders of the past three years had resulted in continual deficits, and many bills and claims remained unpaid. The United States considered this situation a violation of Article III of the 1907 treaty, which provided that the Dominican public debt should not be increased except by previous agreement between the two governments. It had consequently compelled President Bordas to agree in May, 1914, to the appointment of a "financial expert" with authority to control expenditures, and after the inauguration of Jiménez, the United States urged him to strengthen the position of this official and also to place the internal revenues as well as the customs under the receivership. Reforms in the army and in the public-works service, to be carried out under the direction of American officials, were also proposed. Jiménez had agreed to some at least of these reforms while he was a candidate for the presidency, but he proved less amenable after he came into power, and in December, 1915, he refused a blunt demand for the appointment of a financial adviser with wide powers and the creation of a constabulary under American officers.

The internal political situation had meanwhile grown worse. The President was too old and infirm to deal effectively either with his subordinates or with his opponents. As the result of a preëlection bargain, Desiderio Arias had been made Minister of War, and he had used this position chiefly to enrich himself and his followers. He even seemed to be encouraging local political disorders, which increased the influence of the army and usually ended when the malcontents were bought off at the expense of the treasury. The United States repeatedly offered to send troops to repress these disorders, but the President declined to accept such assistance.

In April, 1916, Jiménez apparently decided to check Arias' growing power. He imprisoned two of the latter's chief lieutenants and the Minister of War promptly seized control of the capital. This was a direct challenge to the United States, which had repeatedly stated that it would not tolerate further revolutions. American marines promptly occupied Santo Domingo City, forcing Arias to withdraw into the interior, and soon afterward American forces were sent to other ports and to the more important inland cities. At the capital Jiménez preferred to resign rather than to remain in power with foreign aid, but the remaining members of his cabinet carried on the government until July 25, when the

Congress elected Dr. Francisco Henríquez y Carvajal as Provisional President.

The United States withheld recognition from the new government pending an agreement on the reform measures which had been proposed to Jiménez. In August it even instructed the Receiver General of Customs not to pay over any funds to the Dominican authorities. Since the receivership in the meantime had taken over the collection of the internal revenues as well as the customs, this made the Provisional President's position all but impossible. Dr. Henríquez nevertheless remained in office, without funds, and vainly endeavored to obtain some modification of the American demands. In November he precipitated a crisis, probably unintentionally, by asking the electoral colleges to replace members of Congress whose terms were expiring. It was known that the electoral colleges were controlled by followers of Desiderio Arias, who was openly pro-German, and the imminence of war with Germany made it impossible for the United States to acquiesce in an increase of his influence. President Wilson therefore reluctantly authorized the American naval commanders to take full control, and on November 29, 1916, Captain Harry S. Knapp issued a proclamation establishing an American military government.

The American Occupation

For nearly eight years the country was again under foreign rule. The Military Governor exercised legislative as well as executive authority. His American subordinates headed the various departments, though the majority of the other offices, including those in the judiciary, continued to be held by Dominicans. A native constabulary was trained by American officers. In 1917 and 1918 this force and the American marines had to suppress disturbances in the eastern part of the country, but after that there was no serious armed opposition. The maintenance of order, combined with the wartime demand for sugar, brought a temporary prosperity that made it possible to inaugurate ambitious programs of education and public works, but these were just getting under way when sugar prices collapsed in 1920.

The resultant depression intensified Dominican hostility to the military government. The occupation had been bitterly hated even when it seemed to be benefiting the country economically, and the maintenance of martial law and a stupid censorship of the press also aroused much criticism in other countries. The tactless and arbitrary conduct of some of the American officials aggravated an already bad situation. The United States of course never had any desire to exercise permanent control over the Dominican Republic, and after the war it sought to extricate itself from a situation in which it had been involved more by bad management than by design.

In December, 1920, President Wilson announced that the occupation would soon be withdrawn. Six months later the Harding administration proposed that the Dominicans should elect a government which would assume power after ratifying a convention embodying only a part of the demands that the United States had presented in 1915. The Dominican political leaders, however, refused to coöperate in the plan, and in June, 1922, an agreement was reached in Washington under which the country was to recover its independence without giving the United States any control over its military forces or any financial powers beyond those conferred by the 1907 treaty. A provisional president, selected by the Dominican party chiefs, was to take over part of the Military Governor's authority, and under his administration a constitution and other new laws were to be adopted in preparation for the election of a permanent president. A "convention of evacuation" was to validate the more important official acts of the military government, in order to protect vested interests created by them.

This plan was carried out, though not without difficulty. Juan Bautista Vicini Burgos was inaugurated as Provisional President in October, 1922, but further progress was delayed for some time by quarrels and intrigues among the various party leaders. The difficulties were finally overcome through the tact and persistence of Mr. Sumner Welles, the personal representative of the President of the United States, and in March, 1924, General Horacio Vásquez was elected constitutional President. Upon his inauguration four months later the military government ceased to exist and all the American forces were withdrawn.

The next six years, as in most of the Latin American countries, were a period of prosperity and political tranquility. Party bitterness had faded out during the occupation, and Vásquez was able to win the support of many of his former enemies. He no longer had to contend with the restless greed of local military leaders, for the new army, trained by American marines, was an efficient, well-disciplined force. It was not until the end of his six-year term that political difficulties again arose.

The "Era of Trujillo"

The President's announced candidacy for reëlection had already given rise to much political agitation when a serious illness temporarily incapacitated him and brought on an acute rivalry between members of his own government who hoped to succeed him in power. There was bad feeling, especially, between General Rafael Trujillo, the head of the army, and Vice-President Alfonseca, who was a candidate for reëlection and would presumably head the government if General Vásquez should die. The army consequently offered no resistance when a small force of revolutionists seized the fort at Santiago and then marched on Santo Domingo City in February, 1930. By an agreement effected through the good offices of the American Legation, Vásquez and Alfonseca resigned and Rafael Estrella Ureña, the opposition candidate for the vice-presidency and the leader of the revolution, became Provisional President. The opposition parties, however, gained nothing by the change, for General Trujillo promptly announced his own candidacy for the presidency and was elected in May with the support of the army.

The new President was a professional soldier who had risen from the ranks while the constabulary was being trained by American marine officers and had been given command of the force, now converted into the "army," when the marines withdrew. Once in office, he made himself the absolute ruler of the country. Persons who openly opposed him were severely treated. Many are said to have been killed, among them the veteran trouble-maker Desiderio Arias; and many others, including the chief leaders of the hitherto existing parties, went into exile. An effective secret service made conspiracy dangerous. On the other hand, the enforcement of internal peace made it possible for the country to recover rapidly from the world depression, which had severely affected it, and the Trujillo government was able to do more than any preceding administration in building roads and public works and encouraging agriculture. Its efficiency was demonstrated when it became necessary to reconstruct much of the capital city after the terrible hurricane of September, 1930. The name of the capital was changed from Santo Domingo to Ciudad Trujillo in 1936.

General Trujillo was reëlected in 1934, but in 1938 he declined to be a candidate for a third term. He nevertheless continued to be the acknowledged ruler of the country during the administrations of Jacinto

Peynado and of Dr. Manuel de Jesús Troncoso de la Concha, who took office after Peynado's death in 1940. In 1942 he returned to the presidency, and in 1947 he was elected for a fourth term. On this occasion he overwhelmingly defeated the candidates of two "opposition" parties which had been organized at his request.

One of the important achievements of the Trujillo government was the complete elimination of foreign financial control. The American customs collectorship was abolished by a treaty signed in 1940, and the outstanding bonds were paid off in full in 1947. Another treaty, signed in 1935, settled the long-standing and always troublesome question of the boundary with Haiti, but did not, unfortunately, prevent the massacre two years later of thousands of Haitians living on the Dominican side of the frontier.[1]

General Trujillo has encountered little effective opposition since he first assumed office. Economic conditions have on the whole been good, and the government's policies have brought about an increase and a much needed diversification in agricultural production. The masses of the people have shown little disposition to revolt. His dictatorial methods, on the other hand, have exposed him to much criticism abroad, and several other Caribbean governments, under the influence of liberal political groups, have been openly hostile to his regime. The most formidable attempt thus far made to overthrow him was organized in Cuba in 1947 with the apparent connivance of some high officials in that country, but the projected expedition was broken up by the Cuban government. Early in 1950, after General Trujillo had again accused the governments of Cuba and Haiti of fomenting movements against him, the Council of the Organization of American States intervened to prevent a conflict.

[1] See above, p. 527.

Part IX

꧁꧂

LATIN AMERICA AND THE UNITED STATES

THE story of inter-American relations begins before either portion of the continent achieved independence. In the seventeenth century persons who were interested in the Plymouth Colony were also promoting settlement and organized piracy in the Spanish Main. Colonial questions were involved in each of the European wars of the seventeenth and eighteenth centuries, and each of these wars was fought in part on the western side of the Atlantic. It was partly a desire to end the frequent involvement of the Western Hemisphere in Old World conflicts that led President Monroe in 1823 to issue his famous warning against any further attempt by European powers to control the destinies of the newly independent Latin American republics.

The Monroe Doctrine, as time went on, became one of the fundamental principles of American foreign policy. On several occasions—in Mexico, in Santo Domingo, and in Venezuela—it helped to preserve the independence or the territorial integrity of a Latin American country, despite European unwillingness to recognize its validity. Until relatively recently, however, the United States was chiefly concerned with the application of the Doctrine to Mexico and the Caribbean area. It was less important from the standpoint of national defense, and more difficult from a military point of view, to oppose European aggression in southern South America than in regions nearer to us. The American government consequently took no action to prevent such occurrences as Great Britain's occupation of the Falkland Islands and the Anglo-

French intervention of the 1840's in the River Plate. In fact its general relations with the countries south of the equator, during the greater part of the nineteenth century, were relatively unimportant. They, like ourselves, had far closer economic, cultural, and even political ties with Europe, to which they looked to provide markets for their goods and capital for the development of their resources.

Today the situation is entirely different. Inter-American trade is of great importance to all of the countries of the Hemisphere, and political events in one country may affect the welfare and the safety of each of the others. The problems that confront the American Republics in their relations with one another are perhaps even more difficult and complicated than they were fifty years ago, but the Organization of American States, working within the framework of the United Nations, is an increasingly effective agency for dealing with matters of common interest.

28

Inter-American Relations Before Pearl Harbor

Earlier Pan-American Conferences

Toward the end of the nineteenth century, after a long period of apparent indifference, the United States Government began to show an increasing interest in what was then called "Panamericanism." The larger South American countries were by that time achieving a measure of stability and commercial importance, and the United States was reaching a point in its economic development where it was interested in new markets for its industrial products and in the importation of larger amounts of raw materials for its factories. A desire to promote trade was the chief objective of the earlier inter-American conferences.

The first Pan-American conference met in Washington at the invitation of the American government in 1889. Its chief accomplishment was to set up the International Bureau of American Republics, later renamed the Pan American Union, which has since become one of the important organs of inter-American coöperation. Another result was a convention for the compulsory arbitration of pecuniary claims, a first step in the creation of the peace machinery which was to occupy much of the attention of later gatherings. Extradition, uniform customs and commercial regulations, sanitary problems, and monetary and exchange questions also received attention, as they did at subsequent conferences, but most of the resolutions adopted, like many of the acts of later conferences, had little effect because few of the signatory governments were sufficiently interested to ratify them.

The Second and Third Pan-American Conferences, held at Mexico City in 1901-2 and at Rio de Janeiro in 1906, followed much the same pattern and achieved little of consequence. At Mexico, however, the nations represented agreed that similar gatherings should be held every five years. At Rio de Janeiro they set up a Permanent Commission of Jurists to study the problem of codifying international law. The Fourth Conference, held at Buenos Aires in 1910, dealt, like its predecessors, with a wide range of commercial and sanitary problems, and adopted conventions for the protection of copyrights and patents which were ratified by most of the American states.

The First World War

Neither the measures adopted at these conferences nor other efforts to promote inter-American trade had any very notable results before 1914. Meat and grain from the River Plate republics and nitrate from Chile continued to go to Europe. The people of those countries, and even the Brazilians, who sold much of their coffee to the United States, continued to buy chiefly in European markets, to send their children to Paris and other old-world centers to study, and to travel east rather than north for recreation. Since there was no good direct steamship service, the most comfortable route from New York to Rio de Janeiro or Buenos Aires was by way of Europe. British, French, and German business men controlled much of the export and import business, the banks, the railroads, and many other enterprises. Little United States capital had been invested south of the Caribbean area, and North American residents were few and relatively uninfluential.

This situation changed during the First World War. As it became more difficult to buy goods in Europe, there was a great increase in trade with the United States. American banks established branches throughout Latin America, and there was a greater inflow of American capital. Furthermore the events of the conflict made the American nations aware that they had common interests distinct from those of Europe. President Wilson's stand for democracy against imperialism and militarism met with warm support in many circles in Latin America, and a new feeling of solidarity found practical expression after the United States became a belligerent. Brazil, Cuba, Panama, Haiti, and all of Central America except El Salvador declared war on Germany. Five other countries severed diplomatic relations. On the other hand, Argentina, Chile, Mexico, Colombia, Venezuela, Paraguay, and El Salvador remained formally neutral.[1]

[1] P. A. Martin, *Latin America and the War*, p. 1.

After the war, European trade recovered only a part of its former importance. Great Britain and the continent were still the principal markets for South American exports because the United States was in no position to buy large quantities of products like meat, grains, copper, or petroleum of which it was itself an exporter. In the import trade, on the other hand, American manufacturers retained an important position and supplanted the Germans as the chief competitors of the hitherto dominant British. The goods that they sold were paid for partly by bond issues that most of the Latin American governments floated in New York. During the same period much United States capital went into mines, public utilities, and other enterprises. By 1928 North American investments in South America were estimated at $2,294,212,100, and in Latin America as a whole at $5,587,494,100.[1]

Trade and investment, unfortunately, did not in themselves promote more friendly relations. During the post-war period the feeling toward the United States in the larger southern republics left much to be desired. This was partly the result of inadequate representation of American interests. Many of the firms that entered the South American field during and just after the war were inexperienced and a few were unscrupulous. Too many failed to send representatives who spoke Spanish and were otherwise qualified to win the respect and friendship of the local community. Even the United States Government did not seem to realize the importance of appointing diplomats who were competent and whose character would command respect. These shortcomings were corrected to a great extent as time went on, but not until much harm had been done.

American Policy in the Caribbean

Still more detrimental to good relations was the Latin Americans' dislike of our policy in the Caribbean, and the suspicion and fear that this policy aroused. We have already discussed the Roosevelt corollary to the Monroe Doctrine and have described the interventions in several of the Central American and West Indian republics. To the foreign observer, our conduct in the Caribbean seemed to grow more and more imperialistic in the period between 1904 and 1929.

In Theodore Roosevelt's administration, the United States intervened only when immediate action seemed necessary to correct a bad situation. The Dominican customs receivership was established to avert the ap-

[1] Winkler, *Investments of United States Capital in Latin America*, p. 278.

parently imminent seizure of one or more ports by European powers. An American provisional government was set up in Cuba after the constituted authorities refused to continue in office, but it was discontinued as soon as needed reforms were effected and a new election held. In Central America international conflicts were ended by North American and Mexican mediation, and relations between the five countries were placed on a new basis under the Washington treaties. The Taft administration, with Mr. Knox as Secretary of State, went farther. Under the so-called "preventive policy" it constantly interfered in the internal affairs of Caribbean countries on the theory that it was better to remedy conditions likely to cause civil war or foreign complications than to wait for crises to arise. It did not hesitate to threaten the use of force when its advice was not heeded, and its armed intervention in Nicaragua involved the United States in responsibilities which were troublesome for many years to come. It especially sought to extend to other countries the same sort of financial control that until 1911 had apparently been successful in the Dominican Republic. The period 1909–13 was the era of "Dollar Diplomacy," though the treaties which would have set up customs receiverships in Nicaragua and Honduras failed of approval in the United States Senate, and other attempts to effect financial reforms were equally unsuccessful. In general the "preventive policy" accomplished little, except perhaps to make worse the already bad situations in Nicaragua and the Dominican Republic.

The Wilson administration expressed disapproval of "Dollar Diplomacy" but continued to interfere in Caribbean affairs. If there was less emphasis on the protection of foreign rights and interests, there was more insistence on the maintenance of constitutional forms and democratic practices. Governments that came into power by methods openly illegal were refused recognition and in some cases were forced out of office by American opposition. Acting on the same principle that underlay President Taft's "preventive policy," the Department of State attempted to strike at the roots of the Caribbean political and social problem by bringing about the establishment of efficient police forces, the reform of financial administration, and the adoption of broad programs of economic rehabilitation, all under the direction of North American advisers. When these objectives could not be accomplished by diplomatic pressure, there was a resort to force. Haiti was occupied by American forces in 1915, and the Haitian government was compelled to sign a treaty giving the United States control of several important branches of its administration. A year later a military government was set up in the Dominican Republic. American intervention in the Caribbean had reached its high point at the end of President Wilson's term in 1921.

Thereafter there was a gradual change in policy. In the decade that followed the World War, when no European power was in a position to challenge the Monroe Doctrine, the Roosevelt corollary lost much of its significance. It became apparent, furthermore, that the policies hitherto followed were repugnant to Latin American public opinion and were becoming increasingly unpopular in the United States. Gradually the responsibilities already assumed were liquidated. There was less active interference in the internal affairs of Cuba and Panama, and the American forces were withdrawn from the Dominican Republic in 1924 and from Nicaragua in 1925. Unfortunately the second intervention in Nicaragua in 1926 and the continuance of the treaty regime in Haiti tended to obscure the fact that a change in policy was occurring. North American "imperialism" still provided material for the propaganda of European commercial interests and other unfriendly groups. Even the great American press services, which had recently established themselves in South America, contributed to the misunderstanding by reporting sensational and often misleading articles and speeches by anti-imperialists in the United States.

The Santiago and Habana Conferences

These and other obstacles to continental solidarity were evident in the proceedings of the Fifth and Sixth Pan-American Conferences. The Fifth Conference, which met at Santiago, Chile, in 1923, was more concerned than its predecessors with political questions. It met under a cloud because Peru and Bolivia, still at odds with Chile over questions arising from the War of the Pacific, and Mexico, whose government had not been recognized by the United States, refused to attend. During the sessions there were several indications of unfriendly feeling toward the United States and this feeling was not diminished when the American delegation blocked proposals for a reorganization of the Pan American Union designed to pave the way for the eventual establishment of an American League of Nations, and insisted that the United States must retain the right to interpret and enforce the Monroe Doctrine as it alone saw fit. There were at the same time disagreements between the larger South American countries themselves, and no accord was reached on the proposal for disarmament which was the most important item on the agenda. The chief positive accomplishment of the Conference was the Gondra Peace Treaty, which provided that any inter-American dispute not settled by diplomacy should be submitted to a commission of inquiry, and that no hostile move should be made until six months after the commission's report had been rendered. At the Sixth Conference, which met in Habana in 1928, the unfriendliness of several Latin American countries toward the United States was even more manifest, and efforts to bring about the adoption of a resolution condemning intervention by one state in the affairs of another, clearly directed at North American policies in Nicaragua and Haiti, were blocked only after a series of rather painful incidents.

The Abandonment of the Intervention Policy

Soon afterward it became clear that the Caribbean policies that had been the target for so much criticism both in North and in South America were definitely being abandoned. President Hoover, in the first year of his administration, took steps to terminate the intervention in Haiti, and in 1931 the American officials were withdrawn from the majority of the treaty services there. By 1934 American forces were out of Haiti and only the finances remained under foreign control. In Nicaragua the marines were withdrawn early in 1933. At the same time the policy of the United States changed in other respects. Except in Central America, where the treaties of 1923 created a special situation, the United States abandoned the use of non-recognition of revolutionary governments as a means of discouraging disorder.

President Franklin D. Roosevelt's Good Neighbor Policy went considerably farther in the same direction. In December, 1933, when the Seventh International Conference of American States met at Montevideo, the American delegation signed, though with reservations, a Convention on Rights and Duties of States which provided that "No state has the right to intervene in the external or internal affairs of another." [1] President Roosevelt himself declared a few days later that "the definite policy of the United States from now on is one opposed to armed intervention," and that if a breakdown of law and order in any American country affected other nations, it was the joint concern of the whole

[1] Article 8 of the Convention on Rights and Duties of States.

continent and not of the United States alone.[1] In the years that followed
the United States modified several treaties that contained provisions in-
consistent with the non-intervention principle. The Platt Amendment
was abrogated in 1934, and American rights in the Canal Zone and in
the Republic of Panama were curtailed in the new treaty which was ratified in 1939. In 1941 the customs receivership in the Dominican Republic
and the office of the Fiscal Representative in Haiti were abolished. The
American government thus extricated itself from practically all of the
responsibilities that it had assumed in connection with the internal affairs
of its smaller neighbors.

Economic Nationalism in Latin America

The abandonment of intervention was but one aspect of President
Roosevelt's "Good Neighbor" policy. There was also an effort to avoid
controversies and friction, especially in cases where American financial
interests were involved. The protection of these interests had become
more difficult during and after the world depression because there was
a strong movement throughout Latin America to eliminate or reduce
foreign economic influence.

During the first century of independence commerce and business
affairs throughout the countries south of the Rio Grande had been
almost entirely in foreign hands. European merchants controlled most
of the export and import trade and the small shopkeepers were generally
Chinese, Syrian, Italian, Spanish, or Portuguese. Since practically all
capital came from abroad, railroads, mines, factories, and banks were
managed by representatives of the investors. The natives of the country
were more interested in agriculture and in politics, and in any event
could rarely compete with the more active and aggressive immigrant,
who had better connections abroad and more business training. Those
who obtained positions in business enterprises found that all of the better
jobs and higher salaries went to foreigners. This, and the privileged position which many foreign firms claimed under concessions obtained from
the local governments, caused much jealousy. The eagerness with which
foreign capital had been welcomed when it was needed for the building
of railroads and the opening of mines or factories was forgotten when
the benefits that it brought began to be taken for granted; and Latin

[1] Speech before the Woodrow Wilson Foundation, December 28, 1933.

American statesmen increasingly felt that alien control of such important sectors of their countries' economic life was an unwholesome situation.

Measures designed to break down this control, ranging from a natural and proper regulation of foreign enterprises to outright confiscation, were consequently adopted in most of the Latin American countries. Among the more important were laws restricting the proportion of foreigners who might be employed by any one company and in each branch of a company's work—laws which opened up many new opportunities for native engineers, executives, and technicians. There were also efforts to promote local industry as a means of becoming less dependent on imports. These efforts received a great impetus during the depression, when the difficulty of selling goods abroad and the consequent lack of foreign exchange made it difficult to obtain goods from foreign countries. Another manifestation of economic nationalism was the reluctance to resume service on the foreign debts which had gone into default in the depression years.

These nationalistic policies caused heavy losses to American investors, but the questions which they created were treated with a forbearance indicative of a new spirit in American foreign policy. Even the seizures of the American oil properties in Mexico and Bolivia were not permitted to cause such acute diplomatic tension as they would have caused a few years earlier. Efforts were made to obtain at least a measure of compensation for the owners, but it seemed clear that the State Department's policy was influenced more by a desire to maintain friendly relations with the other American governments than by its concern for the protection of property rights. This attitude was criticized by those whose interests were injuriously affected, but it did much to allay dislike and distrust of the United States in Latin America.

The Shadow of the Second World War

With the growing aggressiveness of fascism in Europe, inter-American relations entered a new phase. The regimentation of the large German and Italian colonies in Latin America to act as agents of fascist policy, and the subversive activities of native fascist and communist parties, supported in some cases at least from outside, were offensive to Latin American nationalism and alarming to those who believed in democratic ideals. The Nazi occupation of Austria and Czechoslovakia showed the Latin Americans that they could not be secure in a world where violence took the place of civilized methods of settling international problems. They, like ourselves, began to perceive that the new forces that had been let loose in the world were a danger to free institutions everywhere.

As early as 1936, the Inter-American Conference for the Maintenance of Peace, meeting at Buenos Aires, adopted a convention in which the American republics pledged themselves to consult with one another if the peace of the continent were menaced by strife within or by attack from without. Their determination to stand together for the defense of their common ideals and interests was made still more evident when the Eighth International Conference of American States met at Lima in December, 1938. A "Declaration of American Principles" stressed the principle of non-intervention, the settlement of international disputes by peaceful means, and the faithful observance of treaties, and proscribed the use of force as an instrument of national or international policy. Other resolutions, obviously directed against the totalitarian powers, denied the validity of the acquisition of territory by force and condemned persecution on account of race or religion. The most important act of the conference was the Declaration of Lima, in which the governments of the American states reaffirmed "their continental solidarity and their purpose to collaborate in the maintenance of the principles upon which the said solidarity is based" and "to defend them against all foreign intervention or activity that may threaten them."

Neutrality, 1939–41

When the World War broke out in Europe, the procedure of consultation was promptly invoked. Representatives of the foreign ministers of all of the American republics met at Panama in September, 1939, and laid down general standards that their governments proposed to follow in maintaining their neutrality. In the "Declaration of Panama" they demanded that the belligerents refrain from any hostile act in the waters near the American continents—a demand with which the warring powers did not always comply. The meeting also dealt with economic problems, and set up the Inter-American Financial and Economic Advisory Committee to study the urgent problems created by the dislocation of foreign trade.

The German conquest of the Netherlands and France in 1940 confronted the American states with new and still graver problems. Both countries had colonies in the Caribbean. The situation was less acute in the case of the Dutch possessions, which were held for the government in exile by British forces, than in the case of the French, which remained under the control of the Vichy regime; but even Britain's ability to hold out seemed uncertain, and it was necessary to consider what might happen to her possessions. In June, 1940, the United States informed Germany and Italy that it "would not recognize any transfer, and would not acquiesce in any attempt to transfer, any geographic region of the Western Hemisphere from one non-American power to another non-American power," and at the same time Secretary of State Hull proposed that another meeting of foreign ministers be convoked at once.

The conference of foreign ministers which met at Habana in July, 1940, marked an epoch in the development of inter-American relations and in the history of the foreign policy of the United States. For the first time the American republics agreed on a concrete program for joint action if there should be a challenge to the Monroe Doctrine. The "Act of Habana" provided that any European possession in the Americas which was "in danger of becoming the subject of barter of territory or change of sovereignty" might be placed under the government of a provisional regime representing the American republics. This regime would end when the territory in question was ready for self-government, or when it was restored to its former status, "whichever of these alternatives shall appear the more practicable and just." The Act set up an Emergency Committee to assume the administration of regions which might be attacked or threatened, but it also authorized any American state to act in its own defense if the danger should be too urgent to permit delay.

The Habana Conference dealt with other questions which had become urgent during the past ten months, such as the spread of subversive totalitarian propaganda. It urged the American governments to prevent foreign diplomatic or consular agents from carrying on activities dangerous to the peace and the democratic tradition of America, and pledged the governments represented to prevent groups or individuals in their territory from carrying on such activities. One of its most important acts, in the light of later events, was a resolution which declared that:

Any attempt on the part of a non-American state against the integrity or inviolability of the territory, the sovereignty or the political independence of an American state shall be considered as an act of aggression against the states which sign this declaration.

and provided for the negotiation of bilateral or other complementary agreements "to organize coöperation for defense and the assistance that they shall lend each other in the event of aggressions."

As the war in Europe progressed, the need for coöperation to defend the common interests of the American states became more and more evident. The problem had both military and economic aspects, but at first the economic aspect seemed the more urgent. More than half of the exports of the Hemisphere went to Europe in normal times. The bulk of this comprised foodstuffs and raw materials for which no other market could well be found. The United States might take additional quantities of some Latin American products, but it could do little to provide new outlets for goods of which we ourselves had a surplus or for commodities like coffee, sugar, and copper, of which the supply exceeded our normal consumption. In the First World War, after an initial period of dislocation, a greatly increased demand from the Allies had brought prosperity to most of Latin America, but at that time great markets were open on the continent of Europe as well as in the British Isles. In 1940, all of the continent was blockaded and British purchasing power was restricted by lack of funds and ships. As a result surpluses piled up, and the inability to export caused a shortage of foreign exchange which made it difficult to purchase the imports which the United States was still able to furnish.

This situation not only endangered the important commercial and financial interests of the United States in Latin America but threatened to diminish the effectiveness of inter-American coöperation for political and military defense. Many Latin American countries faced an economic crisis which might easily facilitate the work of subversive elements, both fascist and communist, which were working with outside help to destroy the whole idea of Pan-American solidarity. Joint action to improve the economic situation seemed one of the surest means to strengthen this solidarity and to assure the Latin American states' ability to resist eventual military aggression.

Through the Inter-American Financial and Economic Advisory Committee and its subsidiary bodies, moderately successful efforts were made to find new products which might be sold by Latin America to the United States and to increase trade in other ways. The shortage of shipping was to some extent relieved when several countries decided to make use of vessels, lying idle in their ports, which belonged to Axis or occupied countries. One very important achievement of the "IFEAC" was the Inter-American Coffee Marketing Agreement, which was signed November 28, 1940. Coffee producers, who had already suffered so many vicissitudes, were especially hard hit by the closing of European markets. The United States could not take their surplus, but it did agree to limit imports to a quota from each country, thus restricting competition and assuring a relatively high price for the amount purchased. The arrangement was not unlike that already in force for sugar, and the cost of maintaining economic stability in the countries benefited fell in both cases on the American consumer.

The United States Government itself was meanwhile extending financial aid to many of the other American countries through the Export-Import Bank, a government institution established in 1934 to aid American exporters. In September, 1940, the amount of loans which this Bank might have outstanding at any one time was increased to $700,000,000 and the Bank was authorized to make loans to foreign governments, corporations, or individuals. By the end of 1941 it had extended aid in one form or another to most of the other American republics, emphasizing especially loans for the improvement of transportation systems, both railway and highway, as part of a program to increase the delivery of strategic raw materials to the United States. Among the projects financed was the intensification of work on the Pan-American Highway between Mexico City and the Canal Zone. The United States Treasury granted large additional credits to several Latin American governments from its stabilization fund, and corporations organized by the United States Government spent or agreed to spend several hundred million dollars in Latin America for strategic raw materials.

As the possibility of an actual military attack on the Hemisphere became less remote than it had seemed in 1939, the Latin American countries, like the United States, began to build up their armed forces. Most of them employed missions from the United States Army or Navy to give technical advice, and many obtained North American arms. The United States, with its new bases in the British possessions in America, was increasing its ability to defend its own shores and the

Caribbean region, but it was clear that it would need the coöperation of other American powers if it were to make good its announced policy of preventing aggression against any other part of the continent. Several of the other American countries, despite the natural reluctance to permit the use of national territory by a foreign power, and the internal political dangers involved, permitted the United States to establish air or naval bases at vitally important strategic points in their territory. One serious potential danger was diminished when most of the axis-controlled air lines in Latin America were taken over or eliminated by the countries in which they operated.

Even more dangerous, perhaps, than an actual military attack was the possibility of espionage and sabotage in Latin America. It was well known that Axis diplomatic and consular agents were encouraging these activities and in some places fomenting actual subversive movements. Almost everywhere the influential German business colonies had been converted into carefully organized, effective agencies for the furthering of German policy. In several countries there were many German immigrants: several hundred thousand of them in Brazil, a considerable number in Argentina, and smaller but compact and largely unassimilated groups in Chile, Uruguay, Paraguay, and other republics. How far these permanent settlers had been converted to Nazi doctrines it is difficult to say, but they were clearly a source of potential trouble. So also were certain elements in the native population. The communists, a small but aggressive faction, coöperated with Axis agents until Hitler's attack on Russia, and in a few countries fascist groups had a not inconsiderable following. Many army officers were admirers of the German system, and German prestige tended to increase with each Axis victory. Fortunately the majority of intelligent public opinion in Latin America seemed to support the governments in their policy of coöperation with the United States.

29

Inter-American Relations, 1941–1950

The Test of Pan-American Solidarity

Between 1939 and 1941 the American Republics' hope of remaining aloof from the European conflict had given way to an increasing sense of the danger that threatened their common interests. At Habana they had declared that they would regard an attack on any of them as an attack on all, and immediately after Pearl Harbor every other nation of the continent assured the United States of its support. Haiti, the Dominican Republic, and all of Central America declared war on Japan the same day that the United States acted. Cuba and Panama did so a day or two later. Mexico, Colombia, and Venezuela broke off diplomatic relations with the Axis powers, and Mexico agreed in January, 1942, to the creation of a joint Mexican–United States defense commission. Brazil emphatically proclaimed its solidarity with the United States.

A third meeting of the ministers of foreign affairs of the American republics convened at Rio de Janeiro on January 15, 1942. The great majority of the governments represented felt that all diplomatic relations with the Axis powers should be terminated immediately, but Argentina, where the government was not friendly to the democracies, opposed a declaration urging such action, and was supported by Chile. The resolution finally adopted recommended that all of the American states break off relations, but with qualifications that left each government free to delay action if it wished. At the same time the resolution reaffirmed the determination of the American nations to coöperate for mutual defense. All except Argentina and Chile severed relations with the enemy during or immediately after the conference, and Chile finally did so in January, 1943.

The foreign ministers also recommended measures for the "economic mobilization" of the continent, to provide an adequate supply of strategic materials and basic commodities for military and civilian use. They expanded the functions of the Inter-American Financial and Economic Advisory Committee and urged the termination of commercial and financial intercourse with Axis-dominated territories. One resolution stressed the need to suppress espionage, sabotage, and subversive propaganda, and proposed the creation of an Emergency Advisory Committee for Political Defense, which was soon afterward set up in Montevideo. Another body established as a result of the conference was the Inter-American Defense Board.

During the next three years the Latin American nations made an invaluable contribution to the allied war effort. We have seen that some of them had already permitted the United States to use parts of their territory for naval or air bases. Several others now did so, greatly facilitating the campaign against the submarine and aiding in the defense of the Panama Canal. The operations in North Africa and the Mediterranean would have been much more difficult had it not been for the flying fields in Brazil. Equally important was the strenuous effort to increase the supply of urgently needed strategic commodities. Tin from Bolivia, copper from Peru and Chile, nitrate from Chile, and quartz crystals from Brazil were only a few of the Latin American products that were indispensable to the war plants in the United States. Large coöperative programs were undertaken to increase the supply of rubber, quinine, and other products which had formerly been obtained from countries overrun by Japan. A greatly increased flow of goods to the United States was made possible not only by governmental coöperation but also by the coöperation of the people who worked in the mines and other enterprises, and enemy efforts to sabotage war production were for the most part frustrated by governmental action supported by public opinion. Most of the Latin American states took effective action against enemy agents, deporting or interning dangerous aliens and seizing Axis-owned properties. Two of them, Brazil and Mexico, went farther and actually sent troops to the fighting fronts.

At the same time the United States gave very substantial help to Latin America. In addition to technical and financial assistance in developing war production, it endeavored, despite the shortages in this country, to supply the most essential needs of the civilian population in the other countries of the hemisphere. The Export-Import Bank increased its loans to other American countries, and this financial aid not only encouraged production for export, but also made possible the expansion of local industry to supply civilian needs. The Office of the Coördinator of Inter-American Affairs carried on an extensive program, in coöperation with local officials, to improve public health and increase food production in several countries.

Relations with Argentina and the Mexico City Conference

The only Latin American state that did not coöperate in the war effort was Argentina. We have already mentioned the secret negotiations which the dictatorship in that country carried on with Germany.[1] The full extent of these activities was not known at the time, but it was clear that the military government was making no real effort to interfere with the work of enemy agents and was encouraging subversive activities against neighboring governments that were friendly to the democracies. The United States and most of the other American countries refused to recognize the Farrell regime after the *coup d'état* of February, 1944. It was difficult to impose more effective sanctions, because Argentine meat and wheat were indispensable to the democracies, and especially to Great Britain. The situation was also a delicate one for some of the South American countries that were vulnerable to Argentine economic and military pressure. On the other hand, the Argentine authorities too apparently found their position uncomfortable as it became clearer that Germany would be defeated.

The reëstablishment of normal relations with Argentina was thus one of the chief questions that came up at the Inter-American Conference on Problems of War and Peace that met at Mexico City in February, 1945. Since invitations were issued only to countries coöperating in the war, Argentina was not represented, but the Conference invited her to adhere to the agreements that it adopted and thus to signify her willingness to join with the other American states in measures for hemisphere defense.

The Conference adopted a number of measures designed to make the joint participation in the war effort more effective, and it attempted to foresee some of the problems that would arise with the coming of peace. To provide for a closer coöperation between the American republics, it adopted an "Economic Charter of the Americas" and a de-

[1] See above, p. 190.

tailed agreement for strengthening the machinery of the inter-American system. Still more significant was the Act of Chapúltepec, which provided that any act of aggression against an American state during the war period should be treated as an aggression against all and should be met by common action agreed on after consultation. One purpose of this defensive alliance, directed against American as well as non-American aggressors, was to support democratic governments in resisting the sort of pressure that the Argentine regime had been exerting against some of its neighbors.

The government at Buenos Aires not only accepted the invitation of the conference to adhere to its final act, but declared war, in March, on Japan and Germany. All of the other American countries resumed diplomatic relations with it, and when the United Nations conference met at San Francisco the other American governments, despite strong opposition from Russia, insisted that Argentina be invited to participate. Unfortunately, however, it soon became clear that there had been little real change in the policies of Colonel Perón and his associates.

The Mexico City conference marked a high point in inter-American coöperation. With the end of the war there was a reaction. The United States necessarily tapered off its purchases and discontinued some of its development programs. The Latin Americans, struggling with post-war inflation and other difficult problems of readjustment, began to feel that the American government had lost interest in them when it no longer needed their help. The officials at Washington were in fact preoccupied with the European situation and the rapidly developing "cold war," and there were periods when Latin American relations seemed to receive little attention in the Department of State.

It was especially unfortunate that renewed tension between the United States and Argentina delayed for two years the realization of one of the most important projects agreed on at Mexico City, the adoption of a permanent treaty to take the place of the war-time Act of Chapúltepec. There was a strong desire for such a treaty among the other American countries, despite the existence of the United Nations, because they preferred the settlement of inter-American questions through the machinery of the inter-American system where each state had an equal voice. The United States, however, insisted that it could not participate in the proposed conference if Argentina also attended, and the conference was consequently delayed until some of the differences between the two governments were adjusted.

The Inter-American Treaty of Reciprocal Assistance

The conference finally met at Rio de Janeiro, where the Inter-American Treaty of Reciprocal Assistance was signed on September 2, 1947. Under this treaty, the American states agreed to endeavor to settle all controversies between themselves by inter-American procedures before referring them to the Security Council or the General Assembly of the United Nations. The treaty further provided that an armed attack by any state against an American state, if it occurred within a zone surrounding the American continents, "shall be considered as an attack against all the American states and, consequently, each one of the said Contracting Parties undertakes to assist in meeting the attack in the exercise of the inherent right of individual or collective self-defense recognized by Article 51 of the Charter of the United Nations." In the event of an aggression outside of the American security zone, or in any other situation threatening the peace of America, the signatories agreed to consult with one another, first through the Pan American Union and then as soon as possible through a meeting of foreign ministers. Under the treaty, no country can be compelled to use armed force without its consent, but where other measures against aggressors are involved decisions binding on all parties to the treaty can be taken by a two-thirds majority. This latter provision, almost unprecedented in international arrangements, is a striking demonstration of the mutual confidence of the partners in the inter-American system.

The Rio Treaty is a regional arrangement within the framework of the United Nations, and provides for the exercise of the right of self defense reserved in the charter. It recognizes the superior authority of the Security Council when, and if, that body chooses to act, but it gives assurance that neither the paralyzation of the Security Council by a veto, nor the opposition of a small minority of the American states, can prevent the nations of the Hemisphere from helping one of their number that is the victim of aggression.

The Bogotá Conference and the Organization of American States

A further strengthening of the machinery for coöperation among the American nations was one of the important items on the agenda of the Ninth International Conference of American States, which met at Bogotá in March, 1948. The decisions on this subject reached at Mexico City required formal action by a regular inter-American conference before they could be fully effective.

The Conference did its work under somewhat discouraging conditions. Several of the Latin American governments had apparently hoped that the meeting would give them an opportunity to obtain further financial help from the United States. Secretary Marshall announced at one of the sessions that President Truman had asked Congress to make half a billion dollars available for loans to Latin America by the Export-Import Bank, but this amount seemed small by comparison with the great sums being spent in Europe and the statement was received in stony silence. At a later stage, all of the work of the Conference was disrupted by the terrific outburst of mob violence which destroyed much of Bogotá.[1] On the whole it seemed the least successful inter-American gathering since the inauguration of the Good Neighbor Policy.

The Conference nevertheless achieved its principal task, the adoption of the Charter of the Organization of American States. This set up a new international entity which had as its declared objectives the peaceful settlement of questions arising among its members, the organization of "solidary action" against aggressors, and the promotion of the economic, social, and cultural development of the continent. The supreme authority in the Organization is the Inter-American Conference, which is to meet every five years. In the intervals, urgent problems will be dealt with by "meetings of consultation" of the Ministers of Foreign Affairs, which may be called at the request of any member of the Council of the Organization. The Council, which is the former governing board of the Pan American Union, may act as an organ of consultation in emergencies. It also directs the work of the Inter-American Economic and Social Council, the Inter-American Council of Jurists, and the Inter-American Cultural Council, and it supervises or maintains liaison with the great number of inter-American agencies that have been set up to promote coöperation in various fields. The Pan American Union, now headed by a Secretary General, is its central permanent organ and secretariat.

The increase in the political functions of the Pan American Union was made possible by changes approved at the Mexico City Conference

[1] See above, p. 369.

and put into effect after that meeting. Before 1945 the Director General of the Union had always been a North American and the Governing Board had been composed of the Latin American ambassadors at Washington with the Secretary of State as chairman. This had led to a feeling that the Union was too subject to the influence of the United States, and it had been agreed at Mexico that the chairmanship of the board should rotate and that the Director General, serving for a ten year term, should never be succeeded by a person of the same nationality. A distinguished Colombian, Dr. Alberto Lleras Camargo, was chosen Director General in 1947, and continued as Secretary General under the new charter.

The creation of the Organization of American States was an important step toward more effective inter-American coöperation. In conjunction with the treaty signed a year earlier at Rio de Janeiro, it provided machinery through which the American states could work together both for their common defense against external dangers and for the improvement of internal economic and social conditions. The Organization, through its subsidiary organs, deals with a wide range of matters where joint action can be helpful. Within a few months after the Council of the Organization had assumed its new rôle, it successfully met its first test in the political field by terminating a conflict that threatened to cause armed strife between Nicaragua and Costa Rica. In 1950 it dealt successfully with two other disputes involving the Dominican Republic and several of its neighbors.

The Bases of Pan Americanism

The American states have been able to build up the most effective system of international coöperation that the world has thus far seen in spite of serious obstacles. Besides the differences in language and culture and inherited traditions, the builders of the Inter-American System have had to contend with suspicion and jealousy on the Latin American side and with prejudice and sometimes indifference in the United States. To many observers "Pan Americanism" has seemed little more than a vague sentiment based on a not very clear understanding of geography.

The events of the past fifteen years have shown that inter-American solidarity rests on a solid basis of common ideals and of opposition to political philosophies repugnant to these ideals. This is especially evident in the field of international relations, where the American republics have supported such concepts as the equality of states, the rule of law as opposed to force, and the peaceful settlement of international disputes. Except in a relatively few cases, they have succeeded in applying these principles in their relations with one another. There have been many wars in Latin America but most of them were simply internal political feuds that crossed state lines. Few were real conflicts between nation and nation, and fewer still could be called wars of aggression or conquest. Disputes between governments, including the troublesome boundary controversies which involved every one of the twenty republics, have in most cases been settled by diplomacy or arbitration, even though armed clashes sometimes occurred before a settlement was reached. A great part of the attention of recent Pan-American conferences has been devoted to the creation and perfection of machinery to prevent war.

The effort to achieve internal political democracy has of course been less successful, and skeptics have questioned the sincerity of inter-American declarations emphasizing democratic ideals because many of the governments adhering to them were in reality dictatorships. It is true that only a few of the Latin American nations have thus far succeeded in making republican institutions a reality, but it is also true that the determination of their statesmen and of their people to attain true republican government has been one of the outstanding facts in their history.

To understand why they have not been more successful, we must consider some of the obstacles that they had to surmount. In the period just after independence, the first need of the new republics was internal peace, without which neither efficient government nor economic progress was possible. Political inexperience, local jealousies, violent controversies over the relation of the State to the Church, and apparently irreconcilable social conflicts made the achievement of peace difficult, but conditions gradually improved as new ideas and increased contacts with the outside world made the issues that had divided the people into hostile factions seem less important. Responsible people realized more and more that revolutions were an intolerable nuisance. An increasing number of merchants and miners and planters were disposed to support any government that promised to maintain order, and the more important Latin American countries consequently enjoyed a relative stability in the last years of the nineteenth and the first part of the twentieth century.

During this period, foreign trade increased rapidly and much foreign capital was invested in mines, railways, and plantations. This economic development was not only a result but to some extent a cause of the establishment of peace. It did not really start until political conditions began to improve, and when it started it was a powerful factor making for further improvement, for any government is more secure in its position in times of prosperity.

In many countries, however, the change simply made it easier for one man or one group to remain in power without much progress toward real republican government. Powerful economic interests were more concerned for the maintenance of peace than for the achievement of democracy, and large revenues made it easier to purchase the support of troublesome political leaders and to pay the army regularly and generously. More important still, the army could be better equipped. New weapons and techniques of warfare made a revolt more difficult than in the days when untrained civilians, armed with the small stock of rifles that each *caudillo* had hidden away at the end of the previous war, could face the equally ill-equipped regular army on fairly even terms. With the introduction of the machine gun, and later of the airplane, and with the improvement of discipline in the permanent military forces, the government had an overwhelming advantage. It became increasingly difficult for a revolutionary movement to succeed unless at least a part of the army joined it, or unless it received substantial help from some outside source.

In the countries with large Indian or Negro populations, elections continued to be little more than a form. Though all the outward aspects of constitutional government might be carefully observed, the president in fact chose all other officials including members of congress, and named his own successor when he did not wish or dare to remain in power himself. Even the courts had no independence where any question involving politics was at stake. The governments differed from those of the first years of independence chiefly in that they were more efficient autocracies, normally set up and overthrown by factions in the army rather than by the older and more destructive type of civil war.

Similar conditions prevailed in some of the other countries. Where the masses of the people are of mixed blood the gulf between the upper and the lower class is not so wide, but the establishment of democratic institutions is still difficult. The *mestizo*, naturally intelligent and quick to learn, has shown much political capacity where prosperity has helped him to improve his situation, but in countries where geographical isolation or lack of natural resources have prevented economic progress he has remained in a state of ignorance and poverty. In such countries the forces which worked elsewhere for stable government were less in evidence. Politics continued to be the chief interest of the ruling class, government jobs the most attractive form of employment, and revolution the normal way to obtain them. When revolutions became more difficult because of changing techniques of warfare dictatorships were the natural result.

But even in countries where social and economic conditions offered the most serious obstacles, the better type of Latin American statesmen continued to work for the ultimate attainment of republican government. They were supported by a strong body of public opinion in the upper and middle classes, and they made progress despite occasional setbacks. For a time during the first quarter of the twentieth century they seemed measurably nearer their goal in many parts of the continent. More recently the depression and the troubled international situation have caused a resurgence of dictatorships, but it would be a mistake to assume that these are dictatorships on the totalitarian model. The press may be muzzled and political opposition suppressed, but there is probably no Latin American country where the government would dare to attempt the regimentation of public opinion which is an essential feature of totalitarianism. The most autocratic rulers are usually compelled by popular sentiment to observe the outward forms of republican government and to give lip service at least to democracy. In many cases it is more than lip service, for there is no necessary inconsistency between the acceptance of dictatorship as the best government for a given country under existing circumstances and a belief in democracy as the ultimate goal.

In several Latin American countries increasing prosperity, a more homogeneous population, and a healthier social organization have permitted greater progress toward the development of truly republican institutions. In Costa Rica and Uruguay, and in the more important sections of Argentina, the Indians, never numerous, have been virtually exterminated. In Chile and Colombia they have been assimilated. None of these countries, therefore, has to contend with the social problems created by the presence of a subject race. In other respects they differ much from one another, and it is necessary to study the history of each to understand the factors that have entered into its political development. In all of them revolutions, though they still occur, are unusual events, and governments are normally established by the vote of the people rather than by force. If elections are still often characterized by bribery and fraud and intimidation, they are nevertheless held under conditions immeasurably better than half a century ago.

Similar progress will be difficult in many of the other countries until something has been done to raise the masses of the people from the oppressed and dependent condition in which they have been since colonial times. The Mexican Revolution was the first great attempt to accomplish this, with what success it is yet too early to say; and in some of the other predominantly Indian countries far-seeing members of the ruling class are apparently beginning to give more attention to social problems. In Peru, Bolivia, Ecuador, and Guatemala, the establishment of social and political democracy will be a slow and difficult process. In the *mestizo* countries, on the other hand, political progress will be chiefly a question of economic development and education.

Anti-Democratic Forces

Acts of inter-American conferences have repeatedly expressed the determination of the American governments to combat ideologies repugnant to democratic ideals. In many of the nations of the continent the challenge to democracy comes from elements within the country as well as from outside propaganda. Some members of the old ruling class, reluctant to give up their power and special privileges, have been inclined to embrace fascistic ideas and to respond sympathetically to propaganda emanating from the Franco regime in Spain. The Army frequently interferes with the operation of republican institutions, though the professional officers are often divided among themselves on political matters and many of them are identified with radical groups. The most dangerous opponents of democracy, however, are the communists.

The communists were active in Latin America in the 1920's and increased their strength during the depression. Their chief success was with such groups as the port workers, miners, and factory employees, who formed a small part of the population but were increasing in number with the progress of industrialization. Organized labor offered a fertile field for their activities. The workers' unions, which had hitherto been regarded as at least potentially subversive groups, became more influential after the First World War, but their leaders, usually intellectuals or politicians rather than men who had come up from the ranks, were often more interested in power or personal profit than in the welfare of labor. Under such conditions, small, disciplined groups, trained in tactics of infiltration, had little difficulty in taking control of the unions. By 1938, when the Mexican Marxist Lombardo Toledano organized the *Confederación de Trabajadores de la America Latina*, most of the national member confederations were communist-controlled. This gave the local communist parties a small but reliable nucleus of voting strength in those countries where elections were relatively free.

The communists increased their political influence in some of these countries when they adopted the popular front policy and coöperated with the socialists and other leftist groups during the late 1930's. Their open support of the Axis between 1939 and 1941 discredited them somewhat, but with the German attack on Russia they turned to a policy of full coöperation in the war effort, and their influence with the workers did much to assure the steady flow of war materials to the United States and its allies. When the *Comintern* was abolished in 1943, most of the local parties changed their names and became ostensibly national organizations in an effort to free themselves of the stigma of subservience to a foreign power. Nevertheless, all of them suddenly and abruptly changed their attitude when the party line changed in 1945 and they have since been the most outspoken and active enemies of coöperation with the United States.

By 1945 some of the local parties were an important factor in politics. The most striking cases were in Brazil, where they cast 800,000 votes in the local elections of January, 1947, and in Chile, where they obtained three seats in González Videla's cabinet after they had made possible the leftist victory in 1946. In both of these countries, however, the communist party was outlawed and forced underground in 1948. In other countries, including Cuba and Venezuela, government intervention has destroyed its control of organized labor. Today the party functions openly and legally only in a minority of the Latin American countries, and in none of these does it apparently control a large proportion of the popular vote. The expulsion of the Marxist leader Lombardo Toledano from the Mexican Labor Confederation [1] must inevitably affect the situation of the Latin American Labor Confederation, of which he is still the leader. A further challenge to this communist-dominated organization appeared with the formation of a new Inter-American Federation of Labor, in which the United States A. F. of L. is participating, in January, 1948.

Economic and Cultural Coöperation

It is clear that the communist menace cannot be destroyed merely by repression. Their propaganda, carried on openly or secretly, will continue to have a powerful appeal so long as a great part of the people of Latin America suffer from abject poverty with its concomitants of malnutrition and disease. The more enlightened political leaders appreciate this. Many of them feel that the chief obstacle to economic and political progress is the continuance of a "colonial economy," with its dependence on the production of a few agricultural or mineral raw materials, and that the best means to raise standards of living is by diversification of production and particularly by industrialization. Several of the Latin American governments have adopted ambitious programs to achieve these objectives.

In these programs they will need outside help, particularly in the forms of new capital and technical assistance. One of the objectives of the policy of the United States has been to make his help available. The Export-Import Bank has already lent more than $700,000,000 to Latin American countries, and other agencies of our government have coöperated with these countries in health and food supply programs. President Truman's "Point Four" proposal to make technical aid and capital available on a larger scale to underdeveloped countries should make possible further steps in the same direction.

Governmental assistance, however, can supply only a small part of the new capital that will be needed, and one of the most important problems facing Latin America today is the creation of conditions that will encourage the inflow of private capital. This is difficult because the spirit of economic nationalism makes it hard to overcome local opposition to foreign enterprise and at the same time causes distrust abroad. Expropriations, exchange restrictions that prevent the transfer of profits,

[1] See p. 426 above.

laws restricting the employment of foreign technical help, and defaults on contractual obligations, have all helped to discourage foreign investors. If the Point Four program is to be a success, it will be necessary to find a means of reconciling the investors' demand for assurance of fair treatment with the Latin American governments' desire to retain control over their countries' economic life.

In addition to an increasingly close coöperation in political and economic affairs, there has been substantial progress toward a better understanding between the peoples of the two sections of the continent. A convention providing for the interchange of students and professors was signed at the Buenos Aires Conference for the Maintenance of Peace in 1936, and this idea has since been carried further with the help of private individuals and institutions as well as governments, until a large number of Latin American students are now receiving financial help to study in the United States and many North Americans are studying in Latin America. In 1938 a Division of Cultural Relations was set up in the Department of State at Washington to concern itself not only with student exchanges but with a broad program of intellectual coöperation in the fields of literature, art, music, and moving pictures. This work was further expanded by the Office of the Coördinator of Inter-American Affairs, established in 1940 under the direction of Nelson Rockefeller. A large number of distinguished Latin Americans were brought to the United States as guests of the Federal Government to visit universities and other institutions, and a still larger number of young people were brought to this country for technical training of various sorts. At present, activities of this sort are carried on by another agency of the United States Government, the Institute of Inter-American Affairs.

Our Policy Today

In September, 1949, Secretary of State Acheson set forth the policies that guide the United States in its relations with Latin America.[1] He said that "the primary objective of any government is necessarily the security of its territory and people. The Monroe Doctrine is an acknowledgement that the security of this hemisphere is indivisible." The United States is therefore vitally interested in the security system that the American republics have set up within the framework of the United

[1] Address before the Pan American Society of the United States in New York, September 19, 1949.

Nations. It is also interested in the development of democracy in the Americas. "We always deplore the action of any group in substituting its judgment for that of the electorate. We especially deplore the overthrow by force of a freely elected government. . . . We realize, however, that the attainment of the democratic ideal in any country depends fundamentally upon the desires and efforts of the people of that country. The nature of democracy is such that it can be achieved only from within." If a new government comes into power by illegal means, we may recognize it, in order to have a channel for the conduct of relations and the protection of American interests, but this does not imply approval of its policies.

Since a "healthy and prosperous people is a far more fertile field for the development of democracy," we are deeply interested in the economic welfare of Latin America. Our government has for some years been participating in important coöperative programs for the economic development of other American countries, and this work will be continued and expanded. It has made much money available through the Export-Import Bank. "Loans of public funds, however, can only be supplementary to the efforts of private capital, both local and foreign." "We hope that the flow of private capital can be stimulated also by the negotiation of treaties to create an atmosphere favorable to increased private investment abroad." "Progress will come most rapidly in countries that help themselves vigorously. Economic development, like democracy, cannot be imposed from outside."

"These then," Mr. Acheson said, "are our three major objectives— the security of our nation and of the hemisphere; the encouragement of democratic representative institutions; and positive coöperation in the economic field to help in the attainment of our first two objectives."

Reading List

The reading list given below includes but a small fraction of the great number of books dealing with Latin America. It is intended to serve as a guide to additional reading and not as an aid to scholarship. Only works in English, and works which seem likely to be of interest to the student who is not a specialist or to the general reader, are included. No effort has been made to list government documents, articles in periodicals, or monographs which are primarily of interest to the professional historian. On the other hand, most of the popular and journalistic books, of which so many have appeared in recent years, are also omitted.

An invaluable guide to current scholarly publications is the Handbook of Latin American Studies, edited by a group of American scholars, which has been published annually since 1936 by the Harvard University Press.

I. The Indians Before the Conquest

Those who wish to know more of the Mexican Indians before the Conquest will find G. C. VAILLANT's *The Aztecs of Mexico* (1941) and S. G. MORLEY's *The Ancient Maya* (1946) especially interesting. Another important book is a symposium entitled *The Maya and Their Neighbors* (1941). There are many other books dealing with ancient Mexico and the Maya region, among them: A. F. A. BANDELIER, *On the Social Organization and Mode of Government of the Ancient Mexicans* (1879) and *The Gilded Man* (1893); BERNARDINO DE SAHAGÚN, *A History of Ancient Mexico* (translated by Fanny R. Bandelier, 1932); L. SPENCE, *The Civilization of Ancient Mexico* (1912) and *The Popul Vuh* (1908); H. J. SPINDEN, *Ancient Civilizations of Mexico and Central America* (3rd ed., 1928); J. E. THOMPSON, *Mexico Before Cortez* (1940) and *The Civilization of the Mayas* (2nd ed., 1932); J. E. THOMPSON and T. W. F. GANN, *The History of the Maya* (1931); M. W.

JAKEMAN, *Origins and History of the Mayas* (only Part I, published, 1945).

Among the best accounts of the history and civilization of the Incas are: P. A. MEANS, *Ancient Civilizations of the Andes* (1931); SIR C. MARKHAM's fascinating though less up-to-date *The Incas of Peru* (1910); the first part of PRESCOTT's *Conquest of Peru;* and the great source of our information about Peruvian society, *The Royal Commentaries of the Incas*, by the Inca GARCILASO DE LA VEGA, a translation of which was published by the Hakluyt Society in Vols. 41 and 45 of their original series. EDGAR L. HEWETT's *Ancient Andean Life* (1939) and OTFRID VON HANSTEIN's *World of the Incas* (translated from the German, London, 1924) should also be mentioned. T. A. JOYCE's *Mexican Archaeology* (1914), *Central American and West Indian Archaeology* (1916), and *South American Archaeology* (1912) are more technical but contain much to interest the general reader.

II. The Discovery and Conquest of America

The outstanding works in English are R. B. MERRIMAN's *The Rise of the Spanish Empire in the Old World and the New* (4 vols., 1918 to 1934) and E. G. BOURNE's *Spain in America, 1450 to 1580* (1904—American Nation Series, Vol. 3). There are also W. H. PRESCOTT's great classics, *The Conquest of Mexico* and *The Conquest of Peru*, which are available in several editions. Of very great interest are several contemporary accounts of the Conquest. BERNAL DÍAZ DEL CASTILLO's *True History of the Conquest of Mexico* should be read by every student. English editions have been published in New York in 1927 and in the Broadway Travellers Series (London, 1928), the latter under the title *Discovery and Conquest of Mexico, 1517 to 1521.* A translation will also be found in Vols. 23, 25, 30, and 40 of the publications of the Hakluyt Society, 2nd series. Among other important contemporary accounts published in translation by the Hakluyt Society are: *Expeditions into the Valley of the Amazons* (Vol. 24, 1st series); *Pascual de Andagoya* (Vol. 34, 1st series); *Reports on the Discovery of Peru* (Vol. 47, 1st series); J. DE ACOSTA, *The Natural and Moral History of the Indies* (Vols. 60, 61, 1st series); *The Conquest of the River Plate (Voyage of Ulrich Schmidt and Commentaries of Alvar Núñez Cabeza de Vaca)* (Vol. 81, 1st series); PEDRO SARMIENTO DE GAMBOA, *History of the Incas* (Vol. 22, 2nd series); PEDRO CIEZA DE LEÓN, *Chronicles of Peru* (Vols. 33, 68, Part II, 1st series; Vols. 31, 42, 54, 2nd series); *Select Documents Concerning the Four Voyages of Columbus* (Vols. 65, 70, 2nd series).

PEDRO PIZARRO's *Relation of the Discovery and Conquest of the Kingdoms of Peru* (2 vols., 1921) and PEDRO SANCHO's *An Account of the Conquest of Peru* (1917), both translated by P. A. Means, will also be of interest. Other books which should be mentioned are C. S. BRADEN, *Religious Aspects of the Conquest of Mexico* (1930); J. Fiske, *The Discovery of America* (2 vols., 1899); R. B. CUNNINGHAME-GRAHAM, *The Conquest of New Granada* (1922), *Conquest of the River Plate* (1924), and *Pedro de Valdivia, Conqueror of Chile* (1926); F. A. KIRKPATRICK, *The Spanish Conquistadores*

(1934); SIR CLEMENTS MARKHAM, *The Conquest of New Granada* (1912); P. A. MEANS, *The Fall of the Inca Empire* (1932); G. P. HAMMOND and A. REY, *Narratives of the Coronado Expedition* (1940); S. E. MORISON, *The Second Voyage of Christopher Columbus* (1939) and *Admiral of the Ocean Sea: A Life of Christopher Columbus* (1942); G. ARCINIEGAS, *Knight of El Dorado* (1942); M. BISHOP, *The Odyssey of Cabeza de Vaca* (1933); S. DE MADARIAGA, *Christopher Columbus* (rev. ed., 1949); F. A. McNUTT, *Fernando Cortés* (1909); and the same author's *Letters of Cortés* (2 vols., 1908).

III. THE SPANISH COLONIAL SYSTEM

Among the best books dealing with the Spanish colonial system in general are C. H. HARING, *The Spanish Empire in America* (1947); and B. W. and J. W. DIFFIE, *Latin American Civilization: Colonial Period* (1945). See also W. ROBERTSON's classic *History of America* (1777, 1796); W. G. F. ROSCHER, *The Spanish Colonial System* (translated by E. G. Bourne, 1904); BERNARD MOSES, *The Establishment of Spanish Rule in America* (1898), *The Spanish Dependencies in South America* (2 vols., 1914), *Spain's Declining Power in South America, 1730–1806* (1919), and *South America on the Eve of Emancipation* (1908). S. DE MADARIAGA, *Rise of the Spanish American Empire* and *Fall of the Spanish American Empire* (both 1947); S. ZAVALA, *New Viewpoints on the Spanish Colonization of America* (1943). Chapters in the books by BOURNE and MERRIMAN mentioned above cover the earlier part of the colonial period. BERNARD MOSES, *Spain Overseas* (1929); C. E. CHAPMAN, *Colonial Hispanic America—A History* (1933), and A. C. WILGUS (ed.), *Colonial Hispanic America* (1936), also deal with the subject. On the political and religious institutions of the Spanish colonies see A. S. AITON, *Antonio de Mendoza, First Viceroy of New Spain* (1927); C. H. CUNNINGHAM, *The Audiencia in the Spanish Colonies* (1919); L. E. FISHER, *The Intendent System in Spanish America* (1929), and *Viceregal Administration in the Spanish-American Colonies* (1926); H. C. LEA, *The Inquisition in the Spanish Dependencies* (1908); L. U. HANKE, *The Spanish Struggle for Justice in the Conquest of America;* A. F. ZIMMERMAN, *Francisco de Toledo* (1938). J. F. RIPPY and J. T. NELSON, *Crusaders of the Jungle* (1936) deals with the work of the Spanish missionaries, and R. B. CUNNINGHAME-GRAHAM, *A Vanished Arcadia* (1901) deals with the Jesuit missions in Paraguay. L. B. SIMPSON's *The Encomienda in New Spain* (1929), and *The Repartimiento System of Native Labor in New Spain and Guatemala* (Ibero-Americana No. 13, 1938) are indispensable to any student of Indian relations. For other aspects of colonial society see J. T. LANNING, *Academic Culture in the Spanish Colonies* (1940); B. MOSES, *Spanish Colonial Literature in South America* (1922); A. P. WHITAKER (ed.), *Latin America and the Enlightenment* (1942); F. A. McNUTT, *Bartholomew de las Casas* (1909). The authoritative work on the colonial commercial system is C. H. HARING, *Trade and Navigation between Spain and the Indies in the Time of the Hapsburgs* (1918). For the activities of interlopers and pirates, see C. H. HARING, *The Bucca-*

neers in the West Indies in the XVII Century (1910); P. A. MEANS, *The Spanish Main, Focus of Envy, 1492–1700* (1935); A. P. NEWTON, *The European Nations in the West Indies, 1493–1688* (1933); and especially A. O. EXQUEMELIN, *Buccaneers of America*, written by a man who sailed with the pirates. The book is available in English in various editions, one published in New York, 1924. E. J. HAMILTON, *American Treasure and the Price Revolution in Spain, 1501–1650* (1934); W. L. SCHURZ, *The Manila Galleon* (1939); R. D. HUSSEY, *The Caracas Company, 1728–1784* (1934); and A. P. WHITAKER, *The Huancavelica Mercury Mine* (1941) deal with special topics that throw light on Spanish colonial policy. A few of the contemporary travelers' accounts that are available in English are of special interest, among them: THOMAS GAGE, *A New Survey of the West Indies*, an English Dominican friar's account of experiences in Mexico and Central America in the seventeenth century; F. R. J. DE PONS, *A Voyage to the Eastern Part of Terra Firma* (1806); and JORGE JUAN and ANTONIO DE ULLOA, *A Voyage to South America* (translated from the Spanish, 1806). ALEXANDER VON HUMBOLDT, *Political Essay on the Kingdom of New Spain* (English translation, 1811) and *Personal Narrative of Travels to the Equinoctial Regions of the New Continent During the Years 1799–1804* (1814–1829) give two of the best contemporary accounts of conditions at the very end of the colonial period.

Several excellent books deal with the colonial period in its relation to the history of our own west and southwest, among them: H. E. BOLTON, *The Spanish Borderlands* (1921); PHILIP BROOKS, *Diplomacy and the Borderlands: the Adams-Onis Treaty of 1819* (1939); C. E. CASTAÑEDA, *Our Catholic Heritage in Texas, 1519–1936* (4 vols., 1936–1939); H. I. PRIESTLEY, *The Coming of the White Man 1492–1848* (1929); and the publications of the Quivira Society.

IV. THE WAR FOR INDEPENDENCE

The causes of the war are dealt with in many of the books listed under the colonial period. For further material see L. E. FISHER, *The Background of the Revolution for Independence in Mexico* (1934) and B. MOSES, *The Intellectual Background of the Revolution in South America, 1810–1824* (1926). Most of the material in English on the war itself is in the form of biographies. W. S. ROBERTSON's *Rise of the Spanish American Republics as Told in the Lives of Their Liberators* (1918) covers the whole period of the conflict, and the same author's *The Life of Miranda* (2 vols., 1929) is the best biography of that leader. There are several books on Bolívar, especially G. MASUR, *Simón Bolívar* (1948), and V. A. BELAÚNDE, *Bolivar and the Political Thought of the Spanish American Revolution* (1938). A part of B. MITRE's *Life of San Martín*, translated by W. Pilling, was published in London in 1893 under the title, *Emancipation of South America*. See also T. COCHRANE, *Narrative of Services in the Liberation of Chile, Peru and Brazil* (2 vols., 1859); R. B. CUNNINGHAME-GRAHAM, *José Antonio Páez* (1929) and A. HASBROUCK, *Foreign Legionaries in the Liberation of Spanish South*

America (1928), and for the relation of the United States to the war see: F. L. PAXSON, *The Independence of the South American Republics* (1903), C. C. GRIFFIN, *The United States and the Disruption of the Spanish Empire, 1810–1822* (1937); A. P. WHITAKER, *The United States and the Independence of Latin America, 1800–1830* (1941).

V. LATIN AMERICA SINCE INDEPENDENCE

Some of the more important books dealing with groups of countries or with Latin America as a whole are:

History

F. GARCÍA CALDERÓN, *Latin America: Its Rise and Progress* (translated by Bernard Miall, 1918); C. H. HARING, *South American Progress* (1934); J. L. MECHAM, *Church and State in Latin America* (1934); A. C. WILGUS (ed.), *Argentina, Brazil and Chile since Independence* (1935), and *South American Dictators During the First Century of Independence* (1937); W. R. SHEPHERD, *The Hispanic Nations of the New World* (1920); F. TANNENBAUM, *Slave and Citizen, The Negro in the Americas* (1947).

There are also several one-volume histories, among them: W. S. ROBERTSON, *History of the Latin American Nations* (revised ed., 1943); H. G. JAMES and P. A. MARTIN, *The Republics of Latin America* (1923); M. W. WILLIAMS, *Peoples and Politics of Latin America* (revised ed., 1945); J. F. RIPPY, *Historical Evolution of Hispanic America* (revised ed., 1945); F. A. KIRKPATRICK, *Latin America: A Brief History* (1939); D. R. MOORE, *A History of Latin America* (1938); T. JONES, *An Introduction to Hispanic American History* (1939); A. C. WILGUS, *The Development of Hispanic America* (1941); C. E. AKERS, *A History of South America from 1854* (1930); J. A. CROW, *The Epic of Latin America* (1946); R. A. HUMPHREYS, *Evolution of Modern Latin America* (1946); and J. F. BANNON and P. M. DUNNE, *Latin America, An Historical Survey* (1947).

Geography

C. F. JONES, *South America* (1930); R. H. WHITBECK, *Economic Geography of South America* (3rd ed., 1940); PRESTON JAMES, *Latin America: A Human Geography* (1942).

Political and Economic Problems

JAMES BRYCE, *South America* (1917); S. G. INMAN, *Latin America, Its Place in World Life* (revised ed., 1942); L. C. JANE, *Liberty and Despotism in South America* (1929); D. M. PHELPS, *Migration of Industry to South America* (1936); Royal Institute of International Affairs, *The Republics of South America* (1937); W. L. SCHURZ, *Latin America, A Descriptive Survey* (revised ed., 1949); F. TANNENBAUM, *Whither Latin America?* (1934); A. C. WILGUS (ed.), *Modern Hispanic America* (1933); H. C. HERRING, *The Good Neighbors* (1941).

In the field of government, see especially: A. F. MACDONALD, *Latin American Politics and Government* (1949); and for the texts of constitutions, R. H. FITZGIBBON *et al.*, *The Constitutions of the Americas* (1948).

On economic problems: G. WYTHE, *Industry in Latin America* (2nd ed., 1949); S. E. HARRIS, *Economic Problems of Latin America* (1944); J. F. RIPPY, *Latin America and the Industrial Age* (1947); P. R. OLSON and C. R. HICKMAN, *Pan American Economics* (1943); and G. H. SOULE, D. EFRON, and N. T. NESS, *Latin America in the Future World* (1945).

International Relations

W. H. KELCHNER, *Latin American Relations with the League of Nations* (1930); P. A. MARTIN, *Latin America and the War* (1925); J. F. RIPPY, *Latin America in World Politics* (3rd ed., 1938); and also the books listed below under Paragraph X.

Education, Literature, Art

H. L. SMITH and H. LITTELL, *Education in Latin America* (1934); C. C. GRIFFIN (ed.), *Concerning Latin American Culture* (1940); I. L. KANDEL, *Education in Latin America* (1942); W. R. CRAWFORD, *A Century of Latin American Thought* (1944); A. TORRES-RIOSECO, *The Epic of Latin American Literature* (1942); W. D. FRANK, *America Hispana* (1940); I. GOLDBERG, *Studies in Spanish American Literature* (1920), and *Brazilian Literature* (1922); A. L. COESTER, *The Literary History of Spanish America* (1916); A. S. BLACKWELL, *Some Spanish American Poets* (2nd ed., 1937); ALFONSO CASÓ and others, *Twenty Centuries of Mexican Art* (1940); ELEANOR HAGUE, *Latin American Music, Past and Present* (1934).

Travelers' accounts

Travelers' accounts are a valuable source of information, especially for the earlier period. Besides those listed below under individual countries, the following are of interest: B. HALL, *Extracts from a Journal, Written on the Coasts of Chile, Peru, and Mexico, in the Years 1820, 1821, 1822* (new edition, 1851); A. CALDCLEUGH, *Travels in South America, During the Years 1819, 1820, 1821* (1825); G. BYAM, *Wanderings in Some of the Western Republics of America* (1850); SIR WOODBINE PARISH, *Buenos Aires and the Provinces of the Rio de la Plata* (2nd ed., 1852); T. J. PAGE, *La Plata, the Argentine Confederation, and Paraguay* (1859); CHARLES DARWIN, *Journal of Researches into the Geology and Natural History of the Various Countries Visited During the Voyage of H.M.S. Beagle Round the World* (Everyman's Library, 1906); W. B. STEVENSON, *A Historical and Descriptive Narrative of Twenty Years' Residence in South America* (3 vols., 1825).

VI. THE RIVER PLATE AND CHILE

Argentina

There are two good one-volume histories: RICARDO LEVENE, *A History of Argentina* (translated and edited by W. S. Robertson, 1937), and F. A.

KIRKPATRICK, *A History of the Argentine Republic* (1931). J. F. CADY's *Foreign Intervention in the Rio de la Plata, 1835–1850* (1929), and M. BURGIN's *Economic Aspects of Argentine Federalism* (1946) deal with particular periods, as does M. W. NICHOLS' *The Gaucho* (1942). A. F. MACDONALD, *Government of the Argentine Republic* (1942), and L. S. ROWE, *The Federal System of the Argentine Republic* (Washington, 1921) are able studies of governmental institutions. For economic problems see M. S. W. JEFFERSON, *Peopling the Argentine Pampa* (1926); E. Tornquist and Co., *The Economic Development of the Argentine Republic in the Last Fifty Years* (1919); V. L. PHELPS, *The International Economic Position of Argentina* (1938); S. G. HANSON, *Argentine Meat and the British Market* (1938); C. C. TAYLOR, *Rural Life in Argentina* (1947); F. J. WEIL, *The Argentine Riddle* (1944). Y. F. RENNIE, *The Argentine Republic* (1945) deals with more recent history. For relations with the United States see C. H. HARING, *Argentina and the United States* (1941), and the State Department's *"Blue Book"* published in 1946. Other books recommended as vivid pictures of life in Argentina at different periods are SIR F. B. HEAD, *Rough Notes Taken During some Rapid Journeys across the Pampas and among the Andes* (new ed., London, 1861); D. F. SARMIENTO, *Life in the Argentine Republic in the Days of the Tyrants* (translated from the Spanish, New York, 1868); and W. H. HUDSON, *Far Away and Long Ago* (New York, 1918).

Uruguay and Paraguay

Uruguay has been grievously neglected by writers in English but S. G. HANSON, *Utopia in Uruguay* (1938), is an excellent study of contemporary conditions there. Conditions a century ago are portrayed in W. H. HUDSON's historical novel, *The Purple Land*, which is available in Everyman's Library.

There are more books on Paraguay, but except for A. E. ELLIOTT, *Paraguay: Its Cultural Heritage, Social Conditions and Educational Problems* (1931), and H. G. WARREN, *Paraguay, An Informal History* (1949) they deal chiefly with the Francia regime and the period of the Paraguayan war. The more important are: P. H. BOX, *The Origins of the Paraguayan War* (1929); J. P. and W. P. ROBERTSON, *Letters on Paraguay* (3 vols., 2nd ed., 1839); J. R. RENGGER and LONGCHAMP, *The Reign of Dr. Joseph G. R. de Francia in Paraguay* (1827); G. F. MASTERMAN, *Seven Eventful Years in Paraguay* (2nd ed., 1870); C. A. WASHBURN, *The History of Paraguay* (1871); EDWARD LUCAS WHITE's fascinating historical novel, *El Supremo* (1916); and W. E. BARRETT, *Woman on Horseback* (1938).

Chile

There are surprisingly few scholarly works in English on Chile. LUIS GALDÁMES, *A History of Chile* (translated and edited by I. J. COX, 1941) is the best history. See also A. V. HANCOCK, *History of Chile* (1893). G. M. McBRIDE, *Chile—Land and Society* (1936) is important for an understanding of social institutions. H. C. EVANS, JR., *Chile and Its Relations with the United States* (1927) and W. J. DENNIS, *Tacna and Arica* (1931) deal with international relations. For the first years of independence see AUGUSTÍN EDWARDS, *The Dawn* (1931); and for a more recent period: J. R. STEVENSON, *The Chilean Popular Front* (1942), and P. T. ELLSWORTH, *Chile, An Economy in Transition* (1945).

VII. BRAZIL

Of the very few books on the colonial period in Brazil, ROBERT SOUTHEY's *History of Brazil* (3 vols., 1817–1822) is the best. More easily accessible is the section on colonial Brazil in Volume I of T. C. DAWSON's *South American Republics* (1903–4). E. PRESTAGE, *The Portuguese Pioneers* (1933) deals with the period of discovery. L. E. DA COSTA, *Rio in the Time of the Viceroys* (translated by Dorothea H. Momsen, 1936) describes life in the colonial period. There are two translations of contemporary accounts: *The Captivity of Hans Stade of Hesse in A.D. 1547–1555 Among the Wild Tribes of Eastern Brazil* (Hakluyt Society's publications, 1st series, vol. 51) and PERO DE MAGALHÃES DE GANDAVO, *The Histories of Brazil* (Cortés Society, 1922). A. MARCHANT, *From Barter to Slavery* (1942) is a good study of Indian relations in the 16th century.

For the history of Brazil since independence see J. P. CALOGERAS, *A History of Brazil* (translated and edited by P. A. Martin, 1939); H. G. JAMES, *Brazil after a Century of Independence* (1925); JOHN ARMITAGE, *History of Brazil* (1836) which deals with the early years of the Empire; and M. W. WILLIAMS, *Dom Pedro the Magnanimous* (1937) which is a good biography covering another long period. Another book of special interest is MANOEL DE OLIVEIRA LIMA, *The Evolution of Brazil Compared with that of Spanish and Anglo-Saxon America* (1914). G. FREYRE, *Brazil* (1945); L. F. HILL (ed.), *Brazil* (1947); and ROY NASH, *The Conquest of Brazil* (1926) are general descriptions. For political conditions see H. G. JAMES, *The Constitutional System of Brazil* (1923); E. HAMBLOCH, *His Majesty the President of Brazil* (1936); and especially K. LOEWENSTEIN, *Brazil Under Vargas* (1932). L. F. HILL, *Diplomatic Relations Between Brazil and the United States* (1932) is a history of relations with the United States. For economic problems see R. C. SIMONSEN, *Brazil's Industrial Evolution* (1939); J. F. NORMANO, *Brazil; A Study of Economic Types* (1935); A. K. MANCHESTER, *British Preëminence in Brazil* (1933); Brazil, Ministry of Foreign Affairs, *Brazil 1939/40; An Economic, Social, and Geographic Survey* (1940); M. L. COOKE, *Brazil on the March* (1944); and H. W. SPIEGEL, *Brazilian Economy* (1949). Two good sociological studies are: G. FREYRE, *The Masters and the Slaves* (1946), and T. L. SMITH, *Brazil, People and Institutions* (1946). H. TAVARES DE SÁ, *Brazilians, People of Tomorrow* (1947) is a more popular description. P. E. JAMES, *Brazil* (1946) is largely geographical. E. DA CUNHA, *Rebellion in the Backlands* (translated by Samuel Putnam, 1944) is an historical classic.

Among the travelers' accounts are ROBERT WALSH, *Notices of Brazil in 1828 and 1829* (2 vols., 1831); H. KOSTER, *Travels in Brazil* (1816); H. W. BATES, *The Naturalist on the River Amazons* (Everyman's Library, 1910); D. P. KIDDER and J. C. FLETCHER, *Brazil and the Brazilians* (9th ed., 1879);

M. Graham, *Journal of a Voyage to Brazil* (1824); J. Luccock, *Notes on Rio de Janeiro* (1820); and J. Mawe, *Travels in the Interior of Brazil* (1812).

VIII. The Central Andean Countries

Here again the material in English is scanty. Sir Clements Markham, *A History of Peru* (1892) is useful, as is Graham H. Stuart, *The Governmental System of Peru* (1925). G. M. McBride, *The Agrarian Indian Communities of Highland Bolivia* (1921), and W. S. Rycroft (ed.), *Indians of the High Andes* (1946) are studies of contemporary Indian problems. A. B. Franklin, *Ecuador* (1943) is a description of that country. N. A. N. Cleven, *The Political Organization of Bolivia* (1940) describes the government and gives some information regarding history. M. A. Marsh, *The Bankers in Bolivia* (1928) deals with one aspect of relations with the United States. For travelers' accounts of early conditions in the Andean countries see T. J. Hutchinson, *Two Years in Peru* (2 vols., 1873); A. S. Duffield, *Peru in the Guano Age* (1877); H. Bingham, *Inca Land* (1922); and F. Hassaurek, *Four Years among Spanish Americans* (4th ed., 1892). The latter gives a good picture of Ecuador seventy-five years ago.

IX. The North Coast Countries

J. M. Henao and G. Arrubla, *History of Colombia* (translated and edited by J. F. Rippy, 1938) is the best history of Colombia. Relations with the United States are dealt with in E. T. Parks, *Colombia and the United States, 1765–1934* (1935) and J. F. Rippy, *The Capitalists and Colombia* (1931). P. J. Eder, *Colombia* (1913) and W. L. Scruggs, *The Colombian and Venezuelan Republics* (1900) are general descriptions, and Francis Hall, *Colombia* (1825) is an early account. There is no general history of Venezuela in English, but Thomas Rourke (pseudonym for D. J. Clinton), *Gómez: Tyrant of the Andes* (1936) and P. M. Arcaya, *The Gómez Regime* (1936) give contrasting pictures of one important period. Mary Watters has written *A History of the Church in Venezuela, 1810–1930* (1933). For general descriptions see H. J. Allen, *Venezuela, A Democracy* (1940); J. M. Spence, *The Land of Bolivar* (2 vols., 1878); W. E. Curtis, *Venezuela* (1896) and L. V. Dalton, *Venezuela* (1912). For lighter reading, Richard Harding Davis, *Three Gringos in Venezuela and Central America* (1896) and T. R. Ybarra, *Young Man of Caracas* (1941) are suggested.

X. Mexico

There is a wealth of material on Mexico. For the Republic's history see H. I. Priestley, *The Mexican Nation* (1930); W. H. Callcott, *Church and State in Mexico, 1822–1857* (1926) and *Liberalism in Mexico, 1857–1929* (1931); H. H. Bancroft, *History of Mexico* (6 vols., 1883–88); Justo Sierra, *Mexico: Its Social Evolution* (English trans., 2 vols. in 3, 1900–4);

Ernest Gruening, *Mexico and Its Heritage* (1934); L. B. Simpson, *Many Mexicos* (1941); H. B. Parkes, *History of Mexico* (1938); and the following biographies: W. H. Callcott, *Santa Anna* (1936); R. Roeder, *Juárez and His Mexico* (2 vols., 1947); U. R. Burke, *Life of Benito Juárez* (1894); E. C. Corti, *Maximilian and Charlotte of Mexico* (English translation, 1928); José Luis Blasio, *Maximilian, Emperor of Mexico; Memoirs of his Private Secretary* (translated from the Spanish, 1934); David Hannay, *Díaz* (1917); J. Creelman, *Díaz, Master of Mexico* (1911); C. Beals, *Porfirio Díaz* (1932).

Probably the best description of the period since 1910 is F. Tannenbaum, *Peace by Revolution* (1933). The recent period is also dealt with in J. Vasconcelos and M. Gamio, *Aspects of Mexican Civilization* (1926); Rippy, Vasconcelos, and Stevens, *Mexico* (1928); M. Saenz and H. I. Priestley, *Some Mexican Problems* (1926); Annals of the American Academy of Political and Social Science (March, 1940), "Mexico Today" (edited by A. P. Whitaker); C. L. Jones, *Mexico and Its Reconstruction* (1921); V. Prewett, *Reportage on Mexico* (1941); N. and S. C. Weyl, *The Reconquest of Mexico* (1939); and in Section I of the *Survey of American Foreign Relations*, published for the Council on Foreign Relations in 1931. An excellent, very recent book is F. Tannenbaum, *Mexico, The Struggle for Peace and Bread* (1950).

Especially important are three books on the agrarian problem: G. M. McBride, *The Land Systems of Mexico* (1923); F. Tannenbaum, *The Mexican Agrarian Revolution* (1929); and E. N. Simpson, *The Ejido—Mexico's Way Out* (1937); also Robert Redfield's studies of life in rural communities: *Tepoztlán; A Mexican Village* (1930), and *The Folk Culture of Yucatán* (1941); N. L. Whetten, *Rural Mexico* (1948).

There are many books on relations with the United States, including G. L. Rives, *The United States and Mexico, 1821–1848* (1913); J. H. Smith, *The War with Mexico* (2 vols., 1919); G. M. Callahan, *American Foreign Policy in Mexican Relations* (1932); J. F. Rippy, *The United States and Mexico* (1926); F. S. Dunn, *The Diplomatic Protection of Americans in Mexico* (1933); C. W. Hackett, *The Mexican Revolution and the United States, 1910–1926* (1926). For some of the more controversial issues of recent years see P. E. Calles, *Mexico Before the World* (1927); R. B. Gaither, *Expropriation in Mexico* (1940); Government of Mexico, *Mexico: The True Facts about the Expropriation of the Oil Companies' Properties in Mexico* (1940); and the Standard Oil Company of New Jersey, *Present Status of the Mexican Oil "Expropriations"* (1940).

Good pictures of Mexico at different periods are Joel Poinsett, *Notes on Mexico* (1824) and F. E. Calderón de la Barca, *Life in Mexico* (1843, available in Everyman's Library). C. M. Flandrau, *Viva Mexico!* (1908) is one of many books dealing with conditions at the outbreak of the revolution.

XI. The Caribbean

For two good studies of United States relations with the Caribbean Area, see D. Perkins, *The United States and the Caribbean* (1947); and W. H. Callcott, *The Caribbean Policy of the United States, 1890–1920* (1942). Other books dealing with the Caribbean area as a whole are: *Survey of American Foreign Relations*, prepared for the Council on Foreign Relations by Charles P. Howland, 1929, Section I, *The Caribbean;* H. C. Hill, *Roosevelt and the Caribbean* (1927); C. L. Jones, *Caribbean Interests of the United States* (1916); *The Caribbean since 1900* (1936); D. G. Munro, *The United States and the Caribbean Area* (1934); J. F. Rippy, *The Caribbean Danger Zone* (1940); W. A. Roberts, *The Caribbean* (1940); and A. C. Wilgus (ed.), *The Caribbean Area* (1934).

Panama and the Canal

The best book on the history of the Republic is W. D. McCain, *The United States and the Republic of Panama* (1937). For the history of the Isthmus in general and the canal project see M. W. Williams, *Anglo-American Isthmian Diplomacy, 1815–1915* (1916), an important scholarly study; and the following books: C. L. G. Anderson, *Old Panama and Castilla del Oro* (1911); W. F. Johnson, *Four Centuries of the Panama Canal* (1907); M. P. Duval, Jr., *Cadiz to Cathay* (1940), and *And the Mountains Will Move* (1947); G. Mack, *The Land Divided* (1944); D. C. Miner, *Fight for the Panama Route* (1940); J. H. Kemble, *The Panama Route, 1848–1869* (1943); H. M. Fast, *Goethals and the Panama Canal* (1942); P. Bunau-Varilla, *Panama: The Creation, Destruction, and Resurrection* (1913); I. E. Bennett, *History of the Panama Canal* (1915); F. Bishop, *Panama, Past and Present* (1913); and N. J. Padelford, *The Panama Canal in Peace and War* (1942).

Central America

Among the best books on Central America are the older travel accounts: J. L. Stephens, *Incidents of Travel in Central America, Chiapas and Yucatan* (2 vols., 1841, new ed. 1949); E. G. Squier, *Nicaragua* (1852) and *Honduras* (1870); and Thomas Belt, *The Naturalist in Nicaragua* (1874, and Everyman's Library).

For history see H. H. Bancroft, *History of Central America* (3 vols., 1883–87) and D. G. Munro, *The Five Republics of Central America* (1918). C. L. Jones, *Guatemala, Past and Present* (1940) is an excellent work on that country and his *Costa Rica and Civilization in the Caribbean* (1935) is also good, though briefer. C. D. Kepner and J. H. Soothill, *The Banana Empire* (1935) and C. D. Kepner, *Social Aspects of the Banana Industry* (1936) are studies of one important economic problem. J. B. and M. Biesanz, *Costa Rican Life* (1944) is a good social study.

For the Walker episode see W. O. Scroggs, *Filibusters and Financiers:*

The Story of William Walker and his Associates (1916). This is an excellent account. See also WILLIAM WALKER's own story, *The War in Nicaragua* (1860). A more modern type of soldier of fortune is the subject of H. B. DEUTSCH, *The Incredible Yanqui: The Career of Lee Christmas* (1931). PAUL BURGESS, *Justo Rufino Barrios* (1926) is a biography of one of the important figures in Guatemalan history.

For the American intervention in Nicaragua H. L. STIMSON, *American Policy in Nicaragua* (1927) and "The United States and Nicaragua," a pamphlet issued by the Department of State in 1932, are indispensable statements of facts from the official point of view. R. DE NOGALES, *The Looting of Nicaragua* (1928) is interesting chiefly as an example of Latin American anti-imperialist propaganda. I. J. COX, *Nicaragua and the United States, 1909–1927* (1927) is a more scholarly study, and H. N. DENNY, *Dollars for Bullets* (1929) is the work of a well-informed journalist. See also R. R. HILL, *Fiscal Intervention in Nicaragua* (1933).

Cuba

The best history of Cuba since 1900 is C. E. CHAPMAN, *A History of the Cuban Republic* (1927). For earlier periods see I. A. WRIGHT, *The Early History of Cuba, 1492–1586* (1916) and W. F. JOHNSON, *History of Cuba* (5 vols., 1920).

Of the numerous books on Cuban-American relations the following are recommended: J. M. CALLAHAN, *Cuba and International Relations* (1899); F. E. CHADWICK, *Relations of the United States and Spain (diplomacy)* (1909), and *Relations of the United States and Spain (war)* (2 vols., 1911); R. H. FITZGIBBON, *Cuba and the United States, 1900–1935* (1935); H. F. GUGGENHEIM, *The United States and Cuba* (1934); L. H. JENKS, *Our Cuban Colony* (1928); D. A. LOCKMILLER, *Magoon in Cuba* (1938); P. G. WRIGHT, *The Cuban Situation and Our Treaty Relations* (1931). *Problems of the New Cuba* (1935), the report of the Foreign Policy Association's Commission on Cuban Affairs, is a very useful study. See also J. A. WRIGHT, *Cuba* (1910), and F. ORTIZ, *Cuban Counterpoint* (1947).

Haiti

The only history of Haiti in English is H. P. DAVIS, *Black Democracy* (rev. ed., 1936). T. L. STODDARD, *The French Revolution in Santo Domingo* (1914) is excellent on the revolutionary period. P. WAXMAN, *The Black Napoleon* (1931) is a biography of Toussaint Louverture, and J. W. VANDERCOOK, *Black Majesty* (1928) a very readable picture of Christophe. JONATHAN BROWN, *History and Present Condition of St. Domingo* (2 vols., 1837) and CHARLES MCKENZIE, *Notes on Haiti* (2 vols., 1830) give valuable information about Haiti in the first part of the nineteenth century. SIR SPENSER ST. JOHN, *Hayti or the Black Republic* (1884) is an unsympathetic description of conditions at the later period, to which J. N. LÉGER, *Haiti—Her History and Her Detractors* (1907) is a Haitian reply. For another contemporary account see M. B. BIRD, *Republic of Hayti and Its*

Struggles (1867). There are two first-class histories of Haitian-American relations: L. L. Montague, *Haiti and the United States, 1714–1938* (1940) and R. W. Logan, *The Diplomatic Relations of the United States with Haiti, 1776–1891* (1941). A. C. Millspaugh, *Haiti Under American Control, 1915–1930* (1931) is a scholarly study of the period of American intervention, and E. G. Balch (ed.), *Occupied Haiti* (1927) discusses the same period from an anti-imperialist point of view. C. Kelsey, *The American Intervention in Haiti and Santo Domingo* (Annals of the American Academy of Political and Social Science, 1922) is a first-hand report of conditions in 1921 by a competent observer. Important for an understanding of present conditions in Haiti are: M. J. Herskowitz, *Life in a Haitian Valley* (1937) and J. G. Leyburn, *The Haitian People* (1941).

The Dominican Republic

Sumner Welles, *Naboth's Vineyard—The Dominican Republic, 1844–1924* (2 vols., 1928) is the best history; Otto Schoenrich, *Santo Domingo* (1918) is also good. C. C. Tansill, *The United States and Santo Domingo, 1798–1873* (1938) is an important work dealing with earlier diplomatic relations with the United States, and M. M. Knight, *The Americans in Santo Domingo* (1928) discusses the American intervention. See also M. L. E. Moreau de St. Méry, *A Topographical and Political Description of the Spanish Part of Saint Domingo* (translated from the French, 1796); Samuel Hazard, *Santo Domingo, Past and Present, with a Glance at Hayti* (1873); *Report of the Commission of Inquiry to Santo Domingo, 1871* (Sen. Ex. Doc. No. 9, 42nd Cong., 1st Session); A. C. Hicks, *Blood in the Streets* (1946); and The Brookings Institution, *Refugee Settlement in the Dominican Republic* (1942).

XII. Relations Between the United States and Latin America

The most important historical works by North Americans are: S. F. Bemis, *Latin American Policy of the United States* (1943); G. H. Stuart, *Latin America and the United States* (Revised ed., 1943); and W. S. Robertson, *Hispanic-American Relations with the United States* (1923). See also J. H. Latané, *The United States and Latin America* (1920); and C. E. Hughes, *Our Relations to the Nations of the Western Hemisphere* (1928). The early period is covered by H. Bernstein, *Origins of Inter-American Interest* (1945), and J. B. Lockey, *Pan Americanism: Its Beginnings* (1920). For the most recent period see L. Duggan, *The Americas* (1949); E. O. Guerrant, *Roosevelt's Good Neighbor Policy* (1950); M. M. Ball, *The Problems of Inter-American Organization* (1944); J. P. Humphrey, *The Inter-American System* (1942); and the five annual volumes, *Inter American Affairs*, edited by A. P. Whitaker and covering the years from 1941 to 1945.

Of the numerous books on the Monroe Doctrine, D. Perkins' three volumes, *The Monroe Doctrine, 1823–6* (1927), *The Monroe Doctrine, 1826–67* (1933), and *The Monroe Doctrine, 1867–1907* (1937) are the most authoritative. The same author's *Hands Off* (1941) is a briefer account which brings the story to a recent period. For other discussions of the Monroe Doctrine see A. ÁLVAREZ, *The Monroe Doctrine* (translated from Spanish, 1924); H. BINGHAM, *The Monroe Doctrine: An Obsolete Shibboleth* (1913); J. R. CLARK, *Memorandum on the Monroe Doctrine* (published by the Department of State, 1930); A. B. HART, *The Monroe Doctrine—An Interpretation* (1916); and GASTON NERVAL (pseudonym for Raul Díez de Medina), *Autopsy of the Monroe Doctrine* (1934).

Economic aspects of inter-American relations are dealt with in J. W. GANTENBEIN, *Financial Questions in United States Foreign Policy* (1939); W. FEUERLEIN and E. HANNAN, *Dollars in Latin America* (1941); M. WINKLER, *Investments of United States Capital in Latin America* (1928), and some of the books listed under V above. There is also a considerable amount of useful material in publications of various departments of the United States Government.

A few of the books in English expressing Latin American points of view are R. REYES, *The Two Americas* (1914); M. UGARTE, *The Destiny of a Continent* (1925); J. ROA, *Positive and Negative Factors in Inter-American Relations* (1940); L. QUINTANILLA, *A Latin American Speaks* (1943); and Carlos DÁVILA, *We of the Americas* (1949). For a North American study of the Latin American attitude, C. H. HARING, *South America Looks at the United States* (1928) is especially important, though written several years ago. A more recent book is C. BEALS, B. OLIVER, H. BRICKEL, and S. G. INMAN, *What the Latin Americans Think of Us* (1945).

XIII. Periodical Literature

The *Hispanic American Historical Review* is the important publication in the historical field. *Inter-American Economic Affairs*, a newer quarterly, contains much valuable scholarly material. From time to time there are good studies of Latin American problems in *Foreign Policy Reports*. *The Americas*, published by the Pan American Union, and the *Pan American Magazine* are of a more popular nature. For current events in Latin America, see the *Hispanic World Report*, published monthly at Stanford University; *Noticias*, published weekly by the Council for Inter-American Coöperation; and the *Annals of the Organization of American States*, which contains documentary and other official material.

Index

Date Due

MAR 2 7 '61			
APR 1 6 '62			
MAR 2 6 '63			
APR 9 '63			
APR 2 4 '63			
MAR 1 7 '64			
AUG 7 '64			
RESERVE			
RESERVE			
AUG 12 '65			
JAN 1 2 '68			
ℬ	PRINTED	IN U. S. A.	